POLYMER CLAY JEWELRY

The Art of Caning

Library of Congress Control Number: 2013938833

Type set in Iwona/Cicle

ISBN: 978-0-7643-4456-5
Printed in China

Published by Schiffer Publishing, Ltd.
4880 Lower Valley Road
Atglen, PA 19310
Phone: (610) 593-1777; Fax: (610) 593-2002
E-mail: Info@schifferbooks.com

For our complete selection of fine books on this and related subjects,
please visit our website at **www.schifferbooks.com**. You may also write for a free catalog.

This book may be purchased from the publisher. Please try your bookstore first.

We are always looking for people to write books on new and related subjects. If you have an idea for a book, please contact us at **proposals@schifferbooks.com**.

Schiffer Publishing's titles are available at special discounts for bulk purchases for sales promotions or premiums. Special editions, including personalized covers, corporate imprints, and excerpts can be created in large quantities for special needs. For more information, contact the publisher.

In Europe, Schiffer books are distributed by:
Bushwood Books
6 Marksbury Ave.
Kew Gardens
Surrey TW9 4JF England
Phone: 44 (0) 20 8392 8585; Fax: 44 (0) 20 8392 9876
E-mail: info@bushwoodbooks.co.uk
Website: www.bushwoodbooks.co.uk

POLYMER CLAY
JEWELRY
The Art of Caning

Mathilde Brun

Photography by Thierry Antablian

Schiffer Publishing Ltd

4880 Lower Valley Road • Atglen, PA 19310

CONTENT

Introduction to Polymer Clay 6

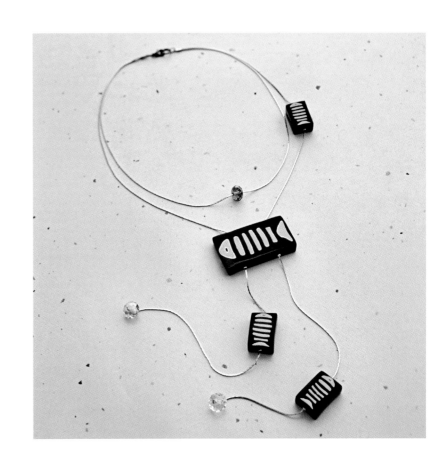

Introduction to Polymer Clay

Polymer Clay (Fimo Clay) is a PVC, plasticizer-based synthetic modeling material. Flexible and pliable, it permanently hardens without shrinking thanks to low temperature curing (266°F/130°C) in a domestic oven.

Presentation

Polymer clay is generally presented in 2-ounce (60g) blocks, but some colors are available in bigger blocks. A large array of colors exists – complementing mat colors, white nacre paste, translucent colors, fluorescent, luminescent, and various colors in metallic (glittery or shiny) – that are ideal to create marbling.

Translucent clay also exists that is only transparent in a thin layer. It gives some volume to the other colors, heightens the contrast of the patterns, and allows for the insertion of other materials. Easy to blend, these materials allow for the creation of all sorts of shapes, colors, and patterns. Elements can also be included, such as pigments, colored sand, and metallic leaves.

Polymer clays also offer different consistency:

Fimo "Soft"

Very supple in consistency, it is ideal for mixing colors and allows for very fine work. If the clay is too soft, just put it in the fridge to harden it a bit.

Fimo "Classic"

Harder than the Soft, it demands a longer mixing but allows more precision, because it resists better to the pressure exerted by the fingers or tools during the modeling. It is ideal for cane work. If the clay is too hard, you can warm it with your hand.

Fimo "Effect"

It enhances the "Soft" range with, for example, some metallic shades very close to reality. You can blend it to match all the other clays. With all the colors being miscible, it is possible to blend them with simple mixing, therefore creating new shades. It is interesting to research your own colors to harmonize them with the other elements of the jewelry being created or to the colors of an outfit. To achieve pastels or darker tones, do not hesitate to add white or black to the mixtures.

Precaution of Use

Polymer clay is not suitable for children under eight. For older children, adult supervision is necessary during the baking to avoid the risk of burns. This material should not be ingested. It is advised to keep children clear of the workplace, to keep the clay out of reach of infants, and to thoroughly clean all the utensils after use.

The curing takes place in a domestic oven. Do not use a microwave. The baking temperature should not exceed 266°F (130°C) and should last no longer than 30 minutes. Beyond that time, toxic gas may emanate.

For gas ovens or those that do not have a precise thermostat, use an ordinary oven thermometer (bimetal for example). Do not use a glass thermometer.

Storing

Unused clay can be stored for years at room temperature in its original packaging or tightly sealed in plastic wrap or aluminum foil inside a glass jar or metallic box.

The Material

Tools and Materials

1. Polymer clay blocks

2. Oven thermometer

3. Varnish

4. Stamp to create patterns

5. Metal leafs

6. Pins to pierce the clay: wooden sticks, needles, metal wire

7. Shaping tools

8. Blades to cut the clay: They must be particularly thin so as not to crush the clay during the slicing

9. Glitter, sequins, or beads

10. Colored sand

11. Soft paintbrush for varnishing

12. "Clay shaper" to smooth

13. Work surface plate glass to work or cut the clay on

14. Soft cloth to polish

15. Fine sandpaper to rub down (400 to 1200)

16. Glass or Plexiglas roller (jar or bottle)

17. Pasta maker machine to roll the clay into thin sheets and for mixing and blending colors

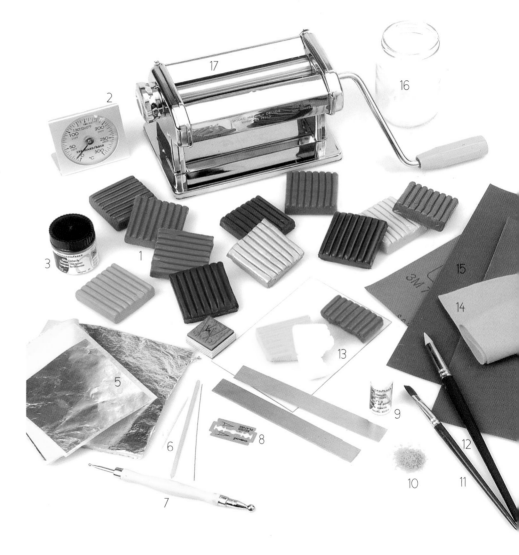

NOTE: In each project's material list and step-by-step instructions, "wire" can also be headpins, needles, or wooden sticks (see #6 above).

Findings for Jewelry Creation

Bent chain-nose pliers: to hold small elements, flatten crimp beads, open and close rings. Round nose and cutter pliers: to create loops in eyepins and to cut wire cables, headpins, and eyepins.

Scissors

Soft metal choker, small metal chain, and beading wire.

Tubular rubber cord

Hook wires and lever back earrings

Brooches pads

End crimp/caps

Clasps

Jump rings: to articulate jewelry or to link elements. They are of different diameter. They are open rings that you can open and close with pliers (see p. 17)

Adjustable flat ring pads

End caps for clasps and crimp beads
(see p. 17)

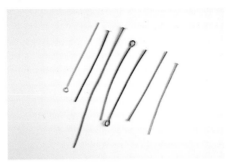

Eye pins and headpins (stems with head) in metal. The stems allow creating articulated jewelry. The headpins block the beads and allow creating charms (see p. 17)

Glass beads, faceted beads, and seed beads

Crystal beads
(ovals, cubes, rice grains, rounds)

Conditioning of the Clay

The quantity of clay necessary for jewelry making is indicated with the list of materials and is counted in blocks of clay. A purchased block equates to a slab of approximately 2 ounces (60g) squared shape (see no. 1, p. 7). We frequently use 1/2, 1/4, 1/8, even 1/16 of a block. Thanks to its square shape, it is easy to divide a block into 2, 4, 8, or 16 parts. For smaller sizes, we will use a nut, a chickpea, a pea, and even a rice grain of clay for comparison.

The idea is to work the clay on a non-porous and clean work surface plate (plate in glass or PVC). During the modeling, the outline will be smoother and the clay can be cut with a blade.

Wearing latex gloves is recommended, as it considerably reduces fingerprints on the formed surfaces. In addition, some colors can stain the skin and require cleaning your hands before handling another color.

Softening the Clay

To be easily pliable, the clay must be softened. It simply needs to be kneaded for a few minutes with your hands. The smaller

the portion is, the easier the kneading. The clay can be molded and re-molded as often as you wish as long as it has not been baked in the oven. Some products exist to soften clay that has become hard with age.

Shaping

All sorts of bead shapes are achievable in modeling. They can be classics (balls, cubes, slices, spinners, tubes), born from the imagination or inspired by our environment (coffee beans, hearts, leaves, sweets, etc.). Some molds exist to help create regular beads, but modeling by hand is more rewarding.

To start with, it is best to practice the creation of beads of simple shapes from a ball of clay and pierce them in order to thread them.

Tip!
Use clay leftovers to create the inside of the beads or the pendant's underpinning sheet. You only need to cover it with the external chosen color.

A Ball

1 Take a clay nut and roll it between the palms of your hand into a ball.

2 Finish by rolling the ball on the table to smooth the surface well.

A Flattened Ball

Slowly flatten a ball with a glass plate applying a regular pressure.

A Cube

1 Flatten a ball between the thumbs and index fingers. The fingers of one hand apply a perpendicular pressure to the fingers of the other hand.

2 Level and square the sides with the aid of the glass plate.

A Flattened Cube

Slowly flatten a cube with a glass plate, applying a regular pressure.

A Bi-cone

1 Place a ball on the table. Place a glass plate on the top of it without applying any pressure. The plate must be horizontally leveled, parallel to the table.

2 Start rotating the plate on the ball; be sure to always maintain the plate parallel to the table.

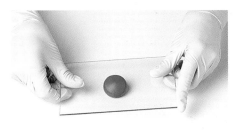

3 Press lightly but firmly on the plate while continuing to rotate it. The movement and pressure must be consistent.

4 After few seconds we obtain a bi-cone.

A Log

1 With your fingers, roll a clay ball on the table to give it an elongated cylindrical shape to the required diameter.

2 To obtain little logs, keep the cutting blade really perpendicular to the table and cut the log into sections.

A Pyramid

1 Take a log section and flatten it between the thumbs and index fingers. The fingers of one hand apply a perpendicular pressure against the fingers of the other hand.

2 Once the shape is achieved, even it out and smooth it with the fingers.

A Sheet

By hand: Flatten a clay ball with a roller, preferably a glass one (bottle or jar), until obtaining the desired thickness.

By pasta machine: We obtain thinner sheets of a regular thickness much easier.

1 Insert a flattened clay section and turn the handle.

2 To obtain very thin clay, roll it through the machine few times.

Skinner Blend

1 Flatten with a roller (or pasta machine) the three clay colors you wish to use for your color blend, in 2/25" thick (2mm) sheets. Go over with the roller to join the colors between them.

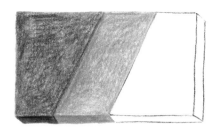

2 Fold the sheet in half and flatten it with the machine to obtain the same surface as before. Repeat the process about ten times to obtain an evenly graduated blend.

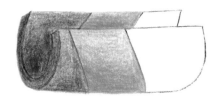

3 Stretch the sheet with the machine to 7" to 13" long (20–35cm), depending on the quantity of clay used and the creation, and then fold it into pleats.

4 Depending on the cane you are creating, you will be able to flatten the pleats after landing it on its edge, to create some sheets to insert in a millefiori (see later)...

... or compacting it to give a cylindrical shape and wrap it with a strip of clay to hold it.

Colors and Patterns

Color Mixing

The colors are miscible, so only a good kneading is necessary to obtain new, uniform shades.

Here is a green from a blue and yellow mix.

Pattern Imprint

It's possible to create texture, or relief, on the bead's surface with the help of stamps, but you can also use anything that has relief: buttons, shoe sole, textile, metal grids, rice grain, etc.

You can create your own stamp by taking an imprint of the desired relief from a piece of leftover clay and baking it.

Millefiori

1 Start with superimposing different color sheets.

2 Flatten with a roller.

3 Cut the sides to obtain a regular sheet.

4 Cut into sections.

5 Superimpose again.

Repeat steps 1 to 5 as many times as desired. As an example, this pattern will be used to make an angel's body (see picture p. 15).

The Canes

A "cane" is principally built with some thin sheets and logs. It allows for creating a pattern in the mass that will not disappear with rubbing. From a cane, identical beads can be cut for a set of jewels.

By stretching a cane by hand or with a roller, the pattern is reduced and it becomes a delicacy impossible to realize with a brush or a pencil.

Cover a Log with Sheets

1 Create a sheet the same width as the log to cover. Cut the side of the sheet diagonally.

2 Turn the sheet, place the log on the on the bevel edged side and wrap.

3 Unroll a bit to see the print of the bevel-edged side on the sheet, and then cut diagonally on this mark.

4 Close the sheet again and roll the log to mesh the elements together, but be careful not to use a lot of pressure. Continue by adding the desired amount of sheets.

Example of a Cane

1 Start with a sketch of the pattern using simple shapes. Inscribe this pattern in a circle or square, depending on the required shape of the sections.

2 Draw these shapes in perspective: it helps to visualize their layout in three dimensions.

3 Create each of the shapes of the pattern: two blue logs in a teardrop shape wrapped with a thin black sheet; a yellow log wrapped with a thin blue sheet; a black log wrapped with a thin blue sheet; and a log "millefiori" (see p. 13), cone-shaped, wrapped with a blue and then a black sheet.

4 Assemble the pattern elements.

5 Shape and cut some small black logs the same length as the patterns.

6 Fill the space between the pattern elements with the help of the thin logs. Tighten them all together.

7 Finish with some black sheets to obtain the desired shape, here a square, and let it stand in a cool place (fridge) for a few hours before stretching it.

8 To stretch a cane, press it between the fingers to elongate the pattern while keeping the square shape of the frame.

9 Continue to stretch by flattening each side of the square section with a roller.

10 Finish by using your fingers.

11 Cut the cane in slices after removing the ends, which were deformed by the pressure.

Piercing the Beads

To create the beads, the clay needs to be pierced all the way through before baking. It is necessary to consider the final design of the piece before piercing the beads, as this will determine the placement of the holes. In a same way, the thickness of the link used will determine the thickness of the holes. For the piercing, needles, toothpicks, skewers, etc. can be used.

Place the piercing tool on one side of the bead and an index finger at the desired exit point on the other side. Using the piercing tool, start to bore through the bead, carefully directing it toward the index finger's exit mark; again, do not use too much pressure.

Remove the tool before the bead is pierced completely, flip it over, and push the tool through to perforate the bead from end to end. To cover an undesirable hole, gently rub the bead surface with a fingernail.

Curing

See "Precaution of Use," p. 6

1 Preheat the oven to 130°C.

2 Place the items to bake on an oven tray covered with foil or sulfurized paper.

3 Put the tray in the oven and bake for 20 to 30 minutes, depending on the item's size.

4 Once cooked, place the items in water to harden them and cool them down.

Tip!
To accentuate the color contrasts and transparency effects, dip the items in ice-cold water or directly into ice.

Coming out of the oven, the items are still supple. The hardening will be definitive only after cooling.

Ring supports, brooches, earring clips, glass and metal beads, wool, leather cords, etc. can go in the oven without problem at this temperature.

Sanding and Buffing

Polishing items gives them an incomparable finish. By removing any ruggedness, an extremely smooth surface is achieved. The "plastic" effect of the polymer clay is also reduced. Depending on the roughness that is to be smoothed, use sand paper of 400 to 1200, finishing with the finest grain.

1 Smooth and buff the piece with very fine sand paper.

2 Wet the paper using water with a bit of soap added to it and then polish with a soft cloth.

Varnishing

1 Hold the items to be varnished with the help of pliers or a cloth peg.

2 Using a clean brush, cover with one coat of varnish.

3 Dry per the manufacturer's instructions. For the cleaning of the brush, use an adapted thinner (acetone for example).

Tip!
To varnish beads, you can string them on a stretched thread.

Then block a bead by slightly inserting a piercing tool in the hole of the suspended bead.

Turn the tool with one hand, rotating the bead, and varnish with the other.

When finished, push the varnished bead along the thread and move on to the next one.

Set Up

This is the last step: The display of the beads! You can use all sorts of threads to create jewelry (see material, p. 8–9). The beads made from polymer clay will be enhanced by additional elements: beads made of glass, rock, crystal, stone, pearl, metals, wood, etc.

Fitting a Clasp with Crimp Beads

This set up is suitable for wire, nylon, or copper thread. After the last bead, thread a crimp bead through the string and pass the string through the clasp. Next, thread the string through the crimp bead again, in the opposite direction now, and through some of the other beads. To finish, crush the crimp bead with flat-nosed pliers and cut off the excess thread.

Opening and Closing a Ring

With the help of two pliers, open the ring by pulling one of the ring ends toward you and the other in the opposite direction. Close the ring with the opposite movement.

Mounting Beads on Wire and Headpins

After inserting a headpin or wire into a bead, cut the excess, leaving a 1/5" (6mm) allowance, and form a loop at one end with the round-nose pliers for the headpin, and a loop at each end for the wire.

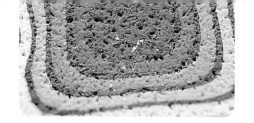

Nautilus

Creation of Beads

Material

CLAY

- Sahara beige (soft 70): 3/8 block
- Chocolate (classic 77): 1/4 block
- Black (classic 9): 1/4 block
- Translucent (soft effect 014): 3 x 1/6 block
- Nacre (soft effect 08): 1/16 block
- Green leaf (classic 57): 1/16 block
- Terracotta (classic 74): 1 rice grain
- Ochre (classic 17): 1 rice grain

FINDINGS

Necklace

1 choker
1 ring (3/10" or 8mm)
3 jump rings (1/5" or 4mm)
1 headpin
2 eyepins

Brooch

1 brooch support (length = 1" or 2.5cm)
2 jumprings (1/5" or 4mm)
2 headpins
1 eyepin

Hair Barrette

1 support for flat hairclip
2 jumprings (1/5" or 4mm)
2 headpins
1 eyepin

OTHER MATERIALS

Grey sand
Metallic wires for piercing
Extra strong glue

"Snail" Beads

1 Take the 3 parts of translucent (3 x 1/6 block). Mix the first to a rice grain-sized piece of terracotta, the second to a chocolate one, and the third to an ochre one. Add a pinch of sand to each mix.

2 Shape a log from each mix (1/2" or 1.5cm) and wrap it with the black. Give them a rectangular shape and stretch them to a length of 1–4/5" (4.5cm) by 2/5" (1cm) of width.

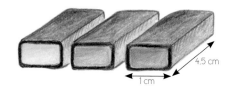

3 Using 1/8 of the chocolate block mixed with a rice grain-sized piece of black clay, make strips of 4/5" by 2–4/5" (2x7cm), with a thickness of 1/25" (1mm), and then make identical strips with 1/8 of a Sahara beige block. Stack them, alternating the colors, to obtain a millefiori (see Introduction p. 13) and cut eight sections of 1/2" (1.5cm).

4 Mix 1/16 of the chocolate block with 1/6 of the nacre and a rice grain-sized piece of black clay, then flatten it into a strip of 1/2" x 4-7/10" (1.5 x 12cm). Cut three sections of 1/2" (1.5cm) from each log created in Step 2. Assemble them on the strip, alternating them with seven sections of millefiori. Reduce the height of the last few sections and add the rest of the millefiori.

5 Create a thin strip, 1/2" (1.5cm) wide, with 1/16 of the Sahara beige block and another of the same size with a chickpea of the black. Position the black strip on top of the Sahara beige one, and then position both beneath the previously assembled strip.

6 Roll into a spiral starting with the sloped part and finish by adding some Sahara beige (1/16 of the block). Let the cane set in a cool area.

7 Stretch the cane to reduce it to 1-1/5" diameter (3cm). Cut two 1/5" (5mm) slices, and from them remove the Sahara beige section placed previously in Step 6. Pierce the two "snails."

8 Continue to stretch the cane to obtain a square section of 1/2" (1.5cm) across. Cut three 1/5" (5mm) slices and pierce them.

"Spiral" Beads

1 Flatten 1/8 of the Sahara beige block and a 1/16 of the green leaf block in sheets (thickness 2/25" or 2mm). Arrange them diagonally and join together with the roller. Flatten with a machine to obtain a thin sheet, fold it in half, and pass through the machine again. Repeat about ten times to obtain a blend (see Introduction p. 12).

2 Stretch the sheet to 8-3/5" long (22cm) with the machine. Fold it to obtain a regular strip 1-1/5" wide (3cm).

3 cm

3 With 1/8 of the chocolate block, make a similar sheet. Place it on top of the blended color strip. Roll into a spiral, starting with the green side. Let the cane set in a cool area.

4 Stretch the cane to obtain a square section of 4/5" (2cm) across. Cut four slices of 1/5" (5mm) and pierce them. Press them (without rubbing) against coarse sanding paper (60) to texturize them with little holes.

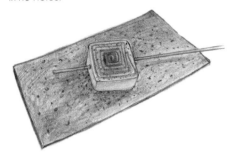

5 Bake the beads after removing the wires. Once cooled down, proceed to the sanding and buffing (see Introduction p. 16). Only varnish the snail-shaped beads.

Assembly

Necklace

Mount a square "snail" bead onto a headpin, and the big round "snail" bead and "spiral" bead on eyepins. Link them together with some jumprings, and attach this combined piece to a 3/10" (8mm) ring with a jumpring. Thread the trinket on the choker

Brooch

Mount a square "snail" bead and big round "snail" bead onto a headpin, and a "spiral" bead onto an eyepin. Link them together with the jumprings. Glue the brooch pad to the back of the big "snail" bead.

Barrette

Mount two "spiral" beads onto headpins and a square "snail" bead onto an eyepin. Link them together with the jumprings and glue the hair clip pad to the back of one of the "spiral" beads.

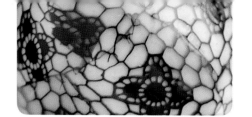

Lace

Creation of Beads

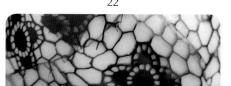

Material

CLAY

- [ ] White (classic 0): 1-1/2 block
- [ ] Translucent (soft effect 014): 1 block
- [x] Lilac (classic 6): 3/4 block
- [x] Black (classic 9): 2/3 block
- [x] Turquoise (classic 32): 1/2 block

FINDINGS (SILVER)

Necklace

3-3/5" (110cm) black ribbon (width 1/25" or 1cm)

1 clasp

2 elongated jumprings

2 flat end crimps

Long necklace

4-1/5" (130cm) fine ball chain

1 fancy box clasp (2 loops)

4 jumprings (Ø=1/10")

4 end caps

OTHER MATERIAL

Metal wires for piercing

Toothpick

The Cane

1 Shape a log with 1/4 of the black block, and then another with 1/4 of the translucent blocks. Wrap the latter with a chickpea-sized piece of the black.

2 Stretch the bicolor log to reduce its diameter to 1/10" (3mm). Cut this into sections one at a time to surround the black log. Wrap the assemblage with a chickpea-sized piece of the black.

3 Stretch the cane to have 1-1/5" (3.5cm) of usable patterns and divide it in 3 equal sections. Cut 2 of these sections vertically. With a finger, press concave the cut side of the half-logs, and assemble them around the one that remained undivided.

4 Shape a log with the rest of the translucent block and wrap it with the remainder of the black block. Stretch it to reduce it diameter to 3/10" (7mm). Cut about thirty sections the same height as your pattern. Cut one of them in four vertically, and use these pieces to fill the gaps in the pattern where the curves meet.

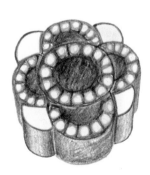

5 Arrange the other log from Step 1 around the pattern. Stretch the rest of the log from Step 2 to 2/25" (2mm) of diameter and divide it into sections to fill in the external gaps of the pattern. Let the cane set in a cool place, and then stretch it to obtain a square section 2/5" (1cm) across.

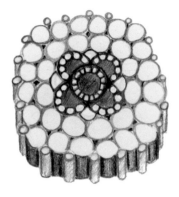

The Beads

1 Divide the turquoise clay in four to shape 4 balls, the lilac in six to shape 6 balls, and the white in eleven to shape 11 balls.

2 Cover the beads with wafer-thin slices of cane. Be sure to avoid any overlap (otherwise cut the surplus with your blade). Thoroughly roll the balls before flattening them into large, oblong pellets. Pierce them with a wire and enlarge the holes with a toothpick.

3 Bake the pellets. Once they have cooled, proceed to the sanding, buffing, and varnishing steps (see Introduction p. 16).

Assembly

Necklace

Thread 7 white beads, 6 lilacs, and 2 turquoises on the black ribbon, making a knot between each. Finish by placing a flat end crimp to each end of the ribbon. Link the flat end crimps to the clasp with the jumprings.

Long Necklace

Thread a white bead and 2 turquoises on a chain length of 1-3/5" (50cm) and 3 white beads on a 2-3/5" length (80cm). Place an end cap to each end of the chain and link them to the clasp with the jumprings.

Koï

Creation of Beads

Reserve the clay leftovers as you go along. They can be used to create base sheets and the inside of beads.

"Lily Pad" Cane

1 Shape a log 3/5" (1.5cm) in height with the green leaf and divide it into 8 unequal sections. Remove one section.

2 With one pellet of black and white each, create two very thin strips, 3/5" x 5" (1.5x13cm). Overlay them and cut 6 parts of 1/5" (5mm). Insert them in the ridges between the pieces. With the rest, wrap the leaf.

3 Flatten the removed green section with a roller and make a 3/5" (1.5cm) wide strip. Wrap the leaf with it.

4 Wrap again with the white sheet, then the black, and replace the missing wedge with some of the black. Wrap the assemblage with a last strip of black, and let the cane set in a cool area.

"Fish" Cane

1 Crumble the red, orange, turquoise, and 1/8 of the white. Shape a block without mixing the colors too much. Divide in two. With one half, shape the fish body 3/5" thick (1.5cm). With the other, form a cube.

Material

Clay
- Green leaf (classic 57): 1/8 block
- Black (classic 9): 2 blocks
- White (classic 0): 3/8 block
- Red (classic 2): 1/8 block
- Orange (classic 4): 1/8 block
- Turquoise (classic 32): 1/8 block
- Gold (soft 11): 1/16 block

Findings

Pendant
1-3/5" (50cm) craft bead wire
1" (30cm) tubular rubber cord (Ø=2/25" or 2mm)
1 lobster clasp
1 ring (Ø=1/25" or 1cm)
2 crimp bead
2 little jumprings
4 little red beads (Ø=1/5" or 4mm)
2 orange tube-shaped glass beads (length=4/5" or 2cm)
4 flat tinted glass beads (length=7/10" or 1.8cm)

Pearl Necklace
1-3/5" (50cm) craft bead wire
4" (10cm) tubular rubber cord (Ø=2/25" or 2mm)
1 lobster clasp
1 ring (Ø=1/25" or 1cm)
2 crimp beads
2 little jumprings
6 flat tinted glass beads (length=4/5" or 2cm)
4 cylinder tinted resin beads (Ø=1/25" or 1cm)
8 little red beads (Ø=1/5" or 4mm)

Brooch
1 brooch pad (length=1" or 2.5cm)

Other material
Metallic wires for piercing
Cotton buds and extra strong glue

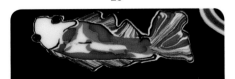

2 Shape the head with 1/8 of the white block (3/5" or 1.5cm thick). Carve out the eyesocket with a cotton bud. With a pea-size ball of the black and the white, make two very thin strips, 3/5" wide (1.5cm). Overlay them and roll into a spiral (Ø=1/5" or 4mm), with the white on the outside. Stretch the spiral to 1-1/5" (3cm) and cut in half. Position the eyes.

3 With 1/6 of the white and the black blocks, make two very thin strips 3/5" x 9-4/5" (1.5x25cm) with the machine. Overlay them, using the strip to surround the head. Split the body in half and insert some of the strip. Attach the head to the body, and surround the body with the bicolor strip.

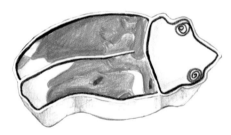

4 Flatten the multi-color cube from Step 1 to obtain a 1/2" x 2" rectangle (4x5cm). Cover with a gold sheet and then a white one.

5 Stretch out the rectangle double its length, divide in two, and overlay. Do it 3 times to obtain a 1-1/5" x 1/2" block, 3/5" thick (3x4cm, 1.5cm). Divide again and reserve one section. Divide the other section into two parts and overlay both parts with a cavity in the middle for the tail.

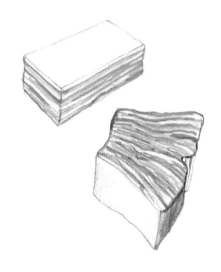

6 Divide the section reserved in Step 5 in 3 parts of 2/5" x 2/5", 3/5" thick (1x1cm, 1.5cm). Cut them diagonally to make 6 fins and position 3 on each side of the body. Attach the tail. Wrap the fish (except for the head) with the black and white strip.

7 Surround the fish with some black pieces to shape a rectangular cane, starting with the spaces between the fins. Let your cane set in a cool area.

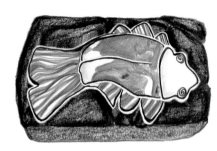

Stretching of the Canes

Stretch the "lily pad" cane to reduce its diameter to 2/5" (1cm), cut it in half, and stretch one section to 1/5" diameter (5mm). Stretch the "fish" cane to reduce the rectangle length to 1-2/5" (3.5cm). Divide it into two bands. Stretch one half to reduce it to 4/5" (2cm). Divide it in two again and stretch one half to reduce it to 3/10" (1.2cm).

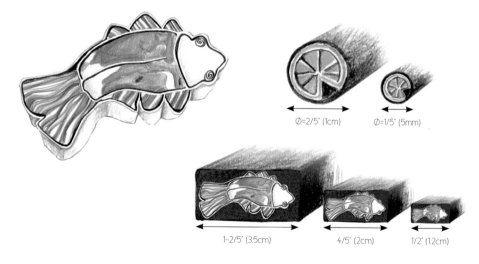

The Pendant and Brooch

1 Divide the remainder of the black into three. Flatten one section into a 5-1/2" x 4" sheet, 1/25" thick (14x10cm, 1mm). Cut some very thin cane slices and arrange them on sheet, starting with the bigger patterns. Trim their outlines so that they interlock and overlap. Flatten with a roller.

3 Divide the pattern sheet into two rectangles of 2-1/2" x 2-1/5" (6.5x5.5cm) for the pendant and 1-4/5" x 1-1/2" (4.5x4cm) for the brooch. Place the top of the pattern for the pendant on the base sheet, 1/5" (6mm) above the wire. Remove the wire and join the sheets without crushing the groove. Do the same for the brooch, but without the groove. Cut the edges straight.

2 From the canes, cut some very thin pattern slices and press them onto the black beads. Trim the outlines again if needed to interlock them. Roll the beads well so that the pattern ingrains without thickness. Pierce the beads with a wire.

The Beads

2 For the base sheets, spread 2 blocks worth of leftovers into a 4-3/10" x 2-4/5" sheet, 1/10" thick (11x7cm, 2.5mm). Mark the groove in which the craft bead wire will run by pressing a piercing tool into the clay with a roller. Leave the wire in place.

1 With the leftover clay, shape a log 2-2/5" long (6cm). Divide into sections: 1 of 4/5" (2cm), 2 of 1/2" (1.5cm), 4 of 2/5" (1cm), and 2 of 1/5" (0.5cm). Shape them into balls. Divide the remaining black from Step 1 "pendant" and "brooch" steps in the same proportions as above. Wrap each ball in black and roll them well.

3 Bake the beads and the sheets after removing the wires. Once cooled, proceed to the sanding, buffing, and varnishing steps (see Introduction p. 16).

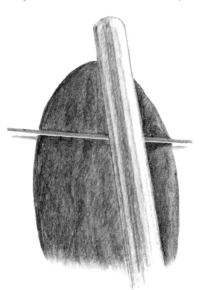

Assembly

Pendant

1 Thread the sheet on the craft bead wire and then, on each side, one red bead, one in tinted glass, one orange, 6" (15cm) of rubber Buna cord, one tinted glass bead, and a red one.

2 Make a loop at each end of the wire. Slip on a jump ring and position a crimp bead. Link each ring to a part of the clasp.

Bead Necklace

Thread the biggest bead on the craft bead wire and then, on each side, one cylindrical bead between 2 little red beads. Next, thread 4 beads, from medium to small, alternating with the glass ones. Finish with 2" (5cm) of rubber Buna cord between 2 red beads. Next, proceed as Step 2 opposite.

Brooch

Glue the back of the sheet to the brooch pad.

Graphic

Creation of Beads

M a t e r i a l

CLAY

- ■ Turquoise (classic 32): 1/2 block
- □ Translucent (soft effect 014): 1/2 block
- □ White (classic 0): 2/3 block
- ■ Green (classic 5): 1/8 block
- ▨ Golden yellow (classic 15): 1/8 block
- ■ Orange (classic 4): 1/16 block

FINDINGS (COPPER)

Pendant

19-1/2" (50cm) craft bead wire
1 barrel clasp
2 jumprings (3mm)
2 crimp beads
22 white "cat eyes" beads (3mm)
3 white "cat eyes" beads (1.2cm)
2 metallic green beads (4mm)
2 metallic green beads (8mm)

OTHER MATERIAL

Metallic wires for piercing

Reserve 1/4 of the white block for the white beads.

The Cane

1 Shape a log 1/2" long (1.5cm), 3/10" wide (1cm) from 1 chickpea-sized of the turquoise. Wrap it with strips 2/25" thick (2mm) of the white, orange, and then white again. Mix the green, yellow, and 1/4 of the white block. Wrap with a green strip. Finish with a thinner white sheet. Let the cane set in a cool area before stretching it to reduce its diameter to 3/10" (8mm).

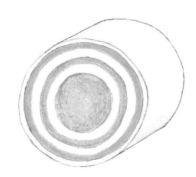

2 Take the white block reserved at the beginning and divide it in four to shape 4 balls.

3 Mix the rest of the green mix with 1/4 block of the translucent, and the rest of turquoise with 1/4 of the translucent block. Divide each color into four and shape 8 balls.

4 Cut some thin cane slices and arrange them on the beads. Roll well to join the patterns and to smooth them over.

5 Roll 2 green beads and a white and a blue into a capsule shape to elongate them. Stretch the ends until pointed and roll these to round them off. Pierce the beads with a wire.

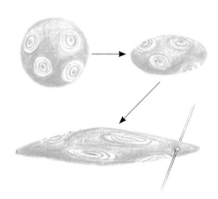

6 Bake the beads after removing the wires. Once cooled, proceed to the sanding, buffing, and varnishing steps (see Introduction p. 16).

Assembly

Thread the beads as in the picture. Next, add a jumpring to each end, fold the wire, and place a crimp bead. Link the jumprings to the clasp.

Go Fish!

Creation of Beads

Material

CLAY

■ Black (classic 9):
1 block + 1 pellet

☐ White (classic 0): 1/2 block

■ Ochre (classic 17): 1/4 block

☐ Translucent (soft effect 014):
1/8 block

FINDINGS (SILVER)

Necklace
60" (150cm) serpentine chain
1 lobster clasp
1 ring (1cm)
2 elongated jumprings
2 end caps
7 crimp beads
3 crystal faceted beads (1.2cm)

Earrings
2 fishhook earwires
4/5" x 4" (2x10cm) serpentine chain
2 elongated jumprings
4 crimp beads
2 end caps
2 crystal faceted beads (1.2cm)

OTHER MATERIAL
Metallic wires for piercing
Toothpick

1 Make 5 sheets 1-1/2" x 1-1/5" in size and 2/25" thick (4x3cm, 2mm): 2 whites (1/8 block), one translucent (1/16 block), one mix of white and ochre (1/16 block each), and one with the remaining ochre. Stack them as per the diagram.

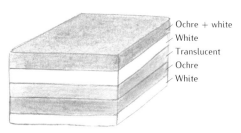

Ochre + white
White
Translucent
Ochre
White

2 Stretch the stack with a roller to 3-1/2" long (9cm). Cut in half and overlay the two sections. Repeat, and stretch the stack again to 2" (5cm).

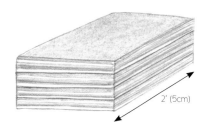

2" (5cm)

3 Cut in half once again and put one section aside for the body. Trim the edges of the other section straight and divide into two unequal parts. Superimpose them and trim into a pyramidal shape.

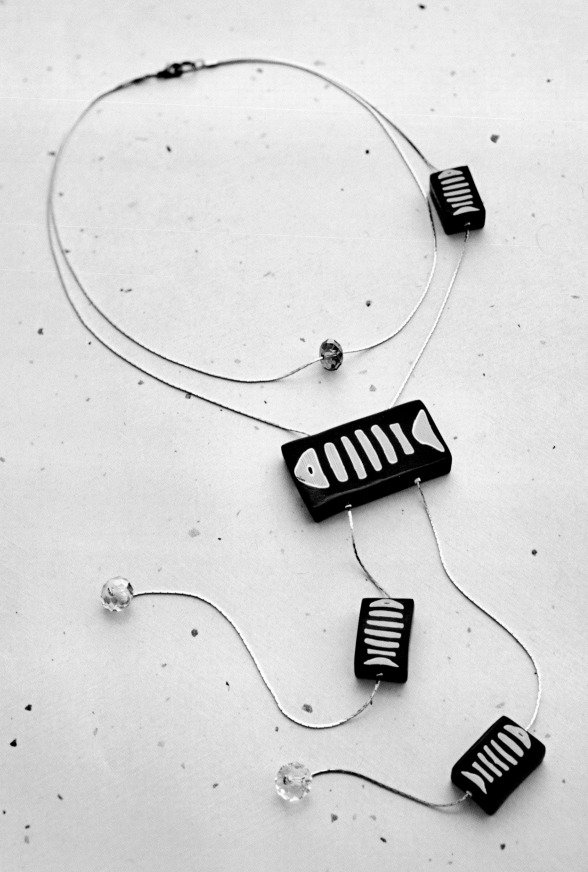

4 For the fish eye, shape a little log 1/5" long (5mm) from a black pellet and wrap it with white.

5 Cut the pyramid into two sections, and then cut one of them vertically. With a toothpick, dig a groove into the base to insert the eye and close the pyramid.

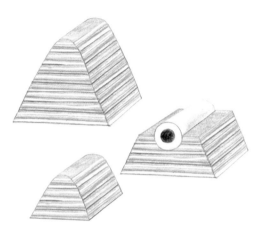

6 Curve the other section to make the fish tail. With 1/8 of white, make a sheet to surround the two sections.

7 Take the section set aside in Step 3 and stretch it with a roller to 2-2/5" long (6cm). Wrap it with a white strip and then a translucent one. Wrap the other two sections with translucent as well.

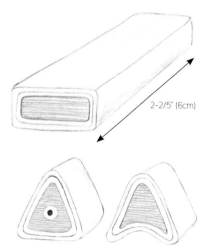

2-2/5" (6cm)

8 Cut 8 sections from the long block for the fish body. Adjust their width so that the body is rounded. With 1/8 of black block, make a long strip 3/50" thick (1.5mm) and the same width as the heights of the fish parts. Wrap each item with it.

9 Add some black around the fish to create a rectangular cane. Fill in the spaces with some little logs. Let the cane set in a cool area.

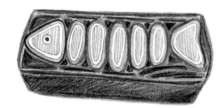

10 Stretch the cane to reduce the pattern to 2-1/5" long (5.5cm). Cut a 1/5" (6mm) slice for the big necklace bead. For the small beads, stretch the cane to reduce the pattern to 1" long (2.5cm) and cut 5 sections of 2/5" (1cm).

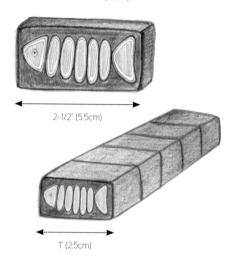

2-1/2" (5.5cm)

1" (2.5cm)

11 Pierce the little beads vertically through their length and the big bead in its width in two parts.

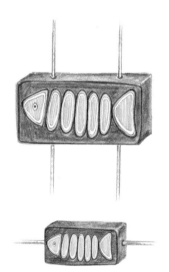

12 Bake the beads after removing the wires. Once cooled, proceed to the sanding, buffing, and varnishing steps (see Introduction p. 16).

Assembly

Necklace

1 Thread the big bead on two chains 19-1/2˝ long (50cm). Support the bottom of it with 2 crimp beads. Thread a smaller bead above the big bead and two underneath it. Block them in the same way. Add a crystal bead at the bottom of each chain and block them.

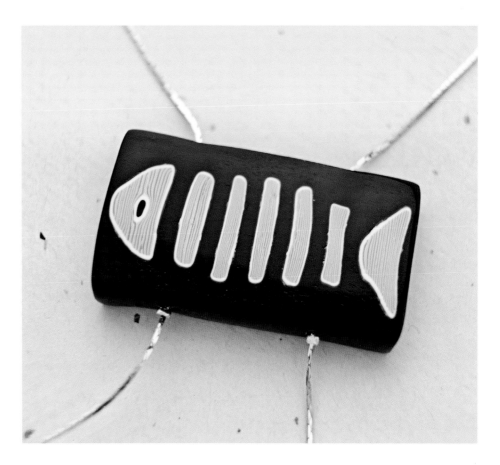

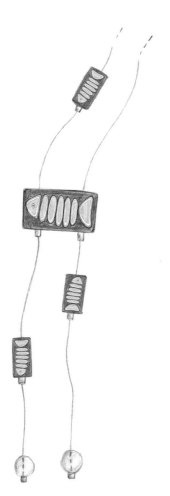

2 Thread the third crystal bead in the middle of a new chain 19-1/2˝ long (50cm). Place an end cap at the end of the chain and link the clasp elements with the jumprings.

Earrings

Thread a little bead on each 4˝ (10cm) chain and block it with a crimp bead. Add a crystal bead at the bottom and block it the same way. Insert the other end of the chain in an end cap. Link it to the ear wire with a ring.

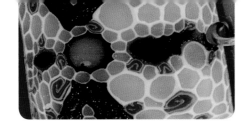

Dragonfly

Creation of Beads

Material

CLAY

- ☐ Translucent (soft effect 014): 1.75 block
- Sahara Beige (soft 70): 1/4 block
- Burgundy (classic 23): 1/4 block
- Metallic sapphire blue (soft effect 38): 1/8 block + 1 chickpea
- ☐ White (classic 0): 1/8 block
- ☐ Nacre (soft effect 08): 1/8 block
- Turquoise (classic 32): 1/16 block
- Black (classic 9): 1/16 block
- Magenta (classic 21): 1 chickpea

FINDINGS

Necklace

19-1/2" (50cm) serpentine chain
2 end caps
1 lobster clasp
1 ring (3/10" or 8mm)
2 little jumprings (1/10" or 3mm)
18 rings (1/2" or 5mm)
12 metal square beads (1/5" width or 4mm)
5 metal round beads (7mm)

(Continued on p. 38)

"Dragonfly" Cane

1 Mix 1/8 block of the translucent with 1/16 of the blue sapphire (mix A). Next, mix 1/16 of the turquoise block with 1/16 of the blue sapphire (B), and then mix 1/16 of the black block with 1 chickpea-size of the blue sapphire (C).

2 Shape two logs using 1/8 of the translucent block. Wrap one with half of mix A and stretch to 8-1/5" long (21cm). Wrap the other with one-third of B, and stretch to the same dimensions.

3 With the rest of A, make a 1-2/5" x 5-1/2" sheet, 1/25" thick (3.5x14cm, 1mm). With the rest of B, make a 1-2/5" x 2-3/4" sheet (3.5x7cm), and then with 1/16 of the translucent block make a 1-2/5" x 2-3/4" sheet (3.5x7cm) one.

4 Divide each log into 6 sections of 1-2/5" (3.5cm). Cut some 1-2/5" (3.5cm) squares in each sheet. Stack everything as shown in the diagram below.

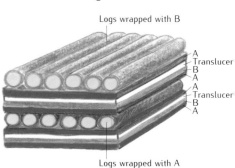

Logs wrapped with B

A
Translucent
B
A
A
Translucent
B
A

Logs wrapped with A

5 Flatten with a roller and trim the edges straight. Divide into two and superimpose the two parts. Pinch the sides to obtain an oblong shape and wrap it with a thin sheet created with half of C.

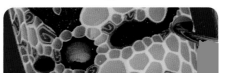

Bracelet

6-3/10" (16cm) serpentine chain

2 end caps

1 lobster clasp

2 little jumprings (1/10" or 3mm)

6 rings (1/5" or 5mm)

3 rings (3/10" or 8mm)

20 metal square beads
(1/5" width or 4mm)

5 metal round beads (3/10" or 7mm)

Cufflinks

2 cufflinks pads

OTHER MATERIAL

Metal wires for piercing

Extra strong glue

6 Stretch the cane to 2-2/5" long (6cm) and divide into 4 sections (between 2/5" and 3/5" thick, 1–1.5cm). Stretch them, pressing one side to create the wings.

7 With a chickpea of C, shape a log the same height as the wings. Wrap it with translucent. Make another one with one chickpea of translucent wrapped with C. Shape the rest of C in drop and bind with translucent.

"Alveolus" Background

1 Mix 1/4 of the Sahara beige block with 1/8 of the nacre and 1/8 of the white (D). Mix 1/4 of D with 1 chickpea of magenta (E). Finally, mix half of E with a chickpea of burgundy (F).

2 Make some 1/25" thick (1mm) sheets. With 1/4 of the translucent block, make a 4/5" x 7" (2x18cm) sheet. Next, make three sheets of 4/5" x 2-2/5" (2x6cm): one with E, one with F, and one with a chickpea of burgundy. Cut the translucent into three 2-2/25" (6cm) sections and stack everything as in the diagram shown.

3 Flatten half the length with a roller and wrap altogether in a spiral. Shape one translucent block into a log and wrap with D. Stretch both to reduce their diameter to 1/5" (4mm).

4 Fill the spaces around the dragonfly with sections from the two logs. Adjust their diameter, stretching them again to fill the smaller gaps, thus creating a rectangular background. Let the cane set in a cool area.

Cane Stretching and Bead Creation

1 Stretch the cane into a 4/5" square (2cm) section. Cut 13 slices, 2/25" thickness (2mm). For the necklace pendant, superimpose 3 slices on top of each other. Next, superimpose the remaining 10 next to each other. Go over with a roller to join them together.

2 With 1/8 of the burgundy, mold a 1/10" wide strip, 2/25" thick (3mm, 2mm). Cut them lengthways and use them to "hem" the long sides. Go over with the roller again and separate the 10 superimposed beads.

3 With the wires, pierce two holes in the pendant sheet and one hole in each of the 10 beads. Bake the items after removing the wires. Once cooled, proceed to the sanding, buffing, and varnishing steps (see Introduction p. 16).

Assembly

Necklace

Set up one set of 3 rings (1/5" or 5mm) on each "dragonfly" bead and two sets of 3 rings on the pendant. Thread the pendant, and then the beads symmetrically, as in the diagram. Position an end cap at each end of the chain and link them to the clasp with the jumprings.

Bracelet

Set up one 3/10" (8mm) ring and one 1/5" (5mm) ring on 2 "dragonfly" beads and two 1/5" (5mm) rings on 2 other "dragonfly" beads. Thread the beads, alternating them regularly. Position an end cap at each end of the chain and link them to the clasp with the jumprings.

Cufflinks

Glue a bead on each cufflink pad.

Tip!
Should there be a cane length leftover, you can thread beads on a long necklace in some burgundy fashion wool.

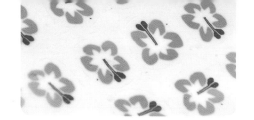

Hibiscus

Cane Creation

M a t e r i a l

CLAY

☐ White (classic 0): 2 blocks
▦ Orange (classic 4): 1/16 block
▦ Magenta (classic 21): 1/16 block
▦ Red (classic 2):1/16 block

FINDINGS (SILVER)

Strand of Pearls
17-7/10" (45cm) craft bead wire
1 fancy clasp
2 jumprings (1/5" or 5mm)
2 crimp beads
27 red mini seed beads

Choker
1 choker
1 ring (1/2" or 1.2cm)
2 rings (3/10" or 8mm)
2 jumprings (1/5" or 5mm)
1 metal flowers charm

Earrings
2 flat pads leverback earring

Brooch
1 brooch pad (length=1" or 2.5cm)

OTHER MATERIAL

Metallic wires for piercing
Round cutters (4/5" or 2cm, 1-1/5" or 3cm, and 1-1/2" or 4cm)
Cottonballs
Extra strong glue

1 Mix 1/6 of the magenta block with 1/16 white and 1/16 of the orange block with 1/16 white. Take 1/8 of the white block. In each color, shape a log 4/5" (2cm) in height. Remove a pie slice-shaped piece from both and replace them with a white piece.

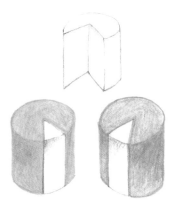

2 Divide the rest of the white log into two and wrap the colored log with them. Stretch to 2-3/4" long (7cm) and divide into 5 sections of 1/2" (1.4cm).

7 cm

3 For each flower, shape a 1/2" in height log (1/5" or 5mm) from a white pellet. With another pellet, shape a log, stretch it to 2-3/4" (7cm), and divide into 5 sections of 1/2" (1.4cm). Arrange the items as shown in the diagram.

4 Flatten a rice grain-sized red block and a little bit more white in 1-1/5" x 2/5" (3x1cm) strips. Divide the red into two and the white into three. Stack them, alternating the colors. Stretch the block to 1-1/5" long (3cm) and divide into two.

5 With a pellet-sized red block, shape a 3/5" in height log (3/10" or 8mm). Wrap it with a thin white strip and stretch to 2-2/5" (6cm). Pinch the sides to obtain an oval section and divide into 4 parts of 3/5" (1.5cm) after removing one side.

6 Make an incision in each flower between 2 petals, and insert a part of the striped strip and 2 oval sections for the stamen.

7 For each flower, take 1/8 of a white block and shape some mini logs to fill the gaps between the petals and obtain some round canes. Surround with a white strip and let it set in a cool area.

Beads and Sheets Creation

The Beads

1 Stretch the magenta cane to reduce its diameter to 2/5" (1cm) and the orange to 1/5" (6mm). With 1 white block, shape 1 log of 5-1/2" long (14cm) and divide it into 28 sections of 1/5" (5mm).

2 Roll each section into balls and on them position 2 cane slices of each color. Roll well to join together and smooth the pattern over, then pierce them.

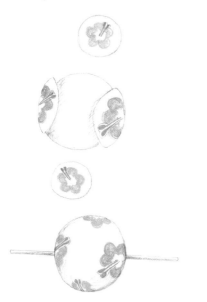

The Sheets

1 With 1 white block, make a thin-layered sheet 4" x 3" (10x8cm). Cut some thin magenta cane strips and arrange them on top of the sheet in lines. Space them by 1/5" (5mm). Smooth over with a roller. Turn the sheet over and repeat with the orange flowers with 1/10" (2.5mm) spacing.

2 With the cutters, cut from the sheet 3 oblong shapes of 1-1/2" (4cm), one of 1-1/5" (3cm), and 2 of 4/5" (2cm). Pierce one hole in two of 1-1/5" shapes with a cotton ball and two holes in two of the 1-1/2".

3 Bake the items after removing the wires. Once cooled, proceed to sanding, buffing, and varnishing steps (see Introduction p. 16).

Assembly

Bead Necklace

On the craft bead wire, thread 28 beads, alternating them with the mini red beads. Thread one jumpring at each end, fold the wire, and position a crimp bead. Link each ring to a part of the clasp.

Choker

Link 3 shapes – 2 of 1-1/2" and one of 1-1/5" (4cm or 3cm) – with the 2 rings of 3/10" (8mm). Next, link the trinket to the choker with the 1/2" (1.2cm) ring. Mount the metal flower charm between the 2 big shapes with 2 rings of 1/5" (5mm).

Earrings and Brooch

Stick the two little shapes on the earring pads and a 1-1/2" (4cm) shape on the brooch pad.

Tokyo

Cane Creation

Material

CLAY

☐ White (classic 0): 1.5 block

☐ Translucent (soft effect 014): 1 block

☐ Gold (soft 11): 1/3 block

☐ Black (classic 9): 1/3 block

☐ Dark flesh (classic 45): 1/8 block

☐ Blue (classic 37): 1/16 block

☐ Metallic blue sapphire (soft effect 38): 1/16 block

☐ Red (classic 2): 1 chickpea

☐ Magenta (classic 21): 1 pea

FINDINGS (BRONZE)

Pendant

37-1/2" (95cm) black chain
1 eyepin 2-2/5" (6cm)
2 headpins
4 jumprings (1/5" or 4mm)
2 matching blue bobbles

Necklace

19-1/2" (50cm) craft bead wire
2 x 12 Buna tubular black rubber cord (2/25" or 2mm)
1 lobster clasp
2 crimp beads
2 jumprings (1/5" or 4mm)
6 blues beads
18 red beads "coral imitation"
2 little red beads

Brooch

1 brooch pad (length=1-1/2" or 4cm)

OTHER MATERIAL

Toothpick
Metallic wires for piercing
Extra strong glue

"Flower" and "Leaf" Canes

1 Mix 1/8 of the white and magenta blocks. Reserve a half for Step 6. Mix 1/8 of the dark flesh block with a gold pea. Flatten those mixes and 1/4 of the white block into sheets of 2/25" thick (2mm) with a roller. Arrange them as shown in the diagram and join together with the roller.

2 Flatten with the machine to obtain a very thin sheet, fold in half, and then flatten with the machine again. Repeat about ten times to obtain grading (see Introduction p. 12).

3 Elongate the sheet with the machine to 11-4/5" long (30cm) and fold into 1-1/2" (4cm) pleats. Compact the accordion into a log and wrap it with a black sheet (1/16 block). Stretch the cane to 11" (28cm).

4 Mix 1/8 of the white block with a chickpea-size of the blue, a pea-size of the black, and 1 of the blue sapphire. Shape a 1" long log (3/5" or 1.5cm). Wrap it with 1/16 of the blue sapphire, white, and then black. Stretch it to 7" (18cm) and flatten one side with the roller to shape a teardrop.

5 Cut in 9 sections of 4/5" (2cm). Flatten the first cane using a mix of black and magenta with the roller and cut into 4/5" (2cm) sections. Shape the leaf of the flower (with a little rose log at the heart) and the bud.

6 Using the magenta block reserved in Step 1, shape into a log and wrap with a mix of red (1/16 block) and gold (1 pea). Next, wrap the log in black (1/16 block). Stretch to 9-2/5" (24cm), flatten with a roller, and cut into 4/5" (2cm) sections. Insert them between the petals.

7 Mix 1 translucent block with 1/8 of the gold block and 1/8 of the white block. Add bits of this mix around each of the 3 patterns to create the canes. Let them set in a cool area.

"Waves" Cane

1 Mix 1/8 of a white block with 1 chickpea of blue, 1 rice grain-size of blue sapphire, and 1 black. Divide into two and mix 2 rice grain-sized black to one of these parts. Next, divide each part into four and, taking one of the parts of each, divide into two.

2 Shape one log from a white pellet and wrap with a little part of both blues. Make 2 long thin sheets (gold and black) of the same width and superimpose them. Wrap the log with a piece of the sheet, with the black on the outside.

3 With a toothpick, mark 5 grooves into the log and then fill each of them with a thin white log.

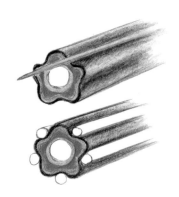

4 Wrap a part of the log with white and then the whole log with light blue, dark blue, and then the gold and black strip.

5 Repeat Steps 3 and 4. Stretch the log to 6-3/10" (16cm) and cut into 4/5" (2cm) sections. Divide each section in four lengthways and arrange them as in the diagram shown. Let it set in a cool area.

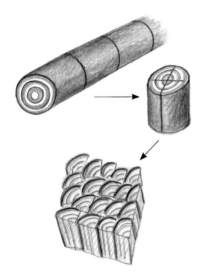

Cane Stretching

Stretch the "flower" cane to reduce its diameter to 1" (2.5cm), the "leaf" cane to 3/5" (1.5cm), and the "bud" cane to 2/5" (1cm). Next, cut the "flower" cane into two and stretch one half to obtain a smaller flower (about 3/5" or 1.5cm).

Beads and Sheets Creation

Necklace Sheet

1 Flatten 1/4 of a white block into a 4" x 4-7/10" sheet, 2/25" thick (10x12cm, 2mm), for the background.

2 Cut some wafer thin slices of each cane and create your arrangement on the background sheet. Trim their outlining edges so that the patterns interlock and the background remains concealed. Use the leftovers cut from around the patterns to fill in the gaps. Flatten regularly with a roller. From your sheet, cut a 2-4/5" x 2-4/5" square (7x7cm).

3 Cut some thin slices into the "waves" cane to create a strip of the same thickness as the sheet created in the previous two steps.

4 Gather all the leftovers. Mix them and flatten them into 2 sheets of about 1/20" thick (1.2mm), wider than the pattern. Cut off the top of one of them and position the two parts on the first one to create a groove, which will allow for the threading of the craft bead wire.

5 Position the sheet with the flowers on the background, with one covering the groove that must be situated 2/5" (1cm) from the top. Lay out a 2/25" wide (2mm) black strip underneath and then position the wave's sheet. Trim the sides straight.

6 With 1/16 of the black block, shape a long strip equal to the sheet's thickness. Position as shown in the diagram and push a metal wire into the groove to pierce the black strip, maintaining the shape with your fingers to avoid distortion.

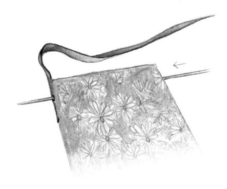

7 Remove the wire, finish the wrapping of the black strip, and reinsert the wire into the groove to pierce the other side of the strip in the same way.

8 From a rice grain–sized black, shape two slightly flattened pellets, pierce them, and position one on each of the sheet's hole.

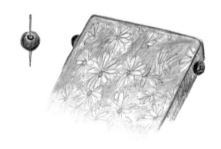

Brooch Sheet

Proceed as you did for the necklace, creating a 2-4/5" x 2-4/5" square (7x7cm) sheet with a groove, but without piercing with a wire or a double background.

Pendant Beads

1 Shape a big bead with the leftover clay and cover with the cane patterns. Roll it well so that the patterns stick and smooth them over.

2 Mold into a rectangular shape with the roller and pierce it from side-to-side with a wire.

3 Bake the items after removing the wire. Once cooled, proceed to the sanding, buffing, and varnishing steps (see Introduction p. 16).

Assembly

Necklace with Sheet

Thread the sheet onto the 19-1/2" (50cm) craft bead wire and then on each side: 3 red beads, one blue, 3 reds, and one blue. Next, thread a 4-7/10" (12cm) Buna tubular cord, followed by a small red bead, and position a crimp bead after folding the wire. Link each side to the clasp with a ring.

Pendant

1 Mount the pendant onto the wire. Link the top to a 31-1/2" (80cm) length chain with a jumpring and the bottom to 2 chains of 4" (10) and 2" (5cm) length.

2 Mount each tassel onto a headpin and link them to the end of the chain with a ring.

Brooch

Glue the brooch pad to the back of the sheet.

Ivory

Creation of Beads

1 Make 2 strips of 1–1/2" x 2–2/5" (4x6cm): a thick one with 1/4 of the translucent block and a thin one with 1/16 of the Sahara beige block. Position the translucent strip on top of the beige, divide into three lengths, and stack them to obtain a 1–1/2" x 4/5" block (4x2cm).

2 cm   4 cm

2 Flatten the block with a roller to 3" long (7.7cm) by 4/5" wide (2cm). Divide the length into 7 parts and superimpose them.

3 Divide into two in length to obtain 14 cubes. Align the blocks and squeeze one end into a slope. Make two strips with a beige pellet and a white one. Layer them underneath the alignment after tilting it.

4 Roll into a spiral, starting with the flattened side. Mix 1/2 teaspoon of brown sand to 1/4 of the translucent block to surround the snail and obtain a 1–1/2" (4cm) square cane. Let set in a cool area, and stretch to reduce its width to 1/2" (1.2cm) across.

M a t e r i a l

CLAY

Sahara beige (soft 70): 1 block

Translucent (soft effect 014): 3/4 block

White (classic 0): 3/4 block

FINDINGS (GOLD)

Necklace

4/5" x 7" (2 x 18cm) fancy gold chain

1 clasp

8 jumprings (1/5" or 4mm)

5 stems

OTHER MATERIAL

Brown colored sand

Round cutter (about 2–1/2" or 6.5cm, depending on wrist size)

Metallic wires for piercing

5 Cut a 3-7/10" (9.5cm) "snail" cane section. Make 2 blocks of the same thickness with the beige and white leftovers. Position them on each side of the section and smooth over with the roller, without pressing too hard, to join the elements together.

6 Flatten 1/4 of the translucent block into a very thin sheet double the size of the piece. Cut into two and cover each side of the piece with it. Smooth over with the roller to join the elements together.

7 Cut some very thin "snail" slices and arrange them on the translucent sheets. Without crushing it, smooth the surface on each side with the roller. Cut one 2/5" wide (1cm) slice for the necklace middle bead.

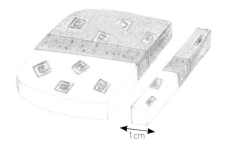

8 With the cutter, remove the center to create the bracelet. Trim the outlines to obtain a slightly rounded square.

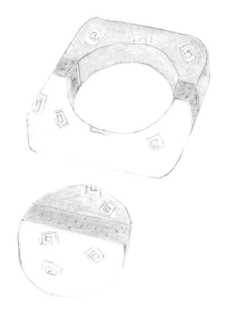

9 From the scooped out central part, cut the 4 other necklace beads. Bevel the ends of the fifth one set aside in Step 7. Pierce the 5 beads through the beige part with a wire.

10 Bake the items after removing the wire. Once cooled, proceed to the sanding, buffing, and varnishing steps (see Introduction p. 16).

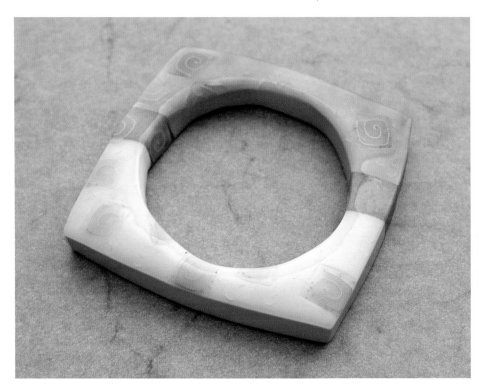

Necklace Set Up

Mount each bead on an eyepin and link together with the 4 jumprings. Link the piece to the chain and then the chain to the clasp with the other jumprings.

Patchwork

Creation of Beads

Material

CLAY

- ■ Black (classic 9): 1.25 block
- ■ Turquoise (classic 32): 2/3 block
- ■ Dark flesh (classic 45): 1/2 block
- ■ Burgundy (classic 23): 1/4 block
- ■ Leaf green (classic 57): 1/8 block
- □ White (classic 0): 1/8 block
- ■ Metallic blue sapphire (soft effect 38): 1/16 block
- ■ Gold (soft 11): 1 pea

FINDINGS (COPPER)

Pendant

4/5" x 9-4/5" (2 x 25cm)
    craft bead wire
4/5" x 8-4/5" (2 x 22.5cm)
    Buna black tubular rubber cord
1 fancy clasp
3 rings (2/5" or 1cm)
4 crimp beads
1 copper chain bobble
4 small irregular copper beads
4 rings (1/5" or 6mm)

Long necklace

33-4/5" (86cm) copper chain
8 long eyepins
    (length=2-2/5" or 6cm)
16 rings (1/5" or 6mm)

Brooch

1 brooch pad (length=1-1/2" or 4cm)

OTHER MATERIAL

Metallic wires for piercing
Cotton balls
Extra strong glue

Reserve leftover clay as you go along. They can be used to create base sheets.

Jacquard Pattern Cane

1 Mix 1/8 of the leaf green block with 1/8 of the dark flesh block. Shape a cube and trim the sides to obtain acute angles. With 1/16 of the turquoise block, use the pasta machine to create a thin strip, beveling the ends for wrapping (see Introduction p. 14). Surround with a black strip in the same way.

2 With 1/4 of the dark flesh block, shape a cube the same size as the one in Step 1. Cut into four diagonal cubes and frame the first green cube to obtain a cane 1–1/5" wide by 4/5" high (3cm x 2cm).

3 Using the leftover clay, superimpose a thin green strip and a turquoise one between 2 black strips. Cut the cane diagonally, place half the strip in the middle, and reshape the cane. Cut it again diagonally and insert the other half of the strip. Reshape the cane and let it set in a cool area.

Woven Pattern Cane

1 Mix 1/4 of the turquoise block with a pea of sapphire. Flatten half of it into a square sheet, reserving the other, and cut diagonally. Make two strips with a mix of 1/8 of the flesh and gold blocks and a strip with 1/16 of the white block. Arrange the piece per the diagram and join together with a roller.

2 Put the sheet through the machine and fold it in half to obtain the same surface as in Step 1. Repeat ten times. Fold one last time and divide its length into five.

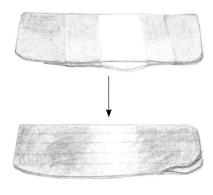

3 Stack the five strips, cut them in the middle, and then stack the two parts. Compress them to obtain a square cane 4/5" across (2cm) and then compress the longest part of the cane to stretch it the other way.

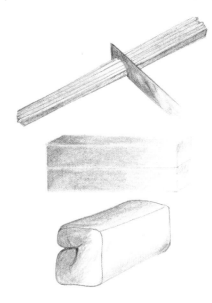

4 Divide the cane into two, lengthwise, and recreate it, with square sections making up the white parts in the middle.

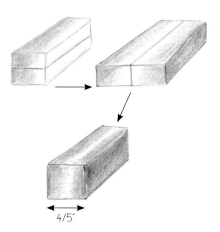

4/5"

5 Stretch the cane to 1–1/2" long (4cm) and cut it into four. Assemble the parts as per the diagram.

Spiral Pattern Cane

1 Shape a log with the blue leftovers. Wrap it in white, burgundy, white, and then with half of the green leftovers. Stretch it to 3″ long (8cm), flatten it, and roll into a spiral.

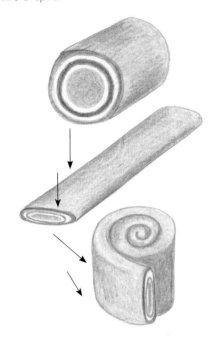

2 Stretch to about 4″ long (10cm), remove the end pieces, and cut into 4 equal sections. Assemble them into a square cane and let set in a cool area.

Patchwork Pattern Cane

With the leftovers and a pellet of the burgundy and black blocks, shape and assemble some thin logs into a square cane. Stretch and cut into four, placing them into a square cane. Let the cane set in a cool area.

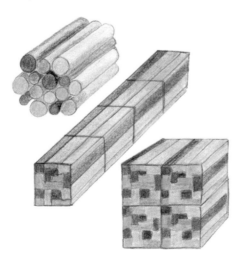

Hound's Tooth Pattern Cane

1 Shape a square cane 2/5″ x 2/5″ (1x1cm) with 1/8 of the dark flesh and burgundy blocks. Divide them in two. Take a half of each color and cut them into four diagonally. Assemble the parts to make 2 bicolor canes.

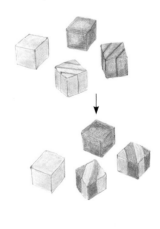

2 Assemble the 4 pieces as shown in the diagram below, and then stretch the cane. Divide it into four and assemble the pieces to obtain the Hound's tooth pattern. Let the cane set in a cool area.

Cane Stretching and Sheet Creation

1 Stretch the 5 canes to obtain sections of 2/5" (1cm) and trim the edges again. Cut 1/25" (1mm) slices and, for each pattern, align them side-by-side to form a sheet. Depending on the patterns, you will obtain different size sheets.

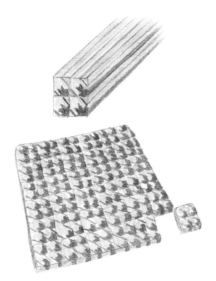

2 Use a rolling pin to smooth over and bond the elements. Cut a strip 1-2/5" wide (3.5cm) from each pattern. Reserve the leftovers to create the pendant and brooch.

Long Necklace Beads

1 Mix all the leftovers to make a 1-1/2" x 13-4/5", 2/25" thick (4x35cm, 2mm) sheet. Cut some different size pieces from some pattern strips and arrange them together, alternating and separating them with some black strips. Straighten out the sides and bevel them.

2 With some of the black block, shape a log the length of the strip. Surround it with the strip, closing the bevel end together. The diameter must correspond to about 3/10" (8mm). If the strip turns out to be too narrow, stretch the black log out to reduce it.

3 Cut this long log into eight pieces to obtain 1-1/2" long (4cm) beads. Pierce them lengthwise with a wire.

Pendant and Brooch Sheets

1 Create a base sheet 4-7/10" x 2-7/10" and 4/5" thick (12x7cm, 2mm) with the clay leftovers. Arrange the remaining patterns on it for the necklace rectangle 2-2/5" x 2-1/5" (6x5.5cm) and the brooch 1-4/5" x 2-1/5" (4.5x5.5cm). Insert some thin black strips between the necklace patterns. Go over with the roller and trim the edges. Surround the pendant with a black strip and pierce 3 holes into it using the cotton balls.

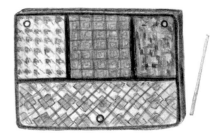

2 Bake the items after removing the wires. Once cooled, proceed to the sanding, buffing, and varnishing steps (see Introduction p. 16).

Assembly

Long Necklace

Thread each bead onto an eyepin. With the rings (1/5" or 5mm), mount a 2–2/5" long (6cm) chain piece between each bead. Finish with a 17–3/10" (44cm) chain piece.

Pendant

1 Mount a ring in each of the sheet holes, and link the trinket directly to the bottom ring.

2 Thread each craft bead wire onto a Buna tubular black cord and add an irregular copper bead to each end. Thread a crimp bead and a jumpring to the end, and fold the wire into the crimp bead.

3 Link one end to the top sheet rings and the other to a part of the clasp.

Brooch

Glue the brooch pad to the back of the sheet.

Snapshot

Creation of Beads

(Continued on p.62)

"Face" Cane with the "Z" Nose

1 For the cheeks, flatten 1/8 of a porcelain block and a mix of the magenta and dark flesh blocks. Arrange per the diagram. With a roller, smooth and join together the colors. Create a grading with the machine.

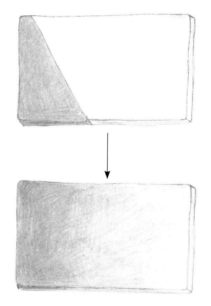

2 Roll this sheet into a 3"-long (8cm) log starting with the pinkest side so that it ends up in the middle. Divide into 6 parts of about 1/2" (1.3cm), and then put them aside.

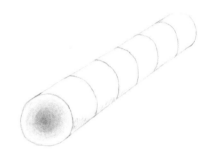

3 For the eyes, wrap a log made from a little black pea with some of the turquoise. Remove a little pie-shaped piece and replace it with some white. Wrap the log, first with some of the porcelain (1 chickpea) and then with some of the black. Stretch the log to 1-1/2" long (4cm), divide into two, and wrap the parts with some of the porcelain.

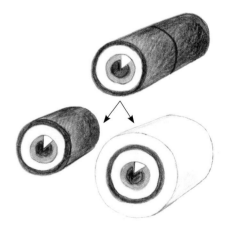

Bracelet

4/5" x 7-4/5" (2 x 20cm) bead wire
2 crimp beads
1 lobster clasp
1 ring (2/5" or 1cm)
2 faceted transparent beads with copper reflects (3/10" or 8mm)
30 irregular copper beads (1/5" or 4mm)
1 big cream bead (4/5" or 2.2cm)

Earrings

2 earwires
2 headpins
2 jumprings (1/5" or 4mm)
2 medium cream beads (3/5" or 1.7cm)
2 little metallic red beads (1/10" or 3mm)
2 flat copper beads (1/5" or 4mm)

Rings

2 rings with flat pad

Brooch

1 brooch pad (length=1" or 2.5cm)

OTHER MATERIAL

Toothpick
Metallic wires for piercing
Extra strong glue

4 For the face feature, flatten with the machine 1/8 of the black and copper blocks into thin strips of 1/2" x 6" (1.3x15cm). Superimpose them. You will probably need to make some more afterwards for assembling the face. For the eyelashes, shape a piece of the porcelain to curve around the eye. Cut it into four and insert 3 strips.

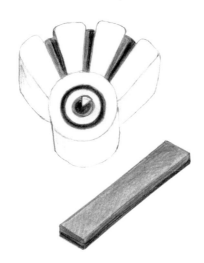

5 Arrange the eyelashes and the eye on a porcelain slice of the same thickness. Let it set in a cool area before stretching the cane to 1-1/2" long (4cm). Divide into three equal sections.

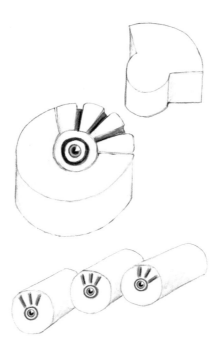

6 Put an "eye" section aside. With the two other ones, start at the top of the face by arranging two "cheek" sections below. Cut some of the black and copper strip parts in a Z shape for the nose. Add some porcelain parts and thin logs to fill in the spaces between the eyes, nose, and cheeks.

7 Shape the mouth with a mix of 1/16 of the red and one rice grain of the copper blocks. Mark out the upper lip's bow with a toothpick, and then cut the mouth in half to separate the lips, sketching a slight smile.

8 Cut 4 grooves into the upper lip and 5 in the lower lip. Cut some parts out and then flatten a little bit of the black into 1" wide (5mm) strips to insert into the grooves.

9 Surround the lips with some black and copper strips. Insert pieces of it between the lips and add a little bit of black. Enclose the mouth with some porcelain segments.

10 Let the cane set in a cool area and then stretch to 2" (5cm). Cut out a 1/5" (4mm) slice and set it aside, and then cut the cane into 3 equal sections. Position one below the base of the nose. Add a black and copper spiral strip at the corner of the lips.

11 Fill in the shape with some porcelain segments to obtain a round face. Surround the face with a black and copper strip, followed by a quite large porcelain strip.

Square Nose "Face" Cane

1 Using the "eye" and "eye + eyelash" pieces that were set aside, wrap the eye without eyelashes and trim them to the same height, if needed. For the eyebrow, add a part of the black and copper above the eye without eyelashes.

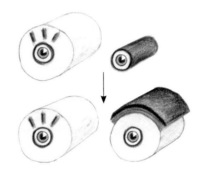

2 For the nose, shape a porcelain log into a square the same height as the eyes. Wrap it with the black and copper strip, and position it below the eyes. Add a porcelain strip around the cheeks; trim some with straight sides for each side of the nose.

3 Position the mouth. Add some porcelain segments to obtain a very round face. To finish, surround it with a black and copper strip, followed by a thick porcelain strip.

Eyes Shut "Face" Cane

1 For the shut eyes, shape a porcelain segment the same height as the mouth and the two remaining cheeks. Cut it into two dome-size pieces and position a black and copper strip on the domed half.

2 Divide the other half in six and insert some black and copper segments for the eyelashes. Reconstruct the eye. Wrap it with a porcelain strip, stretch it to 1–1/5" long (3cm), and then divide it into two.

3 Form the face like the two previous ones, positioning some of the black and copper strip for the nose.

Cane Stretching and Bead Cutting

1 After letting them set in a cool area, stretch the 3 "face" canes to 4" (10cm). Cut off the ends to obtain some very straight sections.

2 Put a 1/2" (1.5cm) slice aside for the square beads. Next, cut 7 slices of 1/5" to (5–6mm) in each cane. With a wire, pierce the beads, top to bottom, apart from the one for the ring. Pierce the mouth and set aside.

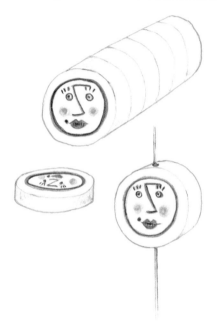

3 With the 3 face sections set aside, compose the family. Trim the sides of the faces to bring them closer. Add porcelain segments to obtain a cane with square sections.

4 Flatten 1/4 of the black block into a thin sheet. Surround the cane with one part, setting the longer part aside.

5 Spread out 1/4 of the black and porcelain blocks in sheets 1/5" thick (5mm). Cut some strips lengthwise and assemble the cane border by alternating them. Smooth with a roller. Cut some slices to surround the cane and wrap the piece with the thin black strip reserved in Step 4.

Assembly

6 Let the cane set in a cool area, and then stretch it to obtain a 1-1/5" x 1-1/5" (3x3cm) square section. Remove the edges and cut five slices 1/5" (5-6mm). Pierce the 3 bracelet beads from side to side, 1/5" (5mm) from the edge. Wrap the bead for the ring with a strip made from a mix of the red and copper.

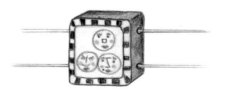

7 Bake the items after removing the wires. Once cooled, proceed to the sanding, buffing, and varnishing steps (see Introduction p. 6).

Necklace

Thread the cream beads and the faces as you like, positioning one to three smaller beads in between. On each side of the clasp, thread these beads: one faceted, 3 irregular copper, one medium cream, 3 irregular copper, one medium cream, and 3 irregular copper.

Bracelet

Mount the beads as shown in the diagram.

Earrings

On each headpin, from top to bottom, mount the following beads: a red, a medium cream, a copper flat, and a face. Link the headpin to the clasp with a ring.

Rings and Brooch

Glue the beads to their support pads.

Blossom

Cane Creation

Material

CLAY

- ☐ Translucent (soft effect 014): 1.25 block
- ■ Violet (classic 61): 1/2 block
- ■ Magenta (classic 21): 1/3 block
- ■ Orange (classic 4): 1/3 block
- ■ Leaf green (classic 57): 1/4 block
- ☐ White (classic 0): 1/4 block
- ■ Green (classic 5): 1/16 block
- ☐ Nacre (soft effect 08): 1/16 block
- ☐ Golden yellow (classic 15): 1 chickpea

FINDINGS

Choker

1 violet choker
2 tube glass bead (1/2" or 1.4cm/length=1" or 2.5cm)
2 rings (3/10" or 8mm)
1 mauve bead (3/10" or 7mm)
1 elongated green bead (length=2/5" or 1cm)
1 headpin (2-2/5" or 6cm)

(Continued on p. 68)

Leaf" Cane

1 Mix 1/16 of the green block with 1/16 of the white and 1 chickpea of the yellow (mix A). Afterwards, take 1/16 of the leaf green (B) and the nacre blocks (C).

2 With a roller, flatten colors B, C, and half of A into sheets of 2/25" thick (2mm). Arrange them as shown in the diagram, and then join together with the roller.

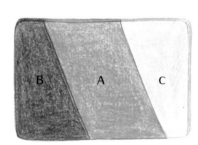

3 Put the sheet through the machine to make it very thin. Fold it in half and put it through the machine again. Repeat the process about ten times to obtain a grading (see Introduction p. 12).

4 Using the machine, elongate the sheet to 9-4/5" (25cm). Fold it over itself if necessary to obtain a 1-1/2" wide (4cm) sheet, and then fold in pleats about every 2/5" (1cm).

1-1/2" (4cm)

2/5" (1cm)

5 Position the accordion on its edge and flatten it with a roller to obtain a 4-7/10" x 1" (12x2.5cm) strip. Cut the strip into four 1-1/5" (3cm) lengths.

Long necklace

19-1/2" (50cm) silver chain

14-1/2" or 37cm (15+12+6+4) craft bead wire

4 elongated jumprings

1 ring (3/10" or 8mm)

2 eyepins (1/5" or 5-6cm)

4 crimp beads

19 elongated green beads (length=2/5" or 1cm)

Assortment of embroidery mini-beads (green, pink, red, white, etc.)

2 red beads (3/10" or 8mm)

1 orange bead (1/10" or 3mm)

1 mauve bead (3/10" or 7mm)

1 orange bead (3/10" or 7mm)

Hatpin

1 pin with clasp

1 white bead (3/10" or 7mm)

1 elongated green bead (length=2/5" or 1cm)

OTHER MATERIAL

Wooden skewers

6 Make a 3-1/2" x 1" strip, 1/25" thick (9x2.5cm, 1mm) from the following colors: second half of A, 1/16 of the translucent block and 1/16 of the leaf green block. Cut them into 1-1/15" lengths (3cm).

7 Shape the translucent into a 1" long (2.5cm) log. Wrap it with the white and leaf green and stretch to 11-4/5" (30cm) to reduce its diameter to 1/10" (3mm). Cut into 6 sections, placing them next to each other. Flatten slightly to reduce the thickness to 2/25" (2mm). Cut the sheet in two lengthwise.

8 Arrange the items as in the diagram.

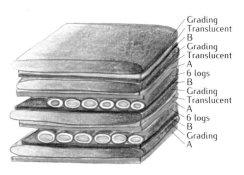

Grading
Translucent
B
Grading
Translucent
A
6 logs
B
Grading
Translucent
A
6 logs
B
Grading
A

9 Flatten this block to 1-1/2" long (4cm). Divide it into two and stack the two parts. Repeat the process over again. Compress the stack to obtain a square cane 1-1/5" (3cm) across.

10 Roll the sides to round off the section and obtain a 1-1/5" (3cm) diameter log. Wrap it partially with a very thin leaf green strip. Let the cane set in a cool area.

"Petals" Cane

1 Using a roller, flatten 1/8 of the violet, orange, and translucent blocks in 2/25" thick (2mm) sheets. Arrange them as in the diagram and join together with a roller.

2 Proceed as in Steps 3 to 5 of the "leaf" cane to create a 4" x 1–4/5" (10x4.5cm) sheet. Divide it into four 1" (2.5cm) lengths.

3 Repeat the same process with 1/8 of the violet, magenta, and translucent blocks.

4 Make a 5" x 1–4/5" strip, 1/25" thick (12.5x4.5cm, 1mm) using 1/8 of the following colors: violet, white, and translucent. Cut them into five 1" (2.5cm) lengths.

5 Shape 1/16 of a translucent block into a 1" (2.5cm) height log and wrap it with the white and magenta. Make a second one, replacing the magenta with orange. Stretch to 15–7/10" (40cm), cut into 4 equal sections, and place them next to each other, alternating the colors. Divide into four lengthwise. Flatten slightly to reduce the thickness.

6 Arrange the elements as in the diagram.

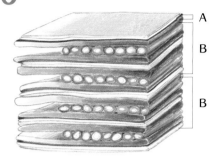

Translucent	
White	A
Violet	
Orange grading	
6 logs	
Magenta grading	
Violet	
White	
Translucent	B
Magenta grading	
6 logs	
Orange grading	
Violet	
White	
Translucent	

7 Flatten this block to 2" long (5cm). Divide it into two and stack the parts. Repeat once more, and compress the stacks into a rectangular cane 2" long (5cm).

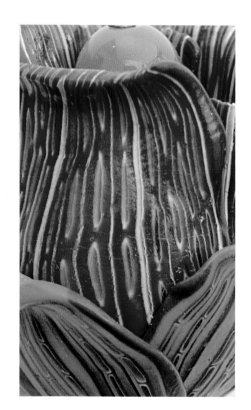

8 Pinch the sides to give an oval shape to the section. Partially wrap it with a thin violet strip. Let the cane set in a cool area.

Bead Creation

The "Big Flower"

1 Shape a ball from some of the translucent block and spear it onto a skewer. Wrap it with three thin slices cut out of the "flower" cane to closely hug the shape of the ball. Position three more petals, staggered on the firsts.

2 Cut 4 thin slices from the "leaf" cane and cover the petal base.

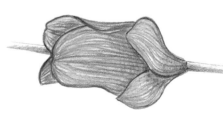

The "Two Medium Flowers"

Cut the rest of the "petal" cane into two, creating a curved edge. Reduce the "leaf" cane to 4/5" (2cm) in diameter by stretching it. Shape two translucent balls (1/8 of a block each). For each flower, cut out 8 petals and 4 leaves. Arrange them on the ball, starting with 3 petals, then 5, with 4 leaves layered over.

The "Little Flower and the Bud"

1 Shape 2 translucent balls (1/16 of a block each). Cover the first one with 3 petals and 4 leaves (the little flower) and the other with 2 batches of 3 leaves (the bud).

2 Bake the items in hanging on the skewers. Once cooled, proceed to the sanding, buffing, and varnishing steps (see Introduction p. 16). Remove the skewers.

Assembly

Choker

Mount a medium flower onto a headpin with a mauve bead at the heart and a green one above the petals. Link the flower to the choker with the 2 rings. Thread a tube bead on either side.

Long Necklace

1 Thread the big flower onto two lengths of 8-1/2" (22cm) bead wire. Stagger the wire by 4/5" (2cm) and mount the beads as shown in the diagram. Fold the craft bead wire ends above the green beads and secure with a crimp bead.

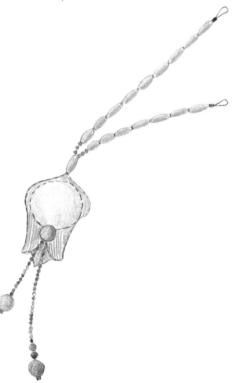

2 Mount a medium flower and a bud as shown in the diagram.

3 Link the flower and the bud to the big flower pendant using the rings (3/10" or 8mm for the flower). Next, link the pieces to the chain with two elongated jumprings.

Hatpin

Thread a white bead, the little flower, and a green bead at the end of the pin. Secure them with a drop of glue inside.

Spring

Sheet Creation

"Grass" Cane

1 Mix the green and the yellow and shape a log. Wrap it with a very thin sheet of the leaf green, and stretch it to 1-1/5" (3cm) diameter. Cut it into two. Flatten each section into a teardrop shape. Cut their base straight.

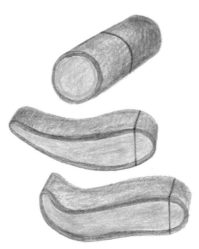

2 Surround with the translucent to obtain 2 rectangular canes. Let them set in a cool area.

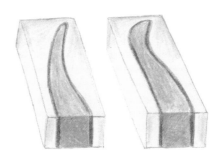

3 Stretch the canes, cut some thin slices, and stretch again to shorten the grass heights. The grasses should be different heights, ranging from 1-2/5" to 1/2" (3.5-1.5cm), to arrange one way or another.

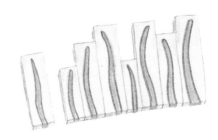

"Butterfly" Cane

1 Divide half of the black into four. Shape the body, two wings, and the head in such a way that their heights measures 1/2" (6mm). Surround them with the translucent to create a rectangular-shaped cane.

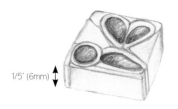

1/5" (6mm)

2 Let your cane set in a cool area before stretching it so that the rectangle length is 2/5" (1cm). Cut a slice and continue to stretch the cane to reduce the length to 1/5" (5mm).

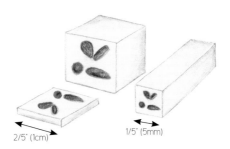

2/5" (1cm)　　1/5" (5mm)

The "Flower" Cane

Take 3/4" of the red chickpea and shape it into a log. Wrap it with a thin white sheet, followed by a black one, a white one, and then a red one. Let your cane set in a cool area before stretching it to reduce its diameter to 1/10" (2.5mm).

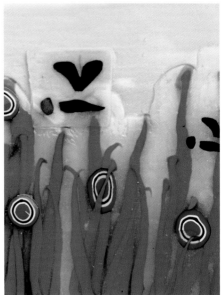

Sheet Making

1 Position the grasses to create a 1/2" x 6" (4x15cm) sheet. Smooth the sheet regularly to join everything together. Add the butterflies and flowers. Superimpose the patterns. Overlap them to add some depth.

2 Mix the white and the turquoise, and then spread it into a thin sheet. Arrange the composition on top of it, keeping a part of the sky above the grasses. Add 1 or 2 butterflies in the sky, including the biggest.

3 Cut the sheet into two (necklace, 3-3/10 or 8.5cm long; brooch, 2-4/5" or 7cm). Wrap each part with the remaining black. Pierce two holes with a cotton ball at the top of the necklace sheet.

4 Bake the sheets. Once cooled, proceed to the sanding, buffing, and varnishing steps (see Introduction p. 16).

Assembly

Necklace

1 Take the two lengths of chain, 2-1/2" and 2-1/10" (6.5 and 5.5cm), and mount 2 trinkets as in the diagram – one with the butterfly bead, the other with the green bead.

2 Thread each craft bead wire through a tubular cord, with 3/5" (1.5cm) protruding on either end. On the clasp side, thread a little green bead, make a loop, place a crimp bead, and link with a ring. On the pendant side, thread the trinket and a green bead. Make a loop and place a crimp bead. Link with the big ring.

Brooch

Glue the brooch pad to the back of the sheet.

Romance

Creation of Beads

The "Rose"

1 Mix some of the white with 1/16 of the magenta and a little pea of the black (color A). Next, mix 1/8 of the white with a rice grain of the black (B). Separate 1/8 of the white (C). Finally, mix 1/16 of the violet with a rice grain of the black (D).

2 Flatten the colors C and D, as well as 1/16 of the magenta, in 2/25" thick (2mm) sheets. Arrange them as shown in the diagram and join together with a roller.

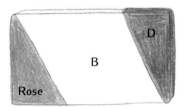

3 Flatten the sheet so that it is very thin. Fold in half and smooth over again. Repeat the process about ten times to obtain a grading (see Introduction p. 12).

4 Stretch the cane to 11-4/5" long (30cm). Fold it to obtain a 1/2" wide (1.5cm) strip, and then fold in pleats every 1/2" (1.5cm). Compact the accordion into a log and wrap it with the white (1/16 block) and then the black (1/16 block).

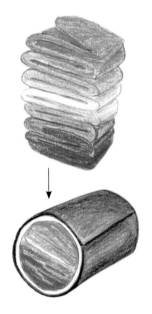

5 Stretch the cane to 7-4/5" long (20cm). Using a roller, flatten it to a 1/2" (1.5cm) width. Cut one section 1-1/5" long (3cm) and ten sections 1/2" (1.5cm).

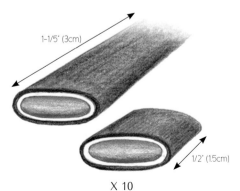

1-1/5" (3cm)

1/2" (1.5cm)

X 10

Material

CLAY

☐ White (classic 0): 1 block
■ Black (classic 9): 3/8 block
■ Magenta (classic 21): 1/8 block
■ Violet (classic 61): 1/16 block

FINDINGS (SILVER)

Necklace
23-1/2" (60cm) fancy cotton bias tape
2 flat bead tips (width=1/2" or 1.2cm)
1 clasp
2 elongated jumprings
3 rings (3/10" or 8mm)
1 headpin (2" or 5cm)

Bracelet
10-1/2" (27cm) fancy bias
4 flat bead tips (width=1/2" or 1.2cm)
1 clasp
10 elongated jumprings
8 rings (3/10" or 8mm)
6 headpins

(Continued p. 76)

Brooch

1 brooch support pad
   (length=1" or 2.5cm)
2" (5cm) fancy bias
1 flat bead tip (width=1/2" or 1.2cm)
4 elongated jumprings
1 ring (3/10" or 8mm)
1 headpin

Ring

1 rectangular ring pad support

Earrings

2 earwires with bows
2 elongated jumprings
2 headpins

OTHER MATERIAL

Metallic wires for piercing
Extra strong glue

6 Crush an end of one of the 1–1/5" (3cm) pieces and then roll it into a spiral so that the violet side of the slice is on the inside. Assemble 4 little parts around the spiral, keeping the violet toward the inside.

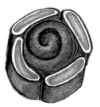

7 Continue to shape the rose. Position the 6 other petals as shown in the diagram. Place some black little logs in between them. Your patterns should measure about 1" or 1–1/5" (2.5x3cm).

The "Leaves"

1 With the color B (pale grey), shape a 1/2" (1.5cm) high leaf and cut the base very straight. Next, cut in six, following the lines of the leaf veins.

2 Flatten some of the white (1/16 block) and the black (1/16 block) to create 2 thin strips of 1/2" x 7" (1.5x18cm). Superimpose them, and cut out some pieces for the leaf veins and the outline. Set the rest of the strip aside.

3 With 1/16 of the white block, shape the second leaf. Cut out a central vein and insert the white and black strip inside, and then surround its outline. Position the two leaves on the rose's side.

The Cane

1 Shape some thin logs with the A color (mauve) and start to surround the flower with it (reserve some of this color for later). With 1/16 of the white block, shape some little logs to place between the mauves. Continue until obtaining a 1–2/5˝ x 1–4/5˝ (3.5x4.5cm) rectangular cane. Surround with a mauve strip. Let it set in a cool area.

2 For the brooch, cut out a 1/10˝ thick (4mm) slice from the cane after removing the first slice to let the grading show. Pierce a hole for the fastening. Stretch the cane to obtain a 9/10˝ x 3/5˝ (2.3x1.7cm) section and cut out a 1/5˝ (6mm) slice for the ring. Stretch the cane again to 1/2˝ x 2/5˝ (1.5x1cm) for the beads.

The Beads

1 For the bow necklace, gather some leftovers (1/2 block) and shape a ball. Cover it with some thin mauve slices (A), followed by some thin pattern slices. Roll over tightly to join together the pieces. Flatten the ball to 1/2˝ thick (1.5cm) and shape the heart. Pierce it diagonally.

2 For the 3 flat beads and the 2 smaller hearts, divide the rest of the mauve into 5 parts and flatten them. Take the equivalent of 1/4 block of the leftovers and shape 5 balls. Cover them with very thin pattern slices and flatten them. With 2 of the flattened balls, shape the 2 hearts.

3 For the 2 square beads of the earrings and the 2 of the bracelet, cut out 8 very thin pattern slices and 4 cane parts of 2/5˝ (1cm). Apply 2 patterns to each part. Pierce all the beads.

4 Bake the items after removing the wires. Once cooled, proceed to the sanding, buffing, and varnishing steps (see Introduction p. 16).

Assembly

Necklace

Mount the heart onto the headpin. Make a very nice bow in the middle and place an end tip at each end. Link them to the clasp with the little rings. Link the pendant to the textile bow with the 3 rings of 3/10" (8mm).

Bracelet

1 Cut a bias length of 7-4/5" (20cm) and two of 1-2/5" (3.5cm). Place an end tip to one end of the little lengths and cut the other on a diagonal. Tie 4 knots in the 7-4/5" (20cm) piece.

2 Mount the 3 flat beads, 1 little heart, and 2 square beads onto the headpin. Link each bead and the 2 little bias pieces to a jumpring and then a 3/10" (8mm) ring. Mount the trinkets onto the bracelet. Keep a flat bead to mount with a 3/10" (8mm) ring on the round part of the clasp. Place an end tip at each end. Link them to the clasp with the little rings.

Brooch

Mount the remaining heart onto a headpin and place an end tip at one end of the bias. Cut the other end so that it is pointed. Link the elements to the brooch pad with a 3/10" (8mm) ring and some jumprings. Glue the pad support to the back of the sheet.

Earrings and Ring

Mount the 2 square beads onto a headpin and link them to their earwires with a ring. For the ring, glue the rectangular bead onto its support pad.

1995 DRAFT SOFTWARE ORDER FORM

Software Package:

Check One [ ]

DOS (r) version (excludes some features)   [   ] $49.95 + $2 S&H   _____

Windows (r) version - Many new features, including GRAPHS, $49.95 + $2 S&H   _____
customized stat categories. AVAILABLE 2/1/94   [   ]

DATABASES:

> **The Low Price of $49.95 includes one forecast database, your choice of dates.**

Check at least one: [   ]

Any one	Included	Jan. 30	[ ]
Second one	$14.95	Feb. 13	[ ]
Each Add.	$9.95	Feb. 27	[ ]
		Mar. 13	[ ]
		Mar. 27	[ ]
		April 3	[ ]
		April 10	[ ] total _____

S&H for data bases ----- Total Number of Databases_____ X $2.00 each   _____

Disk size and Density: 3.5 HI_____   3.5 LOW_____   5.25 HI_____   5.25 LOW_____

Software Package subtotal $51.95

Additional Databases subtotal   _____

Total Draft Software Order   _____

NAME_____ADDRESS_____

CITY_____ST_____ZIP_____PHONE_____

Please send CHECK or MONEY ORDER to: **Diamond Library**
196 Danbury Road
Wilton, CT 06897

JOHN BENSON'S DRAFT SOFTWARE FOR 1995

- You may now choose DOS(r) or WINDOWS(r) to run your software, each $49.95.

- The 1995 WINDOWS software offers a variety of new features. These include

+ New Stat Categories
* Select from 17 Hitting Categories
(AB,PA,AVG,SLG,OPA,OPS,Hits,Singles,2B,3B,HR,RBI,RUNS,SB,CS,BB,SO)
* Select from 11 Pitching Categories
(G,IP,W,L,Saves,Hits,ERuns,BB,SO,ERA,RATIO)
* Combine the basic stat categories to create YOUR OWN custom categories, up to 2 Custom Hitting Stats plus 2 Custom Pitching Stats. Just add, subtract, multiply and divide the 28 given categories to create just about any stats you like.

+ More Stat Years
* Projected 1995
* 1994 Stats
* 2nd Half 1994 Stats
* 1993 Stats
* 1992 Stats
* 3 Year Average Stats (1992-1994)

+ New Graphics
* See Yearly Bar Charts for each stat category for each player
* See Bar Charts for player profiles

+ Improved User Interface
* Mouse Support and all of the other features that Windows provides.
The Windows version requires the following:
* 386 computer
* VGA Display (color or black & white)
* 2MB of Hard Disk space
* Microsoft Windows 3.1

-Note the DOS(r) version does not include these new Windows features but includes a couple of improvements:
+ UT slot for NL Leagues
+ Inflation can be turned off

For both the DOS(r) and the WINDOWS(r) versions, we are offering a larger selection of forecast database issue dates to match your needs precisely. You may choose any one or more among January 30, February 13, February 27, March 13, March 27, April 3 and April 10. Note these dates reflect the day the disks are mailed, the actual database is from 1 day earlier. The disks are mailed from California via U.S. Mail. Choose one or more to suit your own schedule for preparation and drafting. The first database is included in the $49.95, the second is $14.95, and each additional is just $9.95.

Free Bonus for Early Orders: **"STRIKE GUARANTEE"** ... if the beginning of the 1995 season is delayed by even one day, we will mail every early buyer, **FREE**, a new forecast database two weeks before regular play resumes.

THE 1995 ROTISSERIE® BASEBALL ANNUAL

**DIAMOND
LIBRARY**

Executive Editors:

Alan Boodman, Marc Bowman, and Lawr Michaels

Associate Editors:

Lary Bump and Bill Gray

Layout and Design:

Stephen Wade Lunsford and Brian Weaver

Library of Congress Cataloging-in-Publication Data:
 Benson, John
Rotisserie Baseball Annual 1995
1. Baseball -- United States -- History
2. Baseball -- United States -- Records
I. Title

ISBN 1-880876-16-7

For information address: Diamond Library.

Published by Diamond Library, a division of Diamond Analytics Corporation, with offices at 196 Danbury Road, Wilton, Connecticut, 06897.
Telephone: 203-834-1231.

PRINTED IN THE UNITED STATES OF AMERICA

Cover photography by David Price, Wilton, CT
Cover design by Stephen Wade Lunsford

Rotisserie League Baseball is a registered trademark of The Rotisserie League Baseball Association, Inc. For information contact R.L.B.A. at 370 Seventh Avenue, Suite 312, New York, New York 10001. Telephone: 212-629-4036.

Statistics are provided by STATS, Inc., 8131 Monticello Ave., Skokie, IL 60076
Telephone: 708-676-3322.

Rotisserie salary data courtesy of Heath Data Services, 228 N. Lynnhaven Road, Suite 106, Virginia Beach, VA 23452. Telephone: 804-498-8197.

TABLE OF CONTENTS

PREFACE

The Astros and Padres made a 12-player trade with far-reaching impacts. Many players, including a couple dozen who weren't even involved in the trade, will have different roles in 1995 as a result. One of my main activities in life is to contemplate such events and comment on their implications. My boss would tell you this activity is a "principal accountability." But right this minute, the boss is telling me it's that time of year again: time to write down what I think. Writing takes time, of course. While I'm writing, things change. I was already near the end of this year's writing when the Astros-Padres trade occurred. Should we stop and revise all that material? No, let's not. While we were writing about those changes, more changes would occur. That's one wonderful aspect of this subject: it never stops moving. So here it is ... the seventh annual edition. And there is an update on that Astro's/Padres trade!

Doing an annual project for the seventh consecutive year gives one a sense of longevity. Not much lasts for seven years, especially not in the business world, and most especially not in the sports publishing business. When our first annual book went to the printer, Ronald Reagan was in the White House, there were no such publications as *USA Today Baseball Weekly*, or *The National*, or *Fantasy Baseball Magazine*. *The Sporting News* had not yet launched their *Fantasy Baseball Owners Manual*. Obviously, the world has changed since then.

In 1988 I got this idea to write a book about baseball, for people who compete in Rotisserie leagues. At the time there were a couple of books about how to play Rotisserie, and naturally these books got into the subject of baseball, but the depth of baseball coverage aimed specifically at Rotisserie readers simply didn't go very far. To get baseball knowledge, as opposed to Rotisserie knowledge, you had to go to other books, especially books such as the Bill James Abstracts and the Elias series, and to the popular preseason guides which are really annual magazines rather than books. And the problem with all of this material was that it tended to emphasize questions like why the Royals didn't win the pennant, and why certain pitchers do better in night games, and which major league team has the best defensive outfield -- all of which was very interesting but not particularly helpful to those readers who just want to pick the best players for the coming season. And so I got some writers who understand baseball AND understand Rotisserie to start answering the questions that we really want to know about, and this book came into existence.

It is my hope, of course, to reach many new readers with each edition. But to be realistic, I expect that most of the people reading this book have seen it before, in previous years. In 1992, I began the practice of writing two separate introductions, one for new readers and one for return customers.

All readers will be interested in one aspect of the 1995 Annual which is a shift in emphasis. There is a whole new section on Rotisserie Strategies, and the detail descriptions of every position on every team have been shifted to emphasize Rotisserie strategies and their implementation. This change is in direct response to reader requests, and a reflection of the changing world that I have been mentioning in the above paragraphs. Back in 1989 it made excellent sense for me to tell you who was going to play every position on every team, and kind of leave it at that; it was a worthwhile project in itself, because no one else was doing it. Now we have so many daily and weekly periodicals catering to people concerned with such questions, that it's more appropriate for me, in January, to give you more background information about why and how various players are being chosen to receive playing time -- what the manager is thinking and what the GM is planning, and why -- and how you can use that information regardless who gets hot, or not, or injured, during spring training. I hope you like the new emphasis.

For the good old readers, I don't have any earth-shaking announcements in this year's edition. This book is assembled and packaged about the same as last year's except as noted in the preceding paragraph. Most of you know that I do market research, especially in the form of customer opinion surveys asking questions about the content and format of this book and my other products and services. Wherever any major changes in this book have been tested for popular appeal, the overwhelming answer from my readers has always been, "Leave it the way it is." Even the question of lowering the price of this book, amazingly, elicits the response, "Don't change." One reader gave me the rhetorical question: "Would you rather win your Rotisserie league, or save $10?" In every league it seems there are some people who don't want to shell out $22. They never win, and the rest of the people in their league think that's just fine.

In addition to the opinion surveys, I read all my mail, which is a lot. From these sources I am always looking for new ideas, ways to give you more of what you want. Your message to me for 1995, concerning this book, was the same as a year ago: that I shouldn't change it much -- and I haven't. Oh, there are always some good suggestions that have been incorporated (and I thank the people who gave me the ideas), but long-time readers will find the product essentially continuing in the same tradition: a preseason baseball guide with comprehensive comments from the Rotisserie perspective.

The biggest change in the last three years isn't even within this book. In doing the market research, I found a large number of readers who also wanted a traditional, alphabetic arrangement of "all" players including minor leaguers -- not in place of this book, but in addition to it, so they could find any player quickly and get a sentence or two saying who the guy is, and what's expected from him in the coming season. So I made two books, starting in 1993. The "A to Z" book came out about a month before this one. The 1995 edition has profiles on over 2000 players. I am not writing this fact because I'm trying to sell you a book -- although it would be OK with me if you wanted to buy it -- I just know that many of my readers want comprehensive collections of what I write every year, and that A-Z player guide now takes a lot of my effort every year and definitely complements this book. Look inside the back cover if you want more information.

I sincerely hope you find this 1995 edition to be what you want. I am grateful to every individual who buys this book, making it possible for me to earn a living in this unusual line of work. If anyone had told me, seven years ago, that I would soon be spending my winters writing preseason baseball guides for serious contests to pick the best baseball players, I never would have believed it. Never. Sometimes I still don't believe it. So, thanks. Thanks for caring about the game. And thanks for caring about what I think. I care what you think. Write to me any time. You can be sure that your thoughts and opinions will be considered, and appreciated.

JB

ACKNOWLEDGMENTS

What can I say? Anyone flipping through the pages of this book can see that most of it is not "by John Benson." Oh, sure, I did a lot of writing in here, and I spent most of my last thousand work-hours editing and fine-tuning what others had written; but the point is: this isn't really my book. It belongs to the many fine people who gave it their creative energy and careful attention to detail, over months and months of preparation, scouting, research and expository writing.

If I could put more time and effort into any section of this book, it would be these acknowledgments. Some day I want to tell the whole chronicle about the writers, analysts, and aficionados who joined together several years ago, and continue working year after year, to make this annual project such a marvelous sharing of talents and insights -- but every year at this time, I seem to be in too much of a hurry to get the book off to the factory.

The following individuals have been on board ever since the first edition was conceived in 1988: Alan Boodman, Marc Bowman, Lary Bump, Bill Cunningham, Mike Dalecki, Greg Gajus, and Bill Gray. These experts are all intelligent, hard-working individuals who never cease to amaze me with their high quality work, energy and creativity, consistently delivered on time without reminders.

In succeeding years, numerous outstanding individuals have joined the team that produces this book. I always hesitate when it comes time to give specific credits where due, because inevitably one or more of the large and brilliant contributions will get insufficient praise. Sitting in my position, a person gets spoiled. The talent and energy that flows through my office and into these pages is just immense. Let me name just a few of the contributors who did even more than I expected: Tony Blengino, Marc Bowman, Bill Gilbert, Bill Gray, Fred Matos, Lawr Michaels, John Perrotto, and Stuart Shea all accepted major responsibilities and delivered the goods, and more, and more. You get the idea. Every writer was a star this year again. It's an All-Star team, and a pleasure for me to be on it. Brian Weaver and Stephen Lunsford worked long hours on design and layout, with effort and results both much appreciated. Lary Bump remains one of the world's most prolific writers on minor leaguers. Gosh I could go on and on, but the time to let go is approaching rapidly. Thanks to every writer and contributor; I owe you more than words can tell.

All of the writers have by-lines throughout the text. The presence of their work indicates my enthusiasm and respect for what they have to say. Every year we have two or three "volunteers" to cover most teams and write about strategies. Everyone who's work gets into this book is a true winner in my estimation.

One of the more difficult aspects of editing this book is choosing what gets in and what doesn't. Space problems are not always resolved 100% on the basis of merit. Sometimes when you have to cut an eighty page section down to forty pages, with just one day to do that job, good writing can fall by the wayside. Some of the best material that didn't fit in this year's Annual will be appearing in the *Benson Baseball Monthly* during the next few months -- another reason to get that publication, not for my benefit, but to do justice to the writers and analysts who have so much to tell you.

STATS Inc. deserves a special word of thanks. Years ago, when I first thought I might like to try writing some baseball essays (this was supposed to be a hobby that would consume a few hours a year), I called a phone number in one of the old Bill James Abstracts, and found myself talking to a man named John Dewan. One thing led to another, as you can see.

-- John B., January, 1995

A FEW WORDS ON STRATEGIES FOR 1995

Where to begin? If I start out by assuming that all of the readers here have been following my work for years, then I am going to leave some folks disoriented right out of the starting gate. On the other hand, if I start at the very beginning, some long-time readers are going to yawn and ho-hum and wish I would get to the point faster.

Let's try this method, and see how it goes: say we're all at spring training, and we just had dinner at that barbecue place behind the stadium in Fort Lauderdale, and at this gathering there are a few dozen Rotisserie enthusiasts, including a some novices, but mainly a group with experience and insight. And one of this group says to me, "Hey, John, how about saying a few words on the subject of Rotisserie strategies?" And I say no, there's really not much you don't know already; but the group is growing insistent, and so I must proceed. So my method is: try to focus on some subjects that won't hurt anyone by being reminded, if they know them already, yet move along at a steady pace that everyone can follow.

This is, I guess, no time to be modest. I could write a book on the subject of Rotisserie strategies, have written a book in fact, have written two books on the subject (Rotisserie Baseball Volumes 1 and 2 - see inside back cover). So for this current exercise, rather than roll out the encyclopedia, I will try to focus on selected items that seem to come up frequently in conversation, in calls to my advice line over the last year or two, since those books first appeared. And I will try to focus mainly on items that are new, newly interpreted, possibly subject to misunderstanding or forgetfulness, or just newly verbalized. Some of the most stimulating conversations that I have on the phone include the revelation, "Gee, I never said this in words before, but I have always known it intuitively, and acted on it, and since you asked such a good question, I can now state it clearly ..."

GENERAL PLANNING CONSIDERATIONS

> Always have an objective

Consider these two calls from advice-seekers ...

Caller #1 - Should I trade a $15 Luis Polonia for a $15 Jay Buhner?
JB - What's your objective?
Caller #1: I need more power and have excess speed.
JB - Yes go ahead and do that. You could ask for more, but the deal accomplishes your objective. And ...
Caller #2 - Should I trade a $15 Jay Buhner for a $15 Luis Polonia?
JB - What's your objective?
Caller #2 - I need more speed and have excess power.
JB - Yes go ahead and do that. You could ask for more, but the deal accomplishes your objective.

Whether you are working within the tiny context of a tactical trade negotiation, or designing your whole draft strategy for the coming year and beyond, you will do better if you clarify your objective before taking any steps. Winners tend to focus early and stay focused a long time. Losers tend to lack focus much of the time and to change their focus frequently.

Following are some examples of clear objectives for the coming season:

- "Finish first, no matter what it takes."
- "Finish in the money this year, and save enough future value to finish in the money again next year."
- "I just want to finish higher than this one chump who bugs the heck out me."
- "Build for 1996 and beyond."

As illustrated in some of the examples below, finishing first is a goal which requires an early focus and

constant attention. Becoming clear about the goal is the first step to achieving it.

> **Stick with your determined objective as long as possible.**

After a winter of planning and strategizing based on the belief that your team is good enough to win this year, it's unlikely that your chances for winning can be ruined by a tough start. Even a lackluster draft and weak April performances by key players are unlikely to crush a team that was good enough to focus on first place on April 1. One of the wonderful aspects of the baseball season is its great length. Luck has a tendency to balance out, over time.

One helpful metaphor for me is to think of strategy as a large ship on a charted course. Concepts like putting on the brakes, making sharp turns, and reversing direction simply do not apply. The decisions that you make before and during the draft will have a definite momentum as the season unfolds. Very rarely is it a good idea to fight that momentum. Minor shifts in direction, yes. Major changes, no.

For years I played in a league with a guy nicknamed "Squid" (don't ask me; it's probably akin to "Flounder" from the film Animal House) and his style led to a strategic characterization that we affectionately called the Squid Phenomenon.

Squid begins every year, and I mean every year, with the hope-springs-eternal optimism that can only exist in baseball during the month of March. Squid was always convinced that he would not only win the league, but would win by a wide margin.

Every youngster on his farm roster was going to blossom in spring training and win a full-time job and become Rookie of the Year. If you asked Squid if he would trade Jason Bates in March 1994, he would say no, Bates is going to be Rookie of the Year. If you asked him for Ricky Bottalico, that too would an impossible deal because Bottalico was also going to be ROY. How all these players could be Rookie of the Year in the same year was a question that Squid never answered, or even considered.

And of course during March, every one of Squid's faded veterans was going to stage a magnificent comeback, and all his injured players were going to recover completely, even the rotator cuff pitchers listed as "out until July at the earliest" would be Cy Young candidates in Squid's estimation.

All this optimism evaporated every year by late April. If Squid was capable of drafting a good team, the optimism might last all summer, but he came out of every auction with a roster that had "can't win" stamped all over it in big letters. Through some annual metamorphosis, Squid's perceptions changed in regard to almost every player on his roster. Around the fourth week of April, all his rookies and established stars, rehab projects and healthy 160-game stalwarts, all of them turned into bums (except the few off to hot starts, and I mean few).

Thus in early May every year, Squid launched his annual rebuilding campaign. We had an unwritten rule in this league, by the way, that no one was allowed to take advantage of Squid to such an extent that would seriously alter the course of the pennant race. The three strongest competitors, in fact, wouldn't even trade with Squid unless it was necessary to prevent him from giving his whole team away to a middling contender, and then we would be scrupulously fair. The top three spent much of their time trying to assure Squid that his players hadn't all dropped $20 in value since draft day, and urging him to be patient.

Starting to rebuild in May is not a bad idea. It's clearly better than starting in July -- but not as good as starting before the draft. The Squid phenomenon, however, is not just an early shift toward next year; it also involves premature panic. When established veterans are performing below their career norms in early May, and there is no reason to suspect physical problems or other definite causes of these slow starts (and their jobs aren't threatened), then you have to expect that established players will return to their career norms, and stick with them through May and June. Premature panic in 1991 drove Squid to trade me Barry Bonds, then hitting about .180, for Andre Dawson, even up. You get the idea.

So the Squid method is to dump all your high-priced stars, or least as many as you can, for younger players and lower salaries. Squid did this every year around May 15, although he would cling stubbornly to any flagrantly high-priced stars who happened to be playing over their heads on May 15.

Phase Two of the Squid method began annually around the All-Star break, and was stimulated by three phenomena. First is that some of the established players that Squid wasn't able to trade away (remember, some of us in this league were scrupulous about taking advantage) would begin performing around par, perhaps delivering player-of-the-week box scores here and there. Secondly, the faster-starting players whom Squid wouldn't trade away would still look good on paper, even if they had slumped back toward career norms. Third and finally, more owners began to focus on next year and would be offering their high-priced stars around in trade.

Squid's reaction to these developments was always to jump back into the pennant race, reversing the strategy that he adopted in May, which reversed his strategy on draft day. Except for one year, in which Squid finished a miraculous fifth with this method (only because all but four owners dumped early), it never worked or even came close to working.

The Squid Phenomenon is the antithesis of the "win a year, lose a year" method which has become so popular among the smarter owners. Squid goes in both directions every year, and never gets anywhere with his efforts.

Although Squid is a rare case, the mistake he keeps making is not all that unusual. Lots of people make the mistake of changing their objective too frequently, or too early, which brings us to a couple of corollary rules ...

> Set your objective as early as possible.

Like everything in life, starting early correlates with success when it comes to Rotisserie competition. Especially in a zero sum game, where it's important for you to get players before the opposition, and generally do unto them before they do it to you, waiting and waiting to formulate a clear objective will cost you, eventually.

> Develop an integrated set of actions.

To a large extent, this strategy will take care of itself once you have defined a clear objective. If you consider each tactical decision in terms of how it fits your grand plan, then the collected tactical maneuvers and each step along the way will become an integrated set of actions. Until this concept becomes habit, and even for us elderly veterans who think we never forget it, wisdom dictates thinking of detail actions collectively.

For example, if your plan is to finish first at all cost, then you can see a number of necessary steps before you get to them. You know you will be trading away some low price youngsters for some high price veterans as soon as the draft is over, so you may as well start talking along those lines as soon as possible, even before the draft. You know you will need to make life difficult for your arch rival(s), so you better plan before the draft how to do that: bring up the players he needs early, when everyone has lots of money and open roster slots (or in the case of a straight draft, put the squeeze on catcher or shortstop or ace reliever or whatever the other guy needs and you don't need).

Going for first place at all cost, you will need an information edge. If you are thinking about subscribing to a new periodical, or getting on-line access to box scores, or adding any other weapons to your arsenal, do it as early as possible if your intention is to win. Especially on the information front, playing catch-up can be fatal.

> You may change your objective once in each season, never twice.

Simple as this rule sounds, it's amazing how frequently it gets violated, and by smart people who should know better. This rule is closely tied to the maxim of following an integrated set of actions.

The world has changed. Just five years ago, it was possible for an astute owner to dominate a league year after year, cleaning up on draft day with superior knowledge that kept a steady flow of high-value players coming into the franchise at low prices. That kind of broad dominance is no longer possible, unless you play in one of those leagues that allow you to keep star players forever (which can be fun, but it sure isn't standard).

Every year, more and more, victory in each league goes to the one owner who is most single-minded about winning the current year. Once you become 100% clear that winning the current year is your only objective, then all sorts of integrated actions begin to jump at you. Take freeze lists, for example. You look at all the marginal cases where you're not sure whether to extend a player for another year at an additional $5 salary, and all those cases where you're torn between two years at $10 or three years at $15, and settle all those questions in favor of having more money of draft day (i.e. when in doubt, don't extend). If you can find just three cases where you save $5 apiece, that's $15 more for draft day, enough to buy one whole healthy everyday productive outfielder instead of a pure zero on your roster. That much value is enough to lift any team from third to first in the typical highly competitive league.

That single-minded focus will actually accelerate during the season. Undoubtedly anyone strong enough to set a goal of winning this year will emerge from the draft with some bargains here and there. Trading those bargains early, to get higher-priced stars in return, becomes a matter of some urgency. Why? Because the sooner you get the high-price stars onto your roster, the more impact those players will have for you. Getting a $55 Barry Bonds when his owner throws in the towel on July 31 isn't nearly as good (in fact, it's less than half as beneficial) as getting the high-priced Barry in mid May. Trading later, you get two months of benefit. Trading earlier, you get four and a half months of benefit. How much is that two and a half month difference worth? Often about two and a half places in the standings!

Some of the following strategies will flesh out exactly which integrated actions should come into play, depending on your selected overall objective, but those examples are enough to show the theme. Obviously the owner who gets focused on his objective early and single-mindedly is going to do better than an owner who takes a "see what happens" approach on draft day and then sits on his roster inactively until late July when he finally decides whether to go for this year or next year; by then it's too late to do very well in either race, because others have already gotten off to big head starts in both directions.

Finally, on the question of when it's appropriate to change strategies, there has to be some break point. Playing for first place all year, when your best pitcher has gone out with a torn rotator cuff, and your best hitter has been traded to the other league, can be just plain stupid. But how do you know when to turn pessimistic? I look at it this way: all year, I keep asking myself, "What would take to win?" If the answers are plausible, such as I need to trade one gem keeper for a $30 slugger within the next month, and I need a couple of my problem pitchers to start performing around their career norms, and then I can win, surely I will stick with the current year objective. But when I start getting answers like, I need Dan Wilson to hit .300 with 20 homers and I need all three of my setup relievers to inherit closer roles within the next week or so, then it's obviously time to get realistic and start thinking about the longer term.

BEFORE THE DRAFT

> Know the four stages of competition.

Long ago, I proposed that Rotisserie competition can be viewed in terms of four component parts: (1) scouting and forecasting, (2) player valuation and rankings, (3) conduct of the draft, and (4) managing your roster during the season. The roster management aspect (if you retain players) then continues through the winter and into the next year, starting the cycle again.

These four components will all be critical, no matter whether you are going for this year or building for the

long-term future. The strategy just provides focus within each component. For example, when scouting and forecasting for the current year, you want to identify players likely to be high value in the current year, hopefully from opening day immediately. When working on a three-year plan, your scouting and forecasting time can be dedicated to rookies, prospects, and minor leaguers.

> **Spend the most time on scouting and forecasting.**

The "information edge" is the key to winning. That fact applies in midsummer as well as during draft preparation, but it's most important early in the season.

Even as our game has changed, so it's no longer easy to find any high-value players at low prices on draft day, still the information edge is as powerful as ever. Now that leagues are tight and "everybody has the same information," a tiny edge in information can yield a big edge in standings points. With all teams packed tightly together on the standings, finding an extra five stolen bases or a half a dozen home runs overlooked by the other owners, can have just as big an impact on standings as finding a $25 for $5 might have done a few years ago.

I urge everyone to look behind published dollar values, to understand as much as possible about what's happening in every player's career and -- just as important -- what's happening in every manager's and GM's mind. That's why we dedicate so much of the Rotisserie Baseball Annual to manager-viewpoint coverage of every position on every team. Even if the players change, management thinking about WHY these players were selected (or not) will carry over and be considered in handling whoever gets onto the roster, and in deciding who's on the roster.

Following are just a few of many methods that I employ to get an edge in scouting and forecasting. These illustrative examples will point the direction to other insights and considerations.

> **Look for meaning behind every winter deal.**

Even if Rotisserie owners change direction every month or two, real major league teams tend to stay on a steady course within each season and year after year. Teams that go for low budget .500 rosters will stick with that method and generally favor younger players and be extra willing to experiment. Teams that shell out big bucks to become contenders are likely to keep playing their high-priced veterans even after they are falling out of contention.

Winter deals point the direction that each team is going. The Astros, for example, will be more willing to try younger players (e.g. Phil Nevin) in 1995 than they were in 1994. The Padres will be more intent on fielding a credible competitive team in every game, and are now less likely to let any prospect get on-the-job training and develop as a player while taking away from the potency of the lineup.

> **Be wary of emerging youngsters in spring training.**

Management "announcements" during spring training, especially when they relate to younger players challenging veterans, are often issued for reasons other than informing the public about who's really going to play. It is a widespread source of disinformation, to say that a bright young rookie is on his way to displacing a proven veteran, when the real situation is little more than management's desire to see the veteran become less complacent and work harder.

> **Use spring training "games finished" to search for saves.**

It's flattering to see how many emerging experts have acquired this method, which I first published five years ago. One problem with the spring training schedule is that it doesn't provide enough games for saves to be a meaningful statistic. Some ace relievers get zero saves, or one or two, during spring training. Some middle relievers can get three or four saves just by pitching in the right place at the right time, saving split squad games, pitching the day after the ace reliever pitched, etc.

One stat that does come up frequently enough to be meaningful, is the game finished stat. Every game has a "GF" while a save can only occur in a victory, with a close score. Besides being more common, the GF is also useful because it sheds light into each manager's thinking. During spring training, the manager will routinely send out his ace reliever to pitch the ninth inning (and only the ninth inning) every other day during the last two weeks before opening day. Thus an ace reliever can be expected to accumulate six or eight games finished.

On days when the ace reliever doesn't work, the manager will send out another short reliever, theoretically someone worth getting a look as a closer. These pitchers will accumulate GF stats and will stand out, by the end of spring training, as the obvious alternate closers in the manager's thinking. Such information is useful not only on draft day but throughout the season. In 1994, following GF stats would have alerted watchers to Darren Hall of the Blue Jays for example. Even though Hall got sent down to Syracuse, he left evidence in GF's, showing that Cito Gaston had at least considered him as a possible closer. And that information, as it turned out, was worth over $20 to anyone who drafted Hall onto an Ultra roster, or grabbed him as soon as he was called up to fill in for Duane Ward.

> **Scrutinize spring training box scores.**

Experimental and tune-up games in Florida and Arizona tell more about managers' thinking than any lengthy essays could accomplish. Who's batting cleanup, who's leading off, who's been relegated to batting eighth ... all these little clues speak volumes about future value.

> **Especially watch split squad games for clues.**

There is a definite culture at work when a manager decides which players are home when the team plays a split squad game, and which players get on a bus and ride to another stadium that day. The standard method is to send a famous starting pitcher and one top star on the bus, just so the fans in the other town can feel

that they are watching real competition, not a "B" game. Sometimes one other obvious star will make the trip, but most of the established veterans will stay at home and play that day.

This tradition can help you see whether a marginal player is being viewed as a starter or a backup. If a player on the brink of a starting role rides the bus with the famous pitcher and the obvious superstar and the busload of backups, that's a bad sign.

Another clue for split squad games can be watching for pairs of middle infielders. Managers like to have the real shortstop and the real second baseman work together. So if you hear that a rookie is winning a starting job at one of these positions, but the two veterans keep playing together in every split squad game, you can suppose the manager is blowing smoke about the rookie breaking into the lineup.

> **Watch for batting order changes.**

The lion's share of team RBI usually belong to batters hitting in positions three, four or five. If a hitter is moved closer to 3-4-5 his opportunity to drive in runs will improve. Farther away from 3-4-5, the opportunity will diminish. When Barry Bonds hit leadoff for Pittsburgh he never had more than 59 RBI. The season he moved down in the order; 1990, he had 114 RBI, a 93% improvement over the previous year. Mike Stanley's career took off when he moved up from number eight to fifth/sixth in the Yankees' order.

Often the spring training box scores will tip you off to a change in batting order before it happens in games that count.

> **Look at your freeze list as part of the auction.**

It's amazing how many people follow separate lines of thinking for freezing versus buying players on draft day. It is the same question: do you want this player on your roster now, for $X? If you would gladly buy the player in a draft, then go ahead and freeze him. If you would hesitate early in the auction, because

similar players at better prices are likely to be available later, then you should hesitate from freezing also.

The freeze and the auction are two parts of the same process: you give up money, to get players, to fill roster spots.

> Build trade opportunities into your freeze list.

As for setting your objective early, there is no better way to get started on next year, than to begin work before this year's auction. The two-year plan on draft day can put you in a race by yourself.

Often I have observed that, in all leagues that allow trading of players and allow retention of players from year to year, there are always two races going on simultaneously on the same race track: this year and next year. As fate would have it, the competitors who do best in each race are those who get started earliest and help each other during the season -- and they get started early helping each other, too. For example, the faster the "next year" guy can trade away his high-priced stars, the more benefit will accrue to the "this year" owner who gets them. Remember: five months of Barry Bonds is worth more than twice as much as two months of Barry Bonds, so the price can (and will) be twice as high early in the year.

Trades will be fundamental to success, regardless which race you choose to run in, this year's or next year's. Visualizing these trades before the draft will ensure that you have a good draft.

Freezing a $50 Barry Bonds often makes fine sense even when you're going for next year. Don't forget you can trade Bonds for three gem keepers right after the auction. Similarly, freezing a $10 rookie, who isn't expected to play much and might even get sent down, can be a fine move even when going for this year. If that youngster is likely to be attractive to the rebuilding teams, then he is a trade asset and merits consideration as a freeze.

> Watch roster size when freezing.

Often people call me with a long list of possible keepers at low prices, and I say "yes" to each individual name, until we get so far down the list that we have, say, five outfielders being retained. The classic case is a bunch of solid $12 everyday players at prices of $1 to $5. Then when we get to the end of the list, I say wait a minute, we better go back and take another look at those guys.

The question can become one of using up roster slots, more than a question of using up money. Aside from the fact that it's a tactical advantage to have one outfield slot open until late in the auction, just in case a gem bargain floats by, it is also wise to make sure you get your fair share of high-value outfielders. Freezing five $12 players at $5 apiece could be a path to disaster, if there aren't enough high value players (and roster slots) available to get the benefit of that extra cash.

> View your freeze list as a lifeboat.

The freeze list allows you to carry a number of players from one year to the next. In most leagues, this number is limited, and in some leagues it is extremely limited. The key point is understanding that anyone who doesn't fit into your freeze list "lifeboat" cannot help your team, at least not actively. Yet there are many useful ways to get value from those wasting assets.

> With a strong freeze list, make two-for-one and three-for-one deals.

Say your 15th-best freeze has a $6 implicit profit, your 16th best has a $4 profit, and your 17th best has a $2 profit. You can only keep 15. So you trade all three of them to another team with a weak freeze list, and you get back in trade one freeze with a $10 profit. You're happy because your lifeboat has $4 more value (that 15th freeze's profit went from $6 to $10). The other trader is happy because (assuming he didn't have 15 good freezes but only 12 or 13) his lifeboat went up in value by $2 (the one +$10 freeze changed into a $6, a $4, and a $2).

> **If you can't trade away excess freezes, "place" them.**

Suppose in the above example you couldn't find any trade like the one illustrated. Do you give up and just release the +$4 freeze and the +$2 freeze? Heck, no. You trade them to your buddy Joe, for two over-priced bums (or better yet, not two bums, but two good yet overpriced players you would like to see coming back into the auction). Joe is happy to be getting two more freezes, and you're happy because those two players won't hurt you in the standings, especially if you pick the right kind of players to park on Joe's roster. And of course Joe might remember that you did him a favor, and be more inclined to trade with you rather than your arch rival in the coming year.

> **Offer marginal freezes around in trade.**

What you're doing here is collecting free information. Nobody says, just because you offer a player in trade to see what gets offered back, that you have to make any trade. So if you have a $10 Pedro Munoz, and with inflation in your league, you figure Munoz is worth $12 or $13 and has upward possibilities if Steve Dunn doesn't work out and Kevin Maas has a bad spring and Scott Stahoviak doesn't blossom, etc., and the bottom line is you would be willing to pay $11 for Munoz if the auction was going on right now. Should you freeze him? Maybe. Offer Munoz to three owners who should appreciate his value. If they all scoff at you, then it appears you have a good chance to get Munoz for under $10 on draft day, so you may throw him back (I am assuming you have a good freeze list anyway). If you end up paying $11 for Munoz, so it cost you a buck. But if you buy him for $6 late in the draft, then you have gained $4. Play the odds.

> **Shark tip: deceive people who offer marginal freezes around in trade.**

In the above example, scoff at the guy who's thinking of freezing Munoz for $10, then bid $11 or more after he's thrown back.

> **When in doubt, don't freeze.**

Consistent with the roster-slot-has-value theory, be aware that every roster slot filled is an opportunity lost. If you freeze (or buy) a player with a $1 profit, you are giving up any opportunity to get a $5 or $10 profit in that roster slot. Most of the people reading this book are pretty astute scouts and bidders, and roster slots are worth more in their hands than in the hands of less knowledgeable folks. So if you don't feel pretty sure that a freeze is a good idea, throw the player back and see what happens. You might like it a lot.

> **Don't estimate inflation, calculate it.**

It's astounding how many people pay me good money to go over their freeze lists and plan a draft strategy, and they don't know the inflation rate in their league. Rates commonly range from 10% to 50%. Many leagues, enough for you to consider the possibility, have negative inflation (everybody freezes everybody) and many have inflation over 80%!

If you're looking at a $30 player (and of course most leagues are won or lost based on the handling of $30 players) the normal range of inflation will be $3 to $15 on that player. Obviously, guessing is going to lead to disaster.

The numbers you need are all there. The Draft Software does this for you, but if you don't have it, then get out a paper and pencil and a calculator, and do this exercise:

(A) How much money is in your auction? Take (for example) $260 per team, times the number of teams, minus the salaries of frozen players.

(B) How much value is in your auction? Again, take salary per team (e.g. $260) times the number of teams, and subtract the value of frozen players.

Then divide (A) by (B). An answer of 1.25 means 25% inflation, and you need to increase all values to 25% before your auction begins.

> **Mark your values list up/down before the auction.**

Even if you don't use my Draft Software, you can get a leg up on your opponents by tinkering with dollar values (in writing) to suit your league, before the draft. If your league counts runs, for example, don't just go to the auction with a vague notion that you are going to bid aggressively when leadoff batters come up for bid. Write your estimated values on the papers that you will bring to the auction with you, and those adjustments will be one less factor that you have to remember during the heat of the auction. If you're in a straight draft, rearrange priority lists before, not during, the auction.

> **Keep studying right up until the last moment before your draft.**

Having access to a good sports radio station and/or checking on-line wire services just before your draft will yield good results. Remember: tiny edges pay bigger dividends now than they did just a few years ago. Knowing who's hurt and who's healthy is critical. Even a tiny item, like knowing which backup catcher just hit a three-run home run, can make the difference between first place and second place, when it comes to October and you're tied in home runs with your arch rival.

> **But don't overstudy.**

There are really two points here: (1) get a good night's sleep before draft day, and (2) don't overload the info circuits. Think of draft day as something akin to taking the Law Boards. Staying up all night cramming may add a few words to your memorized vocabulary, but losing the edge from fatigue will more than offset the benefits. And topping off the knowledge tank with details like spring training caught stealing percentages will fill up valuable brain cells with useless data.

ON DRAFT DAY:

> **Watch the Littlefield Effect.**

There is an implicit tip underlying this advice: go back and read every edition of Glen Waggoner's RLB books, if you haven't already. If you have done that homework, then you know about John Littlefield, the Padres reliever who got two blow-em-away saves during the first week of the 1981 season, and thus had two saves by draft day, and -- you guessed it -- never got another save in his entire career. Littlefield sold for the price of all other obvious ace relievers on draft day, about $30.

It isn't just the obscure hot-start players who mani fest the Littlefield Effect. The biggest factor to watch isn't the little snares and pitfalls here and there. The biggest factor is the massive undervaluation of established stars in every league every year. And I do mean every league. Even the most experienced and most dispassionate competitors tend to pay too much attention to the first couple weeks of stats; it's a natural result following a winter of starving for stats and box scores. Whatever comes in first gets over-scrutinized, rather like the New Hampshire primaries.

Last year I won an all-champions invitational league, which drafted about three weeks into the season, by loading up with big stars off to slow starts: Barry Larkin, Bip Roberts, Tony Gwynn ... you get the idea. Eleven highly astute owners sat there and let me get away with it. It's just human nature to look in the paper and believe what you see.

> **Don't be afraid to pay top prices for top players.**

On draft day your two major goals are (1) profits -- get bargain players at low prices, and (2) value - acquiring your fair share of reliable, high-value players. While engaged in bargain-hunting, too many competitors forget the fair share question. Consider this caricature: Filling a roster with 23 players worth $10 each, with salaries of only $5, might sound good, but you'll have $150 to spend on your 23rd player, and of course you will lose.

See the essay Practical Auction Budgeting for more (in that two-volume set).

> **Don't pursue specific players.**

It just amazes me how many well-prepared competitors blow months of study by losing perspective on draft day. They call me and ask the question: "Who should I go after this year?" If you ever catch yourself thinking along the lines of "go after" when planning for draft day, and that's your main line of draft preparation, then you must stop yourself and rethink the purpose of the draft in your path to victory.

Targeting a specific player is only appropriate as a narrow tactical maneuver, after you have ensured having enough bargains on your roster, after you have thought through who is available at each position, after you have decided which positions and which stat categories offer the best and most opportunities for bargains, and after you have designed tactics to interfere with your arch rivals accomplishing their objectives. I won't say you should never target a specific player, because I have done it myself, but only after careful study.

> **For every purpose in the draft, list as many names as possible to help accomplish that purpose.**

Thinking of specific names is the final step of draft planning, and when you get to that step, you want to be making long lists of acceptable players, not short lists of must-get players. Whether you need speed, or saves, or a middle infielder, or a starting pitcher, always begin by thinking about that general need and probing everywhere before forming a plan to fulfill that need. The answer my be two players, not one. The answer may be a post-draft trade, not an acquisition on draft day. And whatever the answer is, it should be developed with a long list of players who can help.

> **Deviate from published dollar values when appropriate.**

There are two points here. Published dollar values are never precise. Would you take investment advice from a stock broker who tells you he is certain that the Dow Jones average a year from now is going to be 3849.67 because his computer model say so? Or would you be more comfortable with a guru who says that, based on his understanding of technical and fundamental trends (which he can explain, if you like) the DJIA is likely to be in the 3800-3900 range a year from now? The former expert is clearly deluding himself and anyone who listens to him. The latter has a better grip on reality.

All kinds of forces can operate to make calculated dollar values more or less appropriate in any auction, or at different moments within the same auction. Several of these are presented in our introduction to the forecast stats and values: optimal bidding, draft inflation, budgeting moves, etc.

My advice is NOT to disregard or disrespect published values, just to put them into context. A dollar or two in any direction means nothing. A five dollar adjustment -- even when you believe the underlying forecast stats and value calculation -- may be perfectly appropriate for a given tactical situation, and I don't mean an inflation adjustment; I mean a deliberate departure from calculated value including inflation.

My advice is simply to have a reason, and to know it, and to be able to explain it to yourself (not to others, please) if you had to. Then it's OK to deviate from published values.

> **Early in the auction, nominate the type of players you don't need.**

If you go into the auction with two ace relievers, it should help your cause immensely to nominate all the remaining ace relievers before nominating any players you really need. This step will accomplish several purposes. First, you will help the natural market forces to prop up the price of all remaining ace relievers, while everyone has plenty of money and plenty of vacant roster slots. No one will beat you by getting a proven ace for half of true value, as might happen later in the auction when money and roster slots have dried up. Another purpose you will accom-

plish will be flushing money out from whoever has it, thus increasing your chances to get bargains on the types of players you do need. Third, the maintaining of igh prices on all ace relievers will prop up the trade value of your two aces; it wouldn't help if you freeze two aces at $35 apiece and then the auction makes it look like they were worth only $25 each. Finally, bringing up the type of players you don't need will put the squeeze on everyone who does need them.

This tactic works with any stat category and any position. Whatever you don't need, bring it up and make others pay. Whatever you do need, wait, save your money, and look for bargains.

> Early in the auction, bring up players who are difficult to value.

The wonderful aspect of this game is that people have different opinions. The same player may appear like a $20 star to one owner, while he's nothing more than a $5 speculation in the eyes of another owner. Obviously in such cases we are not talking about healthy, established star hitters; we are talking about players with questions or problems of some kind: rookies, players with insecure roles but high potential, player rehabbing from injuries, fading veterans possibly poised for a comeback, etc.

The more of these hard-to-value players you can bring up early, the more money you will flush out. Just bringing up all the rookie starting pitchers is a fine method to get you through the first ten rounds of any auction. Obviously, however, you don't want to bring up the guys you like yourself, the ones who might be real sleepers from your point of view.

> Nominate players your arch rival needs, early.

The flipside of nominating what you don't need is focusing on specific needs of your arch rival(s) and making sure they pay top dollar to fill their needs. If your toughest competitor is dying for a power hitter, and you're OK in that department, then just say the name of the top home run threat still available, every time it's your turn.

> In 1995, pursue stolen bases.

The offensive explosion of 1994 lifted every offensive category except one: stolen bases. Obviously, neither manager is going to be inclined to try one-run tactics when the score resembles a football game, like 7-0 or 10-3 or 14-7, as happened frequently in 1994. The relative scarcity of steals, versus home runs, simply hasn't sunk in yet. Most of the preseason forecasts and published values for 1995 don't fully reflect the new reality.

> When rebuilding, look at each player in terms of how good he might become.

Here is a very important case where having an objective affects how you bid and build your roster. Everybody has the same $260, but if you decide that you aren't going to spend any of your money for so-so mediocre middle-age talent at full prices, then you can allocate more money to young players for the future and high-price genuine stars whom you will trade away for more youngsters as the season unfolds.

One of the nice aspects of rebuilding is that a future star won't hurt you by flopping in his rookie season. You may decide to throw him back rather than keep him at the end of the year, but the harm done to you is minimal compared to what that player would have done to a contender who shelled out $15 for $2 worth of production.

> Weakness loves risk; strength loves certainty.

Rebuilding isn't the only viable strategy for a weak team. Surprises do happen. Some of the most satisfying victories in this game come from taking a weak freeze list and managing it all the way to first place.

To succeed this year, weak teams need to take chances. Getting more rookie starters, more rehab cases, and more high-potential kids with weak track records, all increase your chances of getting lucky. They also increase your chances of getting burned, of course. Strong teams stay away from such players. But if you want to win this year, and the outlook is

gloomy, buy a few players who could be characterized as lottery tickets: low price, slim chance of success, but with a big payoff if they do hit.

Strong teams lean the opposite way. The stronger your team, the more you want to get players who have no questions, no problems, no injuries, no controversies. A player who is worth about $10, and you know it, can be a better investment than a rookie who will be worth $20 if he clicks but only $2 if he flops. For some teams, Jeffrey Hammonds, Brian L Hunter, James Mouton, Tony Tarasco, and Rondell White are the right kind of outfielders. For another team these players may be all wrong, while less exciting guys like Brian McRae, Jay Buhner, Al Martin, and Orlando Merced are more appropriate.

> Be contrary.

Having a good draft is simple. Just refuse to move with the herd. When everyone is bidding up the price of power hitters, spend your money on speedy leadoff men. When everyone else is shunning expensive starters, buy a solid five-man rotation. Whatever everyone else is overvaluing, stay away from it. It's a fact that when too much money goes into one commodity, then other commodities must be available at bargain prices.

Having a solid foundation in valuation methods (or a wonderful, accurate list of values from a source authority) is the first half of being a successful contrarian. The other half of the battle is liberating your thinking about specific details concerning what you must accomplish on draft day.

> You don't need a balanced roster on draft day.

Often people approach the draft with unbearable anxiety about some scarce commodity. People often call me with comments like, ''There are only three good starting pitchers available and everybody needs one, so I must plan on spending $30 or more to get one,'' or ''With only two big home run hitters in this year's draft, I'm going to pay up to $55 for Fred McGriff because I need power badly.'' Such thinking misses the fact that each season is six months long.

You don't have to finish the draft with a balanced roster. You could finish the draft with only one starting pitcher, trade for two more starters in May-June, and then get more starters in July. One year I went through the month of September with eight starters, to reach a stringent IP minimum of 1,170. Just because your league rules steer you toward having at least five starters, doesn't mean you must have five starters on May 1.

Confined thinking is a major cause of suffering in Rotisserie baseball, and it's almost always self-imposed. Your opponents may help to create discomfort, but you can keep a clear mind by simply asking yourself ''why'' repeatedly, whenever you find yourself thinking about what you ''must'' do on draft day. It's a long, long season, offering plenty of time to shift your roster toward whatever you need.

After the draft, you can change your starter/reliever mix, or your power/speed balance, or whatever. You can spend 90% of your money on hitting, or 90% on pitching on draft day, and then trade for what you need later.

Understanding this flexibility is the key to the flexible strategy that guarantees a strong draft: be contrary. It astounds me how many smart competitors lock themselves into rigid thinking and then get battered on draft day, feeling at the mercy of external forces throughout the auction, not enjoying the draft, sweating and worrying, and not getting the young and improving players that make an owner feel good about his roster. Many people who fall into this trap come to the draft with excellent preparation and a deep knowledge of the player population, but then they get derailed on their way to picking a good team because they let the herd stampede them, and because they won't let go of their preconceived notion of what their post-draft roster must look like.

> Spend whatever you want on hitting versus pitching.

''But I must spend 65% of my money on hitting, and 35% on pitching; you say so yourself.'' Wrong. I never said that. What I have been saying for seven

years is an observable fact: in all leagues as a group, worldwide, year after year, all owners as a group spend 65% of their money on hitting, consistently. And it doesn't vary much. Every year 99% of all leagues fall within the range 61% to 69%, and 80% of leagues fall within 63% to 67%. Within these leagues, however, there will be individual teams that may spend over 80% on hitting, or under 50%.

Opportunities present themselves in every draft, because not all owners will use exactly the same rational, dispassionate methods of valuation and bidding. In addition, each league tends to have a unique culture when it comes to valuation, generally following the personal prejudices of individual competitors who have been successful over the years. If the smartest and most successful competitors lean passionately toward home runs, the rest of the league will usually follow them, imagining they're pursuing the one true recipe for victory. If the perpetual winners favor stolen bases and saves, the other owners will shift their thinking along those lines, too, by observing and imitating.

> **You have to be lucky with starting pitchers.**

While it often makes fine sense to fill up your hitter slots with solid value at fair prices, it is rarely wise to do that with starting pitchers. The unspoken understanding of this fact of life is part of the reason why each league in total spends only 35% of its money on pitching every year.

If you pay full value ("fair value") for any player, you deny yourself the opportunity to get lucky with that player; the best you can do is to get what you pay for. Getting what you pay for is a worthy objective in the case of reliable star hitters; it is also a worthy objective for some (but not all) of your starting pitcher slots. Why? Look at any winning roster, and you find a big surprise in the starting pitcher department [if you don't believe me, go and look at the roster of last year's winner in your league]. Sometimes you find two or more big surprises among the starting pitchers on a first place roster.

Every year there is at least one starting pitcher who comes out of nowhere and produces $25 or more in value. In a tight league with everyone going for this year, the lucky owner who gets that pitcher for $2 is likely to finish first. A $23 windfall profit is usually just too big for the other contenders to overcome.

The windfall profit phenomenon among starting pitchers may occur in two or three cases, or even more, in each league each year, lifting two or three owners above the others. When there are multiple cases of windfall starting pitchers, having just one of them may not be enough to ensure victory; but you can say this much: any owner who does not get even one of them will have a darn hard time beating those who do get them. To win, you have to be lucky with starting pitchers. Filling all your starting pitcher slots with high value players at high (fair) prices, you cannot win, because you cannot get lucky. Always give yourself an opportunity or two to get lucky with starting pitchers.

> **Know the valuation culture in your league.**

Even if you're a new owner, you can tell which way the league is going to lean, by looking at prices paid in past auctions. Before you start bidding, you want a plan based on understanding of how those around you are going to conduct their auction. It would be nice to know each individual owner's tendencies and to use that information to your benefit; but even just knowing the general tendency of the league will help you in designing and building your roster. Some leagues love home runs. Others feast on rookies; they would rather prove their knowledge by getting this year's rookie-of-the-year, at any price, than by finishing in the money. Considering the culture ahead of time will help you be contrary, and thus help you win.

Study previous drafts. What are the various individual owners' draft tendencies? What conclusions can you draw? If a competitor has a history of going for a particular player or always tries to build his team around closers or power hitters, hit them where it hurts and bid aggressively for their "must have" players. You could cause them to over-spend, which will hurt them later in the auction, or you may take

their favorite player away. Even if you over spend they may become desperate and divert from their strategy. And if you have their favorite player it won't be long until they approach you for a trade. When they come to you, you own them.

> Downplay wins when bidding on starting pitchers.

More than any other stat, wins by pitchers are caused by factors other than the individual athlete's performance. The variability and unpredictability of wins are among the major factors that lead bidders to discount pitcher values. If you like wins, look for overlooked starters for teams that win a lot (Kent Mercker is a good example). If you just want pure value, perk up when a starter with a consistently good B/I ratio comes up for bid.

> Look for the "Cherry Picker" of The Year.

Almost every year, some nondescript middle reliever ends up racking up seven or eight wins. Bill Risley of the Mariners was a good example of the breed in 1994. Rarely do these middle relievers duplicate their success in consecutive years. It's a matter of managerial preference (using that pitcher in a tie game, or down by just a run) and in most cases these guys are found on a team with a very good offense, so they can score runs when your guy is in the game, and you get the cheap wins. Because they are middle relievers, they are almost always available cheap, or as a free agents during the season.

> Build around batting average.

Most people tend to downplay the importance of things they don't understand. Batting average is somewhat more difficult to value than home runs, stolen bases, and RBI, because you can't look at a player and see immediately that he has "twice as much batting average" compared to another player, as you can look at a 30-homer guy and see he gives you twice as much in that category as a 15-homer guy.

The minor mysteries surrounding batting average

and its value can be easily removed with simple arithmetic, as you can see in my Volume Two, Playing for Blood. Unfortunately, not many competitors have the time or disposition to work through this arithmetic.

Even more unfortunate, some of the earliest writers who took a stab at BA valuation built their work upon a completely false premise, and so any useful arithmetic that may have applied, from that illogical starting point, shed no light on the subject but rather just obscured it further.

I am referring of course to the primitive notion that the "average batting average" must be worth zero. If the average batting average in a Rotisserie league is .265, with half the teams over .265 and half under, then a .265 hitter is utterly neutral, neither helping nor hurting, and therefore his batting average must be worth zero. This theory suggests you could take the population of hitters on rosters in any standard league, and "see" that the upper half of this group is helpful by performing above average, and therefore adds value, while the lower half can be said to create a drag on batting average, and thus take away value. The conclusions of this theory are, therefore, that average batting average is worth zero, and the sum total of all hitters' contributions in BA must also add up to zero.

The clearest debunking of this myth was presented by Mike Dalecki, phrased in the form of a question printed by me five years ago: if the average batting average is worth zero, then how do you explain the fact that a Rotisserie team with the average batting average doesn't score zero, but scores six points in that category? Obviously, the average batting average is not worth zero, and all arithmetic built on that premise is nonsense.

Value in batting average begins to accrue when your team gets lifted above the bottom of the league in the BA category, and your team begins to score points in batting average. The point of reference for zero value in batting average must therefore be the lowest TEAM batting average in your league, not the average team batting average.

Almost everyone now understands and accepts the Dalecki Principle of batting average valuation, but effects linger from the dark ages. While that ancient notion, that the sum of all batting averages must be zero and the whole category itself must be worth zero, has fled from the enlightening fact that even below-norm teams score positive points in the BA category, the lingering subjective impact of that notion, that batting average is a soft and suspect source of value, continues to affect perceptions and bidding.

I can suggest one more reason for the lack of appreciation of batting average, in addition to the effects of that old false premise which got into print, and the demands for somewhat more arithmetic to achieve full understanding of this category compared to others. The additional consideration is the fact that a player's batting average can go down, while his homers and RBI cannot. We have all known the experience of having a .295 on our roster in July, and feeling the value from that asset, and then watched that hitter slump to .260 by year end, and we felt his value going down. A batter with 15 home runs in July may slump and finish the year with only 19, but we don't view that part of the slump as causing an actual drop in value (although we should because there was surely a standings impact there, too).

The disappointment of a shrinking BA is obviously akin to the feeling one gets when a pitcher's ERA goes up. The similarity of these feelings causes many to perceive the batting average category as unreliable, like ERA and B/I ratio, with the implication that batting average values should be discounted, the same as we do when assigning only 35% to pitchers in the total valuation picture. The facts, however, show that batting average is far more consistent than ERA from year to year. Batting average should not be discounted for this perceived risk, but in fact that discounting occurs every year.

The obvious strategic implication is that you can take advantage of everyone else's misunderstandings, by loading up with high average hitters. I do that every year, in every league (just by using my own calculated

values and believing) and the method works marvelously.

Tony Gwynn and Wade Boggs have been bargains for many years.

> The stronger your team, the more you need players with high batting average.

One of the elusive aspects of batting average value is that every team has a different reference point. Because I love average so much (so many good thing come with it!) often I have had teams with a .290 average as late as June. With such a roster, I must view with disdain a player with a .270 average, because he will drag me down, closer to the next lower team with their .286. A .270 hitter may actually cost me points, while a low-standing team with a .255 average could get a lift of a couple of standings points by adding a solid .270 hitter in June.

The same logical arithmetic applies during the draft while you are building the roster that will produce those team stats. If you plan to build around strong hitting, then a .270 hitter is worth less to you than to another owner. Without getting too elaborate, just bid more aggressively on .290+ hitters and bid more passively on those expected to hit .265 or lower, and your roster will build itself rather nicely.

> Watch park effects when pitchers change teams.

Many successful pitchers owe much of their good fortune to their home ball park. A pitcher who induces hitters to hit flyballs outs in a big stadium, could turn sour if traded to a smaller park. Sid Fernandez in 1994 was a vivid example. In spacious Shea Stadium, Fernandez was one of the leagues best pitchers. When he moved to Baltimore and to the smaller parks of the American league his former flyball outs often left the park. Fernandez gave up 26 homers in only 109 innings in 1994 and he had the worst season of his career. Consequently starting pitchers crossing from the AL to the NL will generally be more effective because of the bigger parks and absence of designated hitters.

If you believe a pitcher might be affected by a change in venue, consider whether or not the pitcher in question is a fly ball pitcher who would be more effected by the distance to the fences, or if he is a ground ball pitcher who would be more affected by his new team's infield defense. A perfect example of this is the transformation of Tom Glavine into a Cy Young pitcher. In 1990, Glavine's ERA was 4.28. In 1991, the Braves installed Rafael Belliard at short-stop, Terry Pendleton at third base and Sid Bream at first base - Glavine's ERA dropped to 2.55, he won 20 games and a Cy Young award. So it isn't just the ''ballpark'' factor; it's also who's in the ballpark.

> Get your last hitter from Colorado or Boston.

Often when choosing a $1 middle infielder at the end of the draft, it's wise to pick a team rather than a player. Even a banjo hitting shortstop is capable of hitting a home run or two, and carrying a .280 average, in Colorado. The thin air makes it a hitters paradise, and a nightmare for pitchers. Wrigley Field is generous as well (lots of day games with sunshine to see the ball well, and close fences, and sometimes the wind is blowing out). Avoid Shea Stadium and Dodger Stadium. In the American league, the friendly parks include Detroit and Boston. So when in doubt about that last hitter, get Rockies or Red Sox.

CONCLUSION

The above tips will get you well-prepared for draft day and help you emerge from the draft with a solid team well on the path to your desired objective. There is more to the game, of course. We have just touched here and there on the ubject of in-season roster management. (There will be plenty of advice on this subject, linked to current events as they unfold, during the regular season in the pages of my Baseball Monthly.) And there is a much-neglected aspect of strategy at year-end: review and analyze. And that step of course gets you started again on planning for next year. But hey, just get through 1995 first!

SECOND HALF STATS

If you already use second half stats as basis for predicting performance in the following season, you can skip this chapter this year. If you're not sure what I'm talking about, keep reading.

Baseball information comes in annual doses, and then gets filed away under annual classifications. We can say simply "1969 Mets" or "1986 World Series" and people can immediately visualize specific players and accomplishments. Almost everything significant in baseball gets a year attached to it, and almost every year has its signature personalities. Try free association, either way: 1951? Bobby Thompson. Roger Maris? 1961.

Statistics, in particular, are stated in terms of per-year totals and averages. If you say, "Joe Bimbleman had 25 homers" that means 25 in one year. If you say, "he has 25 homers" that means this year. Almost all of the big questions in baseball are questions about one year: Can Cecil Fielder hit 50 homers again? Will anyone ever hit 60 homers again? Does the team have a 20-game winner? Are there any "40/40" players left in the game today? You don't have to say "per year;" everyone knows that's what you mean.

During any given season, there is a natural tendency for observers to focus on whatever evidence has become available so far "this year" and to attach undue significance to these partial results, as if they were just as important as any previous annual results. When Scott Erickson was leading the league with a 1.83 ERA half way through 1991, he got just as much attention and respect at that point, as he would have earned in October by posting a 1.83 ERA for a full year. There was no other evidence available to contradict or modify the stated results up to that point in time. Indeed, many people in mid 1991 were looking back at Erickson's 1990 performance and noting the 1.35 ERA during September as confirmation that the new superman was for real.

Nobody was saying, "Hey, it's only half a year of great performance ... he will probably finish the season with an ERA around 3.00." Everyone was inclined to believe that "so far this year" was synonymous with "this year in total."

Early results stick in our memory. Take April for example: I still remember that Graig Nettles once hit nine home runs in April. Ron Cey got 11 jacks in April one year. It was big news at the time. Did you ever hear about how many homers anybody hit during July? Nobody gets national attention for hitting nine homers during July. By midseason, you would need a dozen dingers in a month just to get anyone to lift an eyebrow. If you hit 12 homers in April, people would scream and roll in the aisles and talk about the Hall of Fame.

We get a steady flow of numbers during the season. On April 30 we look at April stats and think about them. On May 31 we look at April-May stats and reflect further. On June 30 we look at April-May-June numbers, and on July 31 we look at April-May-June-July. The cumulative effect of all this looking at numbers is that April gets over-emphasized in our thinking. So does May. And June.

When do we stop and look at every player's isolated July-August performance? Or August-September? The later months just don't ever get the whole national population of fans looking at their results, but April-May results get that kind of scrutiny in print and broadcast media, because on May 31 all the stats they have to talk about are April-May stats.

Many years ago, before these numbers were commonly available, I took a liking to second half stats. To some extent I liked them because they were the "underdogs" of the statistical world. They were ignored, overlooked, and under-appreciated. Another reason why I liked second half stats was that they

gave me an advantage over the people who didn't know about them. Although they are under-appreciated, second half stats are potentially more important than first half stats.

I didn't invent the idea of looking at second half numbers, of course. It is an old baseball axiom that a rookie's true value is measured in his second tour around the league, after pitchers have had time to study him -- during the second half of his rookie season. Matt Nokes hit .289 as a rookie, but his performance changed during the season; he hit way over .300 in the first half, and .250 in the second half. He has been a .250 hitter ever since.

If you want to win Rotisserie baseball, you better get used to the idea of studying second half numbers. Many magazines and annuals have started focusing on second half numbers, just as I predicted they would when I started including them in my annual book in January 1989.

Last year's second half numbers are, after all, more recent evidence than the first half numbers that get so much attention. The anecdotal evidence is endless. You can find many stories in the older editions of the Rotisserie Baseball Annual. But the point is already clear: second half stats are surely worth a long, hard look, as part of your annual effort to forecast player performance for the coming year.

Why is the Second Half so important? Several reasons:

(1) The second half of the preceding year is chronologically closer to the period that we are trying to predict.

In a baseball forecast context, events that happened ten years ago are meaningless. A two year old event is possibly meaningful, but is still suspect because of its age. Events just one year old are more relevant than two year old events, and things that happened late last year are usually more meaningful than those that happened early last year. Second Half stats give us a picture, a valuable little snapshot, in which the more remote events of the previous year (i.e. April, May and June) have been eliminated.

(2) IF SOMETHING HAPPENED during the preceding year that changed a player's abilities and output, that "something" will be more heavily reflected in the second half numbers than in the full year numbers. If whatever it was that happened, happened on July 4th, that event will be fully reflected in second half statistics, 50% reflected in full year statistics, and not-at-all reflected in first half statistics of the preceding year.

Some events get into the news, and some don't. As we all know, many things can happen during the long baseball season. A hitter may be moved in the batting order. The players batting in front of him or behind him in the batting order may change, or be changed. The player's whole team may be changed. Opposing defense may be relocated to a hitter's disadvantage, or his own fielding position may be shifted and have an adverse, or favorable, effect on his hitting. All these factors affect statistics even when a player's innate skills, attitude, concentration, and total playing time remain exactly the same.

(3) Skills can change, too. A young hitter may learn (finally!) to lay off the high fastball, or to go the other way with an outside pitch. He may learn such things gradually over the course of several years, he may learn them during one season, or he may learn them suddenly on July 4th. An older hitter may lose some speed and get to first base on time less often, or he may lose his ability to get around on a fastball. Or pitchers may simply LEARN that the old man can no longer jerk their fastball into the seats. Word spreads fast among pitchers around a league.

(4) Rookies, not veterans, are most susceptible to opposing pitchers and managers learning something that is going to impair their hitting performance. As noted above, the cornerstone of the "second half theory" is the old baseball axiom that a rookie's true ability can be seen in his second tour around the league, i.e. in the second half of the season.

Through the miracle of STATS, Inc. we were able to split the 1994 season in half precisely, at June 7. Following are the $ values earned by every player in the true second half.

HITTERS 1994 SECOND HALF VALUES

NAME	TEAM	VALUE	NAME	TEAM	VALUE
Kenny Lofton	CLE	$55	Sean Berry	MON	$22
Barry Bonds	SF	$52	Joe Carter	TOR	$22
Jeff Bagwell	HOU	$52	Eric Young	COL	$22
Albert Belle	CLE	$42	Reggie Sanders	CIN	$22
Dante Bichette	COL	$40	Sandy Alomar	CLE	$22
Craig Biggio	HOU	$37	Shane Mack	FA	$22
Sammy Sosa	CHC	$37	Mo Vaughn	BOS	$22
Marquis Grissom	MON	$36	Eddie Williams	SD	$22
Fred McGriff	ATL	$35	David Justice	ATL	$22
Paul Molitor	TOR	$35	Jim Thome	CLE	$21
Brady Anderson	BAL	$33	Cal Ripken	BAL	$21
Chuck Knoblauch	MIN	$33	Paul O'Neill	NYY	$21
Ken Griffey	SEA	$32	Jose Canseco	BOS	$21
Derek Bell	HOU	$32	Jeff Conine	FLA	$21
Larry Walker	FA	$32	Edgar Martinez	SEA	$20
Moises Alou	MON	$31	Tim Raines	CHW	$20
Barry Larkin	CIN	$31	Luis Gonzalez	HOU	$20
Frank Thomas	CHW	$31	Alex Cole	MIN	$20
Glenallen Hill	CHC	$30	Eddie Murray	CLE	$20
Tony Gwynn	SD	$30	Todd Zeile	STL	$20
Wil Cordero	MON	$30	Mike Kingery	COL	$20
Vince Coleman	FA	$29	Tino Martinez	SEA	$20
Carlos Baerga	CLE	$28	John Valentin	BOS	$20
Matt Williams	SF	$28	Brett Boone	CIN	$19
Gary Sheffield	FLA	$27	Mark McLemore	TEX	$19
Lance Johnson	CHW	$27	Manny Ramirez	CLE	$19
Mark Whiten	STL	$26	Mike Piazza	LA	$19
Felix Jose	FA	$26	Jay Bell	PIT	$19
Otis Nixon	TEX	$26	Luis Polonia	NYY	$18
Bernie Williams	NYY	$25	Mike Blowers	SEA	$18
Kirby Puckett	MIN	$25	Cecil Fielder	DET	$18
Andres Galarraga	COL	$25	Geronimo Pena	STL	$18
Hal Morris	CIN	$25	Deion Sanders	CIN	$18
Rickey Henderson	OAK	$25	Delino Deshields	LA	$18
Ruben Sierra	OAK	$25	Wade Boggs	NYY	$18
Bip Roberts	SD	$24	Junior Felix	FA	$18
Chad Curtis	CAL	$24	Omar Vizquel	CLE	$17
Chili Davis	CAL	$24	Carlos Garcia	PIT	$17
Tony Phillips	DET	$24	Kirk Gibson	FA	$17
Brett Butler	FA	$24	Tim Wallach	LA	$17
Gregg Jefferies	PHI	$23	Jose Valentin	MIL	$16
Mike Stanley	NYY	$23	Roberto Kelly	ATL	$16
Rafael Palmeiro	BAL	$23	Stan Javier	OAK	$16
Greg Vaughn	MIL	$23	Bobby Bonilla	NYM	$16
Bob Hamelin	KC	$22	John Olerud	TOR	$16
Ivan Rodriguez	TEX	$22	Geronimo Berroa	OAK	$15
Kevin Mitchell	FA	$22	Dave Nilsson	MIL	$15
Juan Gonzalez	TEX	$22	Orlando Merced	PIT	$15

HITTERS 1994 SECOND HALF VALUES

NAME	TEAM	VALUE	NAME	TEAM	VALUE
Chuck Carr	FLA	$15	Jeffrey Hammonds	BAL	$12
Dean Palmer	TEX	$15	Jim Eisenreich	PHI	$12
Rico Brogna	NYM	$15	Tom Brunansky	FA	$12
Rusty Greer	TEX	$15	John Kruk	FA	$12
Darren Lewis	SF	$15	Wally Joyner	KC	$12
Raul Mondesi	LA	$15	Pedro Munoz	MIN	$11
Ray Lankford	STL	$15	Ozzie Smith	STL	$11
Cliff Floyd	MON	$15	Juan Samuel	FA	$11
Harold Baines	FA	$15	Dick Schofield	FA	$11
Dave Clark	PIT	$15	Brad Ausmus	SD	$11
Mickey Morandini	PHI	$15	Wayne Kirby	CLE	$11
Spike Owen	CAL	$15	Luis Alicea	BOS	$11
Robin Ventura	CHW	$15	Jerry Browne	FA	$11
Danny Tartabull	NYY	$15	Lou Frazier	MON	$11
Roberto Alomar	TOR	$15	Leo Gomez	BAL	$11
Chris Hoiles	BAL	$15	Jody Reed	FA	$11
Mike Lansing	MON	$14	Chris Gomez	DET	$11
Terry Shumpert	BOS	$14	Bernard Gilkey	STL	$11
Ken Caminiti	SD	$14	Vinny Castilla	COL	$11
Jacob Brumfield	PIT	$14	Mark Grace	FA	$11
Brian McRae	KC	$14	Ozzie Guillen	CHW	$10
Travis Fryman	DET	$14	Dave Martinez	FA	$10
Chris Sabo	FA	$14	Jeff King	PIT	$10
Tony Fernandez	NYY	$14	Scott Brosius	OAK	$10
Darrin Jackson	FA	$14	Jose Lind	KC	$10
Matt Mieske	MIL	$14	Jim Leyritz	NYY	$10
Terry Steinbach	OAK	$14	Milt Thompson	FA	$10
Paul Sorrento	CLE	$14	Bo Jackson	FA	$10
Pat Kelly	NYY	$13	Ryan Klesko	ATL	$10
Tim Salmon	CAL	$13	Benito Santiago	FA	$10
Charlie Hayes	FA	$13	Todd Benzinger	FA	$10
Eddie Taubensee	CIN	$13	Jeff Blauser	FA	$10
Kevin Seitzer	MIL	$13	Steve Buechele	CHC	$10
John Patterson	SF	$13	Kevin Bass	FA	$10
Steve Finley	SD	$13	Jeff Kent	NYM	$10
Lou Whitaker	DET	$13	Joe Girardi	COL	$9
Shawon Dunston	CHC	$13	James Mouton	HOU	$9
Royce Clayton	SF	$12	Derrick May	CHC	$9
Bret Barberie	BAL	$12	Tony Eusebio	HOU	$9
Randy Velarde	FA	$12	Troy Neel	OAK	$9
Al Martin	PIT	$12	Ed Sprague	TOR	$9
Craig Shipley	HOU	$12	Randy Knorr	TOR	$8
Felix Fermin	FA	$12	Don Mattingly	NYY	$8
Greg Colbrunn	FLA	$12	John Vanderwal	PIT	$8
Lee Tinsley	BOS	$12	Rey Sanchez	CHC	$8
Will Clark	TEX	$12	Gary Gaetti	FA	$8
Brianr Hunter	CIN	$12	Darrin Fletcher	MON	$8
Jay Buhner	SEA	$12	Kevin Stocker	PHI	$8

HITTERS 1994 SECOND HALF VALUES

NAME	TEAM	VALUE	NAME	TEAM	VALUE
Mike Huff	TOR	$8	Henry Rodriguez	LA	$5
Eric Anthony	FA	$8	Rich Rowland	BOS	$5
Darren Daulton	PHI	$8	Darryl Strawberry	SF	$5
Todd Hundley	NYM	$8	Nelson Liriano	PIT	$5
Devon White	TOR	$7	Jim Edmonds	CAL	$5
Joey Cora	FA	$7	Alex Diaz	FA	$5
Eric Karros	LA	$7	Rondell White	MON	$4
Joe Orsulak	NYM	$7	Oddibe McDowell	FA	$4
Kurt Abbott	FLA	$7	Kevin McReynolds	FA	$4
Greg Gagne	KC	$7	Lloyd McClendon	FA	$4
Jim Lindeman	NYM	$7	Orlando Miller	HOU	$4
Jt Snow	CAL	$7	Damon Berryhill	FA	$4
Chris Turner	CAL	$7	Andy Vanslyke	FA	$4
Mariano Duncan	FA	$7	Mark Carreon	SF	$4
Mike Bordick	OAK	$7	Jeff Reboulet	MIN	$4
Mike Macfarlane	FA	$7	Mark McGwire	OAK	$4
Billy Hatcher	FA	$7	Mike Lavalliere	CHW	$4
Mickey Tettleton	FA	$7	Walt Weiss	COL	$4
Jeff Branson	CIN	$7	Jeff Cirillo	MIL	$4
Ricky Gutierrez	HOU	$7	Mike Gallego	FA	$4
John Jaha	MIL	$7	Carlos Rodriguez	BOS	$4
Andujar Cedeno	SD	$6	Lenny Webster	FA	$4
Jose Oliva	ATL	$6	Jeff Frye	TEX	$4
Andre Dawson	FA	$6	Steve Scarsone	SF	$4
Chris James	FA	$6	Tony Longmire	PHI	$4
Dwight Smith	FA	$6	Bill Spiers	NYM	$4
Thomas Howard	CIN	$6	Ryan Thompson	NYM	$4
Scott Hemond	FA	$6	Scott Cooper	BOS	$4
Scott Leius	MIN	$6	Alan Trammell	FA	$4
Mike Greenwell	BOS	$6	Ruben Amaro	CLE	$3
Luis Lopez	SD	$6	David Hulse	TEX	$3
Tom Pagnozzi	STL	$6	Reggie Jefferson	SEA	$3
Manuel Lee	FA	$6	Milt Cuyler	DET	$3
Rick Wilkins	CHC	$5	Scott Servais	HOU	$3
Howard Johnson	FA	$5	Dave Winfield	FA	$3
Brian Jordan	STL	$5	Charlie O'Brien	ATL	$3
Gerald Perry	FA	$5	Juan Bell	BOS	$3
Don Slaught	PIT	$5	Scott Fletcher	BOS	$3
Pat Meares	MIN	$5	Mike Felder	FA	$3
Dave Howard	KC	$5	Dave Valle	FA	$3
Terry Pendleton	FA	$5	Luis Sojo	SEA	$3
Ricky Jordan	FA	$5	Mike Kelly	ATL	$3
Esteban Beltre	TEX	$5	Brent Gates	OAK	$3
Wes Chamberlain	BOS	$5	Norberto Martin	CHW	$3
Scott Livingstone	SD	$5	Lenny Dykstra	PHI	$3
Mark Lemke	ATL	$5	Randy Ready	FA	$3
Tony Tarasco	ATL	$5	Gerald Young	FA	$3
Brian Johnson	SD	$5	Mario Diaz	FLA	$3

HITTERS 1994 SECOND HALF VALUES

NAME	TEAM	VALUE	NAME	TEAM	VALUE
Jeromy Burnitz	CLE	$3	John Cangelosi	FA	$1
David Segui	NYM	$3	Dave Magadan	FA	$1
Tim Naehring	BOS	$3	Brianl Hunter	HOU	$1
Brian Harper	FA	$3	Phil Plantier	HOU	$1
Dave Henderson	FA	$3	Turner Ward	MIL	$1
Brent Mayne	KC	$2	Tom Foley	FA	$1
Darnell Coles	FA	$2	Todd Pratt	FA	$1
Rene Gonzales	FA	$2	Robby Thompson	SF	$1
Denny Hocking	MIN	$2	Karl Rhodes	CHC	$1
Kirt Manwaring	SF	$2	Rob Natal	FLA	$1
Dan Wilson	SEA	$2	Tim Bogar	NYM	$1
Gerald Williams	NYY	$2	Keith Mitchell	FA	$1
Jose Oquendo	STL	$2	Kevin Roberson	CHC	$1
Mike Benjamin	SF	$2	Billy Ripken	FA	$1
Steve Pegues	PIT	$2	Jose Vizcaino	NYM	$0
Greg Myers	CAL	$2	Mike Matheny	MIL	$0
Harold Reynolds	FA	$2	Craig Grebeck	CHW	$0
Bj Surhoff	FA	$2	Melvin Nieves	SD	$0
Jose Hernandez	CHC	$2	Chris Jones	NYM	$0
Warren Newson	CHW	$2	Lenny Harris	CIN	$0
Bill Pecota	FA	$2	Eric Fox	FA	$0
Mitch Webster	FA	$2	Ray McDavid	SD	$0
Rex Hudler	CAL	$2	Francisco Matos	OAK	$0
Chris Gwynn	FA	$2	Rich Becker	MIN	$0
Midre Cummings	PIT	$2	Pat Borders	FA	$0
Lance Parrish	FA	$2	Daryl Boston	FA	$0
Rich Amaral	SEA	$2	David McCarty	MIN	$0
Chad Kreuter	FA	$2	Danny Bautista	DET	$0
Tony Pena	FA	$2	Garey Ingram	LA	$0
Troy O'Leary	MIL	$1	Danny Sheaffer	FA	$0
Eddie Zambrano	CHC	$1	Junior Ortiz	FA	$0
Jerome Walton	CIN	$1	Carl Everett	NYM	$0
Jeff Tackett	FA	$1	Garret Anderson	CAL	$0
Javier Lopez	ATL	$1	Rafael Bournigal	LA	$0
Sid Bream	FA	$1	Gary Varsho	FA	$0
Mike Lieberthal	PHI	$1	Jeff Reed	FA	$0
Dave Hansen	LA	$1	Mike Maksudian	FA	$0
Alex Rodriguez	SEA	$1	Butch Davis	FA	$0
Gary Disarcina	CAL	$1	Jesus Tavarez	FLA	$0
Mark Parent	FA	$1	Alex Arias	FLA	$0
Kelly Stinnett	NYM	$1	Jeff Treadway	LA	$0
Rick Wrona	FA	$1	Torey Lovullo	CLE	$0
Phil Clark	SD	$1	Domingo Cedeno	TOR	$0
Tim Hyers	SD	$1	Randy Milligan	FA	$0
Kim Batiste	PHI	$1	Carlos Hernandez	LA	$0
Chip Hale	MIN	$1	Luis Rivera	FA	$0
Ron Karkovice	CHW	$1			
Damion Easley	CAL	$1	PLAYERS NOT LISTED HAD NO VALUE		

PITCHERS 1994 SECOND HALF VALUES

NAME	TEAM	VALUE	NAME	TEAM	VALUE
Jeff Montgomery	KC	$42	Andy Benes	SD	$15
John Wetteland	MON	$38	Bob Wickman	NYY	$15
Greg Maddux	ATL	$35	Marvin Freeman	COL	$15
John Franco	FA	$35	David Wells	DET	$14
Rod Beck	SF	$32	Mel Rojas	MON	$14
Robb Nen	FLA	$32	Ben McDonald	BAL	$14
Steve Howe	NYY	$32	Bobby Jones	NYM	$14
Bret Saberhagen	NYM	$31	John Hudek	HOU	$14
Todd Worrell	LA	$30	Zane Smith	FA	$14
Jack McDowell	NYY	$29	Joe Boever	FA	$14
Trevor Hoffman	SD	$29	Jose Rijo	CIN	$13
Dennis Eckersley	FA	$29	Ron Darling	OAK	$13
Doug Jones	FA	$28	Charles Nagy	CLE	$13
Jeff Brantley	CIN	$28	Doug Drabek	HOU	$13
Steve Ontiveros	FA	$27	Melido Perez	NYY	$13
Bobby Ayala	SEA	$26	Alex Fernandez	CHW	$13
Darren Hall	TOR	$25	Darren Oliver	TEX	$13
Rick Aguilera	MIN	$25	Wilson Alvarez	CHW	$13
Rene Arocha	STL	$25	Joe Hesketh	FA	$13
Tom Henke	STL	$24	Pedro Astacio	LA	$12
Randy Johnson	SEA	$23	Josias Manzanillo	NYM	$12
Ken Ryan	BOS	$23	Anthony Young	CHC	$12
Mike Fetters	MIL	$22	Jimmy Key	NYY	$12
Todd Jones	HOU	$22	Danny Cox	FA	$11
Bobby Munoz	PHI	$21	Roger Clemens	BOS	$11
Butch Henry	MON	$21	Jose Deleon	FA	$11
Joey Hamilton	SD	$21	Bill Vanlandingham	SF	$11
Steve Trachsel	CHC	$18	John Smiley	CIN	$11
Roberto Hernandez	CHW	$18	Pete Harnisch	FA	$11
Kent Mercker	ATL	$18	Mark Langston	CAL	$11
Lee Smith	CAL	$18	Tom Candiotti	LA	$10
Dennis Martinez	CLE	$18	Johnny Ruffin	CIN	$10
Pat Hentgen	TOR	$18	Rick White	PIT	$10
Bruce Ruffin	COL	$18	Ramon Martinez	LA	$10
Andy Ashby	SD	$17	Jeff Russell	FA	$10
Shane Reynolds	HOU	$17	Kevin Foster	CHC	$10
David Cone	KC	$17	Jason Jacome	NYM	$10
Mike Mussina	BAL	$17	Hector Carrasco	CIN	$10
Mark Eichhorn	BAL	$17	Randy St.Clair	FA	$10
Pedroj Martinez	MON	$16	Jeff Fassero	MON	$10
Kevin Appier	KC	$16	Gil Heredia	MON	$9
Eric Plunk	CLE	$16	Ricky Bones	MIL	$9
Danny Jackson	STL	$16	Rusty eacham	KC	$9
Jim Bullinger	CHC	$16	Chuck Finley	CAL	$9
Ken Hill	MON	$15	Alan Mills	BAL	$9
Randy Myers	CHC	$15	Scott Sanders	SD	$9
Kevin Gross	TEX	$15	Rich Monteleone	FA	$9
Greg McMichael	ATL	$15	Jon Lieber	PIT	$9

PITCHERS 1994 SECOND HALF VALUES

NAME	TEAM	VALUE	NAME	TEAM	VALUE
Tim Scott	MON	$9	Pat Rapp	FLA	$5
Tom Glavine	ATL	$9	Kevin Campbell	MIN	$5
Cal Eldred	MIL	$9	Jason Bere	CHW	$5
Bobby Witt	FA	$9	Bill Krueger	FA	$5
John Roper	CIN	$9	Juan Guzman	TOR	$4
David West	PHI	$8	Carlos Reyes	OAK	$4
Kenny Rogers	TEX	$8	Billy Brewer	KC	$4
Mark Clark	CLE	$8	Arthur Rhodes	BAL	$4
Todd Stottlemyre	FA	$8	Bob Patterson	FA	$4
Erik Hanson	FA	$8	Frank Castillo	CHC	$4
Woody Williams	TOR	$8	Tim Davis	SEA	$4
Scott Kamieniecki	NYY	$8	Jason Grimsley	CLE	$4
Tony Castillo	TOR	$8	Jose Mesa	COL	$4
Mike Stanton	FA	$8	Sterling Hitchcock	NYY	$4
Tom Gordon	KC	$8	Joe Grahe	COL	$4
Fernando Valenzuela	FA	$8	Jose Mercedes	MIL	$4
Kirk Rueter	MON	$7	Greg Cadaret	FA	$4
Toby Borland	PHI	$7	Tony Fossas	FA	$4
Bud Black	FA	$7	Jay Howell	FA	$3
Jamie Moyer	BAL	$7	Rob Murphy	FA	$3
Bill Risley	SEA	$7	Goose Gossage	FA	$3
Luis Aquino	FA	$7	Mark Gubicza	FA	$3
Mark Williamson	FA	$7	Heath Slocumb	PHI	$3
Steve Avery	ATL	$7	Pedroa Martinez	HOU	$3
Ismael Valdes	LA	$6	Storm Davis	FA	$3
Pete Schourek	CIN	$6	Russ Springer	CAL	$3
Christian Howard	BOS	$6	Mark Gardner	FLA	$3
Bob Scanlan	MIL	$6	Mark Acre	OAK	$3
Dave Veres	HOU	$6	Mike Ignasiak	MIL	$3
Kevin Tapani	MIN	$6	Dave Nied	COL	$3
Mark Portugal	SF	$6	John Smoltz	ATL	$3
Terry Mathews	FLA	$6	Chuck Crim	FA	$3
Vicente Palacios	STL	$6	Rich Scheid	FLA	$3
Mike Dyer	PIT	$6	Steve Reed	COL	$3
Chuck McElroy	CIN	$6	Roger Mason	FA	$3
Mike Gardiner	FA	$6	Chris Bosio	SEA	$3
Aaron Sele	BOS	$6	Mark Guthrie	MIN	$3
Kevin Brown	FA	$6	Mark Leiter	FA	$3
Paul Assenmacher	FA	$5	Buddy Groom	DET	$2
Jeff Shaw	MON	$5	Tim Mauser	SD	$2
Hipolito Pichardo	KC	$5	Daryl Kile	HOU	$2
Jeff Tabaka	SD	$5	Yorkis Perez	FLA	$2
Danny Miceli	PIT	$5	Mike Timlin	TOR	$2
Dave Leiper	OAK	$5	John Briscoe	OAK	$2
Jose Bautista	FA	$5	Rudy Seanez	LA	$2
Curt Schilling	PHI	$5	Ryan Bowen	FLA	$2
Mike Munoz	COL	$5	Kirk McCaskill	FA	$2
John Burkett	TEX	$5	Bill Taylor	OAK	$2

PITCHERS 1994 SECOND HALF VALUES

NAME	TEAM	VALUE	NAME	TEAM	VALUE
Graeme Lloyd	MIL	$2	Rheal Cormier	STL	$0
Mike Moore	DET	$2	Dave Burba	SF	$0
Mike Maddux	FA	$2	Albie Lopez	CLE	$0
Jesse Orosco	FA	$2	Bill Gullickson	FA	$0
Steve Bedrosian	ATL	$2	Bob Welch	FA	$0
Erik Schullstrom	MIN	$2	Mike Harkey	FA	$0
Dave Stevens	MIN	$2	Larry Andersen	FA	$0
Dennis Cook	CLE	$2	Lance Painter	COL	$0
Brian Anderson	CAL	$2	Orel Hershiser	FA	$0
John Habyan	STL	$2	Don Pall	FA	$0
Allen Watson	STL	$2	Mike Trombley	MIN	$0
Jose Dejesus	KC	$2	Greg Gohr	DET	$0
Matt Whiteside	TEX	$2	Sean Bergman	DET	$0
Pat Mahomes	MIN	$2	Pat Gomez	SF	$0
Bill Wegman	MIL	$2	Dwight Gooden	FA	$0
Chris Haney	KC	$2	Carl Willis	MIN	$0
Stan Belinda	FA	$2	Mike Williams	PHI	$0
Willie Blair	FA	$2	Bill Swift	FA	$0
Eric Gunderson	NYM	$1	Rich Delucia	FA	$0
Bob Tewksbury	FA	$1	Brian Williams	SD	$0
Jeff Nelson	SEA	$1	Ross Powell	HOU	$0
Tom Edens	FA	$1	Bryan Hickerson	CHC	$0
Brad Brink	SF	$1	Ricky Bottalico	PHI	$0
Dave Otto	CHC	$1	Omar Daal	LA	$0
Armando Benitez	BAL	$1	Scott Bankhead	FA	$0
Tom Urbani	STL	$1	Scott Brow	TOR	$0
Denny Neagle	PIT	$1	Greg Swindell	HOU	$0
Derek Lilliquist	FA	$1	Heath Haynes	OAK	$0
Steve Frey	SF	$1	John Dettmer	TEX	$0
Bryce Florie	SD	$1	Paul Quantrill	PHI	$0
Steve Cooke	PIT	$1	Craig Lefferts	FA	$0
Joe Ausanio	NYY	$1	Rich Rodriguez	STL	$0
Gary Buckels	FA	$1	John Hope	PIT	$0
Mike Hampton	HOU	$1	Mike Bielecki	FA	$0
Jeremy Hernandez	FLA	$1	Atlee Hammaker	CHW	$0
Mark Wohlers	ATL	$1	Mike Magnante	KC	$0
Jeff Bronkey	MIL	$1	Brad Woodall	ATL	$0
Matt Turner	CLE	$1	Dan Plesac	PIT	$0
Kent Bottenfield	FA	$1	Ravelo Manzanillo	PIT	$0
Gene Harris	FA	$1	Scott Service	FA	$0
Angel Miranda	MIL	$0	Jeff Schwarz	CAL	$0
Bob Wells	SEA	$0	Mike Butcher	CAL	$0
Darren Holmes	COL	$0	Mike Jackson	FA	$0
Blas Minor	NYM	$0	Rick Honeycutt	FA	$0
Jaime Navarro	MIL	$0	Jim Gott	FA	$0
Mike Henneman	DET	$0			
Paul Shuey	CLE	$0	PLAYERS NOT LISTED HAD NO VALUE		
Roger Pavlik	TEX	$0			

UPDATE: Analysis of Astros-Padres Trade
by Bill Gilbert

For the Astros, Derek Bell has been handed the right field job and will bat in the middle of the order. Phil Plantier is ticketed for left field and will probably hit behind Jeff Bagwell. Luis Gonzalez was temporarily left with no clear full-time role, suggesting the possibility of another trade. The club believes Brian Hunter is ready to step in as the starting center fielder. James Mouton is considered the all-around backup outfielder. Milt Thompson appeared to be destined for a pinch hitting role. With all these outfielders, the Astros were not pursuing free agent Kevin Bass.

In the infield, Phil Nevin has been told the third base job is his to win. The club was disappointed with his lack of progress in 1994 and they remain concerned about his range in the field and his lack of power at the plate. Craig Shipley provides insurance if Nevin isn't ready. The Astros now have room under the cap and the agent for Houston area resident, Charlie Hayes was in contact with Astros GM Bob Watson. The starting shortstop will be determined in spring training in competition between Orlando Miller and Ricky Gutierrez. Chris Donnels and Andy Stankiewicz are viewed as utility players.

The Astros believe they improved their pitching depth with the trade. Pedro A. Martinez becomes the top lefthander in the bullpen with Ross Powell and Rule 5 draftee, Nate Cromwell battling for the other slot. Tal Smith is high on Doug Brocail, and he will compete for the number five starting slot with lefty Mike Hampton. Both had outstanding winter campaigns.

A preview of the starting lineup, before further trades:
Hunter CF
Biggio 2B
Bagwell 1B
Plantier LF
Bell RF   Nevin or Shipley 3B
Miller or Gutierrez SS
Servais or Eusebio C
Drabek, Reynolds, Kile, Swindell, Hampton, Brocail SP

The middle of the order is clearly stronger, but the bottom is decidedly weaker than in 1994.

For the Padres, left field is open for either Ray McDavid or Mel Nieves to compete with Bip Roberts (who really wants to play outfield) with Finley in center and Gwynn in right. If Eddie Williams is a one-year wonder, Roberto Petagine should be ready to take over at first base, although he had a very poor winter season. The rest of the infield is set with Roberts (who may remain stuck at second) plus Cedeno and Caminiti.

Brian Williams should challenge for the number five starter slot. He has the arm and athletic ability to be successful at the major league level. Maybe a change of scenery is what he needs to reach his potential. The Padres do not have an established lefthander on the staff, and didn't want to part with Martinez.

They were expected to go after some lefthanded pitching help, particularly in the bullpen.

The Padres potential starting lineup is glaringly short in power:
Roberts 2B
Finley CF
Gwynn RF
Williams 1B
Caminiti 3B
Nieves or McDavid LF
Cedeno SS
Ausmus C
Benes, Ashby, Hamilton, Sanders, Worrell, Williams SP

Both clubs were expected to make more deals, and the magnitude of this trade will stir some movement among other clubs. Incidentally, this was not a father and son deal as had been reported. Bob Watson did the negotiating for Houston. Randy Smith was in Houston for a few days over Christmas, but he was really hurting with an injury to his anterior cruciate ligament (suffered playing basketball) which will require surgery after the first of the year.

CATCHER:
TACTICAL CONSIDERATIONS

The position of catcher offers about as much danger as any position except starting pitcher. It is much easier to find a pitfall than to stay on the narrow path toward true rewards.

Following are the main reasons catcher picks can cause problems:

1. Catchers get injured more than any other position players.

2. Strong defensive catchers often get full-time play despite a puny batting average that can wreck a whole team. The stronger your team, the more they hurt you.

3. The small number of good offensive catchers will make bidding intense.

4. In most leagues there are not enough positive value catchers to fill all the necessary roster slots, so waiting until the very end and picking from the leftovers can be just as dangerous as paying too much early in the auction.

5. Catchers never work seven days a week and need to be rested like pitchers. Often they play hurt, affecting their performance.

Investing in an expensive catcher is about as risky as investing in a high-price starting pitcher. It's wise to make a mental adjustment, when bidding, to consider that pitching gets discounted from 50% to 35% of spending on average. Apply a discount to catcher values as well, to account for the risk of injury and/or continued use while not in peak form.

Don't go too far quantitatively, however. By knocking pitchers down from 50% to 35% of budget, we are implicitly taking 30% off the value of every pitcher's expected performance (15/50 = 30%). For catchers, taking off 10% or 15% is plenty, and if we're talking about a $10 to $15 player based on initial calculations, those adjustments will amount to only $1 to $2. Down around the $5 value level, the adjustment can round off to zero.

Also note that I have helped make part of this adjustment for you already, by imposing caution into the projections for playing time. Even if a catcher has been 100% healthy and playing 140 games a year consistently, I will rarely project any catcher to play more than 130 games, and pencil in most of the full-timers for about 125 games. If you check career stats for several prominent catchers, you will quickly see why this method works. Seasons with a catcher getting over 130 games are unusual, and if you look at the rare cases with about 150 games, you are usually looking at a catcher who becomes a pinch hitter when he's on the bench, so he doesn't really catch 150 games anyway. Finally, note the truism that when a catcher plays excessively, his stats deteriorate from wear and tear; so getting 480 at bats when I projected 440 often leads to the same value.

Obviously I endorse the $1 catcher theory, with some cautions:

1. Be alert for opportunities. There is a difference between going to your draft planning to be very cautious about catchers, versus going with a blind determination to avoid getting a good catcher. There are lots of $1 catcher theorists in every auction, and

the number is increasing every year. If all eleven of your opponents are going the same way, then by all means be contrary, and take advantage.

2. Pursuing cheap catchers is quite different from ignoring the position. While I may spend only 1% or 2% of my money on catchers, I also recognize that about 9% of my roster slots (2/23) are going to be catchers, and I'm likely to spend about 10% of my time studying that position when preparing for the draft, both to look for opportunities and to avoid pitfalls.

3. Make a long list of "acceptable" catchers. The simplest method is just to look at career batting averages. Get the guys who won't hurt you. A catcher with a .270 career average is a prime commodity (if you don't believe me, count them). Some of the other things I look for are high OBP's (that would have put you onto Mike Stanley years ago) and an absence of low batting averages. A catcher who hits .270, .210, .275, .205 over four seasons will be much riskier than a catcher who hits .240, .240, .240, .240, although both may have the same career batting average. The former case is better for a weak team that needs to take chances; the latter case is better for a strong team that wants to minimize risk. Other factors that I look for include improvement in strikeout/walk ratios during recent seasons (just comparing the player to himself, not to other players) and absolute strikeout/walk ratio. For a catcher, 2:1 is not bad; when the ratio gets above 3:1 I begin to worry. Darren Daulton was good by this measure even when he was a .206 career hitter. Most hitters wouldn't be allowed to stay in a lineup with a horrendous K/BB ratio, but catchers are an exception because of the defensive aspect. Dan Wilson was almost 6:1 last year.

4. Watch position eligibility with an eagle's eye. Finding an outfielder who qualifies at catcher can often produce rewards comparable to getting a 15th hitter for free.

5. Use the disabled list to your advantage. This works two ways. Late in the draft, when the list of available catchers will scare you, taking a disabled catcher (even one who is out for the season) will at least protect you from damage. Taking a DL catcher is safer than taking a career .210 hitter. The second benefit comes from the time that you buy to study recent box scores and claim a replacement. My league allows 24 hours after the draft, to reserve disabled players and get replacements whose accumulated stats get credited retroactively. So in the heat of the auction, I may bail out by drafting any DL catcher, then checking that night's box scores (and all others up to that point) for a home run or a couple RBI somewhere; I'll put in my claim using that method. Often one home run or two RBI can be meaningful at the end of the year. Just make sure, if you follow this method, to recognize that your work isn't done for the year; you may want to wait longer to claim your DL replacement and give up those retroactive stats, when there's nobody attractive to claim, to keep your options open.

For the Record:

Likely to be bargains: Carlos Delgado, Dave Nilsson, Rich Rowland, Joe Girardi, Tim Laker, Eddie Taubensee, Todd Hundley.

Likely to be overvalued: Sandy Alomar, Ron Karkovice, Mike Lieberthal, Benito Santiago, Charles Johnson.

AMERICAN LEAGUE CATCHERS

In general, catching jobs are still very much up for grabs around the American League. Many of the better hitting catchers have become free agents and have not yet signed for the 1995 season. Mickey Tettleton, Brian Harper, B. J. Surhoff, Mike Macfarlane and Pat Borders were still free agents in late December. Benito Santiago and Joe Oliver from the National League were also still unsigned for 1995. Any of these front line backstops could end up in any of the unsettled AL catching positions, most notably in California, Detroit, Kansas City and Milwaukee. A lot of catching situations could change dramatically over the next few months as this game of musical catchers is played out.

Baltimore Orioles

Matt Nokes left the Yankees as a free agent after last season and will now compete for a backup job in Baltimore. Nokes is a good power threat but not always a good hitter for average; he has averaged a homer once every 20 at bats over the course of his career, and the move to Camden Yards won't hurt the average. Nokes will win a backup/third catcher role for the Orioles and provide Rotisserie owners with an opportunity to pick up a few cheap homers. Just be warned that he can hurt a team's batting average,

especially if he play a lot; that makes Nokes a better pick for a weak team than for a strong team.

Fred Matos:

Chris Hoiles can usually be counted on for 25-30 homers and 90 RBI. His batting average dipped to .247 last year, down from .310 in 1993, but the power numbers were still up there. There are a couple of reasons for the dip in his average: 1) pitchers were more careful with him as shown by his team-high 63 walks, and 2) he frequently batted with runners in scoring position and first base open, leading to more walks. The cautious pitching caused Hoiles to get anxious and to swing at marginal pitches, resulting in a lower average.

Hoiles can make the necessary adjustments to regain his consistent hitting. If you need good offensive production from your catcher slots, Hoiles is at the top of a very short list.

Jeff Tackett is the backup catcher. He is not much of a hitter, but he can pop an occasional home run.

Gregg Zaun is the best catching prospect that the Orioles have in the minor leagues, and is number three on the major league depth chart. Zaun is a weak hitter, but his good defense may eventually land him

a backup catching job somewhere in the majors.

Lary Bump:

The Orioles' top minor league catcher is Gregg Zaun. The switch-hitting nephew of Rick Dempsey, Zaun batted .237-7-43 in the International League, where he caught almost every day, and seemed to take an inordinate number of foul balls off his person. He'll be 24 in April. A negative is his size - he's listed at 5-10, but he's one of a number of farmhands for whom Baltimore has added two or three inches to their listed heights.

Cesar Devarez, voted the best defensive catcher in the Eastern League, also hit as never before. His .313 average was an aberration after he'd batted just .234 in his first five pro seasons. At age 25, his future in the majors depends on his defense. The best batting prospect among the Orioles' minor league catchers is B.J. Waszgis, who went .282-21-100 at Frederick in the Carolina League. He's 24, so he'll have to make a move in Double-A in '95. Jim Foster, who had a good season as a rookie pro in the Appalachian League in 1993, hit .266-8-56 in the Sally League. He also showed good on-base ability.

Boston Red Sox

Damon Berryhill has moved on to the National League after signing as a free agent with Cincinnati when the Red Sox failed to exercise their option to retain him. The effect here is relatively light since Berryhill had lost the starting job to Rich Rowland anyway. Rowland is one of the better sleeper picks at catcher in either league.

Taking over the backup job will be Bill Haselman, who served the same role for Seattle most of the last two years. Haselman has usually been a decent hitter who won't hurt you much in a limited role.

Alan Boodman:

Damon Berryhill emerged as the starter last year following the departure of disappointing Dave Valle

in June. By the end of the season he had lost most of the job to Rich Rowland, due primarily to providing sub-par offense batting lefthanded. Although Berryhill is a switch-hitter, he has in recent years fared better against lefties; the degree of his ineptitude versus righthanders was unexpected. Berryhill is further hampered by poor defense, particularly in keeping opposing runners from advancing almost at will. His throwing arm and lack of balanced offense will continue to prevent him from maintaining a full-time role. Berryhill's option was not picked up by the Red Sox last winter, and the Cincinnati Reds signed him to play second fiddle to Eddie Taubensee.

The Red Sox also had a desire to get Rowland's powerful bat into the lineup more frequently. Through 1993 he had spent nearly four full seasons at Class-AAA Toledo in the Detroit system, playing solid defense and developing further offensively each year. The Tigers, who had been searching for some time for a backup to Mickey Tettleton, ignored Rowland for three years and finally got a good season from Chad Kreuter in 1993, sealing Rowland's fate. The trade last spring to the Red Sox liberated him.

Rowland is seeing his career get off to a late start (he's 28), and will have to translate his minor league numbers to major league performance in the very near future in order to see it continue. He showed a rookie's eagerness to overswing and was clearly thinking home run far too often in 1994. If he has learned anything from his experience last season, Rowland will cut down his swing just a little and improve his OBP as a result, an important adjustment for future success.

Former first-round pick Scott Hatteberg is the one being groomed for the starting role down the road, but he's 25 and has yet to play a full season at Triple-A. His defensive skills are established, and he has good strike zone judgement (one would think more catchers would), but other offensive attributes haven't yet developed. He posesses a minor advantage in batting lefthanded. Hatteberg should be ticketed for that full Triple-A season in 1995, unless the Sox don't acquire a veteran backup for Rowland.

Eric Wedge could be a contender for some playing time behind the plate, and he is discussed in the Designated Hitter section, which should tell you something about his defensive ability.

For both the Sox and fantasy leaguers, Rowland is the man for 1995. His defense will allow him to stay in the lineup even if his hitting sputters, and his power should offset any minor weaknesses. He may end up sharing playing time with some veteran backup who has yet to appear. With no prospects waiting immediately off-stage, Rowland may inherit a considerable portion of the workload depending on how things work out, and may prove to be a very wise and very inexpensive pick.

Lary Bump:

Scott Hatteberg caught Aaron Sele at Washington State, but he may need to hit better to join Sele in Boston. His .235-7-19 record at Triple-A Pawtucket represented an improvement over his brief trial there in 1993. The other catchers with pennant-winning Pawtucket were journeymen George Pedre (.218-5-25, age 28) and Eric Wedge (.286-19-59). The 27 year old Wedge is better suited to DH or first base at this point. The Red Sox, apparently undaunted by Dave Valle's abject failure, signed another former Seattle catcher, Bill Haselman. The 28 year old had a high-powered 163 at bats (.331-15-46) at Calgary, and went .193-1-8 at Seattle.

California Angels

Hank Widmer:

The probable starting catcher in 1995 will be Greg Myers. Myers drove in just eight runs in 126 at bats, but has turned into a decent defensive catcher which is why he should get most of the playing time.

Fred Matos:

Greg Myers was the Angels top catcher last year, but a plate collision caused a knee injury requiring both surgery and a month on the disabled list. He nearly hit

his career average of .243 last year, and that's the expectation for 1995 with an occasional home run or two.

Chris Turner looked overmatched in his first 56 at bats last year when he hit a puny .143, but he rebounded nicely, hitting .301 over his last 93 at bats. But that average is deceptive as he is not a run producer. Turner is a line drive hitter who the Angels will likely platoon versus lefthanded pitchers.

Jorge Fabregas was called up from the minors and hit surprisingly well. His .283-0-16 in 127 at bats was even more of a surprise considering his .223-1-24 hitting in Triple-A. His defense needs a great deal of work as he has to improve throwing out runners and stopping pitches in the dirt. The .283 looks like a fluke as he has never hit well above Double-A, but he is 25 and could improve. He has never shown any power. Fabregas may spend 1995 in Triple-A.

Mark Dalesandro hit .317 in Triple-A in 1994, earning a promotion to the majors. Hitting .300 in the Pacific Coast League is equivalent to about .240 in the majors. He doesn't have any power either.

Todd Greene tore up the California League last year, leading all of the minor leagues with 124 RBI, and ranking second in home runs with 35. He also led the California League in many hitting categories and was voted MVP. He was converted to catcher only a few years ago, so his defense may impede his upward mobility if he isn't moved to another position. Greene may go directly to Triple-A, and if he continues to hit well, he may join the Angels sometime in 1995.

Lary Bump:

California's annual search for a catcher may end in 1996 or 1997 when Todd Greene will be ready, at least offensively. The Angels moved him behind the plate from the outfield last season and he responded by leading Class-A ball with 35 homers and the entire minors with 124 RBI while batting .302. His assignment for '95 will be improving his defense in the Texas League.

Chicago White Sox:

As injury insurance, the White Sox signed Barry Lyons and Junior Ortiz to minor league contracts; neither is a good hitter and both are useless for Rotisserie purposes. Bob Melvin has become a free agent and is still unsigned.

Mike LaValliere re-signed with the ChiSox and will retain his reserve role behind Ron Karkovice. LaValliere's Rotisserie value is limited, but he hasn't had a bad batting average since 1986 (.234 for St. Louis); so he'd be a fine filler pick.

Stuart Shea:

Despite missing considerable time in 1994 due to injury, Ron Karkovice should be the Sox' regular catcher for several more seasons. He throws spectacularly well, is respected for his game-calling, and provides an offensive contribution. Before he tore a ligament in his right knee, Karkovice was hitting for power and, most importantly, controlling his often-wild swing. (He drew 19 walks in April.)

"Officer Kark" is signed through this year, with an option for 1996 that the Sox will almost certainly pick up. There is little catching help in the system, and if he can rehabilitate the knee and get 30-40 games of rest per season, Karkovice should be a valuable regular for several more years. He probably will never hit much above .240, but draws some walks and has developed significant home run punch.

Mike Lavalliere, Karkovice's backup, still hits line drives and still looks like the Campfire Marshmallow Man. He's a valuable backup, Rotisserie and otherwise, for his ability to hit for average and come off the bench. Bobby Melvin and Ron Tingley were around for a couple of weeks, but probably won't be back. They wouldn't help much anyway.

In the minors, Clemente Alvarez was the regular catcher at Triple-A Nashville. Despite an outstanding arm (which he hurt in 1993), Alvarez will never play a key role in the majors. A prime candidate for the Jim McNamara/Luis Pujols Memorial Catcher-with-a-

Hole-in-His-Bat Trophy, Alvarez has never hit above .235 in any of his stops through the White Sox chain, but keeps advancing because of his defense and the utter lack of competition in his way. (Neither Chris Tremie or Rogelio Nunez, who caught at Double-A Nashville, are a threat to Karkovice).

Lary Bump:

There is little among Chicago's minor league catching corps to get excited about. The Sox went so far as to sign 34 year old Barry Lyons, who was a Triple-A All-Star at Indianapolis (.309-14-66) last season, but hasn't played in the majors since 1991. Clemente Alvarez, 26, has major-league defensive skills, but is a woeful hitter (.215-3-14 in the American Association). The Sox sent Double-A catcher Chris Tremie (.225-2-29) to the Arizona Fall League. At age 25, he is more a project than a prospect. The hope for the future is another strong defensive catcher, Mark Johnson, the White Sox' number one draft pick last year out of high school. The lefthanded batter hit .241-0-14 in the Gulf Coast League in his pro debut.

Cleveland Indians

Free agent Matt Merullo moved on to the Twins, signing a minor league deal.

Rick Wrona signed a minor league contract after finishing last year with the Brewers. Wrona is injury insurance and considering Alomar's history he'll probably get to Cleveland for part of the year. However, Wrona is not a good hitter and would be near useless for Rotisserie.

Tony Blengino:

For Sandy Alomar, numerous things happened on his way to surefire stardom. After being traded to the Indians in the Joe Carter deal, Alomar had a solid rookie season in 1990, hitting .290 and driving in 66 runs at age 24. The next three seasons were an unmitigated disaster - one injury after another forced Alomar to the sidelines, and he could only manage a .300 on-base percentage when healthy. The Indians

stayed the course though, and Alomar rewarded them for their patience in 1994. Despite his annual trip to the disabled list, Alomar had a career year, hitting .288 with 14 homers and a .490 slugging percentage. His defense also bounced back - he threw out an adequate 33.8% of opposing baserunners, but more impressively allowed only .56 steals per nine innings, far better than the league average. Alomar, 29, is the second youngest of the good offensive catchers in the AL (Pudge Rodriguez is 23) and, though he may have peaked in 1994, is worth a modest investment. Expect Alomar to hit .270 with 12 homers in 1995.

Even Tony Pena had a solid campaign for the 1994 Indians. Pena had clearly outlived his days as a viable starting catcher, however he still retained his defensive skills, his ability to handle a pitching staff, and was a wise acquisition who complemented the Tribe's overall youth. He was a lifesaver when Alomar suffered his annual injury. Pena hit .295 in 40 games in 1994, but it would be unrealistic to expect similar production in 1995. Even at age 38, he ranks in the upper third of backup catchers. Pena became a free agent at the end of 1994, and could conceivably call it a career, though the Indians would like him back for one more shot.

Jesse Levis, 27, spent his third consecutive season as the Indians' Triple-A catcher. Offensively, he's a high average hitter with decent power, and better yet, hits lefthanded. His size (5-9, 180) makes him an unlikely everyday catcher at the big league level. He is at the front of the line for the backup job should Pena depart, but the fact that the Tribe brought in Pena, and Junior Ortiz before him, tells you all you need to know about their opinion of Levis' major league future.

Matt Merullo, 29, was the White Sox' backup catcher for parts of four seasons, showing virtually nothing at the major league level. He has always ripped the ball in the minors though and 1994 was no exception. As a full-timer shifting between catcher and designated hitter, he hit .300 and slugged a lusty .463. Like Levis, he's a lefty, but worse defensively. His only hope is as a third catcher, and his major league history

suggests little potential success, even after signing with Minnesota.

After batting .225 and slugging .299 over his first three pro seasons, Ryan Martindale put together a solid offensive season at Double-A Canton-Akron, batting .293 and slugging .431. His defense and size (6'3", 215 pounder) are clearly plusses, but at age 26 he has yet to face Triple-A pitching. He has an outside chance of becoming a major league backup, but the prospects creeping up behind him may necessitate a change of venue.

A glance at Mitch Meluskey's offensive statistics probably wouldn't turn a single head. In three pro seasons, he has yet to hit .250, and has hit a total of seven homers. However, he is solid defensively, is a switch-hitter, and was one of the youngest regulars in the Single-A Florida State League in 1994. At 21, he will likely be the Indians' Double-A catcher in 1995. Don't be surprised if his offensive skills materialize this season.

An even more intriguing prospect is Einar Diaz. Diaz was originally an infielder, but was shifted to catcher in 1993 despite his relatively small stature (5'10", 165 pounds). Obviously a fast learner - he was named the best defensive catcher in the Single-A South Atlantic League by Baseball America. He has excellent power and makes contact, but rarely walks. The Indians' would like to see him bang his way up to Double-A by the end of 1995 at the age of 22.

Lary Bump:

With Sandy Alomar's injury history, the Indians always can use potential fill-in catchers in their farm system. Last year's catchers at Charlotte were just that: potential fill-in major leaguers. Jesse Levis (.285-10-59) is best known as an offensive player, but he showed significant improvement behind the plate last year. He'll be 27 in April, and is one of baseball's slowest baserunners.

Former White Sox catcher Matt Merullo (.300-12-75), like Levis, bats lefthanded, but is 29. He may be better suited to DH. Craig Colbert, a 30 year old

former Giant who also can play third base, hit .258-4-25. Ryan Martindale improved in his second Double-A season (.293-6-41), but he's 26 years old. The Indians also signed 31-year-old Rick Wrona, who hit .251-1-21 for the Brewers' Triple-A club at New Orleans. The best long-term catching prospect is 22 year old Einar Diaz (.279-16-71 at Class A Columbus, voted the Sally League's best defensive catcher.

Detroit Tigers

Mickey Tettleton's unsigned status left the job going back to Chad Kreuter, at least for now. It wouldn't be a big surprise if one of the big name free agent catchers is brought in at the last minute.

Fred Matos:

Chad Kreuter hit .286-15-51 in 1993 and the Tigers believed they had found a solid catcher that could carry them over the next several years. Mickey Tettleton, the incumbent catcher, was even moved to make room for him. But the excellent season proved to be a fluke as the pitchers caught up with Kreuter, holding him to .240 over the last half of 1993 and all of 1994, and .240 is about what you can expect from him in the future. Puny-hitting shortstops were hitting a lot of dingers in 1994, and Kreuter should have feasted. But he posted a very poor .224-1-19 in 170 at bats, finally losing his job to Tettleton and John Flaherty.

Mickey Tettleton was on the trading block before and during 1994, as the Tigers sought starting pitchers. No swap was made and he became a free agent. Tettleton kept up his low-average power hitting, and will continue to do so in 1995. There are only a few players such as Tettleton worth considering if you need good offensive production from your catching slots. Tettleton's value is in the $13-18 area, you can bid higher, even as high as $25, if you have other highly productive players at low salaries.

Flaherty is a weak-hitting backup catcher who managed to get into 33 games last year, hitting only .150. He's really not that bad, as shown by his respectable .258 in Triple-A.

Lary Bump:

John Flaherty is a strong-armed catcher, but during his time in Detroit last season he threw out only 25 percent of those who tried to steal against him, and Tigers' pitchers had a 5.60 ERA with him behind the plate. Offensively, the only skill he has developed is power (7 homers in 151 AB at Toledo). In 131 career major league at bats, Flaherty has a .168 average.

Alan Zinter was a Mets' first-round draft choice as a catcher, but you'll find him under first basemen in this book. In his second Double-A season, 25 year old Joe Perona batted a measly .220-5-26 in 359 at bats.

Kansas City Royals

Free agent Mike Macfarlane was being pursued actively by the Royals in late December. Should he go elsewhere, the catching job would be split between lefthander Brent Mayne and an unnamed righthanded hitter. Mayne would get the lion's share of the at bats, but the righthanded hitter could be valuable as a $1 catcher, if he can hit.

Russ McGinnis was re-signed to a minor league contract, while Nelson Santovenia was not retained. This has thrust McGinnis into the lead as a potential righthanded platoon partner with Mayne. If Macfarlane goes to another team, McGinnis has immediate value as a cheap reserve. McGinnis is a relatively good hitter, but his defense will keep him from ever being a regular behind the plate.

Minor league free agents Henry Mercedes (from Oakland) and Mitch Lyden (from Florida) have been given minor league contracts by the Royals. Both are poor hitters and would need multiple injuries to others if either is to reach the bigs again.

Marc Bowman:

The Royals intended to pursue free agent Mike Macfarlane and, if successful, he'll be their regular catcher. His performance has been very steady over the last few seasons; wherever he plays you can count

on about 20 HRs, 70 RBI, a batting average in the .250s, one SB and 15-20 HBP. He stands on top of the plate, in order to pull everything, and has been among the league leaders each of the last four years in getting plunked. Macfarlane is a below average defensive catcher, so he'll stay in the lineup primarily for his bat. Because he is so one-dimensional, his value can quickly disappear if his power diminishes.

On the other hand, should Macfarlane move on to another venue, Brent Mayne would advance from backup to the regular role. Mayne is a low-power hitter who manages a decent average. He's a better defensive catcher, but not by enough to unseat the power-hitting Macfarlane.

With Mayne in a regular role, the Royals would need to find a righthanded hitter to complement the lefty Mayne (who is a career .165 hitter against lefthanded pitching). Potential backups would come from Russ McGinnis, Nelson Santovenia and Mike Knapp. McGinnis and Santovenia are erstwhile major leaguers who are much better hitters than fielders. McGinnis has a lot of power, but hasn't yet proven that his power extends to the major league fences. Both are past their prime and would be used only to plug a temporary hole.

Knapp is also past his prime and has never really hit much above Class A ball. He's Triple-A roster filler at this point. Lance Jennings and Chad Strickland are who the Royals are eventually counting on to take over as righthanded hitters, and possible regulars.

Jennings suffered through one and a half seasons of serious struggles at Double-A Memphis, then spent the whole 1994 season back in Class A ball where he was unspectacular. Strickland has now passed Jennings and spent the year in Memphis where his .215-6-46 year was a disappointment. Jennings and Strickland are probably two years away, and both must take rapid steps forward to be real threats.

21 year old Mike Sweeney hit .301 with 10 homers for Class A Rockford, but it was his first season hitting for either power or average. He'll need to do it again at a higher level to prove himself. A long-term

prospect may have emerged in Sal Fasano. He connected for 32 HRs and 114 RBI in 435 ABs for Class A Rockford and Wilmington. Fasano isn't considered a good defensive catcher however, so he may end up at another position before reaching the majors.

Macfarlane is worth about $10, Mayne is a safe $1 pick and everyone else has no value for 1995.

Lary Bump:

The Royals have catching prospects, but they're a year or more removed from the majors. If KC could merge defensive whiz Lance Jennings and pure hitter Sal Fasano into one player, they would have one of baseball's best prospects. The 23 year old Jennings dropped back from Double-A to the Carolina League, where he batted .247-7-39 and contributed heavily to the development of an exceptional pitching staff with the minors' most dominating team. Fasano, a 37th-round draft pick who is two months older than Jennings, joined him at Wilmington (.322-7-32 in 23 games) after earning Midwest League MVP honors (.281-25-81).

Nelson Santovenia, who was at Triple-A Omaha last season (.166-3-18), never realized the ability he showed at the University of Miami, and he's 33 now. The Royals' Double-A catcher was Chad Strickland, 23, whose 1994 numbers were .216-6-47, just 13 points below his unimpressive career average. Twenty-four year-old Ramy Brooks was loaned to independent High Desert of the California League, where he went .273-20-76 with 102 strikeouts.

Milwaukee Brewers

With Brian Harper and B. J. Surhoff both still unsigned as free agents, Dave Nilsson had a firm grip on the regular job. It's entirely possible that Surhoff could return and force a shift of Nilsson to first base. Several different scenarios are possible depending upon who signs with the Brewers (if anyone) and where the team wishes to emphasize defense (catcher, first base or third base). This is probably the most

unsettled catching situation in the American League and bears a lot of watching before the 1995 season begins.

Bill Gray:

The Brewers' catching situation resembles a puzzle missing some vital pieces. The Brewers feel that Dave Nilsson could avoid some of his injuries if he played another position. That position could be first base, but a lot depends on B.J. Surhoff, John Jaha, and the free agent market.

Surhoff filed for free agency, as did Brian Harper, leaving only Nilsson and Mike Matheny as experienced catchers. Because of the glut of free agents in the market following the 1994 season, it appears that the Brewers would attempt to sign a free agent catcher if Surhoff leaves. If Surhoff returns, expect the Brewers to make him once again don the "tools of ignorance" on a regular basis.

Meanwhile, Nilsson is a likely replacement for first baseman John Jaha, because Jaha went into the tank at the plate last year. But, if Jaha regains his 1993 second-half form, Nilsson won't be needed at first. Assuming Surhoff is again the first-string catcher, he is instantly more valuable than he was as a third baseman. Surhoff is not quite as good a hitter as Nilsson, and it's not likely he'll steal 10-15 bases as he did as recently as 1991. He's never had a lot of power but his batting average will be OK, about .270. Nilsson, a valuable and productive hitter as a catcher, will drop in value as a first baseman, even more so if he becomes an outfielder.

Mike Matheny played in only 28 games last year. He's not ready to assume the every day catcher's job. Bobby Hughes got the nod to work on his skills in the Arizona Fall League last October. Keep him on your prospects list rather than Matheny.

Lary Bump:

Mike Matheny, 24, was voted the American Association's best defensive catcher. In his big-league trial, he was better than the Brewers' other

catchers in throwing out base-stealers, but still not very good at 24 percent. His offensive numbers were .220-4-21 at New Orleans and .226-1-2 in 53 at bats for Milwaukee. The Brewers' catcher in the Arizona Fall League was Mike Stefanski. The 25 year old has a .300 career minor league average despite tailing off to .263-8-56 in the Texas League last year. Twenty-four year-old Bobby Hughes, a big (6'4", 220 pounds) righthanded batter, batted .252-11-53 in the California League and .278-0-12 in 12 games at El Paso.

Minnesota Twins

James Benkard:

Matt Walbeck will face a spring training challenge to protect his job from the advances of young backstops Derek Parks and Mike Durant. This will not be a position of strength for the Twins in '95, but they are confident the talent they have will thrive in time.

Walbeck will gain at least half of the playing time with his solid defense and a batting average that should reach .240. He converted to switch-hitting comparatively recently (1990), and deserves some more time to learn to hit righthanders after hitting .194 against them in '94. Walbeck will eventually need to hit 10 to 15 home runs a year to earn regular duty and said he would do some bulking up this winter.

Parks might gain 200 at bats if he shows power in the spring, yet he is only a platoon player at this point in his career. The Twins have an interest in seeing him succeed, as Parks was a first round draft choice.

Durant is a solid prospect and might push his way into contention in '96. He has a variety of skills, including some speed. He needs another year at Triple-A to improve his defense and show some power.

Lary Bump:

Light-hitting Matt Walbeck is not an immovable object behind the plate in Minnesota, but the two heavy-hitting catchers at Triple-A Salt Lake City

couldn't match Walbeck's defense. One was 30 year old veteran Tim McIntosh, whose contract was sold to a Japanese team. The other was Mike Durant, 25, whose .297 average was 35 points higher than his career average. He showed little power, with four homers and 51 RBI. He can run a bit, but his defense is suspect. Handling the talented staff at Double-A Nashville was Damian Miller, also 25. He also contributed (.268-8-35) at the plate. In the Florida State League, 23-year-old Rene Lopez hit .264-7-48.

New York Yankees

In 1993 Mike Stanley suddenly found himself, for the first time in his career, in a batting order that had no holes. For years pitchers had worked around him, leading to some impressive walk totals and on-base percentages (for those who cared to look) but never leading to much in the way of hitting. That all changed in 1993 when the pitchers had to consider that walking Stanley would only bring up someone like Pat Kelly (who hit .273 with 50 of his 51 RBI from the ninth slot in 1993) or Mike Gallego (who hit .300 batting eighth in 1993).

Since Stanley already knew patience and discipline, the sudden windfall of pitches in the heart of the strike zone turned him into a fearsome power. The success/confidence/success cycle spun wildly in his favor in 1993, and continued in 1994. Except for a brief trip to the DL with a hamstring pull, and some early nagging bumps and bruises, Stanley was steady in his role as the starting catcher. The pitchers appreciate his game-calling and ability at throwing out runners (42% in 1994). The top role is clearly his going into 1995. Stanley has been moved up in the order since being discovered as the fine hitter he is, now batting fifth against lefties and sixth against righties, with enhanced RBI opportunities. He's come a long way since being just a backup and platooner against southpaws.

Jim Leyritz quietly led the Yankees in home run percentage in 1994. On most teams he could be the starting catcher, while he's strictly a backup to Stanley in New York, but his versatility allows him to do more than just catch for the Yankees. Leyritz is likely to be overlooked in many leagues, because he's been around for years without doing much of anything. Even in New York, where interest should be higher, Leyritz has been the victim of some unfavorable press (they started calling him "too cocky" back in Double-A in 1989, and last year the buzzword was "self-absorbed"). The criticism is unfounded (how could anybody with a big head function so well as a backup?) and it will help to keep his price down even in Big Apple leagues. Leyritz has extra value because of the probability that he will start some games at first base and outfield, possibly even third base in a pinch.

Matt Nokes missed two months of the short 1994 season with a broken hand. He never figured into the catching role prominently, as Stanley and Leyritz were doing such a good job. Nokes became a free agent after the end of the season and was expected to remain in the American League where his lefty bat is a big plus. Nokes' biggest problem, for stat league purposes, has been a weak batting average when he plays regularly. If used selectively, his average should be up, as evidenced by what happened in 1994.

Lary Bump:

By the start of the 1996 season, Jorge Posada will be the Yankees' everyday catcher. Because of his defense, the 23 year old switch hitter could be called up this season. Last year he jumped from the Carolina League to the International, showing some power at Columbus (.240-11-48).

Oakland A's

Steven Rubio:

Terry Steinbach has been very consistent in the '90s, and will continue to be the A's starting catcher for a few more years. He is not a superstar, and is often overvalued by fantasy owners who overdose on theories of position scarcity, but he will give solid, if unspectacular, production.

Scott Hemond is the primary backup, and he has several positive qualities for both the A's and fantasy owners, all related to his odd versatility. Hemond qualifies at both catcher and second base, making him a nice player to have on your roster when you need to adjust the positions of better players. Hemond is not a very good hitter though, so while you might assign an extra dollar or two of value to his positional eligibility, don't be fooled into overspending.

The A's have an amazing surfeit of weak-hitting catchers in their system, none of who would appear to have any useful potential for the future. Eric Helfand, Dean Borelli, Henry Mercedes and Izzy Molina might be the same person in four different uniforms. You don't want them if they surface with Oakland.

Lary Bump:

At Triple-A Tacoma, Henry Mercedes (.190-1-17) and Eric Helfand (.202-2-25) were upstaged by 28 year old Dean Borrelli (.279-3-42), who also played in the outfield. At Double-A Huntsville was Izzy Molina (.216-8-50). The best prospect now may be Willie Morales, a 22-year-old righthanded batter who hit .266-13-51 in the Midwest League.

Seattle Mariners

Reserve catcher Bill Haselman has moved on to a similar role in Boston. The reserve role in Seattle became wide open. Since starter Dan Wilson can't hit much, manager Lou Piniella will have to consider a good bat-off-the-bench type to fill this roster slot. Spring training at Peoria thus becomes a spot to watch for help in the $1 department.

Bill Gray:

In 1994, Dan Wilson hit .239 on the road, .179 at home, .213 vs. righthanded pitchers, and .225 vs. lefthanded pitchers. He walked only 10 times in 239 plate appearances while fanning 57 times. His hitting philosophy? See the ball, miss the ball. Still, this former Red makes one think of Bench. The one in the dugout, not Johnny.

Bill Haselman and Chris Howard also got some PT in 1994. Both struggled to maintain a .200 average. There's little wonder the Mariners' first choice in the draft was Jason Varitek, a three time All-American at Georgia Tech. He was named the top college player of 1994, and Baseball America named Varitek the top catcher in college baseball HISTORY. Last year at Tech, Varitek hit a dingbat-induced .432 with 15 homers, 81 RBI, and 71 walks. Keep your eye on him. There's no reason he can't play in Seattle right now, except for the fact that the Mariners have yet to sign him.

Lary Bump:

Last year at Calgary, 29 year old Chris Howard showed the best power of his seven minor league seasons (.252-11-44). Chris Widger, 23, was named the Southern League's best defensive catcher by Baseball America. He also hit for power (.260-15-69), and played in the Double-A All-Star Game. He'll catch for Calgary this season, and could be breathing down Dan Wilson's neck. The righthanded-hitting Widger has had averages between .259 and .264 in each of his three minor league seasons.

For the second consecutive year, 23 year old Jason Varitek was chosen in the first round but declined to sign. This time, the Mariners failed to meet the former Georgia Tech star's demands.

Texas Rangers

Mike Scioscia, who was injured during all of 1994 and never played for the Rangers, has now retired to take a coaching position. He would not have been a factor in 1995 anyway.

Reserve Junior Ortiz has left via free agency and has been replaced by free agent signee Dave Valle. Valle played for Boston and Milwaukee in 1994 and has been a weak hitter with minor pop for most of his career. He's a better fit in Texas where he can give the Rangers good defense as a reserve and giving Ivan Rodriguez the occasional day off. However, smart Rotisserie owners will avoid the career .235 hitting

Valle, unless they need one home run from a fill-in late in the season.

Peter Graves:

Ivan Rodriguez continues to mature as a hitter. In 1994 he became more selective at the plate, raising his average to .306, walking more frequently, and cutting his strikeouts. His 14 homers were a career high. At the age of 23, Rodriguez is an excellent hitting catcher, but is overrated defensively. The defensive shortcomings, combined with perceived attitude problems and an acute Rangers' pitching shortage, may cause Rodriguez to be traded. Rodriguez will certainly be the number one catcher wherever he plays. If the Rangers trade Rodriguez, they'll need to acquire a catcher to replace him - there aren't any candidates within the organization. He occasionally suffers from lower back pain, but that was not a significant problem last season.

Last season, Junior Ortiz kept a spot warm in the dugout as Rodriguez' backup. Ortiz' ebullient personality and his ability to throw out opposing baserunners should keep him in the league somewhere, perhaps with Texas.

Roger Luce is the only minor league catcher in the Ranger farm system with a chance to see playing time in the majors within the foreseeable future. Luce is a fine defensive catcher who was sent to the Arizona Fall League to work on his hitting.

Lary Bump:

With Ivan Rodriguez on hand, the Rangers don't need young catching prospects. Their best is good-field/no-hit Roger Luce (.283-6-22 at Double-A Tulsa and .237-1-14 after moving up to Oklahoma City). Moving up behind him was Darryl Kennedy (.266-1-22 at Class-A Port Charlotte and .229-1-5 at Tulsa), who at 26 is four months older than Luce. Larry Ephan, 24, batted .248-5-41 in the Sally League.

Toronto Blue Jays

Pat Borders defection via free agency left a gaping hole that will be filled by Carlos Delgado, who began the 1994 season in left field, but finished it behind the plate in Syracuse. He's ready to take over the job full time, but Randy Knorr will still get more at bats than the average reserve catcher, as young Delgado is eased into the job. Knorr has some power, but won't help you in batting average.

David Luciani:

Pat Borders, the Blue Jays' regular catcher since 1990, was a free agent and not expected to be retained. Gord Ash, the newly-appointed Jays' GM, instantly finds himself under pressure to get the team payroll down into a range capable of absorbing an owner-imposed salary cap. He was quoted in October as saying that the club was leaning towards youth at this position.

Borders is remarkably consistent, batting in the .240-.255 range since 1991. His arm has deteriorated to being below average and as always, he rarely takes a walk. He might remain an everyday catcher for a couple more years with another club.

A Blue Jay team without Pat Borders would have Randy Knorr and Carlos Delgado battling for the full time spot in spring training. Most likely, Cito Gaston's managerial style would force a strict platoon (Delgado bats lefthanded, Knorr righthanded). That would see Delgado end up with the bulk of the work.

Delgado started off on a furious pace in 1994 as the Jays' left fielder. He adjusted well to the positional change, considering he had never been an outfielder at any level. Of course, as word spread that he couldn't yet handle major league breaking balls, he struggled at the plate and was ultimately sent to Syracuse in mid-season.

However, there are signs that he will still be a great player and probably immediately: (a) Despite his struggles last year, he still took 25 walks in just 41 games. That's exceptional for a first year player, and

given that his 1994 performance with the Blue Jays was considered to be disappointing, there's no telling how good his strike zone judgement will be. (b) He hit nine home runs in just 130 at bats. That's a 35 home run pace and once again, Delgado was having what the club thought was difficulty adjusting. (c) He did all of this at the age of 22. His prime shouldn't be until around 1998-99. Before long, Carlos Delgado will be the best-hitting catcher in the major leagues.

Knorr also shows promise and has spent the last two years as the understudy to Pat Borders, gaining major-league experience which Delgado doesn't have. Knorr, like Delgado, showed good power over a short time (seven home runs in just 124 at bats) but Knorr will be 26 years old this year and is not likely to improve much more. His history also doesn't imply a future as a regular catcher.

The two combined would put up a season's worth of great numbers. If Pat Borders is not a Blue Jay in 1995, the Delgado/Knorr platoon would be worth getting both ends of, if possible.

Lary Bump:

There's probably no more valuable commodity in baseball than a lefthanded-hitting catcher with power who can throw runners out. That's Carlos Delgado. He started last season hitting balls off the Skydome's Hard Rock Cafe, and finished it as the eighth man in 60 years to hit a ball over the 434-foot center field fence in Syracuse. Back in the minors, he also was able to improve his catching. His 1994 offensive numbers: .215-9-24 at Toronto; .319-19-58 in the International League. Delgado, just 22 years old, is one of the best prospects for 1995 success.

Angel Martinez was voted the Florida State League's best defensive catcher. He'd be a better candidate to become Carlos Delgado's caddy if he didn't also bat lefthanded. At Dunedin, the 22-year-old batted .260-7-52.

NATIONAL LEAGUE CATCHERS

Atlanta Braves

Marc Bowman:

In 1994, Javy Lopez established himself as one of the league's better hitting catchers at the ripe young age of 23. He's likely to get even better over the next few years and his improvement will be most rapid in the next two years if he follows the usual development path for young hitters. Lopez connected for 13 homers in just 277 at bats, but they accounted for the majority of his Rotisserie value. His .245 average was damaging to most teams and his 35 RBI were disappointing considering his homer output; he stole nary a base. His biggest problem is poor plate discipline; Lopez struck out about 22% of the time and had a .299 OBP. As long as he is willing to swing at anything, he's unlikely to see much in the way of hittable pitches.

On the positive side, Lopez's power stroke is only getting better. A twenty homer season is annually within grasp for Lopez and he has had good batting averages in the high minors before (.321 for Double-A Greenville in 1992 and .305 for Triple-A Richmond in 1993). He'll probably be able to improve on the .245 average in the future, but how much he will improve depends upon how much plate discipline he

develops. Lopez will probably get 400 at bats in 1995 and should hit about .260 with 18 homers and 60 RBI. That kind of production at catcher would make him worth at least $12.

Though Charlie O'Brien was the defensive half of the catching team for the Braves in 1994, he added a career high eight homers in just 152 at bats, quite a power surge for a guy who had just 16 career homers before 1994, in over a thousand at bats! No wonder they call it the "Launching Pad"....

It would be unreasonable to expect O'Brien's power to continue and he doesn't give you anything else offensively. He can be a lot worse, too; he hit in the .178 to .212 range for three seasons from 1990 to 1992. Stay away from O'Brien. Don't even try to get him as a $1 catcher; there's far more downside potential here than upside. Look for a .210-3-20 season from O'Brien in 1995.

At Triple-A Richmond, Eddie Perez had a decent season offensively (.260-9-49) but he's two years older and is unlikely to unseat Lopez. If he gets to the majors it'll be for another team (he could be the kind of second string catcher who contributes an occasional homer). He's probably not going to become a regular anywhere. He might get a pinch-hitter/third catcher

role like Francisco Cabrera had for several years should he reach the majors in 1995.

Former catcher of the future Tyler Houston has shifted to first base.

Greenville's regular catcher, Joe Ayrault, is a good fielder but not much of a hitter. If he gets to the majors it'll be in O'Brien's role of defensive caddy. He's not worth anything to Rotisserie owners.

The catcher cupboard is a little bare for the Braves in the low minors. Rich Spiegel led his Rookie league Danville team in homers (9) and RBI (26) but he's years away from the big leagues. Likewise, Pasqual Matos led Rookie league Pioneer Falls with seven homers; he's also several years away.

Chicago Cubs

Stuart Shea:

Rick Wilkins' disappointing 1994 performance will probably make him a cheap pickup in most leagues this year. The big backstop proved in 1993 that he could hit anybody's best fastball and as a result was fed a steady diet of curves and change-ups last season. He could not make steady contact and struggled mightily against lefthanders.

If Wilkins can make some adjustments, he should recapture some of what made him such a surprise in 1993. It's more likely, however, that the weaknesses he showed in 1994 are why he never hit above .253 in a full minor league season. He's probably going to produce numbers somewhere between his 1993 and 1994 totals. Wilkins has a strong arm and is considered a good game-caller, and those things make him valuable if he can hit .240 with 15 homers.

Popular veteran Mark Parent did well in 1994 as Wilkins' backup, but was waived in October and signed with Pittsburgh where he'll compete for a backup role. There is little immediate catching help in the minors. Neither veteran defensive specialist Darron Cox nor former Dodger farmhand Adam Brown did

anything interesting at Triple-A. Mike Hubbard, however, played well at Double-A Orlando. He hit 11 homers (after collecting a total of four in two previous minor league campaigns), batted .281, and showed excellent speed. Despite a decent arm, he may be moved to another position to take advantage of his all-around athletic ability.

Cincinnati Reds

Greg Gajus:

Eddie Taubensee (.283-8-21-2) was made expendable by Houston due to the development of Tony Eusebio and the Reds wisely acquired Taubensee when Joe Oliver went down. He will be, at a minimum, the primary catcher, and could finally get an opportunity to be a full time catcher in 1995. The biggest question about Taubensee is his ability to hit lefthanders as he has never been given that opportunity in the majors. Taubensee has all the positives you could want: he's still young at 26, has good defense, has shown steady offensive improvement, plays in a good hitters park, and has a high likelihood of being undervalued (he's the guy traded for Kenny Lofton). Expect 15-20 home runs from Taubensee in 1995.

Joe Oliver (.211-1-5-0) went on the disabled list in April with a mysterious ankle injury and was still there in August, with swelling problems in both his ankles and knees. Even if he is healthy in 1995, the best he can hope for is a platoon role.

Brian Dorsett (.245-5-26-0) played extremely well filling in for Oliver until June, when his offense disappeared. At age 34, he is just a journeyman with a little power, but he is well-liked by the organization and could beat out Oliver for a platoon role if the Reds choose not to give Taubensee the full time job.

Barry Lyons is the only catcher in the Reds system that could have any impact in 1995. The former Met hit .309-14-66 at Class AAA Indianapolis, a year very similar to Dorsett's season there in 1993. He is older than Dorsett (35) but could get a shot at a platoon/third catcher role in 1995 if the Reds give up on Oliver.

Colorado Rockies

David Smith:

Playing catcher for the Colorado Rockies means being strong on patience and humility, and possessing a sense of humor. How else could you survive eight-run first innings by the likes of Greg Harris and Mike Harkey? If you were going to create the perfect catcher, it wouldn't be Joe Girardi, but managers love the intangible traits he posesses. Girardi won't hurt you with mental mistakes and displays strong defensive skills, leadership on and off the field, consistent hitting and good play in the clutch. No, he's not flashy and doesn't have a lot of pop in his bat, but he's a student of the game, and that's the type of backstop the Rockies want. His .276 average in 1994 was a bonus.

Girardi won't earn you a lot of fantasy league glory, but he'll be starting 130 games for the Rockies in 1995, barring injury. He understands his role, and gladly moved from second in the batting order to the bottom third. Girardi's biggest challenge will be to direct a young pitching staff in the years to come.

Veteran minor leaguer Danny Sheaffer is another student of the game; 1995 might be Scheaffer's last hurrah in the majors. He spent 13 years in the minors just waiting for expansion to arrive, and there are some good prospects who the Rockies won't sit on for 13 years while Sheaffer plays.

Jim Tatum is another veteran of the minors who got some pinch-hitting appearances with the Rockies in 1994 but spent most of the year at Colorado Springs where he hit .351 (second best in the organization) with 21 home runs and 97 RBI. He went to the Arizona Fall League specifically to work on catching. He's got a good chance to make the team with those batting numbers, but Don Baylor told him if he wants to play in The Show he needs to make it as a catcher. He'd be good insurance as a utility fielder, too.

Challenging both Tatum and Scheaffer is the organization's top catching prospect who also saw time in Denver the past two years - Jayhawk Owens.

He's got the pure skills, but needs to work on his hitting.

Florida Marlins

Tony Blengino:

A good sign that an expansion franchise is getting closer to becoming a contender is when it develops its first potential superstar. The arrival of Tom Seaver with the Mets in 1967, George Brett with the Royals in 1973 and Gary Carter with the Expos in 1974 foretold of the future success of those teams. In 1994, the Marlins' first homegrown potential superstar, Charles Johnson, made his first major league appearance.

The Marlins will likely allow Benito Santiago to leave via free agency, and give the catching chores to Johnson. The Expos' top pick out of high school in 1989, Johnson instead chose to play college ball at Miami (Fla.). He became a first round pick for the second time in 1992, when he became the Marlins' initial top pick. Now 23, Johnson is superior both at the plate and behind it. He hit .264 with 28 homers and 80 RBI for Double-A Portland in 1994, posting an impressive .369 OBP and .524 slugging average. Half of his hits went for extra bases in the Eastern League, which is not known for offense. Defensively, he has thrown out close to half of thw opposing baserunners in his minor league career, and nailed the only runner who dared try to steal against him in his four big league games. At 6'3" and 215 pounds, he's durable enough to handle a 150 game workload. Johnson is a leading Rookie of the Year candidate for 1995; expect him to hit .265 with 22 homers and 75 RBI.

Pity poor Benito. After three consecutive years of offensive and defensive decline, Santiago had his best season in 1994 since his 1987 Rookie of the Year campaign, but has little chance to retain his starting role with the Marlins. Offensively, Santiago is a free swinger with better than average power for a catcher. In eight seasons as a major league starter, he has never walked as many as 40 times in a season and his career OBP is a woeful .299. On the flip side,

Santiago has delivered double figure home run seasons in each of his eight years as a major league starter, and roasted lefties at a .345 clip in 1994. His defensive prowess returned somewhat to its previous levels with a fine performance in 1994 when he gunned down 47.1% of opposing baserunners, second only to Tom Pagnozzi in the National League. Now 30 years old, he became a free agent at the end of 1994 and was unlikely to be re-signed by the Marlins. Santiago proved in 1994 that he is still capable of being an above average offensive and defensive catcher. He'll latch on somewhere and hit about .260 with 12 home runs and 55 RBI.

By the end of each of the last two seasons, 29 year old Bob Natal emerged as the Marlins' backup catcher. Natal wasn't even the Triple-A starter when he was recalled after the release of Ron Tingley. He has been a decent part time bat at the Triple-A level, but has been a useless hitter in three major league stints. He won't embarrass himself behind the plate, but his low potential will keep him confined to Triple-A unless injuries open a spot.

One torrid month (September, 1990) made Steve Decker seem like a future star to the Giants. Decker was clearly overhyped, and a string of injuries kept him from lengthy major league time with the Giants (and, later, the Marlins). At age 29, Decker had an awesome Triple-A season for Edmonton, batting .390, slugging .606, posting a .448 OBP with 23 doubles and 11 homers in just 259 at bats. His performance in the hitting friendly Pacific Coast League could vault him to the top of the backup catcher list; Decker could get 200 at bats in that role, hitting .255 with four homers and 15 RBI.

There was another aging journeyman catcher residing at Edmonton in 1994. Mitch Lyden posted scintillating offensive numbers, hitting 21 doubles and 18 homers in only 288 at bats, posting a .552 slugging percentage. Thirty year old Lyden is an unlikely backup catcher due to his subpar defense and his lack of plate discipline (74/12 strikeout/walk ratio in 1994; 817/187 for his minor league career). His ten major league at bats - producing one homer - will remain his career highlight.

20 year old John Roskos was Florida's second round pick in 1993. Injuries have limited him to only 176 at bats over his first two pro seasons, mostly as a designated hitter. Roskos generates enormous, legendary, batting practice power from his stocky 5'11", 198 pound frame; he could be fun to watch once he gets to play in the smaller ballparks of the upper minor leagues. The Marlins would gladly settle for a healthy, full season above Rookie ball from him at this point.

Houston Astros

Bill Gilbert:

Scott Servais began the season as the Astros' catcher in 1994 after beating out Eddie Taubensee in spring training. The team carried three catchers for the first three weeks until Taubensee was traded to Cincinnati. The third catcher, Tony Eusebio, 27, unexpectedly made the team based on a sensational hitting performance in spring training.

Servais, also 27, was essentially an everyday catcher for the first half of the season, because the pitchers were more comfortable with him behind the plate. However, he was not able to generate enough offensive production to hold the job. In the second half of the season, Servais and Eusebio, both righthanded hitters, split the job and both hit lefthanders much better than righthanders. Servais batted .254 against lefties, but only .174 against righthanders in compiling a disappointing .195-9-41-0 log. Eusebio lit up lefties at a .426 rate, compared to .214 against righthanders for an overall record of .296-5-30-0.

The catching job is up for grabs in 1995. Servais had respectable power numbers, but he has to hit for a higher average to be anything more than a backup catcher. He is very vulnerable to outside breaking balls and is most effective in a platoon situation. Eusebio is a slashing style hitter who has some power. Eusebio should get over half of the playing time in 1995 and has some potential for further improvement.

Scrappy Scooter Tucker, 28, had an outstanding season at Triple-A Tucson (.321-14-80-3). He failed to hit in two previous big league trials, but is a more accomplished hitter now and should be a capable backup major league catcher. The Astros have announced plans to reduce the payroll in 1995, so a possible scenario would be to let Servais go with Eusebio becoming the starter and Tucker the backup.

Los Angeles Dodgers

Greg Gajus:

Mike Piazza (.319-24-92-1) is the best catcher in either league. The only negative about his career potential is his late start - Piazza is already 26. Picture Johnny Bench or Gary Carter in their prime and you will have a good projection for this season.

Carlos Hernandez (.219-2-6-0) would probably hit better than he did in 1994 were he to be traded or if Piazza got hurt. Obviously, his opportunities with Los Angeles will be very limited.

Tom Prince, the ex-Pirate hitless wonder, actually had a decent year at Class AAA Albuquerque, hitting .303 with 20 homers. He is 30 and, at best, he might push Hernandez for the 100 at bats that Piazza doesn't get.

Montreal Expos

John Perrotto:

The Expos have one of the deepest catching situations in the game. Lefthander Darrin Fletcher and righthander Lenny Webster were an effective platoon in 1994 with Tim Spehr, a decent player in his own right, stuck as the third string catcher. Furthermore, Tim Laker reestablished himself as a prospect after going back to the minors.

Fletcher hit .260-10-57-0 last season and earned his first All-Star berth. He is one of the National League's better offensive catchers. However, despite making some strides, he is still a defensive liability.

Acquired from Minnesota in a spring training trade, Webster had a fine season in part-time duty, hitting .273-5-23-0. The Twins were once high on him, then soured. He is a good looking player, though, who appears capable of doing more if given an expanded role.

Spehr is an acceptable second string catcher, but is buried behind Fletcher and Webster in Montreal and will soon be overtaken by Laker.

The Expos tried to make Laker their catcher in both 1992 and 1993. While his defense was major league caliber, his light bat prevented him from becoming a full time player. Laker was sent back to Class AAA Ottawa in 1994 where he improved his hitting mechanics and turned in a .309-12-71-11 season. The Expos are always looking to trim payroll costs and with Laker now ready to play in the majors would consider trading Fletcher.

New York Mets

Todd Hundley has been penciled in as the Mets regular catcher for more than two years now and he's still growing into the job. Hundley reached the majors at the very young age of 21 and had a regular role at age 23 (it was largely defense that got him to the majors so early). Except for some obvious power when he bats lefthanded, Hundley has struggled on both sides of the plate when it comes to hitting for average. He lacks discipline and chases too many bad pitches.

The good news for Hundley is that all his hitting problems are in areas that can be learned, and he's a good learner (ask his father, ex-major leaguer Randy Hundley, who taught him a lot). Young Hundley is almost certain to develop into a better all-around hitter as he matures. He looks likely to reach 20+ home runs in a season and he should easily hit in the .250 to .270 range when he's fully developed. I look for this development to come soon, but the truth is, I believed and wrote the same thing a year ago, and

Hundley's progress in 1994 was solid but not what anyone can call rapid. I am sure the best lies ahead.

The bad news for Hundley is the presence of Kelly Stinnett. Most organizations have a knack of getting more of what they already have. The Mets have been deep at catcher for a few years, with Brook Fordyce coming up behind Hundley; but, with a fuzzy picture due to injuries, they got Stinnett from the Indians organization before the 1994 season. He turned out to be a wonderful backup for Hundley and worked himself into a platoon role. However, Stinnett is not likely to hit much better than the .253 he produced last year and he's got only a little pop in his bat and no speed. Stinnett's presence is more of a limiting factor for Hundley than a plus for Stinnett's value.

The strategy is to look for Hundley at a bargain price. He's especially appropriate for a team rebuilding for the long-term, or for a team that needs some good luck to reach the top. So, talk about how Stinnett hit for higher average than Hundley and talk about how Stinnett took time away from Hundley last year. Then try to get Hundley cheaply.

Again, the main caution is Hundley's batting average, which will do more damage to the standings of a good team than it would impair a bad-hitting team. Think about how far .237 will pull down a .280 team average, versus .237 having little impact on a team that hits .250 overall, and you get the idea. Hundley is of course perfectly appropriate for a team that plans to ditch batting average completely - in fact Hundley is among the best catchers for such a strategy.

Philadelphia Phillies

Tony Blengino:

Thirty three year old Darren Daulton was as good as ever in 1994. He led all National League catchers in OBP (.380) and slugging average (.549), nosing out Mike Piazza in both categories. Like most Phils, Daulton's season was shortened by by injury: a broken collarbone limited him to 257 at bats. When Daulton was young and struggling, he was helpless against lefthanded pitching and was a dead pull hitter. Overcoming these problems has keyed his success - he hit .289 against lefties in 1994, and now drives outside pitches the other way with authority.

Daulton's poor throwing in 1994 (26.5% caught stealing rate) coupled with his age and injury history indicates that Daulton is beginning a decline. Expect him to slide back to a .260 average with 15 to 20 homers. He might be tried at first base.

The Phils' top 1990 draft pick, 23 year old Mike Lieberthal got his first shot at the majors in 1994, hitting .266 with just five strikeouts in 79 at bats. Last year he hit just .233 with 17 extra base hits in 296 at bats for Triple-A Scranton-Wilkes Barre. In over 1600 minor league at bats, Lieberthal has just 14 homers and a .261 average. His slight build (6'0", 170 pounds) and poor throwing in the majors make Lieberthal a backup candidate. Expect him to serve as Daulton's backup in 1995, hitting .245 with two homers in 200 at bats.

After posting solid part-time numbers in 1993, 28 year old Todd Pratt almost vanished in 1994. When it seemed Pratt would get his chance, after the injury to Daulton, Lieberthal garnered the majority of the playing time. Don't be fooled, however, by Pratt's miserable 1994 offensive numbers (.196, two homers in 102 at bats): Pratt can hit at the big league level. If given 300 at bats somewhere, he would hit 10 HR and slug over .400. That opportunity will not come with the Phils, Lieberthal's status as a former top draft pick and his better defensive potential should win him the backup job.

The only other Phils' catching prospect of any significance (after the shift of Jason Moler to third base) is 1994 Double-A Reading backstop Tommy Eason. 24 year old Eason missed all of 1993, but has posted averages near .300 throughout his pro career; he slugged nearly .500 at Reading in 1994. Due to the absence of real minor league competition, he will be Scranton's 1995 catcher and could be a future major league backup.

Pittsburgh Pirates

John Perrotto:

Don Slaught has given the Pirates five seasons of good production behind the plate, but expect a changing of the, er, shinguards, after this season.

Slaught slipped a little last season, hitting .288-2-21-0 and going more than two months without an extra-base hit at one point. He is also 36, though he stays in good shape. Slaught should still have one more season left for the Pirates before settling into a backup role somewhere else to wind up his career.

Venerable veteran Lance Parrish rejuvenated his career with the Pirates last season, hitting .270-3-16-0 as Slaught's backup. However, he is a defensive liability and the Pirates allowed him to walk as a free agent at the end of the season. His stellar career is likely over this time.

The Pirates' backup in 1995 will be veteran Mark Parent, claimed off waivers from the Chicago Cubs in October (Parent signed a one-year contract). He hit .263-3-16-0 as Chicago's number two catcher last season and has long been adequate in that role. However, if something happens to Slaught, the Pirates will be in trouble with Parent as their regular catcher.

Converted infielder Keith Osik got off to a hot start with Class AAA Buffalo last season, then crashed to wind up hitting .212-5-33-0. Despite his versatility, Osik projects as a major league backup at best. He'll spend another full year in Class AAA.

The Pirates' catcher of the future is Jason Kendall, their first round draft pick as a high school senior in 1992, and son of former big league catcher Fred Kendall.

Kendall is polished defensively and could handle that part of the game on the major league level now. However, his hitting needs work and he has very little power. He did show progress with the bat last season, though, hitting .318-7-66-14 at Class A Salem then .234-0-6-0 for Class AA Carolina.

The Pirates' hope is that Kendall will be ready to step into the lineup in 1996, when Slaught's contract expires. Kendall will start this season in Class AA and, with any signs of progress, will jump to Class AAA by midseason.

An interesting prospect is Angelo Encarnacion, who hit .291-3-32-3 at Carolina last season before a wrist injury ended his season a month early. He is a little guy with a strong arm and good ability behind the plate. His light bat might keep him from being an everyday catcher in the majors, but he's still worth keeping an eye on.

St. Louis Cardinals

John Perrotto:

Tom Pagnozzi has been one of the National League's top catchers since being given the starting job at the beginning of the 1991 season. He's an outstanding defensive catcher, who handles the pitching staff well and is a steady offensive contributor. He hit .272-7-40-0 last season, though a knee injury and the strike limited him to 72 games.

Pagnozzi's only drawback is that he has undergone knee surgery in each of the past two seasons. To his credit, he has made speedy recoveries each time and loves to play. He's 32 and should have at least two or three more good years left.

The Cardinals continue to search for a reliable backup catcher. Last year, they dusted off Terry McGriff, who finally spent a full season in the majors after his 1987 debut. He hit just .219-0-13-0 and the Cardinals need a better performance from their backup in 1995.

Journeyman Erik Pappas had a solid season in 1993 and played well when Pagnozzi was hurt. However, Pappas crashed and burned in 1994. He hit just .091-0-5-0 with the Cardinals and .199-7-30-2 with Class AAA Louisville. He hit an all time low two days before the strike when the Cardinals recalled him from the minors just so they wouldn't have to pay him. That's a pretty good sign he's not in St. Louis'

long range plans, let alone their 1995 plans.

The Cardinals are thin on catching at the upper levels and have no one in the system ready to back up Pagnozzi.

San Diego Padres

Hank Widmer:

The Padres got solid, if unspectacular work from their two catchers in 1994. Brad Ausmus seems to be the starter for the near future, as there are no catchers in the minor league pipeline ready to fight him for the job. Ausmus did an adequate job defensively and the pitchers seem to like the way he calls a game. Considering how bad the Padres were defensively, any player like Ausmus (who could catch and throw a ball) figured to play a lot. Ausmus has occasional power, with seven home runs in 327 at bats. Over a full year one could expect a little more.

Fred Matos:

Some Rotisserie experts expected Brad Ausmus to steal 20 bases last year, but he swiped only five in the strike shortened season. Actually, such a prediction was not farfetched, as he had stolen as many as 19 in a minor league season. But, his seven home runs last year were a surprise (he has never hit as many as two in a minor league season). As many players do, Ausmus is developing power as he matures. Ausmus is 26 years old and is still improving as a hitter; a .280-12-60 season would not be a big surprise in 1995.

Brian Johnson and minor leaguer Brian Deak are competing for a backup role. Neither of these guys reminds anyone of Johnny Bench.

San Francisco Giants

Steven Rubio:

Kirt Manwaring is regarded by the Giants as one of the finest defensive catchers in the game, and they will live with his awful bat as long as he contributes when the team is in the field. He has no offensive value, and must be avoided by fantasy owners, especially since the Giants will give him plenty of at bats.

The veteran backups, Jeff Reed (who had the backup job last year), and Tom Lampkin, who spent 1994 in Class AAA, are not only long past their prime, but were never very good to begin with. The team's busiest Class AA catcher, Eric Christopherson, is already 26 years old and has yet to prove he can hit minor league pitching, much less major league pitching.

The hottest catching prospect for the Giants is Marcus Jensen. He has established his good defensive reputation at age 22, but he's on a par with Manwaring as a hitter. Jensen is at least a few years away.

FIRST BASE:
TACTICAL CONSIDERATIONS

The key to the first base position is understanding that you are likely to end up with two or even three of these players on your roster. All first basemen swing a mean bat. Every other position on the field will occasionally offer playing time to a good-field, no-hit type of player, but the first base job on a major league roster is never awarded to a defensive specialist. On a typical Rotisserie roster, the starting first baseman will be one of the best hitters on the team.

Furthermore, the corner infielder (1B or 3B) on a Rotisserie roster is also likely to be a first baseman, because all the good-hitting third basemen are taken to fill 3B slots (there are hardly enough decent offensive third sackers to go around, much less a surplus to help fill those corner infield slots). Finally, the DH or utility slot on many rosters will again be a player who qualifies at first base, because real major league rosters tend to carry an extra bat as a DH/1B type. So there is usually an ample supply of first basemen to fit into Rotisserie rosters in various slots.

Facing the acquisition of two or three first basemen, it's wise to consider these selections in terms of a coordinated plan. The task isn't quite the daunting exercise in portfolio management that goes into choosing five outfielders, but there are some clearly-defined strategies to consider.

One of the simplest and most successful approaches to the first base position is to get one star hitter and his natural backup. Those who drafted John Kruk in 1994 were wise to add Ricky Jordan as a late-round pick. Troy Neel went well with Mark McGwire, and Reggie Jefferson with Tino Martinez. When the established player goes down in value, because of an injury or slump that puts him on the bench, the substitute goes up in value.

Remember that backups don't have to come from major league rosters. Roberto Petagine is a good farm system pick for anyone with Jeff Bagwell on their roster, and Matt Franco has been waiting in line behind Mark Grace for more than a year. When you can see that a minor league first baseman is good enough to step directly into a major league starting role if needed, he may actually offer a better insurance policy than the journeyman major leaguer who sits on the bench holding his first base mitt and watching.

Because all first basemen can hit well, the star-plus-backup strategy can pay dividends even when the top guy remains healthy and valuable. Anyone who acquired Ryan Klesko as a backup to Fred McGriff before the 1994 season ended up with a windfall, as did the fortunate owners who thought of Bob Hamelin as a backup for Wally Joyner and then discovered they had a productive regular DH.

The star-plus-backup method, even with its upward possibilities, is still a conservative approach, most appropriate for strong teams that don't need to take a lot of chances to win.

There are some more aggressive approaches to first base opportunities, for those who need to get lucky. One obvious idea is to get two or three obscure players with the hope that one of them will blossom into a high-value player. This crapshoot method can work wonders, as it did last year for lucky owners who got Reggie Jefferson or Bob Hamelin for about $4 apiece on draft day. But this method can also backfire. Ask anyone who used three roster spots to

get the understudy players behind Frank Thomas, Rafael Palmeiro, and Cecil Fielder. There is a reason why no one now can even remember who those backups were -- they never got to play!

If you're serious about filling your first base slot(s) with low-price speculative picks, it's better to focus on unsettled major league situations, rather than hope for an injury to an established star. In 1994, for example, David Segui and Todd Benzinger came out of spring training with first base jobs, but both were under scrutiny because of that principle favoring offense over defense. Noting the uncertain status of Segui and Benzinger, and grabbing their most credible minor league replacements, was a tactic that worked to some extent in both cases, as Rico Brogna and J.R. Phillips both emerged with chances to take these jobs during the season. Only one of the two, Brogna, was a success; but any speculative method with a 50/50 chance of producing a happy outcome is a good method.

Another strategic alternative is to be especially aggressive in pursuing the best-hitting first basemen, even to the extent of trying to put the squeeze on owners who delay filling their required 1B slot. It's a lot harder to corner the market on good hitters in the first base population, than it is to try this ploy with catchers or shortstops, but it can be accomplished when the circumstances are just right. Suppose, for example, in a standard 12-team NL Rotisserie league, every owner, except one, retains their best first baseman. With just 14 major league teams to choose from, that means that all but three of the regular starters have been removed from the pool of available first basemen before the draft even begins. If those three get drafted quickly, or go for high prices early in the auction, then the one owner who didn't get a top-tier first baseman will end up with a part-timer, backup, or platooner in the one roster spot where everyone else has a big hitter. And if that one unfortunate owner happens to be your arch rival, so much the better.

The right strategic approach to first base is the one that best fits your unique league situation. Sometimes the right method is obvious before the draft begins,

as in the case where you can take advantage of the way freeze lists have shaped up. More often, however, the best strategy becomes clear only after the draft is underway, when you can see what your competitors are doing and take advantage of any surplus or shortage.

If you're not pursuing any particular scheme then the reliable, conventional approach to first base includes two steps. First, exercise patience in choosing one of the big hitters. The longer you wait, the better your opportunity for a bargain. Just make sure you get one of the big guns before they're all gone. Second, use your next possible vacancy for pure bargain-hunting. If you get another powerful bat for half what he's worth, fine. If you get a low-value natural backup for the minimum price or in the last round, that's fine too. There are usually enough first basemen in the available pool to offer you a bargain or a perfect roster fit somewhere.

Finally, remember that top-hitting first basemen generally make excellent minor league picks. If you stick to the cream of the crop from the minors --guys like Rich Aude, Tony Clark, Steve Dunn, Matt Franco, Roberto Petagine, and Tate Seefried -- you're sure to end up with some major league talent within a year or two.

For the Record:

Likely to be bargains: Cliff Floyd, Greg Colbrunn, Kevin Young, Steve Dunn, Tony Clark, John Olerud, Reggie Jefferson.

Likely to be overvalued: Don Mattingly, Mark McGwire, Andres Galarraga, J.R. Phillips, and John Kruk.

AMERICAN LEAGUE
FIRST BASEMEN

In contrast to American League catchers, American League first basemen are a very stable bunch. Only three first base jobs are essentially unsettled for 1995 (California, Milwaukee and Minnesota) and all three teams have credible candidates ready to play. Likewise, the free agent pool at first base is very thin. The only regulars from 1994 who were unsigned were Mark Grace, John Kruk and Todd Benzinger. Grace is likely to sign in the National League, Kruk may retire rather than play in 1995, and Benzinger is essentially worthless.

There are not likely to be any ''new'' first basemen available on draft day. But, with the large number of heavy hitters at first base, a winning Rotisserie team needs to have a strong hitter at first base (and probably at corner and DH, too, as discussed in ''First Base Tactical Considerations'' in the upcoming Rotisserie Baseball Annual). Therefore, it is important to load up on good hitting first sackers as soon as possible, even if it means paying full freight for them. The lack of new hitters entering the league at first base will mean an unusually constricted market for first basemen in 1995 Rotisserie drafts.

Baltimore Orioles

Fred Matos:

Though the 1995 season will be Rafael Palmeiro's 10th in the majors, he is only 30 years old. He matured and developed a strong power stroke in 1991, and the annual expectation is now 30 dingers and 100 RBI. He could swipe 20 bases under an aggressive run-oriented manager like new Orioles skipper Phil Regan. Last year, his RBI totals would have been much higher and among league leaders, but the leadoff and second slot hitters were in slumps so he frequently had no one to drive in. Palmeiro loves to hit in Camden Yards, and is one of the best hitters in baseball. His value is over $30, and as high as $37 if he steals 20 bases. But you shouldn't overbid as there are many good hitting first basemen.

The backup slot is a toss-up between Jack Voigt, Jeff Manto and Paul Carey with Voigt having the edge because of his experience and outfield ability. Manto was a tremendous hitter at Triple-A Rochester last year, winning the International League MVP award. He can also play some third base, but is 30 years old and has failed in previous major league trials with the Indians and Phillies. Carey has some power but has not developed into the strong hitter that the Orioles

expected. Carey's advantage is that he is the only lefty hitter among the three.

Lary Bump:

Not having learned from past mistakes, the Orioles have loaded their upper minor league levels with first basemen/left fielders/designated hitters. Last year, the best of them was Jeff Manto. In a league loaded with third base prospects, Manto's bat earned him designation as the league's All-Star third baseman. He has a good chance for a utility/pinch-hitter/DH role.

The Orioles built up their Double-A farm club at Bowie to the detriment of the Triple-A roster. One such move was sending 28 year old Jack Voigt from Baltimore (.241-3-20) to Bowie (.312-6-35).

An arm injury, suffered in 1991, has hindered T.R. Lewis' chances as a third baseman. Last season he batted .305-6-31 at Rochester before suffering a broken wrist, then came back as an outfielder at Bowie (.250-3-8).

Paul Carey missed the start of the '94 season because of a broken wrist. In 47 games at Rochester, he batted .250-8-28. At age 27, he's about out of chances.

Switch-hitting Billy Owens batted just .228 at both Bowie and Class-A Frederick. However, he totaled 17 homers and 71 RBI.

After a big season as a rookie pro in the Appalachian League, Bryan Link struggled in the Carolina League (.242-7-51).

Boston Red Sox

Pork Chop Pough re-signed to the Red Sox minor league system. He's not a real credible major league threat, although he had a good season in 1994 and attracted some favorable publicity. Pough is a classic case of the ''all first basemen can hit well, so big deal'' career path problem.

Alan Boodman:

With all of the quality first basemen around, particularly in the A.L., it's easy to lose Mo Vaughn in the crowd. His partial-year numbers from 1994 project to almost 40 homers, well over 100 RBI, nearly 100 runs scored, and 80-85 walks. There isn't too much more you can accomplish in a season, but in fact several players at his position regularly do just that. Vaughn is in a pack with John Olerud, Rafael Palmeiro and Will Clark, all vying for second best in the league behind the Big One, and as such Vaughn is rarely overbid. He may therefore provide a bargain to his Rotisserie owners.

Vaughn is in the midst of his prime seasons, and can seemingly be relied upon to produce numbers in the range of .300-30-100 each year (keep in mind before you bid that he hasn't actually achieved that yet). His only weaknesses are his defense, which is awful, and his sometimes extreme patience at the plate. Any selective hitter (Fred McGriff comes to mind) runs the risk of experiencing self-induced slumps during the course of a year, simply by the nature of the atapproach. Hitters of the quality of a Vaughn or a McGriff also have the ability to break out of those slumps with a vengeance.

In 1995, Vaughn could optimistically produce in the vicinity of .320-35-120, more likely .300-30-105. And, if your league counts walks or OBP, so much the better. A move to DH couldn't hurt either, and ought to occur if the Sox choose not to give Andre Dawson another shot (which they won't if they're smart - see the Designated Hitter section for Andre).

No designated backup first baseman was needed in 1994, and it remains to be seen just who the starter will be in 1995, much less the backup. Scott Cooper, particularly if his shoulder hasn't healed, could be moved to first to open a hole for Luis Ortiz. Both players are described in the Third Base section.

Mike Twardoski is an aged (30) journeyman who filled the first base slot at Pawtucket in 1994. He lacks the power expected of a first sacker, but gets on base frequently enough to be an offensive plus. He is not

often mentioned as a successor to the Throne of Mo.

Lary Bump:

If Mo Vaughn needs relief, there are veteran fill-ins available in the organization. Mike Twardoski has established himself as a .280-level hitter in nine minor league seasons, including four in the International League. Last season he batted .283-13-49 at Pawtucket. His greatest skill is his pitch selection, which has led to a .407 career on-base percentage.

Guillermo Velasquez earned frequent-flyer miles last season, putting in time in the Mexican League, with the Indians' Charlotte farm (.212) and with the Double-A New Britain Red Sox (.214). The 26 year old averaged the same last year as when he was handed San Diego's first base job in 1993. He is no prospect.

Pork Chop Pough showed power in his seven seasons in the Cleveland organization, including .298-20-66 at Double-A Canton last year. He then batted .214 in 16 games at Charlotte. The 25 year old could get a shot because he bats righthanded.

Twenty-three year old Ryan McGuire had some success (.272-10-73) at Class A Lynchburg. In the Florida State League, Doug Hecker had similar numbers (.276-13-70). Jason Friedman was better there (.328-7-87), but the 25 year old was down from Double-A.

California Angels

Adding to the uncertainty caused by the game of musical chairs in the Angels' infield is the emergence of Luis Raven as a attention-getting hitter. He was added to the Angels' 40-man roster in the winter, and the team will give him a reasonable chance to win a major league job.

Veteran Pedro Guerrero hasn't played in the majors or minors for two years, but signed a minor league contract with the Angels over the winter. It's hard to see Guerrero actually playing in the minors, so the contract really means he's got a chance to make the club in spring training.

Fred Matos:

After going on a hitting rampage in the first half of 1993, J.T. Snow has since been a major disappointment. But he is still young, the potential is there, and he can't be written off completely. In an effort to get him back on track, the Angels have Snow hitting lefthanded only in winter ball rather than switch hitting. They found that he is a more natural lefthanded hitter and has more power from the port side. Snow has a very good glove, and manager Marcel Lachemann likes good defense, so he will get another chance or two at full-time play.

After hitting an encouraging .250 in 1993, Eduardo Perez was overmatched last year and demoted to the minors to improve his plate discipline. Angel management plans on starting J.T. Snow at first and Perez at third in 1995, but sometimes the best laid plans don't work out, and Perez may find himself back at first or even in the outfield.

After spending four so-so years in Class-A and AA, the virtually unnoticed Luis Raven blossomed in Class-AA and AAA last year with a surprisingly solid year, even showing considerable power. Never previously considered a top prospect, he is now a candidate for the Angels' first base job. But Raven will have to win it over some more glamorous prospects.

Chris Pritchett hit .309 last year, but it was in the hitter-friendly Double-A Texas League, and it was his second year in the league. He led the league with a .421 on-base percentage and was second in RBI with 91. The competition for the Angels' first base job is tough, but he can make it if he continues to hit well. It helps that Pritchett is excellent defensively.

The Angels first base position is not the place to look for key Rotisserie hitters. Eduardo Perez could hit some homers and steal as many as 10 bases in a full season, leading to a value of around $10. J.T. Snow will likely go cheaply as he has disappointed many

owners before, but he is worth picking up at $5 in the hopes that he turns his hitting around.

Lary Bump:

One of the success stories of 1994 was Luis Raven. The 26 year old righthanded batter hit just 21 home runs in his first four pro seasons, but turned himself into the Texas League's best power prospect (.304-18-57). He never had hit better than .288, but didn't slow down in the Pacific Coast League (.305-13-59). He has also played the outfield, and could be a DH candidate.

After Raven left Midland, the playing time at first base went to 25 year old lefthanded batter Chris Pritchett. He's a singles hitter who produced runs (.309-6-91) and reached base 42 percent of the time, drawing 92 walks. He was voted the Texas League's best defensive first baseman.

Chicago White Sox

Stuart Shea:

Frank Thomas' defense isn't getting any better. (The relevant question, of course, is "who cares?") He still has problems throwing, and doesn't move well around the bag. It will be interesting to see how much longer he'll have at the position before becoming a full-time DH.

Should Thomas suffer an injury, Julio Franco (if he returns) would probably play more first. Defensively, he's no bargain at the position either, but should get better with more experience. Dan Pasqua has a first baseman's mitt as well, but probably won't be in Chicago this season. The Sox will be looking for bench help in 1995.

Drew Denson has been the Sox' regular Triple-A first baseman now for three years, and isn't any closer to the majors than he was in 1992. Denson has a little power, but doesn't hit for high average and doesn't walk much. Denson may be get a few at-bats in the bigs this year if he gets a break, but really isn't a major league player.

Troy Fryman, Travis' brother, is still prized by the organization for his quick bat, but hasn't turned his skills into results yet. He'll probably stay at Double-A this year.

Lary Bump:

There are few better hot-weather hitters than Domingo Martinez, who was at it again in the Dominican Winter League. Aquired from the Blue Jays, tired of watching him struggle to hit his weight. Last year it was Chicago's turn, and the 27 year old righthanded batter finished strong (.270-22-81) at Nashville.

Lefthanded-hitting Mike Robertson, 24, split time between the outfield and first base, and between Double-A Birmingham (.316-3-30) and Nashville (.225-8-21).

Troy Fryman, Travis' 23 year old brother, struggled at Birmingham (.225-6-43) and in the Arizona Fall League. The first baseman at Class A Prince William was 21 year old switch-hitter Eddie Pearson (.277-12-80).

Cleveland Indians

Tim Costo was acquired from Cincinnati in exchange for shortstop Mark Lewis. Costo isn't a threat to steal time from Paul Sorrento, Eddie Murray or Jim Thome. he could make the club as a pinch-hitter, however. Costo is not worth consideration for active roster purposes, but has enough talent to merit an ultra pick as a backup for Murray (for example).

Luis Lopez slugged .484 for Atlanta's Triple-A affiliate at Richmond, hitting .303 with 18 homers (second on the team to Jose Oliva). But, he had nowhere to go with the Braves as Fred McGriff and Ryan Klesko stood in his way. Lopez signed with the Indians as a minor league free agent. He once played for the Padres and could return to the majors in an emergency situation or as a pinch-hitter. If he gets a chance to play regularly or even platoon, Lopez could be worth a buck or two.

Tony Blengino:

Without taking into account the performance of his peers, one might conclude that Paul Sorrento is a valuable offensive player. In actuality, first base was one of only two positions (the other was shortstop) where the Indians' regular was below average offensively.

Sorrento, 29, has been eerily consistent over the past three seasons - his on-base percentages fit into a narrow window between .340 and .345, while his slugging percentages ranged from .434 to .453. After struggling against lefties in 1992 and 1993, Sorrento batted .270 against southpaws in 1994. However, he received limited playing time against lefties due to the acquisition of DH Eddie Murray, who played first while Candy Maldonado served as DH against most lefties. At his age, Sorrento is unlikely to improve much, and could find himself in a bind in 1995.

Slick-fielding third baseman David Bell, 22, has made incredible strides offensively, and is major league-ready. The insertion of Bell into the lineup would free the Indians to move poor fielder Jim Thome across the diamond. By making this move, the Indians would sacrifice a minimal amount of offense while stabilizing the lefty/righty balance of the lineup and dramatically improving the infield defense.

Herbert Perry, 25, was the Indians' 2nd-round pick in 1991, after playing baseball and football at the University of Florida. Perry continued his solid offensive progress at Triple-A Charlotte in 1994, batting .327 and slugging .505. He strikes out quite infrequently for a power hitter, averaging 51 whiffs over the past two seasons. This righty should fit into the picture in Cleveland in 1995 as a reserve infielder (his ability to play third base could also come in handy). His 1994 season ended early due to a wrist injury, which may have received offseason surgery. Expect him to hit .275 with six homers in 200 at bats.

Chris Cron, 31, is your classic minor league journeyman. He was a first baseman/designated hitter at Triple-A Charlotte, blasting 23 homers despite a .231 average. Cron has now racked up 4424 minor

league at bats and 170 minor league homers. He has struck out over 100 times in five different seasons, and almost 1100 times overall. He's had two feeble cups of coffee at the major league level, going 2 for 25. Cron has now played five consecutive Triple-A seasons for four different organizations, and will likely move on yet again in 1995.

Lary Bump:

Herbert Perry worked hard at learning to hit to right field last season, to the point that he almost stopped pulling the ball. No matter where he hit the ball, it seemed to go for a hit (.327-13-70). When the 25 year old's season ended, because of a broken wrist, Charlotte went into a slump that kept the team from repeating as International League champ. Perry could contribute to a title in Cleveland this year.

Another first baseman at Charlotte was 31 year old Chris Cron (.231-13-72). In 11 pro seasons, the righthanded batter has played just 12 major league games.

Greg Thomas, a 22 year old lefthanded batter, had trouble making contact at Class A Kinston (.191-15-42, 97 strikeouts).

Detroit Tigers

Pedro Guerrero (see California First Basemen) wasn't the only washed up veteran to return over the winter; Franklin Stubbs joined the Tigers via a minor league contract. It's unlikely that Stubbs will unseat Cecil Fielder or overtake a good prospect like Tony Clark, but he could get back to the bigs as an extra hitter. He'll have little Rotisserie value in any case.

Fred Matos:

Top prospect Tony Clark is on his way, and big Cecil Fielder may find himself at DH if Clark develops as expected. The 6' 7" Clark was a college basketball player, and his height and athletic ability should enable him to pick up the first base position quickly. He was the number two overall selection in the 1990

draft. Basketball and injuries have slowed his baseball progress, but he finally turned the corner last year. When discussing his power, some observers mention the Jose Canseco of eight years ago. Clark is capable of hitting 500-foot home runs, but his skills are still very rough. He may need another half-year or so in Triple-A, and is an excellent pick for your farm system.

Fielder is a consistently solid power hitter, and you can expect another season of 30+ home runs and 100+ RBI, with a batting average around .250. The years when 50 homers were expected are long gone. Fielder's Rotisserie value is around $20, and you should be careful not to bid too high because power hitters are usually plentiful.

Mickey Tettleton appeared in 24 games at first base and 53 games at catcher last year. He is discussed in the chapter on catchers. Minor leaguer Ivan Cruz was once considered a top prospect, but has struggled in the high minors in recent years and may have peaked in Triple-A.

Struggling prospect Rico Brogna was traded to the Mets for struggling prospect Alan Zinter in the hopes that a change of scenery and coaches would benefit both of them. Brogna did well with the Mets, but Zinter hit .238-21-58 for the Triple-A Mud Hens while striking out 40 percent of the time. Zinter looks like a minor league version of Rob Deer, but sometimes such wild swingers can develop plate discipline and go on to major league careers.

Lary Bump:

Tony Clark was successful after a mid-season promotion, which is a leading indicator of success. Last year (.279-21-86 at Trenton; .261-2-13 at Toledo) was his first full season of playing baseball after finishing a second career hustling his 6' 7" frame up and down a college basketball court. The 22 year old switch-hitter also showed a good glove after moving from the outfield.

Alan Zinter played most of last season at first base for Toledo (.238-21-58). He stole 13 bases, matching the total for his first five pro seasons. Zinter, acquired in a preseason trade for Rico Brogna, struck out 185 times. The 26 year old switch-hitter also played right field and DH, and was originally drafted by the Mets as a catcher.

Ivan Cruz, 26, failed to hit for average at Toledo for the second straight year, but showed power (.248-15-43).

Mike Rendina, 24, went downhill in his second Double-A season, to .227-11-46. Former Notre Damer Eric Danapilis, who also played in the outfield at Fayetteville, batted .252-23-83 after a .341 pro debut in 1993.

Kansas City Royals

Marc Bowman:

Wally Joyner's contract expires at the end of 1995 and not a moment too soon. Because of Joyner's expensive three-year deal, the Royals allowed Jeff Conine to escape to Florida and now American Association All-Star Joe Vitiello has to move to the outfield in order to get into the Royals' lineup in 1995. Joyner has consistently produced in the lower third of all major league first basemen over the course of his current contract.

Sure, Joyner led the Royals in batting average last year, but it's not like he competed for the AL batting crown. His eight HRs were better than only one regular AL first sacker and he was outslugged by several part-time first basemen. He does a good job of drawing walks but is only barely above average. Joyner's ''excellent'' defense is often overrated and of small value at his position.

Joyner's contract has hung around the Royals' necks like an albatross and his huge salary (he's the seventh highest paid player in baseball) prevents the Royals from being able to trade him. The Joyner era will last just one more year in KC. I'd be very surprised to see Joyner earn more than $15 for his Rotisserie owners in 1995; he'll never go for so little since people often

overbid on Joyner when they remember his days with the Angels.

Bob Hamelin is the backup at first base; he is discussed at length in the DH section.

Vitiello was mostly a first baseman for Triple-A Omaha, but will be asked to wield a rightfielder's glove to play regularly in the majors. Look for details about Vitiello in the Outfielders section.

Glenn Davis was another first baseman for Omaha and had a good power-hitting season reminiscent of his days with the Astros. He finished the year with 28 HRs and 97 RBI with a .282 average. Still, he didn't even get a call-up when Joyner was on the disabled list for two weeks in July. That says what the Royals think of him as a major leaguer. At best he'll probably get back to the bigs as a pinch-hitter.

The Memphis first baseman was George Canale, a journeyman power hitter who has never been able to hit major league pitching and hit .230 in 1994. He's a career minor leaguer.

Larry Sutton is the best prospect in the low minors. He crashed 26 homers with 94 RBI while hitting .306 for Class-A Wilmington. He's a classic lefty power hitter who will start 1995 at Double-A Memphis. At age 24, he'll be pushed through the minors. Look for a late 1996 arrival.

Lary Bump:

Joe Vitiello, a 24 year old righthanded batter, really paid dividends last year (.344-10-61 at Omaha). A first-round draft selection in 1991, he has a good batting eye, which put him among the minor league leaders with a .440 on-base percentage. He may not be ready for the start of the '95 season after undergoing off-season surgery on his left knee. When he returns, he could share time with Bob Hamelin as a first baseman/DH. Vitiello has played the outfield, but not very well.

Larry Sutton was voted the Carolina League's Most Valuable Player over teammate Johnny Damon. At

24, the lefthanded-hitting Sutton is three years older than Damon. Still, Sutton showed good power (.306-26-94 in one of A-ball's toughest parks for hitters) and on-base ability (.406 percentage). He was voted the league's best defensive first baseman. He was less successful in the Arizona Fall League.

19 year old Matt Smith was Kansas City's first-round draft choice in 1994. He was Baseball America's 15th-ranked pitcher entering the draft, but the Royals decided he was a better offensive player, comparing him to Kirk Gibson. They believe Smith can be a 100-RBI guy at first base or in left field. In his pro debut, the lefthanded batter hit .238-1-12 in the Gulf Coast League.

Milwaukee Brewers

Bill Gray:

John Jaha has to be impressive in spring training to win the first base job. Jaha had a big second half in 1993, hitting 14 HR after August 1, and the "second half signals" were indicating a big 1994. When Jaha couldn't find his stroke, he lost his confidence and was sent to the minors to regroup. He returned and seemed to be back on track, but the strike swallowed up what had traditionally been Jaha's best month, so we cannot be sure if Jaha regained his confidence, or if the pitchers locked on to a glaring weakness in his swing.

Certainly, coming off a bad year, Jaha could be a bargain in 1995. I'd rather find bargains among steadily improving players, not risky hitters like Jaha. Jaha's bid price will be lower than in 1994 auctions, and it's probably too early to give up on him. This season will tell the tale. There are safer first baseman out there, and don't overlook the fact that the Brewers are concerned enough to be considering moving catcher Dave Nilsson to first.

For the future, familiarize yourself with the name Scott Talanoa. He is the Brewers' first baseman of tomorrow, and honed his skills in the tough Arizona Fall League. Any time a club sends a youngster to the

Arizona Fall League, pay attention. These are their cornerstone minor league players and the club wants to hasten their development.

Lary Bump:

The Joey Meyer of the '90s is 25 year old Scott Talanoa. The 6'5", 240-pound righthanded batter pounded the ball at a .259-28-88 clip for Double-A El Paso.

Bo Dodson, 24, once an up-and-comer in the Brewers' organization, now has to sit behind Talanoa on their prospect train. The lefthanded-hitting Dodson struggled last season (.147-0-7 at El Paso; .261-2-29 for Triple-A New Orleans).

Also in the rear of the car is 25 year old Leon Glenn (.256-8-32 at El Paso; .239-4-22 at New Orleans). Glenn also stole 15 bases.

Ozzie Canseco, 30, spent some time in the outfield and at DH for New Orleans. His .236-14-67 season was in line with his 10-year minor league norms.

Minnesota Twins

James Benkard:

Kent Hrbek's retirement has opened up the position to David McCarty, Scott Stahoviak, Steve Dunn, or Pedro Munoz. Power is what the Twins will be looking for out of each of these candidates, as the Twins' offense sorely lacks a run producer without Hrbek.

McCarty is nearly ready to be a productive big league hitter, and will be a mild bargain in '95. Expect him to total 400 at bats, and drive in 60 runs with 15 home runs while maintaining his '94 average (.260). A heralded prospect who has experienced some growing pains, McCarty dug a deep hole for himself in his '93 debut, with a .214 showing in 98 games. He has started to climb out of this hole, and had some excellent games in '94.

Stahoviak and Dunn each hit lefthanded and are therefore capable of being platoon mates with McCarty, but each needs some more work in Triple-A. Stahoviak is reminiscent of Dave Magadan, although Stahoviak did have problems making contact in his '93 debut, and also struck out 90 times in Triple-A in '93. He does have some pop, as does Dunn. I expect Stahoviak to total 200 at bats in '95, with a .250 average and five to seven home runs. Dunn will struggle to establish himself.

Down the line, McCarty will play first base for Minnesota, while Stahoviak plays a hundred games per year between third, first, and DH. Dunn can become the regular DH if he can hold off Marty Cordova. Dunn will have to fight to reduce his weaknesses, as he needs either to hit more home runs (15 at Triple-A in '94) or start drawing some walks (24 in 330 at bats in '94).

Lary Bump:

Steve Dunn took five years to get past A-ball, but has made steady progress the last three seasons. The 24 year old lefthanded batter hit .309-15-73 for Triple-A Salt Lake City. He has moved ahead of David McCarty in Minnesota's farm system to become one of two likely replacements for Kent Hrbek.

The other potential replacement is lefthanded-hitting former third baseman Scott Stahoviak, 25. His Salt Lake marks were .318-13-94.

Another 25 year old lefthanded batter, Andy Kontorinis, spent his second season in the Florida State League, producing .288-6-51. His greatest skill is strike-zone judgment (57 walks, 39 strikeouts).

New York Yankees

For real baseball teams, Don Mattingly remains a terrific top star and a valuable leader. For a Rotisserie draft or auction, however, it's unlikely that Mattingly is going to be a good buy. He's got all the wrong characteristics. He's past his prime, career-wise. Maybe he can stay at the same level for years, maybe

not; but he sure isn't going to reach new heights at this point in time. In retrospect, it may turn out that Mattingly's 1994 campaign was his "comeback year." He had his highest average since 1988.

Mattingly is famous, popular, and has been at the very top of the player population for statistical valuation purposes (1985-1986). He had earned and been given due public recognition (MVP, batting title); fans love him. If there is any player in New York likely to attract widespread emotional bidding and drafting, it's Mattingly. Finally, he's marvelous on defense, which will mean extensive pleasure for manager Buck Showalter, for the Yankee pitchers, and for their infielders, for whom Mattingly saves numerous E's each year; but that defense won't help you in a dispassionate stat league competition.

Finally, there is the injury history. Recurring pain and back spasms were the symptoms that took Mattingly's big power stroke away, years ago. More recently he has been on the DL with a strained rib cage muscle (1993) and tendinitis in his wrist (1994). For taking care of himself and staying in shape, there is no more dedicated athlete, but again that's a virtue that should comfort his manager and teammates, but not provide the dispassionate type of confidence that would comfort a portfolio manager. If we forget names and histories, a typical 28 year old who has never been injured makes a better pick.

A bargain? Highly unlikely. Mattingly sold for an average price of $18 in 1994 auctions, and even with the good performance he was worth only $11 when the dust cleared at the end of the season. There is one special situation, however, where Mattingly could be considered as a possible sleeper pick: that's a league where everyone (and I mean everyone) is so dispassionate and so astute that they all dismiss Mattingly for the reasons I just enumerated. At $9, I would be very interested in Mattingly, and that's uninflated of course.

If and when Mattingly is not available (he's missed significant time three of the last five seasons) then Jim Leyritz is the most likely fill-in. Leyritz has value in his own right as a catcher (see that chapter), and he's

risen above some bad raps and organizational hassles to show glimmers of the star quality that he knew in his own heart he possessed years ago.

Lary Bump:

Tate Seefried is literally a hit-or-miss player. To advance to the majors, he'll need to cut down on his long swing that gives pitchers handy holes to hit. Even swinging at half-speed, Seefried has enough power to hit home runs. He set an Albany season HR record, and was voted the Eastern League's best power prospect. The 22 year old lefty hitter's numbers: .225-27-83.

Harvard-educated Nick Delvecchio was off to a great start in the Florida State League (.284-7-18 in 95 at bats), but a broken wrist sidelined him. A negative for the lefthanded batter is his age (25).

Last year's top draft pick, Brian Buchanan, split time between first base and the outfield. You can read more about him in the outfield section.

Oakland A's

Steven Rubio:

Mark McGwire remains one of the finest offensive players in the majors today, but with a total of 219 at bats over the past two seasons combined, it must be admitted that the injury risk is a more important factor than his tremendous hitting. Fantasy players might find a bargain here, but more prudent owners should probably avoid McGwire until he demonstrates he can stay healthy for an entire season.

In McGwire's absence, Troy Neel got the lion's share of play at first base for the A's, and he produced as expected, without embarassing himself in the field. Neel has had the same season at the plate twice in a row, and can now be considered a safe bet for solid production, whether he plays first base or DH. Neel is the choice for the owner trying to solidify an already-strong roster, while McGwire meets the needs of fantasy owners who need to take chances.

Lary Bump:

Marcos Armas has been OK, but no better, in two Pacific Coast League seasons (.287-18-73 last year). The Athletics promoted journeyman Jim Bowie ahead of Tony Armas' younger brother late in the season when Mark McGwire was shut down. Bowie, a 30 year old lefthanded batter, hit .314-8-66 at Tacoma.

The Athletics moved Joel Wolfe, 24, from rightfield to first base at Double-A Huntsville. The righthanded batter produced only .275-5-57, substandard for a cornerman. He stole a career-high 26 bases.

Seattle Mariners

Bill Gray:

Tino Martinez has been productive but never has never reached the ''next level'' that would put him in the class of Thomas, Fielder, Vaughn, or Olerud. Going into the All Star break, Martinez was having a pretty awful year, batting just .228 with but 11 home runs. After the break, he batted .352 with nine home runs in only 88 AB. If he'd been able to maintain that pace over a ''real'' second half Martinez could have produced 30+ homers. Now we wonder if 1994 would have been his career year. My guess is that it was. I still think he'll be good for .265 and 18-22 homeruns, but I do not think we'll see Tino enter the elite among first basemen. Pay accordingly.

Mike Blowers also qualifies with his 20 games at first base. See Blowers in the third base essay.

Lary Bump:

The Mariners could use righthanded-hitting Marc Newfield's bat in leftfield or in a first base/DH platoon with Tino Martinez. The 22 year old Newfield turned in a monster (.349-19-83) season at Calgary, and is one of the majors' best long-term hitting prospects. Greg Pirkl, a 24 year old righthanded hitter, went .317-22-72 in his third season at Calgary and had a power surge (.264-6-11 in 53 at bats) in Seattle. He also could be a DH.

Ruben Santana had a big 1993 at Double-A Jacksonville, but wasn't as successful in his second season there while the Mariners searched to find him a position. Randy Jorgensen, 23, the regular first baseman at Class A Riverside (.264-3-42), also has played the outfield.

Texas Rangers

Peter Graves:

Will Clark certainly didn't have any trouble adjusting to the American League. In mid-June he was hitting .384, then tailed off to finish at .329, seventh in the league. Clark stayed generally injury-free in 1994, and enjoyed hitting between Jose Canseco and Juan Gonzalez for most of the season. While Clark is still somewhat of an injury risk, he remains one of the game's better hitters and should continue to be productive in the foreseeable future.

The most likely backup for Clark is Rusty Greer, who is discussed with the outfielders. If the Rangers dip into the minors at first base, the options are Dan Peltier, Trey McCoy, Rob Maurer and Rob Nelson.

Peltier is a high-average singles hitter, not exactly your prototype major league first baseman. McCoy is a fine hitter with a history of periodically retiring from baseball. He's limited defensively and fits in best at DH. Maurer can't seem to stay healthy long enough to get a look. Nelson had the first base job in Oakland for about a week and a half in 1987, until Mark McGwire replaced him. He wandered through the Padres' system for a few years and resurfaced at Double-A Tulsa last season, hitting a respectable .278 with 11 homers.

Lary Bump:

With Will Clark on hand, Texas first base prospects have their best shot as designated hitters. Rob Maurer, a 28 year old lefthanded batter, hit .258-11-30 in 194 at bats for Oklahoma City. From the right side, Trey McCoy, also 28, batted .306 with 15 homers and 67 RBI.

Toronto Blue Jays

David Luciani:

John Olerud was under great pressure to repeat one of the most valuable seasons in recent memory. Of course it didn't happen. Olerud quietly finished the shortened 1994 campaign with a .297 average, 12 home runs and 67 RBI. That put him on a pace for 17 home runs and 95 RBI, still far above his pre-1993 performance.

Olerud will be 26 this year and most students of baseball would therefore tell you that this year or next should be the best of his career. It will be very hard, if not impossible, for him to repeat the efforts of 1993 but he is a very safe bet for an average in the .325-.335 range with plenty of doubles, walks and RBI. In fact, even in the 1991 and 1992 seasons where he drove in just 68 and 66 runs respectively, he was still on a pace for about 80 RBI. He didn't improve in that category the last couple of seasons so much as he simply played an extra fifteen or twenty games a year (Olerud never played in 140 games before 1993).

Injury problems have been rare for John Olerud, so given his age and accomplishments, bet on him to put up similar numbers to the last two years.

NATIONAL LEAGUE FIRST BASEMEN

Atlanta Braves

Marc Bowman:

Fred McGriff is amazing. For seven straight years he has had at least 30 homers, despite losing 49 games to the strike in 1994. In addition to his team leading 34 homers, McGriff led the Braves with 94 RBI and a .318 average. His .623 OBP was a career high; McGriff placed among league leaders in many offensive categories, including OBP - McGriff has an excellent batting eye. He is annually one of the league's very best hitters both in real baseball and in Rotisserie. He's also somewhat underrated because he isn't flashy and he's so consistent that he has never had the monster year that makes people remember him forever; his best year was 1992 when then-teammate Gary Sheffield overshadowed McGriff with a triple crown bid. For 1995 it'll be more of the same from McGriff - a .285 batting average, 35 homers, 100 RBI, five steals and a Rotisserie salary of about $30. He'll earn it.

Ryan Klesko is really a first baseman in leftfielder's clothes, but he'll be discussed in the Outfielders section anyway.

Formerly of the Dodgers and Indians organizations, Luis Lopez had a fine season for Richmond, hitting .305-18-79-4; his .484 slugging percentage was among the best in the International League. But, Lopez has spent all of the last seven years at Double-A and Triple-A while amassing just 88 major league at bats. At age 30, he's probably not going to push McGriff out of the way to get a big league spot. He's possibly pinch-hitter material, or he may just keep hitting minor league homers. In either case he has no Rotisserie value.

Once thought of as the Braves future catcher, Tyler Houston is now primarily a first baseman. The adjustment wasn't smooth and Houston suffered at the plate, hitting .244-4-33-3. He's still only 24 years old, but his career is quickly slipping away.

24 year old Kevin Grijak was one of Double-A Greenville's better power hitters in 1994, connecting for 11 homers and 58 RBI. He's a good contact hitter who doesn't strike out much and has a little speed. He has put up some very good batting averages in the lower minors. The move to Greenville was a double step up for Grijak, who played for "low" Class A Macon in 1993. Grijak also plays in the outfield and his versatility will help him move up quicker. Still, he doesn't look like a major league regular at this point. Despite his all-around offensive contributions and defensive versatility, Grijak is most likely destined for a utility/pinch-hitting role should he reach the big leagues.

22 year old Ramon Nunez connected for 17 homers for "high" Class A Durham, but also fanned 98 times in 453 at bats. Nunez looks like a good power hitter who could move up quickly should he get his free-swinging tendencies under control.

Lary Bump:

Splitting time as Richmond's first baseman were righthander Luis Lopez, who has just 88 major league at bats despite a .304 average for 11 minor league seasons, and disappointing 1989 first round draft pick Tyler Houston, who bats lefthanded. 30 year old Lopez had a typical season, but the 24 year old Houston, drafted as a catcher, was a disappointment.

Another 24 year old, Kevin Grijak, is likely to move past Houston. In 1994 Grijak batted .368-11-22 in 22 games with Class A Durham, then .270-11-58 at Double-A Greenville.

Chicago Cubs

Stuart Shea:

A little Rotisserie Pop Quiz (no peeking at your neighbor's paper):

Mark Grace:

    a) Is an excellent defensive first baseman
    b) Has a fine batting eye
    c) Makes consistent contact
    d) Can hit for average
    e) Is very popular with teammates and fans
    f) Is overrated
    g) All of the above

The answer is g).

Grace does several things very well. Unfortunately, he lacks power and does not get on base enough to overcome that significant weakness. Among National League first basemen he falls behind McGriff, Jefferies, Galarraga and Bagwell. He isn't clearly better than Morris or Kruk, and in a year or so Grace might not be as good as Cliff Floyd. Still, his ability to hit close to .300 and play slick defense enables Grace to carry the mantle of a star, and to demand big money.

As of press time, the Cubs had not decided to bring Grace back into the fold. Should he opt for free agency, he would probably find a new home but at less money than he wants. It's unlikely that he will ever be a top line player and the Cubs need impact from the first base position.

The Cubs may try to keep Grace for a year or two while waiting for Brant Brown or Brooks Kieschnick to fill the position. Should Grace exit, the team would either look for a short term solution among free agents or trade for one. Nobody on their high minor league teams can yet handle the position on an everyday basis. Triple-A regular Matt Franco hit .275 with 11 home runs and projects as a pinch-hitter at best.

Former Texas Longhorn star, Kieschnick, is probably the Cubs' best position playing prospect. The Cubs' first pick in 1993 has been moved quickly, reaching Double-A Orlando last year. Possessed with outstanding bat speed, he hit .282 with 13 homers after a slow start in his first full professional season. Although he had a mediocre 34/62 walk/strikeout ratio in 1994, he's still learning as a raw professional. In college, Kieschnick was a disciplined hitter. He could be in the Cubs' lineup as soon as late 1995, probably at first base. At the start of his pro career, he played left field, but was shifted in mid-1994. His defense is not good at any position and he lacks good running speed.

The Cubs' second draft pick in 1992, Brown was highly regarded by the Himes administration; we'll see how MacPhail and Lynch handle him. Despite a sweet swing and glowing recommendations, Brown hasn't produced good numbers. He hit just .269 with four homers and 34 walks at Double-A in 1994. In Brown's defense, he's only 23 years old and he's been pushed up the ladder quickly.

Lary Bump:

Matt Franco is next in a line of singles hitting first basemen the Cubs inexplicably keep grooming for their home run park. The irony is that they traded Rafael Palmeiro because they didn't think he had enough power. Franco, a 25 year old lefthander, could see regular playing time in Chicago replacing Mark Grace.

Following Franco is lefthander Brant Brown. In his second year at Double-A Orlando, he showed almost no power (.270-5-37) and stole 11 bases, but was thrown out an alarming 15 times. He's not likely to advance past Franco, let alone Grace.

Cincinnati Reds

Tim Costo is gone to the Indians, in a swap of failed first round picks that brought Mark Lewis to the Reds. Costo's departure came just one day before the announcement of Hal Morris getting a new contract, and signals an ongoing commitment to Morris as an everyday, every situation type of player (as if the money didn't tell that story). Costo's departure also removes some of the squeeze on Cincinnati outfield backups, and punctuates Willie Greene's security at third base (remember the Costo/Greene platoon gibberish that preceded the Tony Fernandez acquisition in March 1994).

Greg Gajus:

Hal Morris (.335-10-78-6) had the best year of his career in 1994, hitting over .360 most of the year before tailing off in the second half. At this stage of his career, Morris is John Kruk as a Rotisserie player - a left handed hitter with a very good average, marginal power for a first baseman, a good RBI total, a handful of steals each year and somewhat injury prone (although Morris was free of injuries for the first time in 1994). The biggest question with Morris is his ability to hit lefthanders. His platoon split was huge again last season (.362 versus right handers, .244 with zero homers against lefthanders), and the late season acquisition of Brian Hunter suggests some platooning in 1995. A platoon could be beneficial to his Rotisserie value, protecting or raising his average at a very low cost in home runs and RBI, in addition to driving down his perceived value at auction time.

Hunter (.234-15-57-0) came over from the Pirates and made an immediate impact for the Reds, homering in his first three games. A classic low average slugger (his career high batting average is .251), Hunter

should again get 250 at bats while spot starting at first base and in the outfield, along with the usual pinch hitting appearances. He is a good late round speculative pick.

Two of the Reds better prospects are first basemen. Tim Belk is a 25 year old right handed hitter who hit .309 at Class AA Chattanooga with marginal power (much like Morris).

Jamie Dismuke, a 25 year old left handed hitter, had a solid year in 1993, but struggled at Indianapolis in 1994 (.266-13-49). He then moved on to the Dodgers via the Braves organization as a minor league free agent.

Tim Costo looked good a couple of years ago, but is now 26 and missed almost the entire Triple-A season due to injuries.

Lary Bump:

Coming up through the Cincinnati system are righthander Tim Belk (.309-10-86 at Double-A Chattanooga; .111 in six games after a promotion to Indianapolis) and Toby Rumfield (.249-29-88 in the hitters' paradise of Winston-Salem). Belk will be 25 in April and needs to advance this season to have a shot at significant major league time. 22 year old Rumfield, another righthander, was once a catcher.

As first base insurance (and a DH at Indianapolis), the Reds signed minor league free agent Drew Denson away from the White Sox. The righthanded batter has driven in 103 runs in each of the last two seasons at Nashville, where he batted .263 with 30 homers in 1994.

Colorado Rockies

David Smith:

Discussion about first base for Colorado starts and ends with Andres Galarraga. As long as the Big Cat is making Big Dough (now in the second year of a three year, $12 million contract) he's batting cleanup

for the Rockies. The concern about Galarraga is injuries. In 1993 he spent 42 games on the disabled list, then went down in July of 1994 with a broken hand. You could say he's found a home in Colorado, though. After his .370-22-98 year in 1993, he was actually hitting for more power in 1994, going .319-31-85.

He kept the free-swinging attitude (his 93 strikeouts led the Rockies) and the open stance, but hey, why mess with things when they're going right? Even teammates in slumps were trying out the open stance. Galarraga will help fantasy leaguers out a lot since he sprays the ball a lot for extra bases, and was among league leaders in RBI and home runs until he was plunked in the hand by John Burkett of the Giants.

It's important to realize, however, that this guy carries the team offensively. Everyone else chips in, but this is the guy you want in clutch time for the Rockies. Unfortunately for number crunchers, the National League has a plethora of first basemen putting up big numbers thereby diminishing Galarraga's relative value.

Given Galarraga's injury record GM Bob Gebhard will be smart to groom one of three fill-ins: Ty Van Burkleo, Jason Smith or Jay Gainer. Van Burkleo and Gainer split time in Colorado Springs in 1994. Van Burkleo suddenly discovered power at age 31, hitting 21 homers and driving in 86 runs.

At age 28, Gainer is hardly a spring chicken. He has marginal power and has hit for a good average at high minor league levels. The lefty Gainer might be a platoon candidate in Galarraga's absence.

Smith had respectable numbers in Class A Asheville and could move up two levels in 1995.

After Galarraga went out of the lineup in 1994, John Vander Wal was one of several who came off the bench to play first. Batting lefthanded helps, but don't look for him in the sports pages too much as he lacks power.

Lary Bump:

With Andres Galarraga on hand, the Rockies wouldn't seem to need help at first base from minor leaguers. Galarraga's injury history, however, provides a wide open window of opportunity.

The leading candidates are well traveled veterans Jay Gainer and Ty Van Burkleo. Both bat lefthanded. In his second season at Colorado Springs, 28 year old Gainer slumped to .247-9-34. 31 year old Van Burkleo, who has played in Japan, earned two games with the Rockies on the strength of his .271-21-86 season at Triple-A Colorado Springs.

Another short term prospect is Jim Tatum (see National League Catchers).

28 year old switch hitter Frank Bolick was an Expo in 1993. He started last season at Buffalo (.263-2-8) in the Pirates' organization. After they released him, Bolick became one of the Eastern League's biggest home run threats in a pitchers' park at New Haven, going .252-21-63.

Another player with power potential is Jason Smith (.258-17-57 in the Sally League; .286 in 14 at bats for New Haven). The 24 year old righthander was drafted as a catcher in the 24th round in 1993. lefthanded.

Florida Marlins

Tony Blengino:

Greg Colbrunn, stolen from Montreal by Former Expos' General Manager Dave Dombrowski, is the man for the Marlins. Reconstructive elbow surgery in 1991 ended Colbrunn's catching career but his good power stroke gave him an addition chance as a first baseman.

Early in 1994, when the Marlins finally tired of Orestes Destrade, Colbrunn was installed as the team's regular first baseman. Colbrunn responded by hitting .303 and slugging .484, but, most notably, he

showed for the first time that he could hit righthanded pitching, batting .283 against righthanders in 1994. When Colbrunn's elbow injuries flared again in 1993, he became expendable to the talent-laden Expos and joined the Marlins via waivers.

Colbrunn has always been able to hit lefties and 1994 was no exception as he bashed them at a .347 clip. Unfortunately, Colbrunn's plate discipline remains poor; he has drawn just 21 walks in 497 major league plate appearances. Such impatience is usually not a good sign and while he should improve in this area over time, Colbrunn would have to hit well above .300 to become a valuable first baseman. For Rotisserie purposes, though, he can provide some cheap power with little batting average risk. In 1995, Colbrunn should be good for a .275 average with 13 homers and 70 RBI.

Long heralded as a future major league power hitter, 27 year old Monty Fariss has hit well in the minors, but struggle in short major league stints. For Edmonton in 1994, Farris slugged .527 with 20 homers. But, Fariss has managed just a .217 average in 226 big league at bats. At this point he's basically a Triple-A hitter without a real position. While he will likely get further short chances in the majors, Fariss is unlikely to win a regular role. Most likely, he'll continue to bounce around in the high minors.

The release of Destrade gave 33 year old Russ Morman another major league cup of coffee. Morman has spread his 163 major league games over six different seasons from 1986 to 1994. He's bench filler stored at Triple-A, where he has been a starting first basemen for ten straight seasons, collecting 3993 minor league at bats. Fariss should pay attention to Morman's fate because that is where his career is headed. There are many more like Morman in the high minors and while he'll probably get another handful of big league at bats, it's about 50-50 that he'll even get 50 plate appearances.

After an explosive Class A season for High Desert in 1993 when he hit .363 with 69 extra base hits and led the minors with 126 RBI, 26 year old Tim Clark came crashing back to Earth for Double-A Portland in

1994. Clark hit .265 with only 14 homers and a .414 slugging average. At age 24 (in 1993), Clark was a man playing among boys in Class A. The true measure of his baseball prowess was apparent when he finally faced players with more experience. Still, the lack of depth at first base in the Marlins' organization and his lefthanded hitting gives Clark an outside chance to join the Marlins in 1995. A more likely scenario has the Marlins looking outside the organization for a backup.

Greg O'Halloran got to the majors for 12 games in 1994 as a third string catcher, but he's primarily a first baseman, and not a good one at that. He was merely adequate as a catcher, but is woefully inadequate as a hitter to ever return to the majors in any useful capacity.

Todd Pridy has mashed 74 doubles in the last two years and while he strikes out frequently and has yet to play above Class A, little stands in Pridy's way within the Marlins' organization. Hitters with outstanding doubles power often become home run hitters at higher levels. Watch the 24 year old Pridy's progress at Double-A in 1995; he has a chance to compete for big league playing time by 1996.

Lary Bump:

The first basemen at Edmonton in 1994 were 32 year old Russ Morman (.350-19-82 for Edmonton, then .212-1-2 in 13 games with the Marlins) and 27 year old Monty Fariss (.285-20-60); both bat righthanded. Fariss also played second base in his never ending quest for a defensive position.

At Double-A Portland, 25 year old righthander Derrick White is more viable prospect. He was released from the Expos' Triple-A farm at Ottawa after a .212-0-9 start and finished at .269-4-34-14 despite a major slump.

The Marlins' homegrown prospect is Todd Pridy, a 24 year old lefthander who hit .251-13-89 in the Florida State League.

Houston Astros

Bill Gilbert:

In last year's book, our comment on Jeff Bagwell was that a reasonable expectation would be .300-20-100-10 for the next ten seasons, with one or two monster years along the way. Anyone picking him up at a price reflecting these values received an immediate dividend as Bagwell had a monster season that in at least one respect rivals anything done in the past 67 years. Bagwell's .750 slugging average is the highest since 1927 when Babe Ruth .772 and Lou Gehrig hit .765.

Bagwell and Frank Thomas will both turn 27 on May 27, 1995 and should be reaching their prime years. Although Bagwell has improved in each of the three seasons since his Rookie of the Year campaign in 1991, further improvement would seem to be unlikely. However, he is a hard worker who has been able to make adjustments to stay ahead of the pitchers and he should be able to retain his spot in the game's very top echelon. He is extremely strong and generates exceptional bat speed. His 1994 numbers in only 109 games, .368-39-116-15, set new franchise records for batting average, home runs and runs batted in.

In each of the past two years, Bagwell's season has ended prematurely after he suffered broken bones in his hand when being hit by a pitch. An aggressive hitting style leaves him vulnerable to inside pitches. While he has apparently not sustained any continuing problems due to the injuries, he could be susceptible to similar injuries in the future.

Sid Bream, 34, was signed as a lefthanded pinch hitter and filled the role extremely well in 1994 while making an occasional start at first base. With his aching knees, he has virtually no chance of ever playing regularly again. Utilityman Chris Donnels, 28, also played a few games at first, but doesn't have a future at the position.

The Astros have an outstanding prospect at Triple-A Tucson in 23 year old Venezuelan Roberto Petagine. He played briefly for Houston in 1994 but failed to collect a hit. He spent some time on the disabled list at Tucson, but recorded a .316-10-44-3 season in only 247 at bats. First base is his only position and, since the Astros are committed to keeping Bagwell, Petagine's major league future would appear to be dependent upon a trade to another organization.

The Astros have another first baseman who had an outstanding year in 1994. Jeff Ball, 25, was one of the leading hitters in the Double-A Texas League with a .316-13-57-9 log at Jackson. Ball plays other infield positions and, with continued improvement, could make it as a utilityman in the majors.

Lary Bump:

Roberto Petagine started the 1994 season by jumping from Double-A directly to Houston, but soon went on the disabled list because of a broken right wrist. Petagine can hit, but he can't overtake Jeff Bagwell at first base, so the lefthander may have to move to the outfield.

Mike Simms returned to the Astros after being released from Buffalo (.236-4-8) and had one of the best 100 game seasons in the minors at Tucson (.287-20-85). However, the 28 year old righthanded power hitter has never come through in 172 major league at bats; his career major league average is .209.

At Double-A Jackson, 21 year old lefthander Dennis Colon hit .276-5-52.

Voted the voted the the Midwest League's best defensive first baseman, 22 year old righthander Eddie Ramos' offense didn't improve in his second season in the league (.254-12-56-17).

Los Angeles Dodgers

Greg Gajus:

Eric Karros (.266-14-46-2) continues to hold down first base for the Dodgers, but he doesn't seem likely to develop into a major star. He hit poorly with runners in scoring position in 1994 (.209) so it would be reasonable to expect some improvement in his

RBI count in 1995. Karros' biggest asset is his reliability. He will play every day and provide some, but not great, power and RBI production. For the long term, the Dodgers might hand one of their many fine outfield prospects a first baseman's mitt to try for a little more production out of first base.

Henry Rodriguez and Cory Snyder (described in the outfielders section) were the backups in 1994 and Rodriguez will probably be back to fill the role again in 1995.

In the minors, the Dodgers have an interesting lefthanded hitting prospect, Don Barbara, who hit .351 with 12 home runs in only 168 at bats at Albuquerque. The regular Albuquerque first baseman, Mike Busch (26), has some power but is not a serious prospect.

Lary Bump:

The Dodgers featured a Barbara-Busch platoon at first base in Albuquerque. The 6'5", 243-pound Mike Busch was a member of the Pacific Coast League champs' all weight lifters team. He still hasn't learned to lay off bad pitches, though. Busch may have more power than Eric Karros, but can't match the batting average of the Dodgers' incumbent. The 26 year old righthander finished at .263-27-83.

Lefthander Don Barbara, also 26, hit for power for the first time in his career (.351-12-37 after a .367-1-10 start in eight games at San Antonio). The power surge may have lifted him above career minor leaguer status. He drove in the final run of the North American baseball season in last year's PCL playoffs.

Barbara can't get too comfortable, because the Dodgers picked up a 25 year old lefthander, Jamie Dismuke, when the music stopped in a game of musical waivers that took him from the Cincinnati organization through Atlanta to Los Angeles. A .300 hitter with 20 homers in the Southern League in 1993, Dismuke started miserably last season before rallying somewhat (.266-13-49 at Indianapolis). He's less interesting as a prospect than for his feet together batting stance, which mirrors that of former Tiger John Wockenfuss.

The Dodgers' Double-A first baseman was 25 year old Jay Kirkpatrick, a lefthander who put together a .296-18-75 season.

Lefthander Doug Newstrom, the Dodgers' seventh round draft pick in 1993, moved from third base back to first base last year (the position that he played at Arizona State). As a result, he was voted the best defensive first baseman in the Florida State League. The 23 year old has a good batting eye (59 walks, 51 strikeouts), but may not have enough power (.289-2-46) to be a major leaguer.

Montreal Expos

John Perrotto:

To live up to the hype leading into his rookie season of 1994, Cliff Floyd would have had to hit .400, break Roger Maris' home run record and drive in 200 runs. And it would have helped if he stole 50 bases, won a Gold Glove and became the first active player ever to win induction into the Hall of Fame.

Expectations were great for Floyd, though he had previously only played one month as high as Class AAA. He didn't quite live up to the hype but he didn't have a bad season either, finishing at .281-4-41-10.

Floyd bounced between first base and leftfield last year and was platooned at times, sitting against tough lefthanders. However, after a year to adjust to the majors, he will be the Expos' regular first baseman in 1995. He has all the tools to become a superstar and he will if people just give him a little time to gain some experience.

Veteran Randy Milligan was Floyd's backup last season and struggled through a .232-2-12-0 season; the Expos released him in October. Once an underrated offensive performer with his good slugging and on base percentages, he is slipping fast and will only hang on somewhere as a pinch hitter.

Lary Bump:

By the end of last season, the Expos' Triple-A first baseman was Hector Villanueva, recycled from the Mexican League (which he led in weight gain). The 30 year old righthander did not shine at Ottawa (.215-4-11).

Also at Ottawa was Oreste Marrero, a 25 year old lefthander who did nothing to dispel his reputation as a good field, mediocre hit first baseman with his .244-7-31 season.

Another lefty swinger, Randy Wilstead had a solid year at first base for Double-A Harrisburg (.294-13-64 with a .414 on base percentage), but he'll be 27 in April.

Montreal acquired Dave Duplessis, a 25 year old lefthander, from the Indians in last year's Chris Nabholz trade. Duplessis (.260-8-58 in the Florida State League) hasn't shown the power that you'd expect from a guy 6'6" and 225 pounds, but his French surname has some appeal in Montreal.

Matt Raleigh was voted the Midwest League's best power prospect after his .274-34-83 season in 1994. Subtracting his 138 strikeouts, he made contact only 260 times and hit home runs in 13% of those at bats. He has a problem common to the Expos' first base prospects: At age 24, can the righthander still advance to the majors? He also played third base at Burlington.

New York Mets

The Mets had an unusual situation around first base in 1994. They began the year with a slick-fielding singles/gaps hitter, David Segui, as their regular first baseman, and ended with a "failed" first round pick (who could be a failure at age 24?) Rico Brogna, emerging from burial in the Tigers farm system to become a minor folk hero in New York. In between, another failed first round pick, Jim Lindeman, made spot starts at first when he wasn't in the outfield.

Brogna is the exciting player here. It's really unfortunate that he started off with such a bang when

recalled June 20 to replace Segui (who had gone on the DL with a hamstring problem). Brogna promptly ran up a 15-game hitting streak, and his 1994 batting average attracts the attention of everyone including the ignorant. Brogna might have been a wonderful sleeper for 1995 if his 1994 performance had been more in line with his Triple-A averages of .220, .261, and .273 from 1991-1993. Before last year, .273 was the highest he had batted in any professional league at any level.

The only way to get Brogna for a fair price is to talk about his .351 average excessively and hope that everyone will take a long enough look to see it as a fluke. If you're the lucky guy who got Brogna last year, trading him as a .351 hitter (after the auction, of course, not before) is a sound tactical move, although keeping him as he develops over the next couple of years could be more fun.

Brogna is finally becoming the star hitter that scouts projected he would be before the 1988 draft and as validated by his Double-A home run and RBI crowns in 1990 at the young age of 20. The Mets certainly did OK getting Brogna in trade for Alan Zinter, even-up. You should be so fortunate.

For the short term, you have to expect Brogna to take a step and reconsolidate before his career blossoms fully. Pitchers are going to be a lot more careful with him in 1995, having learned that you can't throw Brogna a fastball when he's ahead in the count and looking for it. Given a less generous pitch selection, Brogna's impatience will be drawn out. He'll get plenty of homers and RBI, but will never hit .350 again.

Obviously, by the time Segui came off the DL July 5, he wasn't needed at first base any longer, although he did make a few spot starts there before the end of the season. Segui is now mainly a left fielder, with more about him appearing in the outfield chapter, along with more about Lindeman.

Lary Bump:

What in the name of Keith Hernandez is going on

here? The Mets have a phalanx of slick fielding first basemen moving up through their system.

The Mets made one of last year's best trades when they dealt Alan Zinter even up for Rico Brogna. Before last season, the 24 year old lefthander's best year was 1990, when he led the Eastern League in home runs. There is nothing in Brogna's history to suggest that he can repeat his .351-7-20 performance in 1994. He was voted the International League's best defensive first baseman and batted .244-12-37 for Triple-A Norfolk.

In addition to hitting for a high average (.358-5-42 at Binghamton; .242-0-28 at Norfolk), 23 year old righthander Omar Garcia was voted the Eastern League's best defensive first baseman. He doesn't have enough power to make it big in the bigs.

The South Atlantic League's best defensive first baseman, 21 year old lefty Jeff Kiraly neither makes good contact (105 strikeouts) nor hits for power (.242-4-34).

Lefthander Terrence Long was the Mets' second first round draft pick in 1994, out of high school. He showed good power in the Appalachian League, going .233-12-39 and mostly played in the outfield to take advantage of his speed.

Philadelphia Phillies

Tony Blengino:

The Phillies all-time career OBP leader (.403), John Kruk had a typical season in 1994, batting over .300 with an above average number of walks and below average power. Stricken with testicular cancer in spring training, Kruk battled back in 1994, but the warning signs of an imminent downturn are unmistakeable. Kruk has a history of injuries and has had trouble with nagging knee and back problems for years. The oldest starting first baseman in the league (at age 34), Kruk became a free agent at the end of 1994. He is unlikely to re-sign with Philadelphia. He will go elsewhere and has been rumored to be considering retirement. Kruk is an unconventional guy who doesn't require the big bucks of big league ball to be happy and could easily just hang up his spikes if he can't find a situation to his liking.

The Phillies passed on an opportunity to draft Frank Thomas in 1989, instead opting for outfielder Jeff Jackson since the team was "pretty set at first base with Ricky Jordan". Jordan had just mashed 11 homers in 273 at bats in 1988 and seemed destined for glory. However, once pitchers learned to stop throwing strikes to the free-swinging Jordan, he became a flop as a regular. Jordan has drawn just 76 walks in 2152 career plate appearances and is a poor defensive player. A serviceable bench player, the 30 year old Jordan can hit a mistake pitch a long way, but he is far overpriced for his weak, one sided production. He was on the trading block during the strike, then became a free agent after the season. He'll probably not return to Philadelphia.

Several options are being discussed by the Phils' front office, including free agent Gregg Jefferies and the shift of third baseman Dave Hollins across the diamond. Barring an import from outside the organization, the Phillies could turn to 25 year old Gene Schall who blossomed at Triple-A Scranton-Wilkes Barre in 1994 to post career highs of 35 doubles and 16 homers. Like Jordan, Schall has marginal power and poor plate discipline. Most likely Schall will get a bench role in Philadelphia in 1995, batting .260 with four homers in 200 at bats.

Line drive hitting Jon Zuber played for Double-A Reading in 1994. The 25 year old Zuber is a consistent hitter for average (.290s range), but doesn't have good power; his nine homers in 1994 were a career high. He could reach the big leagues as a lefthanded pinch hitter, but little else.

Tape measure homers generated a lot of attention for big Jon McMullen at Class A Spartanburg. The son of major leaguer Ken McMullen is 6'0", 240 pounds and just 21 years old. Caution needs to be taken with McMullen, however, due to a left shoulder injury and McMullen's lack of good conditioning.

Gene Schall was one of the International League's leading run producers (.285-16-89) with its lowest scoring team. The 24 year old righthander seems to be a prophet without honor in his own organization, however. Even though free agent John Kruk isn't likely to resign, the Phillies are talking about moving Dave Hollins or Darren Daulton to first base instead of promoting Schall.

Farther down the food chain, Philadelphia has 25 year old Jon Zuber who batted .293-9-70 with Double-A Reading, 25 year old Jeff Bigler - a .281-5-49 hitter in the Florida State League, and 21 year old Jon McMullen (.297-12-53 in the Sally League); all bat lefthanded.

Pittsburgh Pirates

John Perrotto:

After bouncing back and forth between first base and right field last season, Orlando Merced should find regular work at first base in 1995 unless the Pirates try to deal him for pitching help.

Merced had a solid season in 1994, batting .272-9-51-4. Since giving up switch hitting in 1993 to bat strictly from the left side, Merced has become an everyday player. He isn't a bad player but he's no Triple Crown candidate either. The Pirates can live with Merced. In fact, they've lived without a classic power hitting first baseman for years. No Pirate first sacker has hit more than 18 homers in a season since Jason Thompson went deep 31 times in 1982.

Power hitting prospect Rich Aude batted .281-15-79-9 for Class AAA Buffalo last year. Though the 6'5" Aude possesses raw power and put up decent numbers at the highest minor league level, he is not ready to step into the Pirates' lineup. He needs to tighten up a looping swing and work on his defense. He also hit just one home run after the All-Star break last year. The 23 year old Aude will get another full season in the minors in 1995.

Mark Johnson was the Southern League's MVP in 1994 with Class AA Carolina, hitting .276-23-85-6. Don't get too excited, though, as Johnson is not considered a hot prospect. It was the former Dartmouth quarterback's third season at the Class AA level and he turned 27 in October.

Gigantic Michael Brown, 6'7" and 265 pounds, struggled in his first year of Class AA in 1994, hitting just .249-7-45-3 with Carolina. However, his history shows he has had poor first seasons at every level of the minors before having marked improvement in his second season. He is intriguing at his size and the Pirates will give him another opportunity at Class AA this season. Keep an eye on his stats to see if he follows his normal career progression.

Lary Bump:

Rich Aude started to pull the ball and hit with power in 1993, but was a mild disappointment last season in Buffalo, even though Pilot Field favors righthanders. He was voted the best defensive first baseman in the American Association, which was damning with faint praise.

Lefthander Mark Johnson, voted the Southern League's best power prospect, isn't really a prospect because of his age (27). He has played in the outfield, too.

Also with the Carolina Mudcats was 23 year old lefty Mike Brown. He followed up a 21 homer season at hitter friendly Salem with a .249-7-45 year in Double-A.

The Pirates continued looking for a position for underachieving 1991 first round draft choice Jon Farrell, and settled on first base last season at Salem (.270-11-42-11). The 23 year old righthander will have to advance more rapidly to make it to The Show.

St. Louis Cardinals

John Perrotto:

Even those with a good head for figures can find reading spring training box scores an overwhelming task. They often contain as many as 60 names, half of which are unrecognizable, especially with all the

abbreviations the wire services use.

However, if you want to figure out who the Cardinals' Opening Day first baseman will be, you may have to peruse the Grapefruit League boxes this spring. That's because Gregg Jefferies turned down a $20 million, four year contract last summer and became a free agent. Since the Cardinals failed to re-sign Jefferies, first base is be wide open.

Veteran Gerald Perry was Jefferies' backup in 1994 and posted a fine .325-3-18-1 seasons. Though a fine bench player, Perry isn't the answer as a starter at this stage of his career. Besides, he also became a free agent at the end of last season.

Assuming the Cardinals don't replace Jefferies with another free agent, they will likely look to convert other players into the first base role. Third baseman Todd Zeile may move across the diamond, or Triple-A second baseman Darrel Deak could switch positions and advance to the majors. Nothing is certain at this point; stay tuned for further developments.

It will be most interesting to see what happens to Jefferies career in Philadelphia. After crumbling under the high expectations in New York with the Mets and one nondescript season in Kansas City, Jefferies found a home in St. Louis and blossomed. He hit .325-12-55-12 last year after a 1993 that saw him break through at .342-16-83-46.

Lary Bump:

Due to Gregg Jefferies being lost to free agency, first base is a prime location for the Cardinals to fill via trade, or to shift a player out of their outfield logjam.

The first baseman most frequently on the lineup card at Triple-A Louisville was 34 year old Phil Stephenson. He no longer can run (four stolen bases) but he still walks more often than he strikes out, which increased the value of his .269-8-55 hitting. With Stephenson, there is no upside.

Next in line, at Double-A Arkansas, was Doug Radziewicz (.222-8-40). The lefthander will be 26 in

April, so he has limited potential at best. The top first base prospect in 1994 was 24 year old righthander Aldo Pecorilli (.278-18-78-13 in the Florida State League). A converted catcher, he still needs to improve his defense at first base.

San Diego Padres

Fred Matos:

The baseball rebirth of Eddie Williams was one of 1994's most amazing success stories. A visionary Padres scout found him playing in a local San Diego semipro "beer league" in 1993. Williams responded with a career year of .331-11-42 in 175 at bats.

Great things were once expected from Williams, especially in Cleveland where he once made the cover of Sports Illustrated as part of the Indians bright future. But Williams struggled with the Indians (and other teams) before turning into a true journeyman who played for all sorts of teams all over the world and finally heading back home to San Diego and the beer league.

Be very wary of extrapolating his excellent production over 175 at bats into 30 homers or 100 RBI in 550 at bats. It's difficult to see Williams continuing his hot hitting at age 31. He never hit in the majors before and he could easily revert to his weak hitting form of the past. Once pitchers find his weaknesses word will spread quickly. Because there are so many established power hitting first basemen, Williams must be viewed as a big risk; he's not worth a large bid.

After he posted some solid minor league numbers, the Padres expected slugger Dave Staton to hit 30 homers last year, but he slumped badly and ended up slugging in the minors again. Staton needs another tremendous season in Triple-A to prove himself. Until he has better big league success, he'll just be a typical low average, high strikeout power hitter whose maximum level is Triple-A.

Young Tim Hyers (23) got his major league opportunity when Archi Cianfrocco and Dave Staton failed to produce. He was obtained from Toronto and

did surprisingly well considering his limited experience, hitting .254 in 118 at bats. Hyers doesn't have much power now, but that could come quickly as he matures. His limited but solid minor league record portends good things in his future. Hyers is a nice quiet sleeper, who could payoff big if Eddie Williams turns out to be a one year (or half year) wonder.

Phil Clark hit .330-10-38 in 294 at bats over parts of the 1992 and 1993 seasons, so his .215-5-20 performance in 149 at bats last year was a large disappointment. Clark's versatility will help him get into the lineup more often and also helps him get into games as a substitute at first base, third base, in the outfield and behind the plate; he'll get more chances at the plate than the typical backup first baseman. Clark has had solid hitting seasons in the minors and has proven he can hit major league pitching, so his poor 1994 season is most likely a fluke. Watch for Clark to rebound with a solid season of hitting about .270 with a little power.

Kevin Maas struggled in a comeback attempt in the Padres minor league system. He was released and later signed with the Reds.

Lary Bump:

After hitting just .182 for the Padres, 26 year old Dave Staton went back to Vegas and hit .277-12-47. He has power and can draw a walk, but can't field or run.

The hope for the future (approximately 1996) is 23 year old Jason Thompson. The lefthander went a long way in his first year above Rookie ball. He was voted the best batting prospect in the California League (.360-13-63), and even with a 100 point batting average drop he held his own in the Texas League (.260-8-46).

San Francisco Giants

Steven Rubio:

It is now Year Two of the post-Will Clark era, and it is time to give J.R. Phillips his shot at the job. Phillips has fine power, and his reputation for poor fielding is overblown; he's a better defensive player than initial reports had indicated. J.R.'s offensive numbers are not overwhelming when taken in the context of the offense-crazed Pacific Coast League; he has also had trouble with his bat in his short major league stints thus far. Phillips is likely to be overvalued by fantasy players due to his high profile and exaggerated projections; he's a long shot to impress in 1995.

Darryl Strawberry (discussed in the outfield section) has stated that he would be willing, even happy, to play first base if the team asked him. If Phillips fails, Strawberry might replace him.

Behind Phillips, the best firstbase prospect in the system is Barry Miller. At one point in his career, Miller looked more impressive than Phillips (who was in the Angels' system), but he has not improved as much as the Giants would like and he is now 26 years old. He is unlikely to seriously challenge Phillips at this point.

Lary Bump:

J.R. Phillips could have been San Francisco's regular first baseman last season; instead he regularly failed to make contact. Once released by the Angels, Phillips is one of the streakiest hitters around. When he did hit the ball last year at Phoenix, it usually went far (.300-27-79 with 96 strikeouts in 360 at bats). A broken left forearm ended last season for the 24 year old lefthander.

The regular first baseman at Double-A Shreveport, lefty Barry Miller, made better contact but with less power (.277-12-73) than Phillips; Miller had a better 1993 season in the Texas League.

Andre Keene hasn't reached the power level the Giants had hoped to see (.301-9-37 in the Midwest League; .241-3-40 in the California League), but he did steal 21 stolen bases last year. The 24 year old Keene is a defensive liability who was used almost exclusively a DH last year, not an especially handy position in the National League.

SECOND BASE:
TACTICAL CONSIDERATIONS

The name of the game at second base is watching the changing of the guard. Out with the old, and in with the new. Ask anyone who drafted Ryne Sandberg a year ago. At no other position is the player population so clearly divided into two classes: the young emerging and the old fading.

Not coincidentally, second base continues to be dominated by players who were shortstops when they turned professional: Chuck Knoblauch, Carlos Baerga, Pat Kelly, Brent Gates, Delino DeShields, Carlos Garcia, and many others. Ryne Sandberg and Steve Sax were also shortstops in their earliest professional seasons. There is an arguable case that more raw talent is pouring into the young end of the player population (phase two of the 1993 expansion's impact) and a disproportionate share of the young talent comes in the form of ex-shortstops (consider Gregg Jefferies as a non-2B example of the same phenomenon). What's happening is all part of the phenomenon: the best athlete plays shortstop in high school, with carryover effects into the pros.

My take on this situation is that older players are getting pushed harder at second base than elsewhere, so if you want to give special attention to youth at any one position, second base is it. I recommend favoring youth at every position (excepting of course rookies in general and rookie pitchers in particular) but I can say you are more likely to get burned by going with an old expensive veteran at second than at any other field position.

There are some clear opportunities here for profit, while shifting risk onto others. Many of the more recognizable names at second base are weak and risky, while many of the younger stars are coming off deceptively bad 1994 seasons. So, for example, you may confidently nominate the likes of Robby Thompson, Lou Whitaker, Bret Barberie, even Mickey Morandini and Harold Reynolds if he's around, early in the auction (not in the first round, but right after the rookie starting pitchers and any special situations needing attention in your league) and while everyone has lots of money and plenty of vacant slots at 2B and MI, these players will all go for excessive prices.

Removing money early will be a minor consideration, because most of the fully mature regulars are not stars. The benefit will be filling up other folks' roster spots, and getting them to use whatever meager funds they had budgeted for a second baseman or backup middle infielder. Knocking those owners out of the bidding will then create some juicy opportunities to buy the up-and-coming part of the population later, with less competitive bidding to drive prices up.

There is a long enough list of good young second basemen. Patience is the best general strategy. Just keep waiting and waiting as your list of OK second basemen gets shorter, before bidding aggressively. If you must have a star like Baerga or Biggio, make that determination before the draft begins, not in the heat of the bidding ... and if paying full value for one of the few big stars doesn't fit your budget and needs, then by all means bring up the bigger names early to make sure whoever gets them pays the full price.

For the Record:

Likely to be bargains: Delino DeShields, Carlos Garcia, Roberto Mejia, Geronimo Pena, Bret Boone, Quilvio Veras, Chuck Knoblauch, Pat Kelly, Brent Gates, Terry Shumpert, Ray Durham.

Likely to be overvalued: Robby Thompson, Mariano Duncan, Tim Naehring, Lou Whitaker, Harold Reynolds.

AMERICAN LEAGUE SECOND BASEMEN

Several late-fall trades and signings have shaken up the A.L. second base picture for 1995. The overall result has been to seriously damage the value of the Red Sox Tim Naehring and the Rangers' Doug Strange and Jeff Frye. Mark McLemore has left Baltimore via free agency to join the Rangers. The Orioles filled the vacancy by trading with Florida to obtain Bret Barberie. Boston acquired two second base candidates via trade, getting Terry Shumpert from Kansas City and Luis Alicea from St. Louis.

There are only a few holes left to fill among starting AL second basemen, and even fewer good free agents. Unsettled second base spots exist in California, Chicago and Milwaukee. Both the Angels and the White Sox have multiple candidates for the position while the Brewers have mostly unproven glove men. The only 1994 regular who is still a free agent is Mariano Duncan, who played for Philadelphia last year. Duncan is a decent, but limited hitter. The unsettled situations around the league provide room to maneuver for Rotisserie opportunists.

Baltimore Orioles

The loss of Mark McLemore to free agency was offset by the acquisition of Bret Barberie from Florida.

Barberie is a steadier fielder, so the gain will be mainly to Oriole pitchers. However, McLemore's second life was starting to fade while Barberie is just coming into his prime at age 27. Many observers believe Barberie is ready to blossom into a fine all-around player.

Barberie can hit near .300 again, and Camden Yards won't hurt his home run output. Barberie thus becomes one of the more valuable second basemen in the American League. Because he was not a big star with Florida, many people will not have heard of Barberie or will not have a good idea of his value. His potential for growth and relatively low profile could combine to make Barberie one of 1995's best Rotisserie bargains.

Veteran infielder Tim Hulett is still a free agent, but may yet re-sign with the Orioles. If he moves on, newly acquired Junior Noboa may get Hulett's reserve role. Noboa played a little for Oakland and Pittsburgh in 1994 and signed a minor league contract with Baltimore last fall. As a hitter he is safe (often used as a PH) but won't play enough to have value.

Fred Matos:

Mark McLemore has been in or near the majors since

1986, with four teams, and has failed in numerous trials. But over the past three years, he has shown that he can be a steady player. In 1993, he hit .284 in what has to be considered a lucky year with many ground balls getting through the infield and pop flies falling in for hits. Although he is a switch hitter, he is very weak versus lefties, usually hitting them in the .220 range, but for only a puny .167 in 1994. Thus some platooning is expected.

McLemore is a .250 hitter who will be lucky if he can get 50 RBI in a full season. His Rotisserie value is in his stolen bases, which could be as high as 35-40 under an aggressive manager like new Orioles skipper Phil Regan. He's worth $15.

Utility infielder Tim Hulett was the backup in 1994, before opting for free agency. Hulett is not much of a hitter, but the Orioles liked him for his occasional clutch hitting, and good all-around play.

Talented Manny Alexander, normally a shortstop, was tried at second for Triple-A Rochester last year. The trial was a failure, as he appeared lost, and his hitting was adversely affected. He is out of minor league options so he must stick with the parent club as he is unlikely to clear waivers. Alexander is a good base stealer but a weak hitter.

Lary Bump:

An experiment switching Manny Alexander back and forth from second base to shortstop was a failure. Its purpose was to make him a better prospect as a utility infielder. There's more about him under shortstops. 28 year old Kevin Baez, who couldn't make it with the Mets, was just filling a position alongside Alexander with Baltimore's top farm team last year (.237-2-42). He's no prospect.

A better possibility for some major league playing time is 30 year old Junior Noboa, signed as a minor league free agent after batting .288-0-18 at Buffalo. He also batted .310-0-6 in 42 at bats combined between Oakland and Pittsburgh.

The second baseman at Double-A Bowie, Hector

Vargas, had a career year (.313-8-58), but he's seven months older than Baez.

Boston Red Sox

Just when it was becoming profitable to own Tim Naehring, the Red Sox went out and acquired Luis Alicea and Terry Shumpert. Alicea has a little speed and can help with a decent batting average. Shumpert had a surprising season in 1994 as a fifth infielder for the Royals and showed good power by hitting eight homers in his first 100 at bats last year. Pitchers caught up to his free-swinging tendencies, though, and he slowed to a .240-8-24-18 seasons. Shumpert still has excellent speed, though and can also play across the diamond at third base.

I like Shumpert more, since hearing about his early career from his first pro manager, Bill Champion, while spending time at New Haven during the strike. Shumpert was a big enough college talent (at Kentucky) to be a second round pick, and he is one of those players who reached the major leagues at a very young age and put up weak numbers that hide his talent.

Naehring's value has taken a big hit. From a possible 550 at bat season, Naehring will probably drop to about 300 at bats. Instead of being a ''reasonably good investment for 1995'', he is now a risk where perception can exceed reality

Alan Boodman:

The last time Tim Naehring was designated a starter prior to a season was in 1992, and injuries and his sub-par play combined to remove him from the assignment. Since then, Naehring has continued to battle injuries but has made his way through the competition via solid hitting and good glovework.

His reward is the second base job for 1995. Over a full season, Naehring has the capability of putting up numbers in the neighborhood of .295-12-75, which would make him a prime pick among middle infielders. The trick, of course, is for him to make it through the

season in one piece. View him as a reasonably good investment for 1995.

Scott Fletcher began 1994 as the owner of the second base job, but age and, more specifically, hamstring injuries took an extreme toll. Fletcher turns 37 in mid-season, and last winter became a free-agent, one which the Sox were not likely to retain. Before being overcome by ailments, Fletcher was still doing fine work at the keystone, and could still run somewhat. Unfortunately, his batting ability has deteriorated to the point where it would have been difficult to keep him in the lineup anyway.

Good defensive second basemen have been known to hang around the majors for years beyond their prime, and for years after their offense has evaporated (Jim Gantner comes to mind). Don't be surprised if Fletcher takes a tour of the majors, playing for another 2-3 seasons, for a different club each year. He'll never again be a starter, and his Rotisserie value is just about gone.

The next Sox prospect at second base to hit the big leagues at this position will be Steve Rodriguez, whose performance up to now is reminiscent of Scott Fletcher. Following a .274-3-42-20 season at Class-A Lynchburg in 1993, Rodriguez spent only a brief amount of time early in 1994 at New Britain before skipping to Triple-A Pawtucket and performing well there at age 23 (.293-1-35-19 combined). Except for a possible appearence in Fenway in a utility role, Rodriguez will probably put in a full season at Pawtucket in 1995.

Jose Munoz also spent 1994 at Pawtucket, but is an older (27) retread from the Dodgers' organization whose future is limited regardless of his performance. Munoz is a contact hitter with good speed, but really his primary asset has been his health, and that's only going to take him so far.

Lary Bump:

Steve Rodriguez is a classic overachiever. Last season the 24 year old batted .283-0-14 at Double-A New Britain, and even better (.300-1-21) after a promotion

to Pawtucket. He totaled 19 stolen bases. The 5'9" righthanded batter is drawing comparisons to his predecessors, Marty Barrett and Jody Reed. Greg Litton, 30, was a useful veteran influence for Pawtucket's young players. He batted .272-9-48, but .095 in 21 at bats for Boston. He was a minor league free agent after last season.

California Angels

Free agent Rex Hudler signed a two-year contract with the Angels. He's slated for part time duty at second base and in the outfield and will mostly serve as an extra bat off of the bench.

Fred Matos:

The Angels have said that Damon Easley will be the starting second baseman for 1995. Last year, they moved Easley to third, believing that the physical demands of third base are less of a burden on his legs, (he has a history of shin splints). He played 47 games at third and 40 at second, and is discussed in the Third Base section.

Veteran Rex Hudler spent 1993 with the Yakult Swallows in Japan, but returned to the United States and signed with the Angels last year. He had a solid year, albeit in a restricted role as a utility infielder and outfielder. Hudler is a better hitter than most utility players, and showed some surprising power last year. Rod Correia filled in as a substitute for a few games last year, but he is limited to a reserve/utility role.

Kevin Flora has had some difficulties in the past two years which have limited his playing time. His wife and nephew died in an auto accident in 1993, causing him to lose much of the season, and he had a knee problem in 1994. Flora is very fast and excellent defensively, and he could come back and compete for the second base job. If he plays regularly, his stolen bases can make him a valuable Rotisserie player even if he doesn't hit above .240.

Harold Reynolds was signed mid-year as a temporary solution to the second base problem. His hitting skills

have been declining for several years, and he may have difficulty obtaining a major league job in 1995. He is a second baseman only, so he can't latch on as a utility player. The Angels released Reynolds after last season.

Lary Bump:

Kevin Flora is a good offensive player, with speed, who had trouble picking up the pieces of his career after his wife was killed in an auto accident in 1993. He batted just 84 times, with 15 hits, in the Pacific Coast and California Leagues last season. Flora's play in the Arizona Fall League encouraged the Angels. At 25, he can still be a prospect.

P.J. Forbes played most of the season as Vancouver's second baseman. His .286 batting average matched his average for his five-year career. The 27 year old had just one home run and 40 RBI. The second baseman at Double-A Midland, J.D. Ramirez, had solid numbers (.287-14-58), but he's 28, and spent 1993 in the independent Northern League. To find a second base prospect, you have to go down to the Midwest League, where lefthanded-hitting Aaron Guiel, 21, batted .269-18-82-21.

Chicago White Sox

Stuart Shea:

With Gene Lamont returning to Chicago, Joey Cora's chances of remaining a regular are better than they would be with almost any other manager. Even so, Cora's time may have run out. He's pesky, he hustles, and he really isn't good enough to play every day. Cora's defense is only fair, he doesn't provide much at the plate. He is a fine reserve, and would still be a valuable Rotisserie player in that role. This year, he'll probably be cheap if he loses the starting job in spring training.

The man who will take Cora's job, in 1996 if not this year, is Ray Durham. He turned 23 last November, and was rated the #4 prospect in the American Association for 1994. Durham switch-hits, has good power (doubles, triples, AND homers), hits for average, runs well, and is said to have tremendous defensive skills that are still slightly raw. He does not walk much, and one hopes that Gene Lamont won't put him at the top of the lineup just yet. GET HIM, especially if you play in a league that doesn't count on-base percentage.

Craig Grebeck will probably be around as well. Despite an unexplainable lack of playing time (thanks, Gene), Grebeck remains a fine defensive infielder capable of everyday duty at shortstop, third, or second. He has surprising power, draws walks, and runs the bases well. A scenario exists in which Cora could lose the starting job and Durham could bomb out; should these two things happen, Grebeck might luck into regular duty and would do a good job.

Norberto (Paco) Martin finally made the majors in 1994 at age 29. His defense isn't stellar, and all he can add offensively is a good average. He's really a Triple-A player, but could luck into a utility spot if injuries strike.

Despite a long hitting streak last year, Doug Brady of Double-A Birmingham really isn't a prospect (especially stuck behind Ray Durham). He runs well, but doesn't do much with the bat.

Lary Bump:

Switch-hitting Ray Durham, 23, became a prospect at Double-A in 1993. Last season he was even better in Triple-A (.296-16-66-34). He had hit just three home runs in his first four pro seasons. Durham's power, speed, and defense make him likely to supplant Joey Cora and Paco Martin in '95. Doug Brady also stole 34 bases for Double-A Birmingham, but he's 25, and the switch-hitter batted just .248-4-47. Chicago's best speed threat is Essex Burton, who stole 66 bases in a .284-3-50 season in the Carolina League. However, he's 25 years old.

Cleveland Indians

Tony Blengino:

Carlos Baerga's lack of selectivity at the plate is his only weakness; but, is one that bears watching over upcoming seasons. As long as Baerga remains a .300 hitter, his on-base percentage won't sink low enough to hurt the club. If A.L. pitchers catch on however, and refuse to throw strikes to Baerga, he could get into the habit of getting himself out, diminishing his worth as a player. Players tend to become more selective as they mature, and Baerga is a mere lad of 26. Expect his walk totals to steadily improve in the next few seasons, with a corresponding positive impact on his other stats.

Baerga is the most powerful second baseman in major league baseball. He paced his peers in slugging percentage (.525) and homers (19), and finished only two extra base hits (53) behind the Astros' Craig Biggio. Defensively, he is grossly underrated. Despite relatively high error totals (15 in 1994), he routinely reaches more balls than virtually any other major league second basemen. Baerga advanced through the Padres' system as a third baseman, alongside second baseman Roberto Alomar, to whom he will perpetually be compared and who is universally recognized as a peerless defensive second baseman. For the second straight year, Baerga handled 100 more chances than Alomar, despite playing nearly the same number of innings.

The current baseball strike would have to last about five years to stop Baerga from reaching 3000 career hits, as he has reached 796 hits at about the age that most players are still establishing themselves at the major league level. Expect Baerga to hit .320, with 40 doubles, 25 homers, 105 RBI and runs scored, and 10 steals in 1995, with further improvement possible in 1996 and 1997.

The stock of Triple-A second baseman Miguel Flores has dropped precipitously over the past year. After being named the best defensive second baseman in the Double-A Eastern League in 1992, he was rewarded with a return ticket to Canton/Akron in 1993. In 1994, he could do no better than split time with journeyman Tim Jones for Charlotte. Flores is a spray hitter who rarely strikes out, but his stolen base total declined steeply in 1994. After stealing 112 bases in his first four pro seasons, he dropped off to nine in 1994. His offensive and defensive skills are sharp enough for a major league utility role, but Flores appears limited to second base defensively, reducing his worth relative to that of competitor Mark Lewis.

Jones, like Lewis, is able to play several positions. At 32, he has been a useful number two hitter through most of his minor league career, making contact, bunting, and stealing the occasional base. Due to his versatility, he's got a chance to stick somewhere as a 25th man, but don't bet on it.

Lary Bump:

Playing second base at Triple-A Charlotte was 24 year old prospect Miguel Flores (.274-2-31), who platooned with 32 year old former Cardinal Tim Jones (.263-7-42). Another major league veteran, Rene Gonzales, did his utility thing with Charlotte. He batted .226-2-17, and despite a .348 mark in 23 at bats with the Indians, he is not likely to see much more major league time. There are prospects farther down the farm system. Mike Neal, moved from shortstop, batted .262-5-38 in the Carolina League at age 23. In the Sally League, 22 year old Jesus Azuaje was at .282-7-57 with 21 steals.

Detroit Tigers

Fred Matos:

Lou Whitaker, Chris Gomez and Tony Phillips played second base for the Tigers last season. Sweet Lou had another solid season even hitting southpaws for a .278. It was a juiced-ball year, but it's still worth noting that Whitaker's .491 slugging percentage was a career high, and 70 points over his career average. Now 37 years old, there are no signs that he is slowing down, and he could have another good year in 1995.

Whitaker's hitting against lefties is very unpredictable. He has trouble in some years when it therefore becomes necessary to platoon him, and in his good years, it's best to let him play against everybody.

Sparky Anderson worked rookie Chris Gomez into 30 games at second base and 57 at shortstop. Gomez is covered in detail in the Shortstop chapter.

Lou Whitaker's 1995 Rotisserie value could reach $15, but it would not be a big surprise to see his production drop to around $10. After all, Whitaker is 37 years old.

Shannon Penn is the top minor league candidate to replace Whitaker. He is a very fast singles hitter who improved his batting in Triple-A last year where he hit .284-2-33-45. The bad part about his record is the 96 strikeouts in 444 at bats, or about 22 percent of the time. His speed is his strongest asset, and he was rated both the fastest and best baserunner in the International League last year. Penn can nail down the Tigers second base job in 1995 or 1996 if he continues to improve at the plate.

Penn could be brought along slowly by the Tigers, and if he hits reasonably well, say around .250, he could see a lot of playing time and steal a lot of bases. It's best to be cautious when bidding on Penn because he strikes out a great deal and could be easily overmatched by big league pitchers..

Lary Bump:

Shannon Penn's game is based on speed (45 stolen bases in 1994). That skill has been as useful as breasts on a bull with the Tigers, who wait for home runs for their scoring. Penn also uses his speed wisely; he was voted the International League's best baserunner as well as its fastest. Penn may not hit enough (.284-2-33) to earn a major league job anyway. The switch-hitter is already 25.

Kansas City Royals

The trade of Shumpert to Boston changes the reserve situation for the Royals. Lind still has the full time job, but reserves will come from any of a number of utility infielders. Keith Miller could play second base in a pinch, but would not be good over the long haul. Glove man Jeff Garber could get to the big leagues in a utility role to replace Shumpert. None of the Shumpert replacements will have any value except Miller, and his value is looks quite variable going into spring training.

Marc Bowman:

Chico Lind got a challenge from Terry Shumpert in 1994 and responded with his best offensive season ever, posting career highs in batting average and slugging. He even stole nine bases, his best effort since 1989. Still, Lind is a glove man and valued almost exclusively as such. He hasn't suddenly, at age 30, become a valuable hitter. More likely he just had a good year and will revert back to his usual .245 hitting with little power or speed. If he earns more than $1 in 1995 it would be a small upset.

The Royals had run out of options with Shumpert, so he was shopped in spring training. It's fortunate for the Royals that there were no takers, as Shumpert tore up AL pitching when thrust into a short-lived starting role in May, pounding eight home runs in his first 100 at bats. His aggressive approach at the plate eventually caught up with him as he began seeing fewer strikes. Shumpert's power disappeared and his batting average dropped, but his speed remained. He was third on the team with 18 steals while getting caught just three times.

In order to get regular use, Shumpert also played third base occasionally. His versatility will come in handy as he will get more at bats there in 1995. Shumpert is of much more value to his Rotisserie teams than his major league team. In a part-time role he won't hurt your battng average while he gives you the occasional homer and useful stolen bases. Expect .250-5-35-20 in about 250 at bats and be willing to pay at least $5 for it.

Most of the Royals second basemen at Triple-A and Double-A are utility prospects at best. Edgar Caceres had washed out of the Dodgers, Expos, White Sox and Brewers organizations before hitting .271 for Triple-A Omaha in 1994. He's a good contact hitter with some versatility but is too old (30) to be a real prospect.

Jeff Garber has spent parts of the last five years at Double-A and Triple-A with unspectacular results. He hit .303 for Memphis in 1994, the highest average of his career. Still, he's not a good contact hitter and offers few extras with the bat. Garber could eventually earn a utlity role in KC.

Jose Mota is a career minor leaguer who stole 25 bases for Omaha in 1994 but has no chance of playing regularly in the majors. Another of Manny's sons, Domingo, is a more credible (and younger) player, but has shown little above Class-A ball.

Switch-hitting Kevin Davis is merely roster filler - he's been in the minors over eleven years for three different organizations and can accurately be described as a career minor leaguer.

The better prospects are in the lower minors. 22 year old Ramon Martinez hit .268 for Class A Wilmington. He's a good fielder who could have value if he can keep his batting average up as he advances through the Royals' farm system. Steve Sisco isn't as good with the glove but is still a credible fielder. He is a better hitter though, and has good speed too. He's already 25 years old, and needs to make rapid progress to have a major league chance. Lightning-fast Jeremy Carr stole 52 bases for Class A Rockford in 1994 after swiping 30 bases in just 42 games in 1993. The true test will be how he hits above A-ball. Sergio Nunez, 20, had 37 steals while batting .397 for Rookie league Fort Myers.

Lary Bump:

To find a second base prospect in the Royals' organization, we have to go to A-ball. In the Carolina League, Ramon Martinez batted .268-2-35. He's 22, and not to be confused with the Ramon Martinez

playing second base in the Florida organization, or with Wilmington teammate Felix Martinez, a shortstop who is a hitting prospect. Jeremy Carr is a speedburner (52 stolen bases) who batted .256-1-32 in the Midwest League. He is a leadoff candidate who walked more often than he struck out.

Milwaukee Brewers

The loss of Jody Reed and Bill Spiers to free agency (Reed was still unsigned while Spiers signed with the Mets) leaves the Brewers with a large hole at second base. It's possible that Pat Listach or Jose Valentin could end up there, but both are slated for other positions in 1995 (Listach in center field and Valentin at shortstop).

Considering the lack of quality free agent second basemen and the Brewers' need for cheap alternatives, it's unlikely they will bring in an expensive free agent. Instead, they probably try to fill the hole with a journeyman free agent and the results are predictable. The value of a journeyman glove man for Rotisserie purposes is about as close to zero as you can get.

Bill Gray:

Jody Reed looked to be without a team for 1994 until the Brewers offered him a take-it-or-leave-it deal just before spring training. Reed took it without complaint and produced one of the few complete and productive seasons for the Brewers.

Reed, a solid veteran, is vital to Milwaukee. He doesn't deliver much for Rotisserie purposes, and what he did last year is about as good as he's going to be. He should deliver a .260-.270 batting average, with a handful of home runs and the occasional stolen base.

With shortstop Pat Listach mentioned as a center fielder (Darryl Hamilton goes to left and Greg Vaughn to DH), it was surprising that the Brewers released Bill Spiers. Jose Valentin could fill in at second, but he's better at short.

If Reed is gone, the Brewers must look to acquire a journeyman infielder. There are journeymen out there, but none of them can hit. In a new league it's critical to grab a second baseman VERY early in your auction or draft. If you are in an existing league, Alomar and Baerga are not likely to be available. In that case, Jody Reed is the kind of player who won't damage your stats.

Lary Bump:

The Brewers had some journeymen middle infielders at Triple-A New Orleans last season. Tim Barker, 26, batted .264-5-44. He has been in three organizations, and was eligible to become a free agent. He can get on base (.380 percentage), and steal once he gets there (41 in 58 attempts).

An even better baserunner is 27 year old switch-hitter Greg Smith. In fact, Baseball America named him the best baserunner in the American Association after his .231-1-38 season with 34 steals in 44 attempts. John Finn, another 27 year old, batted .288-2-24. He fell off on the bases to 15 steals in 25 tries.

Forget about Rodney Lofton, also 27, despite his .331-2-54-21 season at El Paso. He has struggled in four brief Triple-A trials.

Minnesota Twins

James Benkard:

Chuck Knoblauch will anchor the Twins' infield for the fifth straight year. He is a fine player, and there is little reason to think he will suffer any catastrophic drop in productivity. His '94 numbers (.312-5-51-35) would have all become career highs if it had not been for the strike, so he might be slightly overvalued in '95.

Knoblauch is a consistent and durable player, so it is possible that he has arrived in the prime of his career as a legitimate .300 hitter. Rated as only the seventh best prospect in Double-A in 1990, Knoblauch has worked hard on his weaknesses; base stealing,

defensive consistency, and power. Only injuries can stand in the way of him assembling a sterling career.

The Twins have others who could step forward and make a contribution if Knoblauch is hurt, or if he leaves as a free agent after the '95 season. If Pat Meares is at short, Denny Hocking could play some second, as could Brian Raabe. Hocking could hit .270 in a hundred at bats in 1995 and might surprise by chipping in a few steals. Raabe, 27, hit .321 at Triple-A and has a very good batting eye, so he could surprise.

Todd Walker, the Twins' first round pick in '94 and a big star at LSU, is the major prospect on the horizon. He had an impressive pro debut in a tough Class A league (.304-10-34-6 in 171 at bats) and will be ready to hit in the big leagues within two years. There is some concern about his defense, which is considered to be marginal.

Lary Bump:

27 year old Brian Raabe, the ultimate contact hitter (81 strikeouts in 1,916 pro at bats), also was the Pacific Coast League's best defensive second baseman. His career year at Triple-A Salt Lake City consisted of .321-3-49. He can steal a base (though he was just 9-for-17 last year), and has played at third, so he could win a utility job.

Also having a career year at Salt Lake was Jeff Carter (.324-5-70-26). The 31 year old career minor leaguer compiled a .438 on-base percentage. The switch-hitter played mostly in the outfield last season. Todd Walker, a lefthanded batter, was the Twins' first-round draft choice in 1994. Did they take him because we would be cheap? Six lower picks signed for higher bonuses than Walker's $815,000. Playing just half the season, the 22 year old led Class A Fort Myers in home runs (.304-10-34).

New York Yankees

For years Pat Kelly has been a great young athlete not getting much in the way of results. Injuries have been

a special problem. Although he's been on the DL only twice, including once last year with a strained thumb, Kelly incurs all sorts of little nagging problems which take him out for a couple of days here and there. He's been prominent for frequent mentions in Buck Showalter's pregame meet-the-press sessions (in answer to the question: who can't play today?). Items like ''a little bit of a groin pull'' have prevented Kelly from ever getting more than 406 at bats in a season.

On the plus side, Kelly's athleticism is at such a high level that he was once given a major league starting job at third base, with no professional experience there whatsoever. That wasn't really a positive development (it was a conflict between time for Steve Sax versus time for Kelly) but it shows how highly regarded Kelly's talent is. Defensively at second base, Kelly is known for being able to make plays that no one else in the league -- except Roberto Alomar of course -- would be capable of making.

Kelly broke through on a number of offensive levels in 1994, with career highs in batting average, slugging percentage, and OBP. He's been visibly more confident at the plate, waiting better on bad pitches and swinging more aggressively at pitches he likes. As he develops further and stays healthy for a full year, Kelly should hit more home runs and steal more bases. Look for a career year in 1995 or 1996. Health will be the key factor.

When the Yankees haven't had Kelly at second base, they have usually turned to Mike Gallego (see shortstops) with either Randy Velarde taking short or Dave Silvestri helping to fill in. There is no minor leaguer likely to press Kelly for the next two years or more.

Lary Bump:

If Dave Silvestri hasn't made it to the majors for extended duty yet, he may never. The 27 year old righthanded batter had a year of .251-25-83-18 in the International League. For the fourth consecutive year, he struck out more than 100 times, but he also walked enough for a career-high .380 on-base percentage. His biggest problem has been finding a

place to play. He also has been at shortstop and third base in the minors.

At Double-A Albany, 23 year old switch-hitter Carlton Fleming went .243-0-37-20. He has a .285 average for his three pro seasons, but may need to prove himself by starting this season back in the Eastern League. He makes good contact, but has no power (no homers in 1,067 pro at bats, just 13 extra-base hits last year). He'll also have to improve his career 65 percent stolen base success rate.

Oakland A's

Steven Rubio:

Brent Gates is one of the most important question marks for the Athletics as they enter 1995. The best prospect on the team, Gates spent most of 1994 on the disabled list and must demonstrate that he can play regularly at second base without getting injured. If healthy, Gates is one of the A's best players.

Scott Hemond, the backup second baseman in 1994, is discussed with the catchers (yes, he qualifies at both positions).

The A's tried a handful of journeymen at second during Gates' absence. Junior Noboa, Mike Brumley, Francisco Matos, and even Steve Sax filled a roster spot for Oakland in 1994; none but perhaps Matos will ever do so again. Mark Sobolewski is an aging prospect who didn't hit much in Double-A. He doesn't have a major-league career in his future.

Lary Bump:

With Brent Gates around, the Athletics may not need second base help from the minors unless Gates is injured again. Closest to the majors is Francisco Matos, who went .307-0-30-16 at Triple-A Tacoma, and hit .250 in 28 at bats for Oakland last season.

The Double-A second baseman was Mark Sobolewski, who moved over from third base. Like Matos the 25 year old righthanded batter, Sobolewski

had a typical .252-8-58 season. He does not have Matos' base-stealing speed (4-for-18 in three years as a pro).

Jason McDonald (.238-2-31-52 in the Midwest League) has much better speed. The 23 year old switch-hitter, a fourth-round draft pick in 1993, should be able to hit better and advance.

Seattle Mariners

Bill Gray:

At times in 1993, longtime minor leaguer Rich Amaral looked like a Rotisserie bargain. He had speed and was a decent hitter. So before the 1994 season began, the Mariners decided to trade Bret Boone and let the 32 year old Amaral handle second base for a few years. Literally and figuratively, Amaral dropped the ball. He erred to such an extent that he was sent to the minors and journeyman Luis Sojo was recalled to play second base, along with Sparky Anderson's favorite player, Torey Lovullo. Go no further with Amaral. At 33 he cannot possibly be expected to improve, and his speed, which was his only asset, appears to be in short supply.

Sojo has not been much of a hitter in the major leagues, but he can play defense. Felix Fermin filled in as well for 25 games. For fantasy leaguers, the only help at second base in Seattle might be Brian Turang (see Turang in the Outfielders chapter).

Lary Bump:

Arquimedez Pozo, 21, was the fourth in the California League batting race in 1993. Last season, he showed that in addition to one of the best baseball names around, he has gap power that will only increase as he matures (.289-14-54-11). The second-best name among Mariners' second base prospects belongs to Giomar Guevara. He was voted the Midwest League's best defensive second baseman, teaming much of the season with Alex Rodriguez. For a little guy (5'8", 150 pounds), the 22 year old Guevara has some pop (.301-8-46). In the California League, switch-hitter

Manny Cora compiled a .302-0-46 season. Brian Turang could resurface as a second base candidate, but you'll find more about him under outfielders.

Texas Rangers

The acquisition of Mark McLemore should give the Rangers something they have lacked since Julio Franco was injured in 1992 - a regular second baseman.

Of course, the values of Doug Strange and Jeff Frye have suffered big blows; neither is now worth more than $1. Should Strange's off-season surgery prove to not be debilitating, he can win a utility role for the Rangers in 1995. Frye will probably return to the minors.

Billy Ripken became a free agent and had yet to sign with any team.

Peter Graves:

Ever since Julio Franco's knees gave out in 1992, the Rangers have been weak at second base. Barring a trade or free agent acquisition, there is nothing to suggest that 1995 will be any different.

Doug Strange, the improbable success story of 1993, proved that his 15 minutes of fame were used up, and faded in 1994 (.212-5-26). Strange's glove is adequate at best, and his chances to reclaim a starting job are nil. He underwent arthroscopic surgery to repair a knee injury at the end of the season, and only his ability to play several positions may help him stick as a utility player.

Jeff Frye was supposed to get the job in 1993, after Franco's injury, but suffered a knee injury himself and missed the entire season. After Strange bombed, Frye was given another chance and made the most of it (.327-0-18-6), despite a hamstring problem that dogged him for most of the season. Frye has been extremely injury-prone, but he can hit for average and steal bases when healthy. He has absolutely no power. Frye is the leading contender to start at second base for the Rangers in 1995.

Bill Ripken hit .309-0-6 in limited duty as a backup infielder. He's still a .243 career hitter, lacking both speed and power, and is of no use to a Rotisserie team. If he returns to the Rangers, it will be in a utility role.

Jon Shave lost whatever chance he had to make the team in spring training when he took a line drive in the throat. After emergency surgery to repair a fractured larynx and remove one of his vocal chords, he recovered well enough at Oklahoma City. He's a scrappy player, but won't hit much in the majors.

Lary Bump:

The ongoing drama that is finding a second baseman in Texas has a supporting cast that includes Jon Shave, who was next to awful (.220-1-31) in his second American Association season; minor league veteran Ever Magallanes (.245-4-41 at Double-A Tulsa); Cuban defector Osmani Estrada (.255-4-30 at Class A Port Charlotte), and former Cardinal Craig Wilson (about whom you'll see more under third basemen).

It's an elderly group - Shave is 27, Magallanes 29 and Estrada 26. Only Magallanes bats lefthanded.

Toronto Blue Jays

David Luciani:

Roberto Alomar should have had a better year. That doesn't mean that he wasn't a great player in 1994. He batted .306, but this was his worst batting average since 1991. He stole just 19 bases which was easily his worst total since he was with San Diego. Alomar's newfound power of 1993 was still there, in the form of eight home runs, but he wasn't driving in runs in 1994. This was the result of an uncharacteristic .229 average with runners in scoring position.

Therefore, look for a revival of sorts in 1995, back to normal levels. Alomar is one of the most valuable players in the league (fantasy or otherwise) and if ever there was an occasion for his price tag to dip just

below true value, it will only be this spring. A leg injury in winter ball last year may have caused what we will eventually call just a lull in his career. Alomar also returned to winter ball this off-season, so barring another injury, look for a return to 40+ steals and at least 60 RBI.

Domingo Cedeno, the older brother of Houston's Andujar Cedeno, is Alomar's emergency replacement. Cedeno continues to struggle at the major league level and his minor league career, unfortunately, shows a consistent .220s hitter (he hit between .200-.235 every year from 1989-1992 at all minor league levels). Cedeno, a switch-hitter, may get a chance in spring training to retain his role as the emergency backup infielder, but the front office was forced to consider a signing free agent as insurance. Cedeno was sent down to Syracuse just prior to the strike in what looked to be a move designed to keep him playing, not a permanent demotion. Cedeno will be 26 this year and looks to be, for now, essentially bench material.

Lary Bump:

Chris Stynes started his career as a third baseman, played second base last year at Knoxville, then was scheduled to be back at third (but played mostly second) in the Arizona Fall League. He can hit enough to play third base (.317-8-79-28 Knoxville), but (despite being voted the Southern League's best defensive second baseman) may not be strong enough defensively to handle second. And the Jays need more help at third. The 22 year old righthanded batter is a definite prospect.

NATIONAL LEAGUE
SECOND BASEMEN

Atlanta Braves

Marc Bowman:

Incumbent second basemen Mark Lemke will soon face a challenge from a hot-hitting, slick-fielding prospect, Tony Graffanino. Lemke has been steadily producing as a regular for the last few years and gradually getting better, too. His .294 average was easily his career best and Lemke has never shown much power or speed. A .250 average with few extras is the most you can reasonably expect from Lemke. At age 29, Lemke has probably peaked. He'll still play good defense for the Braves, but he'll soon have to fight off Graffanino for playing time. The infield defensive anchor for the Braves, Lemke will have another full season as the regular second baseman and hit .245 with five home runs and 40 RBI.

22 year old Graffanino had a fine season for Double-A Greenville in 1994, hitting .300 with some power (28 doubles to lead the team), good speed (29 steals also led the team) and a good batting eye (.371 OBP). He'll have a chance to win a job in spring training, but is most likely to start 1995 at Triple-A Richmond.

Ramon Caraballo, the previous heir apparent at second base has been shifted to shortstop and dropped a level to Greenville in 1994.

After three seasons spent shuttling between Greenville and Class A venues, Jose Olmeda advanced to Richmond in 1994 and hit .230 with 17 steals. The 26 year old Olmeda isn't considered a good prospect and would be major league bench filler if called up. There are no other secondbase prospects to be excited about in the Braves farm system. Gerald Roberson hit .288 with 19 steals in his second rookie league year. He's the best of the lower minors and he's several years away.

Lary Bump:

Tony Graffanino took a G out of his name (before the first N), but that didn't change his prospect status from VG (Very Good). The 22 year old bats righthanded. A Double-A All-Star (.300-7-52-29), he has blown past Ramon Caraballo on Atlanta's organizational depth chart. Next up: Mark Lemke. Caraballo lost his job at Richmond, where he was a regular in 1992 and '93, by batting just .133 in 75 at-bats. He was a little bit better at Double-A Greenville (.239-9-30).

Taking his Triple-A job was 26 year old switch hitter Jose Olmeda. He was voted the best defensive second baseman in the International League, but he is no prospect (.230-4-39).

Another good glove man is Marty Malloy, voted the best defensive second baseman in the Carolina League. The 22 year old lefthanded batter (.264-6-35) also has speed (18 stolen bases) and good strike-zone judgment.

Chicago Cubs

Stuart Shea:

After Ryne Sandberg's retirement, Rey Sanchez stepped into those big shoes and played good ball. Already one of the league's top glovemen at the position, he may still grow as an offensive player. Sanchez has shown a clear ability to hit for average. He makes good contact, runs the bases well although he lacks great speed, and hangs in well against righthanders. Unfortunately, he has absolutely no power and does not walk enough to be useful at the top of the order. If he can hit .280 consistently and find more ways to get on base (he led the Cubs with six bunt hits last year), Sanchez can become a valuable regular if not a particularly exciting fantasy choice.

There is no immediate help in the minors. Todd Haney manned second base for Triple-A Iowa in 1994, but clearly isn't good enough to start in the majors; in fact, he even lacks the skill to fill a major league utility role. Nobody at Double-A will move up soon, either.

Hal Morris' brother Bobby hit .346 for Class A Peoria, finishing second in the league's batting race. He also showed developing extra base power, took 50 walks and swiped some bases. Morris doesn't play great defense right now, but will get the chance to improve his glovework in 1995 in the Florida State League, possibly reaching as high as Double-A next year. He is just 22 years old.

Lary Bump:

Todd Haney was voted the best defensive second baseman in the American Association, where he batted .292-3-35. He was tried and found wanting (.162 in 37 at bats) after Ryne Sandberg's retirement. At age 29, the righthanded-batting Haney isn't about to turn his career around.

Despite an excellent start at Iowa, Cris Colon was not recalled to replace Sandberg. The 26 year old switch hitter tailed off to .272-12-55. He also has played shortstop and third base, so his best ticket to the majors may be as a utility player.

Another switch hitter, 22 year old Chad Tredaway, failed miserably in Double-A (.192-1-15), and wasn't so hot after he was sent back to Class A Daytona Beach (.243-5-28).

The hope for the future is more likely to be Bobby Morris, the 22 year old brother of Hal Morris. The younger Morris, who also bats lefthanded, was setting in batting (.354) in the Midwest League. He added seven homers, 64 RBI and a .443 on-base percentage.

Cincinnati Reds

Greg Gajus:

I would like to know what Bret Boone (.320-12-68-3) did to convince Lou Piniella to give him away, much to the delight of Reds fans. In exchange for a catcher that hit .216 and a mediocre reliever, Lou sent the Reds a 26 year old power hitting second baseman and a solid number three starter (Erik Hanson). Among National League middle infielders, only Jeff Kent and Wil Cordero were in Boone's class as a power hitter, and only Craig Biggio and a healthy Delino DeShields would have more Rotisserie value because of their steals. 18 homers, 90 RBI, and a .300 average are reasonable expectations from Boone in 1995.

In the event that Boone is injured, Jeff Branson (.284-6-16-0) is the most likely replacement. A 28 year old left handed hitter with a little power, Branson did not play well in his only chance at full time play in the second half of 1993. Davey Johnson did a great job in picking the spots for his reserves in 1994; of course, players who do not have a definite role have little value in Rotisserie.

In the minors, the Reds have more suspects than prospects at second base. Casey Candaele, the ex-Astro, hit .282 at Indianapolis but is now 34. 26 year old Brian Koelling hit .280 with 27 steals at Chattanooga, after a cup of coffee with the Reds in 1993. He could get a couple of steals if he makes the team as a pinch-runner.

Lary Bump:

It's a good thing that the Reds have a good young second baseman, because there's slim pickings in the farm system. Keith Kessinger, the 28 year old, switch-hitting son of Don Kessinger, batted just .249-3-48 at Indianapolis. That's better than Brian Koelling's .151 in 53 at bats, earning a demotion to Double-A Chattanooga (.280-3-31-27). He's 25, and bats righthanded. At Class A Winston-Salem, Dee Jenkins, a 21 year old lefthanded batter, hit .243-7-33-19.

Colorado Rockies

David Smith:

It's been an eventful 13 months for Nelson Liriano. Avoiding a plane trip home to the Dominican Republic, he became Colorado's starting shortstop (finishing the 1993 season for injured Freddie Benavides). Liriano then became Roberto Mejia's primary backup when free agent Walt Weiss signed before the 1994 season. Later in 1994, Liriano became the regular second baseman when Mejia was sent to Colorado Springs. After a solid season in Denver, playing good defense and contributing with the bat (.396 slugging and .357 OBP), free agent Liriano signed with Pittsburgh in October where he will serve as the Pirates' primary infield substitute.

With Liriano's departure the Rockies have to look at 1995 as another test for Mejia, whose arrival has been much anticipated since the team's inaugural season. After his mid-1993 major league debut, Mejia soon showed that he had good raw talent, but was an undiscipled youngster who lacked focus. Mejia returned to the minors to spend almost the entire 1994 season awaiting an attitude adjustment. Unfortunately, many reports indicate that such an adjustment still hasn't occured.

Although Mejia will be the favorite to start at second base next year, he could once again be replaced in mid-season by any one of four other infielders: Webster Garrison, Vinny Castilla, Jason Bates or Pedro Castellano. Bates probably has the better long term future, but Castilla and Castellano are more ready to assume a major league role.

Garrison had one of his best seasons last year; unfortunately all have been in the minors. He split time with Mejia at second base in 1994. Garrison isn't outstanding in any particular area and is also older than Mejia.

Formerly a shortstop, Castilla spent the winter learning to play third base, boosting his stock if Charlie Hayes isn't re-signed. His glove is good enough for second base, but he may be a little weak with the bat.

Bates is a rapidly rising prospect who had 76 RBI for Colorado Springs; he also went to winter ball. Most feel his best natural position is shortstop. Bates is still a raw talent, too, but may be the best long-term prospect for second base.

Castellano has also played second base, but was injured for much of 1994. He is probably no more than a utility infielder at best.

Castilla and Bates figure to offer the hottest competition for Mejia at Colorado's weakest position in the field. Should Mejia falter again, the Rockies will go to Bates if he's ready; if not, Castilla may get some starting assignments in Denver.

Lary Bump:

Roberto Mejia showed less power (10 homers and 51 RBI between Colorado and Triple-A Colorado Springs) than in 1993. He raised his batting average in the majors 10 points, to .241. In the field, his range was about average. The Rockies expected more, and they still may get it, for the righthanded batter won't be 23 until April. Webster Garrison again proved he can hit in the Pacific Coast League (.302-13-68), but the 29 year old righthanded batter isn't a viable prospect. At Double-A New Haven, the Rockies had Lamarr Rogers (.266-2-35) and Craig Counsell (.280-5-37). Counsell, a 24 year old lefthanded batter, also has played shortstop.

Florida Marlins

Bret Barberie is out, and Quilvio Veras is in. Veras is a speedy young prospect with a career BA over .300 and OBP over .400 in the minors. He is one of those talents who got cheated out of a September callup by the strike. The Mets would have been showcasing him, however, not giving him a tryout for 1995, because they have a much bigger offensive package in Edgardo Alfonzo coming along just as fast as Veras; and of course they have Jeff Kent also.

While I love Veras for his speed and figure that he's got a long and productive career ahead (and another plus is that batting leadoff he would see plenty of pitches in the strike zone), still I must put a big caution on him for 1995, the danger of a low batting average. Walks could keep him in the lineup and make him a better leadoff hitter than Carr, even while he hits about .220 and ruins his stat league value.

Some day he will be a .270-.280 hitter, but I really don't believe he's there yet, at age 23. Veras makes a good pick for a long-term building effort, and a good source of speed for a weak team or a roster with many shuttles; but he's not a good pick for a smart owner with a strong team. And that's a darn shame, because not many people know about him already, and not many people will be astute enough to look back farther than his .249 Triple-A average to his four .300+ averages at lower levels. He's always been among the youngest players at every level.

Tony Blengino:

Second base has become a weak offensive position in the NL. With the exception of now-retired Ryne Sandberg, few second basemen have had stand out years with the bat. In such company, Bret Barberie would appear to be one of the league's better hitters. Barberie began 1994 as the Marlins' second place hitter but started off so poorly he was demoted to the eighth spot. He then got red hot for two months to raise his average to .301 just before the strike. However, due to hitting eighth, Barberie only managed to score 40 runs and drive in 33 in 396 at bats. Batting eighth also kept him utilizing his speed. Batting near

the top of the order Barberie could steal ten or more bases.

Barberie has doubles power; he would hit at least 30 doubles in a full season. His other numbers would also increase with a move to the top of the order. He's an outstanding defensive player with great range. The outlook is bright for Barberie: he should return to the number two spot in the batting order and is entering his prime. Look for .300-10-60-10 from Barberie in 1995 - the last year when you can get him cheap.

Every team employs players like Rich Renteria. He has almost no major league skills, but he doesn't complain about his playing time and can play almost anywhere. A Mexican League star who initially debuted in the majors with the Pirates in 1986, Renteria is roster filler until younger prospects develop. Expect about 100 at bats and an empty .210 average.

Converted shortstop Ramon Martinez is a speedy switch hitter who has already stolen 166 bases in just over four minor league seasons. The 25 year old Martinez hit just .241 for Double-A Portland and has just 38 extra base hits in 930 at bats the last two years. Because he can play both second base and shortstop, Martinez has a chance to reach the major leagues as a utilityman. His inconsistency prevents him from better projections; Martinez will be the Marlins' Triple-A second baseman in 1995.

21 year old Ralph Milliard hit .297, scored 97 runs and cracked 44 extra base hits for Class A Kane County in 1994, then moved on to the Arizona Fall League for further improvement. Due to the lack of real prospects ahead of him in the Marlins' chain, Milliard has a good chance to advance quickly.

Lary Bump:

Mike Brumley, Edmonton's second baseman after coming over from the Oakland organization, used to be a strong-armed shortstop with a weak bat. Now he hits better (.285-12-41), but at age 31 has been reduced him to playing second base. The switch hitter

has played briefly (617 at bats) with six major league teams. If he ever returns to the majors, it won't be for long.

Mario Diaz had a great start with the Pawtucket Red Sox (.333-3-19), but a clause in his contract made him a free agent when Boston didn't recall him. Diaz, a 33 year old righthanded batter, wanted to return to the Rangers, but the Marlins gave him a better deal. He was valuable (.325-0-11) as a pinch hitter and utility infielder for Florida.

From the Blue Jays, the Marlins obtained 1989 first-round draft bust Eddie Zosky (.264-7-37). The 27 year old righthanded batter was drafted as a shortstop.

In the Eastern League was Ramon Martinez, who has great speed and has shown flashes of brilliance defensively. He went .241-1-44-31 steals in his Double-A debut. The 25 year old switch hitter will have to show more defensive consistency to make it in the majors as a utilityman and pinch runner.

The Marlins' best hope for the future is 21 year old Ralph Milliard, a native of Curacao whom they sent to the Arizona Fall League. The righthanded batter hit .297-8-67 in the Midwest League. He has a good eye at the plate, but was thrown out 10 times in 20 stolen base attempts.

Houston Astros

Bill Gilbert:

With Ryne Sandberg's retirement, Robby Thompson's injury and Delino DeShields' decline, Craig Biggio (.316-6-56-39) has established himself as the top second baseman in the National League. For 1994, he can lay claim to being the best second baseman in baseball as his production exceeded that of Roberto Alomar, Carlos Baerga and Chuck Knoblauch - the American League's best second sackers. Biggio has been a solid performer for several seasons and, at age 28, in 1994 he experienced a career year.

Biggio hit over .300 for the first time in 1994 and was a surprise league leader in stolen bases with 39 in 43

attempts. His baserunning represented a major turnaround from 1993 when he stole only 15 bases while being caught 17 times. His home run output dropped from a career high of 21 in 1993 to six in 1994 which more closely represents his career average. He also established career highs in on base average and slugging average, despite the drop in homers. Biggio tied Larry Walker for the league lead in doubles with 44.

Biggio should continue to be one of the top middle infielders in the game for several more years. Since being converted to second base from catching, Biggio has missed just eight games over the past three years; his durability is a big plus.

Utility infielder Andy Stankiewicz (.259-1-5-1) is a capable backup, but isn't slated to see much action.

Dave Hajek (.324-7-70-12) had a career year at age 26 and was an All-Star for Class AAA Tucson. Fletcher Thompson, now 26, went .263-4-31-28 for Class AA Jackson. Neither are considered strong prospects.

Lary Bump:

Behind Craig Biggio is Dave Hajek, who moved from the outfield to second base at Triple-A Tucson in 1994. He had a career year offensively (.324-7-70) and stole 12 bases, but the righthanded batter already is 27. The only other second baseman in sight is Fletcher Thompson. He's not a writer for Rolling Stone, but a 26 year old lefthanded batter who hit .263-4-31-28 in his second season with Double-A Jackson.

Los Angeles Dodgers

Greg Gajus:

Delino DeShields' (.250-2-33-27) first season with the Dodgers was wrecked by a variety of injuries and he may be undervalued by less astute owners in 1995. He should take over the leadoff position from Brett Butler in 1995, thereby getting even more steal opportunities. DeShields is 26, has great strike zone

judgment, is coming off an aberrant 1994 season, and his steals are extraordinarily valuable right now. Given good health, DeShields will be one of the league's most valuable players in 1995.

Eddie Pye and Garey Ingram filled in for DeShields in 1994. 28 year old Pye is a fringe prospect who has had a few chances with the Dodgers. 25 year old Ingram was a 44th round draft pick in 1989 and hit .258 with eight homers and 19 steals for Double-A San Antonio in 1994. Neither of them will move DeShields out of the way.

Lary Bump:

Garey Ingram, a 24 year old righthanded batter, was voted the Texas League's best defensive second baseman in his second season in the league. Offensively, he hit .258-8-28-19 steals for San Antonio. He played outfield during his two Triple-A games. He hit best with the Dodgers (.282-3-8 in 78 at bats).

Eddie Pye, 28, earned his first 10 major league at bats with a .335-2-42 record in his fourth season at Albuquerque. The righthanded batter can hit singles, but he is no prospect.2B

After Ingram left, Chris Demetral took over as San Antonio's second baseman. The lefthanded batter went .261-6-39. At age 25, he's not a prospect.

Bakersfield's second baseman was speedy Miguel Cairo (.291-2-48-44 steals). He's a 20 year old righthanded batter who also has played shortstop. Last season he passed Eddie Rios (.263-13-79 in the Florida State League). The 22 year old righthanded batter spent part of 1993 in the California League.

Montreal Expos

John Perrotto:

Many Expos' players complained when Montreal dealt Delino DeShields to Los Angeles for Pedro Martinez in the 1993-94 offseason. While DeShields is obviously a quality player, the Expos didn't miss a beat without him.

After playing primarily at shortstop and third base as a 1993 rookie, Mike Lansing stepped in for DeShields and did a credible job. He batted .266-5-35-12, somewhat of a dropoff from his rookie season. Lansing will never match DeShields' flair as he is more of a grinder. However, he is capable of putting up numbers a little better than last season for many years to come.

After failing to stick with Baltimore, Philadelphia or Milwaukee, perennial prospect Juan Bell resurrected his career with the Expos last season. He hit .278-2-10-4 in the major leagues after being called up from the minors early in the season. However, the Expos dropped him from the 40-man roster at the end of the season and he is again searching for a home.

Acquired from Colorado as infield insurance following the DeShields trade, Freddie Benavides had a dreadful year, hitting just .188-0-6-0. Guys like Benavides are easy to find. He can't afford another season like 1994 if he wants to keep playing major league ball.

Lary Bump:

Former Padre Jeff Gardner, 31, batted .257-0-16 in 191 at bats at Ottawa. The lefthanded batter is an intelligent baserunner and has an exceptional batting eye, so he could earn a utility job.

Mike Hardge's prospect status is fading after two weak years with the bat at Double-A Harrisburg (.223-6-42 in '94). He stole 30 bases, but was thrown out 13 times.

Down the road is Jose Vidro (.267-4-49 at Class A West Palm Beach). He's a 22 year old switch hitter. There's more about former University of Miami star F.P. Santangelo under outfielders.

New York Mets

Jeff Kent has emerged as a key figure in the top of the National League middle infield population, especially prominent in 1994 as Ryne Sandberg vanished, Delino Deshields slumped with injuries, while Robby Thompson, Ozzie Smith and so many other long-time stars grew older. Kent is no Sandberg, however, and he's likely to be overbid in any auctions where two or more owners are determined to be solid at all three MI positions. There just aren't enough high-offense middle infielders to go around.

Kent's value is obvious from his stats. Not many second basemen can brag about being career .270 hitters with an average of more than 15 homers per year. And Kent's three seasons have all been shortened, none exceeding 496 at bats. Obviously he can hit 20 to 25 homers in a year.

The problem with Kent is streakiness. His emergence as a hitter depended on increased patience and closer study of the league's pitchers. His natural tendencies lean toward overaggressiveness, and unfortunately he falls back toward his natural tendencies when he gets into a slump, while remaining more patient and confident when he's on a hot streak. The result was never more visible than in April-May last year, when Kent hit .375 with eight homers and 26 RBI in April but then batted only .204 with three RBI in 15 games to begin May. On the whole it was of course a good season, but there's a always risk here that Kent could fall into a prolonged slump and fail to reward those who pay top dollar for a top second baseman.

Personally, for a strong team, I would be willing to pay about fair price (say $18 to $20 uninflated) to flesh out a full roster with a fair share of real talent, but for a weak team that doesn't have profits locked in at other positions, Kent is simply too well-known to be a bargain. He's a classic case of a hot start (April '94) attracting attention that keeps everyone focused on the high potential for years afterward. You will do better by looking for a good middle infielder who was hot in July, or who has never yet had a big hot streak.

The Mets have a crowd of minor leaguers around second base, one of the main factors leading to the trade of Quilvio Veras for Carl Everett. Even with Veras gone, they still had Fernando Vina, who was good enough to get sent to the minors August 10 to keep playing last year, and Edgardo Alfonzo, who might really be the next Ryne Sandberg offensively. Jose Vizcaino and Tim Bogar can also play second base, so there was no place for Veras.

The Veras trade took some of the pressure off the contemplated move of Kent to third base, but the emergence of Alfonzo will keep that possibility alive. Another long-term possibility is that Alfonzo, who has already been moved from short to second to make room for defensive prodigy Rey Ordonez, could be moved again, this time to third.

Lary Bump:

The Mets cleared the way for 21 year old Edgardo Alfonzo to move into their 1996 plans at second base or third base by trading Quilvio Veras. Alfonzo swings a good bat, but his shortstop defense was not good enough to hold off another prospect, Rey Ordonez. Alfonzo had a solid season with Eastern League-champion Binghamton (.293-15-75). The righthanded batter walked more often than he struck out and stole 14 bases, but was thrown out 11 times. Don't confuse him with 27 year old non-prospect Edgar Alfonzo, who had remarkably similar numbers with Bowie in the same league.

Baseball America's poll named Doug Saunders the Eastern League's best defensive second baseman. A major leaguer in 1993, the 25 year old really was with Binghamton to help bring along a young infield. The righthanded-hitting Saunders finished at .284-8-45. By the end of the season, he was watching Alfonzo and Ordonez play. Saunders' future probably is as a coach. Don't confuse him with Binghamton third baseman Chris Saunders, a marginal prospect. The Mets have made a commitment to middle-infield defense.

Behind Alfonzo, is 20 year old Sandy Pichardo, who was voted the Sally League's best defensive second baseman. The lefthanded batter (.257-2-30) also can

run (34 steals), but he has to be more selective on the bases. He was thrown out an unacceptable 28 times.

Philadelphia Phillies

Tony Blengino:

Much of the difference between the excellent offensive performance of the 1993 Phillies and the poorer 1994 version was due to pitch selection. Three hitters (Len Dykstra, Dave Hollins and John Kruk) drew more than 100 walks and Hollins added another 85 bases on balls. In 1994 all four of these players suffered injuries that required lengthy replacements by hitters who are less patient, most notably Kim Batiste, Ricky Jordan and Mariano Duncan. Although Duncan had a productive offensive season and started the All-Star game at second base for the National League, his free-swinging tendencies were indicative of the Phils' offensive struggles in 1994. Duncan has drawn just 175 walks in 3848 career plate appearances.

Duncan started games at all four infield position (although he plays none of them well) and has good power for a middle infielder; he has posted a .400 slugging average four times in the last five years. At age 31 Duncan was the oldest regular second baseman in the league and became a free agent after the season. He is unlikely to command a large offer from the Phillies, however, and should move on to another team in 1995.

With Duncan playing at another position during much of the season, 29 year old Mickey Morandini got additional playing time and made the most of it, producing his best major league season. His .292 batting average, .378 OBP and .409 slugging average were all career highs by wide margins. Morandini has been a very consistent base thief, too, stealing between 8 and 13 bases in each of the last four years, with a commendable 80% success rate.

Although Morandini is often overmatched against lefthanded pitching, Duncan's imminent departure and Morandini's above average defense spell an increase in playing time for Morandini, who should post a .270-4-42-11 line in 1995. He would lose some at bats in a platoon arrangement, but would produce a better overall batting average.

Rookie Kevin Jordan could get the opportunity to platoon with Morandini in 1995. The 25 year old Jordan was acquired from the Yankees as part of the Terry Mulholland trade. Jordan rebounded from a broken leg to hit .290 and slug .481 for Class AAA Scranton-Wilkes Barre. Jordan's power has remained steady while his strikeout rate has declined as he has advanced and, although his defense is just adequate, Jordan's bat is major league ready. In about 300 at bats Jordan should produce respectable .270-8-35-6 numbers in a platoon role - for about $2 million per year less in salary than Duncan would commmand.

Utilityman Randy Ready got playing time due to the rash of injuries in Philadelphia, but, at age 35, is a long shot to return.

Double-A Reading second baseman David Fisher is a good gloveman, but poor hitter who converted from shortstop in 1994. He has no major league offensive potential.

Class A Clearwater second baseman David Doster was selected by Baseball America as the Florida State League's best defensive second base prospect. The 25 year old Doster ranked among league leaders in doubles, but his lack of experience above Class A at his advanced age is a large negative.

Lary Bump:

In the wasteland that was the Phillies' farm system, the second half put together by Kevin Jordan was overlooked. The 25 year old righthanded batter finished at .290-12-57 for Triple-A Scranton despite being limited to 81 games by injury. The speed he showed early in his career in the Yankees' organization is gone, and Jordan is not a good defensive second baseman. However, he has good power, and could even make it as a third baseman.

Anthony Manahan, who also has played shortstop, has been a disappointment in the Seattle organization.

He dropped to .285-4-36 in his second Pacific Coast League season.

At Double-A Reading was 25 year old righthanded batter David Fisher (.250-7-42), a marginal prospect at best. Dave Doster, a 27th-round draft choice out of Indiana State in 1993, is making noises as if he is now a prospect. He was the best defensive second baseman in the Florida State League last year. He also led the Clearwater Phillies in home runs (13) and RBI (74). Age may be against the 24 year old righthanded batter, who finished at .281 with 12 stolen bases.

Pittsburgh Pirates

John Perrotto:

The Pirates hosted last year's All-Star Game at Three Rivers Stadium and Carlos Garcia was the home club's lone representative. Well, someone had to be picked.

It's not that Garcia had a bad year, hitting .277-6-28-18. It just wasn't an All-Star kind of year. Garcia, though, has had only two full seasons in the majors and is capable of more than his 1994 numbers show. He has the power to hit 15 homers and enough speed to steal 30 bases.

Once Garcia learns to relax a little and let his natural ability take over, he should emerge as one of the National League's better second basemen. He also needs to be dropped from the leadoff spot, where he is a liability because of a low OBP (this compounds Garcia's putting too much pressure on himself).

Garcia would be a better sixth place hitter where the Pirates could take better advantage of his power. He will likely drop down in the order this year with Jacob Brumfield being both the heir apparent in centerfield and a top leadoff candidate.

The Pirates' best utility infielder, lefthander Tom Foley spelled Garcia against tough righthanded pitchers during the past two seasons. However, Foley became a free agent after hitting .236-3-15-0

last year and the Pirates had no interest in re-signing the classy veteran.

Switch-hitter Nelson Liriano figures to be Garcia's backup and the Pirates' top reserve infielder after being claimed off waivers from Colorado last October. He should be an upgrade over Foley with a better bat and speed. Liriano was the Rockies' starting second baseman for most of the second half of last season after Roberto Mejia was exiled to the minors; he hit a respectable .255-3-31-0.

The starting job should be Garcia's for a number of years as the Pirates have no minor leaguers close to pushing him.

Lary Bump:

With solid starters and Nelson Liriano added to the middle infield mix, there probably is no place for the journeymen who filled those roles last year at Buffalo -- John Wehner (.303-7-44-21), Dave Rohde (.227-1-23) and William Suero (.235-3-23 after a .325-1-7 start at Double-A Carolina). Wehner, an improving 27 year old righthanded batter, also has played the outfield, and could win a utility job.

Derek Swafford, a 20 year old lefthanded batter, was the Pirates' third-round draft choice in 1993. They're bringing him along slowly. Last year with two Class A teams he hit .375-0-11 for short-season Welland and .190-1-16 for Augusta.

St. Louis Cardinals

The Cardinals picked up Ramon Caraballo as a backup. He goes in at the bottom of the major league depth chart, while Luis Alicea disappears entirely. Caraballo looked very promising as he rose up through the Braves organization, often looking like the heir to Mark Lemke. But Tony Graffanino blew past Caraballo as the starter at Triple-A and the probable heir to the major league job in Atlanta.

Caraballo spent much of last summer trying to learn shortstop back down at Double-A; with hindsight we

can characterize this move as an effort to make Caraballo more attractive on the trade market. If and when he gets to the major leagues, Caraballo will provide speed (good enough to be a pinch runner) with some pop in his bat; and he should be able to hit for an OK average although he failed in that department in 1994.

The big story at second base is of course the handing of the everyday role to Geronimo Pena, filling the void left by Alicea when he went to Boston.

John Perrotto:

Although the Cardinals have been carrying three second baseman for awhile now, they don't seem too thrilled with any of them.

The Cardinals are waiting for Geronimo Pena to blossom. Though he seems to have the tools with a good bat, decent power and some speed, Pena hasn't even fully developed into a regular. He is constantly hampered by injury and weight problems and the Cardinals are tiring of his attitude. He did have a decent year in 1994, finishing at .254-11-34-9, but somehow you always expect more. The Cardinals need pitching desperately and will offer Pena as possible trade bait. The change of scenery certainly wouldn't hurt him.

Luis Alicea has been a fine player but the Cardinals don't appear to have enough faith to give him the job. He hit .278-5-29-4 last year but still often took a back seat to Pena. He is a good little player and is good enough to start in the majors. Maybe the Cardinals will finally do both Pena and Alicea a favor by dealing one of them away to a team that can appreciate their talents and then playing the other in a regular role.

Defensive wizard Jose Oquendo hit a little, too, as evidenced by his .264-0-9-1 mark in limited playing time in 1994. However, a string of injuries has reduced his effectiveness and his career is almost over.

St. Louis had power hitting Darrel Deak playing second for Class AAA Louisville in 1994. He hit

.272-18-73-1 and his bat is ready for the majors. However, the Cardinals feel his range isn't good enough for him to play second base in the majors. On the other hand he could force his way into the lineup with his bat. Deak might be the immediate beneficiary of Gregg Jefferies leap into the free agency pool, by either taking over directly at first base or by playing third with Todd Zeile shifting across the diamond.

Lary Bump:

Darrel Deak, the 25 year old younger brother of perennial catching prospect Brian Deak, has shown consistent power while rising from A ball to Double-A to Triple-A the last three seasons. In '94, he also raised his average to .272 at Louisville to go with 18 homers and 73 RBI. He could break into the scramble for playing time at second base this season, but the slow-moving switch hitter might be more valuable if the Cardinals tear out their artificial turf in '96.

Also at Louisville was 29 year old utility insurance policy Jeff "Whitey" Richardson. The righthanded batter hit .259-4-21 in his sixth Triple-A season. Ramon Caraballo, acquired from the Braves, last year lost his job at Richmond, where he was a regular in 1992 and '93, by batting just .133 in 75 at-bats. He was a little bit better at Double-A Greenville (.239-9-30).

Like Darrel Deak, Joe Biasucci is a better prospect with the bat than with his glove. The 24 year old righthanded batter's offensive output was reduced when he jumped from the Midwest League in 1993 to the Texas League last year (.254-15-48). He's the brother of Colts kicker Dean Biasucci.

Former Virginia Tech shortstop Dee Dalton played second base at Class A Madison. The 22 year old righthanded batter will have to hit for a higher average than his .240-12-77-11 last season. In Jeff Berblinger's two pro seasons, he has been solid both in statistics (.296-8-67-24 at Class A Savannah in '94) and in intangibles. With four more levels of the Cardinals' organization to go through, the 24 year old righthanded batter could be too old to make it in the majors. Or he could shoot through the system in a short time to fill a hole at the top.

San Diego Padres

Hank Widmer:

In Bip Roberts' return to the Padres he gave them respectability in the leadoff spot for the first time since, well, since the last time that Roberts played for the Padres (1991). With the notable exception of Tony Gwynn, Roberts was the Padres' most consistent player, despite actually taking a couple of weeks off due to hitting too well; yes, the stress was getting to him. Nevertheless, Roberts had a fine .320-2-31-21 season.

Fred Matos:

Luis Lopez will likely take over second in 1995 if Bip Roberts both stays and moves to the outfield (as he was scheduled to do in 1994). Lopez isn't much of a hitter, and if he plays a full season, he could hit .255 with five home runs and 50 RBI.

Minor leaguers Billy Hall or Kevin Higgins could get promoted in case of injury. Hall isn't much of a hitter, but he can steal some bases. Higgins hit .221 in 181 at bats for the Padres in 1993, but he's now 28 and has no upward potential.

Lary Bump:

The Red Sox drafted switch-hitting Billy Hall before the '94 season, but returned him to the Padres. He batted .360-1-12 at Double-A Wichita and .264-3-21 at Las Vegas. He also stole 34 bases, but at age 25 it may be now or never for him to make the majors.

Utilityman Kevin Higgins, 28, played some second base in his fourth season at Las Vegas, where the righthanded batter's numbers (.309-2-44) were nothing special.

The Padres' best second base prospect may be Homer Bush, 22. The righthanded batter followed up a big season in Australia by going .335-0-16 at Class A Rancho Cucamonga and .298-3-14 for Wichita. He stole 29 bases in 38 attempts in just 98 games. San Diego sent him to the Arizona Fall League for more playing time.

Mat Witkowski, a 25 year old righthanded batter, may have lost his chance to make the majors when he was demoted from Las Vegas to Wichita (.257-3-27-10). In the Midwest League was Eduardo Cuevas, 21. The righthanded batter may have some future after going .297-2-40-11. He needs to become more patient at the plate, develop some power and run the bases more judiciously.

San Francisco Giants

Steven Rubio:

For the tenth year in a row, Robby Thompson is the Giants' first choice as their starting second baseman. If healthy, he is one of the best second basemen in the game, but this is a big if: he is 33 years old and he hasn't played more than 128 games in a season since 1991. Thompson's health is an important question mark for the Giants in 1995, and a risky investment for fantasy owners.

John Patterson played more games at second for the Giants last year than any other player, but was unimpressive. Injuries have ruined his best years, and while Patterson is a fine utility player, he is unlikely to improve at this point in his career. Steve Scarsone is another useful utility player who will never reach stardom. Scarsone could surprise if Thompson gets hurt, but otherwise isn't worth recommending.

Chris Wimmer is one of the best prospects in the entire system. His glove draws phenomenal reviews, he steals bases and his hitting is consistent if not overwhelming. He is probably a year away, but is well worth your attention, particularly if Thompson is injured again.

Lary Bump:

The lone threat to Robby Thompson's job is Chris Wimmer, a 24 year old righthanded batter. In his second pro season, he improved to .284-4-49 for Double-A Shreveport, but his SB total plummeted from 49 to 21.

Erik Johnson, who has made cameo appearances in San Francisco the last two summers, is no prospect. The righthanded batter, 29, hit .292-1-45 in the PCL.

THIRD BASE:
TACTICAL CONSIDERATIONS

The sooner you focus on the slim pickings in this year's pool of third basemen, the better chance you will have to gain a tactical advantage. One of the obvious early steps toward winning would be trading for a fully-priced, high-value third sacker. There are, unfortunately, not many who fit this description.

What happened to the once-formidable batsmen who play third base? They had a collective bad year in 1994, similar to what happens when heavy rains come too early to the Bordeaux region in France: a very disappointing crop.

In the American League, Wade Boggs had a strong year that surprised many (though it surprised me less than it surprised other people, and I can point to my various rosters which included Boggs, as evidence).

Otherwise, where was there any pleasant surprise who reached a high level? Baltimore split their third base season between Chris Sabo and Leo Gomez; and although Gomez ended up with the job, on a high note, he didn't play enough to have a huge season.

Boston's Scott Cooper had a bad year, as did California's Damion Easley and Detroit's Travis Fryman. Gary Gaetti had a decent year for the Royals but remains far below his career peak of the mid 1980's. Kevin Seitzer, who played third for Milwaukee, has been slipping steadily downward since his rookie year in 1987. The Twins never found a good solution for 3B in 1994, and neither did the Athletics. Ed Sprague was a disappointment for Toronto. Chicago's Robin Ventura had a good year good but didn't blossom big-time as many (including myself) had expected, so you could say he was a disappoint-

ment, too. The same comments apply to Dean Palmer of Texas, who continues to postpone his inevitable arrival among major leaguers who can hit for average.

The National League picture was much the same in 1994.

Talk about going from the Penthouse to the Outhouse! Terry Pendleton and the Braves could well have been in the World Series in 1994. Instead of enjoying the Series, Pendleton spent his October looking for a job as he was cast off by the Braves. Yes, baseball environmentalists, there are unmistakable signs of Global Cooling at the Hot Corner.

The National League third base population presents a number of opportunities for profits, mostly at the small end of the spectrum, a larger number of dangers for overpaying, and a few opportunities to get fair value at a fair price.

My personal approach is going to be working with a short list of opportunistic bids for full-time players, based on who gets the least attention during spring training (like at the top of the list, Willie Greene) and if I can't get a full-time player at bargain price, then I will bail out of the bidding for the well-known third base veteran offensive forces and go with a cheap platooner or even a backup for a buck or two. Jason Bates of the Rockies comes to mind, as does Phil Nevin if he makes the majors but doesn't have a starting role.

If you've become queasy seeing names such as Jeff King and Scott Livingstone, on your roster, there is

a chance to escape! Read and take notes. The quiz starts on draft day. Terry Pendleton's replacement in Atlanta will be Jose Oliva, and he will be a fine player. The usual caution about a young player stumbling a little on his way to stardom applies to Oliva, but even if Oliva fails to hit for a high average, he has power, and power is disappearing from the third base spot. Boomers like Matt Williams are that much more valuable as the scarcity of the long ball hitting third baseman impacts the game.

In 1994, only five of the fourteen National League teams had third basemen who hit more than 15 home runs. In order to hold down a third base job, 15 home run power used to be about entry level, didn't it? The power hitters in the NL were Ken Caminiti (18), Tim Wallach (21), Bobby Bonilla NYM (20), Todd Zeile (17) and Matt Williams (42).

Of that group, Bonilla should be mercifully placed elsewhere on defense, and Wallach was hoping that new life in Colorado could be an alternative to getting put out to pasture.

There will be an opportunity in Cincinnati as Tony Fernandez is gone. Finally, it's time for the Willie Greene Show. This time Greene will be worth it. Power hitting Ron Coomer will feel Dodger Blue coursing through his veins as Wallach's replacement. Coomer just plastered the bejeezus out of PCL pitching in 1994, hitting .338 with 22 homers and 123 RBI. He also did well in the Arizona Fall League against a higher level of competition. Coomer is no kid at 27, very old to be making a debut in the majors. Please note trivia buffs, that Sid Bream once hit 31 homers for the same team; Albuquerque. Coomer could be that one guy who seems to fool a lot of fantasy players. He should have a wide open shot at the job, and his visibility as a Dodger should cause more interest than normal. Bottom line is Coomer probably won't be great shakes in LA. If he was a real prospect he'd have arrived much sooner than age 27. Coomer is keeping the spot warm for a kid named Willie Otanez. Otanez is a real long term prospect at 21, probably just two years away form LA, but a much better third baseman than Coomer, and with surprising power (19 HR at A ball) for a 150 pound

man. Put Coomer up for bid early in the auction. You can either bleed away a lot of early cash, or pick him up cheap.

With so many fading veterans in both leagues, and a decent stock of younger players coming along to challenge, third base is likely to be the position with the most turnover in 1995. Many of the tough decisions will go right down to the wire in spring training. Two obvious homework assignments:

1. Get acquainted with the potential rookie crop now, so that when someone is hitting .350 in Florida or Arizona, you can judge whether it fits the player's career development.

2. Follow the news very, very closely during spring training. Don't miss a single box score when it comes to noting who plays third base for every team every day.

On your draft TO-DO list, write down THIRD BASE real big. Then, either get a good one in a hurry, or don't get a good one. It wasn't so long ago that Terry Pendleton was actually more valuable than Matt Williams.

For the record:

Likely to be bargains: Scott Cooper, Travis Fryman, Leo Gomez, Willie Greene, Dave Hollins, Jim Thome.

Likely to be overvalued: Gary Gaetti, Kevin Seitzer, Steve Buechele, Ron Coomer.

AMERICAN LEAGUE
THIRD BASE

As often happens among infielders, maneuvers at other positions will have an impact upon who plays where and how often. For 1995, the maneuvers primarily involved second basemen but the effect will also be felt by third basemen.

Boston, Texas and Kansas City are most significantly effected, with infielders Terry Shumpert and Luis Ortiz joining to new teams. Pay attention to young Mr. Ortiz, as described by Alan Boodman and Lary Bump under Boston Red Sox's Third Basemen. Ortiz hits for both power and average and has made significant strides in the last two years; he's only 23 years old. He's likely to win at last a part time job for the Rangers, playing either at third base with Dean Palmer shifting to the now-vacant DH role, or taking over part of the DH job himself.

Like the first base situation, there are few interesting free agents still available, so not much is likely to change between December and spring training. The best free agents are Chris Sabo and Terry Pendleton, although there are some rumors of Ken Caminiti being on Houston's trading block, too. The expectation is for Pendleton to remain in the National League and for Sabo to return there after his exile from Baltimore.

Baltimore Orioles

Free agents Chris Sabo and Tim Hulett are still unsigned, late in December. While it's quite possible that Hulett will return to the Orioles in a utility role, Sabo won't be back in Baltimore.

Fred Matos:

Prior to last year, all of the Orioles management, with the exception of owner Peter Angelos, had a low opinion of Leo Gomez. So much so that he was nearly traded into oblivion for a third-rate minor leaguer during spring training. But Angelos intervened and insisted that he be kept. It was the Orioles' good fortune, as Gomez soon won the starting job from Chris Sabo. Gomez did it with his strengths: hard work and clutch hitting.

Gomez has the typical power hitter's shortcoming: streakiness. But he always has a very good work ethic, and can come out of slumps with some nice clutch hits. Although he is a .250-.260 hitter, Gomez is capable of hitting 30 dingers, but a 20-25 figure is a more realistic expectation. He has a Rotisserie value of $12-15.

Utility man Tim Hulett is a candidate for the back-up

role, but he will see strong competition from Jeff Manto, voted as last year's International League MVP following an outstanding season at Triple-A Rochester where he showed considerable power. Manto can play third occasionally, but his defense is so poor that he can't be relied on over the long haul. Manto can also play first, a skill that enhances his chance of landing a job as a reserve.

Chris Sabo became a free agent after 1994. He wore out his welcome with the Orioles because of his poor attitude following the loss of the starting third base job to Leo Gomez. He became an outfielder, substitute third baseman, and DH, and prooduced a number of key clutch hits. Sabo is 33 years old and is capable of having a .260-17-65 year.

Lary Bump:

The best third base prospect in the Baltimore organization is Eric Chavez, who powered his way to a .265-23-82 season in the Carolina League. His negatives are his age (24) and strikeouts (100 last year). Double-A third baseman Scott McClain, a 22-year-old righthanded batter, was at just .241-11-58 in a hitter's park at Bowie last season.

Boston Red Sox

The addition of Terry Shumpert via trade from Kansas City gives the Red Sox some flexibility at third base should Scott Cooper's injuries remain a problem.

However, the trade of Luis Ortiz to Texas should be viewed as a vote of confidence in Cooper at third base. Even with a healthy Cooper in the lineup, Shumpert will spend a little time at Boston's hot corner in 1995.

Alan Boodman:

The reason the Red Sox traded Jeff Bagwell back in 1990 was because they determined that Scott Cooper would be making third base in Fenway Park his home for the forseeable future. And he has, but...

Cooper has become a steady player who perpetually seems to be on the verge of a .300-20-85 season. That season was on its way to becoming reality in 1994 when Cooper's year ended in early August due to shoulder problems. It turned out that all he missed was the final week of the season. Cooper will play 1995 at age 27 - an age when a breakout season has a fair likelihood of occurring. Of course, quite a bit depends on his health, and winter reports were sporadic and not always informative. Spring training will be when we find out the truth.

Even without that breakout season, Cooper can still be a good pick for fantasy leaguers. His 1995 stats should be near .290-15-75 with an upside of .315-22-90. He'll need to achive something closer to the second set of numbers in order to emerge from the middle of the pack among A.L. third sackers. Cooper's a good middle-round pick for fantasy purposes.

1995 has to be the year when the Sox figure out how to get Luis Ortiz into the majors and into the lineup. Ortiz posted a .294-18-81 season at Pawtucket in 1993, at age 23. The only weaknesses that showed then were his fondness for swinging at any and all pitches, and his flailings on defense. Both were taken care of in 1994. Ortiz' strikeout/walk ratio went from nearly 6:1 to 1:1, an amazing turnaround, and the defensive problem was "solved" by moving him to DH. Ortiz would be a potent bat to add to the Red Sox' lineup and will be a good sleeper pick if he makes the club in a role other than mere pinch-hitter.

Stan Royer played both third base and first base last year for St. Louis and Boston. He's a minor league veteran, a non-prospect who's been playing full time at Triple-A for most of the 1990's. Royer has moderate power, at best, very little speed or walks, and would hit about .255 in the majors. At age 27, in 1995, he could have several good minor league seasons left, and may spend some time on a major league bench before he's through. Pass on him for 1995.

Lary Bump:

After Luis Ortiz hit a line drive off pitcher Brad Pennington's head last season, Pawtucket manager

Buddy Bailey said, "I'm afraid he's going to kill someone. He hits the ball that hard." Ortiz actually hit the ball harder in 1993, his first year in Triple-A, than last season (.312-6-36). He didn't regain his power stroke after a brief stay in Boston. Ortiz's defense has held him back, but trade talks involving Scott Cooper have given Ortiz hope during the offseason.

From St. Louis, the Red Sox acquired Stan Royer (.280-16-54 at Louisville; .167 with the Cardinals and the Red Sox). The 27-year-old also plays first base. Bill Selby had the best of his three pro seasons (.310-19-69 at Class A Lynchburg; .262-1-18 with Double-A New Britain), but the lefthanded batter is just 17 days younger than Ortiz.

California Angels

Fred Matos:

Good defense is high on Manager Marcel Lachemann's priority list, so gloveman J.T. Snow will likely get a lot of playing time at first base, with Eduardo Perez moving to third. Perez didn't play any games at third for the Angels, but they sent him to Triple-A to "re-learn" the job and to work on his hitting (he was overmatched in the bigs).

Damon Easley played 47 games at third and 40 at second last year, and the plan for 1995 is to establish Easley as the regular at second base. Following a strong .313 in 1993, his .215 last year was very disappointing. Chalk it up to a bad sophomore slump, even though it was essentially his third year in the majors.

Veteran Spike Owen was acquired by the Angels to play second base, but played nearly all of his games at third. At bat, he had a very surprising year. In 1995, he is likely to revert back to his more realistic .246 career average. Although the Angels have plans for Easley at second and Perez at third, Angel plans don't always work out, as was clear last year, so Owen could get another chance for a lot of playing time.

Eduardo Perez can be valued as high as $10 this year even if he hits .250 because he could steal 10-12 bases in a full season, and pop as many as 10 dingers. Based on his poor 1994 record, Easley should go very cheaply, but could slump again resulting in a near zero value. Owen is likely to revert to a .240 average, and has little or no value.

Lary Bump:

One of the definitions for "mess" in my dictionary is "Angels' infield." Third base is no exception. Again this year the hope is 28 year old Eduardo Perez. His father Tony may someday make the Hall of Fame, but Eduardo won't. Last season the righthanded batter went .297-7-38 in the Pacific Coast League after failing to hit with the Angels (.209-5-16). He also plays first base and the outfield, and has enough speed that he stole 12 bases last year.

Perez's Vancouver teammate was 34 year old lefthanded batter Ernest Riles (.310-14-58). He still has enough on-base ability, pinch-hitting skill and defensive versatility to earn a utility role in the majors. Chris Smith, the 21 year old third baseman for Double-A Midland, batted just .261-3-56. He doesn't have enough power to play third base regularly in the majors, but could move back to shortstop and survive. The best long-range third base prospect is George Arias, who showed a combination of leather and lumber (.280-23-80) in the California League. The 22-year-old will have to reduce his strikeout total (111).

Chicago White Sox

Stuart Shea:

Robin Ventura is not the reincarnation of Brooks Robinson, as some have said, but Ventura helps the White Sox. Ventura will help you, too, if you need walks and RBIs. It's a virtual certainty that he will hit in the middle of the order and benefit from Frank Thomas' on-base ability. While Ventura is slow and has a looping swing, he has improved dramatically against lefthanded hitters and walks as often as he strikes out. Despite some good defensive skills,

Ventura wins Gold Gloves at least partially with his bat. His range is decent and he charges bunts well.

The virtually unknown Olmedo Saenz came up to the big club for a few games when injuries struck last May. Saenz, who is 24, has progressed a great deal in a short time (he spent much of 1993 in class-A) and, despite hitting just .261 at Triple-A Nashville in 1994, Saenz could still make his way back to the majors. He smacked 27 doubles and 12 homers in just 107 games, makes good contact, and has been a patient hitter for most of his career. His glove is reputed to be decent, but not outstanding.

Chris Snopek is 19 days older than Saenz, and is behind him. However, the White Sox like Snopek. In just his third year of pro ball, he hit .263 with 25 doubles and 58 walks at Double-A Birmingham. Snopek walks more than he strikes out, runs decently, and has line-drive power. Despite a hand injury, his 1994 season was encouraging to Chicago brass, and with one more good performance, Snopek will be in the running for a utility job in 1996.

Lary Bump:

After a hot start in his Triple-A debut, Olmedo Saenz, 24, tailed off to .261-12-59 at Nashville. The White Sox liked Chris Snopek, voted the best defensive third baseman in the Southern League, enough to send him to the Arizona Fall League. He has a knack for getting on base, but showed little power (.263-6-54) with punchless Birmingham. The righthanded batter is 24. Geovany Miranda, 25, earned a promotion from the Carolina League (.275-0-18-10) to the American Association (.333-0-8 in 16 games). He is not a prospect: he has no homers in seven minor league seasons, and almost never walks.

Cleveland Indians

Shortstop Mark Lewis was a part-time third baseman in 1994, but has been traded to Cincinnati.

Another shortstop, Alvaro Espinoza, has re-signed with the Indians and will compete with free agent

Torey Lovullo for a reserve role. Lovullo came to Cleveland as a free agent from Seattle after a mediocre year in 1994. Neither Espinoza or Lovullo has any Rotisserie value.

Minor leaguer Rene Gonzales left as a free agent and had not signed. He may return to the Indians but is merely Triple-A roster filler in any case.

Tony Blengino:

Last spring training, amidst all of the seemingly more important news, the signing of Jim Thome to a four-year contract by the Indians was barely noticed around baseball. No one argued about his potential, but conventional wisdom stated that a player had to prove himself at the major league level before earning such a contract. The Indians were smart enough to realize that a 22 year old who hit .332 with 25 homers at Triple-A, as Thome did in 1993, would likely experience great success at the major league level. The long-term contract will prove to be a wise investment, based on Thome's 1994 performance. He crashed 20 homers in only 321 at bats, slugging .523. His only offensive weakness was his inability to hit southpaws (only .167 in 1994). Defensively, well, that's another story. Thome, 24, committed 15 errors in only 94 games at third, most on poor throws. A position switch across the diamond to first base is possible, due to the emergence of David Bell. In any event, Thome should hit .300 with 25 homers and 100 RBI in 1995.

Bell, 22, was the Indians' 7th-round pick in 1990. The son of former major leaguer Buddy Bell, he quickly established himself as a standout defensive third baseman. But in his first three pro seasons, he couldn't manage a slugging percentage better than .336. At each level, though, he was one of the youngest starters in his league. In 1993 and 1994, he blossomed offensively as the level of competition improved. At Triple-A Charlotte in 1994, he nearly equaled his home run total for his four previous pro seasons, nailing 18. With the Indians set offensively, but in need of defensive assistance at third base, the stage could be set for Bell's major league debut. The addition of another righty would add some balance to

the lineup, which went 13-20 against lefties in 1994. Bell wouldn't excel right away in Cleveland, and might have to settle for .260, eight homers, 55 RBI in his rookie season.

Alvaro Espinoza, 33, was the Indians' prime utilityman in 1994, playing all four infield positions. After posting respectable numbers in 1993, Espinoza reverted to his light-hitting ways last season. He actually managed to lower his career on-base percentage to .279. Espinoza can't hit for average or power, and has no speed.

Rene Gonzales also has the ability to play all infield positions, but may even be a worse offensive player than Espinoza. He barely slugged .300 at Triple-A Charlotte in 1994, and, like Espinoza, his only chance to make the Indians' roster depends on the failure of younger players. At least Gonzales has the ability to steal an occasional base, making him a slightly less horrible alternative than Espinoza.

Lary Bump:

Sometime this season David Bell, the grandson of Gus Bell and son of Buddy Bell, will make his kin baseball's second three-generation family. After starting slowly with the bat each of the last two seasons, David finished strong (.293-18-88 at Charlotte in 1994). The 22 year old was voted the International League's best defensive third baseman. In the Carolina League, Epi Cardenas, 23, struggled through a .238-4-33 season. Because his bat is limited, he is a better prospect at second base.

Detroit Tigers

Fred Matos:

Following a few years at shortstop where he struggled defensively, Travis Fryman played only third base last year. He had another solid year at the plate, but his average dropped, his strikeouts increased, and his walks decreased proportionately. The increased strikeouts and fewer walks likely came from swinging for the fences.

Fryman will play 1995 at age 26 with five years of major league experience, a combination where a major breakout career year can be expected: 30+ homeruns, a batting average well over .300, and 100+ RBI with a value over $30. He is a blue-chip player.

The Tigers' high minor league talent is thin, so all-purpose utility man Tony Phillips or even Alan Trammell would likely play third if Fryman was injured or needed a day off.

Lary Bump:

The Tigers' Triple-A third baseman - Steve Springer, who must be in his second career as a career minor leaguer by now - is typical of the organization's prospects at the position. The best prospect is Shawn Wooten, who was a no-great-shakes .269-3-61 in the Sally League. And the 22 year old may be better suited to first base.

Kansas City Royals

After re-signing Gary Gaetti and Keith Miller to minor league contracts, the Royals dealt Terry Shumpert to Boston. Don't be fooled by the "minor league" contract given to Gaetti; he won't actually play in the minors. The contract status was offered merely to get Gaetti into camp for 1995.

The development of this situation means that the Royals are hedging their bets on Joe Randa. Instead of just handing the job outright to the unproven rookie, Gaetti will probably come away from spring training with the regular job.

Gaetti will serve as a tutor to young Randa before turning over the reins later in the year.

Miller will also be a minor leaguer in name only. If healthy (a big "if"), Miller should win a reserve 3B/OF/DH role for 1995. His availability doesn't hurt Randa's playing time much; he merely serves as an emergency third baseman should Gaetti's aging accelerate and Randa be unready for the regular role.

Hensley "Bam-Bam" Meulens has returned from a tour of Japan to sign a minor league contract with the Royals. His chances of getting back to the big leagues are better with the Royals than with other teams, but they are still very slim.

Marc Bowman:

Gary Gaetti held down the third base job for the Royals in 1994 and had a resurgent year. He was their best clutch hitter early in the season before fading gradually over the last two months. Gaetti's .287 average was his best since 1988 and he was one of the team's best power threats for the first half of the year.

However, the cracks in his game are showing. He's a one-dimensional power hitter whose once-good defensive play is eroding. Gaetti's contract option was not renewed and he became a free agent. The Royals might bring him back for one more year, but only if Gaetti is willing to play cheaply. That's unlikely, so he'll probably take his 35-year-old bat elsewhere. It's hard to believe he'll get 500 at bats again wherever he goes. A more reasonable estimate would be 350 at bats with 10 homeruns, 45 RBI and a batting average around .255. Don't pay more than $1 for that kind of performance.

The most likely scenario for the Royals at 3B in 1994 will be to have Joe Randa playing there most of the time with Terry Shumpert and/or Keith Miller spelling him occasionally. Randa is a prospect who has demonstrated good power and batting averages as he has steadily advanced through the Royals' farm system. He has won a number of awards and often been named to <u>Baseball America's</u> prospect lists. He's now 25 years old and ready to play in the big leagues. Randa will probably hit .250 in his first major league season, with better averages to come later as he adjusts to big league pitching. He should be good for 15-20 homers in a few years too, although it is unrealistic to expect more than a dozen dingers in his rookie campaign. Expect .250-8-45-5 in 400 at bats in 1994; Randa could be worth a $1 speculation pick as he's likely to be even better in 1996 and beyond.

Terry Shumpert did some backup work at third in

1994 and should get even more play there in 1995. Look for more detailed comments about him in the Second Base section.

"DL" are his middle initials. Keith Miller has been hurt so much over the course of his career that he can't really be counted on in a regular role; he has played in just 42 games for the Royals over the last two years. When he's in the lineup he's capable of hitting for a good average with speed and occasional power. However, his glove is so weak that he's not able to handle any position regularly. Miller would make a good tenth man who can play almost anywhere on the field, starting occasionally and pinch-hitting often. In such a utility role, Miller would probably hit about .285 with three homeruns and 10 SBs. He's not worth much to a Rotisserie team even if he wins a starting job because he'll eventually get hurt. While he has some value to the Royals, Rotisserie owners would be wise to avoid him.

Gary Caraballo is a lesser prospect who hit .246 with 10 HR and 59 RBI for Double-A Memphis. With Randa advancing to the majors, Caraballo will play 1995 in Omaha. He's 23 years old and must prove he can hit above Class-A to get a shot at the majors.

As with other positions, the Royals' better prospects are in the lower minors. Ryan Long has shown good power and some speed, but needs to develop a better batting eye to advance. He's just 22 years old and was a high draft pick, so he'll get every chance to show his abilities. 24-year-old Lino Diaz hit .316 for Rockford and has good speed. He also needs better plate discipline to advance.

Lary Bump:

Joe Randa most likely will take over as Kansas City's third baseman this season. At age 25, he's really a marginal prospect. Despite a .295 average for his four minor league seasons, he hit just .275-10-51 in his Triple-A debut. He doesn't have much speed, but is an intelligent runner who will pick his spots to steal. The Royals sent him to the Arizona Fall League, where he had a good start.

The third baseman at Double-A Memphis was Gary Caraballo, 23. He increased his power output (10 homers, 59 RBI), but with a resulting decrease in batting average. He moved farther behind Randa in line to replace Gary Gaetti.

The third baseman with Wilmington's Carolina League juggernaut was Ryan Long, a 22 year old righthanded batter. His .263-11-68 season was not bad in a pitcher's park. <u>Baseball America's</u> poll named 24 year old Lino Diaz the best defensive third baseman in the Midwest League. He also has played second base. He makes contact, hits for average and has some speed (.316-4-44-11, .381 on-base percentage), and may be a better prospect at second.

Milwaukee Brewers

B. J. Surhoff is still a free agent, although speculation in late December was that he would return to the Brewers. Surhoff may have more of an impact on the catching situation or in the outfield than at third base.

Bill Gray:

Kevin Seitzer in 1994 reached the .300 mark for the first time since 1988. Injuries and the strike limited him to only 80 games, so the .314 average will fool a lot of people. Seitzer, over the course of a 162 game season, is no longer a .300 hitter. Many players have hit well for half a year, then tanked. Seitzer is more likely to be around .270, and he hasn't the power we want in a third baseman. But power hitting third basemen are growing increasingly rare, so Seitzer will be slightly elevated in value.

B.J. Surhoff (also see the chapter on catchers) spent most of the time playing third in '94. Right now Nilsson to first/Jaha out/Surhoff behind the plate appears to be the direction the Brewers intend to take. Surhoff will be valuable for his versatility as he could qualify at third and catcher. Surhoff wants to catch, and should. He gets better results from the pitchers than Dave Nilsson.

Jeff Cirillo was pressed into service when Surhoff and Seitzer hit the DL. Although Cirillo had hit well in the minors, he hadn't a clue in the majors. Oddly, Cirillo hit much better on the road than in County Stadium, which has always been hitter-friendly. Cirillo is better suited to middle infield play. If the regulars stay healthy, Cirillo will probably return to the minors. He needs the work.

Lary Bump:

Jeff Cirillo, 25, was voted the American Association's best defensive third baseman. Cirillo's bat (309-10-46 at New Orleans; .238-3-12 with the Brewers) could help. Tim Unroe's stock rose as much as any minor leaguer's in 1994. He came a long way from a .251 average in the California League in 1993 to a 1994 season (.310-15-103-4) in which he was Texas League MVP and MVP of the Double-A All-Star Game. The former shortstop has a good arm to go with his bat. There has been talk of moving the 24 year old to first base. A good start at New Orleans could get him to the majors early in 1995.

The Brewers' first draft pick in 1994 was Antone Williamson, out of Arizona State. He showed power, but had trouble making contact in his pro debut (a combined .264-4-26 with 31 strikeouts in 159 at bats from the Rookie to Double-A levels). The lefthanded batter is projected as Milwaukee's third baseman in 1996.

Minnesota Twins

James Benkard:

Scott Leius had a good 1994 season and stands to be the leading candidate for the job in '95. Leius hit well in the power department, smacking 14 home runs and driving in 49. He must back this up in '95 with a higher average, but is unlikely to hit more than .260. The Twins can live with that as long as Leius' power remains and his defense continues to be good.

Rookie Scott Stahoviak has some potential as a hitter, but is unproven in the big leagues and had his 1994 season ended by injury. Despite not being ready

for the majors, he has a decent chance to develop into a regular. He could move quickly if he lowers his strikeouts. Stahoviak could secure the job for the coming years if he tightens up his defense. However, there are not many infielders in the majors who are 6'5", so he might end up competing with David McCarty at first base or with Marty Cordova for the DH role.

Chip Hale is a good bench player if you need a consistent .260 average, just as long as you don't expect fireworks from him.

There are few other immediate options for Minnesota besides the above players, as prospects Paul Russo and Chad Roper faltered in '94 and will need more time in the minors.

Lary Bump:

If Scott Stahoviak doesn't end up at first base, he could be the Twins' starter at third. 25 year old Paul Russo, a big power source in the lower minors, has struggled the last two seasons in Triple-A. As a result, he spent most of 1994 at Double-A Nashville (.227-10-40). At Triple-A Salt Lake City, he was .296-3-17. In his second season at Class-A Fort Myers, Chad Roper, 21, went just .240-4-44.

New York Yankees

Two years ago it looked like Wade Boggs had lost it, but his detractors now have to admit that Boggs is, at worst, a gracefully-aged version of his former self, not some kind of wreck. In 1994 Boggs set an all-time record for batting average by a Yankees third baseman, and that population includes some memorable ghosts. His .433 on base percentage offered more testimony that Boggs is far from being washed up.

Normally a player like Boggs, that is a player past his prime chronologically and one who has reached spectacular heights in the past -- five out of six batting titles 1983-1988 and the only player to hit over .350 four straight years since Ty Cobb and Chuck Klein -- would be a candidate to be overvalued. But since

Boggs is, much like Tony Gwynn, dependent on batting average for so much of his value, and because batting average is so widely misunderstood and underappreciated, Boggs can actually be a bargain in 1995 even if he fades some from his 1994 brilliance. Certainly he was a bargain in most leagues in 1994, when he cost an average of $14 and delivered $20 of value (uninflated).

History will show that Boggs' resurgence last year was partly due to the overall hitting explosion, in which veteran batsmen tended to be more adept at taking advantage of weak pitching, but there's no denying that Boggs is fully recovered from that 1992 season in which he simply lost interest in the game. Figuring .320 with near a dozen homers, you can see a very valuable third baseman, especially as overall batting averages slide gradually downward toward pre-expansion levels.

The Russ Davis factor is not going to take away from Boggs' playing time. There were however occasions in 1992 and 1993 when Boggs sat down against a tough lefty, with Randy Velarde or Mike Gallego appearing at third, and that phenomenon will continue to some extent in 1995. But if Davis (if he's still with Yankees) ends up starting two consecutive games against lefty pitching, don't start thinking that "Boggs is being platooned." That type of role is not even a remote possibility, and that type of general statement in the present tense (so-and-so "is" the new closer, or this guy "is" now a platooner) just cannot be applied to any team managed by Buck Showalter. You can be definite about what happened yesterday and the day before, buy if you make general statements about what any player's role "is" on this team, you will look pretty damn ignorant within another day or two. Showalter manages one game at a time.

Worth watching, especially if and when Davis moves on, will be Andy Fox, the third base prospect who got extensive use in a utility role during the '94 Arizona Fall League, and really blossomed given that opportunity.

Lary Bump:

Wade Boggs' big 1994 season set back Yankees third base prospects, primarily Russ Davis, 25. He hit his stride with ten home runs in August before going on the disabled list because of a broken wrist. He finished at .276-25-69 in the International League. The Yankees' trade talks with just about every team the last couple of years have started and ended with Davis. Now Davis may be expendable, but he may not be as marketable.

The Yanks sent Andy Fox, a 24 year old lefthanded batter, to the Arizona Fall League. He was voted both the best defensive third baseman and the infielder with the best arm in the Eastern League. His offensive numbers were better in his partial '93 season at Albany than last year's .222-11-43-22.

One of the stars with Florida State League champion Tampa was Scott Romano (.303-20-87). The 23 year old also walked more than he struck out, and was hit by 15 pitches, recording a .403 on-base percentage.

Oakland A's

Steven Rubio:

Mediocre is a word that comes to mind when considering Oakland third basemen in recent years. From Carney Lansford's final seasons, through the awful performance of Craig Paquette, to the current job holder, Scott Brosius, the A's have settled for uninspired talent at the hot corner for far too long. Brosius is very consistent. Unfortunately he is consistently mediocre, hitting occasional homers while posting a low batting average. He is now 28 years old and unlikely to improve.

Craig Paquette hit 17 home runs in Triple-A last year, but he is truly a terrible hitter. I have described him elsewhere as Cory Snyder having a bad season, but this is perhaps unfair to Snyder. Paquette failed in an earlier shot at the Oakland job, and he will most likely fail again if he is ever given another chance. Avoid him.

The A's have a couple of intriguing minor-league third basemen who could surface in the near future. Jason Giambi spent time at both Double-A and Triple-A last season, and was chosen by the A's to play in the Arizona Fall League. While he is no superstar, he has the talent to win the Oakland job outright in 1995, and is a good sleeper pick. Further down in the system, Scott Spiezio had a strong season at the plate for Class A Modesto. He is two years younger than Giambi and looks to present the A's with an interesting choice between the two in a few years.

Lary Bump:

If Arizona Fall League assignments are an indication, the Athletics must feel Jason Giambi is their best third base prospect. The 24 year old lefthanded batter came through at Tacoma (.318-4-38) after a promotion from Double-A Huntsville (.223-6-30). Giambi has absolutely no speed.

After spending most of 1993 in Oakland, 26 year old Craig Paquette went back to Tacoma last season (.286-17-48). He went just 7-for-49 with no RBI for the Athletics. In the California League, switch-hitting Scott Spiezio, 22, batted .280-14-68. He isn't fast, but was successful in all five stolen base attempts. He also walked 88 times in compiling a .399 on-base percentage.

Seattle Mariners

Free agent Torey Lovullo joined the Indians over the winter. He would have had to battle for a reserve role in Seattle and now will have to do the same in Cleveland.

Another free agent, Dale Sveum, signed a minor league contract with the Pirates. Like Lovullo, Sveum's role would have been as a reserve.

Bill Gray:

At 32, is Edgar Martinez slipping? When a perennial .300 hitter in his mid-thirties doesn't reach that level,

people talk. Don't sweat it. Martinez' slugging and on-base percentage were about normal for him, and his strikeout to walk ratio was better than his career average. Frankly, I expect Martinez to have a much better 1995. A variety of injuries and an ill-advised comeback limited his play for nearly two years. He was hitting .298 at the All-Star break, but batted only .255 afterwards. Martinez is still a very capable hitter, and can produce for another few years. The .285 average might have taken away some of his gloss, but for the astute player, Martinez is now a possible bargain. Expect vintage Edgar Martinez in 1995.

Mike Blowers also qualifies at first base, and might play more outfield in 1995, He is best remembered for his strong 1993 season when Martinez was injured. Blowers seemed to be on the highlight reel nightly as he reached a career high 15 home runs. Blowers is very effective against lefties, so platooning is a possibility. He will never again reach 15 home runs, but 7-10 is within reason and his average won't hurt you. He is not a first-string player, so buy him only for your bench.

Lary Bump:

Edgar Martinez's job is safe. Dale Sveum left the Seattle organization as a free agent, leaving at Calgary just 30 year old switch hitter Tommy Hinzo (.246-0-13), who isn't even a base stealer any more. Double-A Jacksonville's third basemen were 32 year old journeyman Luis Quinones and Lipso Nava, 26, who produced just .191-3-10 there and .255-0-13 in the California League.

Texas Rangers

The addition of Luis Ortiz lets the Rangers move Dean Palmer to the open DH spot. Or, Ortiz could see time at DH himself. Neither Palmer or Ortiz is exactly a Gold Glove candidate. The chances are that both Palmer and Ortiz will get to play third base for at least part of 1995. Both are good hitters, too, so there is a lot to choose from among third basemen in Texas.

Peter Graves:

Third base is Dean Palmer territory - the only real third base prospect in the organization, Mike Bell, is 20 years old and will begin 1995 in the Florida State League.

Scouts still like Palmer's potential, but the comparisons to Mike Schmidt are becoming a thing of the past. Palmer hit a reasonably productive .246-19-59 last season, but struck out once every 3.8 at bats and committed 22 errors in 91 games. To say that he's streaky is like saying that Bud Selig is thrifty - both are gross understatements. Palmer can carry a team for two weeks, then go one for forty. In the Rangers' search for pitching, he may be one of their more tradeable players, so even though there isn't another third baseman in sight, there is a chance that Palmer could be dealt. Regardless, at age 26, Palmer is a good bet to rise in value next season.

If a stopgap third baseman is needed, Doug Strange would be a likely candidate. He is discussed under second basemen. The Triple-A third sacker was 32 year old former Astro Chuck Jackson, who could also fill in, but would not be a long-term solution. Jackson is a decent hitter with occasional power, but did nothing in two short stints with Houston.

Lary Bump:

The Rangers' third base prospect closest to the majors is 25 year old Mike Edwards, who batted .260-6-37 at Double-A Tulsa. Texas also has Mike Bell - brother of David, son of Buddy, grandson of Gus, and a supplemental first-round draft pick in 1993. The 20-year-old was solid in the Sally League (.263-6-58-16). As a point of reference, David was in the Sally League at age 18, and batted just .230 with similar power numbers. Mike is faster than his older brother, who has just 13 stolen bases in five pro seasons.

Toronto Blue Jays

Reserve third baseman and outfielder Darnell Coles remains a free agent late in December. Coles' value is extremely speculative in any case. Considering the difficulty that Toronto had filling it's leftfield slot in 1994 and that Coles did NOT win the job, it's hard to believe his value will increase in 1995 with a new team.

David Luciani:

Ed Sprague may have just one chance left to prove that he can be as good as so many imagined he would be. After demonstrating in 1993 that he was at least adequate with the glove, his hitting has not been up to standard. While he posted 12 home runs in 1993 and a .260 average, he also has become notorious for hitting into double plays, leading the league in 1993 with 23.

Far worse than any other statistics last year were his incredible 95 strikeouts last year and only 23 walks. When the strike came, Sprague was on a pace for a .240 average with 15 homers and a whopping 134 strikeouts, far from acceptable numbers for the sixth or seventh spot in this batting order.

More serious a threat to Sprague's future is prospect Howard Battle, who has torn up the minor leagues the last couple of years and is waiting patiently for his major league opportunity. With Darnell Coles a free agent and Domingo Cedeno possibly headed back to the minors, Battle leads all candidates to be Sprague's backup. Before long, it is Howard Battle who could find himself in the lineup as the Jays' everyday third baseman.

This, therefore, is the pivotal year for Ed Sprague. It usually takes two consecutive bad years to force a player out of his regular role. Sprague must at least return to his 1993 level if he is to keep his job. Any Rotisserie owner who drafts Ed Sprague should take Howard Battle in the reserve draft.

Lary Bump:

Howard Battle, 23, had his biggest battle last season on defense, mixing brilliant plays with an assortment of boots and bad throws. Battle has the potential to hit more home runs in Toronto than he did in Syracuse (.277-14-75). At Double-A Knoxville, Felipe Crespo also had a defensive struggle after moving from second base, but he continued to hit and steal bases (.269-8-49-20). If he starts this season in Double-A, expect him to earn a rapid promotion to Syracuse. Arrival in Toronto in 1996 is a good possibility.

Tom Evans, 20, did well in his second season in the Sally League (.273-13-48). Kevin Witt was the final player chosen in the 1994 draft's first round. The lefthanded batter, who also has played shortstop, started his pro career hitting .255-7-36 in Rookie ball.

NATIONAL LEAGUE THIRD BASEMEN

Atlanta Braves

Marc Bowman:

1995 will be the changing of the guard at third for Atlanta. In a move designed to cut costs, Terry Pendleton was not offered arbitration and became a free agent. He'll be missed by Braves fans as he, ahead of all others, is most closely associated with the team's Phoenix-like rise to National League prominence. Pendleton joined the Braves in 1991, when they went worst to first and won their first division title in recent memory; Pendleton captured the league's MVP award with a .319-22-86-10 season. His performance has slipped in recent years as age and knee injuries have eroded both his speed and defensive range. Pendleton fell to just .252-7-30-2 last year.

He's only 34 years old, though, so he's not done yet. It's likely that he'll find somewhere to play regularly, although his new venue is probably not going to be as friendly as hitting-haven Fulton County Stadium. Assuming he lands in a neutral park, Pendleton will put up a respectable .260-12-60-3 season worth about $10.

Of course, the Braves have a viable alternative in Jose Oliva. The 24 year old slugger provided a glimpse of what he might accomplish in a short stint for Atlanta in 1994, batting .288 with six homers and 11 RBI in just 57 at bats. He also led Triple-A Richmond with 24 homers and 64 RBI; Oliva slugged .493. He doesn't play defense like Pendleton (not many do), so he'll sit down occasionally when his glove isn't cooperating. Oliva's biggest problem is strikeouts. In 2193 minor league at bats Oliva has amassed 632 Ks, about a 3.5 to 1 ratio. For now it appears that the Braves are willing to live with the whiffs as long as Oliva hits enough out of the park. Look for another low batting average, high power season from Oliva: 450 at bats of .240-20-60 production, worth about $10.

Last year's substitute at third base was utility man Bill Pecota who had a disappointing year at the plate, hitting .214 after a fine .323 mark in 1993. Pecota's versatility is a big plus for the Braves, but his .214-2-16-1 in 112 at bats is a much more common season for him than a .323 batting average; he is a career .249 hitter with little power or speed. Pecota's role is utility and he's good at it. He has no Rotisserie value, however.

With the injury to Chipper Jones during spring training in 1994, the Braves didn't have to deal with the

issue of where to put him in their crowded infield. He'll be back in 1995 and will have to play somewhere. The most likely scenario is that he'll get the shortstop job with Jeff Blauser shifted elsewhere. Blauser has played third base before and may do so again; he'll also see time at second base when the Braves want a little more pop in their lineup. Both Jones and Blauser are discussed at length under Shortstops.

The Braves minor league third base talent is roughly similar throughout their system: moderate power hitters capable of low batting averages and prodigious strikeout rates. Gator McBride may be the most promising of the bunch. After an average rookie season in 1993, McBride awoke to hit .333-13-54-17 for Class A Macon. He's just 21 years old and will move up rapidly with that kind of hitting. McBride did fan 80 times in 296 at bats, though, and will need to put a cap on the Ks to keep his prospect tag.

Other minor league third basemen are generally too old for their level, strikeout too much, or have too little power for their low batting averages; none can really be considered good major league candidates at this point.

Lary Bump:

Jose Oliva had a bad-attitude reputation, but when he was sent down to Richmond in mid-season, he reported the next day. Only Terry Pendleton's return from injury caused Oliva's demotion. He was hitting with power in the big leagues (.288-6-11 in 19 games), the same as in the International League (.253-24-64), where he was voted the best power prospect. The 24 year old righthanded batter is a sure-handed fielder.

With Pendleton out of the way, the only threat to Oliva for Atlanta's third base job, may be 22 year old Chipper Jones, the most natural ballplayer in the minors during 1992 and 1993. When the Braves needed a left fielder last spring, the switch-hitting Jones was just as natural playing that unfamiliar position. Then he tore up his knee and missed the season. His physical condition may not allow him to

play shortstop and steal bases in the majors, but he'll hit enough to play well wherever the Braves decide to use him. Bobby Smith, 20, was voted the best defensive third baseman in the Carolina League. He also showed righthanded power and speed (.266-12-71-18 steals), but will have to make better contact (112 strikeouts) to advance to the majors.

Gator McBride has a name that belongs in a baseball novel -- or in a Southern ballpark. Last season that ballpark was in Macon, where he batted .338-13-54 with 17 stolen bases in 81 games. Even though he was just a 37th-round draft pick in 1993, the 21 year old righthanded batter could find himself someday playing across the state in Atlanta if he can continue to hit as he did in '94.

Chicago Cubs

Stuart Shea:

Despite a good glove, a few homers, and a hard-nosed attitude, the aging and slow-footed Steve Buechele really isn't a very good ballplayer. Both on base percentage and slugging average are far below acceptable levels, especially for a third baseman playing half his games in the friendly confines of Wrigley Field; Buechele hit just .223 on the road last year. Unfortunately, there's no one in the minors pushing him, so ''Boosh'' (who is signed through 1995) may be around awhile. In 1995 he'll probably hit a few homers, bat around .250, steal no bases, draw a below average amount of walks, and strike out a lot... just like he always has.

Cristobal Colon (yes, it is Spanish for ''Christopher Columbus'') was the Cubs' Triple-A third baseman in 1994. Once a Rangers' prospect, Colon hit .265 at Iowa with some power, but he never walks, lacks speed, and has only a fair glove. Most telling about Colon's status is that he never got a callup to the big club last year even though aging veteran teammates Mike Maksudian and Todd Haney did. There's little chance of Colon discovering the major leagues any time soon.

Lary Bump:

Mike Sharperson's Triple-A tour last season ended with the Iowa Cubs (.278-5-16) after a stop with the Pawtucket Red Sox (.298-0-13). It may have been the last go-around for the 33 year old. The best hope for the future is Kevin Orie, drafted in 1993's first round as a shortstop. The 22 year old righthanded batter's '94 season was cut short after just six games (.412-1-5) at Class A Daytona Beach.

Kevin Ellis hit well in the Midwest League (.282-14-67), but at age 23 already, the righthanded batter doesn't have a brilliant future. For more about Cris Colon, look under second basemen.

Cincinnati Reds

Greg Gajus:

The signing of Tony Fernandez (.279-8-50-7) to play third base late in spring training was the most daring of Jim Bowden's many moves preceding the 1994 season. Taking a 32 year old known attitude problem, moving him to a new position, and sending down your number one prospect to make room for him would appear to be a recipe for serious problems except that Davey Johnson made it work, mostly by ignoring Fernandez' incessant complaints about the city, the park, the position and his contract until he finally shut up and played ball. At this point in his career, Fernandez is not much of a basestealer (seven of eleven in 1994) but he makes a small contribution in all four categories. If he ends up in a situation where he will play, he should be undervalued. One warning - Fernandez only played nine games at shortstop in 1994, so in some leagues he may not be immediately eligible there to begin 1995 with the Yankees.

Willie Greene will finally get his chance at the third base job. Only 23, Greene has been waiting for his chance for three years and has nothing left to prove in the minors; in 1994 he hit .285-23-80-8 in 435 at bats for Class AAA Indianapolis. Greene is a lefthanded power hitter with decent strike zone

judgement (which the Reds desperately need to balance their lineup). There is no reason not to expect a solid performance.

Lenny Harris (.310-0-14-7) did a fine job in a limited role and would be a short term replacement in the event of injuries. He can still hit, but won't play enough with the Reds to have much Rotisserie value.

Lary Bump:

A typically slow start in spring training and the signing of Tony Fernandez kept Willie Greene from taking over at third base for the Reds last season. He has been a devastating second-half hitter during his two Triple-A seasons. Baseball America named him the American Association's best batting and power prospect during his .285-23-80 season in 1994. The only question now is whether Greene can handle third base defensively. The 23 year old lefthanded batter could end up as Cincinnati's starting left fielder.

Time may be running out on 27 year old Tim Costo, a former Indians first-round draft pick. He started last spring training in a platoon with Greene for the Reds' third base job, then spent most of the year (.194-0-5) on Indianapolis' disabled list because of a wrist injury. The righthanded batter is a candidate for a platoon role in left field.

Thirty year old Gary Cooper also played some third base at Indy (.323-10-36). He could earn a job as an extra righthanded bat in the majors.

The Reds sent Eric Owens, who also played some shortstop at Double-A Chattanooga (.254-3-36-38 steals), to the Arizona Fall League. Because the 24 year old righthanded batter doesn't have much power, he may be better suited to shortstop -- if he can handle the position defensively.

Colorado Rockies

David Smith:

Charlie Hayes demanded big bucks after his 1993

campaign and the Rockies felt compelled to pay the $3.05 million after a .305-20-80 season where he led the league in doubles. Hayes hired a PR agency to help improve his surly image and became a kinder, gentler player for the 1994 season. Unfortunately, Hayes became a kinder, gentler hitter as well.

Hayes hit just ten homers with 50 RBI, and was dropped as low as seventh in the batting order. His pitch selection was miserable at times, and his fielding, which has always left much to be desired, improved only marginally. If the Rockies sign Hayes in 1995, it will be for less than half his 1994 salary. For the second year in a row, he led the team with 17 errors last year.

The Rockies expanded their options by having Vinny Castilla go to the Arizona Fall League and, later, the Mexican Winter League to learn the hot corner. Castilla spent most of the last two seasons as a utility infielder for the Rockies; he lacks Hayes' power, but he's a better fielder and doesn't have nearly the salary expectations that Hayes does.

Pedro Castellano may also get a chance at third base. Castellano is best suited to a utility role, but may get pressed into regular duty if Hayes is gone and Castilla can't do the job. Castellano is a weaker glove man than Castilla, but has more pop in his bat.

Lary Bump:

When he was healthy -- he played just 33 games at Colorado Springs -- Pedro Castellano pounded the ball (.350-4-24). The 25 year old righthanded batter struggled in his 1993 trial with the Rockies, but he could get a longer look this year. Double-A New Haven's third baseman, Bryn Kosco, had his second consecutive big power year in the minors (.242-22-90). But the lefthanded-hitting son of former major leaguer Andy Kosco already is 28, and never has played above Double-A.

In his second California League season, Tom Schmidt, 22, was a disappointment (.243-9-50-100 strikeouts in 99 games). The righthanded batter will have to show something in Double-A this year to remain any

kind of prospect. Pedro Carranza batted .282-9-52 in the South Atlantic League, but at age 23 he's also old for his level of competition.

Florida Marlins

Tony Blengino:

In mid-1993, the Marlins made a deal for a young, but established offensive superstar whom they hoped would be their third baseman for the next decade. A year and a half later, their third baseman for the ages is now a right fielder, and the minor league first baseman they selected in the expansion draft who became their everyday left fielder for two seasons will now become their third baseman.

Jeff Conine holds the second longest current consecutive games played streak (277), just slightly off the pace of Cal Ripken Jr. Conine's third base training began in the Instructional League instead of the major leagues due to the strike.

Offensively, the 29 year old Conine established himself as a major league impact player in 1994, carrying the Marlins when Sheffield spent an extended period on the disabled list. Conine batted .319 and led the club in RBI (82), hits (144) and doubles (27). While Conine is not nearly as devastating an offensive force as Sheffield, he is a solid, professional, productive player who had a career year in 1994. Conine can be relied upon to remain in the lineup every day and accumulate solid numbers. If Conine can handle the defensive adjustment to third base, his relative offensive value will improve, as the average offensive production of NL third sackers lags behind that of leftfielders. Look for Conine to drop back to .280, with 16 home runs and 80 RBI in 1995.

Jerry Browne was very quietly one of the most valuable Marlins in 1994. After starting the season deep on the bench, Browne eventually worked his way into the starting lineup at second base, third base and in the outfield; he took over the leadoff spot and sparked the Marlins' offense with his .392 on base percentage. However, he also struggled in the field,

committing 15 errors in 62 games at third base; he's much better coming off of the bench than in a starting role. Browne became a free agent after the 1994 season but Florida hopes to re-sign him as insurance for Conine and as a good bench player. Look for a .275-2-25-5 season in 300 at bats by Browne in 1995.

Dave Magadan can do just one thing well: get on base. He doesn't hit for power, run or field well, but his singles and walks add up to a better career on base percentage than Tony Gwynn (.389 to .386). Magadan had just eight extra base hits and no steals in 1994, so his value is totally in his batting average. A free agent after last season, Magadan will probably play in the majors somewhere in 1995 and put up a .280-1-15 season in about 200 at bats.

Veteran Mario Diaz hit .325 in 77 at bats as a pinch hitter and extra glove on Florida's bench, but that batting average is 66 points better than his career average and Diaz has no power or speed. The 33 year old Diaz will again battle for a utility infield role and getting his annual ration of 80 at bats, hitting .220 with no homers.

At the age of 36, veteran Nick Capra had a fine season for Triple-A Edmonton, hitting .304 with 25 steals, while striking out just 25 times in 382 at bats. Capra has garnered just 54 at bats in his lengthy career and hasn't hit a major league homer in 13 seasons (as a rookie for the Rangers in 1982). He's worth a cheer for his perseverance, but is obviously worthless in Rotisserie. Should he get another major league chance it would truly be a Capra-like story - Frank Capra, that is.

A year ago Terry Jorgensen was a top candidate for the Twins vacant third base job. Now, at age 28, he's stuck behind career minor leaguer Capra, playing Double-A ball in Portland. He has failed miserably in three separate major league trials. He should study Capra intently as his career is following the same path.

Selected as the Class A Florida State League's best defensive third baseman by Baseball America, Lou Lucca is a good average hitter and has some doubles

power. He has the kind of power stroke that should increase home run output at higher levels. Lucca has yet to play above Class A.

Lary Bump:

Victor Rodriguez, who played some third base for Triple-A Edmonton last year (.278-6-46) deserved mention solely for persevering through 18 minor league seasons, including 12 in Triple-A. He had 28 major league at bats in 1984 and 1989, with a .429 average to show for the experience. He's still only 33, but clearly not a prospect.

Terry Jorgensen, who was a teammate of Rodriguez with the Twins in 1989, was the regular third baseman at Double-A Portland (.289-14-72). The 28 year old righthanded batter has spent the last five seasons with Portland -- 1990-1993 at Portland, Oregon, and last year at Portland, Maine.

Lou Lucca, 24, was voted the Florida State League's best defensive third baseman. He may have the tools to go upstairs, for he can hit for average and righthanded power (.283-8-76) and work for walks.

Houston Astros

Bill Gilbert:

Ken Caminiti was one of three Astro infielders to have a career year in 1994. After three straight seasons with a career high 13 home runs, Caminiti erupted for 18 with 75 RBIs and a batting average of .283. Caminiti's numbers were similar to those of Tim Wallach, Bobby Bonilla and Todd Zeile among National League third basemen. Only Matt Williams clearly had a better year.

In 1995, Caminiti will be 32 years old and in the last year of a contract that will pay him over $4 million per year. Houston owner Drayton McLane has announced his intention to significantly reduce the payroll and Caminiti would appear to be a good candidate for a trade. With his strong defense and productive bat, Caminiti is a valuable player who has much higher

trade value now than he did a year ago.

If Caminiti leaves, the heir apparent is 24 year old Phil Nevin, the top draft choice overall in 1993. After a .286-10-93-8 debut at Class AAA Tucson in 1993, Nevin failed to improve in his second Triple-A season, as he endured a long slump and finished at .263-12-79-3. Nevin has not shown the power that was expected when he was drafted and his defense is not close to Caminiti's standard. The 1995 season is a critical one for Nevin if he is to achieve his potential. At this point, he could still have a successful major league career, but he needs to start producing soon.

Next in line is 25 year old Mike Groppuso, a compensation pick in the 1991 draft. Groppuso hit .264-12-47-6 in his second season at Class AA Jackson. He has shown some improvement each season, but has not hit for a high average because of a tendency to strike out frequently (97 Ks in 352 at bats in 1994). A few years down the road is 21 year old Chris Truby, an undrafted free agent who was the MVP in the New York-Pennsylvania League in 1994. Truby showed four category potential with a .323-7-61-20 log in 76 games.

Lary Bump:

Phil Nevin was the first pick in the entire draft in 1992 out of Cal State-Fullerton. His performance last year (.263-12-79) was hampered by migraines. Nevin, who never has played pro ball above or below Triple-A, was expected to cause headaches for Houston opponents in '94 until Ken Caminiti turned in his big season. The 24 year old Nevin bats righthanded. His best chance this year will for the Astros to dump Caminiti's salary. Juan Guerrero, who showed some promise as a winter-draft-dictated member of the Astros' roster in 1992, spent '93 on a legal sabbatical, then returned to bat .290-7-49 at Tucson. He could have value as a pinch hitter if nothing else.

The Astros sent Double-A third baseman Mike Groppuso to the Arizona Fall League. He batted just .264-12-47 at Jackson, so the fall assignment may have been more to determine whether the 25 year old righthanded batter has a future than to state their faith in him as a prospect.

Los Angeles Dodgers

Giving Tim Wallach another year will deflate the potentially biggest bust rookie of 1995, Ron Coomer. It would have been fun to watch people pay $15 to $20 for the paper slugger Coomer, and then get nine homers with a .260 average from a full-time player, and wonder what went wrong. Maybe Coomer will yet surface some other place and create the opportunity for someone to blunder into him.

Greg Gajus:

Tim Wallach (.280-23-78-0) made many analysts look bad in 1994, producing one of the most astounding comeback seasons in recent memory. While good comebacks are not terribly uncommon, 36 year olds coming off of three consecutive awful seasons to go .280-23-78 is virtually unprecedented. Wallach credited hitting coach Reggie Smith for adjustments that have now extended his career for another couple of years. At his advanced age, a repeat performance is unlikely. Free agent Wallach may also have to take a pay cut in 1995 to get a regular job.

If Wallach does not return, Ron Coomer is considered the favorite for the job. A 28 year old righthanded hitter acquired in a 1993 trade with the White Sox, Coomer hit .338-22-123-4 for Triple-A Albuquerque and was listed as the best defensive third baseman by Baseball America. His offensive numbers appear good, but when you adjust for both the high hitting numbers Pacific Coast League and his advanced age, Coomer is not a great prospect. The most to expect is probably something like Eric Karros - 15 to 20 home runs with a .270 average.

Primarily a pinch-hitter, Dave Hansen (.341-0-5-0) could play third base if Wallach and Coomer were not in the picture. As a regular, Hansen would hit for average without much power.

Jeff Treadway (.299-0-5-1) is still around as a lefty pinch-hitter and infield reserve. Like Hansen, he doesn't play enough to have any Rotisserie value no matter how well he hits.

Lary Bump:

Ron Coomer was considered the Pacific Coast League's best defensive third baseman. He also put up big PCL-type batting numbers (.338-22-123). At age 28, the righthanded batter is not a good long-range prospect, but he could be the Dodgers' 1995 third baseman. Double-A third baseman Henry Blanco, 23, has struggled each of his two seasons at San Antonio. The righthanded batter hit .230-6-38 last year.

A better hope for the future is Willie Otanez, who will be 22 in April. He responded well to a slight demotion from the California League to the Florida State League. He showed very good power (.277-19-72) in a league with big parks. He may be back in the California League this season, but don't be surprised if he jumps to the Texas League and puts up some big numbers.

Montreal Expos

John Perrotto:

Sean Berry is much maligned in Montreal. He is knocked for his glove. He is knocked for his supposed lack of power. However, he had a fine season in 1994 and the Expos could do worse.

Berry hit .278-11-41-14. It wasn't a spectacular season but he put up good power and speed numbers. He's not on the expressway to Cooperstown but it's conceivable he can have a 20/20 season; there's nothing wrong with that.

What might prevent Berry from keeping the job for the long term are shortstop prospects Mark Grudzielanek, Geoff Blum and Hiram Bocachica down on the farm (see Shortstops). One of them could force Wil Cordero to eventually move from shortstop to third base or take the hot corner for themselves. That won't happen in 1995, though.

Shane Andrews had a decent season at Class AAA Ottawa in 1994, hitting .254-16-85-6, but he, too, is

not ready for the majors in 1995.

The Expos tried journeyman Jeff Gardner at third base after he failed in a full season trial as San Diego's second baseman in 1993. Gardner hit just .219-0-1-0 for the Expos and .257-0-16-6 for Ottawa. He has now proven to everyone that he is not a major league player.

Lary Bump:

A 1990 first-round draft pick, Shane Andrews showed great improvement in '94. He made better contact and improved in the field. His home run totals were down each of the last two years, but he will be a big, strong power hitter in the big leagues. At Ottawa last season, the 23 year old righthanded batter's numbers were .254-16-85. He can do even better if he goes back this year. Expect him in the majors before September.

Matt Raleigh, who played both first base and third base, was voted the Midwest League's best power prospect (.274-34-83). With 138 strikeouts, the righthanded batter made contact only 260 times, and hit home runs on 13 percent of those occasions. He's more than a year older than Andrews, so Raleigh's only chance to reach the majors would be in a different organization.

At West Palm Beach, Isreal Alcantara, 21, also showed power from the right side (.285-15-69).

New York Mets

In terms of draft enthusiasm, every player goes through a sort of product life cycle. The trends are especially visible among top players who attract early attention and succeed in developing good major league careers. In the beginning, many players get excessive hype. Top draft picks who bat .340 in the California league suddenly look like can't-miss $30 players, and of course many of them do miss attaining such stature.

Among rising stars, overhype continues into the

rookie season. Usually the player has a disappointing rookie season and "the market" adjusts his value downward immediately (often creating bargains in cases of overadjustment). But in cases of players who reach the star level quickly and stay there for years, the period of decline also contains distinct phases. In early decline, the player's price is sustained by recollections of past glory and hopes for a return to greatness. In late decline, "everybody" knows that the player is past his prime and headed downward, and prices drop sharply in most of the more competitive leagues. Often the late decline period is punctuated by negative press, including qualitative criticisms and profiles focused on attitude and ego. When the press is over-eager, the price drop can come so early as to create a bargain situation.

Bobby Bonilla was not yet a bargain in 1994, costing an average of $30 and delivering more like $20 of value, uninflated. Likewise Bonilla was a disappointment in 1992-1993 because of injuries. But I have to wonder, if the media make him look bad enough (and he sure does get enough unfavorable press in New York and nationally) if a $20 Bonilla isn't a pretty good buy with some upward potential.

Bonilla has been a consistently strong run producer, especially when viewed on a per at bat basis. If the Mets succeed in strengthening their hitting, as moves like the Carl Everett acquisition indicate, Bonilla could be coming to a late peak in his career, at age 32-33. If everyone in your league believes that Bonilla is overhyped and overpriced, paying $20 plus inflation would be an OK move, especially for a team that doesn't need to take chances.

Behind Bonilla, the Mets have Butch Huskey who toiled at Triple-A Norfolk all of last year after reporting overweight to spring training. Huskey went to the Arizona Fall League to play some first and third base and some left field, making him a likely cornerman and outfield backup for the major league roster. Huskey offers good power, some speed, and a better batting average than his minor league record would indicate.

Lary Bump:

The good news in Butch Huskey's '94 season was that he was nowhere near as heavy at the end of the year as he was in spring training, when the Mets sent him to a fat farm. His numbers at Triple-A Norfolk were not good (.228-10-57). He's best known for his power, but he can run despite his size (16 stolen bases) and he is a good glove man. The righthanded batter is just 23.

Philadelphia Phillies

Tony Blengino:

1994 was an utterly wasted season for Phils' third baseman Dave Hollins. After his breakthrough 1992 season (27 homers, 104 runs, 93 RBI), 29 year old Hollins lost part of 1993 to a broken right wrist then started 1994 slowly before breaking a bone in his left hand while sliding into first base. He spent several weeks in rehabilitation, playing rightfield for Triple-A Scranton-Wilkes Barre before re-injuring the same hand in his first game back for Philadelphia.

Hollins' return to his previous level of performance is a gamble as wrist injuries are often slow to heal and can seriously diminish a hitter's bat speed; witness Eric Davis' problems for example. Hollins has now broken wrist bones on three different occasions.

Should Hollins' hitting deteriorate due to his injuries, he's not going to stay in the majors for his fielding ability. He's a poor fielder with a strong, but erratic throwing arm; Hollins has made 38 errors in his last 186 games at third base, mostly on wild throws. While the rightfield experiment with Hollins has ended, he might shift to first base should John Kruk not return.

Kim Batiste's tour-de-force in the 1993 postseason and injuries to Hollins and shortstop Kevin Stocker in 1994 put Batiste in the spotlight. He failed miserably. 27 year old Batiste had a .239 OBP (just one walk in 210 plate appearances), a .278 slugging average and made 12 errors in only 42 games at third

base. To say Batiste has poor plate discipline is like saying Babe Ruth had a little power; Batiste has drawn just nine walks (four of them intentional walks) in 548 major league plate appearances. He also managed his first career stolen base in 1994.

Batiste can't hit, field or run. Why is he still in the majors?

27 year old Tom Quinlan is a slick fielding journeyman who hit very little in short major league stints for Toronto and Philadelphia. He has decent power but strikes out far too much. At the big league level, Quinlan is no more than an extra bat on the bench.

Converted catcher Jason Moler stumbled at Triple-A (.243-2-16-2) and was demoted to Class AA Reading where he hit only six homers after posting solid power numbers in the Class A Florida State League in 1993. At age 25, Moler needs to begin producing in the high minors quickly to remain a prospect.

The best long range minor league prospect is 20 year old Scott Rolen, a second round pick in 1993. The Class A South Atlantic League All-Star third baseman was also selected as Baseball America's best defensive third baseman in the SAL. He put together a .294-14-72-6 year (with 34 doubles) for Spartanburg in 1994. At 6'4", 210 pounds, Rolen should develop power as he matures; lower minor league doubles often become high minors homers as youngsters gain strength and learn to drive the ball. Rolen could be in Philadelphia for a long haul beginning in 1997.

Lary Bump:

Among those available at third base are Craig Worthington and The Human Swing-and-a-Miss, Tom Quinlan. Both bat righthanded. Worthington, who will be 30 in April, batted .288-17-69 with the Cubs' top farm last year, then signed with the Reds and was drafted in December by the Phillies. He last played in the majors with the '92 Indians. Quinlan had just 297 at bats between Scranton (.240-9-23) and Philadelphia, but still had more than 100 strikeouts for the seventh time in eight pro seasons. (He fanned

99 times in 326 at bats at Knoxville in 1988.) Either Worthington or Quinlan could handle a backup job defensively. Worthington would be a possibility for full-time duty if Dave Hollins moves to first base.

Rob Grable, 25, played just 42 games at Reading (.267-2-18) because of injury. The righthanded batter is running out of time to make it in the majors. Kevin Sefcik, a 24 year old righthanded batter, went to the Arizona Fall League after going .285-2-46-30 in the Florida State League.

Down the road is a real prospect. Nineteen year old Scott Rolen, the Phillies' second-round draft pick in 1993, was voted the Sally League's best defensive third baseman, and he batted .294-14-72. His 34 doubles indicate that he could develop more home run power. The righthanded batter could reach Double-A this season, and the majors by the end of 1996. There's more about Jason Moler under catchers.

Pittsburgh Pirates

John Perrotto:

Seven years after making Jeff King, from the University of Arkansas, the top pick in the 1986 amateur draft, the Pirates thought he had arrived in 1993; he drove in 98 runs as the primary cleanup hitter. However, King regressed in 1994, finishing with .263-5-42-3 totals. No longer is he a lock to be the Pirates' starting third baseman.

Economics could push King out of Pittsburgh, which is struggling to survive as a small market club. King made $2.4 million last season and is arbitration eligible. The Pirates are more likely to fire the hugely popular Jim Leyland as manager before gambling $3 million or more on King in 1995. It ain't gonna happen.

The Pirates dispatched failed prospect Kevin Young to Class AAA at last year's All-Star break and told him to play exclusively at third base. Though he shot quickly through the Pirates' farm system, Young

failed as their regular first baseman in 1993. However, third base could be his ticket back to the majors; he will be first in line to replace King.

Young hit .276-5-27-3 with Buffalo. Those are not eye popping numbers but he seemed a completely different player, showing an aggressiveness he lacked during his previous stints in the majors, which included a .205-1-11-0 performance for Pittsburgh last season. Young is an intelligent player and can make the necessary adjustments to play in the majors. He may not reach the superstardom predictions of a couple of years ago but he can become a solid big league player.

Pittsburgh native John Wehner became a hometown hero when he .340 in 37 games as a rookie in 1991. However, that season ended early because of back surgery and he hasn't been the same since. He could still fight his way onto the roster this year as a backup second baseman, third baseman and outfielder.

Give Wehner points for perseverance. He was buried by the Pirates after the 1993 season and wasn't even in the major league camp last spring. However, he hit .303-7-44-21 at Buffalo and was called back to the majors at the All-Star break. He went 1-for-4 with three RBI in two big league games before a broken hand ended his season.

Jay Cranford made 66 errors as a shortstop for Class A Augusta in 1993, then moved to third base in 1994 and had a decent year. He hit .264-13-53-6 for Class A Salem and .186-0-5-0 with Class AA Carolina. The Pirates like his bat but, oh, that glove...!

Ken Bonifay is the nephew of Pirates General Manager Cam Bonifay. Nepotism may have helped him get drafted out of Georgia Tech in the 50th round of the 1991 amateur draft. However, production has kept him around longer than most players chosen so late. After hitting 18 homers for Class A Salem in 1993, Bonifay batted just .249-7-45-3 at Carolina. However, he was plagued by injuries and is still scuffling to keep his big league hopes alive.

Lary Bump:

If the Pirates were to lose Jeff King to free agency, Kevin Young would be first in line for the third base job. The 25 year old righthanded batter simply has not produced in three stints at first base and third base in Pittsburgh. Last year he hit .205-1-11 with the Bucs and .276-5-27 at Buffalo. It may be too soon to write him off, but in another year it may be too late for him to make it.

Ken Bonifay struggled in his Double-A debut (.221-6-28). At age 24, the lefthanded batted might already be out of baseball if he weren't Cam Bonifay's nephew.

Jay Cranford advanced last season from Class A Salem (.264-13-53) to play 17 games in the Southern League. The righthanded batter will be 24 in April.

In December's major league draft, the Pirates selected Freddy Garcia, 22. The righthanded batter hasn't progressed past short-season ball in the Toronto organization. In 1994, he batted .285-13-40 at St. Catharines.

St. Louis Cardinals

John Perrotto:

It seems to be the "in" thing to knock Todd Zeile. Whatever the Cardinals third baseman does, it never seems to be enough. He's always said to be the kind of player who doesn't live up to his potential.

But what, exactly, is so wrong with Zeile? Since being demoted to Class AAA Louisville in 1992 for a refresher course in hitting, Zeile has been an outstanding run producer. Last year he had a fine season, finishing at .267-19-75-1. A lot of clubs would take that. As a converted catcher, his defense is even improving.

Zeile could be on the move again in 1995. The Cardinals are considering the idea of moving him to first base in the likely event Gregg Jefferies leaves as

a free agent. While the Cardinals would fill a first base hole, it would create one on the other side of the infield. They really don't have another third baseman ready to step in.

One possibility would be converting hard hitting Louisville second baseman Darrel Deak (see Second Basemen) to third base.

The Cardinals also have veteran Scott Coolbaugh, who hit .190-2-6-0 in a brief stint in the majors last year and .303-19-75-3 for Louisville. Coolbaugh failed in previous opportunites as a third base prospect with Texas and San Diego; it's doubtful he can win the job at age 28.

Lary Bump:

With Todd Zeile eligible for free agency, the Cardinals faced the possibility of needing a third baseman. Two righthanded-hitting third basemen had good numbers at Triple-A Louisville, but they were 28 year old Scott Coolbaugh and 32 year old Tracy Woodson. Coolbaugh, a minor league free agent, was hot from the beginning of spring training through his time in the American Association (.303-19-75), and earned some time in St. Louis.

The Orioles released Woodson after he started .237-5-36 and made rookie-type mistakes at Triple-A Rochester. At Louisville, he pounded the ball (.348-7-26).

At Double-A Arkansas, Dan Cholowsky, also a second baseman, didn't make contact (.222), but powered 14 homers and 51 RBI and stole 20 bases. The 24 year old righthanded batter is not a strong prospect, unless he can turn things around at Louisville this season.

Another 24 year old righty swinger, Mike Gulan, batted a disappointing .242-8-56 in the Florida State League.

San Diego Padres

Hank Widmer:

Just like they tried to do at first base, the Padres gave opportunities to several players at third base. No one could hold down the job.

Craig Shipley ended up as the starter by default, hitting far over his head (his .333 average in 1994 is 64 points over his career average). But, Shipley is really just a utility infielder and shouldn't get 240 at bats again.

Fred Matos:

When Archi Cianfrocco's weaknesses - hitting breaking pitches and lefties- became a drain on the Padres offense, Scott Livingstone was acquired from the Tigers in a trade for reliever Gene Harris. Livingstone is a singles hitter who can post a good average, but doesn't give you much else. Because of his lack of power, Livingstone is going to have to battle for regular playing time every year. Nevertheless, he is the favorite to open the 1995 season in the Padres' starting lineup. Being a singles hitter with little power or speed makes Livingstone a relative bust in Rotisserie; he's worth less than $10.

Cianfrocco began last year as the Padres starting third baseman, but slumped badly and lost his job when the Padres traded for Livingstone. He finally ended up in Triple-A as an outfielder. He won't be back to the majors until he learns to hit breaking balls.

Veteran utility infielder Craig Shipley stepped in and took over third base occasionally, appearing in 53 games. He hit .333-4-30 in 240 at bats, a very surprising output when compared to his career numbers of .238-5-41 in 495 at bats before last year, compiled over six seasons. Shipley is now 32 years old and his best role is as a utility infielder. He should again revert to his previous .240 level of hitting in 1995.

Career minor leaguer Keith Lockhart also played some third base for the Padres last year. He's now 30

years old and has played at Triple-A for four different organizations over the last four years. He'll be back in Triple-A again in 1995.

Julio Bruno was the Triple-A starter at Las Vegas last year where he hit .260-6-52. He's only 23 and will likely spend another year in Triple-A to improve his hitting.

Lary Bump:

California League pitchers couldn't get out Julio Bruno, 22, the first week of last season (.560-2-7 in six games), so the Padres jumped him all the way to the Pacific Coast League. Batting righthanded, he compiled a .260-6-52 season there. He'll have a chance to do even better at Las Vegas this season.

Twenty-three year old switch hitter Jason Hardtke, moving over from shortstop, bombed in his Double-A debut (.235-5-29). He has averaged .291 in five pro seasons, so there's still hope for him if he starts better this year at Memphis.

Sean Drinkwater, also 23 and also a former short-stop, had similar difficulty in the Texas League (.237-5-39), and didn't do any better back at Rancho Cucamonga (.229-1-12).

Derrek Lee, the Padres' 1993 first-round draft pick, shifted from first base last year. He has held his own in the California League in each of his two pro seasons (.267-8-53-18 in '94). The righthanded batter is still just 19. He's a definite major league power prospect. He could be in the Southern League this season, and could move up fast.

San Francisco Giants

Steven Rubio:

Matt Williams will be holding down the hot corner for the Giants for many years to come. His prodigious power drew special attention as he chased Roger Maris' record in 1994, but Matt has been a tremendous slugger for years and he adds Gold Glove

defense as well. Williams is the type of player who will always be overrated (his on base percentage is awful), but he is nevertheless one of the top power hitters and one of the best third basemen in the game today.

The third basemen in the Giants' high minors, ex-phenom Gary Scott and Joel Chimelis, both appear to be career minor leaguers. They will not unseat Matt Williams.

The team does have an outstanding sleeper, though, in Bill Mueller; he walked more than 100 times in 1994, hit for gap power and was named as the Class A San Jose Giants' Defensive Player of the Year. Mueller is already 24 years old, though, and Williams would seem to block any chance Mueller has of making the majors, but he's extremely promising and well worth watching.

Lary Bump:

Gary Scott, who bombed twice with the Cubs, landed in Phoenix last season (.286-9-56). The righthanded batter is still just 26, and could earn some playing time spelling Matt Williams.

Joel Chimelis twice has batted better than .300 in partial Triple-A seasons, yet the Giants returned him to Double-A for the fourth year in 1994. The righthanded batter hit .295-10-72, but at 27, he no longer is a prospect.

Bill Mueller had a .302-5-72 season in the California League. The switch hitter was a 15th-round draft choice in 1993. He also has played second base and shortstop, and might be better suited to the middle infield or a utility role. He is an excellent leadoff hitter; his 103 walks last season contributed to a .435 on-base percentage. The major drawback is his age (24).

SHORTSTOP:
TACTICAL CONSIDERATIONS

It's not just the Larkin and Ripken show anymore folks! For years it seemed, after Barry Larkin, Cal Ripken and (sometimes) Tony Fernandez were taken, it really didn't matter much who you ended up with. The rest of the shortstop population hit like a butterfly and stung like a flea. Look out! Things are actually changing. Larkin and Ripken have some company, and soon Barry and Cal will be hard pressed to remain among the elite.

The new elite are all young, have good power, and can run. It's almost like having a bunch of good outfielders suddenly eligible at short. In the National League Wil Cordero of the Expos is still a couple years from his prime, but what a sweet young hitter. He's just 23 years old and has more than two major league seasons under his belt. He would've hit 20 homers if the strike hadn't interfered (and he might have gotten to strut his stuff in the play-offs and World Series, which would have wrecked his little remaining sleeper potential). In a perverse way we can thank Bud Selig and his pals for unwittingly helping to keep Cordero under wraps.

In 1995, with Larkin beginning to fade, Cordero should emerge as the best offensive shortstop in the National League. Larkin still is brilliant. His power is holding up, and he is still able to steal bases almost at will, and his batting average will help any team. Shawon Dunston was a comeback pick of the year in 1994. He had missed large parts of two consecutive years, but he came back strong and kept playing hard just like his former self.

On the youth list in the NL, add Royce Clayton right after Cordero. Also keep hoping for Andujar Cedeno to show more of the power and excitement that he

teased us with back in 1991 when he was just reaching age 22.

In the American league, the wealth of newcomers is even more promising. Alex Gonzalez gets another try in Toronto and will very likely succeed this time. Alex Rodriguez has a clear shot to be the best/youngest player in many years, as the Mariners regular shortstop. All he needs is a solid spring training to come north with that role. Then there is Derek Jeter of the Yankees, no slouch in the developing picture of superstars for the year 2000. John Valentin had a wonderful season in Boston. The batting average was a bit inflated but the power is real and should produce double digit home runs this year. He isn't in the class of Rodriguez, Gonzalez, and Jeter, but he's a safer bet for 1995.

In both leagues this year, I advocate a "$1 shortstop approach." This is because the famous veterans will be bid out of sight with so many unknown quantities around them, and the future superstars will be bid to the full value of their future value (remember: it takes only two bidders to drive the price up). Look into the middle ground, the second and third year players who haven't yet done anything fantastic. Bargain hunting can go into the $10 range (uninflated) for a player like Andujar Cedeno.

For the record:

Likely to be bargains: Gary DiSarcina, Denny Hocking, Mark Lewis, Chipper Jones, Andujar Cedeno, Royce Clayton, Walt Weiss.

Likely to be overvalued: Greg Gagne, Pat Listach, Cal Ripken, Ozzie Smith, Orlando Miller.

AMERICAN LEAGUE
SHOPTSTOPS

With the advent of so much young talent entering the majors at shortstop, many veterans are being pushed aside. Rookies are likely to win regular jobs at shortstop (or at least part-time jobs) in Seattle, Texas, Toronto, and Atlanta, with other future stars soon on the way with the Yankees, Expos, Cardinals and Padres.

The displaced veterans won't just disappear, however. Many will serve as tutors to usher in the rookies before moving on to greener pastures. Others will shift other positions or move on to new teams.

For Rotisserie planning, owners should realize that most of the regular shortstops in both leagues will change teams or positions or have significantly reduced roles in the near future. Added together with the advance of the young shortstops, these changes mean it is unwise to look for a long-term, veteran solution at shortstop. In particular, signing an expensive veteran to a long-term contract hurts in two ways: 1) if the veteran's role changes his value could drop dramatically and 2) the opportunity is reduced for grabbing a cheap youngster whose value could climb through the roof.

Remaining free agents include Jeff Blauser (from Atlanta) and Alan Trammell (from Detroit), although both are expect to re-sign with their original teams. The biggest free agent maneuver at shortstop was accomplished when the Yankees acquired Tony Fernandez.

Baltimore Orioles

Fred Matos:

Cal Ripken has played in 2009 consecutive games, and he needs 2131 to break Lou Gehrig's record. If all goes well, he should break Gehrig's consecutive game streak on August 18. The media attention should increase to a level equivalent to that on Pete Rose when he was nearing Ty Cobb's record. The impact of the increased pressure and media attention on Ripken's performance can't really be assessed.

Like the Energizer bunny, Ripken keeps going and going. He had another solid season last year, and he should have another good year in 1995. You can generally figure on .270-18-85, but the RBI statistic depends largely on the abilities of leadoff man Brady Anderson and the second batter to get on base.

Since there is a shortage of good hitters at shortstop, Ripken is overbid in many leagues. If you need good offense from shortstop or the middle infielder slot,

you should go higher than his true $15-18 value, even as high as $30, but only if you have big producers at low salaries to balance things out.

Manny Alexander is a very good prospect who has the misfortune of being behind Ripken. He is a good fielder and a weak but improving hitter who can steal bases. He is out of minor league options, so he must stay with the Orioles in 1995 or be traded as he is unlikely to clear waivers without being claimed. He was tried at second base in Triple-A last year but played very poorly, so a utility infielder job may not work out for him. Alexander was much more comfortable back at shortstop, finishing with a solid .317 average over his last 42 games.

Utility man Tim Hulett has backed up Ripken over the past few years. If the Orioles carry Alexander, Hulett may be looking for another team.

Lary Bump:

Manny Alexander's defense is just what you'd expect from a kid from San Pedro de Macoris. Much of his '94 season was wasted as the Orioles shuttled him between shortstop and second base in an attempt to make him a utility infielder. His defense and offense (.249-6-39) both suffered. His bat is weak; he has good speed (30 stolen bases), but is an inattentive baserunner. He won't have a chance to play shortstop in Baltimore for another 120 games or so.

Boston Red Sox

Alan Boodman:

John Valentin has emerged over the past two seasons as arguably the best shortstop in the American League, a status quite unexpected for a player who had shown almost nothing at the plate until reaching the majors in 1992. He was not overvalued going into 1994, because many fans viewed Valentin's 1993 season as a pleasant surpise, but likely a fluke. Players whose rookie seasons occur at age 26 do not tend to develop much since they are already in their prime. Many such players decline after a solid debut.

But not Valentin. After taking control of the job in May of 1993, only his sometimes grouchy knees have kept him off the field. About the only negatives in his package are those knees and the fact that due to his age, significant further improvement is probably not in the cards. If Valentin simply maintains his current level of performance for another half-decade, Sox fans won't be too unhappy.

Like Jody Reed, Valentin is adept at lining pitches off of the Green Monster. In fact, Valentin's overall offensive attributes are similiar to those that Reed had while in Boston. To predict what Valentin may hit over the next few seasons (knees permitting), take Reed's best seasons (1989-1991) and add a half dozen homers. For 1995, expect something like .295-13-70-4, with substantial doubles and runs scored as well. In the A.L. only Cal Ripken has any real chance to beat those numbers by much.

While Valentin spent time on the D.L. in 1994, Carlos Rodriguez stepped in and performed well enough to earn a shot at a utility spot somewhere, having been released by Boston last December. Rodriguez had been an adequate hitter in the minors, playing at the AA and AAA levels in the Yankees' organization for the previous four years. He lacks both power and speed, but supplements his offense by drawing more walks than the typical Latin ballplayer. Now age 27, his chance for any kind of major league career depends on his ability to maintain a batting average near his 1994 mark of .287 while providing good defense at any position he's asked to play. Wherever he plays, Rodriguez will likely fall short of the 174 AB's he received last year, and is a non-pick for Rotisserie purposes.

Lary Bump:

There is no immediate threat to John Valentin, unless the Bosox decide to rush last year's first-round draft choice, Nomar Garciaparra (all 105 pro at bats of him). The righthanded batter out of Georgia Tech held out a long time before signing. He then played well in the high Class A Florida State League (.295-1-16). He played like a man with much more experience in the Arizona Fall League.

Triple-A Pawtucket used several of its Rodriguezes at shortstop, and at Double-A New Britain was 24 year old Randy Brown (.224-8-30).

California Angels

Tomas Perez, acquired from Montreal, was subsequently sold to the Blue Jays. He's a few years away from the majors.

Hank Widmer:

The best of the Angel infielders is Gary DiSarcina who had his best offensive year in 1994. DiSarcina is a solid player who's not going to produce a lot offensively but he'll play just about everyday. If you can't get any of the top shortstops in the league on your team, you could do worse than DiSarcina.

Fred Matos:

The Angels are very pleased with Gary DiSarcina's play at shortstop, and they signed him to a long term contract. He had a career high .260 batting average last year, and was on his way to setting other career highs but was stopped short by the strike. His walks were up last year indicating that he has improved his patience at the plate (a good sign).

The Angels selected Tim Harkrider in the 8th round of the 1993 draft. He quickly learned to use wooden bats, hitting a surprising .260 in 200 at bats in Class A in 1993, and .271 in the Class AA Texas League last year. He is progressing nicely, especially for an 8th round pick, and should be a candidate to make the Angels in 1996.

DiSarcina is not going to turn into a Cal Ripken type of shortstop and about the best you can expect is .250-.260 with three dingers and seven or eight stolen bases. His peak Rotisserie value is around $6.

Lary Bump:

The one secure spot in the California infield is shortstop. Rod Correia, 27, could return to the majors as a backup to Gary Disarcina or as a utility infielder. Correia batted .274-6-49 in the Pacific Coast League.

Brian Grebeck uses his lack of height (5'-7") to draw walks. He has a .422 on-base percentage in his five minor league seasons. That mark came down a bit last year even though he hit well (.315-1-17 at Double-A Midland; .299-2-18 at Vancouver). At 27, the righthanded batter really is not a prospect.

Tim Harkrider, 23, may have a better chance. The switch hitter, an eighth-round draft pick in 1993, batted .279-1-49 at Midland. He stole 13 bases, but was thrown out 12 times.

A longshot for this season is 21 year old Tomas Perez, selected in the major league draft from the Montreal organization. The switch hitter batted .262-8-47 in the Midwest League.

Chicago White Sox

Stuart Shea:

The Sox' decision to sign Ozzie Guillen to a long-term contract (he is inked through 1997 with an option for 1998) locks the team into his services for several years. Unfortunately Guillen's abilities have diminished quickly. While he still hits for decent average, his speed is gone and his range at shortstop is now only mediocre. Of course, his batting average, lack of power, walks, and stolen bases are very consistent, if consistency is what your Rotisserie team needs. Craig Grebeck is an excellent backup to Guillen, and in reality ought to be the starter.

Brandon Wilson has been on the Sox' short (sic) list for a few seasons. Unfortunately, he played extremely badly for Triple-A Nashville in 1994. Wilson is a gutty player who steals bases, draws walks, and shows fine range. However, with Guillen above him, Wilson's best hope to make the bigs are as a utility man with Chicago or to force a trade elsewhere. Hitting in the low .200s, as he did last year, won't help him.

Lary Bump:

Of the shortstop prospects in the White Sox organization, Glenn Disarcina (Gary's brother) now seems the best. Though Glenn is not a great offensive threat, he led Birmingham in RBI last season (.257-7-57-10). The 24 year old righthanded batter will start '95 at Nashville. Given Ozzie Guillen's injury history, who knows what might happen from there?

While Brandon Wilson flopped in Triple-A (.224-5-26-13), Craig Wilson came on as the Carolina League's best defensive shortstop. He also showed a good batting eye (58 walks, 44 strikeouts) and an ability to drive in runs (.264-4-66). Before we get too excited, let's see how this Wilson, a 24 year old righthanded batter with little speed, does in the upper minors. Don't confuse him with the former Cardinals and Royals utilityman.

A similar type of player to Craig Wilson is Wil Polidor, a 21 year old switch hitter who batted .285-3-36 in the Midwest League.

Cleveland Indians

Mark Lewis was dealt to Cincinnati where he'll back up rookie sensation Willie Greene. The top reserve role will go to re-signed Alvaro Espinoza; he has little Rotisserie value.

Torey Lovullo, described under Third Basemen, has arrived from Seattle. He'll fight Espinoza for a reserve role with the Indians.

Tony Blengino:

Omar Vizquel, 28, is one of the least powerful batters in the majors. He did flirt with .300 for most of the 1994 season, before a pre-strike tailspin dragged him down to .273. His slugging percentage was a meager .325, as he managed only 12 extra base hits. For the third straight season, he reached double figures in steals, with 13. More importantly, he was thrown out only four times in 1994, after being successful on only 50% of his attempts in 1992 and 1993 combined. His

decent speed is the only reason to ever consider drafting him; he is such a good fielder that he will never be removed from the lineup, no matter how poorly he hits. Defensively, he possesses above average range and made only six errors in 1994 - three of them in one game! Expect him to hit .265, with one HR and 15 steals in 1995.

One member of the Indians' organization who was not happy with the acquisition of Vizquel was former number one pick Mark Lewis. Lewis, 25, was first handed the Indians' shortstop job way back in 1991. He performed competently for the last half of 1991 and all of 1992, but lost his job to Felix Fermin in 1993. All involved assumed that this was a temporary arrangement, to last only until Lewis realized that he had the ability to be an outstanding shortstop. After he wasn't rewarded with a promotion for his excellent 1993 season, Lewis responded with a lackluster season at Triple-A Charlotte in 1994. He hit only .259, and though he had always previously displayed good power for a middle infielder, he could only manage a .387 slugging percentage. The Indians are frustrated by Lewis' step backwards in 1994, but traded him to Cincinnati for Tim Cotto in December.

Damian Jackson, 21, was skipped over a level to Double-A Canton-Akron, and ranked among the youngest Double-A regulars. His performance certainly didn't suffer, as he was named the best defensive shortstop in the Eastern League by Baseball America. Offensively, he has hit .269 in each of the last two seasons, and managed 29 doubles in 1994. His chief attribute is his speed - he has 92 steals and an 80% success rate in his three pro seasons. Jackson will be the Triple-A shortstop in 1995, and will be ready to challenge for the big league job in 1996.

When the Indians traded mid-level pitching prospect Shawn Bryant to the Twins in 1993, they somehow managed to extract 17-year old phenom Enrique Wilson in return. Now 19, there aren't many better middle infield prospects in baseball than this guy. He was the second 1994 minor leaguer to reach double figures in doubles, triples, homers and steals, and was named the best defensive shortstop in the Single-A South Atlantic League by Baseball America. There's

more: Wilson's a switch-hitter, and has struck out only 50 times in over 700 pro at bats. Get your mitts on this future four-category player now.

Lary Bump:

Cleveland is high on Damian Jackson. The 21 year old was voted the Eastern League's best defensive shortstop, despite more than 50 errors. The jump from the Sally League to Double-A also doubled his strikeout total (to 121). Jackson's speed is the best part of his game; he had 37 stolen bases at Canton, where he batted .269-5-46, about the same as he'd done in A ball in '93. He was downright awful in the Arizona Fall League, but he has plenty of time to improve.

During the offseason, the Indians obtained Sparky Anderson's buddy, Torey Lovullo, from the Seattle organization. The 29 year old, switch-hitting utility candidate batted .222-2-7 with the Mariners and .294-11-47 at Calgary.

The Indians acquired 19 year old switch hitter Enrique Wilson from the Minnesota organization. He was merely the South Atlantic League's best batting prospect and best defensive shortstop. He has power and speed (.279-10-72-21 steals), and showed excellent bat control (34 strikeouts) for a youngster. He could beat Jackson to the majors in a couple of years.

Another switch hitter, 23 year old Juan Andujar, batted .260-8-46 with 14 stolen bases in his second season in the Carolina League. The former Cardinals farmhand was eligible to become a minor league free agent. In six seasons in the minors, he has played just 12 games above A ball.

Detroit Tigers

Alan Trammell was still a free agent, but expected to return to the Tigers for 1995. With age catching up to Trammell, he's no longer among the best in the league for Rotisserie. Even if he signs elsewhere, it will only be for a partial season's worth of play. He might be a good veteran for teams breaking in youngsters - like the Tigers.

Fred Matos:

Chris Gomez was considered to be a weak hitter, but surprised a lot of people with his bat early in the 994 season. He had a very strong two months and was even touted as a possible Rookie of the Year. The pitchers caught up with him, and he quickly dropped to .257, and would have dropped even further if the season didn't end early. It's doubtful that he can hit better than .250 over the course of a whole season, but he is only 23 and can improve. He was drafted in 1992, so he doesn't have much pro experience. Gomez has a big platoon differential: he hit lefthanders for .349 and righthanders for .219, something that he needs to overcome.

Alan Trammell split the shortstop job with Gomez last year, and if Gomez slumps badly, Trammell will play more. In 1995, you can expect the 37 year old Trammell to decline to the .250 area with reductions in homers and RBI's and very few stolen bases, placing his Rotisserie value around $10. Some people will remember the outstanding years Trammell had in the past and overbid, but caution is the best advice.

Many people will look at Chris Gomez's .257-8-53 and overbid on him. 1994 was a juiced-ball year, and Gomez may not hit eight homers for another three or four years, so it's best to let someone else overbid on him.

The Tigers high minor league teams are thin at shortstop, but weak hitters Jim Givens or Kirk Mendenhall may get call-ups in case of injury. Matt Brunson, the Tigers number one draft pick in 1993, is very fast but needs several more years in the minors to improve his hitting.

Lary Bump:

With Alan Trammell, Travis Fryman and Chris Gomez in Detroit, it doesn't matter yet that the nearest shortstop prospect is at least two years away. Triple-A Toledo's regular shortstop was 33 year old Jeff Kunkel (.249-11-45), in his eighth Triple-A season.

At Double-A Trenton most of the season was good-field, no-hit Kirk Mendenhall (.216-8-35). The 27 year old righthanded batter is an excellent base runner -- he totaled 28 stolen bases in 32 attempts at Trenton and Toledo last season -- but he wouldn't hit enough to get on base in the majors.

The prospects are Yuri Sanchez (.232-1-19 at Class A Lakeland; .205-0-2 in 28 games at Trenton) and Matt Brunson (.216-0-28-50 steals in the Sally League; .179-1-3 at Lakeland). Sanchez, a 21 year old lefthanded batter, was 25-for-33 as a base stealer.

Brunson, a first-round draft choice in 1993, was making his pro debut last season. The 20 year old switch hitter is likely to start this year back in the Florida State League.

Kansas City Royals

Marc Bowman:

The Royals infield glue, Greg Gagne, had an average season at the plate while displaying his usual defensive brilliance. Gagne's .259-7-51-10 season in 1994 was very much in line with his career norms. He's among the better second-tier shortstops (behind Ripken and others), and is worth about $10 to his Rotisserie teams. He's often overlooked in drafts because people focus on his excellent defense and forget that he can hit a little, too. Gagne is the kind of bargain that helps Rotisserie teams win pennants. His 1995 performance should be similar to 1994, and most of the previous years; expect .250-8-55-8 and pay less than $10 for it.

The backup shortstop is the definition of utility infielder. David Howard is probably the weakest hitter in the American League. A career .226 hitter with 23 extra-base hits in 562 at bats and marginal speed, he has no value to Rotisserie teams. The Royals need his versatility and good glove work, though, so expect him to once again be the team's utility infielder in 1995. He'll hit about .226 with no power, so don't even think about bidding on him.

Another weak-hitting utility infielder, Rico Rossy, was Triple-A Omaha's shortstop and his .235 average tells you most of what you need to know about him. He's a weaker fielder than Gagne or Howard though, so he'll only get back to the big leagues in case of an injury. He has no Rotisserie value in any case.

Shane Halter is the most advanced prospect in the Royals system. He's an excellent defensive player but a weak hitter. He has no power and only a little speed and batted .224 for Double-A Memphis in 1994. The 25 year old Halter is probably destined to be nothing more than, you guessed it, a utility infielder.

20 year old Felix Martinez is a speedy switch-hitter, but too much of a free swinger and not a great fielder. He has time to develop further and should advance to Double-A when Halter moves up to Omaha. He may eventually reach the majors as a second sacker instead. Another 20 year old, Mendy Lopez, also displayed good speed in Rookie ball, stealing 19 bases in half a season while hitting .362. He has to work on his plate discipline and fielding skills to have a real shot at major league play.

Lary Bump:

Such was the state of the 1994 American Association that Rico Rossy, the 31 year old ultimate Triple-A mediocrity, was its best defensive shortstop. After a hot start with the bat, he slumped badly (.235-11-63). He's an emergency major leaguer at best.

Twenty-five year old Shane Halter stepped backwards last season at Double-A Memphis (.225-6-35). He is a miserable 19 up, 25 down in stolen base attempts the last two seasons. The Royals sent him to the Arizona Fall League more as a suspect than as a prospect.

In the Baseball America poll, Felix Martinez was voted the Carolina League infielder with the best arm. He has the physical tools needed to advance as a shortstop, but he sometimes gets caught up in styling and hot-dogging in the field. He drew a suspension from his team late last season. At bat, the

20 year old switch-hitter hit .268-2-43-19 steals.

Cesar Morillo started last season at Wilmington (.164-0-4), but was more successful in the Midwest League (.281-2-25). The switch hitter is 21.

Milwaukee Brewers

Billy Spiers isn't really a shortstop any longer, but his free agent defection to the Mets will have an effect on the Brewer shortstop situation. The Brewers intended to play Pat Listach in centerfield and Jose Valentin at shortstop on 1995, but may have to use one of them at second base should they be unable to sign a cheap free agent.

Bill Gray:

Pat Listach played only 16 games before his knee gave out. He tried a rehab assignment and was shut down after only two games, then had surgery to repair his damaged knee. Listach's Patella tendon was removed, and Brewers GM Sal Bando said he thought the surgery should relieve the problem. Listach was scheduled to play winter ball, but he simply wasn't ready. In my opinion, I would simply forget about lusting after the Pat Listach of 1992 and the 54 stolen bases. Looking at his health history, he's had cysts, hamstring pulls, severe knee inflammation, and a patella tendon removal. Something tells me to look elsewhere for speed.

Jose Valentin, despite the shaky batting average, provided power and decent speed and must be seen as even money to be the opening day shortstop. Consider that the Brewers have said that Pat Listach, even if healthy, might play the outfield. Valentin's power is real - he once hit 17 homers in the minors. He has pretty fair plate discipline, and is only 25 years old and improving. As there are precious few shortstops with any power/speed, Valentin is still a sleeper, and a bright light on the Brewers.

Lary Bump:

The shortstop at New Orleans was Greg Smith, who

has played five Triple-A seasons in four different organizations while earning just 52 major league at bats. After his '94 season (.231-1-38-34), the 27 year old switch hitter may never make it.

Late in the season the Zephyrs called up 23 year old Mark Loretta, who had gone .315-0-38 and starred in the Texas League-Mexican League all-star series. At New Orleans, Loretta, a seventh-round draft choice in 1993, batted .210-1-14 and had considerable trouble in the field. In the California League, 21 year old Gab Martinez batted .247-0-32.

Minnesota Twins

James Benkard:

Pat Meares remains the forerunner in the derby for the position, yet he has little job security now. Meares has made admirable progress, and is a living example of the overachieving spirit of the Twins. Still, it is difficult to see him surpassing the levels he reached in '94, and a trade for a shortstop could place Meares in a utility role, which would be more suitable to his levels of production.

There are some alternatives to Meares, such as veteran Jeff Reboulet or rookie Denny Hocking. Reboulet played well in '94 hitting better than expected. He will continue his steady work as a dependable insurance policy. Hocking has some ability and may even earn a shot at the job in the spring. He will divide the year between Triple-A and Minnesota, hitting .250 with a handful of steals in 150 at bats.

Brian Raabe could see some time in the middle of the diamond if Reboulet is injured. The Twins might hold out Hocking at Triple-A for an extended shot at the shortstop job, so Raabe is a better bet to come up for spot duty. Raabe has many of the qualities you look for in a ballplayer: he is durable and handles the bat well, yet he lacks power and speed. At Double-A, the Twins have Mitch Simons, who has almost exactly the same talents and weaknesses as Raabe.

Veteran Jeff Carter is 31 and, with a .324 showing at

Triple-A in '94, is making a late charge at the majors. Young Dominican Andres Duncan hit .254 with a little power and speed in Double-A, but is not certain to develop into more than a role player. Unfortunately for Minnesota, they traded Enrique Wilson to the Indians this past spring for a marginal return, only to watch him post an excellent year in A-ball. Wilson would be their top infield prospect if he had stayed put.

Lary Bump:

Denny Hocking can hit for average and steal bases. He also has what was considered the best infield arm in the Pacific Coast League a year ago, when he batted .279-5-57-13 steals. The switch hitter, who will be 25 in April, should battle Pat Meares to the wire for Minnesota's shortstop job. As he has advanced, Hocking has become less patient at the plate; he didn't draw a walk in 31 at bats for the Twins in '94.

New York Yankees

As I predicted, the Yankees brought in a free agent veteran to ''keep the spot warm'' for Derek Jeter. In perhaps the most important free agent shortstop signing of the winter, the Yankees acquired Tony Fernandez.

Fernandez parted company with the Blue Jays following the 1993 season and remained a free agent almost until opening day last year. Once he joined the Reds, Fernandez did a fine job as a regular third baseman/part-time shortstop, while showing that he can still hit (.279-8-50-12 for the Reds). He should be capable of similar offense for the Yankees, rounding out a potent infield.

Mike Gallego remained a free agent late in December. He has a pretty good chance to sign with one of the teams needing to solidify their infield and should be a cheap Rotisserie bargain, too, wherever he goes.

The Yankees retained Kevin Elster for 1995. If he is still able to play shortstop, Elster would be an emergency shortstop stored at Triple-A where he can also serve as a tutor for Baseball America's minor league player of the year - Derek Jeter.

With Mike Gallego on the free agent market, the Yankees had a vacancy at shortstop in December. Taking Gallego back again was not out of the question. Although he had an off year in 1994, and he's past his prime, Gallego has been a quiet leader on the field and a flexible role-player who got in a full season in 1993 without ever having a regular position.

With or without Gallego, the Yankees have to take a long hard look at Derek Jeter as a prime shortstop candidate for 1995. Jeter shot through all levels of the minor league system and finished in the Arizona Fall League, which he left early because of a sore shoulder (not considered serious).

The Yankees are likely to want a veteran to ease Jeter's arrival, even if he has a big spring training and vaults into the starting role. Using a veteran to keep the spot warm while Jeter gets going at Triple-A for a midseason callup is also a realistic notion.

Jeter is very much the real thing, especially on offense. My only caution on him is the proverbial ''Barry Bonds hit .223 as a rookie'' warning. And I guess it doesn't harm the thinking process to recall that Alex Gonzalez didn't exactly blossom with Toronto when given a chance in 1994.

Randy Velarde is qualified to be the veteran fill-in, although he's never been much a major league shortstop. Velarde's biggest asset, both in the major leagues and in our game, is his multi-position capability. He can play all three infield skill positions and right or left field without weakening the batting order. He is however error prone for a regular infielder and is more likely to continue in his multifaceted role than to hold shortstop for Jeter's arrival.

The Yankees also kept Kevin Elster on their winter roster, along with Robert Eenhoorn. Elster is never going to hit for high average (though his 0 for 20 in 1994 was a fluke) and will pop some home runs if he ever gets to play, but Elster's weakness is a lingering

shoulder problem which, even after surgery, leaves him below average at making long throws. The Yankees interest in keeping Elster can be attributed to the Jeter arrival and the attractiveness of having an assortment of veteran reserves to choose from before leaving Florida.

Eenhoorn is a great athlete who could have been a top soccer pro in his native Netherlands but chose to take an eccentric flyer on the foreign sport of baseball. For years, the Dutch media have been following him around Florida during spring training. If it had worked out, Eenhoorn would have been an exciting story, but even with allowances for the late arrival in the baseball world, he has been a disappointment in terms of development, especially when it comes to hitting.

Wherever he ends up, Gallego will be useful, both in MLB and in our game. Don't look for a star, or even a regular at this stage of his career. But do look for multi-position eligibility and a handful of homers. But for upward possibilities in 1994 and for long term growth, Jeter is as good as any of the newcomers.

Oakland A's

Steven Rubio:

Mike Bordick can't hit. He will probably be overvalued by fantasy owners for the rest of his career, thanks to his .300 batting average in 1992. For this reason you should avoid him. His defensive reputation with Oakland is good, so he'll get plenty of at bats.

Fausto Cruz has shown little in brief callups, but he can hit for average and will take a walk. Cruz has no power and doesn't steal many bases, so his fantasy value will never be terrific, but he is worth keeping an eye on if the A's ever tire of Bordick's anemic bat. Jason Wood is a Double-A version of Mike Bordick. He will be lucky to get a cup of coffee in the majors.

Lary Bump:

Thus far, Fausto Cruz has been proof that a great name won't bring major league success, no matter

how well a player has performed in the minors. He batted .321-1-17 at Triple-A Tacoma, but just 3-for-28 with the Athletics. But some future major leaguers his age (23) were playing in A ball last season, so he has time to develop. Cruz, a righthanded batter, isn't likely to be outstanding in any Rotisserie category.

Jason Wood, the shortstop at Double-A Huntsville, batted .274-6-84. But he already is 25. A possible future righthanded power source is 21 year old Tony Batista (.281-17-68 in the California League). He also has played second base and third base. If he continues to show power in the Southern League, he could be a major league prospect at third or short in 1996 or '97.

Seattle Mariners

Felix Fermin has re-signed for 1995 and will help bring Alex Rodriguez smoothly into the big leagues. He is likely to get the majority of the playing time in 1995, especially to start the year, but should begin to hand the job off to Rodriguez by season's end.

Bill Gray:

Shortstop is a work in progress. Yes, we are all drooling over Alex Rodriguez, but he is going to take a while to arrive. He's not even 20 years old, and it's a tough position to play. Offensively, Rodriguez will be special, but not this year or next. Robin Yount at age 18 hit .250 for the Brewers with only three home runs. Yount was a good hitter, but he really didn't turn into a truly great hitter until he was nearly 25, and after nearly six years in the major leagues. That's when his power arrived, and we need to remember that and not go berserk bidding on this very young player. I'm not about to assume that Alex Rodriguez will be a future Hall of Famer, just as I would not have made that assumption about Robin Yount in 1974. If you are rebuilding, Rodriguez is a good place to start. If you are contending, get a shortstop who is established.

Felix Fermin will continue to play a lot, but he won't bat .324 again, ever. Fermin's hitting is strictly one

dimensional; he has no power or speed.

Lary Bump:

Alex Rodriguez has had an eventful career even though he played his first pro game just last April. He was the first pick in the entire 1993 draft. After highly publicized contract wrangling, he reported last spring to Appleton (.319-14-55-16 in 65 games). He was voted the Midwest League's best batting prospect, the best defensive shortstop, the best infield arm and the most exciting player. Then he was promoted to Double-A Jacksonville (.288-1-8). For a time, he was the Mariners' regular shortstop (.204-0-2 in 17 games) before his 19th birthday. The righthanded batter finished the whirlwind at Triple-A Calgary (.311-6-21).

One of the biggest surprises in the Arizona Fall League was Desi Relaford, who hit for average, stole bases and played good defense. That followed a regular season in which he started at Jacksonville for the second year, but was demoted after a .203-3-11 start. The 21 year old switch hitter tore up the California League (.310-5-59), and totaled 37 stolen bases and a minor league-high 119 runs. With Rodriguez around, Relaford may be shifted to second base.

Andy Sheets, 23, moved around to accommodate Rodriguez and Relaford. A righthanded batter, Sheets hit .270-2-10 at Class A Riverside, .344-2-16 at Calgary, and .220-0-17 at Jacksonville. He'll be back at Jacksonville unless the Mariners try Relaford at second base in Triple-A.

Texas Rangers

The Rangers declined to exercise a contract option on Manuel Lee and he became a free agent, and Jeff Huson was also released.

That leaves Benji Gil and Esteban Beltre as the current shortstops in Texas. It's unlikely that situation will remain static, though. Beltre's marginal defense and weak hitting make him a poor regular and

Gil is unready to take over as a regular in 1995. Look for the Rangers to grab one of the free agents that are still available.

Peter Graves:

The Rangers hold an option on Manuel Lee for 1995, and may need to exercise it as prospect Benji Gil isn't ready for the majors. Lee rebounded in 1994 to have his best offensive season (.278-2-38) since 1988. Always prone to injury, Lee managed to play in 85 of 114 games for Texas, and was basically healthy at the season's end. Defensively, he's better suited to turf than grass, and with the Rangers supposedly emphasizing defense and pitching in 1995, Lee may not fit in. As shortstops go, you can do worse than Lee as long as you don't pay more than a few bucks for him. Esteban Beltre is the incumbent backup. He's a weak hitter; although he hit .282 in limited duty with the Rangers, his lifetime batting average in the minors is .238. Beltre was also erratic in the field. He's insignificant for Rotisserie purposes.

Benji Gil, the Rangers' "shortstop of the future" showed that the future isn't now, hitting .248-10-49-14 at Oklahoma City, with a whopping 113 strikeouts in 444 at bats. Ever since he opened the 1993 season with the Rangers (hitting .123), Gil has been a head case in the minors. Although his potential is still very high, his work ethic is questionable. At the age of 22, Gil is still a definite prospect, but he's nowhere near ready for the big leagues. His defense is particularly suspect. If Gil gets his head screwed on right, he could arrive in one or two years. He has good speed and power potential.

Lary Bump:

The Rangers were concerned early last season when Benji Gil, who was overpowered by major league pitching during a brief exposure in 1993, still wasn't hitting in Triple-A. A hot August dispelled those fears and propelled Gil into the driver's seat for taking over as Texas' shortstop in '95. The former first-round draft choice has been considered a major league fielder for years, and his arm was voted the best among American Association infielders last

year. The 22 year old righthanded batter finished .248-10-55-14 at Oklahoma City. He needs to develop better strike zone judgment (33 walks, 120 strikeouts).

Double-A shortstop Rich Aurilia, 23, batted .234-12-57, and was a disappointment in the Arizona Fall League. He bats righthanded. In three minor league seasons, he has 38 stolen bases but has been thrown out 40 times. In the Florida State League, Guillermo Mercedes failed to hit (.221-0-37). He's a 21 year old righthanded batter. His stolen base efficiency dropped from 71 percent in the Sally League in '93 to 52 percent last year.

Toronto Blue Jays

Dick Schofield has become a free agent and hasn't signed anywhere yet. He'll find a job somewhere because of his steady glove work. A return to Toronto for Schofield would not be a big surprise. Schofield has little Rotisserie value.

Failed prospect Eddie Zosky has been traded to Florida, leaving the shortstop job to Alex Gonzalez for 1995. Since Gonzalez is still unproven the Blue Jays will likely sign a veteran (such as Schofield) to provide steady play in case Gonzalez is still not ready for prime time.

Minor leaguer Tomas Perez was selected off of Montreal's roster by the Angels, then sold to the Blue Jays. He is several years away from big league play.

David Luciani:

Dick Schofield wasn't supposed to be the everyday shortstop. Things just turned out that way. Highly-touted prospect Alex Gonzalez had posted impressive minor league power numbers for a shortstop. Turning 21 years old in April, Gonzalez went on to hit just .151 over 53 major league at bats and his defense looked uncertain at best. Before long, he was hurt, and once healthy was shipped back to the minor leagues for the rest of the season.

Gonzalez gets an identical chance in 1995. Schofield was not offered arbitration in October which left an option open for the Jays to do exactly as they had the year before. If the Jays chose, they could try to sign Schofield to a minor league deal as an insurance policy should Gonzalez struggle again.

If Domingo Cedeno lands a spot on the major league roster, he will serve as a backup on occasion. Without Cedeno and Schofield, the Blue Jays would probably look to the free agent market for insurance. Barring multiple injuries, there is virtually no chance that Domingo Cedeno will ever be the everyday shortstop for the Blue Jays.

Lary Bump:

Alex Gonzalez wasn't ready for the majors last spring (.151-0-1), but he should be this time. He can hit for average and steal bases, and has surprising power (.284-12-57-23 at Syracuse). He was named the International League's best defensive shortstop in the Baseball America poll, even though he was on his way to 30-plus errors. A lack of concentration on routine plays has plagued him in the field, but he'll be just 22 in April, so he has plenty of time to improve.

Another alternative for the righthanded batter could be a move to third base. If he stays at shortstop, he will be a top Rotisserie pick no later than 1997.

Tilson Brito played shortstop for Double-A Knoxville (.267-5-57-33 steals). He's nearly a year older than Gonzalez, but still young enough to be a candidate for a lengthy major league career. If Brito can cut it this year at Syracuse, he could contribute to moving Gonzalez to third base.

NATIONAL LEAGUE SHORTSTOPS

Atlanta Braves

Marc Bowman:

Chipper Jones' knee injury in spring training 1994 postponed the shortstop showdown for a year. Jones is healthy and will challenge Jeff Blauser for the job in 1995. The likely senario is that Blauser will start the year with the regular job but Jones will have it by season's end.

Blauser had an uncommonly poor season at the plate after several years as one of the most consistently good hitting middle infielders in the National League. Still, his .258-6-45-1 season was one of the better years for Rotisserie shortstops at what is still a relatively weak position. Blauser was hurting during the first part of 1994 and should be back to his normal production levels in 1995. But, Jones' presence will mean less playing time for Blauser. Expect a .270-12-65-6 season from Blauser in about 450 at bats.

Switch-hitter Jones should get 350 at bats in 1995 and it is expected that he is completely healed from the serious knee injury suffered in 1994. With a full season of play, he'll start at shortstop, or elsewhere, most of the time. It's unusual for a rookie to start every game in his first season in the majors, so Jones

is likely to suffer some slumps and benchings as the Braves compete for a division title. Jones will be extremely streaky in 1995, so if you draft him, be sure to have the perseverance to ride out the bad times as he's likely to finish 1995 with a .290-10-45 season. Due to the seriousness of his injury it's hard to predict how many bases he'll steal. If he can run normally, he's capable of 25 stolen bases, if not, he may not run much at all.

Switch-hitter Mike Mordecai got a short recall to Atlanta in 1994 as a reward for his excellent hitting at Triple-A Richmond. Mordecai hit .280-14-57-14 in his first really productive season with the bat. He's 27 years old, though, and unlikely to have suddenly learned to hit with authority. His career high in homers before 1994 was five in 1992. Mordecai can run, has a decent glove, and has a chance to win a big league utility role if he can prove to be as versatile as Bill Pecota has been for Atlanta. He's no threat to win a regular job and won't take time away from Blauser or Jones. There's no Rotisserie value here.

Yet another switch-hitter, Ramon Caraballo, was the primary shortstop at Double-A Greenville. Caraballo had been the main challenger at second base in 1993, but changed position and dropped back a level in 1994. He's now 25 years old and taking a step back

is not the best way to get a regular job in the majors. He's headed for a utility role at this rate.

There are no other shortstops of any interest for several years to come. Most of the remaining shortstops are defensive specialists with weak hitting skills. 20 year old Danny Magee may be the best prospect at this point. Magee hit .272 with 13 steals for ''low'' Class A Macon, but struck out four times as often as he walked. Magee's batting eye will have to improve as he advances.

Lary Bump:

A year ago, Chipper Jones appeared in line to be Atlanta's left fielder in 1994 and its shortstop in 1995. The knee surgery that wiped out last season for him now could move him to third base to replace Terry Pendleton. Jones will have a place in the Braves' lineup, perhaps batting as high as third. And he's such a good player that they'll find a position for him and work the rest of the defensive alignment around him. He can hit in the majors, but he may no longer steal bases. However, 22-year-olds like this switch hitter heal better than older players, so it's possible he'll still be able to run.

Mike Mordecai had a big year at Triple-A Richmond (.280-14-57-14 steals), but the switch hitter already is 27. He's a utilityman at best in the majors. Danny Magee, a 1993 sixth-round draft pick out of high school, had a solid season with Class A Macon (.272-1-34-12 steals). The 20-year-old righthanded batter will have to develop some power to become a prospect.

Chicago Cubs

Stuart Shea:

Back injuries aside, Shawon Dunston has always been a talented but flawed player. His inability to lay off lousy pitches has kept him from fully utilizing his tremendous bat speed. However, he has always been a good defensive player and chips in a bit with the bat. In 1994, he came back from his back problems and

put together an inspiring performance. Dunston still doesn't know the strike zone from the ozone, but played hard every day, hit .278 and launched 11 homers. Realistically, his back problems could recur at any time (Dunston needed frequent rest last year). In addition, he was less than at 100% when playing on artificial turf.

Apparently Jose Hernandez will eventually inherit the job. Frankly, it's hard to understand what the Cubs see in this guy. His defense is good, but not spectacular. He can't hit his way out of a lunch bag, he lacks great speed, and won't be improving much more as he'll turn 26 this coming July. Hernandez will never be a productive major league regular. However, he can play short, third, and second well, and therefore should stick in a utility role.

Although there's no help at Double-A or Triple-A, Kevin Orie may be in a Cub uniform by late 1996. A 1993 sandwich pick as compensation from Atlanta for the loss of Greg Maddux, Orie missed almost all of last season after tearing ligaments in his hand while sliding, but should begin 1995 in the Florida State League. Orie is expected to hit for average and power, although his defense is questionable.

Lary Bump:

Iowa shortstop Tommy Shields retired after eight minor league seasons and 34 at bats in the majors.

Cincinnati Reds

Considering the injury history of Barry Larkin, it's a good idea to know all the potential backups, and into that picture the Reds have added former number one pick (and second player overall in 1988) Mark Lewis. For $1 I would gladly put him on my roster. Here is a guy who can play second and third base as well, and after his first 700 major league at bats he was hitting .265 with 60 RBI plus a respectable handful of homers and steals. And the guy just turned age 25 in November! Lewis has been handled roughly by the Indians' organization, alternatively being pushed into a major league everyday role before he was ready and

then kept in the minors even after showing he was adequate to fill a major league roster spot. The change of scenery is the first step toward major league success. Now he just needs playing time.

Greg Gajus:

Barry Larkin (.279-9-52-26) suffered from a slow start (hitting under .150 in April) but rebounded to put up a credible season. The Reds' performance in the 90's has been easy to track - when Larkin plays they win, and when he is suffering from one of his frequent injuries they don't. Larkin used to be the top Rotisserie shortstop in the National League by a wide margin, but his dominance is shrinking. He is still one of the best, but he's now 31 (after getting a late start in professional baseball) and entering the period of probable decline. Larkin is extremely intelligent, a great defensive player, and the team leader, but these attributes are not terribly useful in Rotisserie.

In the (likely) event of an injury to Larkin, the probable short term fill-in would be Jeff Branson (see Second Basemen). Kurt Stillwell (.270 at Indianapolis) and Keith Kessinger (.249) were the Triple-A insurance policies in 1994.

The most interesting prospect in the Reds system is 21 year old shortstop Calvin "Pokey" Reese. The Reds top draft pick in 1991, Reese had a terrible season in 1993, hitting just .212 and suffering from several personal tragedies. In 1994 he blossomed, hitting .269-12-49-21 at Class AA Chattanooga and was considered the best defensive shortstop in the league. Reese was rumored to be a September callup before the season ended. Given his age, Reese may be the best prospect in the Reds system (except for Willie Greene) but with Boone and Larkin the Reds appear set at the middle infield for the next several years.

Lary Bump:

No one has ever questioned Calvin "Pokey" Reese's defense. In 1994, he was voted the Southern League's best defensive shortstop and best infiel arm. He also learned how to make better contact and drive the ball

in his second Double-A season (.269-12-49-21 steals). All but the RBI total were career highs. He totaled just 12 home runs in his first three years as a pro. Within a couple of years, the 21-year-old righthanded batter will move Barry Larkin to another position or another team.

The regular shortstop at Triple-A Indianapolis, Kurt Stillwell (.270-8-49), lost the Reds' shortstop job to Larkin seven years ago, and isn't likely to get it back.

An intermediate possibility, or a utility candidate, is Mark Lewis, obtained in a December trade from the Indians. Lewis has played second base for Cleveland, but may be better suited for third base. He is an adequate shortstop both defensively and offensively (.259-8-34 at Triple-A Charlotte).

In the Carolina League was Ricky Magdaleno (.261-13-49). On the one hand, we can't get too excited about the righthanded batter because everyone hit home runs at Winston-Salem and because he was thrown out more often than he stole successfully. On the other, he's only 20, so there's time for improvement.

The shortstop with the Reds' Sally League affiliate was Chris Sexton (.300-5-59-18 steals). The 1993 10th-round draft pick, a righthanded batter, has hit in the lower minors, but he's 23 already.

Colorado Rockies

David Smith:

It looked like Nelson Liriano was going to be the starting shortstop for the Rockies coming into the 1994 campaign. But GM Bob Gebhard stole Walt Weiss for the bargain price of $2.2 million for two years. The off-season pickup worked to perfection when Liriano moved to second to cover for Roberto Mejia (see Second Basemen).

Weiss started 110 of 117 games, batted leadoff most of the time and was the disciplined batter that managers like having at the top of the order. But Weiss's

biggest contribution to the team was to bring consistency to an erratic infield. Offensively, the switch hitter he led the team with 56 walks and posted a .251-1-32-12 year. The twelve steals were a career high and may be too much to expect. Overall, a .260-2-40-8 year is likely for 1995. It's not worth much, but you could bid a buck and get a small bargain here, particularly if he again reaches double digits in steals.

There's no doubt that Weiss will bat leadoff or second and start 99 percent of the Rockies' games in 1995. Last year's super sub, Nelson Liriano has moved on to the Pirates via waivers, so the backup will be one of two utility infielders: Pedro Castellano or Vinny Castilla. Neither would be good for Rotisserie purposes even if they play regularly.

Jason Bates is the most likely to be promoted from the minors. Bates went .286-19-76 for Triple-A Colorado Springs in 1994. He demonstrated good pitch selection, too; Bates was second on the team in walks with 60 and walked more often than striking out in his 458 at bats.

Lary Bump:

For a shortstop, 24-year-old switch hitter Jason Bates is a very good offensive player (.286-10-76 in his second season with Triple-A Colorado Springs). Ask yourself: Do the Rockies need another hitter?

The guy who's considered the Rockies' shortstop prospect is another switch hitter, Neifi Perez. He batted just .239-1-35 in the California League, but he showed some gap power and speed with seven triples, and is just 19.

Florida Marlins

Tony Blengino:

There are two standard ways to build an expansion franchise.

One way is to go for instant respectability, drafting established major leaguers, hoping to hold the organization together until the farm system is established. This method was selected by the Colorado Rockies.

The other is to draft the best young prospects, sacrificing wins in the short term for long term success. Such a method was chosen by the Florida Marlins.

In keeping with their organizational philosophy, the Marlins' allowed their 1993 shortstop, Walt Weiss, to leave via free agency, ironically losing him to the Rockies. This opened a spot for young Kurt Abbott who possesses a mixture of talents and shortcomings.

Abbott has good power for a middle infielder; he slugged .394 in 1994 and has good speed (despite just three steals last year). Hitting at the bottom of the order often kept Abbott nailed to the base.

But, Abbott was hitting low in the order due to one of his chief weakness -poor plate discipline. His .291 OBP, last among National League shortstops came from drawing just 16 walks (with 98 whiffs) in 371 plate appearances. Abbott also was a defensive disappointment with relatively poor range afield.

There is no immediate help in Double-A or Triple-A, so Abbott will again get a full time role next year, and hit .240-10-50-5. At this point the 25 year old Abbott can't be counted on as a long-term shortstop solution, but he's still young enough to improve.

Surehanded utility infielder Alex Arias lacks enough offensive talent to gain a starting role in the majors. The 27 year old Arias played several infield spots for the Marlins in 1994 and has an inside track for a utility role again in 1995. He would be the one to take over at shortstop should Abbott become injured, but wouldn't hit enough to be worth picking up. Expect him to produce a .250-1-18 season in 200 at bats.

28 year old Joe Millette and 29 year old Jerry Schunk were starting shortstops for the Marlins' Triple-A and Double-A teams, respectively. They have accumulated over 5000 minor league at bats between them. Millette's complete lack of power (no extra base hits in 88 major league at bats, 12 short of the

major league record), and Schunk's poor batting eye (a career .299 OBP) ensure more minor league at bats for both in the future. Neither is a threat to Abbott or Arias for major league playing time.

The Marlins' lower minors are teeming with very young shortstop talent.

Defensive wizard Edgar Renteria hit just .253 for Class A Brevard County but is just a pup. He should fill out his 6'1" frame and will soon begin hitting much better. Now just 19 years old, Renteria has been the youngest starter in every league where he has played. He should advance to Double-A in 1995 and will continue to move up as his hitting improves.

Josh Booty was the Marlins' first round pick in 1994, then had to fight LSU for top role. Booty may eventually move to third base with a major league arrival in about 1997.

The Marlins also took another shortstop in the second round, 18 year old Victor Rodriguez. Known primarily for acrobatic fielding, Rodriguez immediately impressed with his bat, too, hitting .333 for Melbourne of the Rookie Gulf Coast League.

Lary Bump:

Josh Booty was drafted fifth overall last year, but received a record $1.6 million bonus. The Marlins had to lure him away from Louisiana State, where he had a football scholarship as one of the best high school quarterbacks ever to come down the pike. He hit a home run in his first pro game, but had his season cut short when he contracted mono. The righthanded batter was at .222-1-2 in 10 Gulf Coast League games, then .250-0-1 in four games in the New York-Penn League.

Houston Astros

Bill Gilbert:

After Andujar Cedeno's breakthrough season in 1993, he appeared to have a chance to move into the top tier of National League shortstops in 1994. He didn't do it. His numbers were respectable (.263-9-49-1), but not enough to move him out of the middle of the pack. At age 25, his best years should still be ahead of him and, with his tools, he could still reach superstar status.

At this point the weight of evidence suggests that Cedeno is likely to fall short of expectations. His batting average dropped 20 points in 1994 and his strikeout frequency increased from 19% to 23% of his at bats. He continued to suffer lapses in concentration both offensively and defensively while, at the same time, showing flashes of brilliance defensively and an occasional burst of offensive power. He's the type of player who could mature and turn in a monster season, but a more likely case is that his inconsistency and relatively poor fundamentals will limit him to a level only slightly above where he is now.

Orlando Miller received his first major league opportunity in 1994. His stay was brief, but impressive (.325-2-9-1), including a two homer game. Considered a more consistent fielder than Cedeno, 26 year old Miller should be capable of handling a major league job if given the chance. Miller appears to have made progress in overcoming temper problems which have held him back in the past.

On the downside, Miller did not hit as well in his second year at Triple-A Tucson in 1994 (.257-10-55-3) as he did in 1993 (.304-16-89-2). Miller has poor plate discipline and will probably have trouble hitting for average in the majors.

Tom Nevers was Houston's first round draft choice out of high school in 1990. Now 23, he has spent two years at Class AA Jackson without putting up numbers that would suggest he is a strong major league prospect; Nevers hit .267-8-62-10 in 1994.

Lary Bump:

Orlando Miller made a splash with two home runs in one game at Wrigley Field during a brief callup. He also batted .325 in 40 at bats for the Astros. He has batted .300 twice in seven minor league seasons,

including 1993, his second year in the Pacific Coast League. Last season he slumped somewhat to .257-10-55. At 26, the righthanded batter is seven months older than Andujar Cedeno.

The shortstop at Double-A Jackson was Tom Nevers (.267-8-62-10 steals). He doesn't make good contact; he has struck out more than 100 times in three of the last four seasons.

Los Angeles Dodgers

Greg Gajus:

Jose Offerman (.210-1-25-2) crashed and burned in 1994, earning an attitude adjustment trip back to Triple-A Albuquerque. Offerman's play at Albuquerque (.330-1-31-9) indicates he is a good bet to make a comeback in 1995. There were reports that the Dodgers were happy with how Offerman responded to being sent down, as the team doesn't have any other reasonable options at shortstop. He's expected to regain the regular job in 1995, and he is young enough (26) to improve, but place special concern on his steal totals which are the biggest part of his Rotisserie value. Given his poor 1994 season, Offerman will start out hitting seventh or eighth, thus limiting his opportunities to run. Offerman stole only 11 bases (combined major and minor leagues) in 467 at bats in 1994.

Rafael Bournigal (.224-0-11-0) is strictly a glove man who received some playing time after Offerman was sent down. He is 29 and has no upward potential or Rotisserie value.

Tommy LaSorda also used Delino DeShields and Cory Snyder for a few games at shortstop in 1994. If DeShields is used there again (he only played ten games there in 1994) it raises his value and flexibility considerably. Cory Snyder stinks regardless of how many positions he plays.

Lary Bump:

Rafael Bournigal hit well enough in the Pacific Coast

League (.332-1-22) that he earned a chance to end the season on the figurative picket line. In the majors, he didn't hit enough (.224-0-11) to keep his job over Jose Offerman or whomever the Dodgers bring in. The 28-year-old, righthanded-hitting Bournigal is a profile in perseverance. In 1991, he was demoted to Vero Beach as a player-coach, but played his way back up through the organization. He can be useful as a major league defensive replacement or as a minor league coach.

Juan Castro, a 22-year-old righthanded batter, didn't do much in his second Texas League season that he hadn't done in 1993. His '94 numbers were .288-4-44.

A better down-the-road prospect may be Wilton Guerrero (.294-1-32 in the Florida State League). He also stole 23 bases, but was thrown out 20 times. The righthanded batter is just 20.

Montreal Expos

John Perrotto:

Patience paid off for the Expos as Wil Cordero blossomed into an All-Star in 1994. He finally began hitting with authority (.294-15-63-16). Also heartening was his improved glove work and concentration at shortstop.

It was all a matter of maturity for Cordero. Now 23 years old, he finally grew into the job of major league shortstop last year. He took the game more seriously and worked hard to overcome his deficiencies. The Expos have long felt Cordero could emerge into one the game's top shortstops. After last season, there is no longer reason to doubt their assessment.

While the Expos have temporarily ceased talking about shifting Cordero to third base, he may eventually be moved out of the way of three top notch shortstop prospects currently in the Expos' farm system.

After being nothing more than a utility infielder prior to last season, Mark Grudzielanek emerged as the

Class AA Eastern League's MVP in 1994. He hit .322-11-66-32 and is an overachiever in the mold of Expos second baseman Mike Lansing.

Geoff Blum, the Expos' seventh round pick in last year's amateur draft from the University of California, hit .344-3-38-5 for short season Class A Vermont. The switch-hitter makes good contact and has gap power, though his speed is only average.

Hiram Bocachica, the Expos' top pick last year from a Puerto Rican high school, also had a fine pro debut as he hit .280-5-16-11 in the Gulf Coast Rookie League. He has exceptional power for a middle infielder and his rifle arm is reminiscent of Shawon Dunston's.

Lary Bump:

In his fourth minor league season, Mark Grudzielanek made himself a prospect. He was the Eastern League MVP in a monster .322-11-66-32 steals season that exceeded his previous career highs by 55 points, six homers, 12 RBI and seven stolen bases. He followed that up by leading the Arizona Fall League with a .365 average and being named its sixth-best prospect by Baseball America. My rule of thumb is that a player who puts good minor league and winter ball seasons back to back is a genuine prospect. The righthanded batter's age (24) keeps him from being rated higher.

He isn't about to beat Wil Cordero out of the shortstop job, but is a candidate to play second base or third or in a utility capacity similar to Mike Lansing's. Remember, Lansing jumped to the majors at age 25 after going .280-6-54 with 46 steals at Harrisburg. Grudzielanek's name is pronounced -- well, just like it's spelled.

The regular shortstop with Triple-A Ottawa was Chris Martin (.238-3-40). The 27-year-old righthanded batter may have reached his highest level.

In the major league draft, the Expos selected Chad Fonville (.307-0-26-22 steals in 68 California League games) from the Giants' organization. At 5-6, 155

pounds, the 24-year-old switch hitter has little power, but can run out extra-base hits if he puts the ball into the outfield gaps. Fonville has made good use of his strengths -- speed and contact hitting -- to get ahead to this point. He may not have time to make it the rest of the way unless the Expos have to keep him on their major league roster this season.

Jolbert Cabrera, who had a solid season (.254-0-38-31 steals) in the Midwest League in 1993, struggled last year (.203-0-13 at West Palm Beach and .248-0-11 with independent San Bernardino in the California League). At 22, the righthanded batter has time to improve. He'll have to, for coming up behind him is highly regarded 19-year-old Hiram Bocachica (.280-5-16-11 steals in 43 Gulf Coast League games).

New York Mets

The Mets have an unexciting interim solution at shortstop, in Jose Vizcaino. This is the same player who moved from short to second base at Albuquerque in 1990 to allow Jose Offerman to take the fast track to the majors. Now back at short, Vizcaino is a steady but unexciting player. He has no upward potential (1993-1994 was probably his career peak) and is always in danger of being pushed aside by another "big" talent like Offerman.

Bill Spiers came over from Milwaukee on waivers in October. Spiers was once a very bright prospect and potential All-Star, but he was felled by a back injury that was apparently worsened by ineffective medical treatment. From November 1991 until spring training 1994 he was never healthy; but here is a guy still just age 28 and with more talent than anyone else mature enough to play at the major league level on opening day. I like Spiers as a $1 shortstop just fine.

In the minors the Mets have defensive whiz Rey Ordonez and the power/speed offensive package Edgardo Alfonzo who has recently been working at second base alongside Ordonez. Fernando Vina, another utility type, was also on the winter roster.

Lary Bump:

Last year's Norfolk manager, Bobby Valentine, was very high on Aaron Ledesma. Coming back from an arm injury, he batted .274-3-56 with 18 stolen bases and was a sparkplug on defense and in the clubhouse. The only advantage the 23-year-old righthanded batter may have over Jose Vizcaino is that he's home-grown.

By 1996, it won't matter whether Vizcaino or Ledesma is at shortstop, because the Mets are projecting that Cuban defensive whiz Rey Ordonez will be ready. As a rookie pro last year Ordonez batted .309-2-40 with Class A Port St. Lucie and .262-1-20 for Double-A Binghamton, with a total of 15 steals. Another possibility for Ledesma could be to join his former manager in Japan.

Philadelphia Phillies

Tony Blengino:

The Phillies' litany of disaster with high draft picks in recent years makes a successful selection like Kevin Stocker (second round in 1991) seem out of place. He was considered a good field, no hit type of shortstop with limited upward potential. Stocker has exceeded those expectations, however, hitting .298 in 530 major league at bats.

Following his .324 average in 1993, a letdown was expected last year, especially since Stocker had never hit for a high average in the minors. After all, Stocker was inserted into the lineup primarily for his defense. But the Phillies had to be happy with his .273 season in 1994, and they were ecstatic about his .383 OBP which led National League shortstops. Stocker's defense hasn't been quite as good as expected, but it is still above average. Expect another .270 season with little power from Stocker in 1995; he could steal 15 to 20 bases if he batted somewhere other than eighth in the lineup.

Kim Batiste (see Third Basemen) and free agent Mariano Duncan (see Second Basemen) are the possible alternatives in the absence of Stocker.

The Phillies' minor league cupboard is virtually bare at shortstop. At Triple-A, converted outfielder Shawn Gilbert is 30 years old and despite good speed he has no future.

Former Expo Charlie Montoyo has a career minor league OBP above .400 last year. He was also at Triple-A Scranton-Wilkes Barre in 1994 and played some at second base, too. A good batting eye and versatility could get the 29 year old Montoyo back to the majors in a utility infield role.

24 year old Luis Brito played for Double-A Reading in 1994, but he's an impatient hitter with little power (13 walks, 11 extra base hits in 1994). His future is dim.

Lary Bump:

At Triple-A Scranton, the Phillies had shortstops who were not just journeymen, but minor league journeymen. Charlie Montoyo, who also has played third base and second, batted .282-9-47. He had a big game that was televised during the strike, but the righthanded batter is 29 already.

Shawn Gilbert, who also played some center field, is even older (30). His eight-year pro career has been built more on hustle than production. The righthanded batter's '94 season (.254-7-52-20 steals) was typical of his career, except that he showed a little more power than usual and was thrown out 15 times trying to steal.

Luis Brito, a 23-year-old switch hitter, had a hot start (.324-1-13) in the Florida State League, but burned out at Double-A Reading (.222-3-21).

Pittsburgh Pirates

John Perrotto:

It has become apparent that Jay Bell is the cornerstone upon which the Pirates plan to rebuild. He is signed

through the 1997 season and, at age 29, should have many good years left. In fact, one can argue he is now the National League's best all around shortstop.

Bell had another solid year in 1994, batting .276-9-45-2. If he were moved down in the lineup, he would probably hit a few more homers and increase his RBI totals. However, Pirates manager Jim Leyland likes Bell batting second. Bell is a good, though paradoxical, number two hitter. He is an outstanding runner and good on the hit and run, although he strikes out an awful lot. He becomes an entirely different hitter with men on base, making better contact. He also has led National League shortstops in total chances for five straight seasons.

Speedy Tony Womack was the starter at Triple-A Buffalo in 1994 and learned he can't steal first base after being named the Pirates' Co-Minor League Player of the Year in 1993. Womack hit just .221-0-18-41 at Buffalo and has to learn to hit the ball on the ground and bunt if he is ever make it to the majors. His legs are his best asset and he must realize this to advance. Womack did hit .333-0-1-0 in two brief stints with the Pirates last season.

Kevin Polcovich, who hit .294-2-33-9 at Class AA Carolina, projects strictly as a major league utility infielder if he gets that far. The Pirates do have two good looking shortstops in the lower minors, even if scouts think both will eventually have to move to other positions.

Lou Collier hit .280-7-40-32 for Class A Augusta and was the MVP of the South Atlantic League All-Star Game before moving up to the Pirates' high Class A Salem club. He hit .266-6-16-5 for Salem. Collier has great speed and the ability to get on base, making him an outstanding leadoff prospect. However, stiff hands and a scattershot arm will probably cause him to move to the outfield.

Mark Fariss was the Pirates' first round draft pick from a Texas high school last June and was immediately thrown into tough competition. He started out with short season Class A Welland and batted .287-1-17-2 in 45 games. He was then promoted to full season

Augusta, where he hit .122-1-2-0 in 14 games. Fariss was a great high school athlete, accepting a football scholarship to Texas A&M as a quarterback before signing with the Pirates. However, some scouts feel he is short on range and will eventually settle in as a third baseman.

Ramon Zapata hit .287-4-25-3 at Salem and .262-1-7-0 at Carolina last year. His bat isn't much to get excited about but his glove could eventually get him to the majors as a reserve infielder.

Lary Bump:

The highest-ranking shortstop in the Pittsburgh organization is Tony Womack. Above Double-A, the 25-year-old lefthanded batter has been successful only as a base stealer (41-for-51 last season at Buffalo). He batted .221-0-18 in 421 at bats in the American Association. His speed and ability to play more than one position (short and second base) could earn the 5-9 Womack some major league playing time.

Lou Collier's arm was voted the best of any infielder in the South Atlantic League (.280-7-40) before he earned a promotion to the Carolina League (.266-6-16). The 21-year-old righthanded batter also is a threat on the bases. He stole 37 times, but was just 5-for-13 after his promotion.

Mark Farris was Pittsburgh's first-round draft pick in 1994. An outfielder and shortstop in high school, the lefthanded batter played mostly third base and designated hitter as a pro (.287-1-17 with short-season Welland; .122-1-2 in 49 at bats in the Sally League). The Bucs signed him away from the Texas A&M football team.

St. Louis Cardinals

John Perrotto:

Ozzie Smith's fabulous career will probably conclude at the end of the 1995 season. Smith has said he is almost certain this will be his last year before heading directly to Cooperstown.

However, Smith isn't exactly fading away from the game. He is still a very effective player and the most entertaining defensive player in baseball. His hitting slipped a little in 1994 but .262-3-30-6 is acceptable for a 39 year old middle infielder.

The Cardinals have two good defensive shortstops who can be considered possible heirs to Ozzie's legacy. Tripp Cromer spent most of last season with Triple-A Louisville, batting .274-9-50-5. Aaron Holbert was Class AA Arkansas' shortstop and hit .296-2-19-9 while battling injuries.

While Cromer has a little bit better bat, Holbert is considered a better prospect with great range and defensive ability. Holbert, the Cardinals' top draft pick in 1990, has been slow to develop and gets knocked for a light bat. However, Smith was knocked for his weak bat at the start of his career and eventually shook that label.

Lary Bump:

Tripp Cromer has had two very similar years at Triple-A Louisville (.274-9-50). But at age 27, the lanky righthanded batter is not a threat to play several seasons as Ozzie Smith's successor.

The highly regarded shortstop prospect is 22-year-old Aaron Holbert. He batted .296-2-19 in an injury-shortened season with Double-A Arkansas. He's a good glove man who most likely will start this year with Louisville. With a good start, he could come up to replace Smith at any point.

The offensive production for Keith Johns, a 23-year-old righthanded batter, fell off in the Florida State League (.228-3-47-18 steals). If he can show more offense in Double-A this season, his glove could give him a chance to be a prospect.

In the Midwest League, Santo Mota batted .276-4-46. The 22-year-old switch hitter also stole 28 bases, but was thrown out the incredible total of 29 times. Who was flashing signs from the third base coach's box for Madison?

San Diego Padres

Fred Matos:

Incumbent shortstop Ricky Gutierrez slumped during the first two months of last season, hitting only .140. He eventually snapped out of it, but then his defense slipped and he lost the starting job to Luis Lopez. His final .240 average is about what people expected, but he again struck out 20% of the time, an alarming rate for such a weak hitter. He is only 24, so he has time to become a consistent hitter, but best you can realistically expect is a .250 average without power or stolen bases.

Rookie Luis Lopez was tabbed as the starting second baseman in spring training but suffered minor injuries, forcing the Padres to insert Bip Roberts at second base instead. Lopez played 43 games at short and 29 games at second, but the Padres recognize that he is not the answer at shortstop; he'll more likely appear at second base in the future.

Ray Holbert is a good prospect who is causing the Padres to re-evaluate plans to acquire a shortstop via trade. He hit well and stole 27 bases for Las Vegas last season, but his career best .300 average must be viewed with skepticism due to the Pacific Coast League's propensity for offense.

Although Holbert has a good glove, he committed 34 errors in Triple-A last year. Nevertheless, his glove and base stealing ability, such as they are, may be enough to earn him the Padres starting shortstop job. Although the 24 year old Holbert probably won't hit much (about .230) in 1995, he should improve in subsequent seasons.

Lopez and Gutierrez have little Rotisserie value, and Holbert's value is all in his stolen base potential.

Lary Bump:

The other Holbert, 24-year-old Ray, made his major league debut after posting the best numbers of his seven-year pro career at Las Vegas (.300-8-52-27 steals). The righthanded batter was injured in the

Arizona Fall League, which could prevent him from being the Padres' regular shortstop in 1995.

Double-A Wichita's shortstop, Scott Bream, also batted exactly .300. He also hit five home runs and drove in 35 runs. If Holbert's playing time is restricted, the switch-hitting Bream, also 24, could get a look this spring.

Roberto DeLeon's 1994 numbers (.253-7-74) were not especially impressive for the California League. In fact, the 24-year-old, who also has played third base, did better in the Midwest League a year earlier.

San Francisco Giants

Steven Rubio:

In Royce Clayton the Giants would like to think they have solved any shortstop problems for the foreseeable future. However, their optimism, which seemed so understandable just a year ago, is now clouded by Clayton's disappointing 1994 season. The team is pleased with Clayton's defense and his fantasy owners were happy with his basestealing, but at an age when he should have been proving just how good he could be, Royce performed below his career averages in virtually every important offensive category.

There are no useful alternatives at shortstop for the Giants. Veteran Mike Benjamin can hit lefties and plays three infield positions with flair, but his career major league batting average is .186. Paul Faries was once a disappointing prospect; now at age 30 he is a decent backup but nothing more. Minor leaguers Clay Bellinger and Kurt Ehmann are both unlikely to hit enough to play regularly in the major leagues. Perhaps the best longshot would be Chad Fonville, a crowd pleasing fielder who can hit for average but has yet to prove himself in the higher minor league levels.

Lary Bump:

With Royce Clayton on board, the Giants are not looking for help at shortstop. In case of an injury to Clayton, Mike Benjamin might have trouble holding off 30-year-old Paul Faries (.280-2-50-31 steals at Triple-A Phoenix). The righthanded batter also has played second base, and could be a major league utility player. He's at just .201 in 214 major league at bats.

Kurt Ehmann, 24, had the best infield arm in the Texas League according to Baseball America's poll. His offensive numbers were weak (.244-1-40); he had much more trouble making contact (85 strikeouts, 27 walks) than he did in A ball in '93. At this point, the righthanded batter's future is cloudy.

Brett King played short for the Giants' farm teams in the California (.250-1-11) and Midwest (.218-5-30) leagues. He also totaled 18 stolen bases, but the 22-year-old righthanded batter, a second-round draft choice in 1993, doesn't project to be a major leaguer offensively.

OUTFIELD:
TACTICAL CONSIDERATIONS

More than any other position except pitcher, the outfield offers a whole separate exercise in portfolio management. If you don't get significant help in homers, RBI, steals, and batting average somewhere among your five outfielders, then your whole roster is likely to reflect the shortcoming.

Approaching the outfield must therefore be different from approaching catcher, third base, or any other position. You can't just take the prudent, patient approach of having a long list of "OK" outfielders and keep bidding conservatively until some time near the end of the auction, you fill your slots with anyone who slips through at a bargain price. Such an approach could produce an outfield, for example, made up of Otis Nixon, Vince Coleman, Luis Polonia, David Hulse, and Brady Anderson, if you see what I mean.

While watching their team take shape, most owners will keep an eye on balance as the draft unfolds. But when filling any particular position, most people don't think of balance. The example that I just gave, with the all-SB outfield, is an extreme example, but the point is cogent. If you suddenly realized that your outfield slots were all filled and you needed home runs from the infield, you would be facing some tough bidding wars.

For those who think I have forgotten the maxim "don't worry about balance on draft day," the answer is no, I haven't forgotten it. There is a question of degree, however. Keeping in mind the corollary rule that roster balance should always be achievable within the scope of one (plausible) block-buster trade, you still don't want to get into a situation where you need to trade Vince Coleman AND Otis Nixon to achieve balance. That danger is more likely to arise through the acquisition of outfielders without reference to stat categories, than through any other tactical mini-blunder.

Outfield is the one position where I spend more time thinking through "what if" situations in my pre-draft budgeting exercise (see "Playing for Blood" Chapter Seven). Budgeting $30 for Vince Coleman, for example, is an implicit statement of intention to get $30 worth of stolen bases somewhere in the outfield. Coleman may come up in the first round and sell for $42 to an owner who realized, weeks after the season ended, that if he had Vince Coleman instead of Jose Canseco last year, he would have finished first instead of third. Situations like that do occur. In such a case, especially in the first round, I wouldn't get into a bidding war over Coleman; I would simply shift that $30 of my budget onto other names, maybe two $15 base stealers, or add $10 to three other budgeted vacancies (maybe two outfielders and one MI) to provide for stronger four-category types. The point is that I would have thought through those alternative names and possibilities weeks before the auction began, with lists on paper at the draft table

yet somewhat committed to memory as well, so that plans can be shifted smoothly and calmly.

The portfolio management exercises that go into stat balance also apply to risk/reward, high and low values, growth versus stability, and other balancing acts. You're never going to get every aspect covered in five outfield slots, but the five outfield slots being fungible creates an opportunity, that doesn't exist with any other field position, to shift money and categories during the draft. For that reason the opportunity can be viewed as a necessity. So don't ignore it.

In the outfield, you must be alert to get your fair share of big-name high-value players, and be willing to bid aggressively. Fortunately there are enough high value players that you rarely face a situation of "must have" Albert Belle or Marquis Grissom or any other individual name. But in many auctions with strong freeze lists, you may find yourself with a short list of, say, only three outfielders, feeling a need to get one of them; and it's much better to consider that need and budget for it before the bidding begins.

Because outfielders are somewhat fungible in real baseball (most center fielders can play right or left, and most right fielders can play left) the bigger shifts in player population tend to show up in the outfield earlier than at other positions. Established regulars in the outfield can be shifted (for example like Roberto Kelly was in New York to accommodate the arrival of Bernie Williams) while a star shortstop or third baseman is more likely to put a stop on the arrival of a youngster as a full-time player.

One of the mega-trends of 1994 that will continue in 1995 is the shift toward more playing time for younger players, and to a lesser extent but still noteworthy, more roster slots for younger players. (If anyone would like to quantify those shifts using comprehensive demographics, I will be happy to publish them in The Monthly.) For that reason, I attach more urgency to the maxim (which applies to all hitters but especially to outfielders): when in doubt about the choice between two apparently equal options, choose the younger player. "Apparently equal"

means, for example, that both have established roles over the last couple of years, or both have lacked established roles. I am not saying that two $9 forecast players are "apparently equal" if one is a rookie who will go back to Triple-A if he goes 0 for April, while the other is a four-year regular. Very often, though, we do face choices between players who appear about the same in every aspect, and in all such cases for 1995, I recommend going in the direction of youth, because that's what real GM's and field managers will be doing.

After strong portfolio management and an emphasis on youth, I would add the general theme of looking for good players coming off bad years, and/or the usual high potential players who haven't yet had their career year, guys like Ray Lankford, Ron Gant, Juan Gonzalez, and Shane Mack.

Finally, the outfield is the last bastion of speed, especially in the American League. The vanishing stolen base problem will be best addressed if you can keep speed in mind every time an outfielder comes up for bid. In the recent past, I would have advised you to be looking for "20/20" guys, but there are so few of them left, this year I would say try to get some 10/10 guys into your outfield.

For the Record:

Likely to be bargains: Bernie Williams, Rich Becker, Juan Gonzalez, Darryl Hamilton, Lance Johnson, Felix Jose, Manny Ramirez, Ruben Sierra, Shawn Green, Carl Everett, Ron Gant, Jacob Brumfield, Midre Cummings, Darren Lewis, Derrick May, James Mouton, Reggie Sanders.

Likely to be overvalued: Mike Devereaux, Jeffrey Hammonds, Wayne Kirby, Junior Felix, Ryan Klesko, Willie McGee, Darryl Strawberry, Andy Van Slyke (think: Von Hayes), Mike Kingery, Billy Ashley.

AMERICAN LEAGUE
OUTFIELD

There are a large number of very good outfielders who were still free agents late in December. Among the better hitters that remained free agents were Shane Mack, Jay Buhner, Felix Jose, Andre Dawson, Vince Coleman, Darrin Jackson, Mike Devereaux and Dave Winfield from the AL and Larry Walker, Kevin Mitchell and Andy Van Slyke from the NL. There are also a large number of teams said to be pursuing top free agent outfielders. In the AL, Baltimore, Boston, Chicago, Seattle and Toronto are all said to be looking for a big-hitting outfielder.

For Rotisserie purposes this means there are likely to be several new faces in the outfield this year, some of whom are relative unknowns.

Baltimore Orioles

Mike Devereaux and Lonnie Smith remained unsigned free agents. Devereaux will probably end up somewhere else while Smith could return to Baltimore but is just as likely to retire.

The Orioles were said to be in hot pursuit of a power-hitting outfielder with Jay Buhner one of the leading candidates. Almost any new power hitter in homer-haven Camden Yards is going to get a boost to his homer totals. This will be a great place to find a "surprising" new power hitter.

Fred Matos:

The Orioles want to add more punch to their lineup, and owner Peter Angelos has indicated his willingness to sign a free agent power hitting outfielder, or acquire one in a trade. Although they have a number of outstanding prospects, the Orioles prefer an established power hitter like Jay Buhner or Jose Canseco, either of whom would fit in very nicely.

Manager Johnny Oates was very conservative when it came to stolen bases, rarely giving the steal sign unless he was sure the runner could make it. Brady Anderson was caught only once in 32 attempts last year, a far better rate than the more aggressive base stealers such as Lofton, Nixon and Henderson, who got caught around 20 percent of the time. New manager Phil Regan prefers more aggressive running and manufacturing runs when needed, and Anderson could steal 60-70 bases this year, increasing his Rotisserie value substantially.

In October, emerging superstar Jeffrey Hammonds underwent a knee operation to replace the anterior cruciate ligament (ACL) that he injured in a high

school football game. ACL rehab usually takes six months to a year, so Hammonds could miss at least half of the 1995 season. If he returns early, he may play cautiously to prevent another injury. Ozzie Guillen and Randall Cunningham have come back from such injuries, although Guillen doesn't steal as many bases as he did before his injury.

A healthy Hammonds has excellent power, base stealing speed, and can hit for a good average. His quick bat makes up for being fooled by pitchers. But he needs to develop more patience at the plate, and he has to learn to lay off high fastballs. He has the physical tools to become an All-Star and a very valuable Rotisserie player. Hammonds is a risk for 1995, but an excellent choice if you are building for 1996.

Mike Devereaux started last season in a slump, but was beginning to come out of it in May when he was hit in the face with a pitch. He then began to bail out on inside pitches, causing another slump, which was followed by extended periods of working with coaches to adjust his stance and mechanics. There are a number of reasons why the Orioles did not extend his contract beyond 1994, but it was primarily because he was overpriced. Devereaux is only 33 years old and is very capable of having a few more good years. He is a good comeback candidate, and because of his poor 1994 season, should go cheaply in many drafts.

There will be open outfield slots to replace the injured Hammonds and Devereaux if he isn't signed. Veteran Dwight Smith plus prospects Sherman Obando and Damon Buford and a possible newly-acquired power hitter are the candidates for the slots. Smith is a valuable lefty hitter who can hit well as a platooner, fourth outfielder, pinch hitter, and occasional DH. He can hit .300 in a platooning role, and can reach 10 homers and 10 steals in 300 at bats. Smith's playing time and Rotisserie value could be high at the beginning of the season as Hammonds is likely to be on the disabled list.

Obando is a righthanded power hitter who was on his way towards an outstanding season and the International League MVP award when he went out for the

year with a fractured shin bone. In addition to being an outfield candidate, he also has a good shot at the righthanded DH role, which is more suitable for him as his defense on flyballs is poor. Obando doesn't have anything more to prove in Triple-A.

Buford is a singles hitter, a speedy base stealer, and a good defensive center fielder. Although his hitting has greatly improved over the past two years, the 15 homers in Triple-A last year were a fluke. He is not a good fit with the Orioles in 1995, as they already have a good, fast center fielder in Brady Anderson, and a big power hitter would be a better fit.

Johnny Oates liked Jack Voigt's versatility as the fourth outfielder, backup first baseman, and pinch hitter, and Voigt came through with a few game-winning clutch hits in 1994. At most, Voigt's role will be the same in 1995, but most likely his playing time will decline because Oates is no longer the manager, and the Orioles may go with a younger guy with more power, like Sherman Obando.

The Orioles have four talented and highly-regarded minor league prospects in Curtis Goodwin, Mark Smith, Harry Berrios and Alex Ochoa. Goodwin is a fast, base-stealing singles hitter and prototypical center fielder who will likely spend most of 1995 in Triple-A as Buford and Anderson are ahead of him. Ochoa is a fine multi-talented prospect, and other teams frequently ask for him in deals. Smith is talented, but he needs to show more authority at the plate. And Berrios is a very promising and exciting hustler who hits like Chad Curtis, but may need another year in the minors. Since the Orioles are looking for an established power hitter and a starting pitcher, one or more of these prospects may be traded.

Lary Bump:

It came as no surprise when Damon Buford was voted the International League's best defensive outfielder last season. The surprise was his power output (.270-16-66, mostly as a leadoff hitter) at Rochester. He is a base stealer (31 in 37 attempts), but the 24 year old righthanded batter doesn't get on base enough

(.329 percentage) to be a major league leadoff hitter. But, oh! Can he play center field! And yes, he is Don Buford's son. Damon's older brother left the Baltimore organization to go to medical school.

Speed also is Curtis Goodwin's greatest asset. The lefthanded batter, 22, was voted the fastest and best baserunner and most exciting player in the Eastern League. A strong finish brought his final numbers (.286-2-37-59 steals) as Bowie's leadoff hitter to about what he did in A ball, indicating that he probably can do the same in Triple-A in '95. He is penciled in for arrival in Baltimore late this season or in '96. For this season, Buford is a better bet to be the Orioles center fielder.

Another excellent young prospect, most likely Rochester's right fielder this season, is Alex Ochoa. The 23 year old righthanded batter seems to hit nothing but line drives, and went .301-14-82-28 steals at Bowie. He has a very strong arm, though he doesn't always seem to know where his throws are going. Ochoa had a poor start last season, or he would have had even better statistics. One thing to remember about the other Baltimore prospects coming up from Double-A is that the assortment of home parks the team played in before Bowie's stadium was completed added up in hitters' favor to the extreme.

Sherman Obando bounced back from a wasted 1993 season in Baltimore as a major league draft choice. The 25 year old is a good righthanded hitter with extra-base power, and has a good arm. Unfortunately, Obando is very poor at judging fly balls. His '94 season ended early because of a broken shinbone, but his numbers at Rochester (.330-20-69-.603 slugging percentage) would have been an excellent full season for most players. If he plays much for the Orioles this season, it will be as a DH.

Mark Smith is a tarnished 1991 first-round draft pick. He showed some power in his second Triple-A season, but his average dropped 33 points (.247-19-66). He has little speed and little arm for a guy who has played mostly right field in the minors. At this point, he may never play his way to Baltimore beyond the three games he played for the Birds last season.

While Smith was declining, Jim Wawruck was hustling his way past the high draft pick on the prospect ladder. Wawruck batted .300-9-53 at Rochester, and stole 17 bases in 19 attempts. The lefthanded batter will be 25 in April. His arm has limited him to left field, but he compensated for its lack of strength with good positioning and charging base hits.

Harry Berrios, a 23 year old righthanded batter, raised his career average more than 100 points in his second minor league season. He batted .333 in 42 games in the Sally League, then .348 in 86 games after a promotion to the Carolina League. He totaled 19 homers, 106 RBI and 56 stolen bases. He's an offensive threat, but not a good defensive player. His teammate at Frederick was Kimera Bartee, 22. The righthanded batter was at .292-10-57 with 44 steals. He also had a fast start in the Australian League. He needs to work on making better contact.

Boston Red Sox

The Red Sox acquisition of Jose Canseco via trade solves their DH dilemma, but opens up a number of outfield holes. Canseco could take over the open rightfield spot or substitute for injured Mike Greenwell, too, but his 1993 shoulder surgery may prevent him from ever playing in the field again, or pitching again either.

With the trade of Otis Nixon to Texas and Jeff McNeely to St. Louis (for Luis Alicea), the Red Sox are without a centerfielder. That job could go to one of the many available free agent outfielders or the Glenn Murray could be rushed into the job. Murray isn't ready yet and would probably hit for a low average.

Tom Brunansky and Andre Dawson remained unsigned free agents; Dawson is unlikely to re-sign with to Boston, but Brunansky could return.

Alan Boodman:

The Red Sox' outfield in 1995 could contain a lot of new faces before all is said and done. Two of the

starters (Mike Greenwell and Otis Nixon) are getting up in years - 31 and 36 respectively - and are coming off of injuries, in Greenwell's case a fairly severe shoulder, and Nixon fought hamstring problems all throughout 1994. Right field was manned by Tom Brunansky for much of last season, and he thankfully left via free agency.

Greenwell has fought his way back on previous occasions, and despite the fact that he seemed to enter the decline phase of his career six years ago, his lifetime batting average remains over .300. Greenwell adds some markers to his average: moderate power (much of it in the form of doubles), RBIs, and walks. His defense has improved from laughable to adequate. Greenwell's 1994 numbers were adversely affected by his sore shoulder, which ended his season just before the strike was called. If (IF!) he's healthy this year, he'll play practically every day and bat .290-13-75, with 30+ doubles and around 65 walks.

Nixon provided the Sox with speed as advertised, and he's not slowing down much despite age and hamstring maladies. His 1994 numbers were all within the range of his established norms and until the speed goes, Nixon should be able to produce enough to remain employed. To remain at the top of the order however, he'll have to keep his OBP up around .350, otherwise he's Vince Coleman, which is to say valueless.

Nixon wasted no time in learning the AL pitchers, with 42 steals in only 103 games, and posted the highest success rate (81%) of his career to boot. Nixon should be able to score close to 100 runs over a full campaign, as long as he continues to get on base frequently. He has little choice but to be a slap hitter who uses the bunt as a primary weapon. So long as Nixon doesn't alter his style, look for .275-1-35-55 for a couple more years.

Wes Chamberlain was scarcely given an opportunity to get off the plane from Philadelphia before Butch Hobson decided to give Tom Brunansky an extended trial in right field in 1994. Bruno, in typical fashion, lit up the scoreboard for about 15 days, and then cruised the rest of the year while Chamberlain rode the bench or sometimes served as DH.

Chamberlain's no candidate to develop into an All-Star, but he's a fine athlete with substantial power whose defense was better than anticipated. His overall lack of plate discipline has been a large factor in the meandering path of his career to date and is also a factor in his inability to consistently hit righthanded pitching. Still, the Sox could do worse than to open 1995 with this guy in right field.

But they might be able to do better. There are some outfielders in the Sox' system who are very close to being ready for the majors: Greg Blosser and Glenn Murray at Triple-A Pawtucket, and Patrick Lennon, Jose Malave, and Matt Stairs, all of whom spent 1994 at Double-A New Britain.

Blosser is a prime candidate to battle Wes Chamberlain for the right field spot. Actually, based on his glovework, Blosser should be more of a candidate for the DH job. The lack of a glove, along with his sometimes Rob Deer-like offensive numbers, are what has slowed his progress so far.

Blosser does whiff quite a bit, and has typically taken more than one season to adjust to a new level. He adjusted to Triple-A in 1994 at age 23, hitting .260-17-54-11 in just 97 games. The lefthanded hitter would strike out well over 100 times in a full major league season, and would be fortunate to have an on-base percentage much over .300. Blosser is in a good spot though; the position he wants is at least partially open, and he's near the front of the line. For 1995, I'd expect a season of about 350 at bats, with .230-15-45 potential. If he hits more, he'll play more; if not, he'll be in Pawtucket and so will not hurt a Rotisserie team much. He has very good upside potential which may begin to show itself as soon as this summer.

Jeff McNeely fell far and fast in 1994. The 24 yearold (now 25) batted just .231-4-34 at Pawtucket, with 17 caught stealings to go with only 13 swipes. Injuries were not to blame either; it was simply a major step back. McNeely was meant to at least provide a token challenge to Otis Nixon for the center field job in 1994, but did not make the team in the spring and

proceeded to slide downhill throughout the summer. He is still considered by some to be a prospect, but has many things on which to work: he strikes out way too much for a non-power hitter, his base stealing clearly needs improvement, and there are rumblings that his attitude may need an adjustment as well. Last winter, McNeely was traded to St. Louis where he will quickly disappear if his turnaround is not swift and complete.

Murray batted only .224 with 134 strikeouts at Pawtucket in 1994, but this 24 year old showed a lot of positives. He has 30-home-run power, speed that is not even hinted at by his mere nine steals, an upbeat attitude, and he covers a tremendous amount of territory in the outfield. Murray was in the over-crowded Montreal organization until the spring of 1994, which explains why it took him 3+ years to escape Class-A. He will probably get another full season at Patwtucket to work on making better contact, but if Murray appears at Fenway you may want to snap him up quickly.

Lennon is a former first-round pick of the Mariners who appears to have overcome both professional and personal problems, at least for the time being. Lennon seemed ready to burst through to the majors after a .329-15-74-12 season at Calgary in 1991 at age 23. Injuries caused him to miss almost the entire 1992 and 1993 seasons, and his attitude once again deteriorated along with his physical condition.

The Sox signed Lennon, who will be 27 in April, to a contract with New Britain prior to 1994, and he performed splendidly: .326-17-67-13. His age and previous Triple-A experience will enable him to move straight to the majors if needed. Lennon must continue to display the positive attitude he showed in 1994, and probably needs to post similarly good numbers at Pawtucket to truly get back on track. He stands a good chance of appearing in the majors at some point in 1995.

Malave will be 24 in May, and is ticketed to spend this season in Pawtucket. Malave has been a consistent .300 hitter over his five year career, and really broke through with a .299-24-92-4 season at New Britain

in 1994. A righthanded hitter with outstanding bat speed, Malave is probably ready offensively for the majors right now. His main drawback is that he has no experience above Double-A, and that his glovework practically mandates his use as a DH.

Stairs is another ex-Montrealer who was trampled by superior prospects in their farm system. On the verge of the majors following good minor league campaigns in 1991-92, Stairs escaped briefly to Japan, but played in 1994 for the Red Sox at New Britain (.309-9-61-10 in 93 games). Now age 26, Stairs is no longer a prospect, but has an excellent chance of making it to the show if he continues to hit at Pawtucket. A solid spring training for Lennon, Malave or Stairs could result in ownership of an opening day roster spot.

Among established backup outfielders at the major league level, Lee Tinsley was kept around for his speed and not much else, and Andy Tomberlin is a journeyman who's frequently hit well in the minors. Neither exactly has a solid grip on a roster spot in Boston.

Lary Bump:

Last season Greg Blosser finally started to play like a 1989 first-round draft pick (1989). His average was up (.260-17-54-11 steals), his strikeouts were down (from 139 to 97) and he played a solid right field in his second Triple-A season. He started last year in Boston, and should be back there in '95. The lefthanded batter is still only 23.

Glenn Murray is an all-or-nothing type of hitter (.224-25-64-134 strikeouts at Pawtucket), but a good left fielder capable of playing center in a pinch. Dan Duquette brought him over from Montreal, which could be a point in favor of Murray's career development. He made need that help, for his on-field performance suffered in his first Triple-A season. The righthanded batter, 24, still has time to develop.

Nine-year minor league veteran Andy Tomberlin, a 28 year old lefthanded batter, earned his second brief major league stint with a monster start at Pawtucket

(.333-13-39-11 steals). He has enough arm to play right field and can play first base, so he is a good utility candidate.

After Luis Ortiz was traded, Jose Malave became the best hitting prospect in the Boston organization. Playing his home games at one of the minors' toughest parks for hitters, New Britain's Beehive Field, Malave was among the minor league leaders in slugging percentage (.563) and extra-base hits (68) while batting .299-24-92. The 23 year old is a righthanded pure line-drive hitter who has really come on after taking three seasons to get past the short-season leagues. His defense needs work.

The overall best outfield prospect is Trot Nixon, Boston's 1993 first-round draft pick. The lefthanded batter, who will be 21 in April, made his pro debut last year in the fast Class A Carolina League. He batted .246-12-43-10 steals in half a season before a back injury sidelined him. He also wasn't ready for the Arizona Fall League season. If healthy, he'll be among the top major league prospects in 1996 or '97.

Taking Nixon's place in Arizona was Paul Rappoli, a 23 year old lefhthanded batter. After spending '93 in the Eastern League, he was sent back to the Florida State League last year (.347-1-12 in 20 games). After returning to New Britain, he batted a solid .279-4-40-18 steals. Rappoli is a fourth-outfielder candidate at best.

Also at New Britain were 26 year olds Matt Stairs and Patrick Lennon. Stairs, a lefthanded batter, was an MVP in the Double-A All-Star Game, but was anticipating both knee surgery and minor league free agency. The lefthanded batter, who also has played in Japan, was at .309-9-61-10 steals. Lennon, the Mariners' 1986 first-round draft choice, batted .326-17-67 with 13 steals.

Another aged outfielder at New Britain was Wayne Housie, 29. He batted .225-5-40, and the one weapon he had -- speed -- deserted him. He stole successfully just three times in 11 attempts.

The major league draft brought righthanded power prospect Benji Simonton, 22, from the San Francisco organization. He batted .270 in the Midwest League and .297 in the California League, with almost identical power numbers that totaled 28 homers and 108 RBI. He stole 10 bases before the promotion, none after. At Class A Sarasota was base stealer Aaron Fuller (.261-2-28-45 steals). The 23 year old switch hitter has the patience needed by a leadoff batter.

California Angels

Bo Jackson remained an unsigned free agent although the Angels are said to have interest in re-signing him. New Angels' manager Marcel Lachemann is not a fan of Jackson and won't play him in the outfield. Until Jackson's role is known it's best to stay away from him.

Hank Widmer:

The Angels outfield is the strongest area of the team. There aren't going to be any surprises like Jim Edmonds was in 1994, but it'll be a good, solid group. Edmonds is likely to move to first base because the Angels will try Garret Anderson in left field. I'm not convinced that Anderson is ready, as he'll be only 22 when the season starts, but the Angels have moved him quickly through the organization. He hit .321 in Vancouver, but the Pacific Coast League is a hitter's haven and there have been a lot of .320 hitters from that league who didn't make a ripple in the majors. Anderson is not a base stealer, so hope for a high batting average and a little bit of power.

Chad Curtis again becomes the default Angel leadoff batter. Curtis has struggled for the last year and a half, finally moving downward in the batting order. In 1994, his on-base average was unacceptable for a leadoff batter (.317) and he was a borderline 69% base stealer (25/36).

Tim Salmon is the best player the Angels have at the moment. He's young, 26 to start the 1995 season, has power, can hit for average, will take a walk, and has a good arm. Salmon seems to be healthy and should

continue to be one of the best rightfielders in the league (Puckett and Carter are probably the only ones better). He won't steal any bases, but he'll help your team in any other category.

Fred Matos:

Tim Salmon had his second consecutive outstanding season in 1994, proving that he is not a one year wonder as some Rookies of the Year turn out to be. He has an unusual platoon differential in that he hits righthanders much better than southpaws. Correcting that situation could make him a consistent .300 hitter. Salmon is 26 years old and has two years of solid major league experience. He could have a big breakout year in 1995, like .300-30-110 which would make him worth about $30.

Chad Curtis had a down year as he imagined himself as a power hitter rather than the pesky get-on-base type. He can snap out of it in 1995 and revert back to his previous form. He could steal as many as 50 bases, but that would be up to new Manager Marcel Lachemann and how much he wants to run. Curtis could be worth $25-35, depending on his batting average and his stolen bases. He gets caught stealing a lot, and that may put a damper on his running. Curtis is worth much less if your league counts net steals.

Jim Edmonds is a line-drive hitter who can hit for a good average and pop an occasional home run. He's not as glamorous or well known as some of the other Angel outfielders, but his steady hitting and good defense may prevail over the long term. He could be worth $10 in 1995.

Bo Jackson did surprisingly well as an outfielder last year, and even hit a career best .279. Jackson can hit 20 homers as a part-time player, but batting over .250 would be a surprise. For 1995, the Angels told me that they will discuss his role and playing time with him as they envision Bo as a part-time outfielder, part time DH, and pinch hitter, a status that Bo may not like. But that was to be his role last year, and he ended up playing a lot of left field. Manager Marcel Lachemann prefers good defense, and he doesn't like Bo in left because of his limited range. Last year,

Lachemann even played Chili Davis in left for a couple of games. Bo's future with the Angels doesn't look good, so he may sign with another team.

Bo's Rotisserie value is hard to figure as both his 1995 team and his role are unclear. He will be overbid in many leagues as many will remember the "old" Bo. At most, he's worth about $5.

Highly regarded prospect Garrett Anderson is a smooth, line drive hitter, but he doesn't have much power. He is an excellent prospect who has a good chance to break into the Angels' starting lineup in 1995. Anderson will be 23 years old in June, and has nothing more to prove in Triple-A.

Steve Hosey was the Giants' first round draft pick in 1989. He had two solid years in Triple-A with the Giants, but was traded to the Angels in April 1993. Last year was his third in Triple-A, but the bad news is it was his worst. The competition for an Angel outfield job is tough, so Hosey will most likely spend another season in Triple-A.

Lary Bump:

Garret Anderson, 22, has extra-base power (.321-12-102-42 doubles in the Pacific Coast League), but not a lot of speed (three steals in six attempts). Those who were impressed with Jim Edmonds' fast start in '94 will be in awe of Anderson, who is two years younger. The lefthanded batter is one of the best prospects coming up to the majors this season. If he doesn't make it in left field for the '95 Angels, he will soon -- and he'll make it big. After failing to crack the Giants' outfield despite being their first-round draft choice in 1989 and posting some impressive Triple-A stats, Hosey moved to the Angels' organization last season with less success (.259-17-60). The righthanded batter will be 26 in April; the Royals' Dwayne Hosey has passed him as a prospect.

Jovino Carvajal, late of the Yankees organization, had a big year at Cedar Rapids (.292-6-54-68 steals). The switch hitter is 26, so his career probably holds the promise of another Midwest League base stealer, Ramon Sambo. Who's he? Exactly.

Derrin Doty started the season as Carvajal's teammate (.323-5-34-20 steals), but wasn't impressive in the California League (.273-7-24-12). The righthanded batter is 24, and can't be considered a prospect.

Also at Vancouver was a 28 year old, lefthanded-hitting journeyman, John Jackson (.293-2-38-18 steals). He's an insurance policy at best. Orlando Palmeiro, 26, has averaged .310 in four minor league seasons, and was at .328 in the PCL. But the lefthanded batter has absolutely no power (two career homers) and is not an effective base stealer (78-for-129, 60 percent, in his career).

A better prospect is 24 year old Marquis Riley (.286-1-29-32 steals in 37 attempts in the Texas League). He's a righthanded batter. Mark Sweeney moved up from the Texas League (.300-3-18) to the PCL (.285-8-49). He's a 25 year old lefthanded batter with little speed or power, and a marginal prospect.

At Double-A Midland was 24 year old Mike Wolff (.290-13-58). He bats righthanded. Robbie Katzaroff, a 26 year old righthanded batter, has spent parts of the last four seasons in Double-A with four different organizations. After a .276-0-11 start at Midland, he went .281-1-33 in the California League. He totaled 35 stolen bases.

The Angels selected speedy lefthanded hitter McKay Christensen out of high school in the first round of the 1994 draft. Don't look for him for a while, for he'll be on a mission for the Mormon church until 1996.

Someone who will help immediately or not at all is Pedro Guerrero, once one of the most-feared hitters in the National League. The free-agent signee was one of the most-feared hitters in the independent Northern League in '94.

Chicago White Sox

Darrin Jackson and Dan Pasqua remained unsigned free agents. Pasqua will go somewhere else (probably to the minors). Jackson may return to Chicago. If not, the White Sox will be in the market for an outfielder and may take on yet another reclamation project such as Ellis Burks (1993) and Jackson (1994). Whomever it is will immediately jump in value as the White Sox have a potent enough lineup to allow the new acquisition to be free of pressure to produce from the start.

Stuart Shea:

He's no longer the best leadoff man in baseball, or even pretty to watch sometimes, but Tim Raines continues to perform productively at the top of the White Sox order. As he as grown older, his extra-base power has increased, his average has dropped, and his stolen bases have fallen. However, Raines still walks a great deal, rarely strikes out, and swiped 13 sacks without being caught last year.

Raines does have his problems. His range and glove have deteriorated, and he could never throw all that well. In addition, lefties make Raines look bad. However, he's going to lead off in 1995, and he's going to get on base, and he's going to score runs. "Rock" is signed through 1996, and considering the lack of quality outfielders at high levels of the Sox system, he's a godsend to the South Siders.

"One Dog" Lance Johnson led the AL in triples for the fourth straight season in 1994, and continued to display outstanding range in center field. He never walks, but does hit for a consistently good average and steals bases effectively. He contributes in some critical areas, and does not make stupid mistakes. His weaknesses (power, walks) are picked up by some of his teammates. As long as Johnson has his speed, he will help the Sox on the bases, and has hit .274 or higher in each of his five regular seasons with Chicago. Consistency is a virtue, and there are few players more consistent than Johnson.

When the Sox signed Darrin Jackson before the 1994 season, they were probably hoping he'd hit for power like he did in San Diego and show off his throwing arm in right field. More pessimistic observers were fearful that he'd just flail at everything as he has in the past and make mistakes in the outfield. However, DJ had surprises in store for everyone.

While he only threw out two runners last year and connected for just 10 homers, Jackson also went the worked hard to put the ball in play and improved his K/W ratio to 2-1. In contrast to his past tendency, Jackson showed more patience at bat, pushed pitches the opposite way, and, as a result enjoyed his best average and on-base percentage ever. He also played well in the pasture.

If the Sox re-sign Jackson, he will probably relapse as AL pitchers make their adjustments to him. He has recovered completely from the hyperthyroid condition that ruined his 1993 season, and is a courageous and likeable player, but Jackson will be hard-pressed to stay at his lofty 1994 level. He'll probably be overvalued in most auctions.

The Sox are thin in the outfield, but that isn't Warren Newson's fault. "The Deacon" (most of the Sox have interesting nicknames, publicized by voluble broadcaster Ken Harrelson) just hits and hits every time he gets his chance. Unfortunately, he doesn't get enough chances. Newson hits righties very well, draws walks, and has surprising opposite-field power. He deserves to play more than he did in 1994, but Newson's pinch-hitting ability threatens to forever typecast him.

Six-year minor league vet Joe "Do it All" Hall finally made his big-league debut in 1994. He started off hitting line drives, but suffered a severe hamstring injury in May that basically ended his season. The versatile Hall may make the Sox again this season due to the club's lack of bench strength, but he's not a .393 hitter, or even a .293 hitter. Don't be fooled. He's a good 25th man for Chicago, but you can find better.

This same lack of bench strength may mean that Bob Zupcic sticks around as well. The former Red Sox outfielder doesn't seem to have a colorful nickname; his play is so bland and unexciting that he doesn't really merit one. If Zupcic was a world-class defensive outfielder, his weak offense would be excused. However, Zupcic is just oh okay with a glove, and has never impressed with his bat. His main marker is that he was a second-round draft choice in 1987. That was

a long time ago, and the Red Sox make mistakes.

Veteran flotsam Dann Howitt and Dan Pasqua will not be back, and will not be missed.

Minor leaguers Jimmy Hurst (big power and improving strike zone judgement at class-A Prince William), Mike Robertson (highly regarded, but hasn't converted his tools into impact offense), and Essex Burton (great speed, but nothing else) won't make impacts in the major leagues this year. Hurst, especially, is a prospect. He turns 23 in March but has made great strides in the last two years.

Previously unheralded double-A outfielder Michael Jordan, a late starter to pro baseball, hit just .202 with no power. However, he showed some plate discipline and good speed on the bases. He has little chance to ever start in the major leagues, but could end up in a reserve role. His physical gifts and 6'6" frame suggest a possible future in basketball; he is rumored at one time to have played professionally.

Cleveland Indians

Candy Maldonado is an unsigned free agent and won't be back with the Indians; he may have trouble finding a major league job in 1995.

After being acquired in a post-strike trade, 43 year old Dave Winfield became a free agent. He was primarily added by the Indians as an extra bat for the playoffs in case the strike was resolved. Winfield will either sign for a lot of money as a DH somewhere or retire. He can still hit, so he'd be a good one-year speculative pick if he goes to an AL team needing a regular DH.

Minor league free agent Mike Humphreys left the Yankees to join the Indians Triple-A club. He has little chance of reaching the big leagues in 1995.

Jeromy Burnitz managed 13 homers for the 1993 Mets, then just three last year. The Indians acquired Burnitz via trade in the off-season. The rightfielder has no chance of supplanting Manny Ramirez, but

could make the big club as an extra outfielder/pinch-hitter. Burnitz possesses a lot of power, but would resemble Rob Deer if given 400 at bats. Make sure he has a well-defined role before taking a chance on Burnitz.

Tony Blengino:

Albert Belle is a certifiable monster. Years ago, it appeared that he was a self-destructive monster, but he has contained his anger and turned it into intensity. Belle has added another dimension to his game in each of his four seasons as a regular. In 1991, he proved he could hit for power, and in 1992 he proved he could stay in the lineup without a major blowup. In 1993, Belle became more patient at the plate, stole more bases and improved his outfield defense tremendously. In 1994, he put together a dominating season that had him in contention for the Triple Crown when the strike reared its ugly head. His 36 homers, 101 RBI and .357 average gave him a shot at .350 with 50 homers and 150 RBI, a combination previously achieved by only Babe Ruth (twice), Jimmie Foxx and Hack Wilson. Belle is an equal opportunity masher - he hit .367 against lefties and .353 against righties. Despite his already impressive career accomplishments, Belle remains the fourth youngest starting leftfielder in the AL Expect another mammoth year in 1995, with a .320 average, 50 homers, 135 RBI and 12 steals.

In Rotisserie circles, though, Belle wasn't even the most valuable outfielder on his own team. That honor goes to Lofton, who in 1994 seized the Best Leadoff Hitter mantle from Lenny Dykstra and Rickey Henderson. Coming into 1994, Lofton had already proven himself as baseball's foremost basestealer and a consistent .300 hitter. The one hole in his game was a glaring lack of power. In 1994, Lofton complemented his .349 average with 53 extra base hits, including 12 homers, for a glowing .536 slugging percentage. Like Belle, Lofton scorched all pitchers, waxing lefties at a .331 clip and hitting .359 against righties in 1994. Despite all those extra base hits, he found the opportunities to steal 60 bases, giving him 196 (at an 84% success rate) over the past three seasons. There isn't a more valuable Rotisserie prop-

erty in baseball than Kenny Lofton. In 1995, he can be expected to hit .340 with 15 homers and 80 steals.

Which brings us to the guy that could well post a better career than either Belle or Lofton, Manny Ramirez. At age 22, the age at which Ramirez arrived as a dominant offensive force at the major league level, Lofton was a Single-A outfielder in the Astros' chain, and Belle was still Joey, his evil twin which prevented Albert from reaching his fearsome potential. After torching the Indians' farm system in 1993, hitting for a .333 average and slugging .613 at Double and Triple-A, Ramirez proved it was no fluke by earning the starting right field job in Cleveland and holding onto it with his sometimes devastating offensive presence. He is far from a finished product, as evidenced by his .205 mark against righthanded pitching. Manager Mike Hargrove rested him occasionally against tough righties, a practice which will certainly diminish over time. Ramirez is a young free spirit who has some growing up to do, so expect some anxious moments waiting for him to reach his immense potential. Expect another glimpse in 1995, with .280, 35 homers and 95 RBI a possibility. In the future, 50 homer seasons and MVP Awards could ensue.

Wayne Kirby, 31, is the good soldier who toiled for nine seasons in the minors before establishing himself at the big league level with a strong 1993 season in Cleveland. Though not nearly the speedster he was as a minor leaguer, his speed is a valuable commodity on a team whose speed otherwise begins and ends with Kenny Lofton. Expect Kirby's playing time to steadily diminish as Ramirez matures into a true everyday player. 250 at bats, with a .270 average and 10 steals, appear to be within reach for Kirby in 1995.

Candy Maldonado, 34, has reached the end of the ridiculous contract he originally signed with the Cubs, and has become a free agent. In 1994, he served as the Indians' DH against most lefties, as Eddie Murray moved to first base and Paul Sorrento sat. Though Maldonado hit only .196 in 92 at bats, 11 of his 18 hits were for extra bases, including five homers. Sadly, his bat has slowed to the point that he is totally useless against righties (.125 in 1994).

Maldonado's career could be at an end, and it is highly unlikely that he will return to the Tribe in 1995.

Ruben Amaro, 30, thought that he had finally caught a break when he was traded by the Phils to the Indians following the 1993 season. Despite an illustrious minor league career, and some periods of success during Lenny Dykstra's injuries in Philadelphia, his career as a Phil had grinded to a halt. The Indians fully expected Manny Ramirez to spend 1994 in the minors, with Kirby and Amaro platooning in right. Well, if you read this book last season, you knew that just wasn't meant to be, and Amaro was the odd man out. A switch hitter, he is strong against lefties, which is also Ramirez' strong suit, leaving nothing but scraps for Amaro. For that reason, he is unlikely to snare even a backup job in Cleveland. If he latches on as a platooner elsewhere, Amaro could reach double figures in steals.

Omar Ramirez, 24, took a major step backwards in 1994, hitting only .232 at Triple-A Charlotte. Ramirez had been a career .294 hitter before 1994, and he possesses good speed (58 steals over the last three seasons) and consistently walks more than he strikes out. The Tribe won't give up on him, but he has clearly dropped behind Giles in the pecking order. Ramirez could have a major league future as a fourth outfielder, possibly not in Cleveland.

Pat Bryant, 22, is a raw prospect who was the Indians' 2nd-round pick in 1990. He skipped a level to Double-A in 1994, struggling to a .236 average, but flashing his power/speed potential, with 12 homers and 23 steals. Bryant has stolen 111 bases in his last three seasons, but hasn't hit above .263. Also on the down side, he has averaged 106 whiffs in his last four seasons. He's still young and has raw ability, so he will likely advance to Triple-A in 1995. Bryant is a solid season away from emerging as a serious major league prospect.

As an undrafted free agent, Marc Marini knows what it's like to be a perpetual underdog. Despite hitting for high averages with decent power in each of his three pro seasons, Marini, 25, has seen prospects race by him. In 1994, Marini slugged .505 at Double-A

Canton-Akron; his Single-A doubles power matured into Double-A home run power (17 in 1994). His status as a lefty should get him to the big leagues as a spare outfielder, possibly in 1995.

Tony Mitchell, 24, finally emerged above Single-A in 1994, and led Indians' minor leaguers in homers with 25. Mitchell was the Pirates' 34th-round pick in 1989, and had routinely hit for good power before fizzling at Single-A Kinston in 1993. His 1994 rebound, plus the fact that he's a switch-hitter, puts Mitchell in the running for the righthanded portion of the Indians' DH job in 1995. More likely, he will start the season at Triple-A, and be waiting in the wings should the Tribe need midseason reinforcements.

Yet more outfield prospects are lurking in Single-A. Lefty Jon Nunnally, 23, hit 22 homers and stole 23 bases for Kinston in the Carolina League. Though he's struck out 233 times over the past two seasons, and has yet to play Double-A ball, his potential should enable the Indians' 1992 number three pick to excel at Double-A in 1995. Alex Ramirez, 20, was signed by the Indians out of Venezuela at age 16. He has established himself as a power prospect, hitting 31 homers in 1993 and 1994 combined. Considering that he did so in pitchers' leagues, and that he's still growing, his best is likely yet to come. Of some concern is his tendency to swing at everything - a 157/39 strikeout/walk ratio over the past two seasons. Watch his development closely over the next two seasons.

Lary Bump:

Brian Giles now is the Indians' leading outfield prospect. The 24 year old lefthanded batter with the weightlifter's physique in six pro seasons has batted better than .300 four times, including .313-16-58 for Triple-A Charlotte in 1994. For its bench, Cleveland obtained International Leaguers Mike Humphreys (.248-8-51-28 steals) and Jeromy Burnitz (.239-14-49-18). Humphreys, a righthanded batter who will be 28 in April, is a utility candidate who can play any outfield position or second or third base. Burnitz, two years younger, is a lefthanded batter who had similar production in 143 at bats with the Mets (.238-

3-15), but with only one steal. He has a good arm in right field. After a career year in Double-A in 1993, Omar Ramirez was a major disappointment in the International League (.232-8-45-15 steals).

He often was platooned with J.T. Bruett, a 27 year old lefthanded batter acquired during the season from the Twins. He was platooned at Charlotte, and contributed little (.252-1-8) to the Knights' offense. He may resurface in the majors as a defensive outfielder and pinch runner, but no more. Even his speed isn't what it used to be. After averaging better than 30 stolen bases a season, he totaled just nine in 110 games between Salt Lake City and Charlotte last year.

Detroit Tigers

Eric Davis, Kirk Gibson and Juan Samuel all remained free agents and none are likely to return to Detroit with the Tigers alledgedly leaning toward a youth movment. Davis has never been able to overcome injuries and its difficult to predict anything for him but a continued slide into retirement. Gibson and Samuel are well past their primes and may wind up unsigned into spring training. Gibson can still provide a little value but is a very tenuous player at this point. Samuel has no Rotisserie value.

Fred Matos:

The Tigers have been known for preferring veterans, so a prospect usually has an uphill battle to get a good shot at starting. Last year the favored outfield vets were Kirk Gibson, Tony Phillips, Milt Cuyler, Eric Davis, Junior Felix, Juan Samuel, and to a lesser extent, Mickey Tettleton and Skeeter Barnes. Danny Bautista was the promising rookie who won a starting job but was injured early in the season. The new Tiger front office has indicated that it's time for an approach based on youth as the Tigers have not contended using the veterans. But the farm system talent is thin, so they will likely fall back on the old vets once again.

Since the infield is solid, Tony Phillips no longer needs to be an all-purpose utility player, so he can again play left field nearly full time as he did last year. With 19 dingers, he looked like a power hitter but it was a juiced ball year. Phillips is a steady and reliable outfielder that you can usually count on to hit around .300 with 10 homers and 10 stolen bases.

The Tigers gave veteran Junior Felix another chance when his career was almost dead. He responded nicely, restarting his failing career with a changed attitude, thanks in part to Cecil Fielder's guidance. Felix took over in right field when Bautista was injured and hit a nice .306-13-49 in 301 at bats. He will contend for a starting outfield slot in 1995, but he has a track record of hot streaks followed by bad slumps, major lapses afield, and attitude problems, making him a risky player both in Rotisserie and real baseball.

Some people had the talented Eric Davis pegged as a future Hall of Famer a few years ago. He showed flashes of brilliance, but everything just didn't come together for him for more than two or three seasons. Barring injury, he is capable of a 20-20 season with about 80 RBI, but .250 is about the highest average you can expect. Davis still commands a big salary, and as a free agent, was not likely to be re-signed by the Tigers.

Unless he steals at least 20 bases, Milt Cuyler has very little value in Rotisserie. He is a singles hitter who hits below .250, and other than the steals, he doesn't give you anything else. His likely roles in 1995 are defensive substitute and pinch runner.

Danny Bautista may go cheaply in many drafts based on his poor .232 last year. He can steal 20 bases or more and hit around .250. Bautista will play 1995 at age 23, and he is still learning via on-the-job-training. He is improving rapidly and may develop some power as he matures. Bautista is a good Rotisserie pick if you can get him below $10.

Juan Samuel is 34 and a reserve outfielder/infielder who may lose his job to a younger player. Kirk Gibson is covered in more detail in the DH chapter, and Mickey Tettleton under catchers.

Prospect Bob Higginson had a solid season in Triple-A last year: .275-23-67-16. He is the top minor league candidate and can take over a starting outfield slot if someone is injured or slumps badly. Riccardo Ingram has a Triple-A bat. Rudy Pemberton showed some power and speed in Triple-A, and could win a job as a reserve outfielder.

Lary Bump:

The Tigers had a solid outfield at Triple-A Toledo. The biggest surprise was Bob Higginson (.275-23-67-16 steals). The 24 year old lefthanded batter played center field for the Mud Hens, but would have to play left or right at Tiger Stadium. Riccardo Ingram, 28, made it to the majors in his seventh pro season after a good start at Toledo (.287-9-56-11 steals). He bats righthanded, as does 25 year old Rudy Pemberton (.303-12-58-30). All three Mud Hens regular outfielders set season highs in stolen bases in manager Larry Parrish's run-and-gun attack.

At Trenton, 23 year old lefthanded batter Brian DuBose crashed in his Double-A debut (.225-9-41). He also has played first base, and is an inefficient base stealer (12-for-22). Justin Mashore, a 23 year old righthanded batter, had a similar year (.222-7-45), but his season was punctuated with 31 stolen bases and 120 strikeouts.

If the Tigers ever become a running team, a key could be 21 year old Tarrik Brock, who advanced during last season from the Florida State League to Trenton. He totaled 18 triples, four homers, 43 RBI and 18 stolen bases. However, the lefthanded batter was overmatched in the Eastern League (.139 in 115 at bats).

In the major league draft, the Tigers took Todd Steverson, who batted .263-9-38-20 steals in the Southern League. He's a 23 year old righthanded batter.

Kansas City Royals

Vince Coleman remained a free agent and Felix Jose refused a minor league assignment to become a free agent. With the budget-conscious Royals looking to reduce payroll costs, there is very little chance they will sign an expensive free agent for 1995. That means left and right field will belong to rookies Michael Tucker and Joe Vitiello.

Switch-hitter Dwayne Hosey's value also increases, assuming he isn't traded. The Royals will probably add a cheap veteran defensive specialist to give their young outfield some stability, but that player would have little or no Rotisserie value. Should Hosey be traded, Tom Goodwin would have a great chance to catch on as a fourth outfielder, a role in which he could steal 20 bases; the steals represent all of his Rotisserie value.

Dave Henderson and Kevin Koslofski have also left the Royals and are unlikely to return. Henderson is on the brink of retirement, but could win a righthanded pinch-hitting role somewhere. Koslofski will probably end up as Triple-A roster filler somewhere.

Marc Bowman:

In 1994, left field belonged to Vince Coleman, who stole 50 bases but had virtually no other value for Rotisserie owners (or in real baseball). His one year contract has expired and the Royals are looking at promoting their most promising prospect, Michael Tucker, to Kansas City in 1995. The 23 year old Tucker has moved quickly from Class-A in 1993 to a full season at Triple-A Omaha where he hit .276-21-77-11 in 1994. A lefthanded hitter, Tucker has struck out a lot (211 Ks in 968 minor league at bats), but has the speed and power to be a 20/20 man in his first big league season. A first round draft pick in 1992, Tucker is likely to be on everyone's hot prospect list, but he's still going to be underrated by most. His batting average may take a small dip as he moves to the bigs, but you can still expect him to put up very valuable numbers for a reasonable price; look for Tucker to produce .250-15-55-15 in 1995 with better numbers later.

Coleman is likely to find somewhere to play in 1995 and, if he retains a full-time role, will again steal about

40 bases with no other positives. Be particularly cautious of Coleman if your league uses OBP, as he has been atrocious at getting on base in recent years. His 1994 .285 OBP was worse than most leadoff hitters' batting averages; his career OBP is .324 and is getting worse each year. Still, Coleman has the ability to steal almost at will, and stolen bases have never been more highly valued than they are right now. Pay $15 for 40 steals, but don't expect any other useful production and pay even less if you use OBP.

Brian McRae gives the Royals solid defense in center field and about two months worth of excellent hitting each year. McRae has historically hit very well in the first half of the year before slowing down, presenting Rotisserie owners with an opportunity to buy McRae cheaply and get almost all of his Rotisserie value by the All-Star break before dealing him away. McRae is likely to hit near the top of the order, and will adjust his hitting approach to get on base more regularly (his .359 OBP in 1994 was a career high). This will cut his power significantly but should also increase his stolen base count. Watch for McRae to hit .270 with 6 homers, 45 RBI and 30 stolen bases, making him worth slightly less than $20.

Joe Vitiello was an outfielder at Double-A Memphis in 1993, then primarily played first base for Triple-A Omaha in 1994. For 1995, the Royals are talking about shifting him once again, this time to right field. He probably has the arm (he was originally drafted as a pitcher/outfielder), but may lack the speed to do the job well. To get a preview of what could happen with Vitiello as a regular outfielder, the Royals need only to watch the struggles that first baseman Ryan Klesko suffered through when playing left field for Atlanta in 1994. Vitiello won't be that bad, but he's going to have some trouble adjusting defensively. Add that to learning how to hit major league pitching, and the Royals may be asking too much from a rookie.

That having been said, Vitiello can certainly hit. His .344 average led the American Association and he added 41 extra-base hits while also displaying a good batting eye. Age 24 as the season opens, Vitiello would probably provide the Royals with Joyner-like offense for a fraction of the cost. If he gets to play

major league ball in 1995, watch for him to be worked into the RF job gradually. In a part-time role Vitiello should be good for a .280 average over 275 at bats with 6 home runs and 35 RBI. With normal progress he should be a regular in 1996 who is capable of hitting in the .280-.300 range with 15-20 home runs. Vitiello is a great sleeper pick as few folks outside of KC or Omaha have heard of him. He could be 1995's Bob Hamelin - a fine $1 special!

Where does that leave Felix Jose? The firing of Manager Hal McRae may have a profound effect upon Jose's playing time. McRae was a supporter of Jose and allowed him to play through shoulder problems in 1993 and attitude problems in 1994. New management may not be so kind. It can't be denied that Jose is a talented player; he has good speed, some power and has hit .295 or better in three of the last four years. Still, he has not been the big RBI bat the Royals wanted when they dealt Gregg Jefferies for him after the 1992 season. Jose has been stung by the criticism levelled at him for lackadaisical play in right field and occasional lack of hustle on the basepaths. If he remains in Kansas City through 1995, it will probably be as the lefthanded half of a platoon with Vitiello. He'll also serve as a fourth outfielder who can spell Tucker and McRae from time to time. Jose is likely to see less playing time than ever before, but may be more productive on a per at-bat basis. Expect a .300-10-50-15 season from Jose in 1995 and pay about $15 for it.

American Association MVP Dwayne Hosey hit .333 with 27 home runs, 80 RBI and 27 stolen bases in 1994. Now 28 years old, Hosey had failed with four other organizations (White Sox, Athletics, Brewers and Padres) before finding a new focus and having a monster year for the Omaha Royals. Unfortunately for Hosey, Tucker and Vitiello are more highly regarded prospects; Hosey may become trade bait.

Former Dodger prospect Tom Goodwin had his career year in 1994, hitting .308 with 50 stolen bases for Omaha. He's also too old (27) to be a prospect, but could fill in should injury strike one of the Royals' regulars. It's highly unlikely Goodwin would get more than about 75 at bats in Kansas City. He can

steal bases well, but doesn't usually hit enough to earn more than a pinch-running/pinch-hitting role.

Kevin Koslofski spent part of the 1992 and 1993 seasons in Kansas City, but was squeezed out of a regular job in Omaha by hot-hitting prospects Tucker, Hosey and Goodwin. He had a bad year and is far back in the line for a major league job.

After starting 1993 as the Royals regular third baseman, Phil Hiatt played himself out of a job at Omaha and dropped back to Double-A Memphis where he became a Southern League All-Star in right field. His .300-17-66-12 season was a good year, but taken in the context of a two-level drop in playing competition it has to be viewed with skepticism. He still strikes out at a prodigious rate (115 Ks in 397 at bats) and it's hard to believe his batting average and power would translate all that well to the majors. Hiatt will be 26 in 1995 and he can still have a big league career, but he's behind a lot of younger and better talent so he's going to have to go someplace else to do it.

1988 first round draft pick Hugh Walker finally had a good year above A-ball with a .260-7-38-12 year at Memphis in 1994. He's now 25 years old and will also advance to Omaha in 1995. He needs to cut his strikeouts and show better power to get a major league shot.

The most exciting prospect in the Royals system is Johnny Damon, a 21 year old lefthanded speedster. Damon has stolen 126 bases in just two and a half pro seasons, but he's more than just a basestealing threat. He hit .316 last year with 6 homers and 75 RBI, while slugging .462. He also has an excellent batting eye, drawing 62 walks against just 55 strikeouts for Class-A Wilmington in 1994. The Royals view Damon as being similar in skills to Lenny Dykstra: a high average, high speed center fielder who also has good plate discipline and some power. Keep an eye on Damon as he advances to Double-A in 1995.

Other long-term prospects include power/speed candidate Rod Myers and power hitter Raul Gonzalez, both years away from the majors.

Lary Bump:

Michael Tucker, drafted in 1992's first round as an infielder, was part of a hard-hitting triumvirate at Omaha last season (.276-21-77) with Dwayne Hosey and Joe Vitiello. Tucker also has some speed (11 stolen bases). With the new grass surface at Royals Stadium, the 23 year old lefthanded batter's gap power will be more valuable than flat-out base-stealing speed. He's penciled in as the regular left fielder in 1995 despite a poor Arizona Fall League season. The 28 year old Hosey has recovered from a checkered baseball past. The Padres, who had younger outfield prospects, let him go before last season as a minor league free agent. The switch hitter became the American Association's most exciting player (.333-27-80-27 steals), and had a brief stay in Kansas City without getting into a game. His Triple Crown numbers were all the best of his eight-year career, and he isn't getting any younger.

Lefthanded-batting Tom Goodwin was voted last year's best defensive outfielder and fastest baserunner in the prospect-poor American Association, where he performed at a .286-2-37 level with 59 stolen bases. At 26, he's no better a major league prospect with Kansas City than he was in the Dodgers organization.

Les Norman was a major non-contributor (.184-1-4) as Omaha stumbled out of the blocks, so Norman went back for a third season at Double-A Memphis (.264-13-55). The righthanded batter had better statistics in 1993, and at 26 seems to be sliding downhill.

Phil Hiatt, 25, appears to be going the same way. He moved to the outfield after failing to impress while playing half of the 1993 season with Kansas City. He went down to Omaha for a third season, and kept going down after a .182-1-2 start. At Memphis, he went .300-17-66-12 steals. Lefthanded-hitting Hugh Walker has made agonizingly slwo progress in seven seasons in the KC organization. Last year at Memphis he finished at .260-7-36-12 steals. He's still just 25, but he hasn't yet reached Triple-A, and is running out of time.

Johnny Damon, 21, was the best long-term prospect in the minors last season. He also was the best prospect of any kind I saw last year, and the best player I've ever seen in A ball. He hits for average, gets on base as a leadoff batter, steals bases and plays a good center field. The bottom lines for the lefthanded batter: .316-6-75-44 steals-.399 on-base percentage. And he'll even develop more power as he matures. He's likely to be in the majors by September. Baseball America's poll named him the best batting prospect, best defensive outfielder and most exciting player in the Carolina League. That all seems like an understatement.

Also at Wilmington were left fielder Roderick Myers (.263-12-65-31 steals) and right fielder Raul Gonzalez (.261-9-51). Myers, a 22 year old lefthanded batter, has moved ahead of the roly-poly Gonzalez, who in two seasons became a fan favorite at whatever they're calling Wilmington's stadium this week. He stole 13 bases in 1993, but went 0-for-4 as a base thief in '94.

Darren Burton cut his strikeouts way down in 1994 (from 111 to 53), but also slipped from .277-10-45-30 steals in the Carolina League to .255-3-37-10 in the Southern League. With so many outfielders in the organization with more talent, the 22 year old switch hitter doesn't project to Kansas City any time soon.

December's major league draft brought an up-and-coming lefthanded power prospect. Jon Nunnally, 23, pounded out a .267-22-74 season with 23 steals for the Kinston Indians of the Carolina League. He's a former second baseman.

Milwaukee Brewers

Alex Diaz was released by the Brewers and signed by the Mariners. The Brewers' outfield picture has changed little since the beginning of the strike.

Bill Gray:

In 1994, Darryl Hamilton's iffy elbow gave out after just 36 games, and he was finished for the year. There are rumors that Pat Listach will replace Hamilton in center, and Hamilton will move to left. Although he doesn't want to play left, Hamilton is a valuable, high-average hitter, with the speed to steal 30 bases. As AL speed guys disappear, it's understandable why Hamilton is causing a lot of anxious moments. After he was disabled, smart Rotisserie owners opted to reserve Hamilton instead of waiving him. If he plays, and I think he will, anybody who made that move has tilted the playing field in their favor.

Matt Mieske was supposed to be head and shoulders above Alex Diaz last year. Mieske can be a better hitter than he's shown, and Diaz was waived, so it's clear Mieske will have a shot at the rightfield job. He can also play center, and given the high degree of uncertainty at all outfield spots, if Mieske just remains healthy, he should play often. At 27, Mieske is getting a late start in the majors. He will be hard pressed to hit .260 and could do far worse. His power is negligible for an outfielder, and he's no great shakes as a base stealer.

Greg Vaughn had rotator cuff surgery for the second straight year and should open the season as DH. He'll never hit for a high batting average, but has legitimate power, and will drive in runs. He's always been a streaky hitter, and many frustrated owners dump Vaughn while he is in a slump.

Turner Ward can fill in anywhere in the outfield. Ward got off to a great start last year, but slumped badly afterward. Of course, he's not good enough to play every day, but is a decent role player. If he ends up on your team, try to trade Ward early while he's hot. Pat Listach might move to center, as has been mentioned before. If he still is capable of accumulating a lot of stolen bases, he will be very valuable regardless of his position. If you've read the shortstop essay, you already know of my reservations about Listach and his health.

If young Duane Singleton makes the team it will be more by default than design. He did OK at the Double-A level, but struggled at Triple-A. He had an abbreviated tour of the majors in August. He did perform very well in the Arizona Fall League and was

among the leaders in batting average and stolen bases. Singleton is a long way from being a good major league hitter at this point, but has good speed and definitely is in the Brewers blueprint for the future.

Lary Bump:

After spending time early in his career on detention and sitting in the corner, Duane Singleton turned the corner last year. The talented 22 year old lefthanded batter went all the way from the California League to a two-game audition in the Brewers outfield. He batted between .278 and .291 in his three minor league stops last season, and totaled six homers, 51 RBI and 31 stolen bases. He'll be in Milwaukee again this year.

Troy O'Leary also earned a promotion with a .329-8-43-10 steals start at New Orleans. The 25 year old is an adequate outfielder in left or right, but can be no more than a platoon player because he can't hit lefthanders.

Derek Wachter's promotion was from Double-A El Paso (.385-0-24 in 117 at bats) to New Orleans (.285-5-39). The 24 year old is a lanky righthanded batter whose power output fell way down after a big '93 season in the California League.

Danny Perez moved up from Stockton (.273-0-3 in nine games) to El Paso (.325-6-73). The 24 year old righthanded batter has averaged .301 for three pro seasons. If he continues to do well this year at New Orleans, he can see playing time at County Stadium.

In 1993, Scott Pose was an original Florida Marlin after a gigantic spring training. After 15 games, he was back in the minors. He spent all of last season at New Orleans (.282-0-52-20 steals). In 1995, the 28 year old lefthanded batter either will be back in Triple-A or out of baseball.

Ozzie Canseco has some of the qualities of his twin brother -- primarily righthanded power and a certain prickliness. Ozzie, who started his career as a pitcher, hasn't been able to make contact and bat for as high

an average (.236-14-67 at New Orleans) as Jose. The lesser-known twin can be a minor league free agent. The brothers will be 31 on Independence Day.

Ken Felder didn't show a lot in the California League (.274-10-60), but the Brewers have invested a lot of money in the 24 year old righthanded batter and will give him every chance to succeed.

Scott Richardson proved effective as a speedy lead-off-type batter at Stockton. He stole 49 bases and walked more often than he struck out. The walks were especially good; otherwise the 24 year old righthanded batter might have to steal first base. He batted just .265-2-33.

Switch-hitting Brian Banks started last season with Felder and Richardson at Stockton (.236-4-28), then was demoted to Beloit (.300-9-47-11 steals). There's not much market for 24 year olds from the Midwest League.

Righthanded power hitter Todd Dunn, also 24, is in the same boat. As a 1993 first-round draft choice, though, he can expect some preferential treatment. He batted just .219 with 23 homers, 63 RBI, 18 stolen bases and 131 strikeouts.

Minnesota Twins

Shane Mack remained an unsigned free agent who is unlikely to return to Minnesota. The centerfield job will be shared by Rich Becker and Alex Cole.

James Benkard:

Obviously, Kirby Puckett will play if he is breathing, and he will post some good numbers. Almost all players start to decline rapidly around Puckett's age, and it is a testament to his talent that he has not slipped. Look for a .290 season, 15 to 20 homers, and 100 RBI.

Since Shane Mack is almost certain to leave via free agency, Rich Becker and Alex Cole will patrol center field. Cole made some firm advances in his game in

'94, and will maintain a stable .270 average with 20 steals for the next two to three years. Becker's 1994 performance, which included a .265 average with some walks and speed, is a good indication of what he will deliver in '95. He possesses a vigorous and aggressive approach to the game, and games of two or three strikeouts will sometimes be the result. My guess is that Becker will win a starting job late in the season, and his talent will bring him minor stardom in four years.

Pedro Munoz surged back into the Twin outfield last season, after a subpar effort in 1993 had jeopardized his career. If he starts the year well, count on him for 400 at bats and close to 20 home runs. It is likely that Munoz will play regularly in 1995 because he has reached his prime age (27). Do recognize his short-comings on defense and consistency when evaluating him.

David McCarty will not play often in the outfield unless due to injury, leaving Marty Cordova as the primary remaining candidate for left field. Cordova has raw power, but has been plagued by strikeouts, and injuries deprived him of two years of maturation time. His career highs in average (.358) and stolen bases (17) in 1994 were encouraging signs. I look for Cordova to construct a career similar to John Jaha's. While Cordova might hit a dozen homers in 80 games in 1995, his average will be .230-240.

Minnesota has no other major outfield prospects close to being ready for the majors. If they had to reach down into the farm system because of injuries they would select Ed Gerald or Steve Hazlett, who hit .272 and .293 respectively in Double-A in '94. Both have a little power and speed and are relatively young. Torii Hunter, the club's top choice in the 1993 draft, impressed everyone with his performance in A-ball (.293-10-50-8) in 1994 and is a potential five tool threat.

Lary Bump:

Rich Becker can be a center fielder in the tradition of Pete Reiser and Lenny Dykstra. That means Becker plays hard and well, but also gets himself injured. His best skills are hitting for average, throwing and patroling the outfield. Last season the 23 year old switch hitter earned some time in Minnesota with a .316-2-38 start at Triple-A Salt Lake City. A warning sign: He totaled just 13 stolen bases, the fewest in his five-year pro career, after tearing up a knee in September 1993.

Marty Cordova's 1994 numbers (.358-19-66-17 steals at Salt Lake), which would look even better if he hadn't started the season on the disabled list with a broken arm, rivaled the 131-RBI season he put together in the California League in '92. Sure, his best performances have been in hitters' parks, but then again the Metrodome isn't exactly Dodger Stadium. Cordova has some speed, but is not a good outfielder. There could be room for a first baseman or DH, and the Twins have considered moving Pedro Munoz to first base. So there very well could be a spot in the lineup for Cordova, a 25 year old righthanded batter.

Bernardo Brito is a certified minor league power source, with 263 home runs. Last year he blasted 29, matching his career high, to go with a .309 average and 122 RBI at Salt Lake. If the 31 year old righthanded batter gets a chance he could become the Geronimo Berroa of 1995. More likely, Brito will continue to be the Crash Davis of the '90s. Baseball America's poll said Juan de la Rosa had the best outfield arm in the Pacific Coast League. That and his .272-4-46 offense weren't enough to keep the righthanded batter, 26, in Salt Lake's regular outfield. He had a big 1992 season in Double-A in the Toronto organization, then bombed out in Triple-A.

David McCarty, 25, who also plays first base, hasn't yet realized his potential in the majors. Last season he actually hit better with the Twins (.260-1-12) than at Salt Lake (.253-3-19). He's one of those rare throws left-bats right athletes.

Brian Kowitz was drafted away from the Braves organization, where he batted .300-8-57-22 steals. The 25 year old lefthanded batter is limited to playing left field.

Twenty-four year old Anthony Byrd jumped from the Midwest League to the Southern League without great success (.2386=7=38). Speed (28 steals) is his greatest asset. The righthanded batter needs to work on making contact (114 whiffs).

Also at Nashville, Steve Hazlett batted .293-14-54. However, the righthanded batter already is 25. Twenty-three year old switch hitter Tim Moore traded the speed he's shown in the lower minors for power (18 homers, 67 RBI), but batted .248, six points below his career average.

Matt Lawton, 23, had a good leadoff-type season in the Florida State League (.300-7-51-42 steals-.407 on-base percentage). He is a lefthanded batter. Righthanded-hitting Keith Legree, a former University of Louisville basketball player is a month younger than Lawton. Legree batted .242-4-15 in just 55 games at Fort Myers.

The Twins' first draft pick in 1993, Torii Hunter, batted .293-10-50 in the Midwest League. The 19 year old switch hitter didn't show good judgment at the plate (25 walks, 80 strikeouts) or on the bases (eight steals in 18 attempts). Kelcey Mucker, a first-round compensation pick, was less successful in the Appalachian League (.238-6-31). The 20 year old bats lefthanded.

New York Yankees

Update: Daryl Boston remained an unsigned free agent who could return to the Yankees as an extra outfielder/pinch-hitter. His role will be limited wherever he goes.

Minor leaguer Mike Humphreys left via free agency to join the Indians. He had virtually no chance of returning to the majors with the Yankees.

Paul O'Neill achieved notoriety as the one and only big-name free agent to sign during the October that had no World Series. Suffice it to say that O'Neill is happy with the Yankees. Although he reached a career high .311 batting average after arriving in New York for 1993, O'Neill was a deep longshot to win the 1994 AL batting title, which he captured after flirting with .400 for several weeks. The big difference for O'Neill was looking for the breaking ball and adjusting to the fastball, a good method for anyone with quick enough hands to approach American League pitchers. Thus O'Neill finally mastered lefty pitching, and his success and confidence soared together.

O'Neill has clearly graduated from platoon to full-time outfielder; and this year when the preseason prognosticators start guessing at who wins the 1995 batting title, O'Neill's name must be among the prime contenders. He sure has come a long way since sinking into the doghouse in Cincinnati three years ago.

Luis Polonia was a 50-steal baserunner while playing with the ultra-aggressive style of Buck Rodgers' Angels, but back in New York he's just a 25-30 stolen base man. No one should be surprised however. That was Polonia's capacity last time around with the Yankees, and he isn't any younger now. Still, if your league doesn't have two owners who want him (remember it takes only two to drive the price up) then I expect Polonia to be a bargain. Most bidders have never fully understood the value of a high batting average, and most have not yet appreciated the new scarcity of stolen bases, especially in the American League, Polonia's defense is a little shaky, and he will often be used in a platoon with Gerald Williams or relegated to a leadoff DH role in spot games, but the danger of Polonia getting under 400 at bats is a non-factor (as long as he doesn't get injured). There aren't many players who can give you a boost in stolen bases and lift your batting average as well. Polonia is a Rotisserie gem.

Bernie Williams is the gem in this outfield. His raw tools have always been fine, but before 1994 Williams played with a visible uncertainty on the field. It was the kind of problem that didn't come across in TV coverage, but if you sat and the stadium and watched Bernie inning after inning, especially when he got on base, you could see that he wasn't comfortable or confident and didn't trust his instincts or his coaches. That all changed last year.

Actually the change started in mid 1993 after Williams got dropped down to sixth in the order, and the pressure to steal bases disappeared completely. But it was 1994 before the confidence spread to all other aspects of his game. Williams set career highs in just about every offensive category. In 1994 he suddenly became more sure about which pitches were strikes and which were balls (as the BB/K stats reflect) and suddenly he started hitting line drives consistently.

Williams is among my top picks to climb farther into the star population in 1995. The decision-makers who moved Roberto Kelly out of center field and then out of New York, to make room for Williams, are going to look smarter every year for a while.

The other Williams, Gerald, on paper is about half way between bench jockey and platoon partner for Polonia. Williams' time will depend on various factors like how well Polonia does in the field, how much time Danny Tartabull spends on the DL, and who else gets hurt. Williams will be a good $1 outfielder, and an above-average fill-in, especially for Tartabull. In any given week, Williams could hit a home run, or steal a base, or both, and those are rates of 26 home run and 26 stolen base per year, which isn't bad.

The Yankees have a wealth of outfield talent on the farm, led by superprospect Ruben Rivera. Next most ready is Lyle Mouton, a free-swinging home run hitter. Jalal Leach looks like a career minor leaguer. Matt Luke has shown good power in the Florida State League but at age 24 will have to show more than that to remain a prospect. Jason Robertson is a third round pick from 1989, stuck at Double-A for two and a half years while trying to learn to make consistent contact. He doesn't have much power for a big strikeout swinger, but can steal well when he gets on base.

Lary Bump:

Lyle Mouton's physical talent always was apparent, but he didn't translate it into results until last season. Nobody hits the ball any harder, but some hit it more often. The righthanded batter started .307-12-42 at Double-A Albany to earn a promotion to Columbus

((.314-4-32). Mouton is a student of the game. His two drawbacks are his age (25) and the Yankees' crowded outfield.

Chito Martinez put his career somewhat back on track with a .277-16-47 season at Columbus. The lefthanded batter is 29, and hasn't stolen a base in two years. He's limited to pinch hitting and DH duty, or perhaps an emergency stint in the outfield or at first base.

Billy Masse is an aging (28) righthanded batter who slipped in his third season at Columbus to .258-5-14 in 71 games. Jalal Leach, 26, was the regular left fielder in his Triple-A debut. He didn't advance his career by going .261-6-56. The lefthanded batter has struck out more than 100 times in each of his four full pro seasons, and stole only 14 bases in 26 attempts for Columbus. Baseball America's poll voted Matt Luke the Florida State League's best power prospect (.306-16-42), and he continued to power the ball in the Eastern League (.284-8-40). His arm is strong enough to play right field. The 24 year old lefthanded batter also has played first base.

Switch-hitting Lew Hill didn't fare well in his first Double-A season, batting .230-9-33. He'll be 26 in April, so his prospect star has all but faded from sight.

Ruben Rivera's luggage has an eventual destination of "Right Field, Yankee Stadium." He isn't the next Mickey Mantle, as the hype from the Arizona Fall League suggested, but he was voted the best power prospect, best outfield arm and most exciting player in the South Atlantic League, one year after topping Baseball America's Top 10 list of New York-Penn League prospects. He also was the MVP in each league. Rivera finished last season in the spotlight of George Steinbrenner's Tampa empire. The 21 year old righthanded batter was at .288-28-81-36 steals in the Sally League, then .261-5-20-12 in the Florida State League.

The Yankees made Brian Buchanan their first-round draft choice in 1994. A power hitter at the University of Virginia, he adjusted slowly to wooden bats in his pro debut (.226-4-26 in the New York-Penn League).

The righthanded batter played mostly outfield, and some first first, after the draft.

Oakland A's

Steven Rubio:

Rickey Henderson continues in left field. The best player of his era is still a fine baseball player who should remain effective at his current level for a few years. If you can find a league who believes Rickey is finished, grab him, but don't pay for what he did in 1980.

In center field, Stan Javier gave Oakland pretty much what they expected last year when they signed him to a two-year deal. Javier is one of the best percentage basestealers in the game, and he can get on base with reasonable frequency. His 10 home runs last season were a fluke, and he is in his thirties and won't get any better than he is now, but he's a decent pick for a fifth outfielder on a fantasy squad.

In the second half of the 1994 season, Ruben Sierra finally started approaching the level of production the A's thought they were getting when they traded for him a few years back. Too many fantasy owners will overvalue him based on his early reputation as a potential Hall-of-Famer, but if you lower your expectations, Sierra can help a fantasy team, especially if you don't count on-base percentage (he still won't take a walk).

Beyond the usual batch of journeymen (and worse) who populate the Oakland bench are several interesting outfield prospects. Ernie Young took forever to blossom, but he is advancing rapidly now and could contend for a job with Oakland in 1995. Scott Lydy was a disaster in a short 1993 callup, and may not get another chance, but has performed well in the minors for a few years now and could surprise. Jim Buccheri hit .304 with 32 steals in Triple-A last season, but he is already 26 years old.

Further down the road, Kerwin Moore is just the kind of player most appreciated by the Athletics' organi-

zation. He has excellent speed and a willingness to take a walk, making him a potential leadoff man in the majors. A football player in high school, Moore is still mastering the sport of baseball, and will thus be a late bloomer if he succeeds (he is 24 years old).

Jose Herrera showed power and speed for Class A Modesto. Stolen from the Blue Jays along with Steve Karsay in the odd 1993 Rickey Henderson trade, Herrera looks to embarrass the Jays somewhere down the line.

Finally, teenager Ben Grieve was the second overall choice in the most recent draft. He had an impressive professional start in Class A, and will be given every possible chance to succeed by Oakland.

Lary Bump:

Only injuries early in Ernie Young's career held him back. This power prospect, who has played center field, produced last season despite being shuttled up and down the Oakland organizational ladder. He totaled .308-20-74 while playing at the top three levels. After stealing 31 bases in 1993, the 25 year old righthanded batter was successful just five times in 16 attempts last year. He holds the distinction of being the last player to bat in the majors last season, striking out against Bobby Witt.

At age 26, Scott Lydy may finally be able to get beyond the fringes of the major leagues. In '94, the 6-5 righthanded batter had his best power year of his career (.315-17-73-22 steals at Triple-A Tacoma). He has enough skills to be a marketable fourth outfielder. Lydy could take the role that seemed traditionally assigned to Eric Fox, who has gone to the Texas organization.

Manny Martinez, a 24 year old righthanded batter, struggled somewhat at Tacoma (.256-9-60-18 steals).

There was talk before last season that Kerwin Moore, a 24 year old righthanded batter, could be Oakland's regular center fielder. Judging from his batting record in the Southern League (.243-5-33-99 strikeouts), he would have been a disaster in the majors in '94. His

blinding speed makes him a base-stealing threat (54 last season, 325 in seven pro seasons), as well as a strong defensive player. He can get on base; his 210 walks the last two seasons make him a leadoff hitter despite his low average.

A knee injury limited righthanded-hitting Damon Mashore to 59 games with Double-A Huntsville. He batted just .224-3-21 and, at age 25, will have to accelerate his progress to reach the majors.

Jose Herrera, 22, acquired by Oakland in the 1993 Rickey Henderson trade, has speed, a little power and the best outfield arm in the California League. The lefthanded batter was at .286-11-56-21 steals. His teammate, David Francisco, batted .277-9-48-29 steals-110 strikeouts. The 23 year old bats righthanded.

Ben Grieve was the first position player taken in the 1994 draft, selected second overall. A son of Rangers executive Tom Grieve, the 19 year old lefthanded batter dominated the Northwest League (.329-7-50 in 72 games).

Seattle Mariners

Jay Buhner remains with the Mariners, and will continue to hit for good power.

Keith Mitchell refused a minor league assignment to become a free agent; he remained unsigned. Mitchell could be a useful extra outfielder for some team but would have limited Rotisserie value.

Free agent Alex Diaz left the Brewers to sign as a free agent with the Mariners. Diaz has an inside track to replace Mitchell in a bench role for Seattle.

Minor league free agents Darrell Sherman (Padres) and Gary Thurman (Tigers) have joined the Mariners' minor league system.

Sherman or Thurman could re-surface with the Mariners at any time but would have a very limited role and no Rotisserie value.

Bill Gray:

Ken Griffey will start in center field. He might not hit 60 homers in 1995, then again, he might. He hasn't reached his peak yet. Before he calls it a career, Griffey should be the greatest home run hitter in the history of major league baseball. 68 of his 140 hits in 1994 were doubles or better. Weaknesses? He could steal a lot of bases if he wanted to, but does not run much. Therefore, he is not a four category Rotisserie performer.

Jay Buhner will start in right field. Underrated is the term usually hung on Buhner, but don't believe it. He might play in Seattle, but he always drives in runs, hits a lot of home runs, and will continue to do so. Overlooked? No. Buhner's put up too many good years, with more to come. If you wait for Buhner, he will be gone. Grab him early in the draft.

Would it be unfair to say Eric Anthony must put up some big numbers this year? Should he remain healthy this season, my expectations remain high. He has seen American League pitching and should benefit from that. He has produced decent power numbers in the past, and he'll be just 27 this year. It's still too soon to write Anthony off. On the down side, I suspect that another nondescript season will push Anthony onto the scrap heap. Shane Mack broke a lot of hearts early in his career, but has been just fine for the last few years. Eric Anthony could do the same. He should be cheap and could be a big bargain.

If you have Eric Anthony it might be smart to get Marc Newfield. Newfield is still too green to make a big impact, but a player with this much talent might surprise us all. Calgary, Newfield's place of employment for most of 1994, is a hitter's paradise, and Newfield enjoyed it immensely, hitting .349 with 19 home runs. Could he make big splash in the majors this year? I don't think so, but in two years I would much prefer Newfield over Eric Anthony.

Keith Mitchell is a decent hitter. However, barring an injury to a starter Mitchell won't get an opportunity wherever he plays. He was a free agent last winter, and is strictly for the reserve list at this point.

Brian Turang destroyed PCL pitching with a .336 average. He played predominately second base for the Cannons. The Mariners used him sparingly at second, preferring to see how he did as an outfielder. Only if he is given a shot at the second base job with the Mariners would Turang be an interesting pick, because his bat would be considered unimpressive for an outfielder. At second base, he has a huge upside for the future. If you buy him at second base as part of your rebuilding strategy, you will do well indeed. It all depends where the Mariners use him. Is this why they traded Bret Boone?

Lary Bump:

The Mariners could use Marc Newfield's righthanded bat in left field, in a first base-platoon with Tino Martinez. There's no question the 22 year old is ready after his .349-19-83 season at Calgary. His defense isn't good, and he has no speed, but Newfield can hit enough to be a major league star. After a gigantic offensive year in the Pacific Coast League, Bragg finds himself only the number two outfield prospect coming up to Seattle, behind Marc Newfield. The two had almost identical years, but the lefthanded-hitting Bragg (.350-17-85) stole 28 bases despite being three years older than Newfield. The Mariners may not be convinced because Bragg's average jumped 86 points in the hitters' haven at Calgary over his 1993 Double-A mark.

Scott Bryant batted .320-20-87 at Calgary. He was the RBI leader on a team on which six players drove in 72 or more runs. However, the righthanded batter is 27, and has no speed and no arm. The next stop for him is likely to be another Triple-A team.

For the first time in seven years, Gary Thurman spent no time in the majors in 1994. His numbers with the White Sox Triple-A farm at Nashville were somewhat off his minor league norm (.264-5-60-20 steals). At 30, he could go back to the majors, but only as a spare outfielder/pinch runner/righthanded pinch hitter.

Terrel Hansen had a big offensive year in the Southern League (.317-22-78), but then he should have,

for the righthanded batter is 28 and he spent the previous three seasons in the International League. His arm is strong enough for right field, but he's running out of time. He also declined in his specialty area, hit by pitch, from 27 in '93 to 16.

Seattle sought speed in the offseason, and picked up Basil Shabazz (.234-0-27 at St. Petersburg and .175-3-10 at Arkansas in the St. Louis organization, but with 57 stolen bases) and Darrell Sherman (.224-0-5 in 28 games for Colorado Springs in the Rockies organization). Shabazz is a 23 year old righthanded batter who has failed to make contact in his four pro seasons. Two years ago, the lefthanded-hitting Sherman was considered the Padres' center fielder of the future. He three times has stolen more than 50 bases in a season, but he's 27.

Another problem child from another organization is Jeff Jackson. The Phillies' first draft pick in 1989 never has made it past Double-A (.177-5-11 in '94 in his third season at Reading) and was reduced to being claimed in the minor league draft by the Mariners. The righthanded batter is still just 23, but he's another strikeout waiting to happen.

Texas Rangers

The addition of Otis Nixon via trade will put a damper on David Hulse's value. Hulse will probably have to go to another organization to get back to the majors in a regular role.

Oddibe McDowell, Chris James and Gary Redus all became free agents during the off-season. The Rangers seem to be interested in re-signing James, but McDowell and Redus will move on to another venue in 1995. James would get a fourth outfielder role for the Rangers and would have a little Rotisserie value in that role.

Rob Ducey was released in the off-season. His future as a ballplayer is extremely uncertain at this point.

Minor league free agent Eric Fox (Athletics) signed into the Rangers minor league system. He could get

a few at bats for Texas in 1995 but has no Rotisserie value; he's mainly injury insurance stored at Triple-A.

Peter Graves:

Left fielder Juan Gonzalez' performance was not up to his usual other-worldly standards in 1994, but .275-19-85 was still a solid season. The power decline gives some cause for concern, especially in a year in which many hitters were on pace to set career highs in home runs. Gonzalez is undeniably talented however, and the magnitude of his achievements at such an early age is impressive. His performance should improve in 1995. The nagging injuries that have led Gonzalez to remove himself from the lineup in the past weren't much of a problem in 1994. The Rangers' desperate need for pitching may force them to try to deal Gonzalez in order to bolster the rotation.

Rookie Rusty Greer won the right field job by hitting .314-10-46 in 53 games with Texas. Greer is a patient contact hitter with sporadic power. Although primarily a first baseman in the minors, Greer is adequate in right field and should see the majority of playing time there in 1995. I think he'll continue to hit well.

David Hulse (.255-1-19-18) was the only legitimate center fielder to play the position for Texas last season. As a hitter, Hulse is very streaky and has trouble with lefthanded pitching, both of which led former manager Kevin Kennedy to banish Hulse to the minors at midseason. The managerial change may help Hulse, who was never a Kennedy favorite. Another development which would help Hulse would be the acquisition of a bona-fide leadoff hitter, so that Hulse's low on-base average could be moved to the bottom of the batting order. His primary Rotisserie value is as a basestealer (he was successful in 18 of 20 attempts last year). Playing most of the time, Hulse could steal 40 or more.

After Hulse was sent down, the Rangers had major defensive problems in center field. Oddibe McDowell and even Greer were tried, but neither is a long-term solution to the problem. Former Loyola Marymount basketballer Terrell Lowery is the centerfielder in

waiting for Texas, and the Rangers may not be able to wait much longer. Lowery, 24, had a strong season at Double-A Tulsa (.277-5-46-32) and would have been promoted to Triple-A and participated in the Arizona Fall League if not for an injured left wrist. Defensively, Lowery is ready now, but he needs experience facing Triple-A pitching. He struck out 110 times in 470 at bats last season. Lowery's power stroke is developing, and he should eventually hit with moderate power. I wouldn't expect much offensively if Lowery is promoted to Texas in 1995.

McDowell made an impressive comeback from oblivion (.262-1-15-14 in 31 games), and is the leading candidate to be the fourth outfielder if he re-signs with Texas. Like Hulse, his primary Rotisserie value is as a basestealer. Even in part-time duty, McDowell could steal 20 bases.

Chris James (.256-7-19) was waived at the end of the season, but the Rangers were trying to re-sign him. Aside from Gonzalez, James is the only righthanded hitting outfielder on the major league roster. James murdered lefthanded pitching last year, and had more extra base hits than singles (19 to 15). With all the lefthanded hitters around, James is a platoon candidate.

Other outfield possibilities: Rob Ducey, 30, squandered another chance to stick in the majors, going .172-0-1 in April and finishing in the minors. At his age, further chances will be hard to come by. Donald ''The Guy The Rangers Drafted Ahead Of Frank Thomas'' Harris continues his excruciatingly slow development at Triple-A; his power numbers are improving, but he is still undisciplined at the plate and will need a change of organizations in order to move up. Butch Davis will be 37 years old, and doesn't figure to get another chance. Desi Wilson, 26, had a solid season at Double-A Tulsa (.289-6-54-15) and will probably spend 1995 at Triple-A.

Lary Bump:

The Rangers have little in the way of young outfield talent in their organization. So what did they do? They acquired 31 year old switch hitter Eric Fox

(.314-3-19 at Tacoma; .205-1-1 in 26 games for Oakland). The great expectations that Dan Peltier aroused after he batted .402 in Rookie ball in 1989 never materialized. In his fourth Triple-A season, he declined to .268-9-60 without a major league callup. The 26 year old lefthanded batter can do a little of a lot of things but not a lot of anything. He has a decent arm in right field, he can draw a walk, but his power and speed are limited.

Similarly, righthanded-hitting Donald Harris has worn a "great athlete, great prospect" like a hair shirt with virtually no production since 1989, when he batted .284 as Peltier's teammate at Butte. (There's a Beavis and Butt-head joke somewhere in there.) Harris' only marketable skill is his defense. Peltier's teammate again at Oklahoma City, the 27 year old Harris batted .243-16-59 with 107 strikeouts. The former Texas A&M footballer can't even use his speed effectively on the bases; he was a miserable 6-for-18 trying to steal last year.

Rob Ducey was at .268-17-65 for Oklahoma City, but at age 29, the lefthanded batter is no prospect.

At age 36, Butch Davis finally retired and signed to be a coach for the Orioles' Triple-A farm at Rochester. Was that a trade for Doug Melvin et al.?

Now the great-athlete-from-another-sport hope is Terrell Lowery, a 24 year old righthanded batter. The former Loyola Marymount basketball star in 1994 had his best pro baseball season (.286-8-54-33 steals at Double-A Tulsa).

Sergio Cairo put together a .273-14-76 season at Tulsa. The righthanded batter is just 24 despite six minor league seasons, but he has little speed.

Toronto Blue Jays

Part-time leftfielder Darnell Coles remained an unsigned free agent. Coles might re-sign with the Blue Jays and, along with Michael Huff, would serve as a limiting factor on any problems Shawn Green might have in 1995.

Former Rule Five selection Willie Canate was released and has yet to find a new home.

Rob Butler failed to win a leftfield job out of spring training in 1994 and has now been dealt to the Phillies where he'll have another shot at the majors.

David Luciani:

Joe Carter was enjoying perhaps the best season of his career when the strike came. He probably would have hit 40 home runs for the first time and also would have mounted a threat to the club record for most RBI in a season (134 by George Bell in his 1987 MVP year).

Just when you thought Carter had abandoned his running game, he stole 11 bases in 1994 without being caught once. Despite the strike, he also drove in over 100 runs for the sixth straight year and eighth time in the last nine years (the remaining year he drove in 98). This is perhaps the most consistent RBI man in the game and no matter how deep he slumps, Cito Gaston will stick with him indefinitely as the Jays' cleanup hitter. After playing much of last April with a broken thumb, Carter proved that he will not be forced out of the lineup because of a minor injury. His fast start showed that even at 35 years of age, his best season may still be ahead of him.

There's no doubt who the everyday leadoff hitter is for the Blue Jays in 1995. He's also one of the best defensive center fielders in the game. Devon White suffered from strained legs last year, which were primary factors in his stealing just 11 bases. He can and will run more in 1995 and his power remains an underrated asset (13 home runs in 1994).

Mike Huff was acquired from the White Sox immediately before the 1994 season in a trade for Domingo Martinez. It wasn't long into the year before Huff paid dividends. Carlos Delgado, who started the season as the everyday left fielder, went from being a superstar rookie to a minor league catcher and it's almost certain that you will never see Delgado back in left field in the major leagues except in an emer-

gency (however, he is discussed in the Catcher section as a future superstar at that position).

Huff, who before 1994 had spent parts of four seasons with the Dodgers, Indians and White Sox, got a chance to play every day and proved that life can begin at 30. He posted a .304 average over 207 at bats and walked 27 times. Unfortunately, his spot in the batting order was still perceived to be weak when the strike came. Perhaps there was fear that Huff might revert to the .230 batting average he had recorded over 427 at bats before 1994.

Shawn Green, a Triple-A superstar last year, has often been compared to a younger John Olerud. He isn't the same hitter as Olerud and certainly doesn't possess the same batting eye. However, Green will get an opportunity to prove that he is better than his major league debut of 1994 (he went just 3 for 33) and he might end up in a strict platoon with Huff in left field or could even win the job outright. Robert Perez was supposed to be a leading candidate a year ago, along with Rob Butler, to be the left fielder. Both foundered in spring training and by opening day of 1994, the Carlos Delgado experiment was in place while Butler and Perez were in the minors. Perez has a similar swing to Joe Carter and will, along with Green, be in Florida looking to just make the team.

Butler, who has been sent to Philadelphia, had essentially become the Blue Jays' left fielder in the winter of 1993-94. His decision not to attend winter ball was quietly frowned upon by some, and a subsequent poor performance in Florida earned him his ticket to Triple-A Syracuse. The chance of him being a full-time player, like Perez, has now diminished.

Lary Bump:

Shawn Green's smooth swing has drawn comparisons to John Olerud. But Green, voted best batting prospect, most exciting player and best outfield arm as well as Rookie of the Year in the International League last season (.344-13-61-19 steals), is a more complete all-around player. He struggled in his major league baptism last season. Even though Green is a good right fielder, he may find himself playing left field for Toronto in 1995. The lefthanded batter is just 22, and he has a bright future even if he doesn't make it this year.

Two other outfield prospects are Robert Perez, 25, who batted .304-10-65 at Syracuse, and Rich Butler (.292-3-22 at Double-A Knoxvile; .242-3-27 at Syracuse). The righthanded-hitting Perez had a shot at the Blue Jays' left field job last spring, but butchered it with poor defense. Butler, a 21 year old lefthanded batter, is a center fielder with some speed who has been a break-even base stealer (47 up, 46 down) in his four pro seasons. Don't confuse him with his brother, Rob Butler, who was traded to the Phillies.

In Syracuse last season, William Canate was known as "William Cannot," and he could not hit (.183-0-10). He was somewhat better in Double-A (.245-0-28-16 steals), but his only further major league possibility would be as a defensive replacement and pinch runner. As a pick in the major league draft, he had to spend all of 1993 with the Blue Jays, and that retarded his development. The righthanded batter is just 23, but it's a safe bet that he will not return to the majors any time soon.

After playing two seasons without showing much improvement in Double-A (.273-4-49-15 steals last year), Brent Bowers is no longer a prospect in a Toronto organization loaded with young outfield talent.

As a minor league free agent, the 23 year old lefthanded batter may have a chance somewhere else. Lonell Roberts was voted the Florida State League's best baserunner. He stole tons of bases (61), even though he rarely got on base (.269-3-31-.316 on-base percentage). The 23 year old switch hitter's only hope as a major leaguer is as a pinch runner.

Shannon Stewart, 21, was voted the Sally League's best defensive outfielder last season. He also hit well (.324-4-25-15 steals in 56 games), but the righthanded batter will need to turn on more power to get a long look from the Blue Jays.

NATIONAL LEAGUE
OUTFIELD

Atlanta Braves

Marc Bowman:

1994 was a season of change for the Atlanta outfield. Gone were Ron Gant, Otis Nixon and Deion Sanders. In their place the Braves added Roberto Kelly, Ryan Klesko, Mike Kelly, Dave Gallagher and Tony Tarasco. For 1995, the outfield mix may also include Chipper Jones. Jones has been discussed as a possible leftfield candidate, but Klesko's good season at the plate should keep Jones on the infield; Jones is described at length in the Shortstop section.

Leftfielder Klesko proved that his minor league power displays did indeed extend well enough to major league power, particularly in hitting friendly Fulton County Stadium. After averaging a homer every 22 at bats over three years spent in Double-A and Triple-A, Klesko cranked out 17 homers in 245 major league at bats in 1994 -- one per 14 at bats. All the while he reduced his strikeout rate slightly and hit for a respectable .278 average while posting his best ever full season slugging average (.563). It was a fine debut for a powerful young hitter.

His power is for real, but the rest of his game is still in doubt. Can he keep his average up in the .270 to .280 range? Probably not over the short haul. Klesko will suffer, as most young hitters do in their second year, because the pitchers will adjust. Can he keep the strikeouts under control? Maybe, but again the pitchers will adjust and Klesko will need time to overcome their new way of pitching him. Can he play leftfield? No, not really. He's an abysmal outfielder but is stuck in leftfield until he can get back to his true position, first base, which is currently manned by one of the game's best, Fred McGriff.

For 1995, it means that Klesko will have some bad spells where he strikes out a lot without producing much. But, he'll also go on a few tears and pound the fences. Rotisserie players would be wise to grab this guy because he's got 30 homer potential as he keeps getting stronger and learns to hit major league pitching. However, do NOT extrapolate his 245 at bats into 600 at bats for 1995 and expect him to hit 45 homers with 115 RBI; he's not going to do it. A more realistic expectation is a .250 batting average with 25 homers and 75 RBI in about 450 at bats. Not MVP territory, but not too bad either for a 23 year old.

Deion Sanders took his act to Cincinnati in exchange for Roberto Kelly, a quieter player, but a better fit for the Braves lefty leaning lineup. Kelly gave the Braves

about what they expected with a .283 average, six homers and ten steals after the trade. The Braves see Kelly as a leadoff type, but his OBP hasn't always been good enough for him to succeed in that role. He has improved in recent years, though, posting an acceptable .350 OBP over the last two years.

Kelly is the kind of player whose front line stats (batting average, homers, RBI, stolen bases) portray him to be a better player than he really is. He hasn't had a good RBI bat when he was tried in that role; Kelly slugged slightly over .400 in a few years when he batted fifth for the Yankees, averaging 65 RBI per year from 1990 to 1992. His power was not what you'd expect from a leftfielder. Likewise, his OBP, while improving recently, hasn't been good enough for him to bat near the top of the order despite his fine speed. Overall, Kelly produces reasonably good stats, but since there's really no good spot for him in the batting order, his overall production is often less than the sum of the individual parts of his offense.

Kelly's also not a good outfielder and is even worse in centerfield. He has begun to bounce around from team to team, as often happens with players who are a difficult fit in the lineup or in the field. For 1995, his playing time may diminish as Mike Kelly gets more opportunities. After 1995 he could easily be gone to yet another team. Look for .295-12-55-25 in about 475 at bats.

The only piece of the outfield puzzle to remain from 1993 was David Justice. The sweet swinging rightfielder was on his way to his most productive season ever in 1994 and his stats look short only because of the strike. Even so, he posted his first ever .300 batting average and had an excellent .427 OBP. Even though he wouldn't have reached the 40 homer plateau like he did in 1993, Justice would have come close to 30 homers and 90 RBI and he actually did finish the year with a better slugging percentage, .531, virtually matching his phenomenal rookie year in 1990.

Justice is set for a big year in 1995. His good batting eye keeps him from swinging at bad pitches, thereby protecting his batting average. His power is still in the 25-35 home run and 90-100 RBI range, although it doesn't look like it with the strike shortening the season by a third. He'll be hitting in an RBI spot in Atlanta's powerful lineup, so he'll have a lot of runners to drive in. Watch for Justice to remain in the upper echelon of NL hitters with a season of hitting .300-30-100-2.

Mike Kelly is the man most likely to pick up extra at bats in 1995. He spent most of the year at Triple-A Richmond, but still managed two homers in 77 at bats for the big club. He's essentially been the same kind of hitter for the last three years, a power hitting, speedy righthander who strikes out in bunches. Kelly has an opportunity to expand his role to a righthanded platoon with Klesko in leftfield. To get that chance he'll need to reduce his whiffs while keeping his good slugging average (.506 for Atlanta, .476 in Richmond). Kelly should get about 200 at bats, hitting .250-8-25-6. If he keeps his strikeouts down he'll get an expanded role in 1996.

Another lefty, Tony Tarasco, spent time as a backup in both leftfield and rightfield, spending a full year in the majors for the first time in his career. He hit about as well as expected, going .273-5-19-5 in 132 at bats. Tarasco has also been a bit too free swinging for the Braves' liking, although he has improved in recent seasons. Because he's lefthanded, Tarasco isn't going to suddenly get a lot of at bats unless something changes among the Braves regulars. If Justice were injured, Tarasco would probably get the first chance to play regularly. Likewise, should Klesko get hurt Tarasco would get the bulk of the platoon at bats opposite Mike Kelly. Also, should Klesko move to first base to replace Fred McGriff, Tarasco's playing time would increase. However, barring any of these unforeseen changes, Tarasco should play the backup and lefty pinch hitter role, getting about 175 at bats and hitting .275-6-30-9. His Rotisserie value is minimal, but he'd be a good selection for your reserve roster as injury insurance should you have a big investment in Justice or McGriff. With his opportunity to advance into a larger role in future years, Tarasco is a fine $1 investment.

Dave Gallagher is an example of a good ballplayer

who has little or no Rotisserie value. Filling in defensively for Ryan Klesko was his biggest role, but Gallagher also gave the Braves a patient bat in pinch hitting roles. He's a steadying influence on the young Braves outfielders, too. With Klesko slated to again get the lion's share of leftfield at bats, Gallagher, or another defensive specialist like him, will be a necessary addition to the Braves roster. Gallagher has hit better than .224 for most of his career and should again hit about .250 with minimal extras in about 150 at bats.

Gallagher's steady play and bench support cost Jarvis Brown a major league role in 1994 and Brown returned to Triple-A. Brown is a speedy outfielder but a poor hitter (career .210 average in 200 major league at bats). He is capable of stealing a few bases, even in a very limited role, but has no value in Rotisserie since he's unlikely to ever get more than 50 plate appearances. Brown is mainly injury insurance stored in Triple-A.

Lefty Brian Kowitz hit .300-8-57-22 for Richmond, all of those numbers were at or near career highs for the 25 year old outfielder. He mostly has doubles power and would hit about .270 as a major leaguer. Kowitz has good speed but has never stolen bases very successfully. One of his more admirable traits has been a good batting eye; Kowitz usually has nearly as many walks as strikeouts (43 walks, 53 strikeouts in 1994). Kowitz isn't considered a great prospect, but could get to the majors in a backup role in 1995 in case of injury.

Former Royals prospect Bobby Moore hit .366-5-18-10 in a platoon role for Richmond after losing nearly all of 1993 to injury. Moore's speed has evaporated since he had a career high of 35 steals for Omaha in 1991. Moore is now 29 years old and has virtually no chance to play major league ball.

Righthander Troy Hughes split 1994 between Richmond and Double-A Greenville, hitting much better at the lower level; Hughes combined for a .240-4-30-10 season. He's 24 years old and is one of the Braves better prospects in the high minors. He needs another (better) year at Richmond.

Kevin O'Connor, Don Robinson and Pedro Swann, all lefties, comprised the Greenville outfield for much of the year. All three have some speed, Robinson and Swann have decent power and O'Connor and Swann have shown they can hit for a good average. Unfortunately, they all have a tendency to strike out a lot. At age 25, O'Connor isn't going to make it to the bigs. Robinson, 23, has a shot, but 24 year old Swann is the better prospect. He's probably two years away from Atlanta.

22 year old Wonderful Monds hit .290 with ten homers for Macon, but struggled in a short stint for Durham. He has good speed (41 steals), but unfortunately for Monds, he's "wonderful" in name only. A fiftieth round draft pick, Monds is hardly a highly regarded prospect.

Jermaine Dye may be the best prospect in the low minors. Dye hit .298-15-98-19 for Class A Macon in 1994, his first full pro season. A righthanded hitter, Dye is just 21 years old and a rapidly rising star.

Chicago Cubs

Stuart Shea:

The Cubs' outfield is like a blindfolded woodchopper: great tools but no discipline. Contrary to popular belief, the offense generated by the Cubs last year was NOT enough to help them win. In fact, the outfield is due a major part of the blame. In addition, the Cubs lack even one outstanding defensive outfielder, and what help there is in the minor leagues doesn't look to change that weakness.

He has great genes and looks like he ought to be better than this, but left fielder Derrick May is proving to be a big time washout. The son of former big leaguer Dave May, Derrick has a nice looking uppercut swing, but he hasn't hit for power or eye popping averages. He rarely walks, adds little on the basepaths, and on defense he can only make observers shake their heads. May doesn't throw well, appears to loaf at times, often misjudging fly balls.

The fans were all over May last summer for various slumps, poor efforts, and his inability and/or unwillingness to bunt or give himself up to move runners along. A classic example of a player with more trade value than actual value, May might be history in Chicago with new GM Ed Lynch invoking a "speed and defense" mantra. His career batting average is .297 at home, and just .265 away from Wrigley Field. He's not likely to bust out in 1995, but he's 26 years old - an age when many youngsters blossom in the majors.

The decision to give Tuffy Rhodes both the centerfield and leadoff jobs in 1994 was based on one year of good numbers (1993) rather than the seven years of prior evidence which suggested that he was unable to play big league ball. After hitting three homers against the Mets on Opening Day, 1994, Rhodes' star dropped like a stone, and by season's end Tuffy was rotting away on the bench. The likeable Rhodes has enough patience and power to be a decent fifth outfielder, but is so bad defensively that the very idea of him in centerfield is ludicrous.

Acquired from Cleveland late in 1993 for Candy Maldonado, Glenallen Hill escaped from an uncomfortable platoon in leftfield with Derrick May to finish the season in centerfield; he acquitted himself well. While Hill lacks a great arm, he is a good outfielder; Hill also did not routinely misplay balls like Rhodes frequently did. At bat, Hill has terrific raw power and improved his plate discipline last year. He is also the Cubs' fastest and best baserunner. Lest one think that Wrigley Field was the reason Hill resurrected his career, let the record show that in 1994 he hit .339 with seven of his ten homers on the road. The Cubs should let the guy play.

Few players in baseball have the bat speed, arm strength, or ability to accelerate on the bases like rightfielder Sammy Sosa. Unfortunately, he seems manifestly uninterested in learning how to use his great talent and remains a big lump of unmined ore. While he is capable of hitting with enough power to carry a team for several games, he can also easily take the Cubs out of games with his costly baserunning mistakes and strikeouts or his studious ability to consistently miss cutoff men.

If somebody can get to Sosa and convince him that he's not half the player he could be with a little patience and control, Sosa would be an All-Star several times over. Of course, in many Rotisserie leagues, Sosa is one of the most valuable players one can own. If walks mean nothing in your league, get this guy. He's probably not going to hit .300 again, but should hang around the .270 level with loads of power and speed.

Longtime minor leaguer Eddie Zambrano finally made a major league roster in 1994 and produced well. He has some power, especially against lefthanders, and was more patient at the plate than expected. However, he is 29, and won't be moving into a regular role anytime soon.

Kevin Roberson, one of the only on field products of the disastrous Jim Frey regime, broke his hand last July fourth punching a wall after a bad at bat, then missed the rest of the season. While active, he mashed three pinch hit homers but again failed to show any mastery of the strike zone. Roberson is strong and plays the outfield well, but probably won't ever be a regular.

Former Pirates prospect Scott Bullett was Iowa's centerfielder in 1994; he hit .304 with 12 homers and 22 stolen bases and impressed defensively. Now for the bad news: he struck out 101 times with just 19 walks. This ridiculous ratio was even worse than Bullett's normal inability to work the strike zone and reflects a weakness that major league pitchers will be eager to exploit. Bullett is also 26 years old. Don't pay much for him if he happens to be on the Cubs roster. The Cubs were touting Bullett as a possible centerfielder this year; it would be idiotic to play Bullett at Hill's expense.

Ozzie Timmons, a decent power prospect, hit .263 with 19 homers last year at Triple-A Iowa, but needs to make better contact to move up. He's just 24, and still has an outside chance to be a major league regular.

Cincinnati Reds

Jacob Brumfield expanded his role as he was acquired by the Pirates and is the odds-on favorite to replace Andy Van Slyke as the Pirates regular centerfielder. He will probably bat leadoff for the Bucs, too, so his stolen base potential is considerable.

Greg Gajus:

Kevin Mitchell (.326-30-77-2) was in his free agent year, and had precisely the kind of year that you would expect from a veteran who realizes that if you want another big contract, you have to show up for most of the games and produce. Mitchell is a Hall of Fame quality hitter when he is healthy, paying attention, and happy with management, but that happy state has been missing for about half of his career. Given his age (33), and his unreliability, the Reds chose to sign Ron Gant rather than extend Mitchell's contract. Base your projection of his performance on the ballpark (Riverfront was very good to Mitchell) and the manager - Mitchell reacted well to the more relaxed style of Davey Johnson. He would probably sulk under a disciplinarian.

Ron Gant replaces Mitchell in both left field and in the cleanup slot. Before his injury, Gant was one of the most valuable Rotisserie players in the National League, a 30/30 player with 100 RBI. Given the nature of his injury (a severely broken leg) and the astroturf at Riverfront, I would expect his stealing to be curtailed, dropping Gant's Rotisserie value considerably. The best thing about Gant is that he will be motivated -- playing with a one year contract and with something to prove to the Braves. Figure the usual solid power numbers with stolen bases dropping to the teens.

Deion Sanders (.283-4-28-38) is a remarkably overrated baseball player but at the same time an underrated Rotisserie player. The key to both is his stolen bases, an increasingly rare commodity in Rotisserie ball but not particularly valuable in real baseball when you get caught 30% of the time. Sanders can't hit left handers, has a poor arm, is shaky defensively (although he outruns many mistakes) but will undoubt-

edly be the regular center fielder. 50 steals in the current hitting environment is an extremely valuable Rotisserie commodity, and Sanders should have no trouble reaching that total if he stays healthy. Anything else is a bonus.

Reggie Sanders (.263-17-62-21) still represents a solid power/speed combination, but he didn't really improve over his 1993 season. The concern with Sanders is declining strike zone judgment - in 1994 he struck out in 29% of his at bats, versus 24% in 1993. Sanders should be at the peak of his career (he is 27 this season) and had Sammy Sosa potential, but Sosa is two years younger so I'm not expecting a significant improvement unless Sanders gets better control of the strike zone.

One of the biggest improvements for the Reds in 1994 was their outfield depth. After going through 1993 with the likes of Gary Varsho, Cecil Espy, Jack Daugherty and Cesar Hernandez, Jim Bowden realized you cannot win without some reserves that you are not afraid to play. The 1994 group of Jacob Brumfield, Jerome Walton and Thomas Howard were considerably more effective than the 1993 crew. Davey Johnson does not platoon, but he picks spots effectively for his reserves and manages to give them enough time to stay sharp. The result is that the reserves perform well but without enough playing time to be particularly valuable for a Rotisserie roster.

Jacob Brumfield (.311-4-11-6) is the best of the group, a 29 year old righthanded hitter who lost two years in the minors to shoulder surgery. He was the 25th man on the roster a good part of the early season, but when Deion Sanders injured a heel, Brumfield stepped in and hit .479 for two weeks in a starting role. He has a little power and good speed (32 steals in 424 major league at bats) and will be a good sleeper now that he found a situation where can expand his role.

Thomas Howard (.264-5-24-4) is a useful role player who switch hits, plays good defense, and can run and hit a little. He does not hit left handers well, which would limit his contribution in a full time role.

Jerome Walton (.309-1-9-1) returned from the dead (actually from Vancouver) after struggling with injuries most of the time since his Rookie of the Year season for the Cubs in 1989. He was the Reds top righthanded pinch hitter and occasional outfield and first base fill in. He never was a power hitter and he has lost his speed (nine steals in the last three seasons at all levels) so his Rotisserie contribution is limited to batting average.

The Reds do have some interesting outfield prospects that are at least two years away. The best prospect is Chad Mattola, a 23 year old power hitter who stalled at Double-A in 1994. Steve Gibralter (22 years old), Micah Franklin (23) and Cleveland Ladell (24) are also candidates who are young enough to have some upside potential. The Reds also have a large number of failed prospects/marginal major leaguers who could make the team as a 25th man if they had a strong spring (Keith Gordon, Doug Jennings, Kevin Maas, William Pennyfeather).

Colorado Rockies

Two of my favorite might-have-beens will get a look in spring training with the Rockies, Ron Jones and Chito Martinez (the invitations to major league camp have not been formally extended yet, but, heck, Eddie Williams started last year in minor league camp, and both are probable to at least get a look with the major leaguers in Arizona. Jones, age 30, has about the best per-at-bat stats of anybody who didn't stick in the majors. He got 239 major league at bats but twice was felled by knee injuries while running on the carpet in the Vet outfield. Normally I don't indulge in pro-rata numbers, but to illustrate Jones' potential, here's 550 at bats of production based on what he actually did: the .272 average, 30 homers, and over 92 RBI. He's been a consistent line-drive contact hitter every time in the majors, and actually carried a .290 average in two callups before the injuries. If Mike Kingery can make it back up through the Rockies system, so can Ron Jones. And because he was gone from U.S. organized ball last year, his sleeper quality is enhanced. Comparisons to Eddie Williams are not unreasonable.

Chito Martinez is the guy who hit 20 homers in 211 at bats at Triple-A Rochester in 1991, got a well-deserved callup to Baltimore, and hit 13 more homers in 216 major league at bats that year. He spent 1992 as a part time major leaguer with fair results and then began 1993 as the platoon right fielder against righthanded pitching; but he had a couple of oh-fers, and the Orioles played a long string of games against lefty starters, so by the end of April Chito was 0 for 15, and that's where his season ended as Mark McLemore took over the right field role and Martinez went back to Rochester. In 1994 he had 16 homers in 300 at bats for the Yankees Triple-A Columbus team. Too many strikeouts have been the problem in his emergence as a major leaguer. He was let go by the Royals for that reason, and now by two more organizations. This spring is last call for a dose of plate discipline, and Chito knows it.

David Smith:

Don Baylor's only question about his outfield heading into 1994 was how to juggle the batting order to satisfy three outfielders with power potential. In leftfield would be Howard Johnson, who figured to use the short porch in leftfield to get out of his two year slump. In centerfield was Ellis Burks, given a three year, $9 million contract and an encouraging report on his back. In rightfield was Dante Bichette, he of the canon arm and quick bat.

But the best laid plans ... well, you know. Johnson staggered out of the box and in the middle of the season (when he was being used as a pinch hitter) asked to be traded. Instead he just got dumped at the end of the season and Eric Young returned to his leftfield position. Johnson's role as a pinch hitter actually suited him best, as he was 10 for 33 with four home runs.

Burks was named NL player of the month in April with a torrid average over .400 and lots of power. Then late in May he sprained his wrist on a checked swing and ended up in a cast for almost two months. In a moment of desperation, Mike Kingery was inserted. Kingery was the person they were thinking of when the word "journeyman" was invented. He

responded with a career in one season hitting .349 while covering a lot of ground in Mile High Stadium's spacious centerfield. One more week of the season and he would have qualified for the batting race and would have been among league leaders. One area that Kingery couldn't keep up with Burks, however, was in slugging percentage. Burks slugged a blistering .678 while Kingery was at .532 (but led the team with a .402 OBP). Baylor has already said the leftfield job is Kingery's in 1994, but the lefty could platoon with Young, a righthanded batter. Burks will be back in center.

In rightfield, Dante Bichette put up great numbers, and was the perfect third place hitter ahead of Andres Galarraga. He swings the bat like a sledgehammer. But when Galarraga went down with the broken hand in July, Bichette went AWOL. His average slipped and his homer and RBI production disappeared. Regardless, his numbers of .304-27-93 are impressive for a short season and the only question about his future in Colorado is if they can afford him. He was especially proud of the fact that he joined the 20/20 club with 21 stolen bases. Management only signed him for one year to see if 1993 was a fluke. Now they'll have to pay if they want an extended contract.

Also seeing time off the bench could be John VanderWal, although he was very average in limited action. Chris Jones gave up and went to Japan. Trenidad Hubbard finally got a chance after a career in the minors. With HoJo gone he's likely to see limited action again, but he has no chance of getting a regular role. If there's a sleeper in the minors it's Quinton McCracken who swiped 36 bases at Double A New Haven and is considered the top outfield prospect after a solid 1993 campaign for Class A Central Valley.

Lary Bump:

J.D. Noland showed he could hit and run last season (.292-3-44-24 steals at Double-A New Haven; .346-3-34-11 after a promotion to Colorado Springs). The lefthanded batter is a bit elderly (26) for a prospect.

Quinton McCracken (.278-5-39-36 steals in the East-

ern League) is the best base-stealing threat in the Colorado organization. The 25-year-old switch hitter can handle center field defensively, and has played second base. His teammate, Mike Case, 26, batted .260-7-39-10 steals. Case bats righthanded.

Angel Echevarria found out the difference between batting in the California League (.302-6-35) and at New Haven (.254-8-32). The righthanded batter is 23.

Another base stealer is righthanded hitting Terry Jones, drafted in the 40th round in 1993. He was at .293-2-34-44 steals, but he was playing in the California League at age 24.

John Giudice, 23, batted .290-9-22 in the Sally League and .282-4-33 in the California League. The 1993 20th-round choice out of Eastern Connecticut State, a righthanded batter, should be closer to home this year at New Haven.

Florida Marlins

The departure of Carl Everett is a big boost for Chuck Carr, who would have faced a serious challenge for time in center field. Carr had been under some pressure to improve his on-base skills in winter ball, and had made no progress, not even getting play much due to administrative problems. Carr can breath easier now, at least until Jesus Tavarez comes along in late '95 or early '96. Also helped by the Everett departure are Darrell Whitmore (who has other problems that put him in the doghouse) and Nigel Wilson, both of whom would have been pressured if Everett didn't just take over the center field job outright.

Tony Blengino:

Baseball insiders were quite impressed when the Marlins pilfered three young outfield prospects in the expansion draft. Two full seasons have passed and Nigel Wilson, Carl Everett and Darrell Whitmore are each at least 25 years old and have cumulatively proven nothing at the major league level. 1995 is

make or break time for all three, as opportunities abound due to the impending shift of Jeff Conine to third base and the tenuous status of Chuck Carr in centerfield.

The only sure thing in the Marlins' 1995 outfield is veteran rightfielder Gary Sheffield. Despite spending 28 games on the disabled list with shoulder injuries, Sheffield led the Marlins with 27 homers and was among team leaders in runs scored and RBI. His .380 OBP and .584 slugging average duplicated his 1992 figures of .385 OBP and .580 slugging when he nearly won the Triple Crown. Sheffield also has good speed and has stolen 24 bases in 159 games for the Marlins. The most frightening thing about Sheffield is that he has accomplished so much at such an early age. 26 years old during the 1995 season, he is just now coming into his prime and is at an age when many young stars turn their performance level up another few notches. While Sheffield is a mediocre fielder with a sometimes questionable attitude and his hitting is less valuable coming from a rightfielder than from a third baseman (his former position), Sheffield is still an enormous offensive talent. Look for a .310-30-115-18 performance from him in 1995.

After a puzzling holdout to begin 1994, 26 year old Chuck Carr started like a house afire, hitting above .300 for the first two months, playing good defense and ranking near the top of the league in steals. Unfortunately, Carr finished the season with a cold spell that was just as extreme, ending the season with a .263 average. Considering Carr's complete lack of power (second worst in the National League among starting outfielders), his poor .305 OBP lowers his value to any major league team. For Rotisserie purposes, his excellent speed (90 steals over the past two seasons) is his only value and he has far more value for Rotisserie than he does in real baseball. For 1995, Carr is in peril of losing his job to Everett; he would then become a spare outfielder whose Rotisserie-valuable steals could quickly evaporate. Plan on 300 at bats from Carr, producing a .240-0-22-25 season in 1995.

A former top pick by the Yankees (1990), Carl Everett can hit for average and power, has great speed and range with an incredible throwing arm, and is also a switch hitter. Everett had a chance to grab Carr's job in 1994, but wound up on the disabled list a week after his recall from Edmonton. Everett's biggest problem is impatience at the plate; he has struck out six times as often as he has walked in his short major league career, in addition to a 3.5-to-1 ratio in the Pacific Coast League last year. While Everett is hardly a sure thing to take over from Carr, he is already Carr's defensive equal and has far more potential than Carr. Everett will get every chance to win the job in spring training. Aged 24 on Opening Day, this may be Everett's breakout year; expect him to earn 350 at bats, hitting .260-10-50-15.

The Marlins' first expansion draft selection was 25 year old Nigel Wilson who was just another outfielder in the deep Blue Jays' system. Wilson has been bothered by chronic asthma in the Florida humidity in addition to recurring quadricep problems. Also, Wilson has been absolutely plagued by a worse problem -- strikeouts. He has fanned 198 times in 700 at bats since joining the Marlins, with just 47 walks. Wilson has good power, having slugged above .500 in each of the last three seasons, but his once good speed (26 steals in 1991) deteriorated to just two stolen bases last year. Still, with Conine moving to third base in 1995, leftfield is there for the taking by Wilson. He's anything but a sure bet to hold the job, though, and should get 200 at bats, hitting .220-5-24 in 1995.

Darrell Whitmore was the third part of Triple-A Edmonton's outfield in 1994, playing rightfield after a miserable performance for the Marlins in the second half of 1993 (.204 average with 72 whiffs in 250 at bats). A 26 year old lefty, Whitmore hit 20 homers with a .506 slugging average, but his .283 average paled compared to his .355 average in 273 Triple-A at bats in 1993. Whitmore's disappointing season was topped off with an on field tirade during which he shoved his own manager and was suspended by the Pacific Coast League (the Marlins later extended the suspension to ten games). Despite his good athletic ability, Whitmore's speed and defense have been a disappointment and he has fallen far in the Marlins' eyes; he may have to move to another organization.

It's unlikely that he'll be a big factor in the majors in 1995; he could get as much as 200 at bats, hitting .240-4-20-5.

After being an offensive force in the Mexican League, 32 year old Matias Carrillo has managed just a .251 average in 191 at bats. He managed no homers, thus underscoring the relative weakness of the Mexican League. Lefthanded Carrillo does nothing particularly well and should lose his roster spot to lefties Wilson and Whitmore in 1995; he may never get another big league at bat.

Eight year minor league veteran John Massarelli hit .259 for Edmonton, but swiped 39 bases and now has 242 in his pro career. He has no power (13 homers in 2330 pro at bats) and he's unlikely to get a major league chance, especially in competition with the abundance of young outfield talent possessed by the Marlins in the high minors. Consider also that all of the other outfielders are younger than the 29 year old Massarelli. But, due to his great speed, keep an eye on this guy if he gets a big league shot since he can quickly pick up a few valuable steals.

Switch hitting Julian Tavarez also made a cameo appearance with the Marlins in 1994. Like Massarelli, 24 year old Tavarez also has excellent speed and plays good defense but completely lacks power. He could be an acceptable fourth outfielder in the majors and may be better suited to that role than Wilson or Whitmore. He should spend part of 1995 in Florida, hitting .200-0-6-3 in 100 at bats.

Farther down the road, watch out for 1993 eighth round pick Billy McMillon. Yet another lefty, he hit only .252 for Class A Kane County, but had 17 homers, 101 RBI and 84 walks. At age 23, he must now produce rapidly to certify himself as an authentic prospect.

Lary Bump:

Darrell Whitmore, a defensive back at West Virginia, may be a bit too intense for baseball. Last season he went into a rage against a Pacific Coast League umpiring crew and his own manager, resulting in 10

days of suspensions -- two by the Pacific Coast League, eight more by the Marlins. A bigger problem is that the lefthanded batter is getting older (26) in an organization with some excellent outfield prospects. He batted .283-20-61-14 steals.

Nigel Wilson, the first player chosen by Florida in the expansion draft, is trying the organization's patience. He was 0-for-his-September-callup in 1993, and the 25-year-old lefty hitter hasn't developed into the run-producer the Marlins envisioned (.309-12-62 at Edmonton).

Houston Astros

Bill Gilbert:

After a .300 season in 1993, leftfielder Luis Gonzalez turned in a .273-8-67-15 log for 1994, which is a good representation of the type of production that can be expected for several more years. Gonzalez is a solid, but unspectacular performer who tends to be a slow starter. He also has an unusually high propensity for hot and cold streaks. A Rotisserie league owner should find at least one opportunity each year to acquire him in a trade with an owner who is suffering through one of Gonzalez' patented cold streaks. Gonzalez is a smart, hard working player who rarely makes baserunning or defensive mistakes. At age 27, he should be moving into his most productive years. Earlier in his career, he struggled against lefthanders, but he has shown in the last two years that this is no longer a problem. He should be an everyday player for several seasons. However, a move to another team is a possibility in view of Houston's need to reduce the payroll and their wealth of promising young outfield prospects.

Steve Finley has held down centerfield for Houston for the past four years. His 1994 numbers (.276-11-33-13) reflect a little more power and a little less speed than he has shown in prior seasons. At age 30, he should retain this level of production for at least two or three more years. At the end of 1994, Finley's future with the Astros was questionable. The Astros are faced with the need to cut the payroll; Finley

would appear to be a candidate to go. With only one year left on his $4.25 million contract, he should be tradeable.

The Astros have a worthy replacement in 24 year old Brian L. Hunter who led the minor leagues in hitting with a .372-10-51-49 season at Class AAA Tucson. Hunter also led the Pacific Coast League in runs, hits, triples and stolen bases. His professional career started slowly but he has now completed six seasons and should be ready. Hunter's primary value to a Rotisserie owner is in his stolen bases; he has stolen over 30 bases in each of the past five years. He didn't have a .300 season in the minors until 1994 and Hunter has just marginal power; ten homers in both 1993 and 1994 represents a career high. He has hit more triples than homers in his career.

Rightfield became the unsettled position for the Astros in 1994 and may remain so in 1995. Rookie James Mouton (.245-2-16-24) won the job in spring training but couldn't hold it after opposing pitchers discovered they didn't have to throw strikes to get him out. Veteran Kevin Bass (.310-6-25-2) started the year as the fourth outfielder but received most of his playing time in the last half of the season and, at age 34, had his best season since 1986. 32 year old Mike Felder saw some action and expected numbers of .239-0-13-3. 36 year old Milt Thompson was obtained from the Phillies two weeks before the strike to strengthen the team for the stretch run. Felder and Thompson are both eligible for free agency and probably won't return to Houston.

For 1995, Mouton would appear to be the best bet in rightfield. At age 26, he may be ready to fulfill the promise that he showed in 1993, when he was the Pacific Coast League MVP, with a sensational .315-16-92-40 year. The key is improving his plate discipline. Mouton is an intense and intelligent player and, with a new batting coach in 1995, he could make the adjustments necessary to succeed at the major league level.

The Astros have several other outfield prospects but none appear to be quite ready for the majors. The brightest are two young Venezuelans, 21 year old

Bob Abreu, who hit .303-16-73-12 for Class AA Jackson and 19 year old Richard Hidalgo, who batted .292-12-76-12 for Class A Quad Cities. Both have excellent tools and have moved up steadily through the organization. Abreu should be at Class AAA Tucson in 1995 and, with a good year, could make his major league debut in September. Hidalgo may be at Class AA Jackson in 1995 and is about two years behind Abreu. Hidalgo set a new Midwest League record with 47 doubles and made the All-Star team before missing the last week of the season with a broken bone in his hand.

Chris Hatcher is a big powerhitting outfielder who has been hampered by injuries throughout his career. He hit .298-12-73-5 in his first year at the Triple-A level in 1994 and will probably be there again in 1995. At age 26, he needs to demonstrate that he can produce over a full season and cut down on his strikeouts to get a major league opportunity. 24 year old Gary Mota was once one of the brightest prospects in the organization, but has turned in disappointing numbers over the last two years (.239-10-54-12 for Class AA Jackson in 1994). He needs a breakthrough year in 1995 to get back on track.

The remaining Triple-A and Double-A outfielders are short on power and don't have enough other positive attributes to rate as strong prospects. This group includes 27 year old Ken Ramos out of the White Sox organization (.300-1-32-22), and 25 year old Ray Montgomery (.256-7-51-5) -- both at Triple-A Tucson; Buck McNabb (.273-0-27-15) at Jackson and Jimmy White - both 22 years old. White hit .304-13-47-10 while splitting time between Jackson and Class A Osceola.

Lary Bump:

Brian Hunter's playing time could depend on whether Houston has traded Steve Finley. The question before last season was whether Hunter could hit. The hunt is over; he can hit (.372-10-51-49 steals at Tucson). The righthanded batter, 24, also can run and play center field. He earned the most top ratings in last year's Baseball America poll -- best batting prospect, best baserunner, fastest baserunner, best

defensive outfielder and most exciting player in the Pacific Coast League.

Chris Hatcher's Triple-A debut was a good one (.298-12-73). The righthanded batter has moved up one level in each of his five pro seasons, but the final step may elude the 26-year-old unless he can be more patient at the plate.

Ken Ramos batted .300 at Tucson, with a .407 on-base percentage. But the lefthanded batter isn't a particularly effective runner once he reaches base, despite his career-high 22 stolen bases. He has no power (one homer, 32 RBI) and is marginal defensively in left field, and is 27 years old already.

Ray Montgomery, 25, matched his career batting average (.256) and on-base percentage (.326) at Tucson. Not good enough to get the righthanded batter to the majors.

Bob Abreu, 21, is the top hitting candidate behind Hunter. The lefthanded batter finished at .303-16-73 for Jackson. He doesn't have a lot of speed, and has been barely a break-even base stealer. He could end up as a first baseman.

Buck McNabb, a big base-stealer in the lower minors, was successful on only 15 of 32 attempts in his Double-A debut at Jackson, where he batted .273. Speed is the 22-year-old lefthanded batter's entire game; he has hit just two home runs in four pro seasons.

Lefthanded-hitting Jimmy White, 22, advanced during last season from the Florida State League (.316-5-21) to the Texas League (.294-8-26), and is one to watch this season if he makes it to Triple-A.

In the Florida State League, 23-year-old Melvin Mora batted .282-8-46-24 steals. The righthanded batter is a former second baseman.

Nineteen-year-old Richard Hidalgo is a couple of years away from a big career, especially if increasing power as he matures converts last year's 47 doubles into home runs. He had the Midwest League's best

outfield arm, and batted .292-12-76. The righthanded batter was a .500 base stealer (12-for-24).

Also at Quad City, Ray Bowers put together a .257-15-63-14 steals season. The 21-year-old righthanded batter will have to make better contact; he struck out 143 times.

Los Angeles Dodgers

Greg Gajus:

The play of Raul Mondesi (.306-16-56-11) made it easy for Dodger fans to say "Daryl Who?" after Strawberry's release. In addition to his strong offensive performance, Mondesi displayed one of the best arms in the league and should be a fixture for the Dodgers in rightfield for many years (he is only 24). However, some decline is expected in 1995. Mondesi has terrible strike zone judgment (16 walks in 450 plate appearances) and pitchers will make him pay for it in 1995. Mondesi is a fine player but his minor league performance suggests that he is not really a .300 hitter. Expect 20 homers and 20 steals with a .270 average in 1995.

Brett Butler (.314-8-33-27) is 38 now, but is the type of player that ages well and there is no reason not to expect a repeat of his 1994 season. The best evidence that the ball was juiced was Butler's eight home runs. He is a free agent, but his likely replacement won't be ready for a year or two so he should be back at least for 1995.

Henry Rodriguez (.268-8-49-0) had the good sense to hit extremely well immediately upon replacing Daryl Strawberry, but he faded as the season wore on. He is strictly a platoon player, who serves as a firstbase substitute in addition to his outfield play.

Cory Snyder (.235-6-18-1), Mitch Webster (.274-4-12-1) and Chris Gwynn (.268-3-13-0) all played a few games in leftfield but are all free agents and in all likelihood, none will not return in 1995.

The early favorite for the leftfield job is Billy Ashley,

a 6'7" 24 year old power prospect who put together a fine year at Class AAA Albuquerque (.345-37-105-6). He led the minors in home runs with 37, raised his average 48 points, and improved his walks despite fewer plate appearances. Ashley has also received press that suggests he cut his strikeouts but it is a statistical illusion; Ashley batted almost 100 times less in 1994 than he did in 1993 at Albuquerque. In both years Ashley struck out 30% of the time. He's a good but not great prospect at this time; the biggest thing in his favor is opportunity. If someone wants to bid on him like he is the next Matt Williams let them (Williams hit .188, .202 and .205 his first three years in the majors). In 1995, Ashley is probably a .250 hitter with some power but with the danger that a slow start would send him back to Triple-A. 1996 or 1997 will be the best year to own Ashley.

The Dodgers have several other outfield candidates who are a couple of years away. Todd Hollandsworth may be the best of the group. A 22 year old lefthander, Hollandsworth combined power with speed to hit .285-19-91-15; he needs to improve his strike zone judgement. Roger Cedeno is a switch hitting 20 year old center fielder who is Brett Butler's heir apparent. He hit .321-4-49-30 for Albuquerque. Jerry Brooks is an old prospect (age 28) but has put together a couple of good years for Albuquerque (.321-16-79-4 in 1994). Brooks could get a backup outfield/pinch hitter role for the Dodgers in 1995.

Lary Bump:

Billy Ashley is a human highlight reel in batting practice. The 6-7, 220-pound 24-year-old had a 1994 season worthy of a Minor League Player of the Year. The righthanded hitter was the Pacific Coast League's MVP at .345-37-105, and he continued to make great improvement in his strikeout/walk ratio. His defense remains iffy, but the Dodgers remain indifferent to that facet of baseball.

A year away is Roger Cedeno proved himself (.321-4-49-30 steals) as one of the youngest players in the PCL. At age 20, the righthanded batter is ready to move into center field at Dodger Stadium whenever Brett Butler is ready to vacate the position. The

question is whether Cedeno still will be a young man when that happens.

In another organization, Todd Hollandsworth would be a hotshot outfield prospect, but he ranks no better than third in the current Dodgers system. The lefthanded batter earned rave reviews in the Arizona Fall League in 1993. Hollandsworth, who will be 22 in April, didn't disappoint in the PCL (.285-19-91-15 steals). He may not have enough arm to play right field in the majors.

Jerry Brooks has had four seasons with at least 11 homers and 71 RBI at Albuquerque, but has just nine major league at bats to show for his efforts. The 28-year-old righthanded batter also has caught to enhance his value as a utlility player, the role he may have to take to another organization as a minor league free agent.

Former Angel Reggie Williams had a good year at Albuquerque (.313-4-32-21 steals), but the switch hitter is 28 already. Lefthanded-hitting Vern Spearman has no homers and just 96 RBI in 415 pro games, including parts of three seasons at San Antonio. His stolen base totals have dropped as he has risen through the Dodgers system, and he was just 21-for-36 in '94. He's 25, and hardly a prospect in this organization.

Chris Latham, the California League's fastest baserunner, did not hit a lick (.215-2-15-28 steals) in a hitters' league, so he went back down to the short-season Northwest League (.340-5-32-33). The switch hitter is 21.

Righthanded-hitting Jim Martin, voted the California League's most exciting player for his speed and all-or-nothing batting style (.267-12-58- one strikeout every four at bats), will have trouble advancing past younger prospects in the organization. He's 24.

Karim Garcia took a step backward to the Florida State League last season, but he batted .265-21-84) and his arm was considered the league's best. The lefthanded batter had 40 minor league home runs before his 19th birthday, last October. Dwight Maness,

a righthanded batter, was demoted from the Texas League (.219-5-20) to Bakersfield (.250-3-26). He totaled 36 stolen bases, but was much more efficient in the California League. He'll be 21 in April.

Another righthanded batter, Mike Moore, went the same way. After a .224-5-32 start at San Antonio, he batted .296-2-8 in 21 California League games. At 24, he's running out of time.

Montreal Expos

John Perrotto:

Few clubs could lose a player the caliber of Larry Walker without being hurt. With their deep farm system, the Expos are one of the few exceptions. Walker became a free agent at the end of last season. Though the British Columbia native wanted to remain in his home country with the Expos, it didn't appear that Montreal could afford him.

Have no fear, though. The Expos' outfield will still be among the game's best. Moises Alou will move over to Walker's rightfield slot while top prospect Rondell White will take Alou's spot in leftfield. They will flank superb centerfielder Marquis Grissom.

Walker hit .322-19-86-15 and White may not be able to equal that production in his first full major league season. White should come close, though, as he is truly a wonderful talent - a five tool guy with the ability to hit for average, hit for power, steal bases, play good defense and throw well.

Alou and Grissom are already two of the top all around players in the National League and are just entering their primes. That's kind of scary to Expos' opponents.

Alou showed no ill effects last season from either a broken leg or dislocated ankle suffered in September, 1993. He hit .339-22-79-7 and really began to realize just how good he can be. He should put up even better numbers this year in making a strong run at the National League's Most Valuable Player award.

Grissom is another guy who always has to be considered an MVP candidate. He hit .288-11-45-36 last season in what could be considered just a slight down year. He is capable of a better season and his steals should increase now that manager Felipe Alou has decided to leave Grissom in the leadoff spot. Grissom was uncomfortable with being shuttled between the number one and number three spots in the batting order and says he feels much better hitting leadoff.

If, for some reason, White doesn't prove to be quite ready for everyday action, the Expos have a real sleeper in reserve Lou Frazier. Many in the Expos' organization truly believe Frazier is the next Otis Nixon, a speedy player who took a long time in the minor leagues to develop before blossoming. Frazier hit .271-0-14-20 in 1994, his second year in the big leagues.

The Expos' crack scouting staff uncovered yet another hidden gem, signing Vladimir Guerrero last summer. The 18 year old Dominican reminds scouts of Andre Dawson with his ultra quick bat and debuted with a .314-5-25-0 season in the Gulf Coast Rookie League. Guerrero won't be in Montreal for a while but is a name worth remembering.

New York Mets

At one point during the winter, the Mets' major league outfield roster consisted of this underwhelming assortment: Jim Lindeman, Tito Navarro, Joe Orsulak, Ricky Otero, and Ryan Thompson (and that was all). Bobby Bonilla, who played third base (see that chapter) throughout 1995, and David Segui, who moved from first base to left field on days when Rico Brogna played first, were listed as infielders but obviously were part of the outfield depth chart.

It's not surprising the Mets went after Carl Everett, a budding star who can play all three outfield positions and who is good enough to displace Thompson from center field. I like Everett as a good source of speed and power. As noted in my outfield tactics essay in this year's Annual, there aren't enough 20/20 guys left available to make it a reasonable goal to

count on getting one or two of them, but there are enough 10/10 guys that you should be very familiar with them before draft day and fairly aggressive when they come up for bid. Everett is easily within reach of 12-15 homers and 16-20 steals. By 1997, that 20/20 mark will be achievable.

At one point during the winter, the Mets major league outfield roster consisted of this underwhelming assortment: Jim Lindeman, Tito Navarro, Joe Orsulak, Ricky Otero, and Ryan Thompson (and that was all). Bobby Bonilla, who played third base (see that chapter) throughout 1995, and David Segui, who moved from first base to left field on days when Rico Brogna played first, were listed as infielders but obviously were part of the outfield depth chart.

It's not surprising the Mets went after Carl Everett, a budding star who can play all three outfield positions and who is good enough to displace Thompson from center field (see Marlins essay for more). I like Everett as a good source of speed and power.

Segui is a slow, singles-type hitter who worked himself up to double-digit home run power to justify his grip and the first base job, but lost that role anyway. Defensively he is clearly above average at first base but only adequate in left field. Given the lack of power and unexciting defensive assets, Segui must be regarded as unsafe to keep a full-time role even if handed one during spring training.

After Everett, the most attractive outfielder is Thompson, a good source of power and speed. Batting average has always been a problem for Thompson, however, and if he doesn't improve his discipline markedly, he will go into the record books with a low peak in his career with something around .240 and 20 homers. The specific problem is that Thompson keeps forgetting the compact swing that he spent so much time and effort learning. He knows he can generate better power with the compact stroke and better overall as well, and yet every time he clocks a few homers, he starts coming out of the compact stance with long, looping swings. The strikeouts pile up, and the batting average drops, and eventually Thompson will allow himself to be coached back into

the disciplined approach, but he's gone through this cycle three times in his career already, leaving doubt as to whether he will ever climb permanently to a higher level.

Thompson presents himself as thoughtful, even articulate for an athlete who went from high school directly to the pros. His play is erratic, however, not just in the hitting ups and downs but even more markedly in occasional defensive lapses. When he first arrived with the Mets he drew criticism for goofy laughing after a misplay in center field in a game against the Cardinals, and last year Thompson got criticized by Bobby Bonilla for loafing after a hit ball and allowing a runner advance that cost a game. My overall impression is that Thompson has great athletic ability -- it's a thrill to watch him run down difficult fly balls with ease deep in center at Shea Stadium -- but after several chances he just doesn't seem able to keep his head in every minute of every game. That flaw will eventually cost him playing time, later in his career if not in 1995. In the excuse department, Thompson did have problems with his quadriceps muscle, ribs and a dislocated finger in 1994; but the main issue is thinking clearly all the time.

Orsulak is a perennial sleeper, because no one gets the least bit excited about him, and yet he keeps producing a .260-.270 average with 40-50 RBI and usually 8 or 10 homers. People keep getting $8 of value for $5. Orsulak has probably been on more of my own rosters than any other player during the past five years. It seemed like he was about age 32 when I first started liking him (he got to majors at age 21 and had a regular role at age 23) but in fact Orsulak is just 32 now, and aging slowly. His ability to play all three outfield positions will keep him in the 300 at bat range for at least another year or two. On the upper end he can platoon against righties and come off the bench for 400+ at bats.

Lindeman is a long-ago number one draft pick from the Cardinals organization, one of the many who got so hot in spring training 1987 that St. Louis figured it would be a good idea to ship Andy Van Slyke to Pittsburgh (for catcher Tony Pena) as a way to open

a full-time slot for Lindeman to blossom. Obviously history differed from the Cardinals' vision of the future. Still, Lindeman has been hitting minor league pitching so hard the last two years, that it just hasn't seemed sensible to keep him on a farm. His defense is only fair.

Navarro is a speedy, no-power ex-shortstop now strictly a defensive asset and pinch-runner type. Otero is a still-developing (age 22) right fielder likely to spend the whole 1995 season at Triple-A Norfolk.

For reserves, the Mets in December added speedster Jarvis Brown, the former backup for the Braves and Padres, and Chris Jones who has been up with the Rockies. Both are past their prime without ever having been given anything close to a full season of regular major league work; but both are useful as short-term pickups. Jones is more likely to come up with one home run in a two week period, and Brown is more likely to give you one stolen base as a fill-in for a DL situation. Both are just as likely to start the season at Norfolk as in New York.

Philadelphia Phillies

The arrival of Gregg Jefferies, purportedly to play left field (which he can do, no problem) is good news for the whole Phillies batting order. Jefferies can both drive in runs and get on base to set the table for others. As a no-holes hitter who cannot be pitched around, he gives the other team's pitcher and defense that much more to think about.

New arrival Rob Butler can get into the outfield picture, at least as a part-timer. Jefferies may end up playing first base, with Dave Hollins staying at third. Do the Phillies really have enough money to get another established star such as Terry Pendleton or Ken Caminiti to play third? I am skeptical. Keeping Jefferies in the infield would create at least a platoon opportunity for Butler, who has fair speed and can hit much better than his .213 career major league average.

Tony Blengino:

The Phils run to glory in 1993 was keyed by relatively good health, career years from their stars, and incredibly productive platoons in left and right field. 1994 was certainly a different story. The majority of their star level players spent time on the disabled list, and their left and right field platoons' production dropped significantly, with half of each tandem eventually being traded.

Len Dykstra had an incredible season in 1993 when he scored 143 runs (the most in the National League since 1932), hit .305, drew 129 walks and reached career highs in homers (19), OBP (.420), and slugging average (.482). The 32 year old Dykstra seemed to pick up right where he left off in 1994 before he was sidelined by appendicitis, the third time in four years that he missed a significant amount of time due to serious, unrelated injuries. When healthy, Dykstra was again among the best leadoff men in baseball, posting a .404 OBP and a .435 slugging average while scoring 68 runs in 84 games. Due to a pre-strike slump, he hit just .273, uncharacteristically low for Dykstra. His diminishing steals (15 in 1994 after 37 in 1993) are a sign of advancing age. But, Dykstra's power and plate discipline are traits that age well and should keep him very productive for several more years. Expect him to have a .280-12-50-25 season in 1995.

Milt Thompson and Pete Incaviglia formed a dynamic platoon in 1993, combining for 28 homers and 133 RBI. Thompson's trade to Houston in 1994 just before the strike left Incaviglia with the full time job, but his performance fell far short of his 1993 season. He hit just .230 and had a poor .278 OBP (due to 16 walks in 260 plate appearances). Despite hitting 13 homers, he managed just 32 RBI. His excellent "clutch" hitting in 1993 fell apart as he hit just .149 with runners in scoring position in 1994. Incaviglia worked hard during the off season to condition himself for the 1995 season, dropping 20 pounds by the end of September. While the Phillies wish to explore other leftfield options, Incaviglia is the incumbent and can be expected to hit .260-18-70 in 1995, assuming he retains the full time job.

Wes Chamberlain and Jim Eisenreich manned the rightfield platoon until Chamberlain was dealt to Boston for Paul Quantrill and Billy Hatcher. Over the last two years Eisenreich, who will be 36 years old in 1995, has played more games than any other Phillie, while playing excellent defense and hitting .311. But, Eisenreich has little power or speed; he was one of only a handful of National League regulars in 1994 who didn't reach double digits in either homers or steals. On the trading block late in 1994, Eisenreich isn't considered irreplaceable by the Phillies. He's most effective in either a platoon role or as a fourth outfielder; should he be a regular in 1995, expect a batting average drop without many extras: .270-5-40.

The Phils' productive bench from 1993 became a place for over-the-hill veterans and failed prospects in 1994. After being acquired from Boston, Billy Hatcher subbed for injured Lenny Dykstra and continued his seven year decline. His .271 OBP and lack of extras in power or speed did nothing to help the Phillies offense. He has become a zero dimensional player and there is no reason to believe that he'll return to Philadelphia in 1995. He's no more than a pinch hitter at this point and a poor one at that.

Plagued by injuries throughout his minor league career, 26 year old Tony Longmire failed to develop into an adequate replacement for Milt Thompson, as the Phillies had hoped. He displayed mediocre defense and a poor batting eye with little power or speed. Most of his power is for doubles, instead of home runs, further lowering his Rotisserie value. Longmire isn't talented enough to become a regular, but could gain a larger role for the 1995 Phillies, getting 150 at bats and hitting .250 with three homers.

Phillies higher minor league clubs featured a noticeable lack of prospects, yet were some of the oldest teams in baseball in 1994. The outfielders for those teams were mostly a collection of older ex-prospects. Few have marginal major league talents in any regards and the best of them have only the potential to become reserves in the majors. Hard nosed grinder Tom Marsh has some pop in his bat but is far too

undisciplined at the plate and is a poor fielder; at age 29 he is no prospect.

25 year old Ron Lockett has spent five years in the minors and his performance has deteriorated annually. Once a decent prospect, 26 year old Tom Nuneviller hasn't been the same since a serious 1992 knee injury.

Dave Tokheim had the best performance of the Phillie minor league outfielders, hitting .301 with 13 homers, but he is now 26 years old and playing only at Double-A. His slow progress is a negative.

Top draft pick Jeff Jackson was selected ahead of Frank Thomas in 1989 and has been a bust. He missed most of the 1994 season with injuries and hit .177 with six extra base hits in 124 at bats. After six minor league seasons he'll likely be released.

Another top draft pick (in 1992), Chad McConnell has hit just .236 in two pro seasons and has suffered from chronic shoulder problems while also suffering from spells of night blindness. It's hard to see 24 year old McConnell reaching the big leagues anytime soon.

Two Phillie minor leaguers have a chance to fit into their plans in 1995. Phil Geisler and Rick Holifield (both 25 year old lefthanders) had similar seasons in 1994, struggling mightily in Triple-A before posting much better numbers in Double-A. After an impressive spring training, Geisler batted .197 at Class AAA Scranton-Wilkes Barre, with no homers before a .276-7-40 year for Class AA Reading. He had a better season in 1993, connecting for 15 homers in the Class A Florida State League while playing all three outfield positions as well as first base. His versatility and power could give him a chance at a backup role in 1995.

Holifield was claimed off of waivers from the overstocked Blue Jays and he had a .510 slugging average in 155 at bats for Reading while leading the club with 21 stolen bases. Holifield hit just .127 in a short Triple-A stint, fanning 19 times in 55 at bats. He has good power and speed but hasn't hit a lick above

Double-A, not a good sign at his age.

23 year old Jeremy Kendall's 62 steals were the second highest total in the minors and he was selected by Baseball America as the South Atlantic League's best and fastest baserunner. He should be able to rise quickly through the weak Phillies farm system.

Pittsburgh Pirates

The Pirates' acquisition of Luis Mercedes puts another dark horse into the annual Pittsburgh outfield sleeper sweepstakes from which one or two players always emerge to give $6 of value for a $1 investment. These marginal players are most worth noting on the rosters of teams managed by Jim Leyland, Bobby Cox, and their proteges, because once a player makes the major league roster he is virtually assured of getting six or eight at bats per week. Although he's reached age 26 without accomplishing much of anything toward a major league career, Mercedes is nonetheless a three-time minor league batting champion: Class-A at age 21, Double-A at age 22, and Triple-A at age 24. The year he didn't win a title, at age 23, Mercedes hit .334 at Triple-A. In an organization with less outfield talent than the Orioles (like Pittsburgh, for example) Mercedes would have seen a lot more major league playing time by now. In addition to the heavy talent at the top of the Orioles (and then the Giants) depth charts, Mercedes' tempestuous personality has also held him back. Leyland is the right manager to get some results here, if Mercedes can just fit onto the roster.

The Pirates also gave another one-year contract to Dave Clark, who doesn't face much a fight to keep a roster spot. Clark bats left and Mercedes bats right, so (at least on a Leyland team) the two can both fit and be useful.

John Perrotto:

Why have the Pirates gone from three time National League East champions to consecutive sub-.500 seasons all within the first five seasons of this decade? Well consider this: The 1991 starting outfield con-

sisted of Barry Bonds, Andy Van Slyke and Bobby Bonilla; the 1995 version most likely will be Al Martin, Jacob Brumfield and Midre Cummings.

The Pirates finished the breakup of their "Outfield of Dreams" at the end of last season by allowing Van Slyke to leave as a free agent. He followed Bonilla and Bonds, ho took similar routes to their home-towns of New York and San Francisco respectively. While the Pirates' new look outfield might not match the production of three perennial MVP candidates, it holds some promise.

In his second full year in the majors, Martin was having a good season until being derailed by a season ending wrist injury in early July. He hit .286-9-33-15 and continues to blossom into a potential 20/20 player with an outside shot at 30/30. He has good power and speed to go with a hungry attitude. He desperately wants to become a star player.

Martin will be 27 on opening day but, in reality, is much younger in baseball terms. He was a football star, accepting a scholarship to play tailback at Southern California, and didn't begin playing organized baseball until his senior year of high school. He has just reached the point of his career where he is ready to become an All-Star.

Acquired from Cincinnati in an October trade, Brumfield has the inside track on replacing Van Slyke in centerfield and will likely fill the Pirates' huge void in the leadoff spot. Brumfield did a fine job in a reserve role with the Reds and has good speed with some extra base power; he hit .311-4-11-6 last season. Brumfield is 29 but he's in great shape and has never received a chance to play full time in the majors. He is a good looking player and appears ready to take advantage of the opportunity in front of him. Pirates General Manager Cam Bonifay wants his club to run more and Brumfield should get the green light from the leadoff spot.

Van Slyke struggled through a .246-6-30-7 season in 1994 and the time had come for the Pirates to sever ties with him and go forward with their youth movement. The five time Gold Glove winner's defense also

slipped noticeably last season. At 34 and with a history of back and knee troubles, he looked like a player on a severe decline.

The Pirates have held high hopes since trading 20 game winner John Smiley to Minnesota for Cummings in the spring of 1992. He has a quick bat, good speed and decent power potential. However, he also gained the rap of being lackadaisical in the minor leagues even though he seemed to perk up when he arrived in the major leagues last July. Cummings missed two months with Class AAA Buffalo because of a back injury last season, hitting .311-2-22-5. He was called up to the majors in late July, and hit .244-1-12-0 before the strike. He could be a star, but really it is all up to him and how hard he decides to work.

Once considered a failed prospect by Cleveland and the Cubs, Dave Clark has found a home in Pittsburgh the past three seasons. Playing strictly against righthanders, Clark might have been the Pirates' MVP in 1994 with his .296-10-42-6 performance. However, Clark's playing time could decrease sharply in 1995 if the Pirates play the Martin-Brumfield-Cummings troika on an everyday basis. The Pirates will probably look to trade him for pitching help when his market value is at its highest.

The Pirates felt they got a steal last July when they signed Steve Pegues as a free agent after he refused a minor league assignment by the Reds. Once a top prospect in the Detroit and San Diego organizations, Pegues hit .361-0-2-1 in brief major league action and .290-6-29-10 with the Reds' Class AAA Indianapolis farm club. He has some power and speed with decent defensive skills, which could make him an ideal fourth outfielder.

The Pirates let Lloyd McClendon (.239-4-12-0 last season) and Gary Varsho (.256-0-5-0 with the Pirates and .333-2-8-1 with Buffalo) leave as free agents at the end of last season. Both are still competent bench players, though the Pirates would rather spend less money on their spare parts.

Trey Beamon emerged as the Pirates' top prospect last season, though he will likely spend the 1995 season in Class AAA. At age 20, Beamon captured the batting title in the Class AA Southern League by hitting .323-5-47-24 with Carolina. A second round draft pick in 1992 from a Texas high school, Beamon is a very smart hitter for his age but the Pirates would like to see him turn on more pitches and add a bit more power. Once he fine tunes his game, he figures to be a .290-.310 hitter in the big leagues.

The Pirates added an intriguing prospect to their organization in October hen they obtained switch hitter Micah Franklin from Cincinnati in a trade. Franklin hit a combined .284-31-84-9 with Class A Winston-Salem and Class AA Chattanooga last year, leading the Reds' organization in homers and RBIs. Franklin was the Mets' third round pick in the 1990 draft out of a San Francisco high school. He was released a year later because of attitude problems. However, Franklin has matured and instantly becomes the Pirates' top power hitting prospect. He will start this season in Class AAA and the power starved Pirates will watch him closely.

Two other prospects, Stanton Cameron and Jermaine Allensworth, had mildly disappointing years in 1994. Acquired late in 1993 from Baltimore in the Lonnie Smith trade, Cameron struggled in his first chance at Class AAA. He hit just .173-4-14-3 for Buffalo, though he did have a .312-11-56-10 season for Carolina.

Allensworth was a supplemental first round pick from Purdue in 1993 and the Pirates pushed him all the way from short season Class A Welland to Class AA last year. He hit just .241-1-34-16 with Carolina and appeared overmatched at times. He most likely needs to repeat Class AA again in 1995.

Two other outfielders who finished last season at Carolina may eventually develop into major league reserves. Ramon Espinosa has speed and hit .268-2-40-12 before a leg injury ended his season six weeks early. Once a top prospect who was dropped from the 40 man roster in 1992 before learning to switch hit, speedy Daryl Ratliff batted .319-1-19-5 at Class A Salem and .277-0-29-11 with Carolina.

St. Louis Cardinals

The Cardinals will try to make a success out of Jeff McNeely, the Red Sox last best hope for a speedy outfielder before the arrival of Otis Nixon. McNeely played his way right off the Boston depth charts by going downhill in almost every category in his second year at Triple-A (stolen bases down from 40 to 13).

McNeely still has fine athletic tools, and his speed is much better suited to the Cardinals than to the Red Sox (with or without Nixon). Making the major league roster on opening day is far from a given, but McNeely's fresh start gives him much better chances than he would have had. Also note the possible vacancy at first base, post-Jefferies, could take considerable pressure off the outfielders for playing time.

John Perrotto:

The Cardinals outfield has the makings to be one of baseball's very best. They have four outfielders with both tremendous ability and youth on their side. Four guys who can hit for power and average, run, and play good defense. Yet, the sum of the parts of leftfielder Bernard Gilkey, centerfielder Ray Lankford, rightfielder Mark Whiten and Brian Jordan never seem to add up to a big enough whole. You expect all four of them to appear in an All-Star Game together but it never happens.

The most gifted is Lankford, who bounced back from a horrid 1993 to lift his 1994 totals to .267-19-57-11 from the previous year's figures of .238-7-45-14. However, it is becoming extremely doubtful that Lankford will ever blossom into the .300-30-100-30 guy some people envisioned. He could be a star for a number of years, but his hopes of turning into a superstar are fading.

While Lankford bounced back last season, Gilkey regressed, dropping from .305-16-70-15 to .253-6-45-15. Gilkey was signed as an undrafted free agent out of high school and was considered a raw talent for many years. He finally looked like the finished product in 1993 but it's now hard to tell exactly which way his career is going. This season should provide the

answer. He is 28 years old and entering his prime.

After disappointing in both Toronto and Cleveland, the highly touted Whiten seemed to emerge after being traded to the Cardinals just before the start of the 1993 season. He hit .253-25-99-15 that year. While he lifted his batting average in 1994, his overall totals fell off to .293-14-53-10. It is also becoming apparent that Whiten is not going to become a superstar, though he should be a solid player for a number of seasons.

Based strictly on potential, Jordan could wind up being better than the other three. A former All-Pro defensive back with the NFL's Atlanta Falcons, Jordan has devoted his time solely to baseball the past two seasons but has been plagued by inconsistency and injury. He hit .258-5-15-4 in limited action last year. One wonders how much heart Jordan is putting into baseball. He is grumbling that he may go back to the NFL once his baseball-only contract expires following this season.

Gerald Young resurrected his flagging career last season after joining the Cardinals' organization. He hit .308-5-35-12 with Class AAA Louisville then .317-0-3-2 with the Cardinals. He is a prototypical St. Louis outfielder with his good speed and could be productive in a limited fifth outfielder role.

The Cardinals figure to restructure their club over the next couple of years as Walt Jocketty has been hired to replace Dal Maxvill as general manager. The Cardinals need pitching and any of the outfielders could be used as a prime trade bait.

What makes it easier for Jocketty to consider trading any of his outfielders is the fact that another good crop is on the way in Allen Battle (.313-6-69-23 with Louisville in 1994), Terry Bradshaw (.250-4-8-5 at Louisville and .280-10-52-13 at Class AA Arkansas) and John Mabry (.304-0-3-0 with St. Louis and .262-15-68-2 with Louisville).

Battle has been compared to former Cardinal and current Chicago White Sox centerfielder Lance Johnson for his defense, speed and ability to make consistent contact.

Bradshaw has completely recovered from reconstructive knee surgery in 1992. He can fly, has gap power and is a Gold Glove caliber centerfielder.

Mabry is atypical of most Cardinals' outfielder prospects because he is not a burner. However, he has good power and a rifle arm. For long range purposes, an outfielder to keep an eye on is Anton French. Though he hit just .221-2-29-21 in the Arizona Rookie League last season, he fits the Cardinals' mold with superior speed.

San Diego Padres

Hank Widmer:

The Padres had two exceptional outfielders in 1994. Tony Gwynn is the more obvious of the two, but Derek Bell, lost in the fanfare over Gwynn, had a great year. Bell not only hit .311 but put together some strong home run (14) and RBI (54) totals. Bell could have been purchased cheaply in most fantasy drafts.

Gwynn always has had decent RBI totals, but he was batting near the top of the order and rarely had any runners on base when he was batting. In 1994 he was on pace to drive in nearly 100 runs and would have easily passed his previous career high of 72 (1990). Gwynn moved lower in the lineup when Bip Roberts was installed as the leadoff hitter; Roberts good OBP gave Gwynn someone to plate.

Fred Matos:

One of the biggest disappointments of the strike-shortened year was that Tony Gwynn was denied an opportunity to hit .400. At age 34, he had his second consecutive .350-plus season and the future Hall-of-Famer keeps getting better. Critics said he was fat and out of shape but he proved otherwise. Gwynn is an intense student of opposing pitchers and now uses a fancy new videotape system to gain the upper hand. For 1995, you can expect another .300-plus season with about 60 RBI.

Talented but flaky Derek Bell has been on the trading block as the Padres are unhappy with his erratic defensive play. Still, Bell was well on his way to a big year with the bat when the strike interrupted. He's capable of 25 homers, 40 stolen bases, a .300-plus batting average, and 80-plus RBI over a full season. At age 26, Bell has over 1000 major league at bats, a combination of age and experience that point to a breakout year.

Phil Plantier's disappointing .220 last year was caused, in large part, by a sore right elbow, the same problem which required surgery at the end of the 1992 season. The elbow soreness causes him to lose strength in his arm, thus effecting his power swing. A healthy Plantier can be a strong offensive force, hitting .270-30-100 in a full season. Like Bell, Plantier is also 26 years old with over 1000 major league at bats, and a big breakout year is very possible if he can stay healthy.

Bell is easily worth over $25, and his value could vault to $35 if he has a year where everything comes together. Plantier's homers and RBI are valuable, but his elbow problem seems to be chronic. His value could be as high as $20 if his batting average holds up around .270 and he stays healthy. Gwynn's value is in the $22-$25 range depending upon how much his batting average exceeds .300.

Many experts expected that talented minor leaguer Ray McDavid would be patrolling the Padres center field by June, but he wasn't recalled until later in the season. Now 23 years old, he may push the Padres to trade Bell. An analysis of McDavid's minor league record indicates that he may not immediately hit for a high average in the majors. Although he's a very fast base runner who has shown some power, his Rotisserie value now is in stolen bases. McDavid has a basketball background reminiscent of Kenny Lofton's and his baseball skills are still a little rough, but things could come together for him literally overnight.

Originally tabbed for outfield duty, Bip Roberts (covered under Second Basemen) instead played primarily at second base after Luis Lopez was injured. Roberts still played 20 games in the outfield, though, so

he'll qualify there in most leagues.

Talented minor league prospect Mel Nieves may earn a starting job in 1995. He is a switch hitter with tremendous power from both sides. But his minor league record shows a characteristic power hitter's weakness: streakiness. He will hit six or seven homers in a week followed by a week or two of virtually nothing. Nieves may eventually be capable of 30-homer seasons; he's a very good pick up for re-building teams.

Veteran Bill Bean was a role playing substitute last year; he is not in the Padres' long range plans.

Speedster Earl Johnson is worth mentioning due to his leading the minors with 80 stolen bases for "low" Class A Springfield in 1994. He can reach the majors in a few years if his hitting continues to improve and would be similar to Lance Johnson.

Older minor leaguers Keith Lockhart and Harvey Pulliam are decent Triple-A players, but nothing more.

San Francisco Giants

Steven Rubio:

Beyond the amazing Barry Bonds, the Giants' outfield is very unsettled as 1995 approaches. Bonds can be described quickly: plagued by injuries and aging gradually, he still hit .312 with 37 homers, 29 steals, great defense and plenty of walks. He'll be in leftfield for the Giants once again in 1995.

In centerfield, Darren Lewis has a record setting glove and an abysmal bat. He worked hard last season to improve his problem areas, drawing more walks than ever before as he struggled to fill a leadoff role for which he is unsuited. Despite the hard work, the great defense, and his excellent speed and baserunning, though, Darren Lewis is still one of the worst hitting regular outfielders in the game today.

In rightfield, Willie McGee is gone, his Giants' career ending with an unfortunate injury during a midseason game last year. Darryl Strawberry joined the Giants soon after McGee went down, and his performance must be judged as inconclusive. He showed glimpses of his earlier successes and seemed to have his act together both on and off the field, thanks in part to the fine support system of the Giants, beginning with manager Dusty Baker. However, even if Darryl's head is intact, his body is still a question mark: he hasn't reached 200 at bats in a season since 1991. A fascinating player for risk taking fantasy owners, Strawberry did well by the Giants in 1994 but his future is still up for grabs. He has offered to move to first base if the team needed him there and they might take him up on it should J.R. Phillips fail to produce.

The young player most likely to break into the Giants' outfield in 1995 is Rikkert Faneyte, who has been destroying Class AAA pitching for two seasons. He is an excellent sleeper pick for fantasy owners and he would make a fine regular in the Giants' lineup. His skills match the Giants' need for a quality leadoff hitter which they lost with the departure of Brett Butler (speed, defense and good OBP). While Lewis and Strawberry would seem to stand in Faneyte's path, he should finally break through in 1995.

Mark Carreon and Mark Leonard are journeymen backup outfielders and nothing more. As for the team's minor league outfield prospects, Dax Jones is a watered down version of Rikkert Faneyte, young enough to improve but unlikely to bust out. Rueben Smiley is a similarly watered down version of Dax Jones. Ray Ortiz is a career minor leaguer, while Brent Cookson aspires to be the next Mark Carreon.

The best prospects are in Class AA. Calvin Murray draws raves for his "tools"; he is improving gradually and is only 22 years old. He has also struggled offensively in the lower levels of the minors and is not yet ready to shine in the major leagues. Marvin Benard is two years older than Murray and lesser known, but is a legitimate sleeper who could surprise. Derek Reid, on the other hand, is unlikely to succeed.

Finally, June draft choice Dante Powell impressed mightily in the Class A Northwest League, showing speed and power while playing good defense. He's likely a few years away from the majors, but is already an intriguing prospect.

DESIGNATED HITTERS

Baltimore Orioles

Fred Matos:

Harold Baines will play the 1995 season at the age of 36, but he still has the sweet swing and can still hit. His knees are slowing him down more each season, and he needs more rest as the years go by. He has now settled into the role of lefthanded hitting DH.

Lonnie Smith and Chris Sabo are gone, so the competition for the righthanded counterpart to Baines is among outfield prospects Sherman Obando and Alex Ochoa, and veteran minor leaguer Jeff Manto. Manto had an outstanding year in Triple-A, and won the International League MVP award, but it looks like his peak is at Triple-A. Ochoa is a top prospect who spent last year in Double-A, and it would take a very impressive spring training for him to win the job. He may need a year in Triple-A to get more experience. Obando is a poor outfielder, so the DH role is his only chance of making the team. He is a legitimate power hitter who hit a very good .330-20-69 in 403 at bats last year in Triple-A before going out with a shinbone injury. He has nothing more to prove in Triple-A. He has the best chance of being the righthanded DH, and could get more playing time if Baines' knees trouble him. Obando could become the fulltime DH later in the year or in 1996.

Boston Red Sox

Alan Boodman:

Andre Dawson has said he would like to return to Boston for a final season, but the reality is that several things are working against such an appearance, primarily Dawson's physical condition. Many of his baseball-related body parts are failing him, and all that is left of this former All-Star and MVP is his desire and his heart.

Dawson has no on-base percentage to speak of, obviously no remaining speed, and his on-field talents have been reduced to bopping an occasional homerun. The acquisition of Jose Canseco seems to seal Dawson's fate here. Jose Malave or Greg Blosser may get a chance at D.H. should Canseco return to his injury-prone ways.

Eric Wedge, ostensibly a catcher, may also get a look. Wedge can't catch but he can hit: .286-19-59 at Pawtucket last year in less than half a season's worth of games.

California Angels

Hank Widmer:

Chili Davis was the best DH in the league last year. There were games that the Angels won only because Davis came through for them. He was an excellent clutch hitter and has been for the two years since his return to the Angels. However, Davis was a free agent and the Angels under the tight reins of Jackie Autry didn't seem to be interested in signing Davis for the three years he wanted. Yes, there should be concern about Davis' age (he'll be 35 to start 1995), but even if he were younger he would be unlikely to get a long term contract from the Angels. Davis is still a productive hitter but his numbers will dip somewhat. He will help whatever team he ends up with, giving Rotisserie teams good numbers in power

and average. If Davis leaves, look for Bo Jackson to be the favorite to take his place as the Angels' DH.

Fred Matos:

Nearly written off after a mediocre year in 1992, Chili Davis has come back very strong with two good years in a row, and he was even heading for his career-best year in 1994 but was interrupted by the strike. Now 35, he hasn't slowed down and should have a few more good years. The Angels have indicated that Davis is in their future plans.

Davis qualifies only at DH, so the bidding usually will not go as high as for a position player because many Rotisserians don't like to lose roster flexibility. His maximum value is around $18, and you shouldn't overbid as he could have a down year. He has a history of having down years every now and then, but it can't be predicted when the next one will come.

The Angels see Bo Jackson's 1995 role with them as a part time outfielder, part time DH, and pinch hitter, a status that Bo may not like. But the same part time status was supposed to be his role last year, and he ended up playing a lot of left field. Jackson is discussed in the outfield chapter.

Chicago White Sox

Stuart Shea:

The signing of Julio Franco worked out well. He lashed extra-base hits around AL outfields, stayed healthy all year, took 62 walks, and even swiped 8 bases in 9 tries. Of course, the penurious Sox let him test the free-agent waters although they have nobody to take the place of "Juice". They are trying to re-sign him at a more advantageous salary, but after his tremendous 1994 performance, why should he give anything up? His RBI count will likely go down this year if he bats anywhere but behind Frank Thomas.

Former Blue Jay farm veteran Domingo Martinez hit 22 homers at triple-A Nashville in 1994. Power is his only marker, and he's not good enough to play

regularly in the major leagues. That doesn't mean the Sox won't give him a chance to come north, however, but it does mean that he's not worth your time.

Cleveland Indians

Tony Blengino:

The Indians' incredible two-headed designated hitter monster has managed to accumulate 6018 hits, 921 homers and 3567 RBI. Both components of this creation will be elected to the Hall of Fame on the first ballot, and both hit significantly more homers on the road than at home in their careers, indicating that their power numbers are even more incredible than they appear. Unfortunately, the strike robbed Indians' fans of their opportunity to see Eddie Murray and Dave Winfield share the designated hitter role for the latter part of 1994. Adding Winfield contributed more veteran savvy to the Indians' youthful mix, but even more importantly, added a powerful bat against lefties, who were 20-13 against the Tribe. Both players are winding down, but Winfield still carves lefties (.342 in 1994), while switch-hitter Murray is better against righties (.275 in 1994).

Murray, 39, is one of the most consistent sluggers in baseball history. With 458 career homers, he stills rates an outside chance of reaching 500. He has accomplished this despite never hitting more than 33 in a season. Murray probably lost about 20 homers to the two strikes in which he participated. He is 15th on the all-time RBI list with 1738, and in non-strike years has never driven in less than 84 runs. Murray has played in less than 150 games in only one non-strike season (1986). He has established a poor relationship with the media, but you'll never hear a teammate, manager or coach utter a negative word about Murray, an unquestioned team leader. His performance has only slightly deteriorated in recent years, and another one or two productive seasons can be expected. Look for a .275 average with 20 homers and 85 RBI in a season split between first base and designated hitter.

Winfield, 43, is 14th on the all-time hits list (3088), 18th in homers (463), and 12th in RBI (1829). He

was acquired from the Twins during the strike, and will likely never play a game for the Indians. Winfield became a free agent after the 1994 season, and the Tribe was only interested in him for the stretch drive that never was. His numbers finally took a turn for the worse in 1994, with 10 homers, 43 RBI, and a .252 average, all career lows. His ability to grind lefties could earn him a spot somewhere as a platoon designated hitter if he wants it. There is also an excellent chance that Winfield will let his career end quietly, a somber alternative to the final blaze of playoff glory that could have been his if not for the Great Strike of 1994.

Detroit Tigers

Fred Matos:

After a very poor second half of 1993 had some people believing he was washed up, DH Kirk Gibson rebounded nicely in 1994, even playing a lot of outfield. Although 1994 was a lively ball year, it still should be noted that Gibson had a very good .548 slugging percentage, a career high.

Gibson is a tremendous competitor and could have another good year in 1995. But he will be 38 in May, and has been considered to be washed up before, and it is very possible that he could have a poor year. It's best to be cautious and not bid more than $10 for him. Another DH may emerge from the Tony Clark and Cecil Fielder first-base pair if Gibson slumps and Clark is not overmatched, or if Clark has an outstanding spring training and wins a job outright. Clark is a rookie power hitter with enormous potential, but he is still very inconsistent and strikes out a great deal. He is covered in more detail in the first base chapter.

Kansas City Royals

Marc Bowman:

Rookie of the Year Bob Hamelin led A.L. rookies in almost every offensive category, but it wasn't really very fair since he was older than every one of the other candidates. Hamelin lost most of four years to back problems and only had his first full season of play in 1993.

The "Hammer" made the most of his opportunity though, becoming the most feared hitter in the Royals lineup. He easily led the team in homers, RBI, slugging and also had the team's best OBP. Hamelin has always had an excellent batting eye. Because he's not prone to chasing breaking balls in the dirt or climbing the ladder after unhittable high fastballs, Hamelin is likely to maintain his level of performance.

After starting the season in a platoon DH role, Hamelin eventually won the full-time job with timely power hitting, then hit even better as a regular. He was at his best during the second half of the year when the Royals were climbing in the standings and was instrumental in launching their 14-game winning streak by hitting a memorable three-run, twelfth-inning homer to beat the White Sox.

Hamelin will again have the regular job in 1995 and ay get some time at first base to spell Wally Joyner. Due to Hamelin's severe platoon differential, he may get benched against the league's tougher lefty pitchers, but that will only serve to keep his batting average in an acceptable range. It won't cut his power; all 24 of his 1994 homers came off of righthanders against whom he slugged a frightening .648. Look for the Hammer to retain his power, but lose a few batting points: .260-25-85-5 is a reasonable guess at his 1995 numbers, making him worth about $20.

Dave Henderson was the righthanded DH who became strictly a pinch-hitter when Hamelin took over full time. He could still get a few at bats at DH, but it will likely be for another team. His days are numbered, and it's unlikely he'll get more than 150 ABs for any team. Should Hamelin become injured, Joe Vitiello could get a few ABs in the lefty role and Keith Miller would probably get the righthanded ABs; they are discussed in greater detail in the Outfield and Third Base sections, respectively.

Milwaukee Brewers

Bill Gray:

Pat Listach played only 16 games before his knee gave out. He tried a rehab assignment and was shut down after only two games, then had surgery to repair his damaged knee. Listach's Patella tendon was repaired, and Brewers GM Sal Bando said he thought the surgery should relieve the problem. Listach was scheduled to play winter ball, but he simply wasn't ready. In my opinion, I would simply forget about lusting after the Pat Listach of 1992 and the 54 stolen bases. Looking at his health history, he's had cysts, hamstring pulls, severe knee inflammation, and a patella tendon removal. Something tells me to look elsewhere for speed.

Jose Valentin, despite the shaky batting average, provided power and decent speed and must be seen as even money to be the opening day shortstop. Consider that the Brewers have said that Pat Listach, even if healthy, might play the outfield. Valentin's power is real - he once hit 17 homers in the minors. He has pretty fair plate discipline, and is only 25 years old and improving. As there are precious few short-stops with any power/speed, Valentin is still a sleeper, and a bright light on the Brewers.

Minnesota Twins

James Benkard:

Dave Winfield has moved on, meaning the winner of the contest for the DH slot might well be the loser of the battle for the first base job. Marty Cordova, who will not be in that contest, has the best power potential of any young Twin besides David McCarty and will get a long look in the spring. If Scott Stahoviak makes the club along with McCarty, who almost certainly will, and Cordova, then Steve Dunn will return to Triple-A.

The DH slot then will be split between whomever is not playing in left field (Pedro Munoz or Cordova) and Stahoviak. If Stahoviak does not make the team, Cordova will be the DH and could play some first base.

I would say McCarty, Rich Becker, and Cordova, who hit well in the Arizona Fall League, will probably make the team. If one of the latter two drops out, Stahoviak can step in and share time at third with Scott Leius, as well as at DH with Munoz. Munoz' defense has to improve to keep him out of the DH slot full time, but it helps him that his main competitor (Cordova) has defensive deficiencies as well.

New York Yankees

The front office acquired Danny Tartabull in 1992 to be a star right fielder, but Paul O'Neill came along in 1993, and Tartabull has continued to have nagging physical problems that make him better suited to the DH job. There isn't much new and different about Tartabull for 1995. He has always been a top RBI producer when healthy. It is significant that the Yankees have kept him in the cleanup slot, where he was generally sandwiched between Paul O'Neill and Mike Stanley in 1994.

Tartabull is unlikely to be a bargain in any league. He is too famous, past his prime, and injury prone. Still he's a decent acquisition for a team that already has bargains in the form of a strong freeze list, or that does very well early in the auction, and just needs to fill out the roster with high value players at high but reasonable prices. When considering a player like Tartabull and noting that he has missed an average of 100 at bats per year during his career because of injuries, it's wise to remember that when he goes on the DL you get the stats of a replacement for the interim. Tartabull's value, or rather the value of his roster spot, has therefore been somewhat higher than the value of what Tartabull produced on his own.

The Yankees will cycle various players through the DH slot as a means of fine-tuning the lineup against specific pitchers and riding hot streaks, etc. The next closest player in the minors, who might become a DH when called up, is Lyle Mouton, a high power, high strikeout type of pitcher. He won't hit for average and won't contribute any speed.

Oakland A's

Steven Rubio:

Geronimo Berroa was one of the delights of the A's season in 1994, pleasing teammates and fans alike with his inspired hitting. He is now 30 years old and unlikely to improve, but he is no fluke, having hit well in the minor leagues for a long time. You can expect him to continue hitting at his current level for a few years, if he gets the chance. His fate is tied to that of Mark McGwire's: if McGwire plays, Berroa will be fighting Troy Neel for playing time at DH.

Marcos Armas is a first baseman/DH who is a lesser version of his brother Tony. Marcos has decent, but not great power, and that pretty much sums up his positives (at least Tony had a good arm).

Seattle Mariners

Bill Gray:

Reggie Jefferson batted .346 against righthanded pitchers, but produced no hits when he faced a lefthanded pitcher (in only nine AB). Jefferson was used almost exclusively as the lefthanded platoon DH, batting .327 with a modest eight home runs. Jefferson is now a role player and his 1994 performance is about as good as he'll ever be. There was a time not so long ago when Jefferson was considered a lock to be a star. He will never reach that level, which will keep many owners from considering him. But he is still useful, and will probably be inexpensive.

Texas Rangers

Peter Graves:

Jose Canseco made an excellent transition to the DH role in 1994 (.282-31-90-15), proving that health and desire are the two most significant variables in determining his performance. Canseco missed only three games, the first time in four seasons that he's been healthy all year. The DH role should help Canseco stay off the disabled list, in which case he should continue to be a productive hitter for Boston.

With Canseco now unavailable, the Rangers could promote Trey McCoy, a fine hitter with limited defensive skills. McCoy, 28, hit .304-13-58 for Triple-A Oklahoma City but was blocked by Canseco. If given a chance in the majors, I believe that McCoy would hit well. He makes good contact and has better than average power.

Toronto Blue Jays

David Luciani:

The best designated hitter in the league enters the final year of his three year contract with the Blue Jays. Paul Molitor has proven that his role as a leadoff hitter in Milwaukee wasted tremendous RBI opportunities. As the Blue Jays' number three hitter, Molitor was en route to another 100 RBI campaign after posting the first such season of his career the year before. He loves to hit at SkyDome (hitting .378 at home in 1994) and can sub occasionally at first base for John Olerud. He's always one of the safest bets to score runs in the league, even without being a leadoff hitter. This is the year that virtually assures Paul Molitor Hall-of-Fame status as he crosses the 2,800 hit mark.

There are no other potential designated hitters on this team. Once in a while, Cito Gaston will flip John Olerud and Molitor as the first baseman and DH but you will not see other players here unless Molitor is hurt. In the unlikely event that this happens, you will see Joe Carter DH with Robert Perez taking Carter's place in right field. Cito Gaston has never been afraid to introduce younger players as a DH, leaving his regulars in their normal positions. Therefore, the hot bat at Syracuse would also be given consideration in the event of an injury.

STARTING PITCHERS:

TACTICAL CONSIDERATIONS
by Marc Bowman

Relative to hitters, pitchers are very unreliable; starting pitchers are even more unpredictable. For Rotisserie purposes, especially, it is hard to predict who will help and who will hurt. So, the phrase "reliable starting pitching" is almost an oxymoron.

Yet, winning at Rotisserie demands ownership of "reliable starting pitching." In leagues with a minimum innings rule, it is usually necessary to have at least three starting pitchers. For a 12-team league, that means a MINIMUM of 36 starting pitchers MUST be selected from either the American League or the National League. Usually the number selected is more than 36, because many owner take four, five or more, further straining the supply.

Unfortunately, only about twenty pitchers in each league have a track record indicating that they pitch enough innings to help their Rotisserie team and have an ERA or baserunner ratio better than Rotisserie league average. That means that a minimum of sixteen starting pitchers MUST come from a group that includes injured pitchers, rookies, and pitchers who will hurt their Rotisserie teams. Any teams that take too many of the latter kind of pitcher inevitably finish in the lower half of the league in both ERA and baserunner ratio.

So, the objective for a successful Rotisserie owner is to obtain three of those twenty good starters on draft day. Since pitchers are highly unpredictable sorts of players, this is not an easy task.

Two criteria need to be met:

1) A minimum number of innings or starts; otherwise the pitcher isn't doing enough to contribute towards the minimum innings. For the purposes of this study, 180 innings or 30 starts are required in each season (for strike-shortened 1994, 120 innings or 20 starts are required instead).

2) An ERA or baserunner ratio that is better than Rotisserie league average. Rotisserie league average is always better than actual AL or NL league averages since the worst major league pitchers are not being used in Rotisserie leagues. The difference is usually about 0.25 less in ERA and 0.05 less in baserunner ratio.

Note that we are trying to build a superior pitching staff, not a mediocre one. By aiming to be above average, we expect to come in somewhere between the middle and the top in pitching quality categories. The "Reliable Starting Pitcher" strategy aims to do well in pitching, not just to score three or four cheap points in ERA and ratio. Also, we know that by aiming higher we allow some cushion for a little bad luck.

Since 1989, 168 different pitchers have met the first criterion, pitching enough to be helpful. Among the

168 are pitchers like Nolan Ryan, who have retired. In determining reliable starting pitchers for 1995, these pitchers are of no use and have been discarded from the following lists. Likewise, pitchers who have met the innings/starts requirement fewer than three times in the last six years have been discarded since they have not yet proven their long-term reliability. This does not mean that these pitchers, such as Aaron Sele or Steve Trachsel, aren't any good; it simply means that they have not yet proven themselves to be reliable over an extended period of time.

Two other pitchers have also been removed due to the probability that they will miss much or all of the 1995 season due to injury: Tom Browning and Frank Viola.

We are now left with exactly 62 starting pitchers who have met the first criteria in at least three of the last six seasons. All 62 pitched in 1994, 37 in the American League and 25 in the National League.

The remaining pitchers can be classified into four groups: - very reliable and very good, - very reliable but not very good, - very good but not very reliable, and the rest who are - neither very good, nor especially reliable.

In the first group, the pitchers we like, are nine AL pitchers and seven NL pitchers who have met the innings requirements in at least five of the last six years and have had an ERA or baserunner ratio better than Rotisserie league average more than 60% of the time. They are the upper crust of starting pitchers (listed alphabetically):

American League	National League
Kevin Appier	Andy Benes
Kevin Brown	Tom Candiotti
Roger Clemens	Doug Drabek
David Cone	Ken Hill
Chuck Finley	Greg Maddux
Jimmy Key	Jose Rijo
Mark Langston	John Smoltz
Dennis Martinez	
Jack McDowell	

In the next group are pitchers who have met the innings/starts criteria in at least five of the last six seasons, but have been better than league average in ERA or baserunner ratio in 40% to 60% of their qualifying seasons (180 innings or 30 starts). They are the next best thing to the upper crust:

American League	National League
Jim Abbott	John Burkett
Tim Belcher	Tom Glavine
Randy Johnson	Greg Swindell
Terry Mulholland	
Dave Stewart	

The third group contains pitchers who have been less reliable in the innings/ starts area, but have been very good during the seasons when they have pitched enough. These nine AL pitchers and ten NL pitchers have all had only three or four seasons out of the last six in which they met the first criterion but have had better than Rotisserie league average ERAs or baserunner ratios in better than 60% of their qualifying seasons. They are the less reliable, but still very good starters:

American League	National League
Chris Bosio	Steve Avery
Ron Darling	Buddy Black
Sid Fernandez	Erik Hanson
Ben McDonald	Pete Harnisch
Charles Nagy	Orel Hershiser
Todd Stottlemyre	Ramon Martinez
Kevin Tapani	Mark Portugal
Bob Welch	Bret Saberhagen
David Wells	John Smiley
	Zane Smith

The remaining 19 pitchers have been better than league average in ERA or baserunner ratio in less than half of their qualifying seasons. These are pitchers who are often referred to as ''workhorses'' and while they still might provide useful pitching in 1995, they have not been helpful in most years.

American League	National League
Jim DeShaies	Dwight Gooden
Scott Erickson	Kevin Gross

Alex Fernandez
Bill Gullickson
Juan Guzman
Greg Hibbard
Jaime Navarro
Kirk McCaskill
Scott Sanderson
Mike Moore
Jack Morris
Melido Perez
Bobby Witt

Danny Jackson
Mike Morgan
Bob Tewksbury
Fernando Valenzuela

Special mention should be made of the last pitcher on this list. Bobby Witt has met the innings/starts requirements in five of the last six years (he had just 16 starts and 88.2 innings for Texas in 1991). Yet Witt has managed to post a useful ERA just once; in 1990 his ERA was 3.36 while all American League pitchers combined for a 3.91 ERA. In every other season, both his ERA and baserunner ratio have been worse than league average. While Witt can certainly help a pitching staff like Oakland's, he will most definitely harm his Rotisserie owners.

Obviously, it would be best to have three pitchers from the very first list. However, this is often impractical due to the high salaries that those pitchers command in virtually all drafts. A more practical approach is to treat these lists like a Chinese menu: get one from each of the first three lists. If you can get two or three from Group ''A'' or one from Group ''A'' and two from Group ''B'' so much the better. A representative sampling of pitchers from each list might yield a starting staff of Chuck Finley, Jim Abbott and Ben McDonald. Over the last six years these three pitchers would provide an ERA better than Rotisserie league average all six years and a baserunner ratio better than Rotisserie league average in four of six seasons with two seasons exactly at league average.

Overall, you'd get about 600 innings each year (596.2 average) with an ERA 0.29 better than Rotisserie league average and a baserunner ratio 0.01 better than Rotisserie league average. Once you filled out your staff with six relievers, your ERA and ratio should be better still. In a twelve team league,

you could reasonably expect to earn from eight to ten points each in ERA and ratio.

These three representative pitchers are not the best from their lists, nor the worst, so overall averages will vary somewhat. The point is that in every season since 1989 you would get above average pitching by using one pitcher from each list while also getting about 600 innings toward your minimum innings requirement.

Spending the popular 35% on pitching, an average team would use $91 in salary for their pitching staff. Allocating $36 to acquiring six relievers, while spending $25 for a pitcher from the first list and $15 each for pitchers from the second and third lists you could acquire, for $91, a pitching staff that should help you place in the upper third of your league in all four pitching categories, generally a happy outcome!

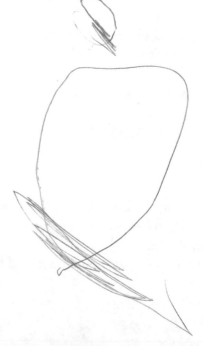

AMERICAN LEAGUE STARTING PITCHERS

While there are a large number of starting pitchers still unsigned, there are very, very few good ones left. The best AL starting pitchers are mostly concentrated in a few teams (Baltimore, Chicago, Kansas City, New York) and that hasn't changed for 1995. So, winter announcements of pitcher signings can safely be disregarded as little will change - the really good pitchers are staying put and the mediocre ones will move around to replace one another.

Of course, there are only about 14 teams in each league that claim to be looking for pitching - "you can never have enough pitching" is becoming more true every year. The bidding for the better pitchers will certainly be intense and will likely come down to the teams who believe they are already contenders. Baltimore, Boston, Cleveland and Toronto stand out as the most ready to grab a top flight pitcher.

Kevin Brown is the most notable exception to the lack of good pitching among the free agents. Brown has been one of the American League's most consistently good pitchers over the last five years, despite his struggles in 1994. When you factor in the hitter-friendly parks in which he has had to pitch, Brown's excellent pitching really stands out.

Baltimore Orioles

Fred Matos:

The Orioles want to win the World Series, and realize that their rotation needs one more top pitcher to get them there. A free agent like Tom Gordon, Danny Jackson or Kevin Brown could be signed for 1995.

Mike Mussina and Ben McDonald were each on their way to 20-win seasons but the strike ruined what looked like their career years. Mussina is one of the best pitchers in baseball, and could win 20 and the Cy Young in 1995. McDonald learned how to pitch and win in 1994, and is also a potential 20 game winner in 1995.

Sid Fernandez was signed to a big free agent contract, and the Orioles hoped that he could provide at least 150 innings and 12 wins. But he was on and off the disabled list, and largely ineffective even when healthy. The Orioles realize that he is overweight, and that presents other possible health problems. Fernandez has the smarts to win even when his good stuff isn't working: in one game last year, he had nothing but fastballs, but he threw four different types and moved the ball around masterfully, keeping the hitters off balance. Fernandez has the potential to win 18 games, but it depends on his health.

Jamie Moyer was frequently beset with first-inning problems last year. He also had some bad luck in turning over Oriole leads in seven games, only to see the bullpen blow them. Normally very effective against righthanders (even better than against lefties) he lost his edge against the righties last year. Moyer is a finesse pitcher who depends on location and changing speeds to keep hitters off balance. The Orioles are trying to acquire another top starter via trade or free agency. If that occurs, Moyer may become the fifth starter.

After years of showing great potential followed by disappointments, Arthur Rhodes was recalled from

the minors in mid-year and pitched two consecutive shutouts. It's the best he's looked so far, but consistency is needed. New manager Phil Regan was formerly a good pitching coach, and he could help Rhodes achieve the Ron Guidry-like greatness that people expect.

Mike Oquist started some games last year, but he struggled and may not ever become an effective major league pitcher. The Orioles have some minor league prospects but none are even close to what the Orioles need in the rotation.

Mussina is the best starting pitcher on the Orioles, and one of the best in the American League. Many people realize that, so he is usually overbid. McDonald usually has a cold streak during the season when his ERA and ratio jump, limiting his value to $20 at most. Fernandez is a risky pitcher because of his health problems, and as a result, should go relatively cheaply. Moyer is not worth much.

Lary Bump:

First, let me cast a dissenting vote on Arthur Rhodes' potential to be a major league star. His 7-5-2.79-1.15 year at Triple-A Rochester looks good, but he still suffered from major lapses of concentration. Buried under that ERA were a whopping 13 unearned runs that came largely in a couple of outings when he blew up on the mound after a teammate's misplay. Nearly a third of the runs he allowed for the Red Wings were unearned; in contrast, just four of the 170 he has given up in the majors were unearned. Until he can get a better handle on himself, I don't see him as better than a fourth or fifth starter.

Rochester's starters weren't bad, but they will soon be passed by the hotshots who made up the rotation at Double-A Bowie and had good numbers despite playing home games in poor pitchers' parks.

Rick Krivda had his moments, but didn't endear himself to an organization running at full-bore paranoia by whining when he wasn't called up during last season. Krivda, an over-the-top lefthander who reminds current Orioles pitching coach Mike Flanagan

of Steve Avery, was 9-10-3.53-1.36 at Rochester.

Barry Manuel started the season as the Red Wings' closer, but after giving up a run an inning for an extended period, he and his 90-plus fastball were moved in desperation to the starting rotation. He pitched well in that role, but not well enough to finish better than 11-8-5.48-1.57 with four saves. At 29, he's hardly a prospect.

Kevin McGehee rebounded from shoulder surgery to win 10 of his final 13 decisions. However, the control pitcher was not really effective. His ERA went from an International League-leading 2.96 in 1993 to 4.76 last season. He went 10-8 with a 1.34 ratio.

Jason Satre probably reached the end of the line last season. He twice flirted with no-hitters early in the year, then had trouble getting any hitters out (6-7-4.97-1.48). The top starting pitching prospect in the Baltimore organization is righthander

Scott Klingenbeck, who showed a major league curve in his one emergency start for the Orioles during a callup from Bowie (7-5-3.63-1.31) last season. Here's a lasting image of Brian Sackinsky from the only live baseball you could see on TV last October. He'd tinker and toy with Arizona Fall League batters and get them out on a succession of grounders and popups. Then he'd lay a fastball over the plate and some guy would belt it over the fence for a solo homer. Jim Palmer gave up a lot of solo homers, too. Sackinsky's greatest asset, and biggest flaw, is his control. He's always around the plate, so batters are always ready to jump on his mistakes. The only thing is, he doesn't make many. He went 11-7-3.36-1.15 at Bowie (despite allowing 24 homers) and 3-1-2.74-1.00 in Arizona. Jimmy Haynes (13-8-2.90-1.15 at Bowie) made an impressive first start in Triple-A, but then was hit hard in two subsequent outings when he seemed to tip off his changeup.

Rick Forney matched Haynes' 13-8 record, but with a 4.62 ERA and 1.36 ratio. Garret Stephenson pitched most of the year in the Carolina League (7-5-4.02-1.18) because he was the least effective starter at Bowie (3-2-5.15-1.58). His Frederick teammate,

Calvin Maduro, went 9-8-4.25-1.25. The 20-year-old righthander's most impressive statistic was his 8.09 strikeouts per nine innings.

In the Sally League, William Percibal was 13-9-3.56-1.48. He needs to work on his control. In the major league draft, the Orioles selected Russ Brock, whose best pitch is a curve. In the Oakland organization last year, he totaled 8-11-3.47-1.36 in Double-A and Triple-A.

Boston Red Sox

Frank Viola, Danny Darwin and Joe Hesketh all remained unsigned free agents. Viola and Darwin may be forced to retire due to injury, age or both. Hesketh has not really been good in a starting role in any case and would only have value if he could take on a long relief/spot starter role for a team with a good starting rotation.

Rookie Nate Minchey was traded, along with Jeff McNeely, to the Cardinals for Luis Alicea. Losing three of their five starters will force the Red Sox to dip into the free agent market or deep into their farm system. Unless they come up with big bucks to sign a first rate pitcher, it could get ugly after Clemens and Sele.

Alan Boodman:

To begin 1995, the Red Sox' rotation will consist of Roger Clemens, Aaron Sele, and three players to be named later. Several members of the 1994 rotation have become free agents (Danny Darwin, Joe Hesketh, Frank Viola), or have become injured in a career-threatening way (Darwin, Viola), or were so ineffective that their chances of remaining in the majors are in serious jeopardy (Nate Minchey, Chris Nabholz).

Roger Clemens recovered nicely from his ailments of 1993, and would have been a more determined Cy Young candidate had he not received the worst run support of any starting pitcher in the American League in 1994. If his performance from last season is any indication, the decline phase of Clemens' career is not imminent. With better offense behind him, he could easily return to the near-twenty win level.

Aaron Sele is not overpowering but posesses tremendous command of four pitches. His level of poise and guile are rare in a pitcher so young (25). Sele has no qualms about pitching inside, a necessary attribute for a hurler in Fenway Park, and stands ready to move into the 15-18 win class. Sele is comparable to Dan Petry at a similar stage in his career, and he has not yet even begun to realize his potential. He is a highly recommended pick for 1995 and beyond.

The Sox are actively trying to sign or otherwise acquire a pitcher in the Jack McDowell or Randy Johnson class. Failing that (but they probably won't fail), there will be a significant drop between the numbers two and three slots in the BoSox rotation. None of the following candidates make good Rotisserie selections for 1995.

Joe Hesketh was a starter for nearly the first three months of 1994, before being yanked from the rotation. Hesketh is capable of starting and relieving, but the bullpen is where he belongs due to a lifelong inability to retire righthanders. With the demise of Viola and the ineffectiveness of Nabholz, the Sox are not exactly long on lefties, so Hesketh may be recycled yet again. Hesketh can win with good run support (who can't?), but is not likely to post quality numbers in other categories.

Chris Nabholz is yet another ex-Montrealite (acquired via Cleveland) that GM Dan Duquette has managed to attract. The Sox are hoping that Nabholz' 1994 was an injury-induced aberration, and his being lefthanded guarantees him an opportunity this spring. Nabholz' best pitch is a sharp-breaking curve which he could alternately neither find nor control in 1994. Better things may be in his future, but for Rotisserie purposes this Fenway Park lefty could be damaging to your team in 1995.

Frank Viola blew out his pitching elbow last May, and required the Jobe surgery to repair it. Even if he returns - a big if - the probability of his success is not great. Danny Darwin's back injury may well have

finished him as well. He is unlikely to return anytime soon, if ever, and his effectiveness had disappeared even before the injury terminated his 1994 season.

Youngsters vying for playing time include Gar Finvold, Nate Minchey, and Tim Vanegmond. Finvold, 27, pitched only 78 innings in 1994 due to being on the roster when the strike hit. He had been steady at all levels prior to his dismemberment in Boston last year. He remains a candidate for the fourth or fifth spot. Minchey, 25, has pitched consistently well in the minors since 1990. He is a large, but not overpowering righthander who has conquered a heart condition. He too, will be battling for exposure in 1995, but will be battling in St. Louis, having been dealt in the Alicea trade. Vanegmond, 26, has taken one step forward each year. His K/BB ratio has usually been much better than he showed in Fenway last year when he was nervous and mistake-prone, but he is ready for major league employment.

Top prospect Frankie Rodriguez pitched solidly at Pawtucket in 1994 despite an 8-13 record. His overall minor league record similarly does not reflect the astounding progress that he's made in his brief career. Only 22, his maturity may be a sticking point, but Rodriguez stands a chance of making an impact in the majors this summer. This is very likely the last time you'll be able to draft him.

Lary Bump:

Boston has acquired pitchers to shore up its staff. Lefthander Brian Looney, who played for general manager Dan Duquette in the Montreal organization, was 7-7-4.33-1.61 with Triple-A Ottawa. Lefthander Vaughn Eshelman (11-9-4.00-1.41), drafted from Baltimore, needs another pitch to go with his fastball. His most promising offspeed pitch is a changeup. During last season the Sox obtained Greg Brummett, a righthanded breaking-ball pitcher acquired from the Minnesota organization. In Triple-A with Salt Lake City and Pawtucket, he was 5-4-5.45-1.70.

Joel Bennett is a strikeout pitcher who depends mostly on a curve. He struggled after his promotion to Triple-A (1-3-6.86-1.48) from Double-A New

Britain (11-7-4.06-1.34), but this season you can expect him to get another promotion -- to the majors.

Rafael Orellano, a 6-2, 160-pound lefthander, threw hard enough to strike out more than a batter an inning in the Florida State League (11-3-2.40-0.96). After a stint on the disabled list, he won his next seven starts. The 21 year old is a comer.

His Sarasota teammate, Jeff Suppan, finished 13-7-3.26-1.17. The 20-year-old righthander was a second-round draft choice in 1993.

An extreme longshot is Dan Gakeler, on his second trip up through the Boston organization at age 30. He was 9-12-4.51-1.42 at New Britain.

California Angels

Oft-injured John Farrell signed a minor league contract with the Indians; he would not have been a major league factor with the Angels.

Hank Widmer:

A lot of people who picked Angels' starting pitchers in their drafts were left with very little at the end of the year. Without exception, Angels brought just about everyone's pitching staff's down.

The best pitcher was Chuck Finley, who got ten wins but with a 4.32 ERA and about a 1.4 ratio. There were times when Finley pitched very well, he just couldn't do it consistently. More than likely he will bounce back to be a quality starter and ace of the Angels' staff.

Mark Langston was even less consistent than Finley, and was hurt for part of the year. Langston's bad year may send his value down for a Rotisserie league. He will be 34 to start the year and I feel less confident in him bouncing back than Finley. Langston got hit pretty hard at times, and while he still struck out almost a batter an inning, he gave up 19 home runs in 18 starts which ballooned his ERA. He didn't have great control either, giving up over four walks per

nine innings. So there is a lot to be concerned about with Langston - proceed with caution.

The other two starters worth considering are Phil Leftwich and Brian Anderson. Both of them got knocked around pretty good, rarely going more than five innings and posting ERA's well over 5.00. However, both can pitch much better than they have shown. Leftwich is the more polished of the two, and at 25 is still young enough to improve. Nothing about Leftwich strikes one as being spectacular, but he could turn out to be a workhorse that goes out to the mound every five days and gives a team some good innings. Leftwich has good control, but isn't a strikeout pitcher. He might be a good pitcher to take a gamble on.

Brian Anderson isn't even close to being a strikeout pitcher, with just 47 K's in 102 innings in 1994. However, Anderson has excellent control (under two and a half walks per nine innings) and was the only Angel starter with a winning record (7-5). He's young, 21, and was probably brought to the majors too quickly but should be a productive pitcher for a few years.

The fifth starters on this team were an absolute black hole of high ERA's, high hit totals, and general ineffectiveness. John Farrell and Mark Leiter were useless, though Leiter improved as a middle reliever. Andrew Lorraine is young and pitched well at Triple-A, but he was lost on the Angels. He's a pitcher who might be ready in a year or two, but wasn't last year.

Which leaves the worst pitcher in the major leagues who received any kind of innings: Joe Magrane. In no start that I can recall, were the Angels ever in the game. And it took 11 starts for the managers to figure out that Magrane was killing them. When Magrane went to middle relief he was just as ineffective.

Lary Bump:

Andrew Lorraine, a fourth-round draft pick in 1993, was in the majors little more than a year later. He was voted the Pacific Coast League's best pitching prospect. His biggest obstacle to sticking with the

Angels is the team's glut of lefthander starting pitchers. The 22-year-old was 12-4-3.42-1.34 at Vancouver.

The major signs pointing Mark Ratekin toward the Angels in 1995 are his mid-season promotion from Double-A (3-4-4.92-1.20) to Triple-A (12-5-5.02-1.61) last season, and the fact that California needs righthanded starters.

Also at Vancouver, righty Mark Holzemer fell off to 5-10-6.60-1.72 in his third PCL season.

Julio Valera underwent Tommy John surgery to repair a torn ulnar ligament. In A, Double-A and Triple-A ball, Valera was a combined 3-4-5.40-1.51

Shad Williams also advanced from Midland (3-0-1.11-0.53) to Vancouver (4-6-4.60-1.51). His problem in Triple-A seemed to be that he couldn't get a strikeout when he needed one.

Oft-injured high draft choice Pete Janicki was demoted to the California League after a 2-6-6.94-1.70 start in the Texas League.

Ryan Hancock went the other way, posting a 3-4-5.81-1.54 record at Midland after a 9-6-3.79-1.28 start at Lake Elsinore.

Chicago White Sox

The trade of Jack McDowell to the Yankees promotes Alex Fernandez into the ace role and forces the White Sox to dip into their well-stocked minor league system for a new starter. James Baldwin and Scott Ruffcorn are the most ready in 1995.

Scott Sanderson will continue his ''Ramblin' Man'' act with a new team in 1995; he remained an unsigned free agent.

Shuart Shea:

Since Jack McDowell left via free agency, the Sox lost a durable and talented pitcher. However, they won't be losing the man who will help them the most in coming years: that man is Alex Fernandez.

The stout Fernandez still has some problems with location, and sometimes throws too many breaking pitches. However, he does have strikeout stuff, fanning 49 in 47 July innings. Fernandez is a second-half pitcher, and likely would have won 18 games if not for the strike. His control is improving, and he's just one step away from becoming one of the AL's best pitchers.

"Black Jack" McDowell started very poorly last season, but finished the year on a 7-2, 1.81 string. McDowell has a beautiful, fluid motion that should help him avoid injury. His stuff is as good as any pitcher in the league, and he has outstanding control. Since McDowell has moved on, he may be even better; the Sox have not given him the outstanding offensive support that the Yanks will.

Jason Bere's fastball is already one of the best in the AL. He can freeze hitters with heat low and outside, or ride it on their fists. Bere also has an off-speed pitch called a "fosh" which fools plenty of opponents. He is still struggling to improve his control, but even so Bere is overpowering enough to be successful. He's not great for ratios, however, so proceed with care. Bere will make 30-35 starts if healthy, and should win 12-15 games.

Fourth starter Wilson Alvarez (nice rotation, huh?) also has excellent fastball, which he is not afraid to throw inside. Alvarez throws four pitches, and is improving his once-unreliable control. As he continues to mature, Alvarez should be a consistent winner, and is good enough to be an anchor on some major league rotations.

Scott Sanderson was last year's veteran plug-in, and he didn't help much. His control was outstanding, but Sanderson allowed 20 homers in 92 innings and won't be re-signed.

Prospects James Baldwin and Scott Ruffcorn, both of whom combine excellent velocity with good movement, will vie for rotation spots this season. Baldwin is the favorite at this point, as Ruffcorn needs to develop more than a good fastball to be a major league starter. He will probably spend another

year at Nashville. Baldwin should be, when he matures, a solid number three major league starter, but will probably have some control problems at the major league level.

Steve Schrenk, a finesse hurler who also pitched well at Triple-A last season, also is seen as a possible major league starter, but it's hard to see how he could pass Baldwin or Ruffcorn anytime soon.

Lary Bump:

Rodney Bolton led the American Association in ERA last season (7-5-2.56-1.23), but he was found wanting in his trial with the White Sox in 1993 and has been passed by better prospects James Baldwin, Scott Ruffcorn and Steve Schrenk.

Another righthander, Robert Ellis, is in the same boat as Bolton. Ellis struggled at Nashville (4-10-6.09-1.72), then went on the disabled list in July. He throws a fastball and a curve, and may need to throw them in another organization to make it to the majors. On the positive side, Steve Olsen was promoted in mid-season from Double-A Birmingham (5-7-3.68-1.25) to Nashville (7-2-3.28-1.22).

Alan Levine also was promoted, after pitching in the Double-A All-Star Game. He was 5-9-3.31-1.41 at Birmingham, then 0-2-7.88-1.88 at Nashville. And the righthander is already 26.

The Sox, somewhat short on lefthanders, picked up 22 year old Keith Heberling in the Jack McDowell trade. Heberling was 11-7-2.92-1.34 in the Florida State League and 1-3-5.66-1.43 in the Eastern League. He's likely to start '95 in Birmingham, but could reach Triple-A by season's end.

Larry Thomas is a sinker/slider lefthander who has to have good control to be effective. He wasn't last season at Birmingham (5-10-4.63-1.47).

Lefthander Scott Christman, Chicago's first pick in the 1993 draft out of Oregon State, went 6-11-3.80-1.38 in the Carolina League.

Another Prince William southpaw was Jason Pierson (14-8-3.33-1.22). He lowered his ERA nearly a run and a half from his '93 season in the Midwest League. Even half of that improvement this year in Double-A would put the 24 year old on the fast track.

Scott Eyre, another lefty, was obtained from the Rangers organization last spring. He started the Midwest League season on the disabled list, but finished strong (8-4-3.47-1.30).

Cleveland Indians

Charles Nagy signed a contract extension and will eventually become the ace of this staff as young prospects enter the scene.

Former Indian and Angel John Farrell signed a minor league contract with Cleveland; he'll mainly pitch at Triple-A as roster filler but could get back to the big leagues as an injury fill-in. He's useless for Rotisserie, despite his admirably perseverance to overcome numerous debilitating injuries.

"Farmer" Jack Morris left as a free agent and went to the Reds. Is there good farmland in Ohio?

Two of the Indians' supposed prospects, Dave Mlicki and Paul Byrd, were included with Jerry DiPoto in the trade for Jeromy Burnitz. Of the three, only DiPoto is a lock to make the Mets opening day roster.

Tony Blengino:

Dennis Martinez is surely the only major leaguer with this career decision to make in the offseason: return to the Indians, or become President of his native land, Nicaragua. American League hitters were largely perplexed by Martinez' assortment of borderline-legal hard breaking stuff, after he spent the previous eight seasons in the NL Martinez averaged over seven innings per start, and only Seattle's Randy Johnson completed more games than Martinez' seven. He has routinely walked less than three batters per nine innings over his career, but he struck out less than five batters per nine innings in 1994 for the first

time in many years. This is a sure sign that Martinez has entered his decline phase, but at age 40, I guess he's entitled. He's got at least a couple more somewhat successful years ahead of him, if he wants them. Expect Martinez to return, going 16-12, 3.65 in 250 innings in 1995.

Charles Nagy, 28, lost the bulk of 1993 due to shoulder surgery. Nagy shrugged off the loss of a couple of MPH off of his fastball, and re-established his pinpoint location around the fringes of the strike zone. Like Martinez, Nagy is extremely durable, also averaging better than seven innings per start, no small feat in a hitters' year such as 1994. Nagy has walked only 2.5 batters per nine innings over his career, and requires pinpoint location to be effective, as he is actually quite hittable. Expect Nagy to stabilize at his current level for another 2-3 years before a swift, painless decline. Pencil him in as the Tribe's ace in 1995, with an 18-12, 3.25 mark.

Mark Clark, 27, was likely saved from an ignominious decline in the second half of 1994 when his wrist was fractured by a line drive, sidelining him for the season. Beneath the glowing exterior of Clark's 11-3, 3.82 mark lurk several reasons for caution. Clark was the recipient of outlandish run support, receiving 6.50 runs per nine innings. Most importantly, young pitchers who are utterly incapable of getting a key strikeout, like Clark and Milwaukee's Ricky Bones, tend to fizzle after just a few trips around the league. Clark relies almost exclusively on his curveball -- he could be the softest-tossing 6'5", 225 pounder ever. Expect the league to catch on in 1995, as he earns an 11-11, 4.15 mark.

In each of the last two seasons, a list of the ten most likely candidates for the Indians' major league rotation wouldn't have included Jason Grimsley's name. In both seasons, Grimsley wedged his way into the picture by season's end, as much by good fortune as by merit. Grimsley's chief asset is a wicked, hard curveball. Unfortunately, his own team's catchers have traditionally had as much trouble handling it as opposing batters. He has thrown an amazing 30 wild pitches in 262 career major league innings. His formerly hideous control has now been upgraded to

mediocre, but once again his only ticket to the Cleveland rotation hinges on the failure of younger, better prospects.

Despite a poor 1993 with Toronto, the Indians threw a sizeable chunk of money at Jack Morris for 1994. Then they threw in 6.52 runs per start for good measure, enabling him to post the most misleading 10-6 mark in baseball history. This didn't stop Big Jack from bailing on the Indians in the pre-strike pennant race, when he placed the annual harvest back home on the farm above the pennant race on his personal priority list. Manager Mike Hargrove, bless his soul, ordered him released.

The acquisitions of Martinez and Morris sentenced top prospects Albie Lopez, Julian Tavarez and Chad Ogea to a full year at Triple-A Charlotte, where they formed one of the most formidable minor league rotations in recent history. For Lopez, 23, and Tavarez, 22, this wasn't a big deal, as they had yet to pitch a full Triple-A season. Lopez made great strides in 1994, going 13-3 at Charlotte and showing flashes of brilliance in a late season trial with the Tribe. In his last start, he threw a complete game shutout with 11 whiffs. Albie Lopez' time has come; expect him to make the rotation and go 13-8, 3.70.

Tavarez is a rakish (6'2", 165 pounds) righty who has dominated at all of his minor league stops, going 34-15 in his three seasons. His out pitch is his curveball, which was selected as the best breaking pitch in the Triple-A International League in 1994 by Baseball America. Tavarez has nothing left to prove as a minor leaguer; for his career, he has a strikeout/walk ratio of nearly four to one, and a career ERA well below 3.00. However, his only-adequate heater leads one to wonder whether he's the next Mike Mussina or the next Jeff Mutis. I'll still lean towards Mussina -- expect Tavarez to make the 1995 rotation, and go 10-7, 4.00.

The omission of Ogea from the 1994 rotation, however, will likely have a profound effect on his development. Ogea, 24, like Tavarez, relies on breaking stuff. His heater only reaches the 85-87 MPH range, slower than Tavarez'. However, coming into 1994, Ogea was clearly ready for the majors, but his hopes were snuffed out by the ludicrous signing of Morris. Surely Ogea could have outperformed Farmer Jack, but Ogea's window of opportunity may now have closed. After a phenomenal start in his second season at Charlotte, Ogea slumped badly in the second half, finishing at 9-10, 3.85. He had a sterling 113/34 strikeout/walk ratio, and now possesses a 41-22 career minor league mark. At this point, he has likely dropped behind Lopez and Tavarez, and a spot in the bullpen may be all Cleveland has to offer. Look for him to go 6-5, 3.65 in a spot starter/ middle reliever role.

Dave Mlicki, 27, was the fourth wheel in the Indians' Triple-A rotation. Some fourth wheel -- he led the staff in strikeouts with 152. His control paled in comparison to his Charlotte teammates, but his top-notch fastball puts him in the running for a major league bullpen spot. He appears fully recovered from 1993 arm surgery.

While Cleveland's Double-A rotation was stocked with decent, if not overwhelming, prospects such as Paul Byrd, Carlos Crawford and Jason Fronio, their next hot prospect appears to be 1993 number one pick Daron Kirkreit. Kirkreit, 22, tore up Single-A while pitching for Kinston, allowing only 132 baserunners in 128 innings, striking out 116 and walking only 40. He was rudely welcomed to Double-A, posting a 6.22 ERA, but striking out better than a batter per inning. Kirkreit's arsenal includes a 90+ fastball, and he has prototypical 6'6', 225 pound size. Look for him in Cleveland by mid-1996.

1993 second-round pick Casey Whitten, 23, has similar stuff, but his big league future could be out of the pen. 1994 number one pick Jaret Wright, 19, throws harder than anyone in the Cleveland organization, but is clearly a work in progress. He has had problems with his weight (6'2", 218+) in the past.

Lary Bump:

Joe Roa could be a case of going from the frying pan to the fire. He was promoted to Triple-A ahead of the harder-throwing, young-stud pitching prospects in

the Mets organization, then was traded to the Indians, who have better-developed prospects ready for the majors. The Indians must have wanted him, though, or they wouldn't have dealt for him. Roa was a combined 10-9-3.31-1.26 at Binghamton and Norfolk. Control is his strong suit.

In the major league draft, the Indians took Jim Lewis. He had some shoulder problems in 1993, then went a combined 3-9-2.84-1.18 last season with Astros farm teams in the Florida State and Texas leagues.

Among the homegrown prospects behind Julian Tavarez, Albie Lopez, Chad Ogea and Carlos Crawford is righthander Daron Kirkreit, the Tribe's first draft pick in 1993. He throws a low-90s fastball good enough to strike out better than a batter per inning in both the Carolina and Eastern leagues last season. His combined '94 record was 11-12-3.62-1.21.

Lefthander Casey Whitten is a strikeout pitcher. He has moved up rapidly since being drafted in 1993's second round. In the Carolina League last season, he was 9-10-4.28-1.25.

Jason Fronio, 25, may have to return to the bullpen to have any chance to make the majors. Last year he went from 5-1-1.98-1.22 at Kinston to 7-6-3.73-1.38 after a promotion to Double-A Canton. His strikeouts/inning pitched ratio dropped significantly.

John Carter struggled to a 9-6-4.33-1.43 season at Canton a year after winning 17 in the Carolina League. Even in a losing season in the Carolina League (4-13-4.44-1.32), Jose Cabrera maintained his typical good strikeout/walk ratio, at better than 2:1.

Lefty Steve Kline, who relies on his control, tore up the Sally League (18-5-3.01-1.14). His teammate, righthander Roland De la Maza, had similar success (13-2-2.96-1.13).

Jaret Wright, Cleveland's number one draft pick last year out of high school, throws a 95 MPH sinking fastball. In four Appalachian League starts, he was 0-1-5.40-1.65. He's the righthanded-throwing son of former major league southpaw Clyde Wright. The main concerns for Jaret are his control and keeping his weight down.

Detroit Tigers

Bill Gullickson faded from the team's ace and Tim Belcher was a huge bust in 1994. Both became free agents and remained unsigned. Gullickson's deteriorating career is typical of soft-tossers and his slide will continue. Belcher can still pitch but will have to change a lot of things to become successful once again. Neither Gullickson nor Belcher are recommended for Rotisserie in 1995.

Fred Matos:

Tigers' management has concluded that they can't contend with the ineffective veteran starters they had last year, and that some young arms are needed. Of the five starters with over 100 innings, only David Wells, with an ERA of 3.96, was below 5.00. Horrendous ERA's were posted by Tim Belcher (5.89), Mike Moore (5.42), Bill Gullickson (5.93), and John Doherty (6.48).

Prior to 1993, Tim Belcher was an effective pitcher with an ERA consistently under 4.00. But he has been very hittable over the past two seasons, and the Tigers were his third team in two years. He will likely sign with a team desperate for 200+ innings without regard to their quality. Belcher's skills have declined, and he should be avoided. An erratic hard-throwing rookie is a better risk.

In 1991 Bill Gullickson won 20 games for the high scoring Tigers, but that was the last year he had an ERA below 4.00. Like Belcher, he is a very hittable Tiger starter and a very poor Rotisserie pitcher. Gullickson has nothing left and may have difficulty getting a contract offer for 1995. Avoid him at all costs.

Mike Moore had an up-and-down season last year, with more starts on the down side. His skills are declining, and he is very susceptible to the long ball, giving up 27 dingers last year (tying for second in the

league). Now 36, he is signed for 1995. Unless your league doesn't count ERA and ratio, Moore is a pitcher to avoid.

John Doherty has limited pitching skills, and needs good run support to win. His ERA of 6.48 was partly due to injuries, but even when healthy, the best you can expect is around 4.50. Although Doherty will go cheaply in most drafts, it's best to avoid him.

David Wells is the best choice of the Tiger starters, but he is noted for his streakiness. He is a tremendous competitor who may have a hot streak with a record like Sandy Koufax, perhaps winning 11 games in a row with an ERA below 2.00. But then everything falls apart. It's best to trade Wells at the end of the streak when he still has a very high value, but the difficult problem is pinpointing the end of the streak.

Greg Gohr, Sean Bergman and Jose Lima are prospects for the rotation, and top 1993 draft pick Cade Gasper from Pepperdine University could move up very quickly. Gohr has failed in several trials in previous years, but he has improved his slider and learned to get ahead in the count and pitch inside. A greatly improved Greg Gohr is still a very risky Rotisserie pitcher.

Sean Bergman had a good record in Triple-A: 11-8 with a 3.72 ERA in 155 innings, while giving up 147 hits and striking out 145. The key statistics (K/IP, H/IP and K/BB) all look very promising, and Bergman could be an effective major league starter -- but maybe not in 1995. All rookie pitchers are risky, so let someone else take the risk on Bergman. If you must take a rookie pitcher to fill out your roster, go with one from a contending team. Such a rookie can't kill you because if he pitches poorly, he will be sent back to the minors.

Jose Lima has a sinking fastball and a very good changeup. Last year in Triple-A, he gave up only 124 hits in 142 innings, and an average of less than a hit per inning is frequently a good indicator of success at higher levels. Nevertheless, Lima is a risky rookie pitcher.

Barring a trade or free agent signing, the Tigers rotation in 1995 will most likely be Wells, Moore,

Doherty, and the most effective two pitchers out of the trio of Bergman, Gohr, and Lima. Of the three, Bergman looks like the best prospect. Overall, Wells is the only Tiger starter worth having on a Rotisserie team, and even Wells is risky.

Lary Bump:

Don't confuse righthanders Felipe Lira and Jose Lima. Lima throws a sinking fastball and a sinker. Lima, who made a brief appearance with the Tigers last season, had a better year at Toledo (7-9-3.60-1.21 to Lira's 7-12-4.70-1.43), but Lira has been better every other year. They have been teammates since breaking into the Appalachian League in '90. I liken their situation to that of Ray Lankford and Bernard Gilkey after the 1990 season. Gilkey had had a better year, but Lankford was the better prospect.

Anyway, if you must take a rookie pitcher -- and if you're so desperate that you have to take a Tigers rookie pitcher -- Felipe Lira is the better choice. You may also be able to pull a Lira-Lima gambit and get a competitor to draft Lima, a not-so-good prospect with a poor team in a hitter's park.

Other Toledo starters were even worse. Ben Blomdahl was 11-11-4.46-1.45, and he averaged only about one strikeout every two innings.

Lefthander Frank Gonzales slid to 6-11-4.77-1.71 in his third season with the Mud Hens. Ken Carlyle started for Double-A Trenton, but pitched mostly out of the bullpen with Toledo. His combined totals were a weak 4-9-4.09-1.44.

Also with last-place Trenton, lefty Trever Miller lost nine consecutive starts and finished at 7-16-4.39-1.43. Shannon Withem took his medicine like a man, going 7-12-3.44-1.28, but averaging better than seven innings per start. Good control keeps him in games despite allowing more than a hit an inning.

Gary Goldsmith was promoted to Trenton (0-4-3.86-1.25) after a 7-7-3.28-1.29 start in the Florida State League.

Lefthander John Rosengren may be the one pitcher in the Detroit organization to keep youe eye on. The former North Carolina Tar Heel was 9-6-2.52-1.25 at Lakeland, then 0-2-7.27-1.85 at Trenton. He should show improvement in the Eastern League this year.

Cade Gaspar, the son of former major league outfielder Rod Gaspar, was the Tigers' first-round draft pick last season, out of Pepperdine U. He went 1-3-5.58-1.17 at Lakeland.

Kansas City Royals

Mark Gubicza re-signed with the Royals and has the fourth starter spot heading into spring training. Still, he must be viewed with caution as he is only a six inning pitcher and control problems could always re-surface. Few power pitchers have much success after becoming finesse pitchers and the success rarely lasts very long.

Bob Milacki refused a minor league assignment and became a free agent. With the desperate state of pitching in the majors he'll find another team for whom to go winless in 1995.

Venerable veteran Dennis Rasmussen again signed to a minor league contract. He probably would have earned a recall in 1994 had the strike not intervened. He'll be in a similar spot in 1995 - waiting in the wings should injuries strike. Rasmussen hasn't had any real Rotisserie value for many years.

Marc Bowman:

The Royals' starting rotation was one of the majors' best in 1994 with a solid one-two punch of David Cone and Kevin Appier and above average three and four spots held by Tom Gordon and Mark Gubicza. They had a lot of trouble finding a reliable fifth starter before getting three wins from Jose DeJesus just before the strike. For 1995 the top part of the rotation remains intact while the fourth and fifth spots will be up for grabs.

Winning the Cy Young award capped a remarkable year for Cone. His 2.94 ERA and 16 wins were among the very best in the league. He was, however, not so much a better pitcher in 1994 than he was a smarter pitcher. Give credit to pitching coach Bruce Kison for preaching efficiency and credit Cone for listening to the advice that he get hitters to put the ball in play and let the Royals' above average defense turn them into outs. The strategy worked as Cone was often able to get into the eighth or ninth innings having thrown just 100-110 pitches instead of his accustomed 140. Throw in a superior effort by the Royals' bullpen and you have a 16-5 record and a Cy Young award.

His 1994 season will serve to make Cone very expensive in 1995 drafts. He'll probably retain a good ERA and ratio for 1995, but wins are impossible to guess for starting pitchers since they rely upon unpredictable run support. The Royals are unlikely to be among the top scoring teams, despite bringing in their fences. The best guess for Cone in 1995 would be: 225 innings of 3.10 ERA, 1.10 ratio and about 15 wins, making him worth at least $30.

In 1994, Kevin Appier suffered for half the season from tightness in his pitching shoulder before recovering to post a 2.57 ERA over his last 14 starts. Weak run support in the second half left him with a 7-6 record, and his first half struggles helped him post a mediocre 3.83 ERA and 1.16 ratio. The important point to focus on is that Appier's numbers after his shoulder problems dissipated were almost identical to his marvelous 2.51 ERA and 1.1 ratio that he had in 1992 and 1993 combined. His off season will have the same effect in 1995 drafts that Cone's down year in 1993 had on bidding in 1994 drafts - he'll go for significantly less than he's actually worth. Appier is among the league's very best pitchers and is likely to pitch 225 innings of sub-3.00 ERA and sub-1.2 ratio while winning 15 to 18 games. This kind of production will be worth at least $35, but smart Rotisserie owners will pay less.

Tom Gordon had another season of both good and bad. His 11 wins were second best on the team, but his 4.35 ERA and 1.4 ratio were below league average. If you want to have Gordon, it's advisable not to actually watch him pitch because he'll alternately

thrill you, then break your heart - often in succeeding innings. It takes a strong constitution to own Tom Gordon. He's scheduled to be the Royals' third starter again in 1995 and should be good for 10-12 wins, a 4.00 ERA and 1.4 ratio over about 190 innings. Pay a small salary and you'll get a small bargain.

Mark Gubicza became a free agent after his best season since 1989. Once a pitcher you could count on to walk a lot of batters (120 in 1987), Gubicza actually led the AL with his 1.8 per nine innings rate in 1994. He has completed the transition from power pitcher to finesse pitcher that was forced upon him due to repeated shoulder injuries beginning in 1990. Because he's only a six-inning pitcher now, it's hard for Gubicza to collect an appropriate number of victories. It's unknown if Gubicza will re-sign with the Royals; if he does he'll have the fourth starter spot to begin 1995. If he goes elsewhere he may have a more important role with his new team.

With a new team, Gubicza might be required to go longer than the six innings to which the Royals limited him; he would then become susceptible to further injury and become a sub-par pitcher who is worthless to Rotisserie owners. If he stays in KC, Gubicza would probably start 30 games, winning 10 with a 4.40 ERA and 1.4 ratio over 175 innings, making him worth a small salary.

The fifth starter spot is up for grabs, but Jose DeJesus made a credible bid for the job with four late season starts in which he managed to win three times. DeJesus is still a very hard thrower who walks more than his share of hitters. He's the same guy who once led the NL in walks allowed (128 in 1991) before he blew out his arm with the Phillies. If he can harness control of his great fastball, DeJesus could win big. Unfortunately that doesn't make him unique. Put him on your "projects" list and pay attention if he suddenly demonstrates unusually good control.

Jeff Granger has a better long range projection. To begin with he's a lefty and the Royals have been practically begging to get a lefty in the rotation (perhaps explaining why they gave Chris Haney six starts). The 23 year old Granger made two spot starts

for the Royals and was overmatched, but he had a good year for Double-A Memphis, posting a 3.87 ERA. He was somewhat erratic but still showed good poise for a player with so little pro experience.

Granger has a great chance to be in the Royals' rotation out of spring training in 1995. Should that happen, he's a poor Rotisserie gamble for two reasons: 1. Rookie pitchers are often so erratic that they will offset a few good starts with one horrific shellacking; and very few of them are good enough to have more than two consecutive good starts. 2. The Royals are so desperate for lefthanded starting pitchers that Granger will get an even longer rope than an ordinary pitcher who is struggling. The Royals need to get Granger acclimated to the majors, but it's unwise to be the poor sap who suffers his stats on your Rotisserie page while he's still in his learning phase.

Bob Milacki got ten starts and won none of them despite pitching quite well in a few of them. He also pitched quite horribly in several starts and earned a trip back to Triple-A. He lacks a good fastball and has to beat the hitters by fooling them with offspeed stuff and good location. Milacki is the kind of pitcher who will keep getting recalled due to the dearth of pitching talent and he'll keep being a disappointment.

Chris Haney is 26 years old and if he's going to be a late-blooming lefty ace he'd better get started soon. If Haney wins a starting role out of spring training and looks good early on, I'd still be skeptical. With his track record he needs to prove himself for a full season. Because the Royals would like to get a lefthander into the rotation, he's going to get every opportunity to succeed, or to fail. Let the Royals experiment, but don't you chance it.

Mike Magnante made one start for the Royals in 1994, but is primarily a reliever. Among the regular starters for Omaha and Memphis were the aforementioned Milacki, DeJesus, Granger and Haney, but Triple-A and Double-A were mostly populated with washouts like Dennis Rasmussen, Rod Nichols, Doug Simons, Paul Abbott, Victor Cole, and Eddie Pierce. While any of them may get to the majors in 1995, none are worthy of Rotisserie attention.

In the high minors the best bets are Mike Fyhrie, Brian Bevil and Brian Harrison. Fyhrie is a finesse pitcher who doesn't impress immediately but might have some success his first time around the league (control pitchers often have early success before getting their clock cleaned later). He had been successful at almost every level before having some problems in 16 starts for Omaha in 1994. Bevil throws pretty hard but finished the year on the DL due to a shoulder tear. He should be back for 1995, but it's hard to predict the effects of the injury.

At Class-A Wilmington, a trio of hard throwers were a combined 33-11. Mike Bovee was the biggest winner, mainly due to his excellent control (5-to-1 strikeout to walk ratio). He's just 5'11", 190 pounds, so he's not your typical overpowering hard thrower. Bart Evans went 10-3 with a 2.98 ERA and struck out a batter per inning and was selected by Baseball America as the league's best pitching prospect. Big Jim Pittsley may be the best of the three; he also whiffed more than one per inning and had a strikeout/walk ratio better than 4-to-1. All three should advance to Double-A in 1995 with an expected 1996 arrival in the majors.

Lary Bump:

Kansas City's pitching staff at Triple-A Omaha resembled a Who Was Who list -- or more appropriately, Who Might Have Been Who. A potent offense was saddled with a pitching staff of has-beens: Rod Nichols (5-10-5.64-1.51), Jeff Parrett (0-3-3.96-1.24), Doug Simons (5-8-4.58-1.28), Dennis Rasmussen (10-7-3.24-1.23). A younger pitcher, 25-year-old righthander Mike Fyhrie, doesn't throw hard, and last season he couldn't get his offspeed stuff over the plate. That resulted in his demotion from Omaha (6-5-5.72-1.56) to Double-A Memphis (2-5-3.22-1.25). The real pitching prospects were with Wilmington's powerhouse in the Carolina League. Dilson Torres was promoted from there to Memphis, and was equally impressive at both levels (a combined 13-2-1.60-. His best pitches are a forkball and a slider.

Hard-throwing righthander Mike Bovee was the biggest winner (13-4-2.65-1.13) with the minors' most dominant team. He also has good control. His

timetable would have him in Double-A this season, Triple-A next year and the majors to stay in 1997.

Jim Pittsley, a 1992 first-round draft pick, struck out a batter an inning at Wilmington (11-5-3.17-1.21). He'll be just 21 in April, and could move up fast after starting this season in Double-A.

Righthander Kris Ralston had a better ERA at Wilmington (10-4-2.39-1.12) than any of the Blue Rocks' Big Three starters. Check to see how he does this season at Double-A Wichita.

Melvin Bunch is a righthanded control pitcher who did well (5-3-3.39-1.10) after coming back from a strained rotator cuff last season.

Milwaukee Brewers

The Brewers chose to pick up their option on Ricky Bones' contract after Bones surprising breakthrough year in 1994. Can Bones continue the above average pitching?

Bill Gray:

Cal Eldred was at his highest value as a rookie. Unfortunately, that was two years ago. That's not to say he is not a good pitcher now. He had a pretty good second half, and could win 12-15 games in 1995. It could get a little ugly, especially if your league counts losses. His ERA could be well into the dreaded 4.00's and his ratio will be close to 1.4. Make sure your other pitchers can help in these areas. As you craft your starting staff, Eldred is good for W's. Period.

Ricky Bones finally had a breakthrough season. He was virtually flawless in the early going, then the hitters began to catch up with him. Still, in a season notable for wretched pitching, Bones did pretty well. Bones has always ranked near the bottom in K's per inning pitched, and last year was no different as he fanned only 57 in 170 innings, or about three strikeouts for every nine innings pitched. Historically, consistently effective pitchers average at least four strikeouts per nine innings.

Was there anything different about Bones in 1994? Maybe. For one, he had never had a major league complete game prior to 1994. In 1994 he had four complete games. We might deduce that Bones has reached a new level of consistency, and if he can improve his ability to keep the ball down, could continue to improve in 1995. Bones' ERA on June 7 was 2.56. When the owners and players decided to "see you in court" on August 12, his ERA was up to 3.43. Bones was a risky pick going into 1994, and let's just say that for now Bones is off the critical list and has become an interesting speculation with moderate downside risk. His ERA might hover around the 4.00 mark, but he should post a decent ratio of around 1.3 with 13-16 wins.

Angel Miranda will be an imposing figure in the near future, and possibly this year. He returned from an injury sooner than expected and pitched just fine. He was dominant in his brief appearances against lefthanded hitters, which is the rule in lefty versus lefty matchups. He did pretty well against righties too. I like lefties, and I'd grab Miranda in a heartbeat. Sharp players should know about Miranda.

Bill Wegman certainly is not old at 32. In 1992 he pitched 261 innings, had a 3.20 ERA and a ratio of 1.2, while winning 13 games. In 1993, injuries limited him to only 121 innings, four wins and a 4.48 ERA. Last year he spent time on the D.L., pitching just 116 innings with eight wins and an ERA of 4.51. Do we assume that injuries have kept him from being sharp? Do we grit our teeth and assume that only because there aren't many good pitchers out there, we should take another shot at Bill Wegman and hope he can hold together? Do we assume that because he still exhibits fine control that he can recover and produce decent quality stats? Yes to all of the above. Buy him. He can still pitch.

I'm not very interested in Bob Scanlan as a starter. He muffed his chance to be a closer last year, yet I still believe he can and will be a good one. That's why I would draft Scanlan even if he begins the season as a starter. What about Mike Fetters? Fetters did fine, and would have to lose the job, which is not impossible to imagine. Then it's back to Scanlan. The data says that Scanlan should be on the mound in LATE INNING SITUATIONS. I think he'll get another chance to win the closer's job in spring training. Scanlan pitched much better in the second half after a particularly rocky April and May. He reduced his ERA from nearly 6.00 to 4.11 in the final 10 weeks of the season.

Jaime Navarro is in jeopardy of being eliminated from the rotation. He's been backsliding since 1992, and there is some young talent on the farm. Navarro still lacks stamina, and he still throws too many pitches, which drains him quickly. Then: Ba-BOOM! Here's a towel and some soap, Jaime. Let someone else take a chance on Navarro.

Lary Bump:

Milwaukee is in need of more pitching help than its farm system apparently can provide.

Marshall Boze went 30-12 in 1992 and '93, but struggled in his Triple-A debut (6-10-4.73-1.49).

Scott Karl is a groundball pitcher most effective when batters beat his changeup and curve into the ground. The lefthander can't throw his mid-80s fastball past many batters. After a 5-1-2.96-1.08 start at Double-A El Paso, he was promoted to New Orleans (5-5-3.84-1.40).

Sid Roberson's name always conjures up an image of El Sid. But Roberson is a slimmer finesse pitcher who showed he knows how to pitch last season at El Paso (15-8-2.83-1.31). The 23-year-old lefty is the best single pitching prospect in the organization.

Righthander Kevin Kloek is one of those pitchers who went to the Arizona Fall League to determine whether he was a prospect than as recgnition that he was a top prospect. He has spent two seasons in the Texas League, including 5-1-3.90-1.16 in an injury-shortened '94.

Joe Wagner, a first-round draft choice in 1993, is a fastball pitcher who will throw inside. He was 13-9-3.93-1.34 in the Midwest League last year.

Another '93 first-rounder, lefthander Kelly Wunsch, struck out five batters in one inning in the Midwest League last season, but he walked so many batters that he went back to the Pioneer League. His combined numbers were 7-12-5.76-1.62. The Brewers had serious injury problems last year. Jamie McAndrew didn't pitch after undergoing off-season surgery.

Lefthander Tyrone Hill, the Brewers' 1991 number one pick, underwent shoulder surgery last June, and is expected to be out at least half of this season. Jeff D'Amico, a 1993 first-round draft choice out of high school, still hasn't pitched in pro ball after undergoing surgery last season to remove a bone spur from his right elbow.

Minnesota Twins

Jim DeShaies remained unsigned as a free agent late in December and is not expected to return to Minnesota. The lefty will land on his feet somewhere but is not recommended for Rotisserie.

James Benkard:

I suspect either Kevin Tapani or Scott Erickson will return (but not both), and that Jim Deshaies will not come back. Pat Mahomes will be in the rotation, and the two young lefthanders, Carlos Pulido and Eddie Guardado, can handle a spot between them. To fill the final two spots, Mike Trombley or Mo Sanford could fill in creditably, and LaTroy Hawkins and Marc Barcelo will be ready by the middle of the season. Minnesota could also shop around for a bargain veteran lefthander to replace Deshaies.

Tapani can be an exasperating pitcher, as he inevitably starts out poorly before making a late rush. Oddly enough, Tapani was vulnerable to righthanded hitters (.314) in '94, yet he still has too many positives to ignore. He is durable, has excellent control, and fields his position well. Tapani could thrive in the National League; his pitches are not a great deal easier to hit than Greg Maddux's. Count on a return to 15 wins with a 3.50 ERA.

Erickson can try an owner's patience even more than Tapani. While young and talented, he has nevertheless had more than his share of poor outings recently. When his sinker is working, Erickson induces ground ball outs, but he falls into trouble when his breaking pitches fail and he must rely exclusively on the sinker. Erickson has improved his control and his conditioning, and could shine if he finds a consistent release point.

Mahomes fashioned an impressive record in 1994 (9-5), and the club guardedly trusts him to take the ball every fifth day. A more relaxed motion enabled Mahomes to work out of some jams with finesse. Despite these gains, real productivity on the mound hinges upon throwing strikes, and Mahomes walked more men than he fanned last year. Long relief is now the best role for Mahomes; expect slow but measurable progress from him.

A strong winter propelled young Carlos Pulido into the rotation in '94. Pulido spots the ball well and has a future. He was pushed past his ability last season. Meanwhile, Eddie Guardado, who has more potential than Pulido, polished his talent at Triple-A. It is difficult to forecast which of the two will be more prepared to chip in during 1995.

I look for Guardado to establish himself in the rotation by the end of '95, with Pulido backing him up in long relief. Guardado could win ten games for Minnesota, but a more likely scenario has him learning by trial and error so he can enjoy successes in the future. Draft Pulido only if the Twins have good fortune with their rotation in the spring and can keep him in the bullpen.

Brad Radke, Oscar Munoz, and Dan Serafini are other prospects who have the potential to become number good starters. Radke has accomplished almost as much as Hawkins since Minnesota chose him in the eighth round, directly after Hawkins, in 1991. He is not overpowering, but mixes his pitches well and has stayed durable. He will also need a full year at Triple-A before challenging for the majors.

Munoz stayed healthy through a difficult year at Triple-A after earning Pitcher of the Year honors in the Southern League in 1993. At age 26, he could help out the Twins with 40 innings and a 4.00 ERA in 1995. Serafini, a first round pick in 1992, performed well (9-9, 4.61) at 20 years of age in a high Class-A league. The Twins' top lefthanded prospect is two years away from the Metrodome.

Lary Bump:

With better prospects coming up behind him, Oscar Munoz may have missed his chance with a poor Triple-A season in '94 (9-8-5.88-1.78). Ditto Mo Sanford, who despite his 95 MPH fastball went 7-5-4.87-1.38 at Salt Lake City. Moving out of the pitching-rich Cleveland farm system didn't help lefty Shawn Bryant, who was 5-9-6.27-1.67 at Salt Lake.

The organization's best prospect, LaTroy Hawkins, shot through the farm system last year, stopping by the Southern League just long enough to be voted its best pitching prospect. His combined totals from A ball to Triple-A were 18-6-3.07-1.24. The righthander should expect to get the ball from Tom Kelly every fifth day this season.

Not far behind Hawkins is righthander Marc Barcelo, a first-round draft pick out of Arizona State in 1993. He was 11-6-2.65-1.16 at Double-A Nashville, and might have finished last season in the majors if not for the strike. The 6-3, 220-pounder will be ready when his slider is.

Mike Misuraca had what was considered the best breaking pitch in the Southern League last season, and as a result equaled the highest win total of his six-year career (8-4-3.63-1.28 at Nashville; 3-5-5.21-1.54 at Salt Lake).

Control artist Brad Radke went 12-9-2.66-1.08 at Nashville. Todd Ritchie, the Twins' first draft pick in 1990, pitched just four times last season (0-2-4.24-1.82 at Nashville) while recovering from shoulder tendinitis. Another high draft pick, lefty Dan Serafini, was 9-9-4.61-1.51 in the Florida State League.

New York Yankees

There is an exception to every rule in Rotisserie science, and the exception to the ''don't pursue wins'' rule is that it's OK to regard Jimmy Key as helpful in the wins category. Key is in the ideal situation with a team that supports him offensively and a manager who watches his usage as if under a microscope. Key's 11-game winning streak in 1994 was a career high.

With Key, the quality numbers are consistently good, too. He's not overpowering but is among the best at working to precise spots and changing speeds with a variety of breaking pitches. How close does Buck Showalter monitor Key's workload? In his only complete game last year, Key threw just 94 pitches.

Back in 1993 Melido Perez looked like he was on the skids, pitching badly when he wasn't sidelined by hip and shoulder injuries. In 1994 he was again healthy and successful. Perez features a dominant fastball in the mid 90's. He likes to throw his heater to get strike one on a hitter, and then throw forkball after forkball until he gets a strikeout or a weak grounder. It's a simple method that works well. Perez has improved his concentration to throw more strikes and let his defense work for him; one of the problems keeping him out of the top tier in past years was a tendency to just plain miss with ball four. The progress in discipline shown in 1994, combined with the physical comeback, leave Perez high on my list of desirable starters for 1995. He's come a long way since going 6-14 and having shoulder surgery.

Jim Abbott had a good year in 1994, but most of his success came early as he began the year going 6-2 with a 2.67 ERA. Abbott has the talent to pitch like that (well, almost) for a whole year, as he showed with back to back seasons of 2.89 and 2.77 with California in 1991-1992. The battle for Abbott in New York has included contending with the unfriendly media; it's not that anyone has picked on Abbott in particular, just that writers in New York are the toughest in the country when it comes to putting everyone on the spot with penetrating questions that may or may not have anything to do with the game on

the field. The team owner hasn't helped, refusing to drop the question of whether time spent working with handicapped children might be detrimental to Abbott's pitching performances.

Behind all this gibberish is a high quality southpaw who can still get the heater up over 90 when he's on, and just needs to throw his curveball for strikes to be a consistent winner. Abbott was among those players whose free agent status depended on strike time counting toward major league service. Away from New York, he would probably pitch better.

Scott Kamieniecki keeps starting the year in the pen or in the minors and ending up with a regular spot in the starting rotation. Last year he took over to help fill the void left by faltering Bob Ojeda and Terry Mulholland. Kamieniecki is a rather ordinary pitcher, working with a superior team. His standard four-pitch repertoire will keep him in the rotation as long as he pitches well, and there is enough alternative talent (and enough urgency about using it), so that Kamieniecki comes with the built-in insurance policy guaranteeing that he will never be allowed to pitch 200 bad innings. That quality can be very valuable in a standard league that doesn't allow "free" moves to dispose of unwanted pitchers.

One of the candidates to press Kamieniecki or whoever else is in the starting rotation, is talented young lefty Sterling Hitchcock. Finally gaining a starter's role late in 1994, Hitchcock finished strong: a team-leading 2.93 ERA in five starts. Hitchcock has a huge and diverse repertoire, but his success in the majors will depend on a straightforward approach featuring his 90+ fastball to get plenty of strikeouts, popups, and flies. Hitchcock is among the Yankees' most promising long-term starter prospects, still just age 23. While he isn't "safe" for 1995, he's got high potential and a great future, and makes a good pick at a low price for a rebuilding team.

Another young gun in the long-term starting picture is Australian Mark Hutton, who got some bullpen work in 1994, including some closer duty at Triple-A Columbus. Conversion to the pen is a possibility, but Hutton is more likely to become valuable as a major league starter before he becomes valuable as a major league closer. Hutton has as a big a mid-90's fastball as any of the Yankee pitchers and will eventually succeed in one role or the other. Like Hitchcock he makes a good pick at a low price for the future-oriented.

Free agent Terry Mulholland was not expected back with New York. The Yankees were apparently wrong in believing that Mulholland had come back cleanly from an assortment of injuries including a hip flexor and knee strain. If he was physically OK in 1994, it didn't show. Mulholland needs fine control to keep his slider and sinker down in the strike zone. His good changeup was a bigger asset in the National League.

Lary Bump:

Andy Pettitte will probably need at least to start 1995 in Triple-A, but the 6-5 lefthander is a good candidate for a mid-season promotion like the one he had last year, when he was a combined 14-4-2.86-1.18 with Double-A Albany and Triple-A Columbus. At just 22, he has excellent control and is the farthest advanced of any Yankees pitching prospect.

Mariano Rivera is a 6-4, 168-pound righthander who was promoted twice during last season and totaled 10-2-2.95-1.19 in the Florida State, Eastern and International leagues. His next promotion would take him to the majors. Kirt Ojala was the Yankees organization's pitcher of the month for April 1994. That could end up being his career highlight -- or he could hang on the fringes of the majors for 10 seasons, because he's lefthanded. His '94 numbers at Columbus were 11-7-3.83-1.37.

Dave Eiland came back to the Yankees organization last season (9-6-3.58-1.24 at Columbus). The 28-year-old righthander probably will be back there as an insurance policy this year.

Jim Musselwhite, the best control pitcher in the Florida State League, earned a promotion to Double-A during last season. His totals were 11-7-2.95-1.04. Brien Taylor missed all of last season after injuring his left shoulder in a barroom brawl. He has a major

league fastball and curve, but needs major work on holding runners and fielding.

Ramiro Mendoza was one of the leading winners (12-6-3.01-1.25) with a Tampa team the Yankees loaded with talent. He's 6-2 and 154 pounds, and if he puts on some weight he can also put some MPH on his fastball.

Matt Drews, the Yankees' first-round draft pick in 1993 out of Sarasota High School, made his pro debut last season (7-6-2.10-1.06 in the New York-Penn League). He and his low-90s fastball should arrive in the majors in 1997 or '98.

Oakland A's

Steven Rubio:

Bobby Witt would be a decent number four starter, but he has been pushed into the role of staff ace with Oakland. Outside of a hot streak last season which included a near-perfect game, Witt was once again safely mediocre, an improvement of sorts over his early years (when he was dangerously erratic).

Ron Darling looked to be finished as a major league pitcher only two years ago, and so his average performance in 1994 was somewhat startling. Darling is a smart pitcher and he may become one of those pitchers who recover some of their old glory in their mid-30s. Caution is advised, of course, but the very fact that I still must write about Ron Darling speaks volumes for the level of his comeback.

Steve Karsay, if healthy, is probably the best pitcher in the A's rotation. Having said that, fantasy owners are advised to recall the axiom that you should avoid injury-prone pitchers until they have proven their health has returned. Karsay is only 23 and has plenty of time to get back on track. His abilities are strong enough that he would make a good choice for risk-taking fantasy owners. But the more prudent owners should wait a year.

Todd Van Poppel is a bust. Last year we spoke of a four year string of control difficulties, and noted that Van Poppel had not yet justified the hype surrounding him. He followed with an ERA above 6.00 and more walks than strikeouts. Avoid him.

Steve Ontiveros rose from the dead in a fashion more surprising even than Ron Darling's. Almost forgotten, Ontiveros returned to Oakland and led the American League in ERA while impressing fans with his competitive spirit and willingness to take on all challenges. Ontiveros also pitched well in 1993, in both Triple-A and the AL (with Seattle), so his remarkable resurgence is likely to be a real one.

Tony LaRussa stated when he signed a new contract to return to Oakland, that one of the deciding factors was how impressed he was with the young pitchers in the A's system. Carlos Reyes had a chance to show his stuff in the majors last year, and while he wasn't often impressive, he rarely embarassed himself. His minor-league numbers are good, and he is still young enough to make his mark in the majors.

Doug Johns led the Pacific Coast League in ERA last season. Although he is already 27 years old, you have to be impressed by anyone who posts a 2.89 ERA in the hitting-crazed PCL, and the A's are speaking highly of Johns at this point. He could be a factor in 1995.

John Wasdin dominated Class-A and Double-A hitters last year, and is now considered one of the best pitchers in the Oakland system. Wasdin is a hard-throwing former number one draft choice who probably needs a year at Triple-A. Russ Brock is a curve-balling righty who has also caught LaRussa's eye. Brock can strike batters out, has impressed at all minor-league levels, and is another A's pitcher who might be a sleeper. Gavin Osteen has pitched well at every stop in his career, with the exception of his three stints in Triple-A. He may have reached the limits of his ability, but his successes in the lower minors mark him as a prospect who could still surprise. Mike Mohler has pitched well in the minors, but couldn't find the plate in an earlier callup to Oakland.

Lary Bump:

The Athletics have an abundance of lefthanded would-be prospects. Mike Mohler experienced some shoulder problems that started him out in A ball, then went 1-3-3.53-1.37 at Triple-A Tacoma. Gavin Osteen was 8-9-5.27-1.50 in the Pacific Coast League. Doug Johns moved from Double-A Huntsville's bullpen (3-0-1.20-1.87) to Tacoma's rotation (9-8-2.89-1.21). His control was much better as a starter. Steve Wojchiechowski was 10-5-3.10-1.19 at Huntsville. While half of the Athletics' ballyhooed four 1990 first-round draft-pick pitchers went down with injuries, 26-year-old Kirk Dressendorfer attempted to come back from his by going all the way back to the Arizona Rookie League. He was 0-1-0.00-0.57 in 12 1/3 innings.

John Wasdin, a 1993 first-round draft choice, was part of a rotation at Class A Modesto that was so loaded the Athletics assigned two starting pitchers to split time in each game. Then Wasdin was promoted, and became one of the Southern League's best pitchers. His totals were 15-4-3.15-1.05. With a good start in Triple-A this year, he'll be in Oakland before fall. Another '93 first-rounder, Willie Adams, was 11-4-3.91-1.25 between Modesto and Huntsville.

Don Wengert went the same route, Modesto to Huntsville, then topped off his year with a strong Arizona Fall League season. His '94 minor league totals were 10-5-3.17-1.20; in Arizona he was 2-1-2.38-1.18. Stacy Hollins was an even greater force in the Arizona Fall League (7-1-2.38-0.96) after a 13-6-3.39-1.31 season at Modesto. Another Modesto mainstay was Bobby Chouinard (12-5-2.59-1.23).

Seattle Mariners

Shawn Boskie was released. He is barely on the fringe as a major league pitcher and is not a good selection for Rotisserie no matter where he goes.

Bill Gray:

Unless you are starting a league, Randy Johnson probably won't be available. Johnson has managed to put up some impressive seasons despite giving up a lot of walks. But he has cut down on the walks to such an extent that his walks per nine innings pitched are now less than four. He allows less than seven hits per nine innings pitched, and opposing batters cobbled together a .216 average against Johnson in 1994. Only Roger Clemens (.204), Greg Maddux (.207), and David Cone (.209) were more effective. There is no need to go to the fine print on Randy Johnson. At his best he is untouchable. Hell, at less than his best he's untouchable.

Chris Bosio is about the only other Mariner starter you might be interested in owning, but Bosio might be slipping a little. Lefties banged him around to the tune of .301 in 1994. Smart field managers usually like to put in a lot of lefthanded batters against righthanded pitching and this is not a good sign for Bosio. I'm a bit wary of his ratio as well; 1.4 is pretty steep for a guy who should be at most 1.2-1.25.

Then, there is Dave Fleming. He should smoke lefthanded hitters, as good southpaws will. Lefties hit him for a .279 batting average, but it was ugly when Fleming faced righthanded hitters. They hit .317 against him last year, up from .298 in 1993. Fleming really needs another pitch that sinks and causes batters to hit grounders. Without one, it doesn't look good for a long career in major league baseball.

Others filling in on the staff were Roger Salkeld, Greg Hibbard, Jim Converse, John Cummings and Shawn Boskie. If Salkeld and Hibbard are healthy enough to pitch much in 1995, either might be an interesting pick. I'd definitely stay away from all the rest with Cummings being a possible exception. I'm not recommending Cummings, a lefty, to anybody at this point, but I do think he is talented enough to be a pretty good pitcher. He is still a work in progress. Just keep your eye on him. Any rookies that make their way to the big leagues should be avoided of course, especially true if they pitch in Seattle.

Lary Bump:

The best pitching prospect in the Seattle organization, righthander Tim Harikkala, gets a star next to his

name as one to watch in '95. He was promoted twice last season, and did about as well in the Southern League as in the Midwest League. He totaled 16-4-2.34-1.18. He is not a strikeout threat, but he apparently knows how o pitch.

Jackie Nickell had the best control in the California League, according to Baseball America's poll. He earned a brief promotion to Double-A Jacksonville after his 9-4-3.79-1.08 start at Riverside. He should reach Triple-A this year, and Seattle in '96.

Derek Lowe has been able to go out every five days, but with mixed results. At Jacksonville, he was 7-10-4.94-1.50. Even though he's 6-6, he doesn't throw hard. At age 21, he still has time to develop some velocity.

Shawn Estes went on the disabled list because of shoulder weakness, and pitched just 10 games in Rookie and A ball (0-5-3.86-1.46). The 1991 first-round draft choice has had control problems.

Texas Rangers

Easily the AL's best free agent starting pitcher, Kevin Brown will probably leave the Rangers for one of the "contending" Eastern or Central Division teams; Baltimore is said to be in hot pursuit. Should Brown join the Orioles (or other strong pitching teams) his value would rise. The pressure to carry the staff would be gone and he won't be in much of a hitter friendly park than he has toiled for much of his career.

Also, the Rangers were dead last in 1994 in the American League with a .976 fielding percentage and ground ball pitcher Brown suffered often at the hands of the sub-par Ranger infielders. A change of scenery can help Brown in many ways and make him, once again, one of the league's very best starting pitchers.

Jack Armstrong and Tim Leary have both become free agent and are still unsigned. Don't be surprised if they stay that way until spring training as both are barely major league pitchers at this point.

Peter Graves:

It's not a pretty sight. The Rangers used 12 different starters last season, compiling a horrid 5.55 ERA. The 1995 season holds little hope of improvement from within, with the top two pitchers in the rotation, Kevin Brown and Kenny Rogers, having become free agents in the offseason. Add in the instability of the Rangers' bullpen, and this group of starters could merit the "don't touch" label we've become accustomed to attaching to teams like Detroit. Expect an overhaul of the rotation via trades and free agent signings before Opening Day.

Kevin Brown is coming off a horrendous season in which he gave up 11.5 hits per nine innings. Only one pitcher in the last 25 years, Lary Sorensen, has been more hittable over as many innings. Brown's 4.82 ERA doesn't even reflect the fact that he also gave up an unearned run every nine innings. Several factors may have contributed to Brown's shocking decline. For the first time in his career, Brown was the designated "staff ace", and he did not react well to the pressure. Brown also may have been distracted by baseball's labor problems; he was one of the more high-profile player reps. Also, Brown may have been physically too strong to throw his trademark sinker effectively. He did a lot of upper body strengthening in the offseason, and struggled frequently in the first inning, when he would be at his strongest.

Another factor was the thin Texas bullpen, which led former manager Kevin Kennedy to leave Brown in games when it was obvious that he was struggling. Finally, while he did induce ground balls, they often found their way through the porous Ranger infield for hits. Brown is not likely to return to Texas; management sees him as a whiner and a bad clubhouse presence. I think he does have a decent chance of pitching effectively in 1995. He is healthy and a change of scenery (especially if he signs with a good defensive team that plays on grass) could help.

Lefthander Kenny Rogers' perfect game against the Angels belied another inconsistent season. Rogers has the best stuff - good fastball, big curveball - of any of the Ranger starters. Over the course of an entire

season, Rogers will have enough outstanding performances to offset the bad ones, but the end result is only slightly above average. He has been a full-time starter for only two seasons, and with talent and good health, Rogers does have the potential to improve.

Roger Pavlik was the Rangers' best pitcher in 1993, but a partially torn rotator cuff ruined his 1994 season. At first the Rangers had Pavlik pitch with the pain, with hideous results. Ultimately, Pavlik was shut down for nearly two months, although he did not have surgery. When he came back in late July, he was finally pitching well, and then the season ended. If Pavlik is throwing without pain this spring, he is a good candidate for a comeback. However his unorthodox, cross-body delivery puts a great deal of stress on his shoulder, and he could have additional problems with the rotator cuff. Even when healthy, Pavlik walks a lot of batters, relying on the strikeout to bail him out of a jam.

The remaining rotation spots are wide open. As for the organization's candidates to fill those spots, we turn to the Not Ready For Prime Time Players. Rookie righthanders Hector Fajardo, John Dettmer and Rick Helling combined for 30 starts in 1994, and they may be needed at the major league level next season as well. Fajardo is the most likely of the three to be in the big leagues in 1995, having nothing left to prove at the Triple-A level. Unfortunately, he has everything to prove in the majors. Fajardo relies on location and changing speeds, and was unable to fool big league hitters with any consistency. He yielded a homer every six innings, and had particular trouble with lefthanded batters. Fajardo is only 24 and could earn a rotation spot with a good spring, or even by default.

The big question about John Dettmer going into 1994 was whether he could handle the big jump to Double-A. That question was answered early in the season, as Dettmer continued the domination that he had displayed in going 26-4 in his first two pro seasons. Then the injury-ravaged Rangers decided to rob the cradle and bring Dettmer up to the big leagues. In his first big league game, Dettmer threw a career-high 137 pitches before losing in the ninth inning. He wasn't the same afterward. Though effective at times, Dettmer was more often overwhelmed. His chief asset had always been good control of an average fastball and slider. That control vanished with Texas, and Dettmer was hammered. His 4.33 ERA is deceptive; adding in unearned runs, Dettmer allowed seven runs per game. He needs a full year at Triple-A and even then might not recover from the damage caused by the Rangers' mishandling.

Rick Helling was the one rookie the Rangers counted on last spring. However, as we all know, you can't ever count on rookie pitchers. Helling was a monumental disappointment. After three decent starts, he fell completely apart. His out pitch, the slider, was high in the strike zone and the ball left the park with astonishing regularity (nearly 2.5 homers every nine innings). Helling was optioned to the minors to work things out, without success. At 24 years of age, Helling remains a solid prospect, and with a good spring he could make it back to the big leagues.

The most likely prospect to get a serious look with the Rangers next season is 22 year old righthander Julio Santana, who went a combined 13-9 at Single- and Double-A. Santana is a converted shortstop who has advanced quickly in his two seasons as a pitcher. He has an excellent fastball and changes speeds well, but needs to improve his breaking pitch. Had it not been for the strike, Santana would likely have spent September with Texas.

The Rangers paid Jack Armstrong $900,000 for his two starts in 1994, when tendinitis in his right shoulder ended his season. If he is healthy and willing to take a substantial salary reduction, Armstrong could resurface with Texas next season. It has been three and one-half seasons since Armstrong has pitched well on a consistent basis. He would probably fare better in the bullpen, but if he's with Texas, they'll probably need him to start.

Righthander Steve Dreyer's 1994 season ended in May with surgery to remove bone chips from his right elbow. Dreyer has been a control pitcher in the minors, but hasn't been able to throw strikes in two major league stints.

Faded lefty prospect Brian Bohanon had fallen so far on the Rangers' depth chart that he was the eleventh starter they used in 1994. He then went out and justified the Rangers' lack of confidence in him, getting tagged by opposing hitters at a .321 clip. The former first round pick was left off the 40-man roster last winter and went unclaimed. He did have a good year at Triple-A, but can't seem to make the jump to the majors.

How bad were things in 1994 for Texas? They signed Tim Leary in July. Leary had been cut twice by the Expos' organization when the Rangers located him, and after a two-inning simulated game, Leary had found a big league job again. After six appearances and an 8.07 ERA, he went on the disabled list with shoulder problems. Leary has virtually nothing left.

The Rangers' other pitching prospects in the high minors all have serious question marks. Righthander Duff Brumley followed an impressive 1993 with a miserable season in which he was tried as a reliever and then switched back into the rotation. Brumley had trouble controlling his slider, and needs another Triple-A season to get back on track. Righthander David Perez turned in a workmanlike season at Triple-A, but isn't highly regarded. The most effective Triple-A pitcher for Texas? Former Met and Oriole John Mitchell, who hasn't pitched in the major leagues since 1990.

Lary Bump:

David Perez is not overpowering, but he can spot his pitches. It took him three years to get out of Double-A, so expect another Triple-A season for him in '95. At Oklahoma City last year he was a workhorse (11-14-4.07-1.39). If he does make it to the majors, it could be as a reliever. He was an Arizona Fall League bust (0-6-5.63-1.58).

Duff Brumley was unsuccessful in a conversion to the bullpen during last season, and lost his slider and his control even after returning to the starting rotation. He finished at 3-6-5.51-1.69 for OK City.

Lefty Ritchie Moody went the other way with the 89ers, switching from relieving to starting for the first time as a pro. That experiment ended with an 0-5-6.00-1.69 record and rotator cuff surgery.

The disarray extended to Double-A. Chris Curtis led the Texas League in losses (3-13-5.36-1.61). Tulsa's ace was converted reliever Lance Schuermann. The lefty was 10-11-4.10-1.31.

The major league draft brought Francisco Saneaux from the Baltimore organization, where he was 4-12-6.54-1.77 in the Sally League. He's considered a live arm, and at age 21 he has time to improve on his 91 walks in 106 innings.

Toronto Blue Jays

With Dave Stewart and Todd Stottlemyre becoming free agents - and with both likely to go elsewhere - the Blue Jays are scrambling to find competent starting pitching behind Pat Hentgen and Juan Guzman. Stewart might really be finished at the age of 38 and coming off of his worst season since becoming a starting pitcher in 1986. Stewart will probably stick it out for another year (or part of a year) before calling it quits.

Stottlemyre can't seem to turn the corner and become the good pitcher everyone seems to think he can be. With a new environment and a new pitching coach his fortunes can change in 1995. More likely, however, Stottlemyre will continue his inconsistent ways and still be though of as an underachiever.

David Luciani:

Pat Hentgen is the ace of the staff and Juan Guzman is the number two man. Beyond that, the 1995 Blue Jays' rotation is very blurry.

Hentgen was en route to his second consecutive 19 win season when the strike hit. He was about to become the first Blue Jay to strike out 200 batters in a season. Early in the year, Hentgen set a new club mark for strikeouts in one game when he shut out the

Kansas City Royals on the strength of 14 strikeouts. At just 26 years of age, Hentgen could have his best season ever in 1995.

Before last season, Juan Guzman had posted a remarkable 40-11 record in his career and had a 3.28 ERA over three seasons. In 1994 he was terrible, recording a 5.68 ERA over 147 innings. He allowed 165 hits and his snails-pace motion betrayed him so much that 23 of 26 base stealers were successful against him. Guzman's 12-11 record was misleading in his favor as the Blue Jays gave him the best support of any pitcher on the team (6.20 runs per nine innings). It's clear that Guzman has reverted to the wildness which plagued him as a minor leaguer before 1991. The Jays can only cross their fingers and hope that he'll either throw hard enough to compensate for it or relearn the control he had from 1991-92. It may be that Juan Guzman isn't as good as everyone thought he was. If he ever gets his control together for an entire year, he will win a Cy Young Award.

Dave Stewart had announced plans to retire after 1994, but the strike soured his intentions and last October he found himself searching for a contract for 1995. Insisting that he would consider only Toronto or a job in Japan, he didn't seem to have any other options. The Jays' rotation, while thin, is moving towards youth now that the streak of winning seasons has come to an end. Signing Stewart to anything other than an incentive-laden contract would be a mistake. The fastball is still okay and the forkball sharp, but hitters now know when each is coming. His 5.87 ERA of last year combined with a 4.44 ERA from the year before doesn't promise great things. The end, unfortunately, may be now.

Todd Stottlemyre filed for free agency and it was hard to tell whether the Jays were interested. Stottlemyre is notorious for his temper tantrums and is therefore his own worst enemy on the mound. Where talk of great potential once dominated descriptions of him, we now see evidence that this mediocre pitcher may have spent his final season as a Blue Jay. Posting a 4.22 ERA in a pitching-poor year will cause the money to come but not likely from Toronto. They know him too well for that.

Al Leiter may also not be kept. The Blue Jays' front office's first priority is to improve the starting pitching and that means building a team around Pat Hentgen, Juan Guzman and three pitchers who weren't here last year. Leiter is wild and although still a hard thrower, he went just 6-7 in his 20 starts with a 5.08 ERA. His career to date, were it stronger, might have justified giving him another chance. More likely, he's headed elsewhere and may be close to an early exit from the major leagues.

Of the unknown starters on the Blue Jays, we will likely see Paul Spoljaric and Brad Cornett at some point in 1995. Both appeared with Toronto briefly last year (and both were ineffective) but Spoljaric has been presumed to be a starter of the future for the last couple of years. He will be offered another chance. Barring a free agent signing, you would see a 1995 rotation of Hentgen, Guzman and Spoljaric with the two best minor leaguers from spring training rounding out the field. More likely, the Jays will sign at least one free agent starting pitcher and it would not be at all surprising to see them sign two well-known starters.

Lary Bump:

Travis Baptist may have hit his ceiling in 1994, when he was an ordinary pitcher (8-8-4.55-1.45) on an ordinary staff. The lefthander will have to pick up his strikeout pace in his second Triple-A season to get a major league shot. Another lefty, Huck Flener, was shut down early after an 0-3-4.62-1.24 start at Syracuse.

Despite having a fastball voted the best in the Southern League, Jose Silva struggled last season (4-8-4.14-1.31) after starting in the Florida State League. The 21-year-old's status was clouded further by an off-season auto accident.

Chris Carpenter, a first-round draft pick out of high school, made his pro debut last season in the Pioneer League (6-3-2.76-1.36). His out pitch is a mid-90s fastball.

NATIONAL LEAGUE STARTING PITCHERS

Atlanta Braves

Marc Bowman:

The Braves pitching staff remains the best in baseball, headed by the best individual pitcher currently in the game - Greg Maddux. The excellent four man rotation of Maddux, Tom Glavine, John Smoltz and Steve Avery was made even stronger by the addition of swingman Kent Mercker as a fifth starter. The five starters combined to go 65-27 with a 3.14 ERA and 1.23 ratio. The success of the past few years means little will change for 1995.

Maddux pitched well enough to earn a third consecutive Cy Young award with his 16-6 record, 1.56 ERA and 0.90 Ratio; he was among league leaders in virtually every category. From a Rotisserie standpoint, Maddux by himself was often good enough to lift a pitching staff into the upper division. His season was worth almost $50 in most leagues, an incredible accomplishment for a pitcher. Because Maddux doesn't rely on just one pitch, he's likely to be more consistent than pitchers usually are. He has pinpoint control and throws several pitches with timing and precision; he rarely beats himself and has never been injured. Since his last losing record (in 1987), Maddux has gone 123-73 with a 2.74 ERA

over 1724.1 innings. More significantly, most of that record was earned while pitching for those lovable losers, the Cubbies (it takes a truly marvelous pitcher to win consistently in Wrigley). Maddux is the best pitcher in baseball and well worth the exorbitant price he'll command in Rotisserie drafts. One caution, however, should be heeded: it's unreasonable to expect Maddux will perform as well over an entire season as he did in four months of 1994. If you expect him to win at least 18 with a sub-3.00 ERA and a sub-1.10 Ratio, you'll be in the right ballpark.

Here's an interesting Rotisserie strategy involving Maddux. Because Maddux is often good enough to put a Rotisserie staff in the upper division in ERA and Ratio by himself, teams that draft him in 1995 can use him for three or four months to build good numbers (and sufficient innings pitched) then trade him to a team that is challenging one of their immediate contenders in ERA and/or Ratio. Even over a third of the season Maddux is enough to help that team beat your opponent; it's the equivalent of gaining one or two points for yourself and might help win a tight race. Of course you should be able to get a quality player or two in return and help yourself in other categories. The result will be excellent pitching that helps you in two categories, a chance to make a devastating late season deal to hurt an opponent, plus

whatever you can get in trade. Of course, you'll have to pay dearly for the opportunity, but it's something to think about for 1995.

The other Cy Young winner on the staff, Glavine had a slightly worse year in 1994, but was still a very successful and valuable starting pitcher. His ERA has steadily climbed since his 1991 Cy Young year, from 2.55, all the way up to 3.97 in 1994, but his four year ERA is still 3.05 over that period in 876.1 innings. Likewise, his Ratio has jumped from 1.09 in 1991 to 1.47 last year, but his four year Ratio is still a fine 1.26. Keep those averages in mind when bidding on Glavine in 1995 because he's likely to come back towards them next year. While Glavine's ERA and Ratio have been rising, they are still very good in relation to the rest of the National League. Also keep in mind that Glavine is 75-34 since 1991, an average of 19 wins per year. The presence of Maddux on the Braves staff may help bring Glavine's Rotisserie cost back into reasonable range. To take advantage of this you must purchase Glavine BEFORE Maddux comes up for bid; once Maddux is gone teams needing starting pitching will focus more attention on Glavine. Bid on Glavine with the expectation of 18 or more wins and 235 innings of 3.25 ERA and 1.30 ratio.

Smoltz suffered his first full season losing record in 1994, then finished the year by going under the knife to correct an elbow problem. His injury is particularly worrisome for two reasons. First, his delivery puts a lot of stress on his elbow; if he isn't completely healed or if he pushes his comeback too quickly he could suffer subsequent, and more serious, injury to the elbow. Likewise, in order to protect the tender elbow, Smoltz's delivery might change slightly and put unusual strain on other parts of his throwing arm or shoulder, leading to injury in those areas. Obviously, the opportunity for additional serious injuries are much larger than before.

Second, Smoltz has thrown a large number of innings at an early age. He'll be 28 years old in 1995, but has already thrown 1358 career innings in the major leagues after 377.1 minor league innings. Since turning pro in 1987, Smoltz has averaged 217 innings per season. Any way that you slice it, that's a lot of work

for a young arm. Pitchers who throw a lot of innings at a young age are much more predisposed to long term injury, and Smoltz may just be the next to break down permanently.

Reports on his surgery were good, but then such reports almost always are positive - when was the last time you heard a club report that surgery has gone badly? Wise Rotisserie owners will take a more cautious approach. Make Smoltz prove that he is ready to return at full strength. Watch the spring boxes to see if he is taking his regular turn and if he is throwing as many innings as Maddux, Glavine and Avery are alloted. Of course, pay some attention to the results, also, but an occasional bad outing isn't so important unless it becomes a chronic situation.

On the other hand the injury situation should help bring his price down and he is still likely to be a better than league average pitcher next year. He is probably going to receive more careful treatment in 1995 and won't be throwing complete games like he has in the past (such as his nine route-going performances in 1992), so 200 innings isn't guaranteed. Assuming he's fully recovered, count on a 13-10 year from Smoltz with a 3.80 ERA and a 1.25 Ratio over 200 innings in 1995.

Avery remains one of the best young lefthanders in the game, even though he had an off year in 1994. But look at that ''off'' year more closely. His 4.04 ERA was better than the league average of 4.21. His 1.20 Ratio was better than the league Ratio of 1.39. He won just eight games, but only 22 pitchers won more often in the strike-shortened season. If Avery, as a fourth starter, can be among the top thirty or so pitchers in wins, and be better than average in ERA and Ratio while giving a team 151.2 innings he must be a very valuable pitcher indeed. And that was in an ''off'' year.

Bidding strategy on Avery is the same as for Glavine. Get him before the top Braves' pitchers are gone. The 25 year old lefty has a lot of experience for a young pitcher and is poised for a breakthrough season in 1995. Twenty wins with an ERA near 3.00 and a Ratio near 1.10 in 230 innings are all well within reach

for Avery. Bid on him with the expectation of about 70% of those numbers you'll get a fine bargain. Among the Braves' front four starters, Avery is the most likely to be reasonably priced and be able to out-perform his salary.

Mercker's fine season in 1994 wasn't a surprise because of his good ERA and Ratio (3.45, 1.20), but due to his excellent pitching as a fifth starter. He began his rotational work with a no-hitter and continued to be very good all year. Still, his sudden transformation into a quality starter may not hold up over the course of a full season. He's really better as a reliever and should again make more appearances in that role in 1995. Don't be surprised to see him in the starting rotation occasionally next year, but Rotisserie owners should be very careful. He's the kind of pitcher that would be excellent for teams needing to take chances with their pitching. But, if you already have a good staff, stay away from Mercker. If he goes back to the bullpen for any length of time, he'd be a safe mid-season pick up, but his lack of innings in that role would mean far less value.

The most likely to join the 1995 rotation is 25 year old lefty Brad Woodall. He topped off an excellend 15-6, 2.42 campaign for Richmond with a start in Atlanta in place of injured John Smoltz. It was his first taste of the big leagues and won't be his last. Woodall throws hard enough and with good enough control to win in the majors, but his fine change-up is his bread and butter pitch. Woodall should eventually be a reliable starting pitcher, but he is to be avoided for Rotisserie purposes in 1995. Because he has a relatively high profile for someone with just one game of major league experience, Woodall could be overbid in many drafts. Besides, drafting Woodall violates the first rule of Winning Rotisserie Baseball - avoid rookie pitchers.

35 year old Mike Bielecki got a start in place of Smoltz, also, but he's primarily a long relief specialist at this late stage of his career. Outside of Woodall, no minor league starters are unlikely to grab a regular major league rotation spot and are therefore worthless for Rotisserie in 1995.

Triple-A Richmond's rotation included Mike Birkbeck (34 years old in 1995), Anthony Telford (29), Kevin Lomon (23), Brian Bark (26) and Chris Seelbach (22); Woodall and Bark were the lefthanders. Birkbeck and Telford are washouts from other organizations (Milwaukee and Baltimore, respectively) and had decent years but are well past the point where they can pitch effectively in the major leagues. They are injury insurance at Triple-A.

Bark had a poor season and was eventually sent to the bullpen. He needs an outstanding season at Triple-A in 1995 to get a major league chance. Lomon did well enough for Richmond, but allows too many hits with too few strikeouts; he seems to be the kind of pitcher who can beat up on Triple-A hitters but won't succeed in the majors. Still, he's only 23 so he's got time to improve. Neither Bark or Lomon are highly regarded prospects.

Seelbach is a better prospect. His 4-6, 2.33 half season for Double-A Greenville earned him a promotion to Richmond where he went 3-5, 4.84. A good year for Richmond in 1995 would give Seelbach a reasonable chance at the majors in 1996.

The best long term prospect is Terrell Wade, a 22 year old lefty who tore up three minor league levels in 1993 (combined 14-4, 2.44 ERA with 208 strikeouts in 158.1 innings, including an 18 K performance to end the season) then went 9-3 with a 3.83 ERA and a strikeout per inning for Greenville. A promotion to Richmond during the 1995 season is likely for Wade, with his major league shot coming late in 1996, assuming he continues his good pitching at higher levels.

Chicago Cubs

Stuart Shea:

Surprise! The Cubs have some real live arms in their starting rotation. How long has it been since anyone could say that?

Willie Banks came over from Minnesota for catcher

Matt Walbeck. The friendly and intelligent Banks has an outstanding fastball and a straight change-up as good as any in the National League (according to Bobby Bonilla, among others). Unfortunately, despite some excellent starts, he suffered a horrific string of bad outings later in the season in which he appeared to randomly lose concentration. His pitches frequently sailed all around the plate without getting near the strike zone. He's got uncommon talent, but needs help. Right now, he's a Rotisserie nightmare who allows a ton of baserunners.

In spring training, the Cubs dealt spare infielder Jose Vizcaino to the Mets for Anthony Young. Despite a terrible big league record and a well publicized record losing streak, Young is a gifted pitcher with excellent sinking motion on his pitches. He thrives when he can induce hitters to beat pitches into the dirt, and dies when his pitches stay up. Young did a good job in 1994, especially against righthanders, but missed the end of the season after tearing ligaments in his pitching elbow. He'll miss most of 1995, too, but when he returns he'll be a good low cost risk.

A Chicago area product (from suburban Evanston), Kevin Foster is a strange but tantalizing case. Despite piling up excellent minor league numbers, both the Mariners and Phillies gave up on him. The hungry Cubs, meanwhile, welcomed the hard throwing youngster into their rotation in June. By season's end, he and Steve Trachsel were the staff aces. Foster has an excellent fastball and a fine change-up, and he throws strikes. Most observers feel that he needs to add another pitch to be a long term success.

Largely unheralded, but surprisingly polished, Trachsel began the season by striking out a high number of hitters. As the year went on, he was inducing more batters to put the ball in play. Trachsel lacks overpowering velocity, but rides his fastball in on hitters and throws strikes. He allows plenty of homers, but fine Cub hurlers from Jenkins to Rick Sutcliffe have shared this tendency and won in spite of it. Not a power pitcher, Trachsel will survive if he can keep men off base. He doesn't have to overpower hitters, just continue to challenge them.

Converted shortstop Jim Bullinger has always had a live arm, but until 1994 hadn't shown any indication of controlling it. He flamed out as a closer, but seemed to find himself last year. He will probably open this season as the fourth or fifth starter. Bullinger will get his share of strikeouts and is improving his previously horrid control. He's an interesting late round pick; "Bully" is durable, strong, and still learning how to be a starting pitcher.

Whither Mike Morgan? The anticipated staff ace had a truly miserable year on all fronts in 1994. Both his parents were sick most of the season, he suffered migraine headaches and got his butt whipped on the mound. In reality, his fluky 1992 season probably won't ever be repeated, but Morgan could be a third or fourth starter if healthy. He is intelligent and durable, but can't survive without better location.

Frank Castillo is still around. He missed much of the year with a finger injury, but fared well in a minor league rehab assignment and made four late season starts with the Cubs. Despite some disappointments in his career, Castillo still has potential to be really good; he should be in the rotation again this season. His control is still excellent and he has a good mix of pitches despite lacking an overpowering fastball. Once a comer, he is already somewhat forgotten now, and so would make a good late round draft.

Oft-injured Jose Guzman made only four starts last year before heading back to the operating table for shoulder surgery. Whether he will return in 1995 is anyone's guess; he has thrown hard in the past, but was inconsistent even when healthy in 1993 and certainly can't be counted on.

Turk Wendell appears to have worn out his welcome in the Cubs organization. Despite problems in the Chicago rotation last year, wacky Wendell got just two starts with the Cubs even though he went 11-6 with a 2.95 ERA for Iowa. If he gets a chance with another team, Wendell could be a decent fourth starter. He's a finesse pitcher with fluctuating control and a good sinker. Wendell would make good trade bait.

There is little capable starting pitching in the minors. The rotation last year at Triple-A consisted mainly of Wendell, Larry Luebbers (6.04 ERA), Rafael Novoa (5.24), Blaise Ilsley (4.42) and Mike Anderson (6.14). The news was no better at Double-A, where highly regarded prospects Jon Ratliff and Derek Wallace regularly got their teeth kicked in and Amaury Telemaco, probably the best pitcher on the staff, came up with a sore arm. The Cubs' top draft choice in 1994, Jayson Peterson is obviously several years away.

Cincinnati Reds

Greg Gajus:

Jose Rijo (9-6, 3.08 ERA, 1.34 Ratio) had what is becoming a typical Jose Rijo year. He received the worst run support of any Reds starter, struggled with a tender elbow, and was one of the best starters in the league not named Maddux. One of the more interesting questions for 1995 is what the impact of lighter pitcher workloads in 1994 will have on their durability. If there is a sudden outbreak of healthy pitchers in 1995, someone like Rijo, who is overpowering when healthy (1.54 ERA during the second half of 1993), would rival Maddux as the best starter in the league.

John Smiley (11-10, 3.86, 1.30) bounced back nicely from a disastrous 1993. Smiley features very good control and good command of all of his pitches, but like many pitchers of this type he is vulnerable to the long ball.

Erik Hanson (5-5, 4.11, 1.30) was very effective until he injured a knee ligament fielding a bunt, ending his season. Hanson's curveball was devasting against National League hitters and he had the best control on the team.

John Roper (6-2, 4.50, 1.30) moved into the rotation after the injury to Tom Browning and did not disappoint, rolling off six wins to go with his 7-0 record for Indianapolis. Be cautious about Roper as a starter as his sparkling record was due in a large part to getting the best run support on the team (6.5 runs

per game). His strikeout rate (5.0 per game) was not very good, he struggled with lefthanders (.321 batting average) and he was vulnerable to homers. Roper will be a good major league pitcher eventually (he is only 23), but I would let another owner pay the price of his development pains.

Tim Pugh (3-3 6.04 1.80) is a candidate (again) for the fifth starter role that he won in 1994. A few atrocious starts and a stress fracture in his back (which Pugh tried to pitch through) ruined his stats, but he pitched well in the Triple-A playoffs.

Pete Schourek (7-2, 4.09, 1.46) was a pleasant surprise for the Reds. Signed after he was released by the Mets, Schourek began the season for the Reds as a lefty situational reliever but was moved to the rotation after the injury to Erik Hanson. He pitched extremely well as a starter, although he usually tired after the sixth inning. Despite his struggles with the Mets, Schourek is the type of pitcher you look for to suddenly increase in value - a lefthanded power pitcher that is young (26) and with a new organization after struggling. For 1995, he looks better than Roper.

Tom Browning (3-1, 4.20, 1.16) started out strong, completing two games (one more than he completed the previous three years) and teasing owners into thinking he might be back. Considering his previous two years, his age (34) and the nature of his injury (a complete fracture of his throwing arm) he is the longest of long shots.

Kevin Jarvis (1-1, 7.13, 1.53) received three starts after Hanson went down and is highly regarded by the organization after a strong season at Class AAA Indianapolis (10-2, 3.54).

CJ Nitkowski was the Reds top draft pick in 1994, and he pitched decently for Chattanooga after the college season (6-3, 3.50).

Mike Ferry, who was protected during the 1992 expansion draft, struggled at Indianapolis. He is a Bob Tewksbury type with extremely good control. Longshot candidates include lefthanders John

Courtright and Blaine Beatty (who was extremely effective for Double-A Chattanooga), and righthanders Terry Bross, Rick Reed and Scott Sullivan.

Colorado Rockies

David Smith:

The starting pitching for the Colorado Rockies is a lot like a bad haircut -with time it's going to get better. Two veterans who figured to help the team were duds. Mike Harkey (5.79 ERA) and Greg Harris (6.65) were both relegated to the bullpen for short stays, and Harkey was even demoted to Class AAA Colorado Springs. They're both gone for 1995, which means even though they were terrible, their 32 starts and 240 innings must be replaced.

The ace of the staff figured to be Armando Reynoso and he started off well enough, going 3-4 with a 4.82 ERA until he tore tendons in his pitching elbow in May and was lost for the year. Reynoso has the best righthanded pickoff move in the NL, so his off-season rehab will be crucial and not rushed.

The other potential staff ace was supposed to be David Nied. He improved in 1994 after a disappointing 1993 campaign when the top expansion draft choice hurt his arm. In 1994 he also had to deal with his wife's premature delivery of their son Tanner. Nied has matured and his 9-7 record with a 4.80 ERA showed it; a 4.80 ERA s good in Colorado. He gave the Rockies an important 22 starts and 122 innings.

The biggest surprise, however, came from the class clown, Marvin Freeman. Another former Braves' pitcher (Nied and Reynoso came from Atlanta, too), Freeman was acquired as a free agent after 1993 and became the fifth starter. He pitched into the sixth inning much of the time; his 10-2 record and 2.80 ERA were far better than any other starters posted. Freeman started 18 games and struck out 67 while walking only 23 - another ratio no other Colorado pitcher enjoyed.

Kevin Ritz filled out the rotation after Reynoso got hurt, and had his ups and downs. After spending much of 1993 rehabilitating an injured elbow, Ritz's 15 starts may be the ticket for him to return to prominence as a prospect.

The question now is, who will be the fifth starter? Assuming that Nied, Reynoso, Freeman and Ritz are one through four, GM Bob Gebhard is hoping that some of the Rockies' amateur draft choices will begin to pay off. The man on the fast track is Juan Acevedo, a righthander who was co-player of the year with the New Haven Ravens. Acevedo tore through the Eastern League with a 17-6 record, 2.37 ERA and 161 strikeouts against just 38 walks. At age 24, he has come out of nowhere, beginning 1993 as the fifth starter at Class A Central Valley; he would have been promoted to Denver in 1994 had the strike not intervened. He hits the mid-90s with his fastball and is worth a dollar or two investment.

The problem with this rotation is that lacks a lefthander. A lefty with experience, Lance Painter started a handful of games over last two years and may take Ritz's spot in the rotation. The next choice to be in a Rockies uniform in 1995 is Mark Thompson. He pitched nine innings of big league ball last year, surrendering eight walks and sixteen hits. Obviously he's got a long way to go but is just 23 years old (Rockies' management will give him plenty of time to develop). The road from Denver to Colorado Springs is so well travelled by Rockies' pitchers that Thompson will probably be up before the All-Star break.

Last, but not least is Doug Million, who made almost that much money as a first round draft pick out of high school. The 18 year old lefty is the top prospect in the organization, already throwing in the low 90s. He fanned 75 batters in just 58 innings with Bend (2.34 ERA) and will go at least to Class A Central Valley in 1995, maybe even as far as Class AA New Haven. Look for him to take the mound for the Rockies in 1997 at the tender age of 21.

Florida Marlins

Proceeds of the Bret Barberie trade: Jay Powell, a number one pick out of Mississippi State in June '93. He played on Team USA with future Oriole teammate Jeffrey Hammonds. So far Powell hasn't done much stat-wise, having produced two Class A seasons with mid to high 4's ERA, more than a hit per inning, and overall less than a 2:1 strikeout/walk ratio. But the Marlins love young pitching, and they love it in quantity. Figure Powell for arrival in 1996 or 1997. He has worked out of the bullpen, too.

Tony Blengino:

Part of the blame for the extensive injuries suffered by the Marlins' relief corps can be laid at the feet of the starting rotation, who averaged just 5.6 innings per start -- last in the National League -- after a 5.9 mark in 1993. The situation won't improve in 1994 as the starter with the most stamina, Charlie Hough, has now retired. Among the remaining Marlins' starters, only Mark Gardner has ever averaged six innings per start in a season, in 1991 while with the Expos. None of the rest of the current major league staff is likely to develop into a workhorse, either.

The most reliable returning pitcher, 27 year old Pat Rapp posted fine ERAs in the hitter friendly Pacific Coast League in 1992 and 1993 (3.05 and 3.43, respectively). Rapp has always handled righthanders well (.213 opponent average in 1994) and has had good control in the minors. But his lack of overpowering stuff has turned Rapp into a nibbler in the major leagues and his walk counts have mushroomed to 4.3 per nine innings. Young finesse pitchers without great stuff tend to have a very limited shelf life. Both Rapp's lack of stamina and ability to retire righthanders could shift him into a middle relief role eventually. For now, though, he's firmly entrenched in the Marlins' rotation and should have a peak season this year or next. Look for a 12-12 record with a 3.90 ERA in 1995.

The strike couldn't have come at a better ime for 29 year old Chris Hammond. As usual, Hammond had an outstanding first half and had spent most of the second half on the disabled list when the strike hit, thus eliminating his usual second half slump. Because Hammond relies on finesse, his change-up has been quite effective the first time around the league each year. Hammond's strength is his control, which has improved in each of his four big league seasons. Although he allows a lot of baserunners (1.43 career baserunner ratio), Hammond survives by minimizing homers, allowing just five in 73 innings in 1994, and by holding baserunners very well; just one runner stole a base successfully against Hammond in 1994. While his health continues to be a question mark he'll be in Florida's rotation for most of 1995, posting a 9-12 record with a 4.00 ERA.

During the first half of 1994, 25 year old David Weathers was the team's best pitcher, maintaining a sub-3.00 ERA into June during his first tour of the National League. The results were considerably different during his second trip around league, as is often the case with rookie starting pitchers. From the middle of June until the end of the season he was hammered and his ERA bloated to 5.27; Weathers allowed 11.07 hits per nine innings (opponents hit .306 against him). His frequent early exits were a concern to the Marlins and he relied almost exclusively on an average fastball as he lost confidence in his breaking stuff. Still, Weather's good start in 1994 after an excellent Pacific Coast League performance in 1993 indicates his potential; it's way too early to write him off yet. While he lacks star potential, Weathers should eventually settle in well at the major league level; he'll be 10-12 with a 3.95 ERA in 1995.

Bizarre injuries and flashes of brilliance mark 27 year old Ryan Bowen's history (he has more frequently been mediocre while with the Marlins). Bowen has a 90-MPH fastball but is just 15-28 with a 5.37 ERA in four major league seasons. Bowen has had a handful of dominating major league performances that continue to tantalize the Marlins and he'll be given yet another chance to make rotation in 1995. An even money gamble for the fifth starter spot, Bowen will go 5-9 with a 4.20 ERA in 120 innings in 1995.

Charlie Hough is to be commended for his work in a Marlins' uniform. In his mid-40s, Hough gave the

team more innings than any other pitcher and was a calming influence on the young Marlins' staff. An arthritic hip made pitching painful and Hough was forced to retire with a career 216-216 record. His leadership will be missed.

33 year old curveball specialist Mark Gardner filled in for both Hammond and Bowen when they were injured in 1994. Though he dazzled in his first handful of starts, his legendary vulnerability to the gopher ball did him in quickly. Over the last two seasons, Gardner has allowed an amazing 31 homers in 184 innings, with an overall 5.53 ERA. Gardner's breaking stuff is very tough on righthanders who hit .233 against him in 1994, making him somewhat of a long relief candidate. His days in the rotation are likely over.

Lefty curveball specialist Rich Scheid turned some heads with five very credible major league starts after his mid-season promotion. But, at age 30, Scheid is no young prospect. Even though he was rated by Baseball America as having the Pacific Coast League's best breaking pitch his major league future is dim. He's basically a poor man's Chris Hammond. He could win a relief role, his lack of a good fastball puts him behind Yorkis Perez and Vic Darensbourg in the Marlins' pecking order. It'll be back to Triple-A for Scheid in 1995 (for the seventh straight season).

The Marlins' first homegrown starting pitcher will likely be 1993 first round pick Marc Valdes. After signing late and only pitching ten innings in 1993, 23 year old Valdes rocketed through the ranks in 1994. After dominating at Class A Kane County early in the season, he skipped a level and jumped all the way up to Double-A Portland. A dropoff in performance after such a jump would be excusable, but Valdes was even more effective at the higher level, chalking up a 2.55 ERA and allowing only 77 hits in 99 innings. Overall, Valdes was 15-8, with a 2.72 ERA and 138 strikeouts with just 60 walks in 175 innings. Valdes is mature beyond his years; he doesn't strive for the whiff at all costs. He is content to spot his 88-90 MPH heater on the fringes of the strike zone, inducing grounders and conserving pitches in the process. Valdes could eventually be the workhorse the Marlins need; in 1995, he could win a spot in the rotation with

a strong spring. Look for an 8-8 record with a 3.75 ERA in 150 innings in 1995, with much better years to follow.

What's wrong with Kurt Miller? At the tender age of 22, he has already been the top pitching prospect in the Pirates', Rangers', and Marlins' chains. Through 1992, Miller was a power pitcher with better than average control. Over the last two seasons, Miller has regressed dramatically, walking 98 in 174 innings with just 77 strikeouts for Triple-A Edmonton since his acquistion by the Marlins. The small Pacific Coast League ballparks probably contributed to Miller's 6.88 ERA in 1994, but his precipitous strikeout decline is what worries the Marlins. Perhaps he is having arm trouble after throwing so many innings at a young age. Among Miller's four big league starts in 1994, one was brilliant and three were awful. Before he gets another chance, Miller will have to improve his control and show a return of his formerly good power pitching.

The Marlins' possible future closer, 24 year old Darensbourg left the bullpen (where he was dominant in 1993 at Class A Kane County) to join Double-A Portland's rotation. The lefty had mixed success, going 10-7 with a 3.81 ERA, 103 strikeouts and 60 walks over 149 innings. He improved dramatically over the course of the season, however, finishing the year with a one hitter. A little small to be a big league starter, Darensbourg will like return to the bullpen in 1995. He'll be a major league pitcher soon, quite possibly on Opening Day, 1995, as the Marlins number two lefty reliever.

One of the Expos' five first round draft picks in 1990, 26 year old Stan Spencer was pilfered by former Expos' GM Dave Dombrowski and added to the Marlins' roster via the Rule Five minor league draft in December of 1992. He has lost two full seasons to injury and is a finesse pitcher with pinpoint control (2.2 walks per nine innings in 1994). He doesn't have the upside potential of Marc Valdes, but Spencer is probably his equal at this point. Spencer will get a shot at a major league job in the spring but will go to Triple-A to start 1995. Spencer or Miller would be the most likely to receive a promotion early in 1995.

Marginal prospects Steve Long (25 years old), Mike Myers (26) and Matt Petersen (25) either struggled or were injured in 1994, but each was sent to the Arizona Fall League, so they still are highly thought of by the Marlins.

Javier De La Hoya, a former Dodger farmhand, went 0-7 for Double-A Portland. The righthander is now 25 years old. Following an excellent 1993 season, Reynol Mendoza allowed 73 baserunners in 37 innings in 1994 before blowing out his arm. Both are longshots at best.

The lower regions of the Marlins' chain contain many good prospects. 21 year old Will Cunnane had professional baseball's lowest ERA in 1994 at 1.43, allowed 133 baserunners in 139 innings while striking out 106 with 23 walks. He doesn't throw hard, though. Another 21 year old, Andy Larkin has struck out 214 with just 50 walks in two pro seasons, but has yet to pitch above "low" Class A ball. Over three pro years 21 year old Tony Saunders has struck out 170 with 54 walks but missed a large portion of 1994 due to injury. He bears watching as one of the few lefthanded starting prospects in the organization.

Houston Astros

Bill Gilbert:

The pitcher friendly Astrodome is usually a good place for Rotisserie League owners to look for starting pitchers, but in 1994, starting pitching was Houston's weak spot. Astros starters recorded an ERA of 4.11, only marginally better than the league average for starters (4.08). Doug Drabek and Shane Reynolds were the only starting pitchers with ERAs lower than the league average for starters.

After his disappointing season in 1993, Doug Drabek rebounded with a season (12-6, 2.84 ERA, 1.07 ratio) consistent with his five straight winning seasons in Pittsburgh before joining the Astros. His curveball regained it's former sharpness, his location was better and he was more effective in changing speeds. Drabek, now 32, was one of the top five starters in the

league in 1994 and he is likely to remain in this group in 1995. His arm is sound and his work habits and demeanor are exemplary.

Shane Reynolds began the season in the bullpen, but finished it as the team's second most effective starter (8-5, 3.05, 1.20). The key to Reynolds' success is a split fingered fastball that evokes memories of Mike Scott. Reynolds' other major asset is excellent control (21 walks and 110 strikeouts in 124 innings). His fastball is average in velocity, but his command allows him to paint the corners and get ahead in the count. At age 27, Reynolds faces a critical year in 1995. He needs to prove that his unexpected success in 1994 was not a fluke. The guess here is that he will do well again in 1995.

Pete Harnisch was the staff ace in 1993, but suffered shoulder problems early in 1994 and was ineffective. After a five week stint on the disabled list, 28 year old Harnisch came back with five strong starts before faltering in his last three outings. His 1994 figures (8-5, 5.40, 1.46) reflect his struggles in the early part of the season. When he returned his arm appeared sound and e was much more effective. Harnisch is not likely to repeat his 1993 success, but he should do much better than his 1994 totals. A reasonable expectation would be 14 wins with an ERA around 3.50 and a ratio in the 1.30 range.

Darryl Kile's breakout success of 1993 wasn't repeated in 1994 (9-6, 4.57, 1.59). Kile's biggest problem was control as he led the league by allowing 82 walks in 147 innings. He finished the season with four strong starts, including the last two without any walks. At age 26, Kile is facing a crossroads season in 1995. He throws hard and has possibly the best curveball in the league. He could still become one of the top pitchers in the game. The key for Kile is to achieve command both of his pitches and the confidence to throw them. Assuming he regains his self confidence, he should be a consistent winner and possibly a dominant pitcher for many years. He will probably be undervalued in 1995 based on his disappointing 1994 season.

Greg Swindell had his second straight disappointing

season after signing a four year contract with the Astros prior to the 1993 season. He had an encouraging start to 1994 with quality starts in his first five outings. However, he struggled for the rest of the year with only seven quality outings in his remaining 19 starts, including an abominable performance in the final game before the strike (when a win would have put the team on top of the National League's Central Division). He finished with an 8-9 record, an ERA of 4.37 and a 1.36 ratio, a record very similar to 1993. There is little basis for expecting improvement in 1995. Swindell has excellent control, but he has been hit hard over the past two years. He can't get his fastball past batters and he does not have another pitch that is good enough to get him out of trouble. Frequently criticized for being overweight, Swindell at appears to be on the downside of his career at 30 years of age.

Brian Williams started the season as the fifth starter, but failed to hold the job. He started 13 games, but only four of them could be considered successful. Williams is an excellent athlete with a strong arm. However, he has not developed the consistency and command of his pitches required to succeed in the major leagues. His 1994 record (6-5, 5.74, 1.95) is not good enough to keep him in the league. At age 26, he will face an uphill battle to get back in the rotation in 1995.

The Astros do not appear to have any strong candidates at the Triple-A level ready to move into the big league rotation. The ace of the Tucson staff in 1994 was 35 year old journeyman Craig McMurtry (8-4, 3.56, 1.21). Other starters on included veterans Eric Bell (31) and Mark Petkovsek (29), overachieving Donnie Wall (27) and Chris Gardner (26) who is attempting a comeback after arm problems. Obtained from the Yankees in the Xavier Hernandez deal, 26 year old Domingo Jean failed to make the major league squad in spring training and spent most of the season on the Tucson disabled list with arm problems. He is a question mark for 1995.

The club has some prospects further down the line. 26 year old Kevin Gallaher split time between Class AA Jackson and Class AAA Tucson and averaged over one strikeout per inning. Chris Holt and Doug Mlicki, both 23, had successful seasons for Jackson and should pitch at Tucson in 1995. Jim Lewis and Jim Waring, both 25 and recovering from arm problems, moved up from Class A Osceola to Jackson during the season and appear to be back on track. The club's brightest pitching prospect is 23 year old lefty Billy Wagner. The Astros' number one draft choice in 1993, Wagner led the minor leagues in strikeouts in 1994 pitching for Class A Quad Cities. However, he still gives up too many walks to be a consistent winner (8-9, 3.26, with 91 walks and 204 strikeouts while allowing only 99 hits in 153 innings). Wagner should climb rapidly through the organization and could have an outstanding major league career if he develops better command of his pitches. He could arrive by 1996.

Los Angeles Dodgers

The departure of Kevin Gross creates an opportunity for someone to move up. In mid December it would be premature to say who gets that job, but the significant fact is that Los Angeles is one of the few places where it's worth spending any time worrying about gets a fifth starter role. I like all Dodger pitchers, and the fifth starter here in 1995 can easily be a $2 gem. If you want to know how much Dodger Stadium helps a pitcher, ask Pedro Astacio, who had the 2.63 ERA at home and 6.31 on the road last year.

Note also that Dodger starters offer wonderful opportunities in leagues that allow you to set a weekly lineup; just pick the home starts for any Dodger SP and you get good numbers. Heck, in 1993 when Kevin Gross had a 4.14 ERA and a 1.47 B/I ratio overall, I got a 2.70 ERA and a 1.18 ratio from him by using the selective starts method.

Greg Gajus:

The Dodger quintet of Hershiser, Martinez, Candiotti, Astacio and Gross have made all but three of the Dodger starts in the last two seasons. This is unusual given that none of them are particularly overpowering and only Astacio and Martinez are younger than 33.

Their collective performances are also similar, with ERA's between 3.60 and 4.29, with parallel ratios and win totals between 6 and 12. Stability is a wonderful thing, but wholesale replacements may be necessary soon.

Orel Hershiser (6-6, 3.79 ERA, 1.39 ratio) is the veteran of the staff but, at age 36, can no longer be considered more than a league average pitcher. He is getting by on guile but was hit hard in 1994 - a .439 opponent slugging average - and lefthanders hit .297 against him. Be very wary if he changes teams in 1995 as almost every park is a better hitter's park than Dodger Stadium.

Ramon Martinez (12-7, 3.97, 1.27) is now the nominal ace of the staff, although he is not back to his 1990-1 form. He is still capable of dominating a game (he led the league in shutouts in 1994) but he doesn't show much consistency. The best run support on the team boosted his Won/Lost record.

Pedro Astacio (6-8, 4.29, 1.27) is 25 years old and is probably the safest pick in the Dodger rotation. He is young enough to improve, but right now he is another league average pitcher who will get his starts. Dodger Stadium protects you from too many really disastrous performances.

Tom Candiotti's performance (7-7, 4.12, 1.39) was damaged when he tried to pitch through a nerve injury that affected his back and shoulder. Knuckleballers often pitch into their forties, and Candiotti is entering the prime years for a pitcher of his type when/if he recovers from the nerve injury. Make sure he is pitching in spring training before making a bid.

It is hard to believe, but Kevin Gross (9-7, 3.60, 1.30) was the most effective Dodger starter in 1994. He had the best ERA, the best control, and of course got stuck with the worst run support of any Dodger starter (3.5 runs per game).

Should the Dodgers make some changes in their rotation, the most interesting prospect is 21 year old righthander Ismael Valdez. Starting the season in

Class AA San Antonio (55 strikeouts and only 9 walks in 53 innings) he was promoted to Class AAA Albuquerque (39 strikeouts and 13 walks in 45 innings) and then brought up to the majors (3-1, 3.18, 1.09). The Dodgers tend to be patient with their pitchers (Even Hershiser spent two years in Double-A and a year and half in Triple-A) so Valdez must be impressing someone to get such fast promotion.

Greg Hansell is a 24 year old righthander who had an excellent year at Albuquerque after a terrible year there in 1993. In 1994, he was 10-2 with a 2.99 ERA and a 3-1 strikeout to walk ratio in both starting and relief roles.

Ben VanRyn was the Dodgers top Double-A prospect in 1993, but failed in his first shot at Triple-A and was sent back to San Antonio where he was again effective. He is only 23, so he has time to develop.

The phenom of the Grapefruit League, Chan Ho Park was put into the rotation at Double-A San Antonio after he was sent down. He was moderately effective (5-7, 3.55 ERA) before being shutdown with a tender elbow. Park was rated as the tenth best prospect in the Texas League but given the massive cultural adjustments he must deal with in addition to baseball adjustments, another two or three years in the minors may not be a bad idea.

Longshot candidates include Brian Barnes, a former Expo curveball specialist and Kip Gross, who was injured most of the year after a good season at Triple-A in 1993.

Montreal Expos

John Perrotto:

All championship teams need a strong starting rotation. While the strike robbed the Expos of chance at championship in 1994, they certainly had good starting pitching. Few clubs have a more formidable trio than righthanders Ken Hill and Pedro Martinez and lefty Jeff Fassero.

Hill bounced back from a frustrating, injury marred 1993 to become one of the National League's top starters in 1994. He was 16-5 with a 3.32 ERA and a 1.222 ratio, prompting one highly regarded National League manager to claim Hill had the best arm in the league. Hill's injuries have always been to his legs rather than his arm, so there's no reason to believe he can't continue to be a big winner for years to come.

Speaking of pitchers who have the potential to be big winners, look no further than Martinez. The Expos drew heavy criticism following the 1993 season when they dealt second baseman Delino DeShields to Los Angeles for Martinez. Many observers felt Martinez was a good set up reliever but lacked the size or stamina to be a major league starter.

An 11-5 season with a 3.42 ERA and 1.106 ratio silenced those critics. Martinez throws hard and possesses one of the league's best change-ups. Furthermore, he isn't afraid to throw inside as evidenced by all the bench clearing brawls he incited last season.

Fassero was bothered by leg injuries last season but quietly had a very good year. He was 8-6 with a 2.99 ERA and 1.147 ration. Discarded by St. Louis, the White Sox and Cleveland, Fassero has blossomed under the tutelage of pitching coach Joe Kerrigan. He should continue to be one of the league's better third starters.

Lefthander Butch Henry proved to be a revelation last season. Cast off by Cincinnati, Houston and even pitching starved Colorado, Henry was promoted from the minors early last year and proceeded to go 8-2 with a 2.43 ERA and 1.090 ratio. The Expos have always had a knack for resurrecting pitchers' careers (such as Fassero's). Henry looks like the next Fassero.

Lefty Kirk Rueter isn't blessed with outstanding stuff but he finds a way to win. He went 8-0 as a rookie in 1993 then followed that up with a 7-3 season last year, though his ERA was high at 5.17 and his ratio was 1.397. Is he lucky or good? It's hard to say but it is very hard to knock a career record of 15-3.

The Expos are high on lefthander Gabe White and righthander Rod Henderson and gave both youngsters brief shots in the major league rotation. Neither did much in 1994 but still have loads of potential and should eventually become good major league starters. White was 1-1 with a 6.08 ERA and 1.479 ratio with Montreal last season and 8-3 with a 5.05 ERA and 1.438 ratio at Class AAA Ottawa. Henderson was 0-1 with a 9.45 ERA and 2.400 ratio with the Expos, 6-9 with a 4.62 ERA and 1.463 ratio with Ottawa and 2-0 with a 1.50 ERA and 0.750 ratio with Class AA Harrisburg.

Lefthander Carlos Perez, younger brother of former Expo Pascual, burst into prominence in 194 with a monster season. He was 7-5 with a 3.33 ERA and 1.437 ratio at Ottawa and 7-2 with a 1.94 ERA and 0.924 ratio at Harrisburg. He throws hard and his pitches have good movement. Though he needs to gain better command and polish his change-up, Perez has a chance to join the Expos' rotation this spring.

Another pitcher who could reach the major leagues fast is righthander Everett Stull, who was 10-10 with a 3.31 ERA and 1.320 ratio at Class A West Palm Beach. Stull's career seemed stalled in his first two pro seasons after being the Expos' third round pick from Tennessee State in 1992. However, he developed a slider and improved his change-up last season to complement his 96-MPH fastball.

Righthander Brian Looney made a meteoric rise from Class A to the majors in 1993 but had a so-so year with Ottawa last season, going 7-7 with a 4.33 ERA and a 1.608 ratio. He was also 0-0 with a 22.50 ERA and 2.000 ratio is a short stint with the Expos. He was probably rushed and needs another full year at Class AAA.

New York Mets

Pete Harnisch (again a free agent) offers a glittering track record and strong signs that he finished 1994 in near-perfect physical condition. Stat-wise, the most impressive fact is that he pitched with a 6-1 record after coming off the DL last year and had a streak of

five consecutive strong wins from June 30 through July 21. The problem that Harnisch had to overcome was a very sore tendon. Diagnosing and treating that problem ended the string of horrible outings that gave him a 7.15 ERA in his first nine appearances; and we can safely believe that just knowing about the problem now makes it near impossible that Harnisch will go out and suffer through another season with a 5.40 ERA. The party line, put forth by both the Mets and the Astros, is that Harnisch successfully found a way to reduce the strain on his arm by modifying his delivery slightly, and that change led to his good streak.

The facts don't quite support the theory that Harnisch was OK after his DL visit last year. In a curiously botched story, the AP reported at the time of his trade that Harnisch had a 2.61 ERA after June 30, to go with that 6-1 record. But in fact Harnisch had a 3.81 ERA with the 6-1 record after June 30. He delivered those five brilliant outings and then struggled three times, giving up 13 hits and five runs in 5.1 innings on July 26, six runs in 5.2 innings on August 1, and four runs in six innings on August 6; and those were the last three times we saw Pete Harnisch. Any pitcher can have three bad outings that mean nothing whatsoever, but when we are examining a pitcher who had a physical problem just recently cured, three bad outings certainly raise the question of a relapse. The bottom line is that I like Harnisch as comeback candidate, but I am not on the bandwagon of those who believe he has already staged that comeback.

The Mets have a long history of just coming up with good starting pitching every year. More intensely during the past ten years, this tendency has made Shea Stadium a good place to look for starters, partly because of the ballpark and strong scouting and emphasis on defense, but mainly because strong pitching breeds strong pitching: when one starter isn't going well, someone else comes along and takes his place. There is no better built-in safety factor with a starting pitcher, than the assurance that his field manager will remove him if he's going badly -- and that means both: remove him from the game on any given day and remove him from the rotation any week or month.

Just one year ago, the Mets didn't have even one starting pitcher who could have been considered a solid bet to have a fine 1994 season. Going into the 1995 season they have a staff with four who could be presented as solid bets. Bret Saberhagen has come back from two injury-riddled seasons to be strong throughout 1994, finishing on a particularly high note. Bobby Jones and Jason Jacome suddenly became two of the most successful soft-tossers in the majors, Jones coming off a two-win late season callup in 1993, and Jacome jumping from the minors to immediate major league success. Added to these three new arrival Pete Harnisch, and the Mets suddenly have a staff to challenge the whole National League, at least on paper.

Into this rosy picture I must interject some cautions. Saberhagen has in fact been OK physically in just one of the last three years. I would love to have him on my team, but I wouldn't assume he's sure to be healthy throughout 1995 just because his most recent season was his healthiest of the last three years. The fact is, he looked healthier three years ago and two years ago, and didn't deliver a full season's performance in either instance. Overall, I love the 11:1 strikeout/ walk ratio, the dominating fastball that can beat any hitter with its precise locations and various movements, and the tendency toward long, lofty streaks that can carry a team for two or three months. I just have observed that since 1989, when Saberhagen produced 262 innings, he has never gotten over 199 again.

The only thing wrong with Bobby Jones is that he has already pitched about as well as he ever will during his career. Jones has strictly mediocre stuff in terms of velocity and movement. He can just barely, and not consistently, get his fastball up near 90, and never blows people away.

What is remarkable about Jones, and what made the scouts love him even when he was in the minors and not throwing nearly as hard as his peers, is simple good sense. Almost every professional pitcher, including those who reach the majors with a ''slow'' fastball in the low 80's, must have been utterly dominant at some time in his past. Kids don't get pro

contracts by merely being in the top 10% of all scholastic athletes; they have to be outstanding. In the pitching profession, one of the major adjustments necessary to move up the career ladder is overcoming the temptation to get through a critical situation by reaching back for just a little something extra, and blowing just one pitch past one hitter. All too often, those temptations will produce a very hard hit ball off the bat of a developing professional hitter who is learning to recognize when a pitcher is about to make that mistake of overoptimism. Jones, according to many close observers, has never made that mistake even once, and that's the main reason he rose through the minors and became a major league success quickly. It is highly unlikely, however, that Bobby Jones will ever pitch in an All-Star game, because he's simply above-average.

Even more than Jones, Jacome is the type of pitcher who is going to have more trouble with hitters who get time to study him and learn his methods. Jacome has not yet been around the league twice. His best pitch is a changeup. His fastball clocks at only 82-85 MPH. Jacome has good control, a couple of good breaking pitches, and a superior knowledge of how to pitch. He is however the type of pitcher that I consider to be a trap for Rotisserians, because he has glittering stats that make him look dominant, which he isn't. Jacome can, and probably will, keep pitching at a high level in terms of good control and good smarts, but his stats just won't be the same after more hitters get used to him.

A major league fifth starter is usually not a good roster spot to be scouting for the purpose of filling your Rotisserie staff, and that rule applies to the Mets rotation for 1995. Often it puzzles me when people call and pay two bucks a minute to ask me the question, who's going to be the fifth starter on this team or that team, and the answer is, if you don't know (as in the case of Kent Mercker last year, everyone knew) then you don't want to know.

Last year the Mets used Mike Remlinger in their rotation after getting him as minor league free agent and watching him pitch well at Norfolk. Remlinger would really be better suited to middle relief work than to starting. His fastball (not the blazer he had as a number one draft pick, but the post-surgery comeback version) is good enough for the minors but not good enough for major league hitters who know it's coming. Remlinger had several starts in which he was very effective for four or five innings but then suddenly found hitters sitting on his fastball and having it timed perfectly. His presence in the Mets rotation last year was more a comment on the lack of alternatives, than a comment on Remlinger's revival. There may be a good short reliever here, but not a good starter.

Pete Smith, a free agent at the end of last year, was in the Mets rotation throughout 1994 (except for time on the DL in late July - early August). Once a bright prospect with the Braves, and at the time one of the rare exceptions to the rule that fifth starters never look attractive, Smith developed shoulder tendinitis, and that recurring condition has prevented him from advancing. Even with the severe pitching shortage of 1994, most teams wouldn't have kept Smith in their rotation when he was so inconsistent. The talent is good; when he's successfully keeping his curve and slider down, Smith can pitch a gem game loaded with groundballs. Too often, though, his fastball is BP material up in the zone, and that problem combined with the tendinitis makes him just plain unreliable.

Dwight Gooden was condemned to miss all of 1995 for drug violations, but Steve Howe's lifetime ban lasted only a few months. It would be a clever move to get Gooden for $2 on draft day and reserve him until 1996 if the suspension holds. When he comes back (very likely not with the Mets, but probably still in the National League) Gooden will again be valuable starter. He has come back from shoulder surgery and still has his big fastball and sharp curve.

Juan Castillo is the Mets' readiest minor league starter. He's likely to surface in the majors some time during 1995, and Mets rookies have an amazing way of doing well when they first arrive. Ask Jason Jacome.

Philadelphia Phillies

Tony Blengino:

In 1993, the Phillies' remarkable overall good health was underscored by the fact that their five primary starting pitchers accounted for 152 starts. Their good fortune was reversed in 1994, as only one Phils' starter pitched enough frames to qualify for the ERA title, and the team employed eleven different starting pitchers in a shortened season. Interestingly, the Phillies' starting pitching actually improved relative to the league in 1994; their cumulative 4.05 ERA ranked fifth in the National League and their 722 innings pitched ranked third.

The unlikely savior for the Phillies was lefty Danny Jackson. Due to an assortment of arm miseries since finishing second in Cy Young voting in 1988, Jackson was ineffective until 1994. Healthy again, Jackson used his trademark slider to strikeout three times as many batters as he walked (129 Ks, 46 walks - a career best ratio) and went at least six innings in all of his 25 starts. However, for the seventh straight season, Jackson allowed more than a hit per inning. pitched. A free agent at the end of 1994, Jackson presented the Phillies with a dilemma. While they would like to keep him in Philadelphia, owner Bill Giles is reluctant to sign pitchers to the kind of long term deals that Jackson will surely command after his 1994 season. Obviously their is suspicion that 1994 was Jackson's best and that he'll fall off next year. Expect 200 innings of 3.75 ERA and a 12-15 record.

After solid seasons in 1992 and 1993, and a dominating postseason performance in 1993, 28 year old Curt Schilling didn't appear to be quite right during spring training in 1994. This wasn't a big concern as Schilling is notorious for starting slowly. He said he was physically fine even as his woes continued into April. Unfortunately, it was not the case and although Schilling tried to pitch through the pain, he underwent mid-season arthoscopic elbow surgery, only to return shortly before the strike. He seemed to be completely recovered from the elbow problems, though, pitching a dominating complete game victory in his last start. Don't be misled by Schilling's final record of 2-8 with

a 4.48 ERA; this guy can still pitch. He owns a 90-MPH fastball and a biting slider, both of which weren't harmed by the surgery. Look for Schilling to rebound with a 15-9, 3.00 ERA season in 1995.

Tommy Greene's story bears some similarity to Schilling's. Like Schilling, Greene owns a 90-MPH fastball and hard slider, and won 16 games in 1993 while contributing to the Phillies pennant drive that year. Again like Schilling, he struggled in 1994 while claiming no physical problems only to eventually succumb to surgery. However, unlike Schilling, Greene wasn't able to return from surgery before the strike; he was scheduled to start August twelfth, the day the strike began, but instead remained on the disabled list. Greene has an extensive history of arm problems, most recently causing him to miss 20 starts in 1992. Greene's major league future appears to be in considerable peril. Watch his health closely. If he's back to full speed, Greene could go 10-10 with a 3.60 ERA, but if not he could quickly fade in 1995.

Jim Fregosi took a huge chance by inserting struggling reliever David West into the starting rotation early in June, 1994, but it paid off big when West led the National League with an opponent batting average of .205. It was a successful conversion despite West's 4-10 record (3.55 ERA). West's control isn't sharp enough for extended rotational success, though, as he has walked 112 in 184 innings with Philadelphia. Still, the Phillies will let West begin the 1995 season in the rotation. The best bet is for West to eventually return to the bullpen in a situational lefty role with a 6-8, 3.80 ERA season.

Obtained in an unpopular offseason trade with the Yankees, 27 year old Bobby Munoz began the year in the bullpen before being demoted to Triple-A where he began working as a starter. Munoz underwent a metamorphasis, mixing a good curveball with 90-MPH heat. He returned to Philadelphia, triumphantly posting a 7-5 record with a 2.67 ERA. It would be easy to get excited about Munoz's promising return, but some caution is required. Despite a huge 6'7", 237 pound frame and a hard fastball, Munoz has never been a big strikeout pitcher. The strike might have hidden a second half stumble as his

ERA climbed almost a full point during his second tour around the league. Also, Munoz has struggled with his control in past seasons and is very poor at holding baserunners (opponents stole 11 bases in 11 tries against Munoz in 1994). Overall Munoz's 1994 debut was similar to Ben Rivera's 1992 start. Expect Munoz to progress similarly, to a 6-10 mark with a 4.00 ERA in 1995.

The similarities between Munoz and 26 year old Rivera are indeed striking. Both are large righthanders who had big first year successes and perpetually struggle with their control. After a 13-9 season in 1993 (helped by a league leading 6.43 runs per game in support), Rivera hit the wall in 1994. The Phillies attributed his terrible start to a tired arm and farmed him out for a rehabilitation stint that was, in reality, an ultimatum to get in shape. Rivera returned shortly before the strike and finished at 3-4 with a 6.87 ERA. His 25-17 career record must make Anthony Young downright angry. Rivera will again challenge for a starting role but can't be expected to succeed. Expect a 5-8 season with a 5.00 ERA.

Viva Fernando Valenzuela. In a suspected publicity stunt, 34 year old Valenzuela joined the rotation when other starters were felled by injury and contributed seven highly professional starts, going 1-2 with a 3.14 ERA. He walked just seven batters in 45 innings and held opponents to a .274 OBP. But, Valenzuela should be added to the list of pitchers saved by the strike as his success was unlikely to continue. He started similarly for the Orioles in 1993 only to get bashed in his second trip around the league. The Phillies will likely invite him to Spring Training and he may actually win a spot. While Valenzuela could be effective in a middle relief/spot starter role, he would be a disaster in the rotation over a full season.

First round draft pick Tyler Green's stock fell precipitously in 1994 when he led all of professional baseball in losses (16) while posting a 5.56 ERA. Green's problems began in spring training when he lost his composure on the mound during a game. Fregosi was not amused and Green subsequently lost his spot in the starting rotation. His knuckle curveball doesn't work on hitters who know he can't throw it consistent for strikes; they prefer to wait on his hittable fastball. He'd be more effective in a relief role, where hitters would only get a look at his out pitch once, but the Phillies don't believe his arm can stand the strain of pitching so often.

24 year old Jeff Juden throws very hard. He began 1994 in the rotation but poor control caused a demotion and his control further deteriorated. A darkhorse candidate for the 1995 rotation, Juden has just two complete games in 128 professional starts, so he might be betters suited to the bullpen.

Dominating in two Triple-A stints before 1994, 26 year old Mike Williams struggled to a 2-7 record with a 5.79 ERA. He may have a future as a middle reliever.

Journeyman lefty Bob Gaddy had a decent year in Triple-A, going 9-12 with a 3.59 ERA; the 28 year old is a stopgap, injury replacement at best.

Former top draft pick Pat Combs has been 6-20 over his last two Triple-A seasons. He's now 28 years old and has no major league future.

The best of a mediocre crop of upper level minor leaguers is 23 year old Larry Mitchell. A fifth round pick in 1992, he struggled with his control for the first time in 1994, going 10-13 with a 3.97 ERA and 103 walks at Double-A Reading. Mitchell went to the Arizona Instructional League and could get a mid-season promotion if he continues to progress.

Pittsburgh Pirates

John Perrotto:

The strike didn't hurt the Pirates last season as far as dashing any post season hopes. However, they could have used the remainder of the year to sort out their young starting pitching.

The Pirates went into 1994 thinking lefthander Steve Cooke and righthander Paul Wagner were ready to

develop into a solid 1-2 punch in the rotation after they had good years in 1993, their first full seasons in the big leagues. However, both regressed. Cooke was 4-11 with a 5.02 ERA and a 1.248 ratio while Wagner was 7-8 with a 4.59 ERA and a 1.554 ratio. Cooke pitched in some bad luck at times but was also hammered at other times. The Pirates now question whether he will ever become more than a competent fourth starter. Cooke's out pitch is his curveball but his fastball is a little weak and he needs to be fine in order to win consistently. He is still just 24 years old and willing to learn. He might not win 20 in a season but he should be able to be consistently give the Pirates 200 innings per year.

Wagner is a puzzle and was dropped from the rotation following his first start after the All-Star break. He has a 95-MPH fastball and an outstanding slider. However, he has yet to grasp the change-up and batters eventually time his pitches because of his lack of off speed stuff. Wagner also becomes timid whenever he runs into trouble and often falls apart. At age 27, he can't be considered a kid much longer and he has to make a move this season. Follow his progress in spring training because he does not go to camp with the assurance of a spot in the rotation.

Righthander Jon Lieber had a good rookie season in 1994 and the Pirates believe he has the best chance of eventually becoming the staff ace. He began the season at Class AA Carolina (2-0, 1.29 ERA, 0.714 ratio) then quickly moved through Class AAA Buffalo (1-1, 1.69, 0.810) to Pittsburgh (6-7, 3.73, 1.298). Lieber has an outstanding, late breaking slider and a sinking fastball. He needs to develop a changeup but he has outstanding control and poise for a young pitcher. The only thing that might hold him back from becoming a consistent 15-to-18 game winner is that he does not place a great deal of emphasis on conditioning.

Lefthander Denny Neagle was a pleasant surprise in 1994 after two nondescript seasons as a middle and long reliever. Acquired from Minnesota as a rookie in the 1992 deal that sent 20 game winner John Smiley to the Twins, he blossomed after being handed a starting job late in the spring training. He went 9-10

with a 5.12 ERA and a 1.343 ratio in 1994. Neagle's best pitch is an outstanding changeup, something he could rarely use out of the bullpen. His fastball, curve and slider are adequate but the change keeps hitters off balance. Neagle is a bright guy and should develop into the kind of starter who will stick around for years because of his ability to outsmart hitters.

Righthander Rick White will also get a crack at a starting job this season after a whirlwind 1994. He was considered a non-prospect before dominating the Puerto Rican Winter League as a short reliever following the 1993 season. He had a big spring, began the season as the Pirates' closer, then was demoted to long relief before eventually moving into the rotation when Wagner was bumped. Overall, he was 4-5 with six saves, a 3.82 ERA and a 1.274 ratio. Though he debuted in the majors as a closer, White has an array of pitches wide enough to be a good starter. He has a live fastball, a decent curveball and slider and a developing change-up. White also isn't intimidated by major league hitters and never gives in.

Lefthander Zane Smith bounced back to anchor the Pirates' young staff in 1994 after having being hampered by shoulder problems the previous two seasons. He was 10-8 with a 3.27 ERA and 1.248 ratio, showing he was back to his old standards. Smith became a free agent at the end of last season and the cost conscious Pirates were trying to find a way to keep him. Smith, though, is a risk. He will be 34 on Opening Day and has now had both elbow and shoulder operations during his career.

After winning just four games over the past two years while suffering from elbow and shoulder injuries, lefthander Randy Tomlin was released at the end of last season. Though he won 14 games in 1992, Tomlin was 0-3 with a 3.92 ERA and 1.597 ratio with the Pirates in 1994, then 2-2 with a 5.30 ERA and 1.642 ratio for Buffalo. Many scouts felt Tomlin's early success was a fluke, the result of his motion across the body fooling hitters. They were probably right. It's extremely doubtful he'll ever reach double digit in wins again.

Righthander John Hope got the chance to take a regular turn in the Pirates' rotation during the final month of the 1993 season and he held his own. However, he spent most of last season at Buffalo, going 4-9 with a 3.87 ERA and a 1.210 ratio. He was also 0-0 with a 5.79 ERA and 1.571 ratio in a brief stint with the Pirates. The 24 year old Hope had elbow surgery early in his pro career, then had arthroscopic shoulder surgery last September. He is still young enough to come back but must be considered a risk until he proves he is healthy again.

The Pirates' post season rookie hero in 1992, knuckleballer Tim Wakefield saw his career continue its downward spiral in 1994. He spent the whole year at Buffalo and was 5-15 with a 5.84 ERA and a 1.676 ratio. The Pirates still hope he can regain the touch of his knuckler but it's starting to look pretty doubtful.

The Pirates are high on other pitchers in their upper minor league levels, most notably righthander Esteban Loaiza who rebounded from arthroscopic elbow surgery in November, 1993, to go 10-5 with a 3.79 ERA and a 1.292 ratio for Carolina last season. He throws 95-MPH with improving breaking and off speed stuff. One big plus: Pirates manager Jim Leyland fell in love with Loaiza while touring the minor leagues during the strike. Loaiza will start the season at Class AAA. However, he could be in the majors quickly if the Pirates have a need in the rotation.

Righthander Gary Wilson relies on changing speeds. He also emerged into prospect status last season. Wilson began the year 3-1 with a 2.31 ERA and a 1.286 ratio for Class A Salem, then was 8-5 with a 2.56 ERA and a 1.117 ratio for Carolina.

Without fanfare, righthander John Ericks wrote an amazing comeback story last season. He was St. Louis' first round draft pick in 1988 but was released in 1993 after a string of shoulder injuries. Healthy in 1994, he was 4-2 with one save, a 3.10 ERA and a 1.192 ratio for Salem, then 2-4 with a 2.68 ERA and a 1.070 ratio for Carolina. How well he progresses this season in Class AA or Class AAA will tell whether Ericks can get to the majors.

Righthander Mariano De Los Santos has a highly developed change-up for a young pitcher but he tends to throw it too often and at the expense of developing his fastball and slider. He was 7-2 with a 3.66 ERA and a 1.329 ratio for Carolina but just 2-6 with a 4.81 ERA and a 1.286 ratio after being promoted to Buffalo. He'll start the year in Class AAA but the Pirates are always looking for pitching and will keep a close eye on him.

Righthander Dennis Konuszewski had a solid season with Carolina, going 6-5 with one save, a 3.59 ERA and a 1.436 ratio. The Pirates thought enough of him to send him to the Arizona Fall League at the end of last season.

Righthander Brett Backlund was the Pirates' seventh round draft pick from the University of Iowa in 1992. He made it all the way to Class AAA that year and went to major league camp as the probable fifth starter in 1993. However, Backlund has never fully recovered from blowing his bid to make the big league club in 1993. He spent a second season with Carolina in 1994 and was 5-13 with a 3.61 ERA and a 1.320 ratio. Now off the fast track, he won't see the majors until 1996 at the earliest.

An interesting guy in the Pirates' system is a little lefthander named Roberto Ramirez. He was on the 40 man roster and in the major league camp last spring, though he spent most of the season in the Mexican League. He was once a jockey in his native Mexico but impressed the Pirates last spring and was 0-1 with a 5.27 ERA and a 1.704 ratio in a brief stay with Carolina.

St. Louis Cardinals

For years I have been telling people that Danny Jackson was overrated (because of his Cy Young type season with 23 wins and 2.73 ERA in 1988) but now he's come back strongly from the Chicago disaster and established himself as a proven veteran. And he's in the good side of my ledger for being a lefty, for being able to throw hard, and for pitching in St. Louis, overall a fine package. There is a trail of

progress worth noting. First is the combination of good luck and better conditioning, which have helped overcome a horrendous injury history. In addition to groin and abdominal muscle pulls, he had shoulder, toe, wrist and forearm woes during his bad season of the early 1990's. The other big part of the good news is that as Jackson leaves Philadelphia, he takes the Johnny Podres changeup with him. Jackson is now far enough removed from the long-ago huge season, and also past the postseason glories which inflated his price in too many auctions. Still, the biggest problem is that he will be frozen in many auctions; lots of astute owners got him for about $5 a year ago.

John Perrotto:

The Cardinals' starting pitching was a mess in 1994. The bad news is that the ace of staff could be gone when 1995 starts.

Right-hander Bob Tewksbury, who has become one of the National League's most consistent pitchers in recent years, became a free agent at the end of last season. With he Cardinals historically reluctant to give out big free-agent contracts, there was no guarantee Tewksbury would be back. He did not have a great season last year, going 12-10 with a 5.32 ERA and 1.362 ratio, but he was better than anyone else the Cardinals.

Without Tewksbury, the Cardinals would have been a team without any ace without the addition of Jackson. The Cardinals have long been high on the potential of left-handers Rheal Cormier, Donovan Osborne and Allen Watson and right-hander Omar Olivares. However, all four come into 1995 as question marks.

Cormier, a control specialist, had his 1994 season ruined by muscle pulls in his back and was 3-2 with a 3.71 ERA and a 1.185 ratio. Osborne, who won 21 games in his first two major-league seasons of 1992-93, missed all of 1994 after undergoing shoulder surgery.

Osborne has the ability to become the Cardinals' number one starter but no one knows for sure if he'll be healthy by spring training. Cormier could be the type to win 10-12 games a year but his health is also in question. Keep on an eye on both during sprig training.

Watson started his major-league career with six straight wins in 1993 but is 6-12 since. Last year, he was 6-5 with a 5.52 ERA and 1.582 ratio. He shows signs of greatness but must begin gaining consistency. He is just 24, though, and has great poise. He is a good bet to turn into a big winner.

Olivares is an enigma. He has talent and pitches well at times. Other times, he looks like he has no business being in the major leagues. Last year he was 3-4 with one save, a 5.74 ERA and 1.643 ratio with St. Louis and 2-1 with a 4.37 ERA and 1.340 ratio for Class AAA Louisville. Olivares and Cardinals manager Joe Torre don't get along well. Almost everyone agrees Olivares needs a new start in another organization to reach his full potential.

A pitcher with an outside shot of making the rotation is right-hander Vicente Palacios, who was 3-8 with one save, a 4.44 ERA and 1.249 ratio last season after spending 1993 in the Mexican League. He pitched better than his record indicated but he will go to the bullpen unless many of the Cardinals' younger starter flop.

Three other young pitchers who could wind up in the Cardinals' rotation at some point in 1994 are right-handers Alan Benes, John Frascatore and Brian Barber.

Benes was the talk of the Cardinals' farm system last season, one year after being the club's top draft pick from Creighton. Benes, younger brother of San Diego ace Andy Benes, began the season by going 2-0 with a 1.48 ERA and 1.167 ratio in four starts with Class A Savannah. He then was 7-1 with a 1.61 ERA and 0.897 ratio in 11 starts with Class A St. Petersburg, 7-2 with a 2.98 ERA and 0.955 ratio in 13 starts with Arkansas and 1-0 with a 2.93 ERA and 0.933 ratio in two starts with Louisville.

The Cardinals' grand plan is to have Benes spend the first half of 1995 at Louisville, refining his off-speed and breaking pitches, then joining the major-league rotation around the All-Star break.

The Cardinals love Frascatore's arm and brought him to the majors last season for one July start, which he lost. He was 7-3 with a 3.10 ERA and 1.167 ratio with Arkansas and 8-3 with a 3.39 ERA and 1.353 ratio with Louisville.

Barber, a prized prospect, suffered a groin injury early last year and suffered through a miserable season. He was 4-7 with a 5.38 ERA and 1.471 ratio with Louisville and 1-3 with a 3.25 ERA and a 1.306 ratio with Arkansas. He is just 22, though, and has been very impressive during outings in major-league exhibition games the past two springs.

One member of the Cardinals' '94 rotation that won't be back is veteran right-hander Rick Sutcliffe. He was 6-4 with a 6.52 ERA and a 1.847 ratio before undergoing shoulder surgery. Though 38 and a free agent, Sutcliffe vowed that he will return to the major leagues again. Someone might give him a shot but he doesn't appear to have anything left.

One prospect that could be ready by 1996 is right-hander Jay Witasick, the Cardinals' No. 2 draft pick in '93 from Maryland-Baltimore County. He was 10-4 with a 2.32 ERA and 1.036 ratio for Class A Madison and has a live fastball with great movement. He injured his back midway through last season but did nor require surgery.

Right-hander Blake Stein, the Cardinals' sixth-round pick from tiny Spring Hill (Ala.) College last year, had an impressive debut with short-season Class A Johnson City. A finesse pitcher who has a wicked split-finger, Stein was 4-1 with a 2.87 ERA and 1.133 ratio.

Right-hander Matt Arrandale was one of the top pitchers in the minors last season, going 15-3 with a 1.76 ERA and 1.000 ratio for Savannah and 3-4 with a 3.05 ERA and 1.288 ratio for St. Petersburg. Despite those numbers, most scouts do not consider Arrandale a prospect because of a below-average fastball.

San Diego Padres

Fred Matos:

Righthander Andy Benes is one of the best pitchers in the National League. Already an excellent pitcher, the Padres are trying to improve his effectiveness even more by having him change speeds more rather than relying solely on his fastball. They could really improve his effectiveness by improving his supporting case; he could become a 20 game winner with a good team. Overbid in many leagues last year, Benes' 6-14 record could turn off a lot of bidders this year. Projected for 15 wins a 3.44 ERA nd 1.22 ratio a year ago, Benes didn't earn his projected $16 salary. But, he is noted for a strong finish and could have come close had the strike not prematurely ended the season. In 1995, Benes could again be worth $16 or even $20 should he get any help at all from his teammates.

After failing miserably in previous trials with the Phillies and Padres, Andy Ashby was one of the biggest surprises in the National League last year. He had always displayed talent, but just hadn't learned how to pitch until last year when he perfected a change-up to go along with his excellent fastball and curve. His deceptive 6-11 record pales beside his 3.40 ERA. Ashby allowed 145 hits in 164 innings while fanning 121 and holding opponents to a .233 average. Now 27, Ashby looks like he has finally arrived, but he has the bad luck of playing on a building team that can't give him enough support.

Talented rookie Joey Hamilton pitched well after a promotion from Triple-A. He has the necessary poise plus an excellent sinking fastball and a good changeup, but his breaking ball may need further refinement. It was written last year that the Padres expect him to be the staff ace in a few years, but don't forget that Hamilton is a rookie, and rookies tend to struggle; even Roger Clemens struggled in his rookie year. Hamilton will likely be highly overbid, and those who acquire him at inflated salaries may regret it. Remember

Benson's First Rule of Winning at Rotisserie: Avoid rookie pitchers.

Statistical wizards who analyze strikeout to walk ratios, hits per inning pitched, strikeouts per inning pitched, and opponent batting averages will likely identify Scott Sanders as being on the verge of a great season. He showed some flashes last year, but mostly struggled before spending time on the disabled list with a rib cage injury. His 4.78 ERA and 4-8 record should drive most Rotisserie players away, but Sanders is a real sleeper. He could fill out your pitching roster very nicely as a cheap fourth or fifth starter. Don't expect a lot of wins in 1995, but his other stats could be very helpful.

The Padres were expecting a good season from young hard-throwing Tim Worrell, but he was felled by serious elbow ligament damage. It may be several years before he can return to his previous form.

Starter/reliever Wally Whitehurst was in the rotation until he came down with bone chips in his elbow that required surgery and a long stint on the disabled list. He was often hit pretty hard, allowing 84 hits in 64 innings. But it's hard to tell how just how much was bad pitching and how much was due to Whitehurst trying to pitch while hurt. He has been reliable at times for the Mets and Padres but is not good for Rotisserie purposes.

Veteran Bill Krueger filled in for the injured starters, but has little left at age 37. He might hang around as a lefty reliever but is not in the Padres' long range plans.

A number of major league teams once saw great potential in Scott Chiamparino, but he always ended up with one kind of injury or another. He pitched effectively in Triple-A in a comeback attempt last year and may have earned another shot in the majors. Like other rookie pitchers, he should be avoided.

Should minor leaguers Kerry Taylor, Doug Bochtler, Mike Campbell, Denny Harriger or Hilly Hathaway reach the majors they are to be avoided at all cost. Pacific Coast League managers rated Taylor as the second best pitcher in the league; he may have some potential but it would be wise to let other Rotisserie owners take that risk.

San Francisco Giants

Steven Rubio:

The Giants' rotation has several question marks as 1995 approaches. Billy Swift has applied for free agency, Bud Black has been released and John Burkett is now in Texas while young Salomon Torres presents one of the more puzzling problems for the team, both now and for the future.

John Burkett does not look anything like Jimmy Key (he is a righty, and he uses a pitching motion which exposes his background as a bowler), but his stat lines are quite similar to Key's. Burkett has excellent control and has already won 20 games once in a season. Burkett could capable of winning 20 games again, if Texas improves its defense.

Mark Portugal had a solid first season for the Giants in 1994, which went mostly unnoticed as the team struggled. A fine third starter who may have to be the second starter this year, Portugal should continue his fine pitching in 1995.

After the Burkett and Portugal the rotation gets dicey. William VanLandingham was the biggest surprise of the season last year for the Giants, showing maturity beyond his years and winning even when he didn't have his best stuff. He is far from established, however, and must be considered a prime candidate for a fall in 1995. Having said that, VanLandingham has proven he has the head and the arm to pitch successfully in major leagues, and is likely to have a fine career in the majors, albeit with occasional ups and downs.

Salomon Torres is quite simply the most puzzling player the Giants have had since the days of Mike "Poison" Ivie. Torres could be the best pitcher in the Giants' organization, and at times he pitches as if this were true. At other times, however, he seems to fall

apart on the mound, losing all sense of purpose. Unfortunately, these lapses are more frequent thus far in his major league career than his high points, and he is likely to continue to both frustrate and amaze the Giants and his fantasy owners for years to come. With unlimited upside and unlimited downside, Torres is the surest definition of a player suited only for the most risk taking of fantasy owners.

Bill Swift is currently a free agent. Should he return to the Giants, he will be their ace, as he has been for the past three years. Swift is an outstanding pitcher who should succeed wherever he pitches, but as an extreme groundball pitcher he is especially susceptible to a weak infield defense. If he winds up with another team he may not be as successful as the Giants have been one of the National League's better defensive teams in recent years.

Trevor Wilson is still around. He is well liked by teammates and fans, but he's hurt pretty much all the time. He's not worth the risk for fantasy owners, although he could pay off for the Giants.

In the minors, Dan Carlson has pitched well for two years in Class AAA; while he's not a future star, he would seem to be capable of solid pitching at the major league level even though the Giants seem curiously hesitant about promoting Carlson.

A better choice is Joe Roselli, perhaps the best pitcher in the Giants' system. Roselli has come back slowly from an old arm injury, but should be pitching well at the major league level within two years.

Steve Whitaker could surprise if he masters his control, an area in which he was much improved in 1994. Doug Vanderweele already has fine control, and could aspire to the level of a John Burkett, but must be considered a longshot. Edwin Corps was pitcher of the year for Class A San Jose and could be a good one farther down the road. Jamie Brewington led the Giants' minor league pitchers in strikeouts and is another name to place on your "futures" list.

RELIEF PITCHERS:
TACTICAL CONSIDERATIONS

Saves create more anxiety than any other statistic. Why? In the first place, they are darn scarce -- twice as scarce as wins by pitchers (every game produces a win, but only half produce a save). If you think about 30 saves being worth as much as 60 wins by a starting pitcher, you begin to get a concept of just how much value gets packed into an ace reliever. Another major factor is that saves tend to be concentrated in one player on each major league team. Imagine one pitcher being the "designated winner" and you begin to get a feel for the desire to know all managerial decisions before they occur. Finally, there is the well-published fact that saves correlate highly with winning Rotisserie leagues. Research indicates that this correlation is not exactly a cause-and-effect type of correlation. Having the most saves doesn't make a team win. But having saves and winning definitely go together. The reason is that people who win are people who appreciate saves and know how to get them. Accordingly, the saves category is very often the front line in battles between the toughest contenders, both on draft day and during the season.

The types of questions that I get about saves tell a lot about the path to success in the saves category. Only rarely does anyone call me before draft day and say, "I need a big saves guy; please suggest one or two." Much more common is the question, "Who are some good, hard-throwing middle relievers and setup men who might be in line for some saves later in the season?" That question of course reveals the winning method to get saves: whatever else you may do with your pitching staff, invest some money in potential future saves. The leverage is great.

About the only time I ever find smart owners suffering in the saves category is when a novice owner trades away his ace reliever(s). Such deals upset the smartest owners the most, because they appreciate saves and the dumb owners don't appreciate them. Other than having a League Entrance Exam in which all prospective owners are required to write a 500-word essay on The Value of Saves, the only way to avoid this type of problem is to keep talking continuously to every owner about his saves, so if and when he gets ready to throw away his aces, you can be there.

In terms of draft day, my message is basically one of good news: there is one calming thought that I bring with me to the draft every year in every league, to help alleviate the fear of being left with no saves: there will be 1200 saves in the major leagues this year. The average major league team will generate 43 saves, and many below-average teams will exceed the average of 43. Weak teams have fewer blowout victories than strong teams; often they have more narrow victories, and thus more saves. Weak teams are also more likely to lack depth in the bullpen and therefore keep going to the same guy over and over in save situations.

For draft strategy, I recommend that choose one of two paths well in advance:

(1) Pay the price for a top established closer, if you have the luxury of affording one, or

(2) Invest heavily in potential; five top setup men at $5 apiece can be a cheaper route to 30 or 40 saves, than paying $40 for a top ace and $10 more for a couple of hopefuls.

Making this decision before the draft will enable you to focus on more detailed aspects of your budget, after settling this one issue, which will very often be your biggest single decision in draft budgeting.

For 1995 I lean somewhat toward a "pay the price" strategy, because 1994 was such a bad year for high-price relievers (Duane Ward, Dennis Eckersley, Bryan Harvey, Mike Perez, Xavier Hernandez, and more). Bottom line is that 1994 was a year when a lot of people got burned following the pay-the-price strategy, so fewer people are going to be going that way in 1995.

For the Record:

Likely to be bargains: Bobby Ayala, Armando Benitez, Billy Brewer, Roberto Hernandez, Steve Howe, Ken Ryan, Toby Borland, Ricky Bottalico, Hector Carrasco, Trevor Hoffman, all Pirates at $1 apiece, Todd Jones, Pedro A Martinez, Yorkis Perez, Mark Wohlers (still just a kid), Todd Worrell.

Likely to be overvalued: Rick Aguilera, Steve Farr, Mike Henneman, Rene Arocha, John Hudek, Bruce Ruffin, Joe Grahe, Randy Myers.

AMERICAN LEAGUE
RELIEF PITCHERS

As always, relief pitchers are a volatile bunch. The number of established closers who lose their jobs, become injured or retire seems to be going up each year. From the end of the 1993 season to winter of 1994 there was bullpen turnover for no fewer than eight AL teams with several of the remaining closers losing at least a share of their full-time closer roles. The prognosis for 1995 is more of the same. New closers will be in place in Baltimore (Armando Benitez), Boston (Ken Ryan), California (Lee Smith), Cleveland (Paul Shuey, perhaps), New York (Steve Howe), Texas (Darren Oliver, perhaps), and Toronto (Duane Ward returns). Turnover could also occur in Detroit, Minnesota and Oakland as the established closers for those teams may move on. Only in Chicago (Roberto Hernandez), Kansas City (Jeff Montgomery), Milwaukee (Mike Fetters) and Seattle (Bobby Ayala) is there any likelihood of stability entering the season.

Among the remaining free agents who are realistic closer candidates, Dennis Eckersley stands out. But, he's close to the end of his long career and must be considered a risk. Nearly all other free agent relievers are unremarkable bullpen filler who are unlikely to garner more than a few saves; the best exception is Joe Boever.

For Rotisserie owners, the challenge and the opportunities have never been greater. With only a handful of closers likely to get 30+ saves, the value of established closers has never been higher, but the challenge of identifying those closers is more acute than ever before. Paying top closer dollars to a guy who is replaced in mid-season is a sure way to lose.

On the other hand, the number of $1 relievers who pay huge dividends will be larger this year than in any season in recent memory. Saves in Cleveland, Detroit, Milwaukee, Oakland and Texas are almost certainly going to be spread around (assuming that Eckersley doesn't return to the Athletics). Any one of three or four candidates with each team could earn a dozen saves. The opportunity and challenge here is to identify the otherwise unknown relievers who have the best chance to get those dozen saves.

Baltimore Orioles

Free agent Lee Smith signed with the Angels, officially signifying that Armando Benitez is the front-runner for the majority of save opportunities in 1995.

Free agent Mark Williamson remained unsigned, but the Orioles are said to want to re-sign him.

Williamson's role is middle relief and he has usually been a steady, if unspectacular reliever.

Fred Matos:

Lee Smith had a tremendous first half last year, but began to fade after the All-Star break, blowing saves and posting an ERA of 8.53. He appeared to be both overused and running out of gas at the All-Star break. Smith doesn't have much of a fastball anymore, getting by with forkballs, sliders, and good location. American League hitters finally began to solve him about mid-year, and it is doubtful if Smith has another good season left in his arm, but he has surprised people before. Smith has signed with the California Angels.

Alan Mills and Armando Benitez are now the top candidates for closer. Mills tried to be another Lee Smith last year, but he was crushed in a few relief outings early in the season and was disappointingly inconsistent overall, uncharacteristicly for him. Nevertheless, he still has a shot at the closer role if Benitez is found to need more minor league experience.

Benitez was promoted from Double-A to the Orioles at mid-season, and promptly began to pitch like an established veteran. His fastball has been clocked as high as 98 mph, and his poise and outstanding stuff make him a leading candidate for the Orioles' closer job. Benitez was sent back to Double-A after the strike, but looked like an entirely different pitcher than the ice-water-in-his-veins reliever that pitched so well for the Orioles. He was cocky and careless, and looked very immature. New Orioles' skipper Phil Regan has 10 years experience managing in Venezuela and other winter leagues, so he may be the ideal manager for the young fireballer.

The Orioles can use an effective lefty reliever as Jim Poole was inconsistent, even against lefthanded hitters who hit .421 against him. Poole was in a catch-22 situation where he needed more work to regain the location on his pitches, but the Orioles couldn't let him pitch to regain his location because he wasn't effective. If he finds his location, Poole can have a good year.

Sidearmer Mark Eichhorn had a very good year as a setup man for closer Lee Smith. He was tough on lefthanded batters, holding them to a .181 average. Pitchers like Eichhorn can be very good for a number of years, but can lose their effectiveness quickly.

Mark Williamson has to fight for a job every year, as the Orioles usually omit him from their plans. His consistently solid pitching usually prevails over some erratic rookie. Williamson throws a fastball and a palmball, and he will continue to be effective if he still has the fastball.

Brad Pennington sadly discovered that his fastball, outstanding as it is, just isn't enough to win in the majors. The discovery occurred when he grooved his best one to Ken Griffey, Jr. with the bases loaded, and Griffey blasted a prodigious home run. Pennington was immediately shipped to Triple-A. He said that he has to learn how to trick people.

Joe Borowski, Steve Chitren, Tom Wegmann and Jim Dedrick are the minor leaguers with the best chance of pitching for the Orioles sometime in 1995. Borowski quietly did a very good job sharing the closer's job in Double-A with the more publicized Armando Benitez. Borowski is a big, hard thrower who has averaged more than one strikeout per inning in his minor league career, a very positive sign.

Once considered the heir-apparent to Dennis Eckersley, Chitren appeared in 56 games for the A's in 1991. But a back injury in 1992 caused a loss of velocity, affecting his progress. The A's eventually gave up on him, and he was selected by the Orioles in the Triple-A portion of the Rule V draft. He spent last year in Double-A as a middle reliever trying to recapture his speed and effectiveness.

Tom Wegmann shared the closer's job at Triple-A Rochester last year, getting eight saves in the process. It was his second full year in Triple-A. His best chance of making the Orioles is as a middle reliever, but the competition is tough.

Jim Dedrick's minor league roles have been long and middle relief. He has been a solid pitcher, and could

break into the majors in 1995, if not with the Orioles, then with another team.

Boston Red Sox

Steve Farr has retired after getting much more from his limited talents than might otherwise be expected. After his worst major league season, Todd Frohwirth has joined the Pirates via a minor league contract. He can help the Pirates as a veteran reliever on a young staff.

Replacing Frohwirth in the Red Sox pen could be free agent signee Bill Wertz. The former Indian righthander lacks outstanding stuff but has always managed to make his limited skills go a long way. Like Farr, he just gets people out. Wertz won't have much Rotisserie value but will still help the Red Sox.

Righthander Ricky Trlicek has been released and is still a free agent. Control problems helped push Trlicek back as far as Double-A last year and have plagued the 26 year old throughout his career. If he returns to the majors it would be in a long relief role.

Alan Boodman:

For the first time, Ken Ryan begins a major league season as the official closer. All indications are that he knows what to do with the responsibility. Ryan put together a very fine season in 1994, despite occasional outbursts of inconsistency, and is poised to place himself among the elite closers in the league.

Ryan is a large fellow who throws reasonably hard, but control had been a minus up until last year when he walked fewer than three men per nine innings, a significant step forward from his previous efforts. The Sox' bullpen is neither deep nor talented, therefore Ryan will have little initial competition for the closer's job. He is capable of reaching 30 saves with an ERA under 3.00, and he doesn't demand a Montgomery or Aguilera-type bid as of yet. However, the fact that Ryan is fairly young (26) and has yet to perform in the role of closer for a full season carries a certain amount of risk, so bid accordingly.

Chris Howard and Tony Fossas were the one-trick lefthanders in the Sox' bullpen. Fossas, now 37, specializes in retiring lefties only, his control has never exactly been tremendous, and his mistakes tend to be hit with authority. If used properly (i.e. sparingly), his ERA may be acceptable, but Fossas has never posted as many as three saves in a season. His value to a fantasy league team is non-existent.

Howard, age 29 and like Fossas a late arrival to the big leagues, showed in 1994 that he can pitch successfully to hitters on either side of the plate. His star potential isn't good, but Howard fared well last year in a protected role, and may do better in a slightly larger assignment in 1995. He probably won't hurt your ratio or ERA, but will still pitch relatively few innings, and isn't likely to garner more than five saves unless Ryan flames out.

With likely free-agent defections from Todd Frohwirth, Jose Melendez, and Sergio Valdez, and the retirement of Steve Farr, the number two righthanded relief spot could go to Cory Bailey. Bailey, 24, has so far received little chance to prove himself at the major league level, but has closed with success everywhere he's been in the minors. A full season in Boston in a long relief role would start him out on the right track, but such a role limits his value Rotisserie-wise. Keep one eye on Bailey for 1996 and beyond.

Rick Trlicek has pitched well for brief periods in the past, but was destroyed in Fenway in 1994. At age 26, Trlicek has plenty of time to figure out what's gone wrong, but until he does he will continue to bounce through the minors, making only sporadic appearances at the major league level. No fantasy value, obviously.

Jose Melendez will long be remembered as the man for whom Phil Plantier was thrown away. Melendez was in line to be the closer in 1993 (over Jeff Russell) before a spring training injury sidelined him for nearly the entire season. Relegated to the minors for most of 1994, Melendez displayed acceptable control but was hammered regularly. He fared even worse in a brief recall to Fenway, and became a minor-league free agent last winter. The Sox will smartly cut their

losses with this guy, but Melendez may resurface somewhere, although probably not with an important role. Let him re-prove himself for a year or two before jumping back on the bandwagon.

Steve Farr announced his retirement last year after an injury-filled and ineffective final season in 1994. He was acquired from Cleveland for Jeff Russell and was expected to at least share the closer's position with Ryan, but Farr never really recovered from his ailments and was frequently bombarded. His career still went a lot farther than most expected.

Todd Frohwirth was kept around last year as insurance, but the policy turned out to be worth very little when it came time to pay off. He's now 32, and did pitch well most of the time for Pawtucket. Frohwirth was a free agent, and has been counted out numerous times before, only to come back surprisingly strong. He has at most one such comeback left, and it won't be in Boston.

Sergio Valdez seems to spend a part of most seasons at the major league level. Like Frohwirth, Valdez performed ably at Triple-A in 1994, only to become an arsonist in the majors. He broke into the bigs at age 20, so he seems older than his 29 years, but has time to catch on somewhere. Valdez has been vulnerable to the gopher ball at all levels and is not a candidate for an expanded major league role no matter where he turns up.

Jeff Pierce is a relief pitcher with excellent control who split the 1994 season between New Britain and Pawtucket, throwing well at both stops. He's 26, rather old to just be reaching Triple-A, but should be the closer there if Cory Bailey sticks with the big club. Pierce might get a look in 1995 at some point, but will have to perform well to stick as he is not high on the prospect list.

Marc Bowman:

Drafted from the Indians, 28 year old Bill Wertz has had four straight excellent years in the mnors but has never been a closer at any level. The righthander posted a 3.14 ERA for Triple-A Charlotte in 1994 while fanning 60 batters in 66 innings. Wertz has a good chance for a regular role in Boston's bullpen in 1995.

Righthanded curveball specialist Heath Haynes was drafted from from the over-stocked Expos system. While the 26 year old Haynes was exclusively a reliever at Triple-A Ottawa (6-7, 4 saves, 2.38 ERA), he may get a shot at the rotation in 1995; Haynes career record is now 29-9.

Righthander Joe Hudson was a middle innings guy at Double-A New Britain, going 5-4 with no saves and a 3.92 ERA. The 24 year old Hudson has decent control, but unremarkable stuff.

California Angels

The Angels have drawn an ace and a wild card with their winter signings. Lee Smith and Mitch Williams will both have a chance to get saves for California's bullpen in 1995; first Smith, then possibly Williams.

At age 37, Smith may no longer have what it takes to be a regular closer. He was clearly not the same pitcher near the end of last season and was routinely hit hard by opponents. Caution is the watchword with Smith for 1995. Even if he starts the season in good condition he could quickly fade before mid-season.

Can Williams find the strike zone? Probably not. Will it matter? Maybe not. Williams has ''succeeded'' as a closer by throwing hard, not by throwing with accuracy. He has the wildness to walk the bases full, but the velocity to then strike out the side. Angels fans will likely see a little of both from Williams in 1995.

Taken in small doses Williams can be valuable both to the Angels and to Rotisserie owners. Keep in mind that Lee Smith may not keep the closer job all year. Williams could have it by the end of the season; he would be a fine late-round selection to fill out your pen. Williams is a must for anyone who owns Smith. Sure, Williams walks a LOT of batters, but he doesn't pitch enough innings to do very much damage to your Baserunner Ratio. As long as he can get some saves

he has positive value. On the down side, Williams value would disappear should his role change even slightly, say to a set-up role. Also, even if he finishes 1995 with the closer job it's unlikely that he'll keep it; the Angels are grooming Troy Percival for the job.

After one of the worst seasons by a closer in recent memory, Joe Grahe has left the Angels to sign a minor league contract with Colorado. Grahe's signing is more of an insurance policy against further flame-outs by the Rockies' closers than a sign of increased saves by Grahe. In 1994, Grahe posted an unreal 6.65 ERA with an equally unreal Ratio of 1.98. At that rate he'd have to get at least twenty saves to stay above zero for Rotisserie. It was a season reminiscient of, well, Mitch Williams' struggles with various other clubs.

Lefty Ken Patterson remained an unsigned free agent and could turn up anywhere. Being lefthanded will help the 30 year old Patterson return to the majors.

Righthanders John Dopson and Jeff Schwarz have both been released. They are marginal major league pitchers at best and their big league future is dim. 31 year old Dopson has failed both as a starter and as a reliever. 30 year old Schwarz is an eleven year minor league journeyman who will continue his minor league journeys in 1995.

Hank Widmer:

While the Angels' starters were underproductive, the bullpen was an arson squad. Without exception (well, maybe Bob Patterson) a trip to the Angels' pen was sure doom, and doom is what anyone felt if any Angel relievers were on their fantasy team.

Fred Matos:

With Joe Grahe, Mike Butcher and a cast of thousands all coming up short, the Angels were unhappy with their bullpen, especially the closers. Trade talks to acquire a top closer were held with other teams, and the cheap Angels were so desperate that they were even considering acquiring Tiger closer Mike Henneman and his big salary.

But the answer to the Angels' closer problem is in their minors. Top prospect Troy Percival had elbow surgery in 1993, but he is now a much stronger pitcher than before undergoing the knife. He throws a mean fastball at 98 MPH and dominated the Pacific Coast League the latter part of last season. The Angels and a lot of Rotisserians have been waiting for Percival's arrival for several years, and he is highly likely to take over the closer job sometime in 1995.

Angels sources told me that they are still looking for an ace closer for 1995 to groom Percival for the closer role for 1996. They believe that Percival is just not quite ready despite his overpowering stuff.

The Angels' plan for the bullpen for 1995 includes Troy Percival, Grahe, Patterson, Springer and Leiter. Joe Grahe's role is middle relief and setup, and the idea of converting him to a starter has been shelved. Russ Springer is an inconsistent starter and reliever swingman who has struggled in the past, but has a very good arm. Veteran Mark Leiter is a good long and middle reliever, and veteran Bob Patterson is the southpaw setup man and situational reliever.

Last year's cast of thousands included Mike Butcher, Craig Lefferts, John Dopson, Scott Lewis, Jeff Schwarz, Bill Sampen, and Ken Patterson. All except Butcher and Schwarz have been either released or are free agents that the Angels do not plan to sign. Butcher is inconsistent because of control problems with his curveball, and Schwarz is a Triple-A pitcher, at best.

For Rotisserie, Troy Percival looks like the reliever to acquire in 1995, but he will be well known in most leagues and will likely be overbid. If the Angels acquire an aging closer like Lee Smith for the transition year before Percival becomes the closer, the bids on Percival will be much lower and he should be acquired for a big payoff in 1996, or maybe in 1995 if the old closer falters.

Marc Bowman:

At age 26, righthander Erik Bennett is behind Troy Percival (and others) in the bullpen pecking order

despite another good year in Triple-A (2.81 ERA, 83 Ks in 90 innings, 3-to-1 K/BB ratio).

Twenty-eight year old righthander Ken Edenfield had his best season above A-ball in 1994 with a 3.38 ERA and nine wins in a team-leading 51 games for Triple-A Vancouver. Edenfield struck out a batter per inning but is not a highly regarded prospect in California; if he reaches the majors it will be in his accustomed long relief role.

A better long-range prospect might be Bill Simas, a 23 year old righthander. After leading Class A Lake Elsinore in saves (13 with a 2.11 ERA), Simas earned a short stint at Double-A Midland. For both clubs he showed remarkable control but doesn't have the overpowering fastball usually desired in a closer. Simas might reach the bigs as a situational/long-relief type in a couple of years.

Chicago White Sox

Serviceable lefty Dennis Cook left the White Sox via free agency to signe with the Indians. With Scott Radinsky's continuing rehabilitation from Hodgkin's Disease, the re-signing of lefthander Paul Assenmacher becomes even more necessary for the White Sox. Until Radinsky returns in full force, Assenmacher would have some Rotisserie value in the White Sox' pen, getting an occasional win or save in a set-up role.

Righthanded 34 year olds Jose DeLeon and Kirk McCaskill remained unsigned free agents in late-December. One of them might return to Chicago in 1995 and would pitch in middle relief. DeLeon has recently gotten his wildness under control and can give the White Sox and Rotisserie owners a small value. Forced out of the starting rotation, McCaskill was successful in a set-up/middle relief role. In a full season McCaskill could manage a sub-4.00 ERA with a useful Ratio and a handful of saves and wins. He'll need to re-sign with some team during the winter - his back-up sport, hockey, is also experiencing some labor pains.

Aging lefty Atlee Hammaker returned from the dead to make two appearances for the White Sox in 1994. He has re-signed with the White Sox and will fill a long relief role in 1995, assuming the 37 year old can still pitch in the big leagues.

Isidro Marquez has re-signed to a minor league contract.

Stuart Shea:

Despite an ugly string last season in which he lost the closer's job, Roberto Hernandez is still the Sox' go-to guy. He still has killer stuff and fine control, and should rack up another 30-35 saves this year, especially if his supporting cast is around to get him to the late innings.

Paul Assenmacher's contract was bought out in October, but the Sox are said to want him back as insurance policy for recovering lefty Scott Radinsky. Assenmacher is still a valuable and durable pitcher, and could be a closer if necessary. Radinsky, diagnosed after the 1993 season with Hodgkins' disease, spent last year taking chemotherapy treatments and staying in shape. He is expected back, but even when healthy had control problems. He is durable and before his illness had terrific heat.

Dennis Cook helped some from the left side, but he was waived in October and claimed by Cleveland. Atlee Hammaker made an unlikely return from years of injuries, and will come to camp this spring with hopes of landing a job. Don't expect much.

Chicago still needs some help from the right side. Kirk McCaskill was occasionally effective in the setup role last season, but had some poor stretches. He loses effectiveness after the first few hitters, and can't claim to have good control. Jose DeLeon is finding success in middle relief, where he can dominate in stretches, but won't help a fantasy team much. He won't expand his role. Dane Johnson, a second-round Blue Jays draftee in 1984 who spent 1990-92 pitching overseas, came up for awhile but showed that he hadn't conquered his career-long control problems.

There isn't much "relief relief" in the minors. Onetime Dodger prospect and Mexican Leaguer Isidro Marquez had a good season at Triple-A in 1994, but he's fringy at best. Undrafted 1991 free agent Chris Woodfin pitched extremely well at Class-A Prince William and just as well in a stint at Double-A Birmingham late in the year. He's a strikeout pitcher despite an average fastball and is worth watching.

Marc Bowman:

Twice a minor league Rule Five draftee, 30 year old Matt righthander Matt Karchner had good control for Birmingham and Nashville in short and middle relief roles. He'll contend for a job in the White Sox bullpen in 1995, but won't pitch in critical situations, so he won't have any Rotisserie value.

Cleveland Indians

With Gerry DiPoto gone in trade to the Mets, Jeff Russell sent packing as a free agent, Derek Lilliquist signed as a free agent by Atlanta, Bill Wertz signed as a free agent by Boston and Matt Turner still out due to a cancerous thyroid, the saves picture for Cleveland is extremely muddled. Rookie Paul Shuey is said to have the inside track, but his hold on the job is hardly set in cement. Eric Plunk, Jose Mesa, Dennis Cook and others will also get some chances to close games for the Indians, a team that could win 100 games in 1995.

Russell remained unsigned and won't be back with Cleveland. He could go to any team as late as the final few weeks of spring training and would have a credible shot at saves wherever he goes. Russell's value is only for any saves he might get, though, as his pitching ability is quickly disappearing.

Mesa has re-signed with the Indians, getting a two year contract with options for two more years. Mesa has successfully converted from a mediocre starter into a useful, high-innings reliever. Due to his ability to pitch often and for several innings, Mesa can get a fair number of wins with a respectable ERA and Ratio. He's a good bet to earn more than the $1 that

smart Rotisserie owners will ante up for him in 1995.

While Larry Casian and Matt Turner have both been released by the Indians, the two are headed in entirely different directions. Casian will find a new team in 1995 and be lucky to get major league work. Turner will be re-signed by the Indians in hopes of his eventual rehabilitation. Turner can pitch and will get another chance with Cleveland in 1995. Since his return is unpredictable his value is nil to start the season.

Veteran lefty Cook re-joins the Indians as a free agent signee after a good year in middle relief for the White Sox. He'll have a similar role for the Indians and could be good for a half dozen wins with a good ERA and Ratio. He'll be worth slightly less than Mesa, but still more than $1.

Tony Blengino:

For the second straight season, Eric Plunk was the unquestioned savior of the Indians' bullpen. Unlike Russell, this guy had a tough job. Plunk, 31, pitched 71 innings in 41 appearances (including several longer than three innings), inherited 42 baserunners (only nine scored), while holding righties to a harmless .171 average. As in 1993, he struck out better than a batter per inning pitched, despite mediocre control. For some reason, Hargrove went to great lengths to avoid using Plunk as his closer, opting for Farr, Russell and Paul Shuey at various points in the season. Like Russell, Plunk became a free agent at the end of the 1994 season. Unlike Russell, he is still a desirable commodity to the Indians' organization. Look for him to return to Cleveland, and get his share of save opportunities as the Paul Shuey experiment begins in earnest. Plunk should be good for 8-5, 3.20 and 10 saves.

Shuey, 24, was the Indians number one 1992 draft pick (number two overall). He was drafted as a starter, but was shifted to the bullpen early in the 1993 season. His fastball has been clocked at 95 MPH, and once he becomes sufficiently confident to challenge big league hitters consistently, he will become a dominant closer at the major league level. Shuey took

...major league trial in 1994, notching an ... le giving up 26 baserunners in 12 ... being recalled directly from Single-A. ...s then dispatched to Triple-A Charlotte, where ...e dominated, allowing 25 baserunners in 23 innings, while whiffing 25 and saving 10. Shuey will get first crack at the major league closer job in 1995. Expect him to endure some more growing pains, but manage to go 3-2, 3.85 with 20 saves.

What should you do with a righty starter who throws hard, but loses it in about the sixth inning each time out? You either farm him out, or hope his stuff proves more effective in smaller doses out of the bullpen. The Indians tried the latter with Jose Mesa, with reasonable success. Like Plunk, Mesa was utilized often and in difficult situations. He was second in the AL in appearances (51), relief innings pitched (73), and inherited baserunners (46). After posting a 285/236 strikeout/walk ratio in his previous pro career, his mark improved to 63/26 in 1994. Mesa held righties to a .244 average, and appears headed for a decent shelf life as an adequate middle reliever. Look for 6-6, 3.85 in 1995.

Derek Lilliquist, 29, has been the token lefty out of the Indians' pen since 1992. Lilliquist was routinely thrown into the fire by Hargrove, inheriting 38 baserunners in only 29 innings pitched. He has become increasingly hittable with each passing season; in 1994, opposing batters hit .304 against Lilliquist, with righties batting a mighty .356. While he still overmatches lefties (.205 in 1994), he has become nothing more than a one-batter pitcher.

Lilliquist's struggles set the stage for the acquisition of fellow southpaw Larry Casian from the Twins. Casian made Lilliquist look like Bruce Sutter in his prime. Check out these numbers: 89 baserunners allowed in 49 innings, including 12 homers; a 7.35 ERA; and an opposing batting average of .356 and slugging average of .613. It's a mortal lock that, despite his hideous 1994 campaign, Casian will somehow latch on with somebody in 1995. Don't touch him.

Jerry DiPoto, 27, was the early line favorite to become the Indians' closer in 1994 before being sidelined after the removal of his cancerous thyroid gland. In truth, DiPoto wasn't that great prior to his illness. His 1993 save total (11) obscured a below average ratio (1.5). DiPoto has fully recovered physically, but was clearly not the same pitcher in 1994. After experiencing moderate Triple-A success, he was strafed in Cleveland, giving up 36 baserunners in 15 innings, with opposing batters raking him at a .406 clip. His power and control are both marginal for a reliever and his opportunity to grab the closer role has seemingly passed. He'll be hard pressed to make the club in 1995, and won't pitch in important situations if he does.

Righty Matt Turner, 28, was obtained from the Marlins for Jeremy Hernandez on the eve of Opening Day 1994. Within three weeks he had been diagnosed with Hodgkin's Disease. The Indians waived Turner during the strike so that he could receive his 1994 salary in full. This is no charity case, either -- the guy can, and will, pitch for the Indians. He had a superb season setting up Bryan Harvey in Florida in 1993, and held righties to a .205 average in his brief tenure in Cleveland. Don't be surprised if a fully-recovered Turner emerges as a valuable middle reliever in Cleveland in 1995.

Calvin Jones, 31, is a forkball specialist who has been a serviceable minor league closer in his two years in the Indians' organization. He could help the Tribe in a pinch, but he appears headed back to Charlotte in 1995. Bill Wertz, 28, did a commendable job in a 34-game stint with the Indians in 1993 before returning to Triple-A as a setup man in 1994. Despite only average velocity, Wertz always manages to strike out nearly a batter per inning. He would make a fine tenth man on a major league staff -- a spot starter/long reliever who will take the ball often.

Pep Harris, 22, was converted from a starter to a closer in 1994, and turned in an excellent season split between Single-A Kinston and Double-A Canton-Akron. Harris earned 20 saves, allowing only 30 hits (but 29 walks) in 53 innings. Harris could open the season as the Triple-A closer, and a similar

performance could earn him a midseason promotion. Harris probably doesn't throw hard enough to be a dominant major league closer. Travis Driskill, 23, was the Indians' fourth-round pick in 1993. He became the closer at Single-A Columbus, racking up 35 saves, striking out 88 in only 64 innings. He relies on a curveball and slider, as he possesses only a slightly above average fastball. His repertoire will be sorely tested by hitters at higher levels, but his progress bears watching.

Marc Bowman:

Lefty Dennis Cook settled into a middle relief job for the White Sox in 1994 after a couple of years as a spot starter/reliever for the Indians in 1992-3. Cook was fairly successful (3.55 ERA), and has a chance to win a bullpen job in 1995. He's not a big strikeout pitcher and is equally successful against righthanders and lefthanders. He would probably be better suited to middle relief than to a set-up or closer role. At 32 years old, Cook isn't going to suddenly blossom into a closer.

Acquired in the off-season from the Cardinals were a pair of set-up candidates, 26 year old lefty Steve Dixon and 27 year old righthander Willie Smith. Dixon throws hard enough to succeed in the set-up role and had a fine season at Triple-A Louisville in 1994 (11 saves, 2.52 ERA); he has fanned a batter per inning in two-plus years at the Triple-A level.

Smith was a speculative closer pick for some NL Rotisserie players in 1994, but instead led Louisville with 29 saves and posted a 2.31 ERA. Smith has been compared to Lee Smith; he also throws hard enough to win a set-up or closer spot. However, 1994 was his first year as a primary relief ace, so his chances to close for the Indians in 1995 have be considered slim at this point.

Detroit Tigers

Joe Boever, Storm Davis and Greg Cadaret remained unsigned free agents late in December. Davis and Cadaret have little chance of getting saves and are mostly useless for Rotisserie. Palmballer Boever could get ten saves in the right situation or he could return to his accustomed set-up role. e has Rotisserie value in either case and is a recommendation as a $1 selection.

Veteran minor leaguer Mike Christopher has re-signed a minor league contract with the Tigers.

Fred Matos:

John Wetteland and John Hudek are two pitchers that the Tigers had on their roster and let slip away in recent years, only to see them become relief aces in the National League. Whoever scouted and recommended signing them deserves a nice bonus and a promotion; the player personnel evaluator responsible for letting them get away deserves to be fired. It's no wonder that the Tiger pitching staff is a disarrayed mess.

The talent-poor Tiger bullpen cannot make up for a poor starting rotation, so Manager Sparky Anderson frequently leaves the starter in a little longer than he would like. The result is that the starter has nothing left and gets hammered and Anderson is forced to go to his pen anyway.

Mike Henneman would be a much more effective closer if the rest of the bullpen would do the job it's supposed to. There was some hope last year as Joe Boever, Greg Cadaret, Mark Gardiner and Buddy Groom were respectable despite their terrible-looking ERA's. It's even more remarkable because of the awful Tiger starters frequently needing relief.

Henneman (and his large salary) were on the trading block last year, but a deal wasn't made. He was also on the disabled list twice, once with an inflamed shoulder. Note that Henneman does not get as many saves as other top closers because Manager Sparky Anderson frequently goes with the hot arm in the bullpen.

Veteran Joe Boever had an excellent year in the Tigers' bullpen, and showed that he can be a closer. He needs to pitch a lot to maintain his effectiveness.

Cadaret, Storm Davis, Gardiner and ' role pitchers. There was some about Gardiner and Davis becoming but they are inconsistent and wouldn't hold the job.

Talented reliever Gene Harris, acquired from San Diego in May, came down with an inflamed elbow very soon thereafter, missing almost two months. Harris has a good fastball and slider, and was San Diego's closer in 1993. Harris can get saves with the Tigers as Anderson will go with him if he's hot.

Phil Stidham developed a new pitching style and made rapid progress last year as he began the season in Double-A, was promoted to Triple-A, and then to the Tigers. He is primarily a reliever, but can earn a starter's job if he continues to pitch well.

The bullpen in the Tigers' high minors was populated with over-the-hill veterans like Wayne Edwards, Drew Hall, Kurt Knudsen and Mike Christopher, all trying to get back to the show. If one of these vets suddenly finds the fountain of youth, he may make the Tigers, but at best it would be as a middle reliever or set-up man.

Rick Greene and John Grimm are talented closer prospects who pitched in Class-A last year. Either or both could move up to the Tigers quickly.

Marc Bowman:

Brian Maxcy's fine season for Triple-A Toledo will attract attention and give him a shot at a bullpen job with the Tigers. The righthander posted a 1.62 ERA with a 2.5-to-1 K/BB ratio and a strikeout per inning.

Lefty Sean Whiteside, 23, was successful in a part-time closer role for Double-A Trenton in 1994 (2.45 ERA, five saves). It was the first season above Class A for the former starter. Whiteside has a chance to have a similar role in Toledo in 1995, with further advancement to the majors as soon as 1996.

Kansas City Royals

Marc Bowman:

No discussion of the top relief aces can be complete without including Jeff Montgomery; no AL reliever has more saves than Montgomery since 1992. His early season struggles in 1994 were attributable to bursitis in his shoulder that left him with just four saves and a 6.17 ERA in mid-May. After a cortisone treatment, Montgomery rebounded to save his final 17 chances and was nearly unscored upon for the last two months of the year.

Montgomery throws hard enough that hitters have to look for the fastball, but also mixes in occasional offspeed stuff to keep them honest. It has been a devastating combination as Montgomery has recorded 168 saves since becoming the team's closer in 1990. He'll again have the relief ace job in 1995 and can be reasonably expected to collect 40 saves in a full season of work. In an era of uncertainty about closers, Montgomery's reliability makes him worth even more than usual.

A pair of fine setup pitchers made Monty's job much easier in 1994. Lefty Billy Brewer and righthander Rusty Meacham formed a good tandem while combining for seven wins and seven saves on their own. Brewer was used as a situational lefty, rarely facing more than three hitters at a time. For Rotisserie purposes Brewer has marginal value since he won't get more than a handful of saves and doesn't pitch many innings. However, he also can't hurt you since any runs he allows are usually the responsibility of other pitchers. Because he'll get the occasional win or save without any ERA or ratio risk, Brewer is worth a late $1 draft pick.

Meacham has a similar role but is more likely to pick up the slack in saves should Montgomery become hurt for any length of time. Meacham would be a good choice for anyone who spends big money on Montgomery. On his own Meacham will also give you a low ERA and ratio but not enough innings to be of much help. Still, he's a low risk proposition who should give you a few wins and saves and is another late $1 draft pick suggestion.

Hipolito Pichardo had Meacham's role early in the season but was shifted to a long relief role later in the year. Pichardo has been a starter in the recent past and could go back to that role if needed, but he lacks the stamina to be effective. Pichardo's fastball lacked its usual movement in 1994 and he was hit hard (opponents batted .309 against him). He's still learning to pitch so he's probably going to make positive progress in 1995. But, being a setup man, Pichardo won't be worth more than a dollar in Rotisserie.

Mike Magnante had the long relief lefty role and also made a spot start. He doesn't really have great stuff and has to be very sharp to succeed. He'll never win a closer role and isn't good as a starter; it'd be wise to avoid Magnante in a Rotisserie draft.

Stan Belinda has fallen from ace reliever to mop-up duty in just one and a half seasons. Once the Pirates closer, Belinda is now the long man out of the pen and he likes that role better. After a 5.14 ERA in 1994, it's hard to see him getting another shot at a closer role real soon. He still has the good fastball but it's still too straight to get by big league hitters regularly. Stay away from Belinda.

Enrique Burgos was Omaha's closer, getting 19 saves with a 2.88 ERA. More importantly, he may have found a way to harness his overpowering fastball. His walks were down to a more reasonable level although they were still too high (5.3 per nine IP), and he still fans batters at an accelerated rate (10.9 per nine IP). Being lefthanded helps, but he won't unseat Montgomery. Pay attention if he gets traded elsewhere as he could quickly earn a closer's role. His major league numbers might look like Mitch Williams' but as long as he gets saves he'd have a lot of value.

Once a starter, Rod Myers became a closer and had good results for Double-A Memphis, posting a 1.03 ERA and limiting opponents to just 45 hits in 70 IP. Hard-throwing Myers has been slowed by injuries in the past and it remains to be seen if his arm can stand the strain of frequent use in a closer's role. If so, Myers may get a major league shot by 1996.

Milwaukee Brewers

Bill Gray:

In early 1994, Atlantis was easier to find than a reliable Brewers closer. Bob Scanlan flunked first, then Jeff Bronkey, then Graeme Lloyd. Finally, Mike Fetters proved that there was indeed a closer in Milwaukee.

Fetters had a fine season, gaining 17 of the Brewers' 23 saves. He was also the only Brewer with saves to have an ERA under 3.00. Scanlan, Bronkey and Lloyd posted ERA's over 4.00. So going into the season, it's safe to assume Fetters is the man. Yet, as I indicated in the Starting Pitcher section, Bob Scanlan, who last year blew his chance at being the closer, is still in the running and will be given an opportunity to win the job again in spring training. Don't bet against him. At the very least, make sure you pick him up if you own Fetters. With one year under his belt, Fetters is not in the premier closer category, and is not likely to reach Eckersley-type numbers in 1995, if ever. Fetters was groomed to be a starter and many feel that's where he will eventually end up.

A couple of years ago for the Cubs, Bob Scanlan had a similar season to Fetters' 1994 effort and, as I noted, Scanlan's pitching was much improved in the last ten weeks of the 1994 season. As for the rest of the bullpen, there is simply not much help here. Rookie Scott Karl will be given a look. He should give Lloyd some competition from the left side, assuming he makes the team. Some lefty will get a handful of saves, probably Lloyd.

Marc Bowman:

Former closer Doug Henry signed with the Mets during the off-season.

A hard thrower, 29 year old righthander Mike Ignasiak has had control problems throughout his career. He bounced between Triple-A and the majors once again and will stick for good once he becomes more reliable. For Rotisserie purposes Ignasiak has little value. Still, with the unsettled Brewer bullpen,

enly good control could earn Ignasiak
-time closer role should both Mike
Bob Scanlan first fail.

Minnesota Twins

Carl Willis was an un-signed free agent. The righthanded, 34 year old Willis had his worst season for the Twins and may have to go elsewhere to return to the big leagues. He has no value wherever he ends up.

Rookie Brett Merriman has left the Twins' organization to sign a minor league contract with the Padres. Merriman is a middle innings candidate with the Padres.

James Benkard:

Veteran bullpen stalwarts Carl Willis and Mark Guthrie should return to the Metrodome in 1995. Joining them is a group including Eddie Guardado, Dave Stevens, Mike Trombley, Erik Schullstrom, Carlos Pulido, and Brett Merriman -- all are maturing into winning pitchers. Trombley will be the best bargain of the group.

Trombley has come a long way since being selected in the fourteenth round of the 1989 draft; people may have dismissed or forgotten about him because of his struggles the past two years. While essentially a control pitcher, Trombley is no weakling, and this should be his year to break out with ten wins and 150 innings out of the rotation and the pen.

Willis and Guthrie are each control pitchers who struggled in 1994. As long as they are healthy, I see no reason why they will not return to productivity. Willis has pitched fine baseball the past few years and still maintains his aggressiveness and control. Guthrie should reclaim his position as a top lefthanded reliever now that he has logged a season of recovery from shoulder woes.

Stevens will spend this season learning about the stopper's job while in setup duty. He has some significant positives: he throws hard, has stayed healthy, and has intimidating size. I expect him to blossom well in '95, with 50 games pitched, ten saves, and a 4.00 ERA. He will be ready to close games in 1996.

Mo Sanford has undergone the transformation from a hot prospect with Cincinnati, to a possible starter with an expansion team (Colorado), to a PCL veteran. He has worked hard on harnessing his control, and can help the Twins with 60 innings and a 3.75 ERA out of the bullpen.

Schullstrom moved from Double-A to being a good reliever in the majors in 1994. Like Pulido, he can thrive if his duties are limited in '95.

Merriman, like Sanford, has bounced around in his career and needs some time to settle down and find his control. It is unlikely this will happen in 1995.

Campbell has battled hard in his nine year career, and reached a worthy level of achievement in '94. He is similar to Willis in how he has succeeded in establishing himself in the majors at 30 years of age. I expect Campbell to pitch 50 good innings over the next three years.

LaTroy Hawkins and Marc Barcelo each have promising futures in the Twin rotation. Hawkins throws with an easy motion and has a deft touch with a changeup, two admirable qualities for a young pitcher. Do not expect to see great results if he makes the team before the middle of 1995. Hawkins needs time to finish maturing physically, and a 2-4, 4.75 record in 80 innings would be a likely result of rushing him.

Barcelo needs a full year in Triple-A to develop. 1994 was his first full pro year, and just staying healthy this year will be a challenge. Also, he only started to pitch over 100 innings for the first time in 1993, his junior year at Arizona State. Nevertheless, Barcelo looks like a number three starter in the making, as he has a varied repertoire, good command, and ideal size (6'3", 210 pounds).

Marc Bowman:

Considering the price that Rick Aguilera is likely to command as one of the premier closers of the last five years, I would be inclined to let someone else have him this year. Aguilera had some biceps soreness in 1994, and the opposition hit .306 off him. Suffice it to say that Duane Ward looked better going into spring training a year ago. With the $40+ it would take to buy Aguilera, you can put $20 of that into hitting (and trade for saves later if you need them) and buy three prime young hard throws in good situations for $6 apiece. You might even come up with this year's Bobby Ayala.

To complete the book on Aguilera, he is still effective when he's on, and his arm injury wasn't regarded as serious. He was on for a few weeks early in 1994. Aguilera has always been the type of pitcher who gets into a groove and becomes unhittable while he's in that groove. His fastball sizzles and moves, setting up his good forkball. If you see him pitching well (with your own eyes) then it's OK to believe he will continue to pitch well. Most likely that won't happen until mid-May, at which time you take him off someone else's roster, along with his $40 salary.

Lefty Rich Robertson was acquired from the Pirates during the winter and will compete for a situational bullpen job in 1995. He has been a starter in the minors and could do some spot start work for the Twins in an emergency. Still Robertson doesn't have any outstanding pitch, so he'll probably settle into a middle innings role.

Journeyman righthander Kevin Campbell led Triple-A Salt Lake City with seven saves but is not a candidate for a closer's job in Minnesota. He's now 30 years old and has spent parts of the last four seasons in the big leagues for Oakland and the Twins. Campbell is a control specialist who could compete for a middle/long relief role in 1995.

Righthander Gus Gandarillas has some closer potential. The 23 year old throws hard enough and has shown good control at lower levels. He was the closer for Class A Fort Myers in the Florida State League, posting 25 saves in 1993, then collected eight saves with a 3.16 ERA for Double-A Nashville in 1994. Gandarillas lost part of last season to injury; his status as a prospect will depend upon how quickly he recovers.

Scott Moten earned a promotion from Fort Myers to Nashville with his fine 2.16 ERA, 8-4, seven save performance in 1994. He has decent control but lacks an overpowering pitch. Moten is not really a closer candidate, but could reach the majors in a middle relief role.

New York Yankees

With Xavier Hernandez leaving the Yankees via free agency to join the Reds and the Yankees re-signing Steve Howe, the closer's job officially belongs to Howe. Although Manager Buck Showalter won't say as much, Howe should get the majority of saves for the Yankees in 1995.

Righthander Scott Bankhead is a valuable long reliever coming off a bad year with Boston. He was acquired by the Yankees during the strike and has re-signed with them for 1995. Bankhead can earn a couple of bucks for his Rotisserie owners.

For years I have been telling people that Steve Howe has good enough stuff to be a full-time closer. It took the failure of all the alternatives on the Yankees staff to produce a true test in 1994. Howe passed the test with flying colors. Another plus is that Howe has withstood some negative press that went beyond harshness and across the line of honesty in 1993, and he has come through that fine, too. The Yankees had an option on Howe for 1995 at about two and half million dollars, and they took that option without hesitation. On the free market, he's worth more than that.

The tools of success for Howe are a 93 MPH fastball and 90+ slider with good movement. He can throw either pitch to precise spots, tending to work lefties in with fastballs and then drop the slider on the low outside corner. Against righties Howe just keeps

on the hands, much reminiscent of
t his best.

...ny negative for Howe is that manager Buck
...nowalter doesn't like to give all the saves to one
hurler, doesn't even like to use the word "closer" to
describe any pitcher's role. Showalter won't say
"bullpen by committee" either. He simply manages
one game at a time, and chooses his pitchers depending
on the situation day by day. The save statistic itself is
the farthest thing from his mind. Showalter has used
the phrase "set up for each other" to describe the
way he uses a left/righty combo, which is of course
a strong possibility for Howe if the Yanks can come
up with a righty half of the combo for 1995.

The pitchers who struggled and thus cleared the way
for Howe in 1994 included Xavier Hernandez, Bob
Wickman, Jeff Reardon, Sterling Hitchcock, and
Greg Harris. Hernandez was the biggest
disappointment and was gone off the roster shortly
after the season ended. He was not the same pitcher
in New York as he had been in Houston, not even
close.

Hernandez was expected to be the top guy in the pen,
righty or lefty, in 1994. In Houston Hernandez had
thrived on the strengths of a sharp split-finger pitch
and an amazing ability to throw it for strikes
consistently. His main problem with the Yankees last
year was simply poor control, which is of course a
fatal flaw in an ace relief pitcher who can't get two or
three strikeouts in a row. In addition to walking too
many in 1994, Hernandez was also too easy to hit,
allowing the opposition a .300 average. He is a decent
candidate for a comeback with another team in 1995.

Although Hernandez was on the DL last summer, it
was the result of being hit on the elbow by a batted
ball, not a direct pitching-related injury. He did have
some shoulder stiffness early in the season but
appeared to get over it, with all the rest he got later.
One plausible theory to explain the poor control is
that Hernandez blossomed two years ago (composite
2.34 ERA in 1992-1993) when given a clearly defined
role and very frequent work. Hernandez had been
much less impressive in his various major league trials

in 1989-1991 when he was tried in various roles and
generally came to the park without a clue about how
he was going to be used. It was very much the same
situation in New York in 1994, except that Xavier
had the added pressure of being expected to pitch
excellently whenever called upon. And his results in
1994 were very much like he had in his early major
league trials. Given a manager who likes defined
roles, and giving Hernandez a defined role that
includes regular work, he can be productive again.

Bob Wickman, who came up as a starter, became a
full-time reliever in 1994. He's a sinker/slider pitcher
who took over the top righty job from Hernandez in
May. While Buck Showalter kept refusing to suggest
that Wickman had become "the closer" and I kept
telling everyone the obvious truth that saves were
wide open, Wickman did hold the top job for more
than a month, getting six saves from mid-May to mid-
June, before Howe took over. Even when Wickman
was getting those saves, his role included being ready
to come in as early as the sixth inning if needed. He
begins 1995 with that same role: whatever is required.
He must be considered number two in line after Howe
for saves, unless and until someone else emerges.

Hitchcock is a talented young lefty who will be cast
as a starter if possible (see Yankees SP section for
more).

Scott Bankhead didn't join the Yankees in time to
figure in the saves picture last year, but he will be
there in 1995. Formerly a gem setup man with the
Red Sox, Bankhead fell into disfavor in 1994, not
exactly relegated to the doghouse but not given much
work in critical situations, either. Boston traded him
to New York during the strike. The Yankees let him
become a free agent but then re-signed him two
weeks later.

Bankhead is a basic fastball/slider short reliever. He's
had to carry a limited workload because of recurring
shoulder problems, and he's long past his prime when
he was a promising young starter with the Mariners
(14-6 with a 3.34 ERA in 1989). Nonetheless
Bankhead has been effective in his limited role, and
whatever he's got left, Buck Showalter will make the

most of it. For $1 in 1995 Bankhead has the makings of a gem sleeper at best, and a fairly harmless filler at worst.

Mark Hutton's 95 MPH fastball has encouraged the Yankees to take a look at him as a closer candidate, but more likely he will be further tried as a starter before that decision is made.

Marc Bowman:

Joe Ausanio has done the closer's job at Triple-A Columbus, but he really doesn't have the stuff to be more than a setup man in the majors and still has one foot firmly planted in the minors.

Another righthander, 26 year old Jeff Patterson joined the Yankees over the winter as a six-year minor league free agent. Patterson has been at Triple-A for most of the last three years, but 1994 was his worst as a pro. He's not a big strikeout pitcher and has occasionally spotty control. Patterson is a long-shot for a lengthy major league stint; he's injury insurance stored at Triple-A.

Righthander Andy Croghan is getting a little old (age 25) to be a great closer candidate, but his numbers for Double-A Albany were exceptional enough to attract attention. In his first season above A-ball, Croghan collected 16 saves in 36 appearances, posting a 1.72 ERA with a strikeout per inning. He'll have a chance to earn a big league bullpen job in the spring but most likely will spend the summer pitching for Triple-A Columbus. Another performance like he had in 1994 will get him to New York quickly.

Oakland A's

All of the saves speculation in Oakland revolves around where free agent Dennis Eckersley winds up. He would have the closer's job should he stay with the Athletics or if he were to join a new team. Without Eckersley, Oakland was looking at Mark Acre, Steve Briscoe, Bill Taylor or any of a number of unproven youngsters. Acre has the inside track but is hardly a good recommendation for saves in 1995.

Steven Rubio:

There are two possible scenarios for the A's bullpen in 1995. If, as expected, Dennis Eckersley returns for one more season, he will be the stopper. Even now, at the end of his career, Eck strikes out more than a batter per inning while rarely walking anyone. He can still pitch, and will give fine value to fantasy owners who don't bid too highly based on Eck's immortal run of a few years back.

If Eck does not return, the question of his successor will merely be moved up a season. There are several intriguing candidates and none have taken clear hold of the perennial "Next Eck" job. Mark Acre is mentioned more often than most by the A's organization as the man who will eventually replace the Eck. He struggled with his control during his rookie season, but otherwise did nothing to damage his reputation. A tall righthander, Acre looks imposing on the mound, which seems to be part of the job description for stoppers.

Bill Taylor was a 32 year old rookie last season, pitching very well (as he had done for many years in several farm systems). Taylor once led the International League in saves, and if he were younger, would be the clear frontrunner to replace Eck, but the age factor may prevent Taylor from ever racking up major-league saves. His 1994 performance was not a fluke, in any event.

If you are looking for a sleeper in this bunch, John Briscoe's name should be on your list. He has been extremely wild for a long time, and although he is making control progress, it is very slow progress indeed. Nevertheless, strikeout pitchers get plenty of chances, no matter how wild they are, and while Briscoe must be considered an extreme longshot to have any major-league success, he is perhaps the one Oakland reliever you can get for $1 in 1995 who might end up becoming the stopper sometime in the future.

Roger Smithberg grabbed seven saves in Class AAA-last season, but didn't really pitch very well, and at 29 is probably unlikely to take over the stopper's job.

...as one of the many pleasing comeback
...land last season, returning to the
...ve-year absence to post a 1.93 ERA.
...ould stick around for a decade as a one-out
...y, but won't rise above that level.

Marc Bowman:

Lefty Vince Horsman has spent most of the last three
years in the A's bullpen but hasn't really distinguished
himself. He'd be able to serve in a situational role if
he could handle lefthanded batters better. 28 year old
Horsman could battle for a long relief job for Oakland
in 1995.

The up-and-down career of 27 year old righthander
Steve Phoenix reached a pinnacle with two big league
appearances in 1994. After three-plus years as a
starter, Phoenix has shown pretty good stuff in a
relief role since the second half of 1993. While he
doesn't have overpowering stuff, Phoenix has
command of several pitches and good control. He'll
have a good chance to win a middle relief role for
Oakland in 1995.

Seattle Mariners

Bill Gray:

You have Bobby Ayala? You have a pretty good
closer. Having watched Ayala a lot in Cincinnati, I
was a bit skeptical that he was up to the task, but he
posted 18 saves and fanned 1.34 batters per inning.
My concern with Ayala was based on his wildness.
He still walks too many batters and closers with this
problem do not last long. But, Ayala was able to just
blow hitters away when he needed to. As long as he
has the big heater he'll be safe, but will likely crash
and burn quickly when the fastball loses some steam.

Bill Risley was a most sought after mid-season
pickup, but as soon as most players became aware of
him, Risley began to be hit hard. He did pitch better
after the All Star break. Fate is the major factor in a
reliever getting a win. It's almost unheard of for a
reliever who wins nine games as Risley did last year

to do it again the following year. There will be some
middle reliever who gets an unusual number of wins
in relief, but it probably won't be Risley. Without the
benefit of wins, he's actually a pretty useless pick.

Jeff Nelson was mentioned as the closer prior to
Ayala's emergence, but he pitched his way back to
the minors for a spell. He looked pretty good when
he came back, at least the numbers did. Nelson last
year (and Carl Willis of the Twins in 1993) seemed to
interest a good number of fantasy players because
they had a decent ERA and ratio. The sad truth is that
pitchers like Nelson and Willis usually come into a
game with a runner or two on base, and one out or
less. Runs that they allow are not charged to them,
they are charged to the previous pitcher. So if you
look at Jeff Nelson's 2.76 ERA and conclude he is a
good pick, you are making a mistake. A 2.76 ERA
over 47 innings pitched will have very little effect on
your total numbers.

Marc Bowman:

Lefthander Kevin King turned to a relief role and
found a niche in the majors as a situational reliever.
He doesn't throw especially hard so the 26 year old
won't be used to close games. Control difficulties
will limit his use and his success; King has walked 21
batters in 27 major league innings.

Righthander Jeff Darwin led Triple-A Calgary with
11 saves and earned a short (two games) stint with the
Mariners. Darwin doesn't have a blazing fastball, but
he throws hard enough with good enough location to
succeed in a limited stopper role. 25 year old Darwin
will compete for an important bullpen role with the
Mariners in 1995.

Righthander Bob Wells had much more success in the
big leagues in 1994 than he had in the minors, posting
a combined 2.00 ERA in seven games for the Phillies
and Mariners despite a 6.54 ERA for Triple-A Calgary.
That poor figure is probably a PCL-induced
abberation, however, as Wells has consistently
produced an ERA of 2.79 or less in parts of three
years at Double-A and Triple-A in the Phillies system.
The 28 year old is not a good prospect for increased

major league time; his best bet is to catch on as the last guy in the bullpen for the 1995 Mariners.

Righthander Jim Mecir was Double-A Jacksonville's righthanded closer, recording 13 saves in 46 outings, posting a 2.69 ERA before finishing up in the Arizona Fall League. At age 25 he's not a great prospect but can earn a big league set-up role with continued good pitching.

Scott Davison is on the 40-man roster for 1995. He's only had 11 appearances over the last two seasons with a 6.14 ERA. He's a big question mark

Texas Rangers

Tom Henke has signed with the Cardinals as a free agent and will earn the majority of saves in St. Louis. In the free-for-all for saves in Texas, Darren Oliver appears to have the inside track. Cris Carpenter and Matt Whiteside could also earn saves for the Rangers in 1995, but both lack the rubber-armed quality necessary for frequent use in a closer's role. The job is probably Oliver's to lose.

Both Rick Honeycutt and Jay Howell have become free agents. Both aging righthanders had very poor seasons in 1994 and remained unsigned. They may both remain that way.

Peter Graves:

The Texas bullpen will be restructured extensively in 1995 by new GM Doug Melvin. Last season's crew complied a shocking 5.28 ERA with 22 blown saves.

Tom Henke's back problems resurfaced last season, contributing to a decline in his effectiveness. At one point around the All-Star break, Henke considered retirement, but returned shortly thereafter and pitched fairly effectively. Henke's 3.79 ERA was his highest in ten years, and he was on a pace to save 22 games, his lowest total since 1989. Can he bounce back with the Cards? It's only been one year since Henke saved 40 games for the Rangers, but at age 37, he could be slowing down.

The only bright spot in the Ranger pen was rookie lefthander Darren Oliver (4-0, 2 saves, 3.42 ERA). The son of former big leaguer Bob Oliver was promoted to the majors in April, but struggled and was sent to the minors. Upon his return to Texas, Oliver was, in the words of one scout, "the most improved pitcher in the league." Oliver has an excellent fastball and a slurve, and when he throws strikes he's tough to hit. Control has been a problem, but Oliver's command improved dramatically during the course of last season.

If Henke returns, Oliver will be the primary lefty setup man; if a closer is needed, Oliver is the most likely candidate from last year's bunch. At a moderately low price, Oliver could pay off handsomely. A word of caution: Oliver had offseason surgery to remove bone chips from his left elbow.

One reason for Tom Grieve's firing was the acquisition of Rick Honeycutt and Jay Howell as the lefty-righty setups for Henke last year. Honeycutt was consistently awful (1-2, 1 save, 7.20), and would have been released had the strike not been looming. Lefties clobbered Honeycutt at a .412 clip: he's done. Howell (4-1, 2 saves, 5.44) never got untracked and may also be done at age 39. Howell did pitch somewhat more effectively after late May (his ERA was above 10.00 prior to then). Neither Honeycutt nor Howell are in the picture for 1995.

The other main righthanded candidates are Cris Carpenter and Matt Whiteside. Both pitchers are tremendously susceptible to overuse, and both were overused last season, with predictable results. Carpenter (2-5, 5 saves, 5.03) was the most effective Ranger reliever against righthanded hitters (.237) and served as the primary closer when Henke was unavailable (he did blow 7 of 12 saves). If used carefully, Carpenter could scavenge enough wins and saves to be worth a minor investment, but in this bullpen he's a gamble. Whiteside (2-2, 1 save, 5.02) is primarily a middle reliever; he won't be used in enough win or save situations to be worth anything.

Lefties Dan Smith (1-2, 4.30) and Brian Bohanon (discussed under starting pitchers) could see some

Smith can't seem to stay healthy for ~ weeks at a time. His latest problem ~rn left rotator cuff.

~ere are a few interesting relievers in the Ranger farm system. Lefthander Ritchie Moody had been one of the more promising relief candidates for the Rangers before they tried converting him into a starter. That experiment lasted only eight starts before Moody underwent season-ending rotator cuff surgery. Righthander Kerry Lacy, who had been one of the more prolific minor league closers in recent years, had only 12 saves for Double-A Tulsa and was supplanted by season's end by sidearmer Mark Brandenburg (1.74, 8 saves, 12 walks, 63 strikeouts at Tulsa). Finally, in the deep minors, college closer Brandall ''Bucky'' Buckles was a man among boys at short-season Hudson Valley (18 saves, 8 walks, 53 strikeouts). Buckles could advance quickly, especially in the depleted Texas system.

Marc Bowman:

Two full years in Triple-A with improving results earned Terry Burrows his one game big league stint. The 26 year old lefty is not a great prospect but has a chance to win a set-up or situational role in a Ranger bullpen lacking in lefthanders. He's in the right place to get a big league role in 1995.

Righthander Jose Alberro throws hard, but has been too erratic to win a promotion to the majors. At age 25 he's ready to make the jump to the bigs if he can show better control. With the muddled state of the Ranger bullpen, Alberro has a chance to emerge with a share of the closer's role, but he has to be considered a long shot at this point.

Double-A Tulsa ERA leader Danny Patterson (1.64) got him six saves. 24 year old Patterson also made one start among his 30 appearances; his strikeout and walk totals were nothing spectacular. It was the first year above A-ball for the righthander; he posted similar numbers for Class A Charlotte in 1993. Further improvement could earn Patterson a middle innings role in the big leagues by 1996.

Righthander Wilson Heredia collected 15 saves for Class A Charlotte in 1993, but moved to long relief role for Tulsa in 1994 with mixed results. Interestingly, Heredia greatly improved his control, from 20 walks and 26 strikeouts in 1993 to only eight walks with 53 Ks for Tulsa. Heredia was susceptible to the long ball in 1994, though. The 23 year old could get to Triple-A Oklahoma City in 1995 with a major league shot by 1996; keep an eye on him should he produce similarly impressive control numbers in 1995.

Toronto Blue Jays

Free agent Danny Cox has re-signed with the Blue Jays and will have a long/middle relief role in 1995. He has limited Rotisserie value because he has no chance for saves and doesn't pitch often enough or get a lot of innings, so any good pitching he does won't be enough to add Rotisserie value.

Dave Righetti has been released and is expected to retire.

David Luciani:

''Duane Ward could start throwing anytime'' was a common phrase in 1994. We heard it all too often and it took until July for most of us to accept that he was not going to throw at all. Well, Duane Ward could start throwing anytime now. This time it's the truth. He is committed to a winter program that will put him on a pace to be back for 1995 at full strength.

Assuming that it is successful, late-1994 surgery will have helped Ward regain his role as one of the top closers in the game. If he is healthy, he will be given every save opportunity. Ward is one of the hardest throwers in the league and the Blue Jays sorely missed his presence. Ward, and Tom Henke before him, provided the backbone to a bullpen that kept the Jays above .500 every year. Without a true closer, they finally stumbled. If ever the organization or the fans needed absolute proof of Ward's value, they got it in a game against the California Angels where Todd Stottlemyre and Mike Timlin, purported in April to be ''co-closers'' in Ward's absence, coughed up a

seven run lead in the final inning. Of course, that experiment was quickly abandoned as Stottlemyre was "demoted" back to the starting rotation and Timlin back to his role as a blowout relief pitcher.

Darren Hall then stepped in from the minor leagues and earned a spot for 1995 as the main setup man to Ward. Hall posted 17 saves with the Blue Jays last year against just three blown opportunities. If nothing else, he demonstrated that over a short run he is a capable replacement for Duane Ward. Given more work as Ward's understudy, he will likely prosper as a reliable backup closer over the next couple of years. His age (30) essentially prohibits him from ever permanently inheriting the main role in the bullpen.

Tony Castillo is the only lefty out of the bullpen for now. He was perhaps the Blue Jays' most effective pitcher in 1994. A 5-2 record and a 2.51 ERA ensured that he will be one of the five or six relief pitchers to be with the club on opening day of 1995. Castillo doesn't throw nearly as hard as he once did, but he allowed just a .237 average to lefthanded batters. He'll never be a closer as shown by four blown saves in five chances last year. Dave Righetti, the other lefty who saw action here last year, was not offered a contract and was facing either retirement or a non-roster invitation somewhere.

Woody Williams will be back in the Jays' bullpen this year. His velocity and movement peaked in 1994 and where others were unreliable, Williams was consistently good, striking out 56 batters in 59.1 innings last year. He allowed just 44 hits and a 3.64 ERA and opponents hit just .205 off of him. He may even be given brief consideration as a starting pitcher, something he has done as recently as 1992 with Triple-A Syracuse.

With the apparent return of Ward and the appearance of Darren Hall, Timlin might be out of chances. The Jays rarely carry twelve pitchers, which would mean there are only five or six spots in the bullpen. Of those, four are taken by Ward, Hall, Williams and Castillo. This doesn't even include Danny Cox, who was so successful in 1993 and was excellent in his injury-shortened year of 1994. Cox might be signed to a new contract (he was not offered arbitration in October). Timlin will compete with Scott Brow for the remaining spot on the club. If Cox is given a new contract or another free agent relief pitcher is signed (a very likely possibility), Timlin's career in Toronto is in peril.

Marc Bowman:

Righthander Tim Crabtree was found wanting in a short trial as a closer for Triple-A Syracuse. The 25 year old also made some spot starts after being exclusively a starter at lower levels. Crabtree is not a strikeout pitcher and allows far too many hits per inning to be considered a major league closer candidate. If he gets to the big leagues it will in long relief.

Lefty Ricardo Jordan led Double-A Knoxville with 17 saves and struck out 70 batters in 64 innings. It was his first full season above Class A and his 2.66 ERA was comparable to previous numbers in A-ball. At age 24, Jordan should advance to Triple-A in 1995 and could get a call-up to Toronto during the season. Jordan will challenge for a lefty set-up job in the majors by 1996.

NATIONAL LEAGUE
RELIEF PITCHERS

Atlanta Braves

Marc Bowman:

Greg McMichael, Mike Stanton, Alejandro Pena, Juan Berenguer, Joe Boever, Bruce Sutter, Jim Acker and Gene Garber. If this were a Jeopardy answer, the question would have to be: Which eight relievers have been single season saves leaders for the Braves in the last ten years?

With eight different saves leaders over the last ten seasons, the Braves relief ace role has obviously had a lot of turnover. The main thing to recognize in this kind of situation is that the status of the current incumbent closer is shakier than that of a liberal Democrat Congressman last November.

Even though the Braves are likely to win nearly 100 games in 1995, it would be imprudent to expect 40 or more saves from any one reliever. Likewise, paying top closer dollars for the current closer is foolish.

A more intelligent approach is to attempt to acquire McMichael early in the draft for a low bid while other "top" relievers (Rod Beck, John Wetteland, Bryan Harvey, Randy Myers, etc.) are still available. An early $20 bid may earn you 25 to 30 saves. But,

should the bidding approach $30, let someone else take the risk.

On the other hand, second tier Braves relievers all have more value than similar relievers with other teams. Each of them can get a handful of saves and each are more likely to pick up wins than a second tier reliever for a team that isn't going to win as often as the Braves. Additionally, there is always the chance (about 90% over the previous ten years) that the Braves will change horses in mid-stream and switch to a new closer. A two dollar bid for a second tier Braves reliever might earn you a dozen late season saves and a new "incumbent" closer.

Going into 1995, incumbent McMichael will start the year with the job but is quite likely to lose it. He had his ups and downs in 1994 but Bobby Cox stuck with him. Should McMichael struggle again next year a bullpen by committee might quickly be installed. While McMichael would probably keep a share of the saves, the rest would probably go to two lefties, Mike Stanton and newly acquired Derek Lilliquist. The biggest threats to McMichael from righthanders would come from Mark Wohlers and Brad Clontz, even though Wohlers appears to be stuck in a long relief role for now. Clontz is a good prospect for the long term but may stay in the minors for most of 1995.

Stanton had a decent season as the primary set up man for McMichael, although he was probably a disappointment to anyone who paid more than a couple of bucks for him after his 27 save season in 1993. Stanton will have to share the lefty set up duties in 1995 because...

A new lefty will be on the scene in 1995. Late of Cleveland, Lilliquist rejoins the Braves staff. He had been with Atlanta for 1989 and part of 1990, primarily as a starter. The club's former first round draft pick (1987) is now a situational lefty and a good one.

Lilliquist's arm hasn't shown the resiliency necessary to pitch on successive days. Therefore, he's more likely to be used on a regular cycle, pitching about every three days. This might hurt his chances to get saves since save situations can't be conveniently scheduled. So, Stanton is more likely to get any leftover saves.

Expect 25 saves for McMichael, eight for Stanton, five for Lilliquist and about five other saves spread around to other relievers. The remaining relief corps is only for setup purposes and has little value to Rotisserie players.

Kent Mercker also did some relief work but was primarily the club's fifth starter. The emergence of another starter (such as Brad Woodall) would push Mercker back into his accustomed relief role where he would have a good ERA but his Baserunner Ratio would be about league average. Mercker would not be likely to get more than a handful of wins or saves in such a role, so has little value. For more on Mercker consult National League Starting Pitchers.

With Stanton, Mercker and now Lilliquist in the Braves bullpen, an obvious question arises: just how many lefthanded relievers do the Braves need, anyway? Of course, lefthanded relief help is always in need and they may need to make a trade late in the year. Hmmm...

Still bothered by the elbow injury which ended his 1993 season, Gregg Olson no longer has snap on his great curveball or the durability to pitch regularly.

The results speak for themselves: a 9.20 ERA and more walks than strikeouts. He'll get another shot to overcome the injury, but his career may indeed be over if he can't recover. Should Olson fully recover he could compete for the closer's job but it's beginning to look like he's finished. He's a very long shot for 1995.

Braves fans (and many Rotisserie owners) are still waiting for Mark Wohlers to establish himself as a fearsome closer. Wohlers spent an entire season in the majors for the first time in 1994, but it could hardly be considered a success. His 4.59 ERA was worse than the 4.50 ERA he posted in 1993 which was a previous career high. Worse still was his control. He walked 50% more batters in almost the same number of innings; his Ratio rose from 1.23 in 1993 to 1.65 in 1994. While his strikeout rate also went up it hardly makes up for his poor control. In his current role Wohlers is asked to come in and throw hard for an inning; usually in a situation where the game is already out of contention. Until Wohlers demonstrates better control it's probably going to remain his role.

Steve Bedrosian served as a righthanded set up man again in 1994. The likable "Bedrock" has overcome personal tragedy to pitch well after unretiring in 1993. Still, he is now 37 years old and the end has to be near for him. Even with a full season Bedrosian is unlikely to grab the closer role and therefore has no Rotisserie value.

Another righthander who is well past his prime, Mike Bielecki handled long relief requests after returning from an injury that ended his 1993 season with Cleveland. The 35 year old Bielecki doesn't throw very hard and is no longer anything special. His role could quickly be taken by any other journeyman reliever.

The most exciting prospect is 23 year old Brad Clontz. After being nearly untouchable for Double-A Greenville (1.20 ERA, 27 saves, 0.93 ratio, 49 strikeouts in 45 innings), Clontz went on to record another eleven saves for Triple-A Richmond with similarly impressive numbers (2.10 ERA, 1.08 ratio,

21 strikeouts in 26 innings). Clontz then led the Arizona Fall League in saves. He's probably ready for a big league shot, but the Braves are likely to start him out at Richmond in 1995.

When considering a bid on Clontz please use caution. Despite his excellent performance in 1994, it is impossible to predict relief fame for Clontz in the big leagues. High save totals in the minors rarely become high major league save totals. For further evidence one need only to look at what has become of Mark Wohlers. With continued good pitching, a late season recall in 1995 is in Clontz's future. Anything more than that is impossible to speculate upon at this early stage of his career.

Despite leading Richmond with 26 saves, Terry Clark has virtually no chance for a useful role in Atlanta. He's a 34 year old righthanded journeyman who last appeared in the majors, for one game, with Houston in 1990. He has nothing that can be considered major league stuff.

The addition of Lilliquist might spell the end for lefthander Pedro Borbon. He is now 27 years old and has done little to distinguish himself in the minors or in his short major league stints. Borbon's future is with another club.

Lefthander Tom Thobe got most of Greenville's saves after Clontz was promoted; he had a good year, going 7-6 with nine saves, a 2.54 ERA and striking out almost as many batters as he allowed hits. At age 25, though, Thobe isn't considered a hot prospect. He's likely to stay at Greenville to start 1995.

Chicago Cubs

Stuart Shea:

Chuck McElroy, Bob Scanlan, Paul Assenmacher Heathcliff Slocumb are in one corner. Mike Anderson, Darron Cox, Larry Luebbers, Mike Carter, Tuffy Rhodes and Jose Hernandez are in the other. Which bunch of ballplayers would you rather have? The Cubs decided that it was more important to dump

salaries than have a bullpen, so the aforementioned relievers hit the trail after the 1993 season began, bringing the second group of warm bodies in return.

As a result, Randy Myers was left with a shifting and ineffective supporting cast. Myers saved what he could last year, although there were precious few contests to nail down. Rumors of his departure ran rampant last season, but he stayed in Cubs stripes all year. 1995 is his free agent campaign and Myers will probably depart for other pastures if the Cubs don't win, or at least contend strongly, in 1995. He's still one of the better closers in baseball, but appeared to have lost a few MPH in 1994. Myers has never pitched well in July and continued that trend last year.

On the other hand, Dan Plesac added some velocity by undergoing a rigorous conditioning and strengthening program before the 1994 season. The former Brewer pitched quite well in April and May, but his frequent use (caused by poor starting pitching in the early months) caused a breakdown when summer came along. Plesac was on a 78 game pace when the strike came and he simply wore out. He won't be a closer again, but still makes lefthanded hitters look bad. Plesac signed with the Pirates for 1995.

Don't look now, but Jose Bautista might be gaining some respect. Despite allowing 12 earned runs in his last 20 innings, the ex-Oriole pitched very well for the Cubs again in 1994. His control was, for the most part, excellent. He, too, wore out under the strain, and tied for second in the majors with his 58 appearances. With a reasonable workload, he's a valuable pitcher, though not of high Rotisserie value.

Another one of Tom Trebelhorn's former Brewers, Chuck Crim came aboard after having spent most of 1993 out of baseball. After Crim was called up in early April, he began well but quickly showed why he hasn't had a good year since 1990: he hasn't got any stuff left. He probably won't return.

Former White Sox hurler Donn Pall hitched his horse to the Cubs wagon just before the strike. His split finger pitch is excellent when it's working; when he

hasn't got control of his elusive out pitch, Pall is meat. In Wrigley Field, he can't really afford mistakes like he could in old Comiskey, and even when on his game Pall isn't anything more than a ninth or tenth man.

Mediocre lefthanders of older vintage, Dave Otto and Blaise Ilsley saw some time with the big club in 1994. Neither did anything to convince cynics that they belong in big league uniforms and won't ever contribute much to big league or Rotisserie rosters. Randy Veres (yet another Brewer castoff) had a good outing or two, but isn't any better than 40 or 50 other righthanders in Triple-A right now.

Crim, Veres, Otto and Ilsley spent some time at Iowa in 1994 and are no better than any other righthanders, lefthanders, ambidextrous throwers, or pitching machines employed by the Cubs' Triple-A club, either. Other members of the illustrious Iowa bullpen included Mark Lee, Mike Walker, Bill Brennan, and Greg Perschke. There isn't much at Double-A Orlando either, as former top draft pick Derek Wallace struggled when converted to short relief and Jesse Hollins was shelved for the second year in a row by a bad rotator cuff. Previously unheralded Jason Hart saved ten, fanned 33 and walked six in 31 innings at Daytona Beach in his first season of pro ball. He posted a fine 1.45 ERA and should advance to Orlando this year.

Cincinnati Reds

Greg Gajus:

One of the characteristics of Davey Johnson as a manager is his willingness to divide up saves among the bullpen denizens. With the Mets, he almost always used co-closers (Orosco and McDowell, McDowell and Myers) and with the Reds in 1994 he had four different pitchers recording saves. While this makes great baseball sense it is a problem for Rotisserie players. Reds relievers make fine second relievers, but if they are your primary closer you will have no chance competing with the guys who have the whole job like Myers and Beck.

The chairman of the Reds' committee was Jeff Brantley (6-6, 2.48 ERA, 1.13 ratio, 15 saves) who had his best season since 1991. Brantley was always a solid reliever, but his value plummetted when the Giants tried unsuccessfully to make him a starter. By the time that experiment failed, Rod Beck had taken the closers role. Look for Brantley to be the chairman again in 1995 and earn 15 to 25 saves.

Chuck McElroy (1-2, 2.34, 1.16, five saves) was rescued from the Cubs and was the top lefthander in the bullpen. Johnson was careful to limit his use to an inning at a time and McElroy responded with his best season. His declining strikeout rate (5.9 per game) is cause for some concern.

The Reds reliever most likely to suddenly increase in value is Hector Carrasco (5-6, 2.24, 1.28, six saves). The spring training phenom of 1994, Carrasco received a few early saves, but Johnson used him mostly as Brantley's setup man. Carrasco became Jose Rijo's protege, and he looks and pitches much like Rijo with a good 90+ MPH fastball and nasty slider. Opposing batters hit only .210 against him.

Johnny Ruffin (7-2, 3.09, 1.20, one save) also pitched well in a setup role, but must outpitch both Brantley and Carrasco to have much Rotisserie value. Like Carrasco, he features a very good fastball and slider. Rob Dibble is probably finished (at least with the Reds). After a couple of appearances in spring training, Dibble returned to the disabled list and was a disaster during a brief late season rehab assignment at Indianapolis (ten walks and a 22.85 ERA in six appearances). At best, he is a late round speculation pick.

Rich DeLucia, Rich Sauveur, Scott Service, Tim Fortugno and the loser of the fifth starter contest will compete for the long relief roles and will have almost no Rotisserie value.

Colorado Rockies

The Rockies picked up ex-Angel Joe Grahe and gave him a minor league contract. Despite getting 13 saves

in 1994, Grahe was horrible, allowing the opposition a .426 on base percentage. His arrival is more of a no-confidence warning about Darren Holmes than it is a plus for Grahe; overall the deal should have no impact except to keep Grahe out of the California bullpen picture.

David Smith:

Darren Holmes may have gone out like a lion, but he came in like a lamb.

To end the 1993 campaign, Holmes converted 21 of 22 save opportunities. He never regained his confidence in 1994, hurt his arm and wound up splitting time between Colorado Springs and the DL. Holmes' numbers reflect his struggles: 6.35 ERA and three saves for the Rockies; 8.22 ERA in four games the Triple-A Sky Sox.

A starter in early 1993, Bruce Ruffin took over as closer and capitalized on the opportunity. He recorded 16 saves with a 4-5 record and 4.04 ERA, finishing a team high 39 games for the Rockies. Ruffin has the job going into 1995.

Two righthanders and another lefty set-up Ruffin: Steve Reed, Willie Blair and lefty Mike Munoz appeared in 61, 57 and 47 games, respectively. When their arms tired in August, righthander Jim Czajkowski was promoted from Colorado Springs.

Reed's sidearm delivery keeps righthanders on their heels. Munoz held opponents to a .223 average with his 93-MPH fastball; the Rockies feel that he can become their closer in the future. Blair had more control problems in 1994 than in previous years but his biggest problem is allowing a high number of hits per inning (11.3 per nine innings in two years with Colorado); Blair has also been touched by the long ball, allowing one every 7.7 innings pitched since he began pitching in the thin Denver air.

Czajkowski was doing well with the Sky Sox (Class AAA) with a 2.71 ERA and eight saves in 63 innings. A nine year minor league veteran, the 31 year old Czajkowski is Triple-A roster filler at best.

Bruce Walton is a good candidate to make the jump to the majors, again. He has spent all of the last six seasons in Triple-A with short stints in the majors in each of the last four years amounting to 34 major league innings pitched. The 32 year old righthander led Colorado Springs with 13 saves but he's hardly a rising star. He'd be long relief help should he reach Denver again.

Holmes is the wildcard in the equation - his spring could determine the future of Blair or Reed. With an effective Holmes, the Rockies would only need one of them. If Holmes is effective it would also probably lock out Czajkowski and Walton from lengthy big league chances.

Florida Marlins

Tony Blengino:

In their first two seasons, Marlins' relievers have pitched 848 innings, an average of 3.1 innings per game. In the National League, only the Rockies, Cards and Expos' bullpens have worked harder. Despite the heavy workload, the Marlins' bullpen was exceptional in 1993 and decent in 1994. However, only one member of the pen has survived both seasons without a serious injury, quite possibly as a result of that heavy workload. In 1994, Marlin relievers combined for a 4.39 ERA, ninth in the National League, mainly due to the struggles of their middle relievers. Marlins' closers were exceptional, though, and blew just seven saves in 37 attempts - easily the league's best record.

Since Marlins' replacement closers performed well, Bryan Harvey's lost season did more to damage his trade value than to the short term fortunes of the team. It's difficult to shop a pitcher who has lost most of the season to injury in two of the last three years. Nevertheless, Harvey's arm is sound and he'll have every chance to reclaim his closer role next spring. But, two things have changed due to Harvey's injuries: first his workload will be cut to about 50 innings in 1995, and the success of the replacement closers will give the Marlins alternatives when distributing save

opportunities. The 32 year old Harvey has a career 2.42 ERA and has struck out three times as many batters as he has walked. For 1995, expect Harvey and his unhittable forkball to make a solid comeback to a 3-2 season with a 2.75 ERA and 25 saves.

Obtained in a steal of a trade from Texas, Robb Nen has always had star potential, but injuries and poor control kept the hard throwing Nen from succeeding in the major leagues. Nen possesses a 97-MPH fastball, but had walked 46 batters in 56 major league innings. He got another chance in 1994 when a series of injuries thrust him into the closers job. Nen responded by fanning 60 with just 17 walks in 58 innings and converting all 15 of his save opportunities; he allowed just one of 28 inherited runners to score in 1994. Nen provides the Marlins with bullpen depth. He can replace Harvey again or serve as a valuable bridge between the starter and closer. At age 25, Nen is destined to be a major league closer. Be wary of a short term relapse of his control problems, but look for an 8-6 season in 1995 with a 3.40 ERA and ten saves in 90 innings.

Nen only got the closers job after 28 year old Jeremy Hernandez went on the disabled list with a bulging disk in his neck. Hernandez managed nine saves in twelve attempts over the first two months of the season, finishing the year with a 2.70 ERA. Although he throws fairly hard, he's not a prototypical closer because he's not a strikeout pitcher. Instead, Hernandez relies on a sinking fastball to induce grounders. His ability to work often and for a lot of innings makes him particularly valuable to the Marlins; Hernandez led the majors with 112 relief innings pitched in 1993. Assuming he recovers from his neck injury Hernandez should be a steady middle reliever, going 6-6 with a 3.20 ERA and three saves in 85 innings.

The Marlins' wanted to have a lefty strikeout artist in the bullpen for situational matchups; they were disappointed with Rich Rodriguez's performance in 1993 and gave 27 year old Yorkis Perez a chance to win the job. Perez responded with 41 strikeouts in 40.2 innings and a 3.54 ERA; he also held lefthanded hitters to a .194 batting average. Perez often entered the game in difficult situations; stranding 29 inherited runners placed him third in the league. He has the inside track for a reprise of the same role in 1995, but may get some competition from Vic Darensbourg (see Starting Pitchers). Expect a 2-1, 3.65 ERA season from Perez in about 40 innings.

Curveball specialist Richie Lewis is the sole Marlins' reliever to survive two full seasons without suffering a serious injury or be traded, demoted or released. Lewis' 1994 performance was hardly respectable, however as demonstrated by his 5.67 ERA over 54 innings pitched mostly in long relief. His always suspect control completely deteriorated in 1994 as he walked six batters per nine innings. The 29 year old Lewis held righthanders to a .224 batting average but had more trouble with lefties (.353 opponent average). For 1995 Lewis will have to fight to retain his bullpen job; at best he is the fourth righthander in the Marlins' pen and unworthy of Rotisserie interest.

30 year old Luis Aquino has served the Marlins well in both a starting and relief role for both seasons. His versatility was helpful to an evolving pitching staff and he posted an ERA below league average in both seasons despite having underwhelming stuff. After limiting opponents to a .210 average in 1994, Aquino became a free agent; he'll probably find a similar swingman role with another club. As usual he'll be mostly overlooked in the spring, barely make the team, then post respectable numbers for the season. He's still worthless for Rotisserie, though.

A starter in the Mets' organization before his expansion draft selection, 26 year old John Johnstone had a terrible season as a starter in 1993 (4-15, 5.18 ERA), then was shifted to the bullpen and reduced his ERA to 4.46 in the offense oriented Pacific Coast League. Most impressive were his 43 strikeouts in 42.1 innings with just nine walks. Johnstone's control abandoned him in his short stint with the Marlins; he walked 16 in 21.1 innings despite fanning 23. Johnstone has a legitimate chance to unseat Lewis in the Marlins' 1995 bullpen, but expect him to work solely in long or middle relief.

Journeyman finesse pitcher Terry Mathews logged

43 generally impressive innings for the Marlins in 1994, walking just nine and limiting righthanders to a .205 average. The 30 year old Mathews has been a starter in his minor league career and also started two games for the Marlins last year; he could fill the hole left by Aquino's departure. Most likely Mathews will return to Triple-A in 1995.

If you need proof that minor league statistics of finesse pitchers mean nothing, examine the career of 28 year old Jeff Mutis. After posting fine ERAs from 1988 to 1991 for Indians' farm teams, Mutis has been less than stellar with a carerr 6.48 ERA in 58 big league appearances. He's only in the majors because he's lefthanded. Mutis allowed 66 baserunners in 38 innings last year and has allowed 25 homers in 143 career innings. Apparently every team has to have a pathetic lefty in their bullpen; Mutis has that job with the Marlins.

A perennial White Sox prospect, 28 year old Brian Drahman pitched well enough in short major league stints from 1991 to 1993. His 4.77 ERA for Class AAA Edmonton wasn't really so bad when you consider it happened in the offense laden Pacific Coast League. He doesn't throw very hard, but still has managed a strikeout per inning in the minors. Drahman will battle Lewis, Johnstone and Spradlin for a middle relief role in 1995.

There are mostly mediocre journeymen in the Marlins' upper minor league levels; 31 year old Willie Fraser and 29 year old Darrin Chapin should never again receive major league meal money. At Double-A Portland, 26 year old Don Perigny had a 3.86 ERA but has better than a 3-to-1 strikeout/walk ratio in his career. However, Perigny doesn't throw hard enough to be a big league closer. He became the closer when Vic Darensbourg was inserted into the rotation. Class A closers Doug Pettit (25 years old), Bryan Ward (23) and Sean Touchet (22) combined for 155 strikeouts in 138 inings; it remains to be seen if they can sustain that dominance at higher levels.

Houston Astros

Bill Gilbert:

Despite the failure of Mitch Williams, relief pitching was one of the Astros' strengths in 1994. The relievers' ERA was 3.66, fourth lowest in the major leagues. The biggest plus was rookie John Hudek (0-2, 2.97 ERA, 1.07 ratio, 16 saves) who started the season at Tucson, before making his major league debut with enough force to be selected to the All-Star team. Hudek was not a complete surprise because he gained attention with an outstanding winter campaign in Venezuela. However, he had a disappointing spring.

He pitched only seven innings for Triple-A Tucson (with 14 strikeouts) before his recall. Hudek has a fastball in the mid-90s and admits to being a one pitch pitcher. After being virtually unhittable in his early outings, there were a few occasions late in the season when he didn't have the usual pop and movement on his fastball and he was hit hard. Such is often the case for pitchers who advance suddenly after pitching well in winter ball.

At age 28, Hudek should start the season as the team's primary stopper. However, Todd Jones, who came on strong in the second half, should get some of the save opportunities and would take over as the closer if Hudek falters. 26 year old Jones (5-2, 2.72, 1.07, five saves) throws almost as hard as Hudek and has a better assortment of breaking balls and off speed pitches. He started slowly and he did not gain the confidence of Manager Terry Collins until midseason.

The only lefthander in the bullpen for most of the season was young Mike Hampton (2-1, 3.70, 1.50), obtained from Seattle in the Eric Anthony deal. The 22 year old Hampton impressed the Astro staff with his poise and pitching repertoire and should receive an expanded role in the future, possibly as a starter. He is not likely to have significant value to a Rotisserie league owner in 1995.

Another pleasant surprise was 28 year old Dave

Veres, purchased from Tucson in May. Veres was not even in the major league camp in the spring and his eight year inor league record did not predict success at the major league level. However, he made the most of his opportunity and was consistently effective as a middle reliever (3-3, 2.41, 1.12, one save). Veres has excellent control and effectively changes speeds and location. However, he is not likely to get many save opportunities with Hudek and Jones ahead of him.

Lefty Ross Powell, obtained from Cincinnati in the Eddie Taubensee deal, spent most of the year at Tucson (4-2, 5.99, 1.59, one save), but was impressive in two brief stays with the Astros (0-0, 1.23, 1.50). The 27 year old will probably be the second lefthander in the Astro bullpen in 1995.

The Astros have three bullpen prospects in the high minors. 27 year old Jim Dougherty has moved up a notch in each of his four years since being drafted in the 26th round out of the University of North Carolina. The sidearming righthander had recorded at least 21 saves each season and had an ERA under 2.00 in each of his first three years. He wasn't as successful in his first year at the Triple-A level (5-4, 4.12, 1.69, 21 saves). He has a chance to make the Astro staff in 1995, but cannot expect to be the closer.

Lefthander Alvin Morman had a disappointing season in 1995 in his first year at Tucson (3-7, 5.11, 1.49, five saves). In his first three years, 26 year old Morman had a 17-2 record with a 2.30 ERA and more than one strikeout per inning. Morman is a hard thrower who appears to need another year in Class AAA. He could have some value in the future.

Once a top prospect in the Giants' organization, 25 year old Rick Huisman had a banner year as the closer at Class AA Jackson (3-0, 1.51, 1.12, 31 saves). Huisman was a starter early in his career before multiple arm problems caused the Giants to give up on him. Huisman is an aggressive pitcher who led the minor leagues in strikeouts in 1991 and still reaches 90-MPH. He has a chance to make the Astro staff in 1995 and should be a successful major league closer in the future.

Los Angeles Dodgers

In one of those deals that normally wouldn't be noticed by anyone, the Dodgers acquired John O'Donoghue from the Baltimore organization, for John DeSilva. O'Donoghue failed in a 20-inning major league trial in 1993, and flopped back at Triple-A in '94, but before that he was highly regarded. His name reached its highest prominence just before the major league expansion draft, when scouts ogled his smooth delivery and poise on the mound. Now converted from starter to reliever, O'Donoghue will get a look both a lefty matchup specialist and as a long man and spot starter. He wasn't effective against either righties (.318) or lefties (.342) in 1994, so his arrival will most likely depend on an overall return to form, which means hitting spots and changing speeds effectively.

Greg Gajus:

1994 was a disaster for Tommy LaSorda's bullpen. While the Dodgers' closer situation is almost always somewhat unsettled, in 1994 no one handled the job. The Dodgers had 20 saves, by far the league's lowest total.

When the season finished August 12th, Todd Worrell (6-5, 4.29 ERA, 1.17 ratio, 11 saves) had the job. He began the year as co-closer, was injured again, then regained the job by August. He turned in an impressive strikeout rate (9.4 per nine innings), but at age 35 and with a long injury history, Worrell looks like a long gamble. He's signed for 1995 and should hold the job going into spring training. After that it's anyone's guess what LaSorda will do to the bullpen.

1993 first round draft pick Darren Dreifort (0-5, 6.21, 2.07, six saves) took over when Worrell was injured and got a few early saves but stumbled badly later. Demoted to Class AA San Antonio, Dreifort worked as a starter before finishing the year on the disabled list. Baseball America rated him as the Texas League's best prospect; he should compete for the closer's role in spring training.

The unpredictable Jim Gott has finally retired after

years of delivering a surprise season of 25 saves every few years to lucky Rotisserie owners. Of course, mixed with those valuable seasons were years of two saves for his unlucky Rotisserie owners.

Roger McDowell (0-3, 5.23, 1.74) became a free agent and is probably finished. He'll move on to become a full time starter for MTV's Rock-N-Jock softball.

The greatest disarray was in the lefthanded set up role. Gary Wayne, Al Osuna, Omar Daal and Brian Barnes all failed in the role before being demoted to Class AAA Albuquerque. While Osuna was the most effective after his demotion, none have much Rotisserie valuable beyond a couple of unpredictable saves.

Besides Dreifort the most interesting prospect in the Dodgers' system is righthander Antonio Osuna who overmatched Double-A hitters at San Antonio to post a 0.98 ERA with 19 saves and was then unscored upon in six Triple-A appearances. Osuna was a free agent signed out of the Mexican League where he once recorded 15 consecutive strikeouts.

Submariner Todd Williams improved on a poor 1993 season to go 4-2 with a 3.11 ERA and a team high 13 saves for Albuquerque. Peter Gammons' favorite Rudy Seanez managed to reach the majors again and actually pitched 8.2 innings without getting injured.

Montreal Expos

John Perrotto:

No team in the National League had a 1-2 bullpen punch like the Expos' duo of John Wetteland and Mel Rojas in 1994. The hard throwing righthanders combined for 41 saves, more than any other National League clubs totaled as a team.

Wetteland suffered through a groin injury and bouts of ineffectiveness but still went 4-6 with 25 saves, a 2.83 ERA and a 1.06 ratio. He just might be the best closer in the game and he's only 28. Despite all that,

Wetteland may not finish 1995 with the Expos. Strapped for cash, the Expos are always looking to unload a big salary. More than anyone on their talented team, the Expos realize Wetteland is the guy who could draw the biggest return because he is the one player who could assure another club of a pennant.

Having Rojas makes it easier for the Expos to consider dealing Wetteland. Despite being greatly overshadowed by Wetteland, Rojas is a fine short reliever in his own right as evidenced by his 3-2 record with 16 saves, a 3.32 ERA and 1.10 ratio in 1994. He could close for a lot of major league clubs. It would be more than a bit ironic if the Expos traded Wetteland and gave the closer's job to Rojas. Rojas has been crying for two years that he should be traded because manager Felipe Alou (who happens to be his cousin) doesn't use him correctly.

The Expos also have a good crew of righthanded set up men, who get lost in the large shadows of Wetteland and Rojas. Tim Scott (5-2, 2.70, 1.29, one save) and Jeff Shaw (5-2, 3.88, 1.07, one save) both throw hard and could be closers in other situations. Gil Heredia was 6-3 with a 3.46 ERA and a 1.30 ratio and became a very reliable middle and long man last year; he was also effective when pressed into starting duty.

Another righthander to keep an eye on is Heath Haynes, a clone of Expos lefthanded starter Kirk Rueter; he also has very ordinary stuff but a knack for winning. Haynes didn't allow a run in a brief major league stints last season and was 6-7 with four saves, a 2.38 ERA and a 1.00 ratio with Class AAA Ottawa. Haynes owns an eye-catching 29-9 career record over four minor league seasons.

The Expos' one bullpen weakness is the lack of a quality lefthander. They went in 1994 thinking rookie Joey Eischen could become their lefty set up man, and hoping that he could even blossom into a closer as they converted him from a starting role. However, Eischen was just 2-6 with two saves, a 4.94 ERA and a 1.52 ratio at Ottawa and 0-0 with a 54.00 ERA and a 6.00 ratio in a brief stay with the Expos. He doesn't seem comfortable pitching out of the bullpen.

A lefty longshot for the bullpen in 1995 is native Quebec son Denis Boucher, who was dropped from the 40-man roster at the end of last season. He was 7-6 with a 3.71 ERA and a 1.29 ratio as a starter with Ottawa last season but 0-1 with a 6.75 ERA and 1.66 ratio with Montreal. The Expos desperately hoped he would become a drawing card in French-speaking Montreal but it just never happened.

Montreal's top relief prospect is righthander Scott Gentile, who dominated out of Class A West Palm Beach's bullpen after beginning the season as an overmatched starter with Class AA Harrisburg. Gentile was 0-1 with a 17.42 ERA and 4.10 ratio with Harrisburg but then went 5-2 with 26 saves, a 1.93 ERA and 0.97 ratio with West Palm Beach. Furthermore, he finished the season with 43 consecutive scoreless innings. He has closer's stuff with a 94-MPH fastball and 89-MPH slider.

New York Mets

While most observers in New York were assuming that the Mets would re-sign free agent John Franco, the front office lined up a large number of alternatives.

Robert Person took five years to get to Double-A as a starter, but then he blossomed as a reliever in the Arizona Fall League in 1994. Said his AFL manager Brian Graham, "Just based on what he's done in this fall league, I would have to say that Person deserves a major league shot in 1995." What Person has done is to convert successfully from a starter to a reliever.

He was held back mainly because of his limited repertoire. Two times through the batting order, and Person has shown all his pitches to all the hitters; sometimes once through the order is about it. In short relief, it's a different story. Person has a "plus" fastball, clocking 91-94 MPH consistently, and a nice sharp slider, but not much more, He's been working on a changeup for years, and it's still in development. "He can be a two-pitch pitcher in short relief," however, says manager Graham. "He's got the resilient arm to work consecutive days, and he has the ability to get loose quickly. The best news is that he comes in and goes right after the batters."

Person isn't the only new face in the Mets pen. Blas Minor, who looked promising as a rookie in 1993 but never matured any further, got demoted and then waived by the Pirates (after a recall during the strike; do you think maybe someone was trying to save money there?) and now Minor is Mets property.

More relief pitching came in the Jeromy Burnitz trade: Jerry DiPoto, Dave Mlicki, Paul Byrd, not to mention the player to be named later. DiPoto is coming back from thyroid cancer, and though he's expected to be OK health-wise, his talent as a pitcher is obviously in question. Mlicki is another major rehab project. He had rotator cuff surgery in 1993. Byrd is the most promising for being relatively free of physical question marks, but he's also the only one the three who got demoted in 1994, from Triple-A to Double-A for most of the year. He still has possibilities as a pen man.

Another winter acquisition was Doug Henry, the former Brewers closer (see Milwaukee) who never developed another reliable pitch to go with his OK fastball. Henry hasn't been an effective reliever in a long time, and last year he walked more than he struck out. His presence with the Mets is part of an obvious effort to try the quantity method as a way of coming up with quality for the bullpen. Henry is highly unlikely to add to his 61 career saves in 1995, or ever.

Mike Maddux, who had the righty setup job before Manzanillo took it away from him last year, became a free agent in October. Maddux got two saves early in 1994, but none after April. He broke his toe kicking an immovable object in the dugout after one bad outing and spent time on the DL. He's essentially a breaking ball pitcher who needs to keep the ball low in the strike zone. Maddux is capable of bouncing back to competence in 1995. Manager Dallas Green won't want him back, but some other team will see the merit in giving him a tryout that should lead to a middle relief or setup role. Still, the best days are clearly behind him.

Philadelphia Phillies

Tony Blengino:

The Phils upgraded their 1994 bullpen situation dramatically in a classic case of addition by subtraction. 1993 closer Mitch Williams was exiled to Houston after his World Series debacle. Grudgingly, the Astros parted with starter prospect Jeff Juden, but would only complete the trade if the Phils would agree to take Doug Jones and his huge salary off of the Astros' hands.

Jones became the bullpen anchor as the Phillies had the National League's second lowest ERA at 3.44. The 38 year old Jones does in a whisper what Williams tried to do with a shout. The difference between Jones' precision, finesse pitching and Williams' wild power pitching was like night and day. Although Jones allowed more than a hit per inning, he walked just six batters in 54 innings and finished third in the league with 27 saves. Jones' saves were more difficult to earn than Williams' 41 saves in 1993; he received 20 inherited baserunners in 47 games, compared to ten inherited runners for Williams in 65 games.

Jones became a free agent at the end of his fine campaign and will earn a high salary, possibly too much for the Phillies to pay. Exercise great caution when bidding on Jones, however, as he followed similarly excellent years in 1990 and 1992 with awful seasons in succeeding years. Expect Jones to tail off to a 5-9 season in 1995 with 15 saves and a 4.00 ERA for some other team.

As a set up man, 29 year old Heathcliffe Slocumb was a pleasant surprise. He seemed to overcome the control problems that have plagued him throughout his career; Slocumb walked 3.5 batters per nine innings against his career mark of 4.7 per nine innings entering the 1994 season. Slocumb has a "heavy" 90-MPH fastball and has allowed just nine homers in 209 career innings, including no homers in 72.1 innings last year. However, his 5-1 record and 2.86 ERA aren't as good as they look. Slocumb's baserunner ratio was 1.42 and he was touched for

nine unearned runs; an unusually high number for a reliever. He'll once again be a middle reliever for the 1995 Phillies, going 6-6 with no saves and a 3.75 ERA.

Ricky Bottalico was annointed as a leading bullpen prospect by many "experts" last year; we chose Toby Borland to make an impact instead. The gangly (6'7", 175 pound) Borland held righthanders to a .224 major league average with his sidearm delivery. The 26 year old Borland has likely arrived in the majors to stay, after finally succeeding in his third try at the Triple-A level in 1994. The Phillies seem reluctant to try him as a closer, though, and he'll probably be a top righthanded set up man in 1995. Expect Borland to go 6-4 with five saves and a 2.95 ERA next season.

At age 42, Larry Andersen may finally be nearing the finish line; he had two disabled list stints in 1994. Andersen also experienced control difficulties for the first time in his 20 year major league career, walking 15 batters in 32.2 innings. He continues to be successful against righthanded hitters, though, holding them to a .193 batting average. Andersen's lack of durability will limit him to a situational righthanded relief role, should he return in 1995.

Paul Quantrill was a big disappointment after his acquistion from the Red Sox in the Wes Chamberlain trade. Expected to serve as Jones' primary set up man, Quantrill instead had a 6.00 ERA and allowed opponents to hit .331 against him. An off speed pitcher who needs absolute precision to be effective, the 25 year old righthander has never been a big strikeout pitcher, but has also kept walks to a minimum. Quantrill was also used in the rotation for Triple-A Scranton-Wilkes Barre, walking just six in 57 innings. A switch back to the bullpen is in the works for Quantrill in 1995. His finesse pitching seems better suited to the American League; lack of a good heater will hurt him in the National League. He should go 5-7 with a 3.80 ERA in 1995.

34 year old Tom Edens is the definitive journeyman, having spent six seasons with five different teams and carrying a mop for all of them. Edens has had four

saves in the last three seasons even though he has finished 49 games in that span. Acquired just before the strike from the Astros in exchange for Milt Thompson, Edens is a long reliever who will make the 1995 team if the younger relief prospects (Borland, Quantrill, Bottalico) fail.

Only by virtue of being lefthanded is 26 year old Andy Carter in the major leagues. He has nothing that can be considered major league stuff, a career minor league ERA of nearly 4.00 and a losing record as a professional with just one save. But, with David West in the rotation, Carter is the only lefty candidate for a bullpen role in 1995. Carter had some success in his first trip around the National League, but was hit harder the second time around; he was demoted when his ERA had reached 4.46 in 20 games. Carter will make the club as a lefty situational reliever, going 2-2 with a 4.15 ERA.

Ricky Bottalico's blistering performance in the 1993 Arizona Fall League sparked exaggerated hyperbole and wild over-bidding for the next "Great Closer". In his first visit to Triple-A Bottalico was anything but great, posting an 8.87 ERA with 54 baserunners in 22 innings. A return to Double-A Reading gave him a chance to rebound; he garnered 22 saves in 28 appearances and struck out more than one batter per inning with fewer than one baserunner per inning.

Bottalico's development parallels that of Borland with Bottalico being a year behind. Bottalico will have to experience some Triple-A success before he gets a big league promotion. But, Manager Jim Fregosi has his heart set on Bottalico becoming his closer, so he must still be considered the team's future closer.

The Phillies took a chance on 32 year old lefty Norm Charlton after his major elbow reconstruction surgery in 1993. The noble gamble failed as Charlton suffered one setback after another despite a looking pretty good early in his rehabilitation. A power pitcher before getting hurt, his only recourse is a return as a finesse pitcher; an unlikely event.

The Phillies' 1993 first round draft pick, 22 year old

Wayne Gomes was put into Class A Clearwater's starting rotation in 1994 in order to "build arm strength" after pitching just 27 innings in his final year of college ball and 15 innings in his Rookie League pro debut. Gomes managed less than five innings per start while walking almost a batter per inning. He also used a 95-MPH fastball to strike out a batter per inning while allowing just 85 hits in 104 innings. Gomes has a lot to learn about discipline and work ethic, but appears to have enough talent to be a big league closer someday.

Eight year minor league veteran Chuck Ricci came on strong late in the season to lead Triple-A Scranton-Wilkes Barre with six saves. The 26 year old righthander has fanned more than a batter per inning over the last two years with a strikeout to walk ratio of almost four to one. Ricci has an outside shot at a situational role in the 1995 Phillies bullpen.

Pittsburgh Pirates

When in doubt, take any $1 arm from the Pirates pen. The odds of any given reliever getting one save (and thus being worth $1) is always better than 50/50 in Pittsburgh. To this mix for 1995, add Todd Frohwirth, the 32-year-old submarine soft-tosser who had some glittering seasons in Baltimore before his horrendous 1994 campaign. If Frohwirth is physically well enough to make the roster, Leyland will find a way to get him a save or two, maybe more.

John Perrotto:

The Pirates' problems finding a quality closer have been well documented. For a refresher, just rewind your memory back to Game Seven of the 1992 National League Championship Series.

The Pirates haven't had a closer with 20 saves since Bill Landrum came out of nowhere to notch 28 in 1989.

However, the Pirates thought they had found their man last season when Alejandro Pena finally appeared to be over the reconstructive elbow surgery that caused him to miss all of 1993. After a few shaky

outings, the righthander was 3-2 with seven saves, a 5.02 ERA and a 1.12 ratio. Then, his elbow blew out again in late June. The Pirates released Pena, likely ending his career.

So, who will be the Pirates' closer in 1995. You just might be the answer. All you need to do is drop by Pirate City in Bradenton, Fla. this spring and ask for a tryout.

OK, the Pirates' bullpen situation might not be that desperate. But it's close. At the end of last season, righthander Mark Dewey had the most career saves of anyone on the staff with eight. He was promptly released after a season in which he was 2-1 with one save, a 3.68 ERA and a 1.56 ratio.

The guy with the most potential is righthander Danny Miceli, a hard throwing 24 year old. He was 2-1 with two saves, a 5.93 ERA and a 1.48 ratio last season with the Pirates and 1-1 with two saves, a 1.88 ERA and a 0.88 ratio with Class AAA Buffalo. Miceli pitched with a lot of confidence in the second half of last season and likes the pressure of taking the mound with the game on the line. However, he does need to develop a second pitch to complement his good fastball; he's working on a slider.

Pirates manager Jim Leyland likes to ease young players into roles, so don't expect Miceli to automatically get 90 percent of the save opportunities this season, even if he starts out strong.

The makeup of the remainder of the bullpen is anyone's guess. Journeyman righthander Mike Dyer resurfaced in the majors last year. It was his first time in the big leagues since spending the second half of 1989 as a starter in Minnesota's rotation. Dyer battled back from nerve damage in his shoulder that threatened his career in 1990-91. He was the Pirates' closer for a few weeks after the All-Star break but couldn't hold the job. Dyer was 1-1 with four saves, a 5.87 ERA and a 1.76 ratio for the Pirates and 3-3 with 12 saves, a 2.34 ERA and a 1.40 ratio for Buffalo.

Another righthander, Blas Minor, wound up back in the minors last season after a solid rookie season with the Pirates in 1993. He was just 0-1 with one save, an 8.05 ERA and a 1.90 ratio for Pittsburgh last season but 1-2 with 11 saves, a 1.98 ERA and a 1.16 ratio for Buffalo. He'll likely get one more chance to stick in the majors in 1995.

Ravelo Manzanillo was the Pirates' top lefthanded reliever in 1994, leading the club in appearances. His story was remarkable. After being released by Toronto in 1991, he spend 1992 in Taiwan and was out of organized baseball in 1993. The Pirates spotted Manzanillo playing winter ball in his native Dominican Republic during the 1993-94 off season and invited him to spring training.

Manzanillo went 4-2 with one save, a 4.14 ERA and 1.74 ratio. His herky-jerky motion makes him tough on lefties but his lack of control makes him tough on Leyland, who despises walks. Leyland won't trust him to close many games.

Lefty Rich Robertson was 0-0 with a 6.89 ERA and a 1.92 ratio after being called up at the All-Star break from Buffalo, where he was 5-10 with a 3.11 ERA and a 1.21 ratio as a starter. At best, he is the 11th man on a major league staff.

Jeff Ballard was a key lefty reliever for the Pirates at the start of last season. However, he was demoted to Buffalo at the All-Star break and his days with the Pirates are almost certainly over. An 18-game winner with Baltimore in 1989, he has never fully recovered from elbow surgery following that season. He was 1-1 with two saves, a 6.66 ERA and a 1.73 ratio with Pittsburgh last season and 3-7 with a 4.82 ERA and a 1.54 ratio at Buffalo. Ouch.

A lefthander to watch is Jason Christiansen, a 6'5" hard thrower. He has put up good numbers in the farm system as a set up man since being signed as an undrafted free agent in 1991. He was 2-1 with two saves, a 2.09 ERA and a 1.13 ratio for Class AA Carolina last season, then went 3-1 with a 2.41 ERA and a 1.03 ratio for Buffalo. The fact that he has never been used as a closer in the minors makes it unlikely he'll be given that role in the majors. However, his

live fastball and good control impressed Leyland during his trip to Buffalo last August.

Lee Hancock is a 27 year old lefty who puts up solid but unspectacular numbers in the minors. He was 4-5 with one save, a 3.43 ERA and a 1.44 ratio for Buffalo last season then was sent to the Arizona Fall League along with Christiansen. An indictment of his potential, though, is the fact that the pitching starved Pirates have never given him a call to the majors over the past two seasons. How good can he really be?

Brian Shouse is another lefty whose value has to be in question. He was placed on the 15-man protected list for the expansion draft in November, 1992, then was dropped from the 40-man roster just ten months later. His 3-4 season with Buffalo in 1994, to go with a 3.63 ERA and a 1.14 ratio, did nothing to really bring him back to prospect status.

The Pirates also sent two big, intriguing righthanders to the AFL, Jeff McCurry and Marc Pisciotta. McCurry was 6-5 with 11 saves, a 3.21 ERA and a 1.28 ratio for Carolina last year while Pisciotta was 1-4 with 19 saves, a 1.53 ERA and a 1.28 ratio for Class A Salem and 3-4 with five saves, a 5.61 ERA and a 1.81 ratio for Carolina. Considering the tattered state of the Pirates' bullpen, it would be no great surprise if either one wound up in Pittsburgh at some point in 1995.

St. Louis Cardinals

Tom Henke has arrived, providing the veteran that St. Louis needed last year. There are questions about Henke's physical condition, however. In 1994 he was hampered by problems with his back and shoulder, and even when he was in his prime years, Henke was susceptible to various muscle pulls. He has a long history of spring training miseries and slow starts, usually taking until mid May to get into prime condition.

Henke's arrival is still bad news for the other would-be ace relievers on the Cardinals' staff. Rene Arocha and his large repertoire could even return to the starting rotation, while Mike Perez will have to come

back from injuries, and pitch at a high level well into the major league season, and see the demise of Henke, before he can again be cast as an ace reliever.

Given the importance of management discretion in the awarding of saves, I would much rather have Henke than anyone else in this pen. And even if he pitches badly, his value could be propped up by the Dave Smith Rule: no matter how bad you pitch, you can get 15 saves if management wants you for the job (Smith got 17 saves with a 6.00 ERA for the Cubs in 1991).

John Perrotto:

New Cardinals CEO and President Mark Lamping insists the club will do whatever it takes to win. The great fans of St. Louis and the Midwest can only hope that Lamping is telling the truth.

For too many years, the Cardinals have worried more about the bottom line than their winning percentage. That is more than a little puzzling since the club is owned by Anheuser-Busch, one of the world's richest corporations.

The Cardinals' penny pinching ways may have hit an all time low late in the 1993 season when they traded Lee Smith, baseball's career saves leader, to the New York Yankees for a minor leaguer because they wanted to get something for him before he walked as a free agent. Smith had saved 43 games for the Cardinals that year and 160 in less than four full seasons in St. Louis. The Cardinals tried to say Smith was at the end of the line but he proved them wrong by leading the American League with 33 saves for Baltimore in 1994.

The Cardinals never really did replace Smith; it was a big reason why they finished tied for third in the five team National League Central in 1994.

The Cardinals gave the job to righthander Mike Perez out of spring training; Perez had been an effective set up man during the previous two seasons. As many expected, that move turned out to be disastrous. Perez had said he didn't want the pressure of closing

in the majors then proved he wasn't up to the task by going 2-3 with 12 saves, an 8.71 ERA and 2.00 ratio. Cuban defector and former starter Rene Arocha then moved into the closer's role and did a decent job, finishing at 4-4 with 11 saves, a 4.01 ERA and 1.39 ratio. However, Arocha's chances of long term effectiveness in the role is debatable. Arocha relies more on changing speeds and using a variety of pitches from numerous arm angles. That approach works better for a starter than a short man, who needs to come in and blow people away. However, he did seem to like the job and handled the pressure much better than Perez.

The Cardinals, though, have no options beyond Arocha. Sure, a lot of relievers in their farm system have put up gaudy save totals but don't be fooled. The Cardinals' minor league closers are almost always older than most of the players in their leagues; they use their experience to overmatch their opponents, not talent. However, few make it to the majors and fewer still are successful. Perez is a perfect example of this; he saved 129 games as a minor leaguer before his 1994 disaster. Another example is Willie Smith, who had 29 saves for Class AAA Louisville last season at 27 years old, but was released at season's end.

The rest of the contenders for bullpen spots are either journeymen or young pitchers who are not considered great prospects.

The journeymen are lefty Rich Rodriguez and righthander John Habyan. Rodriguez was 3-5 with a 4.03 ERA and 1.46 ratio last season while Habyan was 1-0 with one save, a 3.23 ERA and 1.48 ratio. The younger lefthanded candidates are: Bryan Eversgerd (2-3 with a 4.52 ERA and 1.40 ratio for St. Louis and 1-1 with a 4.50 ERA and 1.58 ratio with Louisville last season), Tom Urbani (3-7 with a 5.15 ERA and 1.48 ratio for St. Louis and 4-2 with a 5.77 ERA and 1.410 ratio with Louisville) and Steve Dixon (0-0 with a 23.14 ERA and 4.71 ratio with St. Louis and 3-2 with 11 saves, a 2.51 ERA and 1.33 ratio for Louisville).

The younger righthanders: Frank Cimorelli (0-0 with

one save, an 8.77 ERA and 2.25 ratio with St. Louis and 5-3 with four saves, a 4.01 ERA and 1.38 ratio for Louisville) and Gary Buckels (0-1 with a 2.25 ERA and 1.25 ratio with St. Louis, 7-2 with two saves, a 3.26 ERA and 1.17 ratio for Louisville and 0-0 with 0.00 ERA and 0.50 ratio with Class AA Arkansas).

The only one of the five to get mildly excited about is Buckles, who has a good curveball. However, he is also 28 years old and was out of baseball for the entire 1992 season after being released by California.

As mentioned earlier, it is unwise to get carried away with relievers in the farm system. However, one guy to keep an eye on is righthander Frank Garcia, who had more than twice as many saves as any reliever in the Arizona Rookie League last season. He was 1-1 with 18 saves, a 1.21 ERA and 0.77 ratio. However, Garcia was also 20, two years older than most players in the Arizona League.

San Diego Padres

Hank Widmer:

Acquired as part of the deal for Gary Sheffield, Trevor Hoffman has turned into the kind of stopper the Padres have lacked since Randy Myers left in 1992.

Padres middle relief was nearly as big of a disappointment as their porous defense. They had to use an exceptionally large number of middle innings relievers to bridge the gap from starters to Hoffman, and often the lead didn't hold.

Marc Bowman:

In order for a reliever to earn a save, his team must first earn a victory. Therefore, it stands to reason that closers for losing teams would necessarily suffer in relation to closers of equal ability for winning teams. This isn't always the case. Several things have a larger bearing upon a reliever's save opportunity.

The reliance of a manager upon a single closer is the largest factor in save distribution, of course, but also

figuring into the mix is how often starters are able to throw a complete game, how often games are blow outs (for either team) and the quality of set up relievers.

The best comparison can be made between the Braves and the Padres. The Braves won 21 more games in 1994 than the Padres, yet their ace closer, Greg McMichael, managed just one more save than his counterpart with the Padres, Trevor Hoffman. Indeed, both teams recorded exactly 26 saves for the season. How is that possible?

Two measurable things occured, plus one factor that is more difficult to figure precisely. To begin with, Braves' starting pitchers completed 15 games, compared to just eight by Padres' starters. Also, the Braves were involved in far more blow outs; no team had fewer one-run games than the Braves' 28. Meanwhile, the Padres were at the higher end of the scale with 37 one-run contests.

The intangible factor was McMichael's occasional stumbling. It probably had an effect upon how and when Braves' Manager Bobby Cox went to the bullpen. When McMichael was faltering, Cox might have been more reluctant to go get his ace closer in a tight spot. Hoffman didn't suffer from such a lack of confidence by his manager.

Finally, one more factor keeps ace relievers with winning teams from having a proportionally large number of saves when compared to ace relievers for losing teams. Winning teams tend to have several streaks during the season in which they win four, five, or more games at a stretch. Since few pitchers can pitch effectively more than two days in a row, the top closer can't possibly save every game of the winning streaks; he misses out on some save opportunities when he rests. Closers for losing teams don't run into that problem as much because their teams don't run off as many long winning streaks and the streaks are usually shorter, too.

Because good teams always have lengthier and more numerous winning streaks during the season, their bullpen aces will often save a smaller percentage of their teams' victories. In 1994, the four teams with the best records in the National League (Montreal, Atlanta, Cincinnati and Houston) won 273 games with 128 saves. The five worst teams (San Diego, Chicago, Florida, Pittsburgh and St. Louis) won 250 games with 135 saves. The worse teams recorded saves in 54.0% of their games compared to just 46.8% by the better teams. For further proof consider that Randy Myers set a National League record in 1993 with 53 saves for a team that only won 84 games, seventh best in the league.

Getting a large number of wins for a bad team is difficult, but getting a large number of saves for the same team is far more commonplace. The chances of Andy Benes winning 20 games for the Padres are extremely remote, but the chances of Hoffman recording 40 saves isn't small at all.

Despite the poor set up relief help provided by the Padres, Trevor Hoffman has three things going for him as a closer which will provide him with a lot of save opportunities:
- He is definitely the ace closer so he won't share saves,
- On a pitching staff populated with younger starters, the number of complete games should be lower than average, and
- The Padres are not going to be involved in as many blow outs as other teams; their mediocre offense and decent starting pitching should keep game scores lower and tighter.

Combine these factors with Hoffman's hard stuff (a 95-MPH fastball) and you have a genuine ace reliever; he could quietly get 35 saves in 1995. With the topsy-turvy state of relief pitching, that makes Hoffman one of the better buys for 1995.

Fred Matos:

The Padres bullpen looked like the land of opportunity last year as old veterans were given another chance and many rookies, even 30 year olds, made major league debuts. Trevor Hoffman emerged as the ace closer when Gene Harris wore out his welcome and was traded to Detroit. Hoffman has an outstanding fastball and struck out 68 in 56 innings last year. Now

27 years old and a three year veteran, he will be the relief ace for the foreseeable future. Though the Padres don't have a good team, Hoffman could still collect 35 saves.

Rookie lefthander Jeff Tabaka made his major league debut last year at age 30. Although he had a 5.27 ERA, he pitched well, giving up only 32 hits in 42 innings while holding hitters to a minuscule .213 average, both good signs. He's the lefty setup man for Hoffman and could get a few wins and saves.

Doug Brocail was the Padres top draft pick way back in 1986, finally making it to The Show in 1993 after some rough minor league years. He's been easy to hit over the course of his career, allowing more than a hit per inning every year. Brocail also developed a serious elbow problem last year that required surgery. Brocail is a pitcher to avoid, even when he is healthy.

The Padres have a number of excellent closer prospects in the minors. Talented but erratic southpaw Robbie Beckett was promoted from Class AA to Class AAA in midseason. The Padres' first draft pick in 1990, Beckett has outstanding stuff, including a major league fastball and slider, but has trouble finding the strike zone consisstently; he has walked more than a batter per inning over the course of his five year career. Beckett was wilder at Triple-A than he has ever been, walking 39 in 23.2 innings. More than one observer has labeled him as another Mitch Williams.

The Padres made collegiate starter Dustin Hermanson their top draft pick in 1994 (third overall) and they see him as a future closer. He began last year as a closer for Class AA Wichita, and pitched well enough to earn a promotion to Triple-A Las Vegas. He could be in the Padres bullpen in 1995 and may even become a starter should the rotation fall apart.

Mike Draper was the Triple-A closer last year, but he posted a horrible 6.85 ERA and allowed 92 hits in just 70 innings.

Only Hoffman has any Rotisserie value and should be in the $30 to $35 range. Tabaka might be a good injury replacement during the season.

San Francisco Giants

Steven Rubio:

You start the discussion with Rod Beck, who did not blow a save last season, in an ''off year.'' Keep believing in pitchers like this until they give you a reason to quit trusting them. Beck is one of the best.

Mike Jackson could be gone for 1995. He would be sorely missed by the Giants, as he is perhaps the best setup man in baseball today. He has the tools to be a stopper if given the chance, and is well worth your attention.

Like most teams, the Giants have a potpourri of pitching talent laboring in middle relief. Most of them are unnoteworthy, although Dave Burba has been striking out batters at a phenomenal rate for some time now. Bryan Hickerson is perhaps the most dangerous of these guys for fantasy owners, as his versatility makes him the first choice for a spot start, where he is fully capable of being bombed.

after some good years for Cincinnati before sitting out all of 1994 with an injury.

Once again your attention should be drawn to Kevin Rogers, the one pitcher in this group who could bust out. Rogers missed most of 1994 due to injury, but should be fine for 1995. He has been impressive throughout his career and would make an excellent late round pick for fantasy owners. While he's unlikely to get any saves behind Rod Beck, Rogers can pitch with the best of them. He was also a starting pitcher in the minors and some of us believe he could be surprisingly effective in this role in the majors, although the Giants seem unconvinced.

The most interesting minor league reliever is Stacy Jones, who was made a stopper for the first time in his career in 1994 and responded by setting a single season saves record for Class AA Shreveport. His numbers have ''late bloomer'' written all over them; he is now 28 years old. Kurt Peltzer has been decent for quite a few minor league seasons and probably deserves a shot in the majors to see what he could do.

IN SEARCH OF THE PERFECT DRAFT PICK

1995 marks our sixth year telling you about the ''Age 26 and under, with experience'' phenomenon. The goal is simply to find the perfect draft pick: a player who is going to rise in value in the coming season, exceeding anything he has done in the past, performing at the star level AND yet be undervalued on draft day.

To find these players, we take advantage of three natural tendencies:

(1) Players who have been around the major leagues for a couple years or more don't attract the same attention as rookies and sophomores. After a player has two or seasons in the record books, there is an appearance that he has an ''established'' performance level. Rotisserie leaguers tend to accept these established levels as good estimates of what will happen in the year to come.

(2) Hitters normally peak around age 27 or 28. At age 25 or 26 they are typically going through their years of biggest improvement. Not by coincidence, age 25 or 26 is also the year when most players first win major league jobs, as their skills elevate them to the major league level. Many of the age 25-26 group (the major league newcomers in this group) thus get caught up in the annual hype about each year's rookie class.

(3) Players who become full-time major leaguers at younger ages, say 23 or 24, tend to be far above average. They are already above average in the critical measure of how long it took them to reach major league capability. Players who become full-time major leaguers at age 23 or 24 tend to become stars after they mature further. Players who become full-time major leaguers at age 20-22 tend to becomes superstars. The best athletes reach a point, earlier than other players, where their talent is good enough for the majors -- but that doesn't mean they stop improving, just because they have become successful in The Show. In fact, star players usually keep on improving, just like their less-gifted colleagues, right up to age 27 or 28.

The ''perfect'' draft pick is, therefore, a player who is not yet age 27 (and is thus still in his period of growth and improvement) but also a player who has been in the major leagues long enough to give an impression that he has reached an established level.

In the last two years, the top ten names on our Age 26 lists have included Jeff Bagwell, John Olerud, Gregg Jefferies, Carlos Baerga, Roberto Alomar, Sammy Sosa, Albert Belle, Mo Vaughn, Delino DeShields, and Travis Fryman -- basically, everybody who was anybody in the world of rising young talent reaching new heights in baseball. In prior years we have tabbed Ken Griffey, Barry Bonds, Ron Gant, Larry Walker, Steve Finley and dozens more who fit this pattern of reaching the majors at a young age and then achieving stardom after having rookie and sophomore years that don't show their full potential. (Barry Bonds hit only .223 as a rookie, as I love to keep reminding everyone). You get the idea.

Not everyone on this list automatically soars in value the year we print their names here, of course. Last year's choice as number one the list, Eric Anthony, was a genuine dud. I liked him to be a bargain, unwanted in many leagues because of his .224 career average, and sure enough he was inexpensive on draft day and ''improved'' to .237 and reached a career high in stolen bases; but Anthony played only 79 games due to assorted injuries including knee tendinitis which put him on the DL, and a league suspension. If he played a full season, he would have hit 20 home runs for the first time as I predicted, but he was dreadful compared to previous number one names on the Age 26 list (Jay Bell 1991, Larry Walker 1992, and Jeff Bagwell 1993. The Anthony experience has convinced me to focus more on the talent aspect and less on the low-price bargain aspect, at least when it comes to choosing the top name overall.

For 1995 I feel very comfortable with my number one choice, both for star quality and for a price profit:

(1) WIL CORDERO: If you haven't seen this guy play, and I mean focusing on him throughout a whole game, then you can hardly appreciate how much talent he brings

to the field. He's already a $30 ballplayer. Write these numbers down, and check back in October 1995: 570 at bats, 22 homers, 89 RBI, 20 steals, .297 average, $30. And 1996 will be even bigger.

(2) CHUCK KNOBLAUCH: This guy has been on the same list before. Last year I stared at Jeff Bagwell's name, thinking, yes, the guy could do even better in 1994 than he did in 1993 after appearing as my number one selection; after all, he was hurt during the final weeks of 1993 and missing that time cut into his numbers. Not making the same mistake this year, I am staring at Knoblauch's name and thinking, hey, just because he's been here before doesn't mean I must drop him to the "also noteworthy" group at the bottom of the list. Yes, he could do even better in 1995. At the upper end of the spectrum, we could be looking at a .315 average and 40 steals. At the lower end of the spectrum, maybe just more of what we saw in 1994 -- and that's pretty darn good.

(3) KEN GRIFFEY: Same comments as for Knoblauch. Yes, Griffey at $40 could easily turn out to be a bargain.

(4) BRET BOONE: The change of scenery produced a whole new player in 1994. When I visited with Boone during spring training a year ago, it was hard to believe this was the same player who had looked so tense when he was with the Mariners. The look on his face was more like a confident veteran who had been through a dozen spring trainings before, and here he was in his first go-around with the Reds. What does Davey Johnson know about young players? Where can I buy his book? Expect Boone to hit right around .300 and pop 20 homers. Not bad for a National League second baseman, heh?

(5) ROYCE CLAYTON: Is it possible he had his career year in 1993 at age 23? No way. Clayton took a step or two backward in 1994, but so did the whole Giants team. Look for his average to jump from .236 back into the .260-.280 range, and look for a career high in home runs (topping 6 should be easy). Also look for 50+ RBI, not the anemic level of 1994. And look for the career year in 1996 after a solid year in 1995.

(6) DELINO DESHIELDS: Last year, I didn't exactly strike it rich with injury rehab cases, so there are none in my top five picks this year. If anyone is certain to do better in 1995 than he did in 1994, however, DeShields must be among the prime candidates. Look for a rise in batting average, from .250 up to .270 or higher, and look for the

stolen bases to jump from 27 to 40 or more.

(7) BRENT GATES: Next in line among the injury rehab cases among the young star population. Heck, if he just goes back to what he did as a rookie in 1993 after spending 1992 in A-ball, he will be a high-value bargain. And there's no reason why Gates shouldn't do even better in his third year.

(8) CARLOS BAERGA: Back to my "yes they really can do better" list. Baerga hit .347 in the second half, as I define it, in 1994. His 1993 performance is a baseline (figure .310 or .320, with 20 homers and 110 RBI) upon which he can build with a nice long hot streak.

(9) TODD HUNDLEY: It is remotely possible that Hundley might hit down around .230 again, but the upward possibilities are the intriguing aspect here. For years I've been saying it's just a matter of time until Hundley "soars" to the level of a .250-.270 hitter, and he's obviously got the power to be a valuable catcher. My computer model, which I use as a starting point for all my forecasts, says .239 with 16 homers for 1995. My gut feeling is more like .250+ with 20+ homers. What he looks like in spring training will be the key to how high I push my Draft Day predictions.

(10) BERNIE WILLIAMS: A classic case of star-on-the-rise. Figure 20 homers and 20 steals, with a .285 average, and you get the idea for 1995. There's a .300 hitter in here, waiting to burst out. Remember how the Yankees moved Roberto Kelly out of center field, and then out of New York, to make room for Williams. On the field and in the clubhouse, he's gone from a tense, almost disoriented personality, to blossom into a graceful star.

CLOSE TO THE TOP TEN: Ivan Rodriguez, Andujar Cedeno, Juan Gonzalez, Dave Nilsson, Travis Fryman, Phil Plantier, Gary Sheffield, Dean Palmer, Eddie Taubensee, Brad Ausmus, Pedro Munoz.

* * * * * * * * * * * * * * *

NEW SERVICE: Stay Current All Year

You asked for it ... you got it:

JOHN BENSON'S WEEKLY
Baseball Analysis Message
On Tape

During the baseball season February 26 to October 1:
Updates **EVERY SUNDAY**

During the winter: updates on the 15th of each month

900-737-3707
Just $1.49 / minute

Choose from American League or National League

Who's coming, who's going
Impacts of free agent signings
Who's hurt - and what it means
Winners and losers in trades and other deals

YOU SAY YOU DON'T LIKE "900" NUMBERS ?
Get the same baseball updates by subscription

VOICE MAIL ACCESS - $49 per year for 30 Updates - AL or NL
($79 per year for both - 60 Updates!)
Call as many times as you want, and save $$$ off 900# prices
Phone 800-707-9090 for Mastercard/Visa orders to get your personal access number
Or send $49 (or $79) to Diamond Library, 196 Danbury Road, Wilton CT 06897

THE CURRENT CROP OF TOP DRAFT PICKS

By Jim Callis

Just as major league teams provide for the future through the amateur draft, fantasy league teams do the same through the minor league/ultra draft. There are few greater joys for fantasy league owners than to draft a young prospect and after a couple of years watch him make an impact on their club. Those of you who grabbed Jason Bere before he burst onto the scene with the White Sox, take a bow.

One caveat needs to be stressed. The draft is an inexact science because major league teams have to project the abilities of prospects over time. That's a nearly impossible task, and a reason that one-third of all first-round choices never make it to the major leagues.

The 1994 draft all-star teams below were chosen on the basis of the players' potential impact and the speed with which they'll reach the major leagues. Only 10 of the 26 players came out of high schools, and there's a reason for that. More projection is involved with high schoolers than with collegians, making older players a safer bet. College players also need, on average, one year less of seasoning in the minor leagues. For fantasy leagues who start minor league picks' contracts ticking from Draft Day, that's especially crucial.

AMERICAN LEAGUE

CATCHER: Jason Varitek, Mariners (14th choice overall out of Georgia Tech) Did Not Play Professionally In 1994 Varitek hadn't signed by mid-December, which makes him a risky choice for any owner in an AL-only fantasy league. But he's still notable because he's a switch-hitter with rare offensive potential for a catcher. Baseball America's 1994 College Player of the year should hit for power and turn in a decent batting average as well. Because he has completed his college eligibility, Seattle controls his rights until the 1995 draft. Draft rules are unclear as to whether he would re-enter the draft or become a free agent at that point. ETA in the major leagues: 1997.

FIRST BASE: Matt Smith, Royals (16th overall out of Grants Pass, Ore., HS) .238 AVG, 1 HR, 12 RBI, 1 SB in 101 AB for Rookie-level Gulf Coast Royals Kansas City spent a club-record $1,000,000 bonus to buy Smith away from Stanford University, where he was to play football for Bill Walsh, who considered him a legitimate National Football League prospect as a linebacker. Most clubs liked Smith as a pitcher, but the Royals believed that not using Smith every day would be wasting the talents of a player they considered the best athlete

they've signed since Bo Jackson. Smith is first and foremost a power hitter, and he'll also hit for average. Surprisingly, he's not much of a runner. ETA: 1998.

SECOND BASE: Todd Walker, Twins (eighth overall out of Louisiana State U.) .304 AVG, 10 HR, 34 RBI, 6 SB in 171 AB for Class A Fort Myers Second base is usually a prospect wasteland--see the National League pick--but Walker is an exception. One of the best second basemen in college baseball history, he was the best pure hitter in the draft. He's a future batting champion with line-drive power and the speed and intelligence to steal a 15-20 bases per year. His defense has been questioned, but he'll still be a star at third base if he has to move because of Chuck Knoblauch. ETA: 1996.

THIRD BASE: Antone Williamson, Brewers (fourth overall out of Arizona State U.) .264 AVG, 4 HR, 26 RBI, 0 SB in 159 AB for Rookie-level Helena, Class A Stockton, Double-A El Paso Milwaukee general manager Sal Bando is a former Sun Devils third baseman, and he insisted that his team draft another in Williamson. He's similar to Walker in many respects, a pure hitter with gap power, though he won't steal as many bases. The Brewers have a huge hole at third base, so Williamson should get an opportunity quickly. ETA: 1996.

SHORTSTOP: Nomar Garciaparra, Red Sox (12th overall out of Georgia Tech) .295 AVG, 1 HR, 16 RBI, 5 SB in 105 AB for Class A Sarasota Garciaparra was drafted primarily for his defensive prowess--he's both steady and sometimes spectacular at shortstop--but his hitting has been a pleasant surprise for Boston. After a successful debut at Class A Sarasota, he held his own in the Arizona Fall League with much more advance prospects. He projects as a No. 2 hitter in the major league, good for average and a few RBI if not for homers, and is an instinctual base stealer who can swipe 20 or more bags per season. ETA: 1996.

OUTFIELD: Ben Grieve, Athletics (third overall out of Arlington, Texas, Martin HS) .329 AVG, 7 HR, 50 RBI, 2 SB for short-season Southern Oregon The son of former Rangers outfielder and general manager Tom Grieve, Ben is the most exciting hitter to come out of high school since Gary Sheffield. Grieve made his pro debut in the Northwest League, a circuit consisting mostly of college players, and was one of the better hitters in the league. He's another batting-champion in waiting and also should develop tremendous power. His speed is negligible for fantasy baseball purposes. ETA: 1997

OUTFIELD: Brian Buchanan, Yankees (24th overall out of U. of Virginia) .226 AVG, 4 HR, 26 RBI, 5 SB in 177 AB for short-season Oneonta The best raw power hitter in the draft, Buchanan solidified his status as a first-round draft choice when he homered to beat No. 1 overall pick Paul Wilson of Florida State late in the college season. Buchanan has exciting power, but his ability to make contact will determine how quickly he advances and whether he becomes more than a one-tool player. He's a fairly good athlete, but may wind up at first base if he can't cut it in the outfield. ETA: 1998.

OUTFIELD: Jeff Abbott, White Sox (117th overall out of U. of Kentucky) .397 AVG, 7 HR, 51 RBI, 4 SB in 239 AB for Rookie-level Gulf Coast White Sox/Class A Hickory One veteran scout said he never had seen anyone adjust to pro ball or handle pitches on the outer half of the plate like Abbott, who had one of the best debuts of the draft era. He's a hitting machine who should develop some power once he learns to pull pitches, and he should steal about 10 bases per season. Chicago had one of baseball's best drafts in 1994, and Abbott is the one member of that crop who's on the fast track. ETA: 1997.

STARTING PITCHER: Travis Miller, Twins (34th overall out of Kent U.) 4-1, 2.63 ERA, 62 IP, 55 H, 14 BB, 54 SO for Class A Fort Wayne/Double-A Nashville Overshadowed by No. 3 overall draft pick Dustin Hermanson at Kent, Miller is a prospect in his own right. He was a supplemental first-round choice received by Minnesota after failing to sign Varitek in 1993. Miller isn't overpowering, but he throws strikes and wins. Given the Twins' pitching problems, he probably won't spend too much time in the minor leagues. ETA: 1996.

STARTING PITCHER: Cade Gaspar, Tigers (18th overall out of Pepperdine U.) 1-3, 5.58 ERA, 31 IP, 28 H, 8 BB, 25 SO for Class A Lakeland The son of former major league outfielder Rod Gaspar, Cade didn't become a full-time pitcher until 1993. A year later, he would have been the No. 6 pick in the draft if his bonus demands didn't scare off the cost-conscious (read: cheap) Angels. Gaspar slid 12 picks to the Tigers, who gave him $825,000. In return, Detroit got a pitcher with an above-average fastball and a plus breaking ball. Like Miller, Gaspar is pitching for an organization that needs arms badly. ETA: 1997.

STARTING PITCHER: Jaret Wright, Indians (10th overall out of Anaheim Katella HS) 0-1, 5.40 ERA, 13 IP, 13 H, 9 BB, 16 SO for Rookie-level Burlington The son of former major league pitcher Clyde Wright, Jaret throws harder than any other high school pitcher available in the draft. His first pro season was pretty much a wash because he held out for most of the summer before signing for $1.15 million, but Cleveland is counting on him to progress quickly through the minors. Like most young pitchers, he needs to refine his secondary

pitches and command. ETA: 1997.

STARTING PITCHER: Carlos Castillo, White Sox (89th overall out of Miami Southwest HS) 6-3, 2.15 ERA, 71 IP, 56 H, 12 BB, 74 SO for Rookie-level Gulf Coast White Sox/Class A Hickory Castillo is a relatively unheralded third-round draft pick with an almost-uncanny feel for pitching and four pitches he can throw for strikes. The only concerns Chicago has are his work ethic and conditioning. The downside for fantasy leaguers is that the White Sox aren't exactly in need of pitching, so it's uncertain how early he'll play a major role. ETA: 1998.

RELIEF PITCHER: Jaime Bluma, Royals (79th overall out of Wichita State U.) 6-1, 0.98 ERA, 14 SV, 46 IP, 26 H, 6 BB, 40 SO for short-season Eugene/Class A Wilmington Bluma pitched in the shadow of Darren Dreifort at Wichita State, but like Dreifort is a legitimate closer who won't need much seasoning. Bluma has an effective fastball and slider that are made better by his ability to place them where he wants to, and he has the easygoing, somewhat flaky that many top closers seem to possess. ETA: 1997.

NATIONAL LEAGUE

CATCHER: Paul Konerko, Dodgers (13th overall out of Scottsdale, Ariz., Chapparal HS) .288 AVG, 6 HR, 58 RBI, 1 SB in 257 AB for short-season Yakima Mike Piazza may prevent him from catching in Los Angeles, but no one will keep Konerko's bat out of the major leagues. He debuted by winning the RBI title in the college-oriented Northwest League, and like Varitek is a rare catcher who can hit for both power and average. His defense is somewhat questionable, but as with Carlos Delgado, Piazza's offensive prowess will carry him at another position if needed. ETA: 1997.

FIRST BASE: Bryon Gainey, Mets (64th overall out of Mobile, Ala., Davidson HS) .218 AVG, 8 HR, 35 RBI, 0 SB in 211 AB for Rookie-level Gulf Coast Mets, Rookie-level Kingsport Armed with a surplus of compensation picks, the Mets may have had the best draft in baseball in 1994. Gainey, one of four New York prospects on the NL draft all-stars, is a high school version of Buchanan. He's a raw power hitter who will need to make better contact, though he lacks Buchanan's athleticism. To put it simply, Gainey is a masher. ETA: 1998.

SECOND BASE: Jason Camilli, Expos (44th overall out of Phoenix Thunderbird HS) .255 AVG, 0 HR, 13 RBI, 5 SB in 212 AB for Rookie-level Gulf Coast Expos Most second-base prospects arrive from other positions, and Camilli was a high school shortstop. He makes this team almost by default, because only three other NL draftees from the first 12 rounds play second base. Montreal believes Camilli can become an

all-around player with decent speed and gap power, but to draft him in a fantasy league would be an incredible reach at this point. ETA: 1998.

THIRD BASE: Josh Booty, Marlins (fifth overall out of Shreveport, La., Evangel Christian HS) .231 AVG, 1 HR, 3 RBI, 1 SB in 52 AB for Rookie-level Gulf Coast Marlins, short-season Elmira The recipient of a draft-record $1.6 million bonus, Booty didn't show much in his first pro season because he was sidelined by mononucleosis. USA Today's 1993 Offensive Football Player of the Year and a coveted Louisiana State University quarterback recruit was drafted as a shortstop, but probably will move to third base in the future as he grows. He'll produce average and home runs, but despite his athleticism won't steal many bases. ETA: 1998.

SHORTSTOP: Hiram Bocachica, Expos (21st overall out of Bayamon, P.R.) .280 AVG, 5 HR, 16 RBI, 11 SB in 168 AB for Rookie-level Gulf Coast Expos One of two Puerto Ricans to go in the first round in 1994--the first two from their nation to go that high in a draft--Bocachica is a potential five-tool talent at shortstop. Montreal envisions him becoming another Wilfredo Cordero, the best fantasy league shortstop last season. And as a bonus, Bocachica has the defensive skills to stay at shortstop, unlike Cordero, who eventually will move to third base, perhaps to make room for Bocachica. ETA: 1998.

OUTFIELD: Jay Payton, Mets (29th overall out of Georgia Tech) .357 AVG, 3 HR, 38 RBI, 11 SB in 244 AB for short-season Pittsfield, Double-A Binghamton Payton has the best power-speed combination of any NL outfield draft, and his best tool may be his ability to hit for average. He broke into pro ball by winning the New York-Penn League batting title, and he's a run producer who led NCAA Division I with 102 RBI in 1994. The Carl Everett-Quilvio Veras trade notwithstanding, Payton is on an accelerated course to Shea Stadium. ETA: 1996.

OUTFIELD: Terrence Long, Mets (20th overall out of Millbrook, Ala., Stanhope Elmore HS) .233 AVG, 12 HR, 39 RBI, 9 SB in 215 AB for Rookie-level Kingsport Payton wasn't the only power-speed outfielder drafted by New York. A fine athlete in his own right, Long probably will hit more home runs than Payton while producing an equally fine average and about the same amount of stolen bases. Payton rates a slight edge because he'll arrive in the big leagues quicker. Long played some first base in high school, but probably won't move there unless the Mets develop an outfield logjam. ETA: 1998

OUTFIELD: Dante Powell, Giants (22nd overall out of Cal State Fullerton) .314 AVG, 5 HR, 25 RBI, 27 SB in 169 AB for short-season Everett, Class A San Jose Powell was something of an enigma in college, never quite tapping his

seemingly unlimited potential and consistently underperforming in postseason play. But he had a smashing pro debut, and appears to be the speedy center fielder San Francisco thought it was getting when it drafted Calvin Murray in the first round in 1992. Powell has all the tools and should be a premier base stealer, a useful talent in any fantasy league. ETA: 1997.

STARTING PITCHER: Paul Wilson, Mets (first overall out of Florida State U.) 0-7, 4.56 ERA, 49 IP, 40 H, 21 BB, 50 SO for Rookie-level Gulf Coast Mets, Class A St. Lucie. Don't let Wilson's less-than-scintillating debut scare you off: New York still believes he can contribute on the major league level this year. Wilson's ace potential emerged with Team USA in 1993, and when he developed an overpowering slider to go with his plus fastball last spring, it was almost unfair. As Walker said after Wilson beat Louisiana State at the 1994 College World Series, "It was a college baseball team facing a major league pitcher." ETA: 1996.

STARTING PITCHER: Doug Million, Rockies (seventh overall out of Sarasota, Fla., HS) 6-3, 2.20 ERA, 70 IP, 58 H, 24 BB, 94 SO for Rookie-level Arizona Rockies, short-season Bend Million has, well, a million-dollar left arm (OK, Colorado signed him for $905,000). He was the top lefthander available in the draft, and proved his worth by dominating the college-oriented Northwest League. He has an above-average fastball that will get quicker as he fills out, and an outstanding curveball. Compared to Steve Avery, he'll move quickly for the pitching-hungry Rockies. ETA: 1997.

STARTING PITCHER: Scott Elarton, Astros (25th overall out of Lamar, Colo., HS) 8-1, 2.89 ERA, 83 IP, 51 H, 23 BB, 70 SO for Rookie-level Gulf Coast Astros, Class A Quad City Elarton didn't allow a run in 28 innings of Rookie ball, then went 4-1 in a full-season Class A league, pretty heady stuff for a high school pitcher. Then again, few pitchers can match Elarton's scary combination of size (6-foot-8) and overpowering fastball. Unlike most tall pitchers, such as Randy Johnson, Elarton has no mechanical problems and has a polished arsenal. ETA: 1997.

RELIEF PITCHER: C.J. Nitkowski, Reds (ninth overall out of St. John's U.) 6-3, 3.50 ERA, 75 IP, 61 H, 40 BB, 60 SO for Double-A Chattanooga Nitkowski often is compared to Frank Viola, another St. John's-developed lefthander. Nitkowski probably won't get much better than he is now, but that's not a problem because he's a southpaw who can throw decent stuff, including a knuckle-curve, for strikes. He went straight to Double-A and acquitted himself well, and it's not out of the question that he could make Cincinnati's starting rotation in spring training. ETA: 1995.

RELIEF PITCHER: Dustin Hermanson, Padres (third overall out of Kent U.) 1-0, 1.91 ERA, 11 SV, 28 IP, 19 H, 11 BB,

36 SO for Double-A Wichita, Triple-A Las Vegas The hardest thrower available in the draft, Hermanson also was the only 1994 draftee to reach Triple-A. He'll probably battle Nitkowski to become the first to play in the big leagues. Besides his considerable heat, Hermanson also has the unflappable makeup needed to be a closer. A starter in college, he excelled in short relief with Team USA in 1993. ETA: 1995.

As a supplement to the 1994 draft all-star teams, we also present an evaluation of first-round selections from the previous three drafts. The biggest lesson to be learned from these is just how speculative the draft is. When these players were drafted all were considered potential stars, but a lot can happen on their way to the major leagues.

Just ask Brien Taylor, whose career was jeopardized when he hurt his shoulder in a fight during the 1993-94 offseason. Or Al Shirley, who struck out 208 times in 1994.

GRADING SCALE A--Potential major league star. B--Potential major league regular. C--Potential major leaguer. D--Major disappointment thus far. F--Failure.

1991 DRAFT

1. Brien Taylor, lhp, Yankees	B
2. Mike Kelly, of, Braves	B
3. David McCarty, 1b-of, Twins	B
4. Dmitri Young, 3b, Cardinals	B
5. Kenny Henderson, rhp, Brewers	Did Not Sign
6. John Burke, rhp, Astros	Did Not Sign
7. Joe Vitiello, 1b-of, Royals	B
8. Joey Hamilton, rhp, Padres	A
9. Mark Smith, of, Orioles	C
10. Tyler Green, rhp, Phillies	C
11. Shawn Estes, lhp, Mariners	D
12. Doug Glanville, of, Cubs	C
13. Manny Ramirez, of, Indians	A
14. Cliff Floyd, 1b-of, Expos	A
15. Tyrone Hill, lhp, Brewers	F
16. Shawn Green, of, Blue Jays	A
17. Eduardo Perez, 1b-of, Angels	B
18. Al Shirley, of, Mets	F
19. Benji Gil, ss, Rangers	B
20. Calvin Reese, ss, Reds	B
21. Allen Watson, lhp, Cardinals	B
22. Brian Barber, rhp, Cardinals	B
23. Aaron Sele, rhp, Red Sox	A
24. Jon Farrell, of, Pirates	C
25. Scott Ruffcorn, rhp, White Sox	A
26. Brent Gates, 2b, Athletics	B

1992 DRAFT

1. Phil Nevin, 3b, Astros	B
2. Paul Shuey, rhp, Indians	B
3. B.J. Wallace, lhp, Expos	C
4. Jeffrey Hammonds, of, Orioles	A
5. Chad Mottola, of, Reds	B
6. Derek Jeter, ss, Yankees	A
7. Calvin Murray, of, Giants	C
8. Pete Janicki, rhp, Angels	D
9. Preston Wilson, 3b-of, Mets	B
10. Michael Tucker, of, Royals	A
11. Derek Wallace, rhp, Cubs	B
12. Kenny Felder, of, Brewers	C
13. Chad McConnell, of, Phillies	C
14. Ron Villone, lhp, Mariners	B
15. Sean Lowe, rhp, Cardinals	C
16. Rick Greene, rhp, Tigers	D
17. Jim Pittsley, rhp, Royals	A
18. Chris Roberts, lhp, Mets	B
19. Shannon Stewart, of, Blue Jays	B
20. Benji Grigsby, rhp, Athletics	C
21. Jamie Arnold, rhp, Braves	C
22. Rick Helling, rhp, Rangers	B
23. Jason Kendall, c, Pirates	B
24. Eddie Pearson, 1b, White Sox	B
25. Todd Steverson, of, Blue Jays*	B
26. Dan Serafini, lhp, Twins	B
27. John Burke, rhp, Rockies	C
28. Charles Johnson, c, Marlins	A

*Selected by Tigers in major league Rule 5 draft at 1994 Winter Meetings

1993 DRAFT

1. Alex Rodriguez, ss, Mariners	A
2. Darren Dreifort, rhp, Dodgers	B
3. Brian Anderson, lhp, Angels	B
4. Wayne Gomes, rhp, Phillies	C
5. Jeff Granger, lhp, Royals	B
6. Steve Soderstrom, rhp, Giants	D
7. Trot Nixon, of, Red Sox	A
8. Kirk Presley, rhp, Mets	B
9. Matt Brunson, ss, Tigers	C
10. Brooks Kieschnick, 1b-of, Cubs	A
11. Daron Kirkreit, rhp, Indians	B
12. Billy Wagner, lhp, Astros	B
13. Matt Drews, rhp, Yankees	B
14. Derrek Lee, 1b, Padres	B
15. Chris Carpenter, rhp, Blue Jays	B
16. Alan Benes, rhp, Cardinals	A
17. Scott Christman, lhp, White Sox	B
18. Chris Schwab, of, Expos	C
19. Jay Powell, rhp, Orioles*	C
20. Torii Hunter, of, Twins	B
21. Jason Varitek, c, Twins	Did Not Sign
22. Charles Peterson, of, Pirates	B

------*Jim Callis is editor of Baseball America.*

The Best 100 Prospects for 1995
By Lary Bump

A couple of months ago, John Benson suggested to me compiling a list of the 100 best prospects for next year's major leagues. It sounded like a big job, even for someone who spends as much time studying minor leaguers from every angle that I do. In the first place, it sounded like a lot of players.

One hundred rookies? How many first-year players ever do well in the majors? Well, it turned out that finding 100 candidates was not difficult. That number is, after all, fewer than four players per team. My list grew and grew until it reached 252 names. I toyed with the idea of listing the top 100 playing prospects and the top 100 pitching prospects, but that would mean more than seven players per team, and that many newcomers won't see significant playing time in '95.

Without intending that it would come out that way, the list approximates the 65-35 split that John endorses in allocating Rotisserie League salaries to players and pitchers. The top 100 list includes 58 position players and 42 pitchers. That makes sense because most major league rosters are 44 percent pitchers (11 of 25). There is a crying need for new and better pitchers, but the identity of the marginal candidates to fill them is hard to determine. There is no salary figure attached to these players, so they all are equally attractive prospects in that respect. However, by implication some players have higher value than others on this list. The ones higher on the list are more likely to play a lot and excel in the 1995 majors. The top half of the list is more desirable than the lower half, and hitters form a higher percentage (64 percent, 32 of 50) at the upper level.

It's important to outline the criteria that went into selecting this one-man's-opinion top 100 list. These are not necessarily the best players coming up from the minors, but those with a combination of talent and an opportunity to play. Those are two of the four criteria needed to make it as a major league rookie -- Talent, Skill, Opportunity and Luck -- or to make them easier to remember, LOTS or a SLOT.

Also, the players on the list are not necessarily rookies in the technical sense, but players who had more than half of their at-bats or innings pitched in the minors in 1994.

The list also makes the major assumption that the strike will be settled in time to get in a '95 baseball season. Most of the players listed here would not be playing if the strike continues -- they are on 40-man major league rosters, and members of the Players Association not likely to cross a picket line.

The number in parentheses is the player's age as of April 1, 1995. This is especially important for position players. You'll notice that many of the youngest players on the list are near the top.

1. Carlos Delgado, Blue Jays C (22). Yeah, yeah. He hit the ball all over the SkyDome last April, then bombed out. What you don't realize is how he went back down to Triple-A and worked on his defense behind the plate. He also made more consistent contact at the plate. He also excelled in that leading indicator of success, second-half performance. He was instrumental both in turning Syracuse's offense into the most dangerous in the International League and in keeping a mediocre pitching staff above water.

2. Chipper Jones, Braves SS-3B (22). His physical condition is the key after he sat out a year because of knee surgery. He could play short if the Braves don't re-sign Jeff Blauser, or third to replace Terry Pendleton, or in the outfield. But if healthy, he'll play well.

3. James Baldwin, White Sox RHP (23). He has the best combination of pitching power and savvy coming up. The Sox are in need of starting pitching with Jack McDowell gone.

4. Garret Anderson, Angels OF (22). The Angels can use all the hitting they can get, and Anderson drove in 102 runs despite hitting just 12 home runs in Triple-A.

5. Alex Rodriguez, Mariners SS (19). Felix Fermin is merely keeping the position warm. Rodriguez may not start the season in Seattle, but he'll be back during the summer. More than one Rookie of the Year has come up from the minors during the season.

6. Alex Gonzalez, Blue Jays SS (21). Offensively, there is no question. Defensively . . . he may have to move to third base. He will not be as intimidated by laying in the big leagues as he was last spring.

7. Derek Jeter, Yankees SS (21). His opportunity may be limited by his sore arm and the signing of Tony Fernandez, but if Jeter gets a chance, he'll be every bit as good as the others above him. He shot all the way from low Class A ball to Triple-A last season.

8. LaTroy Hawkins, Twins RHP (23). A leading indicator of a prospect's success is a prior-year midseason promotion in which the player holds his own. Like Jeter, Hawkins was successful last after two promotions.

9. Billy Ashley, Dodgers OF (24). This big guy makes it worth the price of admission just for the show he puts on in batting practice. I was prepared to name Brian Hunter my Minor League Player of the Year until I found that Ashley was the Pacific Coast League's most valuable player. Those people, who saw more of Ashley than I did convinced me: Ashley is my choice as Minor League Player of the Year. That 1994 honor, however, does not make him the best prospect for 1995. It's unlikely any rookie will hit more homers.

10. Brian Hunter, Astros OF (24). Hunter, who's game is speed, rates just behind Ashley. If Steve Finley isn't traded, Hunter's value could decrease.

11. Marty Cordova, Twins OF (25). Minnesota loves hitters, and Cordova just hit and kept hitting after coming off the disabled list last season in Triple-A.

12. Alan Benes, Cardinals RHP (23). Andy Benes' younger brother was successful after each of THREE promotions in 1994.

13. Frank Rodriguez, Red Sox RHP (22). He may be the hardest-throwing pitcher coming up this year. He matured as a professional during last season.

14. Julian Tavarez, Indians RHP (23). The stringbean righthander has been brought along slowly without overtaxing his deceptive buggy-whip delivery.

15. Scott Ruffcorn, White Sox RHP (25). His bottom-line numbers have been better than Baldwin's, but he is not as impressive physically.

16. Charles Johnson, Marlins C (23). I'm not as high on this guy as many others seem to be. Johnson can play defense and hit home runs, but he will not hit for average for at least a couple of years in the majors.

17. Willie Greene, Reds 3B (23). Greene has been a strong closer in each of the last two seasons. His defense may cause him to move to left field.

18. Marc Barcelo, Twins RHP (23). Two Twins pitching prospects this high? Have you seen the Minnesota rotation recently? Barcelo was a first-round draft pick in 1993.

19. Midre Cummings, Pirates OF (23). The best move the Pirates made was bringing in some outfielders with major league experience to push him to a better effort this season. Think he can beat out Jacob Brumfield or Steve Pegues?

20. Albie Lopez, Indians RHP (23). Like the Twins, the Indians have room in their rotation. Lopez does not condition himself as well as Tavarez.

21. Denny Hocking, Twins SS (24). Hocking can switch-hit, bat leadoff, run the bases a bit -- and field better than Pat Meares.

22. Luis Ortiz, Rangers 3B-OF (24). He may end up as a DH, but Ortiz will be in the lineup somewhere. He hits the ball as hard as anyone.

23. Rico Brogna, Mets 1B (24). You may wonder why a guy who batted .351 in last year's major league trial can be this low. He could end up even lower, for he never batted better than .273 in seven minor league seasons.

24. Benji Gil, Rangers SS (22). He's another who, like Alex Gonzalez, is more mature and better prepared than a year ago. Gil finished last season strong in Triple-A, and the Rangers really have no other alternative.

25. Rondell White, Expos OF (23). If there had been no strike, he would have played often and well late last summer. With Larry Walker and possibly Marquis Grissom hitting the free agent trail, there will be plenty of opportunity.

26. Andrew Lorraine, Angels LHP (22). The 1993 fourth-round draft pick made it to the majors with just 22 minor league games. The only negative factor is that California is more in need of righthanders.

27. Brad Clontz, Braves RHRP (23). The sidearmer excelled after a promotion to Triple-A. If Atlanta acquires an experienced closer, Clontz's value goes down.

28. Bill Pulsipher, Mets LHP (21). He probably won't start the season in New York, but the Mets probably can't keep the confident youngster with the devastating cut fastball down for long.

29. Shane Andrews, Expos 3B (23). You won't find him this high on anyone else's list, but I'm telling you the improvement he made last year was palpable. He'll be a slugging star by the end of the century.

30. Russell Davis, Yankees 3B (25). If he's traded, his value goes higher. If he stays with the Yankees, the value will decrease as he sits behind Wade Boggs.

31. Tony Clark, Tigers 1B (22). He has the potential to soar higher, but with just one full season in the minors and 25 games above Double-A, he may take time to adjust.

32. John Dettmer, Rangers RHP (25). No Texas pitcher who came up last season was successful, but the Johnny Oates regime will prepare them better this year.

33. Tim Laker, Expos C (25). Last year he added a bat to his considerable defensive talents.

34. Ray Durham, White Sox 2B (23). The switch hitter has come on strong each of the past two years, with last season even better. He's about Joe Morgan's size, and starting to develop power to go with his speed.

35. Quilvio Veras, Marlins 2B (24). The trade to a warm-weather team should alleviate his slow-starting seasons in cold weather. He'll steal plenty of bases and cover lots of ground in the field.

36. Jose Oliva, Braves 3B (24). He showed great power in last year's major league trial. He has a good glove, and an improved attitude.

37. Dustin Hermanson, Padres RHRP (21). He's the top player on this list from last year's draft. The Padres challenged him by assigning him to Double-A Wichita. By season's end, he was the Triple-A closer.

38. Armando Benitez, Orioles RHRP (22). He's lower on this list than others you might see. He showed an ability to strike out major league hitters in a brief trial last season, but he still has no saves above Double-A. That's a long way from big-league closer.

39. Herbert Perry, Indians 1B (25). He can hit line drives to all fields, and he's a quiet leader.

40. David Bell, Indians 3B (22). There were few hotter hitters in the minors at the end of last season. The third-generation ballplayer also is on the defensive level of his father, Buddy Bell.

41. Roberto Petagine, Astros 1B (23). He's this low only because he may have trouble finding a spot in the lineup behind Jeff Bagwell and his big contract. As a lefthanded thrower, Petagine can play only first or the outfield.

42. Brad Woodall, Braves LHP (25). Fits the description of crafty lefthander. He's an overachiever.

43. Carl Everett, Mets OF (25). Everett already may be the best defensive center fielder in the National League. At bat, he'll make better contact than Ryan Thompson.

44. J.R. Phillips, Giants 1B (24). The job was supposed to be his last year. Back in Triple-A, he improved. Another year of Todd Benzinger is inconceivable.

45. Ernie Young, Athletics OF (25). He tore up the Southern League, did well in the Pacific Coast League and struggled with Oakland. He can hit, run, throw and play defense.

46. Antonio Osuna, Dodgers RHRP (21). People who confuse him with Al Osuna will miss out on a power-pitching bullpen prospect

47. Rich Becker, Twins OF (23). He would rank higher if he could keep himself from getting hurt. A knee injury took away a significant part of his speed in the field and on the bases.

48. Marc Newfield, Mariners 1B-OF (22). He can hit. All he needs is a position. He could even be the DH to get his bat in the lineup.

49. Ron Villone, Mariners LHRP (25). A strong performance in the Arizona Fall League almost assured him of a closer's job in Seattle.

50. Darren Dreifort, Dodgers RHP (22). He would rank higher if he were healthy, and probably should rank lower because he could miss a large portion of the season. His talent is not in question.

51. Alan Embree, Indians LHRP (25). He has been resurrected as a reliever after surgery derailed a promising career as a starter.

52. Mike Kelly, Braves OF (24). He has been a disappointment so long that few people realize he has the talent and the time to carve a productive big-league career.

53. Jason Giambi, Athletics 3B (24). The job is his if he can produce. He did better in Triple-A than in Double-A last year.

54. Danny Bautista, Tigers OF (22). Sparky Anderson's effusive praise doomed him to failure last year. But he could come back to star at any outfield position in Detroit.

55. Joe Vitiello, Royals 1B (23). He's a pure hitter, but not much of a fielder. Hence, he's a first baseman.

At the very least, he could platoon with Bob Hamelin or Wally Joyner.

56. Michael Tucker, Royals OF (23). He may have more speed and power than Vitiello, and he may be assured of the left field job, but Vitiello ranks slightly higher.

57. Joel Bennett, Red Sox RHP (25). He has been a strikeout pitcher at every minor league level. He may not reach the majors until midseason because he has pitched just four games above Double-A.

58. Luis Raven, Angels 1B-OF (26). Nobody knew about this guy until he proceeded to tear up the Texas League, and then the PCL.

59. Juan Acevedo, Rockies RHP (25). He was one of the best pitchers in the Eastern League. The big question is how he will fare going from a pitchers' park to the high altitude of Denver or Colorado Springs.

60. Allen Battle, Cardinals OF (26). After the White Sox selected him in the 1993 winter draft, they returned him to St. Louis, and the Cards are glad they did. He was among the American Association leaders in almost everything. He will be held back because the major league team has so many solid outfielders. If Battle should be traded, his value would increase.

61. Chan Ho Park, Dodgers RHP (21). He may have a better season than Dreifort just because he'll pitch more. The Dodgers aren't sure whether either is a starter or a reliever, but the bullpen is where they need help.

62. Oscar Munoz, Twins RHP (25). He had a disappointing '94 season, but he can pitch.

63. Damon Buford, Orioles OF (24). He's an excellent center fielder and a smart baserunner. Don Buford's son added some power last year.

64. Dan Carlson, Giants RHP (25). It's a mystery why the pitching-poor Giants have hesitated so long

to bring him up. With John Burkett, and probably Bill Swift, gone, they'll have to give Carlson a chance.

65. Kevin Jarvis, Reds RHP (25). He wasn't successful in his major league trial last year, but even if he has to start the '95 season at Indianapolis, he'll be back.

66. Pokey Reese, Reds SS (21). An excellent glove man, he learned how to hit last year and is continuing to mature physically. He rates this high because of Barry Larkin's injury history.

67. Kevin Jordan, Phillies 2B (25). A broken leg cut into his playing time last year, but when he came back, he smoked the ball. The fact that he isn't a good defender doesn't seem like a major drawback with the Phillies. Jordan also has played third base.

68. Gene Schall, Phillies 1B (24). I have Schall rated higher than even the Phillies. He is an excellent run producer who can help some team. If he's traded, he shoots up this list.

69. Mark Thompson, Rockies RHP (23). He's a product of the Rockies' first draft, so they will give him every opportunity to advance. Pitching in Colorado will hurt his Rotisserie numbers.

70. Scott Klingenbeck, Orioles RHP (24). He's an intelligent breaking-ball pitcher who filled in capably in an emergency start with the Orioles last season. You'll see other young Baltimore pitchers ranked higher elsewhere.

71. Ray Holbert, Padres SS (24). The job can be his after Ricky Gutierrez quite literally kicked it away a year ago.

72. Dave Silvestri, Yankees 2B (27). He's too old to be an exceptional prospect, and too good a hitter to be left off this list. Silvestri's glove has shuffled him from shortstop to third base to second. He'd do better if he was traded.

73. John Frascatore, Cardinals RHP? (25). The Cardinals need pitching. This guy was as good as any

at Louisville last year, so he will receiver an opportunity.

74. Sid Roberson, Brewers LHP (23). He's a lefthander named Sid, but doesn't throw as hard or have the heavy pitches that Fernandez does.

75. Terrell Wade, Braves LHP (22). You've probably heard of Wade, a strikeout artist in the lower minors who held his own after a late-season promotion to Triple-A. But where would he fit into the Atlanta staff?

76. Greg Gohr, Tigers RHP (27). Another player who ranks higher with my than others like me who think they know prospects. Gohr is a former high draft pick whose time finally seems to have come. Pitching at Tiger Stadium won't help his stats.

77. Jeromy Burnitz, Indians OF (25). He doesn't figure to play regularly, but he could fill in as part of a platoon or a defensive replacement for Manny Ramirez, and Burnitz can run the bases. He also is not helpless against lefthanders.

78. Rikkert Faneyte, Giants OF (26). San Francisco isn't likely to continue to try to get by with two-thirds of an outfield. The Dutchman should be practicing his throws from right field.

79. Jason Bates, Rockies SS (24). He has been a good hitter in good hitters' parks in the minors. The Rockies' new stadium shouldn't be much different.

80. Darren Bragg, Mariners OF (25). His '94 statistics at Calgary were almost identical to Marc Newfield's. But while Bragg has more speed, he's also three years older.

81. Glenn Dishman, Padres LHP (24). With just two Triple-A games under his belt, he may not start the season in San Diego, but they'll be needing pitchers before the season gets too old.

82. Jeff Granger, Royals LHP (23). KC's number one draft choice in 1993 has had two cups of coffee in the majors, though he has been just a .500 pitcher in A and Double-A ball. He's likely to come up to stay some time after opening day.

83. Matt Grott, Reds LHP (27). Unlike many of the pitchers on this list, Grott is a junkballer. In six minor league seasons, he has learned how to pitch. He also was impressive in the Arizona Fall League.

84. John Wasdin, Athletics RHP (22). He's another 1993 draft pick, but he exploded last season, even after a promotion to Double-A. Mark him down for mid-season arrival in Oakland.

85. Ismael Valdes, Dodgers RHP (21). The number of Dodgers pitching prospects on this list just underscores their need. A stronger bullpen could solidify their standing as the NL West team to beat.

86. Ray McDavid, Padres OF (23). In the minors, McDavid has established himself as a .270s level hitter with double-figure power and speed. He could do about the same in the majors.

87. Lyle Mouton, Yankees OF (25). He's not as big as Billy Ashley, so he doesn't hit the majestic home runs, but Mouton hits line drives about as hard as Ashley or Luis Ortiz. Mouton started realizing his potential last year, when he had a successful in-season promotion to Triple-A and a good Arizona Fall League season.

88. Rick Holifield, Phillies OF (25). He opened plenty of eyes by leading the Arizona Fall League in stolen bases. He has cut down his swing to sacrifice some power, and he can play right field or center.

89. Bob Higginson, Tigers OF (24). He came along to have a good Triple-A season at Toledo. He played center field there, but would have to play left or right in Detroit.

90. C.J. Nitkowski, Reds LHP (22). He and Hermanson are the only 1994 draft choices on this list. Nitkowski was in Double-A last year, and can be a mid-season major leaguer with a good Triple-A debut.

91. Steve Schrenk, White Sox RHP (26). He was next in line behind Baldwin and Ruffcorn on the Nashville staff. Not bad, a 14-game winner as a Triple-A team's number three starter.

92. Sherman Obando, Orioles DH (25). You'll see him listed as an outfielder, but he cannot play in the field in the majors. But, boy, can he hit!

93. Enrique Burgos, Royals LHRP (29). Burgos, who came back from pitching in Taiwan in time for the '93 season, throws as hard as anyone. He doesn't always know where the ball is going.

94. Gabe White, Expos LHP (23). In contrast, White is a finesse pitcher. But he can sneak fastballs past unwary batters.

95. Greg Blosser, Red Sox OF (23). He might have been higher on other lists a year ago, but he's a much better player now. After he was sent down from Boston, he became more skilled, especially in the field.

96. Jorge Posada, Yankees C (23). If anything happens to Mike Stanley, the switch-hitting Posada will be ready to fill in. He's an excellent defensive catcher.

97. Duane Singleton, Brewers OF (22). He managed to get himself in trouble continually, but was more focused last season, when he was promoted three times, from A ball to the majors.

98. Mike Lieberthal, Phillies C (23). The Phils' former number one draft pick already has part of three Triple-A seasons under his belt. He's a good catcher, and not an automatic out.

99. Mark Grudzielanek, Expos SS (25). He's higher on other lists, and he would be here if he had a greater opportunity to play. He was the Eastern League MVP and the Arizona Fall League batting champ. He can't dislodge Wil Cordero from shortstop, but could end up at third.

100. Brien Taylor, Yankees LHP (23). He hasn't pitched since 1993, or above Double-A. But if his shoulder surgery didn't damage his arm too much, he could be in the majors soon after a re-indoctrination in Triple-A. He has the physical pitching tools, but needs to work on the finer points of fielding and holding baserunners.

SCOUTING REPORTS and EXPERT ANALYSIS

Lary Bump's prospecting tips and advice are now available on an ongoing basis -- four ways, with new and different information in each source.

- Who's movin' on up and who's stock is goin' down
- Minor league injury reports
- Prospects to watch
- Players most likely to get a callup, and how they will perform

** FANTASY FARM PHONE **

GET 30 (or more) WEEKLY MESSAGES ON TAPE
Just $49/year -- 1995 service starts February 18
Updates every Saturday through the baseball season
Call 800-707-9090 or 203-834-1231 for information on how to order from the U.S. or Canada

** John Benson/STATS Inc. Live Advice Line **

Lary Bump's extension:
Call 900-773-4440, Ext. 8857
Monday-Saturday, Noon-3 p.m., year round $1.99/minute
To schedule conferences at other times, call 203-834-1231

** Benson's Baseball Monthly **

Includes Lary Bump's views on prospects --
how he sees them, and how you can identify them
See the ad in this publication or call 203-834-1231 to subscribe

** Bump's Best Bet Ballplayers **

Weekly on-line reports on the USA Today Information Center
Type GO MINORS, then select Columns
For information, call 800-826-9688

THE PRICES IN THIS BOOK ARE **NOT** RECOMMENDED BIDS

YOU MUST ADJUST FOR:

OPTIMAL BIDDING, INFLATION, AND BUDGETING

Three concepts that we pioneered and explained in these pages, years ago, have a big impact on what you should bid on draft day. Other than failure to do homework, there are no mistakes more common than forgetting these three vital elements. Consistent with the introductions in the front of this book, we are not going to write the lengthy "how to" explanations in this Annual again every year. Detailed essays covering all three subjects -- Optimal Bids, Draft Price Inflation, and Auction Budgeting -- appear in the volumes *Rotisserie Baseball Playing for Fun* and *Rotisserie Baseball Playing for Blood*, which belong in your library if you want to win (these books of course cover many other topics as well).

For those who need a quick refresher, these are the key concepts:

OPTIMAL BIDS

Optimal bids are the bids most likely to yield the biggest profits on each player. The lower you bid, the bigger will be the "value profit" (V) if you buy the player in question. If you buy a $20 player for $15, that's a "V" of $5. The lower your bid, the higher your V will be. However, low bids have a poor probability of success in acquiring the player. The higher you bid, the better will be your probability (P) of getting that player. If you bid half or less of the player's value, you will have a low P. If you bid 100% or more of the player's value, you will have a high probability of getting that player (but little or no value profit). We know the actual probability that certain bids will succeed, by examining hundreds of actual auctions, to see what each player actually sells for (in most cases it is a normal bell curve distribution). Since we know the probability and know the value of

each bid, we can calculate the expected result. Your overall expected profit from each bid is the probability P, times the value of the purchase V, or P x V. Optimal bids are based on calculations of the actual P x V for various types of players.

To summarize the results briefly, the optimal bid for an established star hitter or an established healthy ace reliever is about 85% of the player's value. The optimal bid for a solid star starting pitcher or an average everyday position player is about 70% of value. The optimal bid for an average starting pitcher or a hitter with an obscure role is about 60% of nominal value. The optimal bid for a rookie starting pitcher, or a middle reliever, or mediocre hitter with an injury history, is about 40% of nominal value.

DRAFT PRICE INFLATION

In leagues that retain players from one year to the next, owners tend to keep those players that have high salaries relative to expected value, such as Barry Bonds at $22 or John Wetteland at $10 or Brady Anderson at $2. Each one of these retentions removes a great deal of talent (value) from the draft pool, but only removes a small amount of money from the total auction spending allowance. The result is that lots of money remains in the auction, but not much talent, and prices must rise.

It is easily possible to calculate draft price inflation for your unique league. Simply take your total auction allowance (e.g. 12 teams x $260 = $3120 total) and subtract the total salaries of players being retained ("frozen") or expected to be retained. The balance is the money in your auction. Then subtract the value of players being retained (use my values in

this book, or use your own) and subtract that amount from your auction allowance. That is the value of the players remaining in your draft pool.

For example, if your league freezes $1200 worth of players, at salaries of $900, then your money in the auction equals $3120 minus $900, or $2220; and your value in the auction equals $3120 minus $1200, or $1920. Divide the money by the value (2220/ 1920) and the inflation rate in this example is 15.6%. The actual average inflation rate in most auctions is about 15%, but can vary from a negative amount (if owners freeze players at salaries higher than true values) or can go as high as 80% or even 100% in extreme cases. DO NOT USE ESTIMATES OR AVERAGES. CALCULATE THE ACTUAL INFLATION RATE FOR YOUR LEAGUE. Your bids could be off by as much as 50% if you don't adjust for inflation, and adjust correctly. Once you know your league's inflation rate, you should increase every value in this book by that percentage.

It is an unfortunate coincidence that the average inflation rate (+15%) is often equal to the optimal bid discount (-15%). That coincidence hides these offsetting factors and leads to a great deal of misunderstanding and unsuccessful auctions. Please: do your homework! I hate for people who read my books to do poorly in their leagues. I want you to win. OK?

The world's top expert on draft price inflation, in my opinion, is Mike Dalecki. Almost everything you ever see or hear about DPI derives from Mike's work, often without credit given where it is due. Mike wrote the first explanations, and the best and clearest.

AUCTION BUDGETING

A somewhat more elusive concept than optimal bids and draft inflation, auction budgeting cannot be "calculated" and requires the use of judgment. Budgeting works this way: make sure you spend all your money and get your fair share of big talent. Early in the auction, it's fine to sit back and stubbornly refuse to bid higher than the optimal bid times the inflated value. You must, however, pay attention as

the talent disappears.

Make a list of those players you hope to acquire at each position, with an estimate of the price you are willing to pay; and when the list gets short you must bid more aggressively (higher). And for people who have a really good freeze list with a lot of profits locked into star players: forget optimal bids altogether. Once you have more profits than anyone else in your league, your only concern is getting your fair share of the talent in your league.

Like I said, all of these concepts are worthy of deeper exploration, and I hope you will look in to them. Just please: don't look at my dollar values in this book and think they are ''recommended bids'' -- because they're not. There is much more to this game than calculating values.

POSITION SCARCITY

If you compare the dollar values in the alphabetical listing of hitters with the dollar values in the ranking by position, you will see that I have added $1 to the value of several catchers (and $2 to a couple more). The reason that I do this is to provide 24 catchers with a value of $1 or more. Personally, I make this adjustment mentally during the auction; but for the sake of those who have enough to think about already, I have given you lists with 24 "+" value catchers in each league.

FREE AGENTS

Finally, you will see that my rankings by position include free agents listed in both leagues. You can see what a player would be worth IF he ended up playing in that league. In a few cases there is a difference of $1 or even $2. Forecast stats are based on the league in which a player last played; so for example a pitcher moving from the AL to the NL should be expected to have a lower ERA and fewer baserunners per inning.

DOLLAR VALUE "ADJUSTMENTS" --
TRYING TO USE STANDARD VALUES
IN NON-STANDARD LEAGUES ?

This essay will save you some money if you were planning to call 900-773-7526 and ask me how to "adjust" standard dollar values. Many people call me to talk about player values and valuation methods. Especially during the winter, when the stats finally stop changing long enough to do some in-depth analysis. People get their stats on disk, load 'em into the computer, and start calculating.

Many of the questions that people ask are not susceptible to short answers; certainly they not well suited to discussion at $2.49/minute. For example:

> "My league uses both AL and NL players. How do I adjust your values so I can use them in a mixed league? Do I just take 50% of your values?"

> "My league uses strikeouts as a category. How do I adjust your values to include strikeouts?" [Same question for runs scored, innings pitched, etc. as additional categories.]

Everybody wishes they could simply adjust the standard dollar values. "Give me a formula," they say, "and I will do the arithmetic." The formula is in those permanent advice books just presented on the previous page ("Blood" if you care to know which one). The only way to calculate dollar values is to begin with the raw baseball stats.

When you build a house, you start with the foundation; you don't buy a pre-fab roof and then build the pieces underneath. To build a truck, you start with a chassis; you don't start with a car and then take off some parts while adding others. When you build Rotisserie dollar values (for any league using any rules) you start with baseball stats. You can't take dollar values that were founded on different rules and adjust them to your league, unless you want to un-calculate everything, and then re-calculate everything. Trust me: it's easier to start from scratch.

Take the Mixed League case for example. Here's what I tell people who want to know why they can't quickly change one-league values into both-league values:

1. THE PLAYER POPULATION

Standard Rotisserie rules and dollar values are based on a population of 552 active major league players, 276 National League and 276 American League. Standard value methods therefore provide 552 names with a positive value. In a mixed format with, say, 10 teams and 23 players per team, you only need 230 players with positive value. If you have 240 or 250,

that's no big problem, but with 552 "valuable" players on your list, you're going to be making some weird bids.

Cutting all values in half will not cut the number of positive-value players in half. In fact, cutting every value in half won't have any significant impact on the number of players valued $1 or higher. A tiny number of players previously valued at $1 will drop below 50 cents and fall off your list, but all of the players worth $2 or more will continue to look valuable, even though they are nowhere near good enough to be selected in a 230-player league.

One major concern in a 230-player league is the 230th player. If you take standard dollar values and cut them in half, the 230th player on your list is going to be worth about $5. If you pay $5 (or even $4 or $3) for the 230th player, you are making a stupid purchase, and you are going to lose. The 230th player is never worth more than $1, because there is only one bidder.

About this point in our $2.49/minute conversation, most of the mixed-leaguers introduce one hopeful assertion before giving up: "Well, I can just count 230 players, and if the last guy is worth $5, then I can subtract $4 from every player. And then I can add up the total value of all the positive-value players, and make it conform to my league's auction allowance. If my league allows $260 per team and the total spending limit is $2600, then I just look at the total positive value for my 230 top players, and if it's $1000 for example, then I just multiply every value by 2.6. Wouldn't that work just fine?"

For those who are determined to minimize their work effort, the method: "divide by two, subtract X, and multiply by Y" will get you an answer. But you will end up doing almost as much work as you would have done by starting from scratch, and your answers will not be nearly as accurate. And you will *surely* lose you league. I can even tell you what your team will look like! Your starting pitchers will all be American Leaguers. Your hitting will feature speedsters from the AL (like Lance Johnson and Kenny Lofton) and you will have a disproportionate share of home run hitters from the National League (like Fred McGriff

and Matt Williams). If you have tried the divide-subtract-multiply method for your mixed league, look at your roster and see for yourself if I didn't describe it pretty well. The problem is that you forgot to consider ... .

2. LEAGUE CONTEXT

To value a starting pitcher for an AL Rotisserie league, you compare that pitcher to his peers in the AL population. You don't compare him to National League pitchers. The average ERA in the American League in 1993 was 4.32. In the National League in 1993, the average ERA was 4.02. Very often the difference between the two leagues is nearly half a run in ERA. How much is half a run in ERA worth in the standings in your league? About five or six points? And then consider the same difference in ratio, and you can see that 10 or 12 standings points depend entirely on league context. If you ignore league context, you lose, unless you have twelve points to throw away on just two pitching categories.

If you just divide-subtract-multiply standard dollar values and think you are getting anything useful for a mixed league, think again. The same distortions occur in the hitter population. A stolen base is worth more than a home run in the American League, but the opposite is true in the National League. Your simple method will gloss over these AL/NL differentials, put you in the dark, and give a huge advantage to your opponents who know how to deal with these factors and take the time to do it right. Conversely, if you do the work and your opponents don't, you get a huge advantage for yourself.

Now consider your mixed league context, and the differentials get even bigger. If you are making ten 23-man rosters using both AL and NL players, a pitcher with a 3.90 ERA can actually be a liability! Your rosters need 90 pitchers in this mixed league. Assume that the ace reliever from each of the 28 major league teams will be selected by somebody. And assume that a few co-closers and top setup men also get chosen. Suppose only about one third of the 28 major league teams have a co-closer or setup man worth choosing. That makes 10 more relievers, or 38

relief pitchers in total. For your league with 90 pitchers, you need only 52 starters for your ten teams, less than two starters from each major league team, on average. Many of the "good" number three starters, worth about $10 in a standard American League, will be zero value or even negative in your league. How are you going to "adjust" for that, without doing the arithmetic, the hard way? If you try to take a pitcher's standard value, and "convert" it to fit your league, you will go nuts. Take my advice. Start with baseball stats. Compare them to the stats in your league. Count the numbers of players needed, and compute real values. Don't try to ''convert'' or ''adjust'' anything.

THE EASY WAY OUT

For Just $49.95 you can buy my draft software which will do all these calculations for you: mixed leagues, non-standard rosters, and 25 different baseball stats to choose from. There is an ad shamelessly promoting this product in the back of the book -- but it's there bexause it will help you win. I want my clients to win! Seriously, software experts tell me this program should sell for $200 or more, but we are crazy enough to give it away cheap.

Questions and answers about player valuation appear in every issue of my Baseball Monthly. If you don't see what you need in the preceding essays, and don't want to invest $2.49/minute calling me, you can always write a letter to the editor and get a free answer in the monthly.

Finally, all my valuation methods appear with examples in the ''*Playing for Blood*'' book advertised inside the back cover. So you can do it yourself from scratch, use the software, or call me. Your choice.

1995 12-TEAM "MIXED" LEAGUE HITTER VALUES

NAME	TEAM	VALUE	NAME	TEAM	VALUE
Kenny Lofton	CLE	$52	Juan Gonzalez	TEX	$16
Barry Bonds	SF	$42	Delino Deshields	LA	$16
Jeff Bagwell	HOU	$40	Rickey Henderson	OAK	$16
Ken Griffey	SEA	$38	David Justice	ATL	$15
Albert Belle	CLE	$35	Chad Curtis	CAL	$15
Frank Thomas	CHW	$34	Felix Jose	FA	$15
Marquis Grissom	MON	$34	Jose Canseco	BOS	$15
Sammy Sosa	CHC	$29	Brett Boone	CIN	$15
Craig Biggio	HOU	$28	Wade Boggs	NYY	$15
Gregg Jefferies	PHI	$28	Lance Johnson	CHW	$15
Fred McGriff	ATL	$28	Travis Fryman	DET	$14
Deion Sanders	CIN	$27	Shane Mack	FA	$14
Carlos Baerga	CLE	$27	Luis Polonia	NYY	$13
Paul O'Neill	NYY	$27	Ray Lankford	STL	$13
Paul Molitor	TOR	$26	Ruben Sierra	OAK	$13
Moises Alou	MON	$26	Manny Ramirez	CLE	$13
Roberto Alomar	TOR	$25	Tim Salmon	CAL	$13
Larry Walker	FA	$25	Luis Gonzalez	HOU	$13
Rafael Palmeiro	BAL	$25	Tony Phillips	DET	$13
Dante Bichette	COL	$25	Ivan Rodriguez	TEX	$12
Kirby Puckett	MIN	$24	Chili Davis	CAL	$12
Derek Bell	HOU	$24	Jeff Kent	NYM	$12
Chuck Knoblauch	MIN	$24	Tim Raines	CHW	$12
Wil Cordero	MON	$24	Vince Coleman	FA	$12
Brett Butler	FA	$23	Devon White	TOR	$12
Hal Morris	CIN	$23	Mark Grace	FA	$11
Tony Gwynn	SD	$22	Robin Ventura	CHW	$11
Mike Piazza	LA	$22	Edgar Martinez	SEA	$11
Andres Galarraga	COL	$22	Wally Joyner	KC	$11
Will Clark	TEX	$22	Brian McRae	KC	$11
Gary Sheffield	FLA	$22	David Hulse	TEX	$10
Bernie Williams	NYY	$21	Stan Javier	OAK	$10
Mo Vaughn	BOS	$21	Cliff Floyd	MON	$10
Roberto Kelly	ATL	$20	Jim Thome	CLE	$10
Bip Roberts	SD	$19	Derrick May	CHC	$10
John Olerud	TOR	$19	Bobby Bonilla	NYM	$10
Jeff Conine	FLA	$18	Charlie Hayes	FA	$10
Otis Nixon	TEX	$18	Brent Gates	OAK	$9
Barry Larkin	CIN	$18	Geronimo Pena	STL	$9
Brady Anderson	BAL	$17	Mark Whiten	STL	$9
Reggie Sanders	CIN	$17	Steve Finley	SD	$9
Raul Mondesi	LA	$17	Cecil Fielder	DET	$9
Ellis Burks	COL	$17	Greg Colbrunn	FLA	$9
Darren Lewis	SF	$16	Chuck Carr	FLA	$8
Matt Williams	SF	$16	Greg Vaughn	MIL	$8
Lenny Dykstra	PHI	$16	Bernard Gilkey	STL	$8
Joe Carter	TOR	$16	Ken Caminiti	SD	$8
Kevin Mitchell	FA	$16	Jeffrey Hammonds	BAL	$8

1995 12-TEAM "MIXED" LEAGUE HITTER VALUES

NAME	TEAM	VALUE	NAME	TEAM	VALUE
Jay Buhner	SEA	$8	Mark McLemore	TEX	$3
Don Mattingly	NYY	$7	Danny Tartabull	NYY	$3
Brianl Hunter	HOU	$7	Sandy Alomar	CLE	$2
Mike Stanley	NYY	$7	Leo Gomez	BAL	$2
Cal Ripken	BAL	$7	Bret Barberie	BAL	$2
Carlos Garcia	PIT	$7	Andujar Cedeno	SD	$2
Sean Berry	MON	$7	Tony Tarasco	ATL	$2
Mike Greenwell	BOS	$7	Terry Steinbach	OAK	$2
Mike Lansing	MON	$7	Wayne Kirby	CLE	$2
Carl Everett	NYM	$6	Shawon Dunston	CHC	$2
Harold Baines	FA	$6	Pat Kelly	NYY	$2
Darryl Hamilton	MIL	$6	Greg Gagne	KC	$2
John Kruk	FA	$6	Dave Clark	PIT	$2
James Mouton	HOU	$6	Geronimo Berroa	OAK	$2
Todd Zeile	STL	$6	Andy Vanslyke	FA	$2
Royce Clayton	SF	$6	Willie Greene	CIN	$1
Lou Whitaker	DET	$6	Orlando Merced	PIT	$1
Darren Daulton	PHI	$6	Ron Gant	CIN	$1
Eddie Murray	CLE	$6	Alex Gonzalez	TOR	$1
Chris Hoiles	BAL	$6	Ozzie Guillen	CHW	$1
Al Martin	PIT	$5	Jim Edmonds	CAL	$1
Eddie Williams	SD	$5	Rico Brogna	NYM	$1
Jay Bell	PIT	$5	Shawn Green	TOR	$1
Dave Nilsson	MIL	$5	Eric Karros	LA	$1
Scott Cooper	BOS	$5	Sherman Obando	BAL	$1
Ryan Klesko	ATL	$5	Marc Newfield	SEA	$1
Rich Becker	MIN	$5	Brian Jordan	STL	$1
Darrin Jackson	FA	$5	Javier Lopez	ATL	$1
Eric Young	COL	$5	Ozzie Smith	STL	$1
Alex Cole	MIN	$5	Milt Thompson	FA	$1
Carlos Delgado	TOR	$5	Alex Rodriguez	SEA	$1
Kevin Seitzer	MIL	$4	Brian Harper	FA	$0
Dean Palmer	TEX	$4	Dwight Smith	FA	$0
Jacob Brumfield	PIT	$4	Phil Plantier	HOU	$0
Chipper Jones	ATL	$4	Don Slaught	PIT	$0
John Valentin	BOS	$4	Omar Vizquel	CLE	$0
Glenallen Hill	CHC	$4	Reggie Jefferson	SEA	$0
Tino Martinez	SEA	$4	Kirk Gibson	FA	$0
Jeff Blauser	FA	$4	Eric Anthony	FA	$0
Pedro Munoz	MIN	$3	Mark McGwire	OAK	$0
Bob Hamelin	KC	$3	Jeff King	PIT	$0
Paul Sorrento	CLE	$3	Mickey Tettleton	FA	$0
Mariano Duncan	FA	$3	Mike Macfarlane	FA	$0
Dave Hollins	PHI	$3	Jose Oliva	ATL	$0
Alan Trammell	FA	$3	Mickey Morandini	PHI	$0
Troy Neel	OAK	$3	Ray Durham	CHW	$0
John Jaha	MIL	$3	Jim Leyritz	NYY	$0
Tony Fernandez	NYY	$3	Tim Wallach	LA	$0

1995 12-TEAM "MIXED" LEAGUE HITTER VALUES

NAME	TEAM	VALUE	NAME	TEAM	VALUE
Rondell White	MON	$0	Mark Lemke	ATL	-$3
Mike Blowers	SEA	$0	Henry Rodriguez	LA	-$3
Jim Eisenreich	PHI	$0	Kevin Stocker	PHI	-$3
Midre Cummings	PIT	$0	Jose Valentin	MIL	-$4
Randy Velarde	FA	$0	Scott Brosius	OAK	-$4
Benito Santiago	FA	$0	Ryan Thompson	NYM	-$4
Walt Weiss	COL	$0	Scott Fletcher	BOS	-$4
Joe Orsulak	NYM	$0	Brad Ausmus	SD	-$4
Junior Felix	FA	-$1	Jeff Frye	TEX	-$4
Joe Girardi	COL	-$1	Billy Hatcher	FA	-$4
Ricky Jordan	FA	-$1	Rich Rowland	BOS	-$4
Bj Surhoff	FA	-$1	Phil Nevin	HOU	-$4
Terry Pendleton	FA	-$1	Bill Spiers	NYM	-$4
Joey Cora	FA	-$1	Rey Sanchez	CHC	-$4
Jerry Browne	FA	-$1	Matt Nokes	BAL	-$4
Kurt Abbott	FLA	-$1	Dave Hansen	LA	-$4
Gary Gaetti	FA	-$1	Todd Hundley	NYM	-$4
Rick Wilkins	CHC	-$1	Jody Reed	FA	-$4
Denny Hocking	MIN	-$1	Oddibe McDowell	FA	-$4
Rusty Greer	TEX	-$1	Manuel Lee	FA	-$4
Luis Alicea	BOS	-$2	Todd Benzinger	FA	-$4
Bo Jackson	FA	-$2	Eduardo Perez	CAL	-$4
Thomas Howard	CIN	-$2	Jose Lind	KC	-$4
Eddie Taubensee	CIN	-$2	Scott Leius	MIN	-$4
Robby Thompson	SF	-$2	Lenny Harris	CIN	-$4
Pat Listach	MIL	-$2	Jose Vizcaino	NYM	-$4
Kevin Bass	FA	-$2	Kevin McReynolds	FA	-$4
Tim Naehring	BOS	-$2	Andre Dawson	FA	-$4
Chris Sabo	FA	-$2	Chris Gomez	DET	-$4
Karl Rhodes	CHC	-$2	Rich Amaral	SEA	-$4
Steve Buechele	CHC	-$2	Ed Sprague	TOR	-$4
Lou Frazier	MON	-$2	Scott Livingstone	SD	-$4
Juan Samuel	FA	-$2	Luis Sojo	SEA	-$4
Terry Shumpert	BOS	-$2			
Matt Mieske	MIL	-$2	PLAYERS NOT LISTED HAVE NO VALUE		
Roberto Mejia	COL	-$2			
Dave Winfield	FA	-$2			
Mike Kingery	COL	-$2			
Wes Chamberlain	BOS	-$2			
Danny Bautista	DET	-$3			
Willie McGee	FA	-$3			
Tom Pagnozzi	STL	-$3			
Mike Bordick	OAK	-$3			
Darrin Fletcher	MON	-$3			
David Segui	NYM	-$3			
Ron Coomer	FA	-$3			
Alex Diaz	FA	-$3			
Dave Magadan	FA	-$3			

1995 12-TEAM "MIXED" LEAGUE PITCHER VALUES

NAME	TEAM	VALUE	NAME	TEAM	VALUE
Rod Beck	SF	$36	Paul Shuey	CLE	$9
John Wetteland	MON	$35	Mark Portugal	SF	$8
Lee Smith	CAL	$31	Roger Clemens	BOS	$8
Greg Maddux	ATL	$31	Duane Ward	TOR	$8
Jeff Montgomery	KC	$28	Tom Candiotti	LA	$8
Bobby Ayala	SEA	$26	Charles Nagy	CLE	$8
Randy Myers	CHC	$25	Kent Mercker	ATL	$8
Doug Jones	FA	$25	Erik Hanson	FA	$8
Roberto Hernandez	CHW	$25	Orel Hershiser	FA	$8
Ken Ryan	BOS	$25	Andy Benes	SD	$7
Trevor Hoffman	SD	$25	Steve Trachsel	CHC	$7
Rick Aguilera	MIN	$24	John Burkett	TEX	$7
John Franco	FA	$24	Ben McDonald	BAL	$7
Tom Henke	STL	$24	Joey Hamilton	SD	$7
Bret Saberhagen	NYM	$23	Pete Harnisch	FA	$7
Dennis Eckersley	FA	$22	Darren Hall	TOR	$7
Jose Rijo	CIN	$21	Wilson Alvarez	CHW	$6
Jimmy Key	NYY	$18	Armando Benitez	BAL	$6
Steve Howe	NYY	$16	Butch Henry	MON	$6
Greg McMichael	ATL	$16	Kevin Brown	FA	$6
Jack McDowell	NYY	$16	Bruce Ruffin	COL	$6
Mel Rojas	MON	$15	Steve Avery	ATL	$6
Mike Mussina	BAL	$14	Eric Plunk	CLE	$6
Bill Swift	FA	$14	Pedro Astacio	LA	$5
Hector Carrasco	CIN	$13	John Hudek	HOU	$5
Todd Worrell	LA	$13	Danny Jackson	STL	$5
Jeff Brantley	CIN	$13	Steve Cooke	PIT	$5
Pat Hentgen	TOR	$13	Marvin Freeman	COL	$5
Ken Hill	MON	$12	Johnny Ruffin	CIN	$5
Todd Jones	HOU	$12	Mark Wohlers	ATL	$5
Robb Nen	FLA	$12	Mark Langston	CAL	$5
Mike Fetters	MIL	$12	Pedroj Martinez	MON	$5
Shane Reynolds	HOU	$12	Darren Holmes	COL	$4
Doug Drabek	HOU	$11	Jon Lieber	PIT	$4
Bryan Harvey	FLA	$11	Steve Ontiveros	FA	$4
David Cone	KC	$11	Mike Stanton	FA	$4
Randy Johnson	SEA	$10	Rick White	PIT	$4
Kevin Appier	KC	$10	David Wells	DET	$3
Alex Fernandez	CHW	$10	Jim Gott	FA	$3
Xavier Hernandez	FA	$10	Chris Bosio	SEA	$3
John Smiley	CIN	$10	Bobby Jones	NYM	$3
John Smoltz	ATL	$9	Curt Schilling	PHI	$3
Tom Glavine	ATL	$9	Mike Jackson	FA	$3
Dennis Martinez	CLE	$9	Derek Lilliquist	FA	$3
Zane Smith	FA	$9	Mark Eichhorn	BAL	$3
Jeff Fassero	MON	$9	Aaron Sele	BOS	$2
John Farrell	FA	$9	Ricky Bones	MIL	$2
Mike Henneman	DET	$9	David West	PHI	$2

1995 12-TEAM "MIXED" LEAGUE PITCHER VALUES

NAME	TEAM	VALUE	NAME	TEAM	VALUE
Mark Clark	CLE	$2	Bob Tewksbury	FA	$0
Jason Jacome	NYM	$2	Norm Charlton	FA	$0
Chuck McElroy	CIN	$2	Tim Mauser	SD	$0
Steve Farr	FA	$2	Stan Belinda	FA	$0
Rene Arocha	STL	$2	Mike Morgan	CHC	$0
Graeme Lloyd	MIL	$2	Darren Dreifort	LA	$0
Jose Bautista	FA	$1	Frank Castillo	CHC	$0
Jeremy Hernandez	FLA	$1	Dwight Gooden	FA	-$1
Ramon Martinez	LA	$1	John Habyan	STL	-$1
Darren Oliver	TEX	$1	Pete Schourek	CIN	-$1
Bob Wickman	NYY	$1	Chris Hammond	FLA	-$1
Billy Brewer	KC	$1	Ricky Bottalico	PHI	-$1
Mike Maddux	FA	$1	Vicente Palacios	STL	-$1
Chuck Finley	CAL	$1	Trevor Wilson	FA	-$1
Jeff Russell	FA	$1	Roger Mason	FA	-$1
Gil Heredia	MON	$1	Joe Boever	FA	-$1
Rheal Cormier	STL	$1	Kevin Rogers	SF	-$1
Albie Lopez	CLE	$0	Mark Dewey	SF	-$1
Tommy Greene	PHI	$0	Mark Guthrie	MIN	-$1
Pedroa Martinez	HOU	$0	Greg Hibbard	SEA	-$1
Greg Swindell	HOU	$0	Steve Frey	SF	-$1
Mike Gardiner	FA	$0	Jim Bullinger	CHC	-$1
Donovan Osborne	STL	$0	Heath Slocumb	PHI	-$1
Bill Vanlandingham	SF	$0	Jose Melendez	BOS	-$1
Gene Harris	FA	$0	Brian Anderson	CAL	-$1
Bobby Munoz	PHI	$0	Mike Perez	STL	-$1
Dave Stevens	MIN	$0	Alan Mills	BAL	-$1
Mike Butcher	CAL	$0	Bob Scanlan	MIL	-$1
Bill Risley	SEA	$0	Tim Davis	SEA	-$1
Cris Carpenter	FA	$0	Tony Castillo	TOR	-$1
Jim Abbott	FA	$0	Rich Monteleone	FA	-$1
Jason Bere	CHW	$0	Tom Edens	FA	-$1
Kenny Rogers	TEX	$0	Larry Andersen	FA	-$1
Kevin Tapani	MIN	$0	Steve Phoenix	OAK	-$1
Jeff Shaw	MON	$0	Steve Reed	COL	-$1
Rusty Meacham	KC	$0	Toby Borland	PHI	-$1
Sid Fernandez	BAL	$0	Bryan Hickerson	CHC	-$1
Jeff Nelson	SEA	$0	Terry Mathews	FLA	-$1
Kevin Foster	CHC	$0	Rich Rodriguez	STL	-$1
Jay Howell	FA	$0	Fernando Valenzuela	FA	-$2
Paul Assenmacher	FA	$0	Scott Bankhead	FA	-$2
Jamie Moyer	BAL	$0	Kirk McCaskill	FA	-$2
Anthony Young	CHC	$0	Matt Turner	CLE	-$2
Gregg Olson	FA	$0	Brad Clontz	ATL	-$2
Tim Scott	MON	$0	Mitch Williams	HOU	-$2
Josias Manzanillo	NYM	$0	Steve Bedrosian	ATL	-$2
Danny Cox	FA	$0	Bob Patterson	FA	-$2
Frank Viola	FA	$0	- PITCHERS NOT LISTED HAVE NO VALUE -		

HITTERS 1995 FORECAST STATS AND VALUES

NAME	TEAM	$VALUE	AGE	AB	AVG	OBA	SLG	HR	RBI	RUN	SB	CS
Kurt Abbott	FLA	$8	25	418	.252	.300	.383	9	44	50	9	4
Mike Aldrete	OAK	$1	34	226	.250	.327	.363	5	23	28	1	1
Manny Alexander	BAL	$0	24	112	.230	.258	.321	1	9	12	4	3
Edgardo Alfonzo	NYM	$0	21	100	.252	.310	.370	2	12	15	2	1
Luis Alicea	BOS	$6	29	261	.272	.356	.421	5	34	36	5	4
Roberto Alomar	TOR	$30	27	520	.310	.392	.456	11	62	96	29	11
Sandy Alomar	CLE	$11	28	415	.270	.321	.427	13	52	48	6	5
Moises Alou	MON	$31	28	542	.308	.367	.544	26	97	92	14	7
Rich Amaral	SEA	$2	32	161	.272	.337	.373	2	16	26	5	2
Ruben Amaro	CLE	$0	30	71	.242	.317	.437	3	9	11	3	1
Brady Anderson	BAL	$26	31	599	.259	.347	.419	16	67	100	38	6
Garret Anderson	CAL	$2	23	195	.263	.310	.400	4	24	26	1	1
Shane Andrews	MON	-$1	23	100	.220	.306	.330	2	12	11	1	1
Eric Anthony	FA	$9	27	410	.250	.313	.424	16	58	52	6	4
Alex Arias	FLA	$0	27	167	.253	.319	.323	1	17	13	1	1
Billy Ashley	LA	$3	24	238	.245	.276	.416	9	33	28	2	1
Rich Aude	PIT	$0	23	133	.260	.311	.398	3	18	15	1	1
Brad Ausmus	SD	$6	26	413	.252	.310	.354	8	31	48	7	2
Carlos Baerga	CLE	$31	26	587	.316	.342	.509	24	105	101	9	3
Kevin Baez	FA	-$3	28	50	.200	.262	.260	0	5	6	0	0
Jeff Bagwell	HOU	$42	26	575	.329	.415	.610	36	125	118	15	5
Harold Baines	FA	$14	36	416	.286	.351	.462	18	67	57	1	0
Bret Barberie	BAL	$10	27	449	.287	.337	.383	5	39	49	5	2
Skeeter Barnes	FA	$0	38	94	.267	.303	.372	2	15	15	2	3
Kevin Bass	FA	$5	35	232	.273	.331	.418	5	35	36	4	3
Kim Batiste	PHI	$0	27	249	.243	.258	.317	3	24	20	1	1
Howard Battle	TOR	$0	23	130	.240	.296	.362	3	12	11	3	2
Danny Bautista	DET	$6	22	332	.251	.303	.370	6	43	40	8	7
Billy Bean	FA	-$1	30	138	.224	.258	.304	1	15	10	1	2
Rich Becker	MIN	$13	23	414	.271	.365	.403	9	57	54	13	6
David Bell	CLE	$0	22	93	.258	.309	.398	3	11	10	0	1
Derek Bell	HOU	$30	26	557	.294	.338	.440	19	71	74	27	9
Jay Bell	PIT	$14	29	568	.278	.353	.424	11	55	90	7	3
Juan Bell	BOS	$1	27	173	.239	.312	.329	2	17	22	5	2
Albert Belle	CLE	$38	28	553	.307	.381	.629	45	125	101	13	8
Rafael Belliard	ATL	-$2	33	148	.234	.267	.297	0	10	12	0	2
Esteban Beltre	TEX	$0	27	105	.255	.310	.305	0	8	8	2	4
Freddy Benavides	FA	-$1	28	110	.230	.265	.318	1	10	10	1	1
Mike Benjamin	SF	$0	29	93	.215	.267	.366	2	11	13	4	1
Todd Benzinger	FA	$4	32	298	.263	.301	.386	7	33	30	1	1
Geronimo Berroa	OAK	$9	30	234	.292	.357	.466	9	43	37	4	1
Sean Berry	MON	$15	29	404	.269	.340	.455	15	55	57	14	3
Damon Berryhill	FA	$1	31	234	.255	.302	.402	5	31	24	0	1
Dante Bichette	COL	$30	31	540	.295	.323	.500	24	98	83	20	9
Craig Biggio	HOU	$34	29	590	.295	.381	.432	(11)	66	105	40	10
Lance Blankenship	OAK	$1	31	242	.224	.345	.293	2	19	35	10	4

HITTERS 1995 FORECAST STATS AND VALUES

NAME	TEAM	$VALUE	AGE	AB	AVG	OBA	SLG	HR	RBI	RUN	SB	CS
Jeff Blauser	FA	$13	29	508	.271	.347	.404	11	63	82	7	5
Greg Blosser	BOS	$1	29	190	.237	.320	.400	6	21	21	3	1
Mike Blowers	SEA	$7	30	291	.275	.341	.426	9	46	38	2	3
Tim Bogar	NYM	-$1	28	105	.223	.275	.314	2	11	10	2	1
Wade Boggs	NYY	$20	36	515	.321	.408	.433	10	65	81	2	1
Frank Bolick	FA	-$2	28	50	.221	.301	.340	1	6	6	0	0
Barry Bonds	SF	$45	30	504	.310	.430	.617	41	103	108	35	11
Bobby Bonilla	NYM	$18	32	525	.276	.365	.493	26	88 95	80	2	4
Brett Boone	CIN	$21	25	523	.299	.340	.470	18	88	78	5	5
Pat Borders	FA	$3	32	423	.248	.283	.359	7	43	35	1	1
Mike Bordick	OAK	$6	29	489	.259	.326	.331	2	45	51	8	5
Daryl Boston	FA	$1	32	152	.229	.294	.388	6	21	21	3	3
Rafael Bournigal	LA	-$1	28	100	.237	.300	.290	0	9	4	1	0
Darren Bragg	SEA	$0	25	99	.258	.329	.394	2	10	15	3	2
Jeff Branson	CIN	$1	28	135	.262	.295	.400	4	15	18	1	0
Sid Bream	FA	$0	34	94	.271	.352	.394	2	11	10	2	1
Rico Brogna	NYM	$10	24	395	.273	.306	.461	14	48	33	2	1
Scott Brosius	OAK	$6	28	344	.239	.290	.404	13	47	37	5	5
Jarvis Brown	NYM	-$1	28	62	.227	.289	.371	1	3	9	2	1
Jerry Browne	FA	$6	29	342	.282	.370	.374	3	32	42	3	1
Jacob Brumfield	PIT	$11	29	293	.287	.353	.444	6	25	57	14	8
Tom Brunansky	FA	$1	34	224	.232	.314	.402	8	35	24	1	2
Steve Buechele	CHC	$7	33	467	.249	.324	.403	16	66	48	1	1
Damon Buford	BAL	$1	24	110	.246	.285	.373	3	12	16	4	3
Jay Buhner	SEA	$16	30	508	.268	.378	.498	27	90	89	1	3
Scott Bullett	CHC	$2	26	203	.245	.270	.365	4	18	24	6	3
Ellis Burks	COL	$22	30	408	.312	.382	.527	20	71	85	8	5
Jeromy Burnitz	CLE	$5	25	305	.234	.336	.393	11	40	52	6	4
Brett Butler	FA	$28	37	567	.305	.399	.407	6	40	101	32	14
Rob Butler	PHI	-$1	24	122	.225	.298	.320	2	9	17	2	2
Ken Caminiti	SD	$17	32	531	.275	.341	.437	17	85	76	6	4
Willie Canate	FA	-$1	23	94	.232	.274	.287	0	7	10	3	1
John Cangelosi	FA	$0	32	97	.247	.338	.289	0	5	12	4	1
Jose Canseco	BOS	$22	30	453	.275	.371	.519	29	93	86	11	9
Ramon Caraballo	STL	-$2	25	80	.210	.245	.338	1	7	8	1	1
Chuck Carr	FLA	$17	26	484	.261	.305	.339	4	34	69	32	12
Mark Carreon	SF	$2	31	170	.269	.319	.406	5	29	17	1	0
Matias Carrillo	FA	$0	32	118	.253	.295	.339	1	9	12	2	2
Joe Carter	TOR	$24	35	535	.268	.319	.514	32	120	89	10	2
Vinny Castilla	COL	$1	27	142	.270	.303	.415	3	17	15	2	2
Andujar Cedeno	SD	$11	25	491	.267	.326	.409	12	61	60	6	3
Domingo Cedeno	TOR	-$2	26	102	.212	.278	.294	0	10	13	2	2
Roger Cedeno	LA	$0	20	99	.240	.302	.303	0	8	10	3	2
Wes Chamberlain	BOS	$5	28	300	.264	.306	.423	9	39	30	2	2
Archi Cianfrocco	FA	$1	28	291	.237	.264	.371	6	31	25	2	0
Jeff Cirillo	MIL	$0	25	129	.245	.306	.380	2	13	17	1	1

HITTERS 1995 FORECAST STATS AND VALUES

NAME	TEAM	$VALUE	AGE	AB	AVG	OBA	SLG	HR	RBI	RUN	SB	CS
Dave Clark	PIT	$9	32	298	.278	.350	.470	13	54	47	2	2
Phil Clark	SD	$3	26	235	.255	.281	.421	8	29	25	2	2
Tony Clark	DET	$0	22	105	.253	.330	.438	5	18	11	0	1
Will Clark	TEX	$26	31	528	.313	.410	.502	21	102	96	6	2
✳ Royce Clayton	SF	$16	25	550	.255	.307	.356	7	56	62	25	6
Greg Colbrunn	FLA	$16	25	457	.289	.326	.449	15	80	48	4	4
Alex Cole	MIN	$13	29	329	.274	.354	.368	3	21	59	22	9
Vince Coleman	FA	$21	33	490	.250	.295	.347	2	34	74	46	11
Darnell Coles	FA	$0	32	171	.230	.284	.374	4	19	19	1	0
Jeff Conine	FLA	$24	28	568	.305	.361	.495	22	93	79	2	2
Ron Coomer	FA	$4	28	225	.272	.297	.396	5	35	28	2	2
Scott Cooper	BOS	$13	27	501	.281	.341	.429	14	67	65	2	3
Joey Cora	FA	$6	29	297	.270	.349	.360	2	30	51	9	4
✳ Wil Cordero	MON	$29	23	570	.297	.355	.484	21	89	88	20	5
Marty Cordova	MIN	$0	25	96	.278	.330	.406	2	10	10	2	1
Rod Correia	CAL	-$1	27	81	.258	.318	.309	0	4	11	1	2
Tim Costo	CLE	$0	26	91	.268	.330	.396	1	10	10	2	1
Tripp Cromer	STL	-$1	27	90	.240	.288	.356	1	8	8	1	1
Fausto Cruz	OAK	-$2	23	110	.249	.300	.330	0	6	6	0	1
Midre Cummings	PIT	$9	23	456	.258	.297	.384	10	40	49	9	5
Chad Curtis	CAL	$24	26	551	.265	.332	.387	11	59	83	35	17
Milt Cuyler	DET	$2	26	204	.237	.299	.328	2	18	34	9	4
Darren Daulton	PHI	$14	33	394	.268	.375	.497	20	76	62	5	1
Butch Davis	FA	-$1	36	45	.243	.274	.356	1	4	6	1	0
Chili Davis	CAL	$20	35	506	.279	.378	.486	26	97	79	4	2
Eric Davis	FA	$4	32	203	.215	.308	.360	6	30	26	12	4
Russ Davis	NYY	$3	25	278	.248	.315	.417	9	44	30	1	0
Andre Dawson	FA	$4	40	290	.252	.278	.421	10	40	33	1	1
Steve Decker	FLA	$0	29	125	.256	.310	.392	3	14	11	0	0
Carlos Delgado	TOR	$13	22	360	.278	.395	.489	20	58	48	2	2
Delino Deshields	LA	$23	26	464	.276	.373	.384	5	42	73	37	10
Mike Devereaux	FA	$4	31	452	.236	.289	.372	12	58	56	2	2
Alex Diaz	FA	$5	26	299	.258	.288	.314	2	22	31	10	9
Mario Diaz	FLA	$0	33	132	.260	.301	.364	1	16	17	1	0
Gary Disarcina	CAL	$4	27	462	.251	.282	.318	3	41	55	5	6
Chris Donnels	HOU	$0	28	86	.255	.342	.384	2	6	11	1	0
Brian Dorsett	FA	$0	33	156	.250	.314	.365	4	19	15	0	0
Rob Ducey	FA	$0	29	121	.237	.300	.372	2	11	14	2	3
Mariano Duncan	FA	$12	32	473	.265	.293	.397	10	61	64	11	3
Steve Dunn	MIN	$1	24	293	.235	.257	.437	6	41	39	1	0
Shawon Dunston	CHC	$10	32	437	.272	.305	.414	12	42	52	6	8
Ray Durham	CHW	$10	23	445	.241	.320	.375	10	39	75	18	9
Lenny Dykstra	PHI	$23	32	490	.287	.408	.451	11	44	105	27	7
Damion Easley	CAL	$5	25	399	.243	.309	.341	5	38	52	9	7
Jim Edmonds	CAL	$9	24	391	.280	.345	.389	7	50	45	4	3
Jim Eisenreich	PHI	$7	35	329	.272	.337	.389	5	44	43	6	2

HITTERS 1995 FORECAST STATS AND VALUES

NAME	TEAM	$VALUE	AGE	AB	AVG	OBA	SLG	HR	RBI	RUN	SB	CS
Kevin Elster	NYY	-$1	30	40	.210	.275	.325	1	4	4	1	1
Alvaro Espinoza	CLE	$0	33	192	.243	.263	.318	1	16	23	1	2
Tony Eusebio	HOU	$1	27	135	.270	.305	.415	3	24	15	0	1
Carl Everett	NYM	$14	24	390	.279	.330	.418	10	44	54	14	9
Jorge Fabregas	CAL	$0	24	212	.247	.286	.307	0	25	20	3	2
Rikkert Faneyte	SF	$2	25	277	.248	.329	.404	4	33	28	4	2
Mike Felder	FA	$0	32	139	.241	.278	.317	1	11	13	5	2
Junior Felix	FA	$7	27	273	.269	.321	.458	10	41	45	3	4
Felix Fermin	FA	$3	31	488	.255	.282	.311	1	43	58	4	4
Tony Fernandez	NYY	$11	32	393	.275	.348	.405	6	47	53	11	8
Cecil Fielder	DET	$19	31	571	.258	.343	.483	35	120	86	0	0
Steve Finley	SD	$17	30	514	.277	.324	.414	11	44	78	18	8
John Flaherty	DET	-$2	27	69	.217	.244	.290	1	5	4	0	1
Darrin Fletcher	MON	$6	28	374	.255	.314	.398	10	64	32	0	0
Scott Fletcher	BOS	$5	36	297	.252	.308	.360	4	26	46	9	3
Cliff Floyd	MON	$18	22	492	.271	.318	.441	15	71	63	16	7
Tom Foley	FA	$0	35	173	.238	.295	.341	3	20	17	0	0
Eric Fox	FA	-$1	31	68	.221	.269	.302	1	4	10	2	1
Matt Franco	CHC	$0	25	90	.256	.328	.389	2	11	10	0	0
Lou Frazier	MON	$4	30	129	.263	.339	.310	0	12	20	13	3
Jeff Frye	TEX	$3	28	241	.280	.336	.407	1	19	36	4	1
Travis Fryman	DET	$22	26	597	.281	.348	.484	23	101	90	6	3
Gary Gaetti	FA	$6	36	311	.264	.304	.431	11	49	44	1	2
Greg Gagne	KC	$11	33	486	.263	.309	.391	9	58	55	10	13
Andres Galarraga	COL	$27	33	507	.308	.339	.535	28	89	79	7	4
Dave Gallagher	FA	$0	34	203	.251	.336	.350	2	21	33	1	2
Mike Gallego	FA	$5	34	419	.249	.332	.370	9	52	55	2	2
Ron Gant	CIN	$10	30	310	.258	.322	.448	14	51	48	8	6
Carlos Garcia	PIT	$16	27	545	.271	.302	.376	10	42	70	18	11
Jeff Gardner	FA	-$1	31	122	.248	.321	.344	1	7	15	1	1
Brent Gates	OAK	$16	25	506	.298	.360	.407	7	62	62	7	2
Kirk Gibson	FA	$9	37	312	.250	.331	.446	14	58	59	6	5
Benji Gil	TEX	$3	22	239	.234	.280	.351	6	26	27	7	5
Bernard Gilkey	STL	$17	28	515	.272	.339	.404	10	59	75	17	11
Joe Girardi	COL	$7	30	416	.276	.322	.361	4	38	50	4	5
Chris Gomez	DET	$4	23	314	.249	.321	.366	5	46	33	5	3
Leo Gomez	BAL	$12	28	494	.257	.348	.453	22	85	72	1	1
Rene Gonzales	FA	$0	33	100	.269	.334	.370	1	11	13	3	1
Alex Gonzalez	TOR	$9	21	269	.264	.315	.428	7	25	38	15	9
Juan Gonzalez	TEX	$23	25	513	.280	.327	.540	33	103	77	5	3
Luis Gonzalez	HOU	$20	27	517	.279	.350	.445	14	80	72	16	14
Curtis Goodwin	BAL	$0	22	64	.245	.286	.320	0	5	9	5	2
Tom Goodwin	KC	$0	26	50	.240	.286	.380	1	2	12	4	3
Mark Grace	FA	$18	30	547	.304	.378	.428	9	69	75	3	2
Tony Graffanino	ATL	$0	22	89	.249	.311	.337	1	9	10	3	2
Craig Grebeck	CHW	$1	30	177	.273	.354	.350	2	15	25	1	1

HITTERS 1995 FORECAST STATS AND VALUES

NAME	TEAM	$VALUE	AGE	AB	AVG	OBA	SLG	HR	RBI	RUN	SB	CS
Shawn Green	TOR	$9	22	271	.280	.300	.406	6	40	33	8	4
Willie Greene	CIN	$11	23	404	.255	.335	.478	19	55	51	6	4
Mike Greenwell	BOS	$15	31	469	.286	.357	.454	13	63	74	5	3
Rusty Greer	TEX	$6	26	305	.267	.351	.439	11	41	34	1	0
Ken Griffey	SEA	$41	25	571	.318	.399	.634	46	112	111	14	5
Marquis Grissom	MON	$39	27	590	.287	.342	.422	14	64	106	55	9
Ozzie Guillen	CHW	$10	31	468	.278	.301	.348	3	50	52	7	5
Ricky Gutierrez	HOU	$3	24	429	.246	.324	.329	4	33	61	5	6
Chris Gwynn	FA	$0	30	81	.274	.332	.395	2	11	10	0	1
Tony Gwynn	SD	$25	34	540	.330	.392	.476	10	73	89	8	1
Chip Hale	MIN	$0	30	170	.254	.335	.359	2	19	20	1	2
Joe Hall	CHW	-$1	29	90	.211	.263	.356	2	16	19	0	0
Bob Hamelin	KC	$13	27	453	.254	.366	.490	23	82	77	4	4
Darryl Hamilton	MIL	$14	30	393	.285	.347	.377	4	40	59	16	6
Jeffrey Hammonds	BAL	$15	24	413	.283	.325	.472	14	64	61	9	5
Dave Hansen	LA	$3	26	190	.284	.369	.389	4	24	18	0	1
Shawn Hare	FA	-$1	27	70	.243	.311	.386	2	7	11	1	0
Brian Harper	FA	$8	35	366	.285	.316	.396	7	48	36	1	2
Lenny Harris	CIN	$2	30	149	.285	.330	.349	1	16	17	4	2
Bill Haselman	BOS	$0	28	147	.233	.272	.401	4	15	22	2	0
Billy Hatcher	FA	$5	34	345	.255	.295	.348	4	34	44	7	6
Charlie Hayes	FA	$17	29	536	.284	.337	.459	18	72	63	5	6
Eric Helfand	OAK	-$2	26	50	.220	.287	.320	1	6	6	0	0
Scott Hemond	FA	$1	29	186	.231	.301	.339	3	20	22	6	5
Dave Henderson	FA	-$1	36	50	.220	.278	.400	2	7	6	0	0
Rickey Henderson	OAK	$23	36	387	.270	.414	.411	12	37	85	36	8
Carlos Hernandez	LA	-$1	27	96	.240	.259	.354	2	8	7	0	0
Jose Hernandez	CHC	-$1	25	113	.234	.278	.327	1	6	12	1	2
Phil Hiatt	KC	$0	25	92	.238	.311	.370	2	13	12	3	3
Glenallen Hill	CHC	$11	30	303	.274	.335	.416	9	43	42	12	6
Denny Hocking	MIN	$6	25	245	.261	.295	.420	6	26	25	9	4
Chris Hoiles	BAL	$14	30	416	.264	.377	.500	27	71	68	2	1
Ray Holbert	SD	$0	24	125	.239	.290	.312	1	9	11	4	1
Todd Hollandsworth	LA	$1	21	151	.245	.288	.404	4	21	19	2	1
Dave Hollins	PHI	$12	28	470	.267	.361	.423	15	80	80	3	2
Sam Horn	FA	$0	31	77	.244	.290	.429	3	11	9	0	0
Dwayne Hosey	KC	$1	28	106	.243	.310	.387	3	10	12	5	3
Steve Hosey	CAL	$0	25	55	.248	.307	.400	2	7	6	2	2
Chrish Howard	SEA	-$2	29	50	.202	.270	.300	1	7	6	0	0
Dave Howard	KC	$0	28	91	.227	.315	.308	1	14	11	3	2
Thomas Howard	CIN	$6	30	259	.263	.306	.382	5	30	34	8	4
Rex Hudler	CAL	$1	34	136	.257	.290	.426	4	16	17	2	3
Mike Huff	TOR	$1	31	157	.270	.355	.401	2	19	23	2	1
Tim Hulett	FA	$0	35	136	.252	.324	.363	3	16	17	1	1
David Hulse	TEX	$18	27	453	.278	.323	.333	2	29	83	29	5
Todd Hundley	NYM	$5	25	389	.239	.291	.405	16	52	49	2	1

HITTERS 1995 FORECAST STATS AND VALUES

NAME	TEAM	$VALUE	AGE	AB	AVG	OBA	SLG	HR	RBI	RUN	SB	CS
Brianl Hunter	HOU	$14	24	396	.288	.317	.292	6	40	42	15	8
Brianr Hunter	CIN	$4	27	310	.227	.274	.455	16	60	39	0	0
Butch Huskey	NYM	$1	23	176	.238	.310	.364	4	5	19	4	3
Jeff Huson	BAL	$0	30	120	.232	.312	.317	2	9	17	4	2
Tim Hyers	SD	-$1	23	102	.243	.297	.280	0	7	11	2	0
Garey Ingram	LA	$0	24	50	.282	.341	.420	2	5	6	0	0
Bo Jackson	FA	$6	32	281	.252	.316	.434	15	50	29	1	1
Darrin Jackson	FA	$13	31	441	.279	.322	.422	13	57	50	6	2
John Jaha	MIL	$12	28	442	.257	.328	.410	19	66	71	7	6
Chris James	FA	$2	32	202	.254	.338	.510	8	27	31	1	0
Stan Javier	OAK	$19	31	500	.268	.344	.394	10	61	91	23	7
Gregg Jefferies	PHI	$31	27	535	.320	.387	.471	14	74	72	23	8
Reggie Jefferson	SEA	$8	26	305	.281	.340	.443	10	44	36	1	1
Derek Jeter	NYY	$1	20	95	.270	.344	.380	1	9	12	5	2
Brian Johnson	SD	$0	27	119	.255	.293	.409	2	16	10	0	0
Charles Johnson	FLA	$3	23	327	.230	.296	.404	14	48	36	1	0
Howard Johnson	FA	$1	34	252	.233	.346	.391	6	31	30	3	4
Lance Johnson	CHW	$22	31	546	.282	.325	.391	2	58	72	30	8
Chipper Jones	ATL	$13	22	484	.267	.316	.397	13	59	59	9	4
Chris Jones	NYM	$0	29	81	.257	.294	.425	2	8	10	2	2
Ron Jones	COL	$0	30	50	.270	.314	.400	1	11	10	0	0
Brian Jordan	STL	$9	28	320	.266	.318	.445	10	40	35	9	6
Ricky Jordan	FA	$6	29	254	.286	.308	.458	8	39	33	0	0
Felix Jose	FA	$22	29	495	.289	.346	.434	12	60	68	21	15
Wally Joyner	KC	$17	32	501	.297	.376	.447	12	73	72	5	5
David Justice	ATL	$22	28	515	.288	.392	.518	30	92	85	3	5
Ron Karkovice	CHW	$3	31	335	.224	.312	.421	16	46	49	2	4
Eric Karros	LA	$11	27	541	.258	.304	.421	19	74	66	2	1
Mike Kelly	ATL	$2	24	201	.242	.261	.458	7	29	26	3	3
Pat Kelly	NYY	$11	27	438	.265	.310	.394	6	53	53	12	9
Roberto Kelly	ATL	$27	30	552	.290	.339	.428	14	61	87	27	12
Jeff Kent	NYM	$20	27	545	.283	.333	.464	23	96	75	3	5
Jeff King	PIT	$9	30	471	.262	.324	.387	9	64	55	5	3
Mike Kingery	COL	$4	34	222	.280	.345	.527	3	29	39	4	5
Wayne Kirby	CLE	$9	31	273	.278	.328	.388	5	34	46	12	5
Ryan Klesko	ATL	$13	23	409	.270	.341	.494	22	71	62	2	0
Chuck Knoblauch	MIN	$29	26	564	.301	.366	.413	4	58	105	35	9
Randy Knorr	TOR	$0	26	111	.244	.303	.429	5	16	16	0	0
Kevin Koslofski	FA	-$1	28	50	.255	.369	.360	1	4	10	0	1
Chad Kreuter	FA	$0	30	147	.241	.338	.371	3	18	17	0	1
John Kruk	FA	$13	34	407	.294	.403	.449	9	60	63	5	2
Tim Laker	MON	$1	25	145	.265	.332	.379	3	15	13	1	0
Ray Lankford	STL	$22	27	524	.268	.364	.454	20	73	100	20	15
Mike Lansing	MON	$15	27	507	.270	.325	.368	5	46	59	21	9
Barry Larkin	CIN	$25	30	548	.289	.375	.428	12	71	91	23	4
Mike Lavalliere	CHW	$1	34	168	.271	.353	.321	1	24	9	0	2

NAME	TEAM	$VALUE	AGE	AB	AVG	OBA	SLG	HR	RBI	RUN	SB	CS
Manuel Lee	FA	$4	30	372	.263	.315	.340	2	37	46	4	2
Scott Leius	MIN	$4	29	322	.248	.318	.401	10	40	50	3	4
Mark Lemke	ATL	$5	29	384	.273	.349	.351	4	34	43	1	3
Patrick Lennon	BOS	$0	26	50	.280	.356	.420	1	6	6	1	1
Mark Leonard	FA	-$1	30	50	.251	.364	.420	1	8	6	0	0
Jessie Levis	CLE	-$2	26	50	.222	.238	.280	0	3	5	0	0
Darren Lewis	SF	$25	27	568	.268	.334	.359	4	41	90	43	16
Mark Lewis	CIN	$1	25	180	.247	.273	.332	2	16	17	4	1
Jim Leyritz	NYY	$7	31	264	.267	.357	.516	15	52	38	0	0
Mike Lieberthal	PHI	$0	23	295	.239	.267	.367	3	37	27	1	0
Jose Lind	KC	$5	30	416	.257	.291	.321	1	41	41	7	5
Jim Lindeman	NYM	$1	33	134	.266	.296	.440	5	18	16	0	0
Nelson Liriano	PIT	$1	30	222	.259	.359	.401	2	26	33	2	2
Pat Listach	MIL	$5	27	180	.272	.333	.333	1	14	27	11	5
Greg Litton	FA	-$1	30	50	.244	.297	.360	1	6	6	0	0
Scott Livingstone	SD	$3	29	259	.277	.309	.367	3	23	23	1	2
Kevin Lockhart	FA	-$1	30	55	.219	.286	.349	1	6	5	1	0
Kenny Lofton	CLE	$53	27	555	.325	.398	.495	12	61	120	70	14
Tony Longmire	PHI	$0	26	115	.240	.289	.314	1	14	10	2	1
Javier Lopez	ATL	$10	24	455	.266	.307	.426	16	54	46	2	3
Luis Lopez	SD	$1	24	201	.265	.309	.379	1	16	21	2	2
Torey Lovullo	CLE	$0	29	91	.235	.309	.361	2	8	11	2	1
Scott Lydy	OAK	$0	26	101	.240	.322	.347	2	10	14	2	1
Kevin Maas	MIN	-$1	30	50	.220	.260	.400	2	8	6	0	0
John Mabry	STL	$0	24	50	.304	.360	.440	0	7	4	0	0
Mike Macfarlane	FA	$9	30	385	.257	.328	.473	18	58	59	1	2
Dave Magadan	FA	$5	32	369	.274	.385	.338	3	36	46	1	0
Mike Maksudian	FA	-$1	28	50	.252	.310	.340	0	8	11	0	1
Candy Maldonado	FA	$0	34	133	.224	.326	.412	7	19	18	1	1
Jeff Manto	BAL	-$1	30	50	.240	.280	.360	1	6	6	0	0
Kirt Manwaring	SF	$3	29	406	.255	.313	.337	3	39	39	2	2
Tom Marsh	PHI	-$1	29	62	.227	.255	.381	1	7	6	1	0
Al Martin	PIT	$13	27	356	.276	.347	.466	11	42	56	13	7
Norberto Martin	CHW	$1	28	119	.268	.315	.366	1	13	16	3	2
Chito Martinez	COL	-$1	9	50	.240	.280	.380	1	7	7	0	0
Dave Martinez	FA	$1	30	182	.252	.318	.368	3	19	19	3	3
Edgar Martinez	SEA	$17	32	449	.298	.394	.470	15	62	73	6	3
Tino Martinez	SEA	$13	27	436	.263	.327	.475	22	72	54	2	3
Mike Matheny	MIL	-$2	24	65	.220	.261	.340	1	4	4	0	1
Francisco Matos	OAK	-$1	25	50	.250	.267	.300	0	4	2	2	0
Don Mattingly	NYY	$14	33	497	.296	.380	.422	11	70	75	0	0
Derrick May	CHC	$17	26	499	.290	.341	.423	12	75	66	7	3
Brent Mayne	KC	$3	26	316	.248	.310	.345	5	40	33	3	2
David McCarty	MIN	$2	25	240	.250	.288	.392	5	28	31	3	3
Lloyd McClendon	FA	$0	36	140	.241	.301	.379	4	17	16	0	2
Ray McDavid	SD	$3	23	197	.240	.286	.355	4	23	30	8	5

Handwritten notes near John Mabry row: 500, .266, 16, 70

HITTERS 1995 FORECAST STATS AND VALUES

NAME	TEAM	$VALUE	AGE	AB	AVG	OBA	SLG	HR	RBI	RUN	SB	CS
Oddibe McDowell	FA	$3	32	163	.254	.353	.331	2	13	27	9	2
Willie McGee	FA	$4	36	200	.283	.338	.380	3	23	23	4	2
Fred McGriff	ATL	$32	31	547	.303	.383	.587	40	113	101	7	4
Terry McGriff	FA	-$2	31	99	.219	.299	.343	2	10	9	0	0
Mark McGwire	OAK	$8	31	292	.256	.405	.503	19	58	50	0	1
Jeff McKnight	FA	-$2	32	80	.227	.290	.288	1	7	8	0	0
Mark McLemore	TEX	$12	30	426	.264	.350	.331	3	43	59	18	8
Jeff McNeely	STL	$0	25	96	.240	.318	.271	1	6	12	4	2
Brian McRae	KC	$19	27	556	.271	.343	.383	8	59	85	24	10
Kevin McReynolds	FA	$4	35	296	.252	.331	.416	8	37	36	3	1
Pat Meares	MIN	$2	26	225	.261	.295	.333	1	23	26	4	2
Roberto Mejia	COL	$6	22	325	.251	.319	.440	10	34	41	7	2
Bob Melvin	FA	-$2	33	50	.230	.259	.320	1	6	5	0	0
Orlando Merced	PIT	$10	28	449	.272	.354	.405	9	63	59	4	2
Luis Mercedes	PIT	-$1	27	50	.280	.340	.360	0	6	8	1	0
Matt Merullo	MIN	-$2	29	50	.220	.259	.300	1	5	4	0	0
Matt Mieske	MIL	$6	27	320	.250	.306	.406	11	43	47	5	5
Keith Miller	FA	$0	31	114	.246	.291	.325	1	8	14	3	1
Orlando Miller	HOU	$1	26	143	.233	.269	.343	4	32	11	3	2
Randy Milligan	FA	$0	33	156	.255	.381	.391	4	20	20	0	1
Keith Mitchell	FA	$1	25	178	.242	.335	.365	5	20	24	2	1
Kevin Mitchell	FA	$22	33	452	.292	.387	.573	32	96	72	2	1
Paul Molitor	TOR	$31	38	585	.310	.384	.472	16	89	101	20	2
Raul Mondesi	LA	$24	24	575	.289	.315	.473	17	78	82	16	10
Kerwin Moore	OAK	$1	24	86	.233	.316	.320	1	7	15	8	3
Mickey Morandini	PHI	$8	28	382	.271	.339	.382	3	32	51	10	5
Hal Morris	CIN	$26	34	561	.326	.379	.467	12	87	74	7	3
James Mouton	HOU	$15	26	447	.258	.318	.385	10	40	63	23	7
Pedro Munoz	MIN	$11	26	399	.280	.329	.466	16	57	60	1	1
Eddie Murray	CLE	$15	39	534	.262	.313	.427	20	89	67	6	4
Glenn Murray	BOS	-$1	24	90	.210	.282	.389	4	11	11	1	0
Greg Myers	CAL	$1	28	231	.251	.300	.359	5	24	19	2	2
Tim Naehring	BOS	$5	28	296	.273	.338	.402	6	39	37	2	2
Rob Natal	FLA	-$1	29	50	.260	.328	.380	1	3	2	1	0
Troy Neel	OAK	$11	29	371	.270	.353	.464	18	58	54	3	3
Phil Nevin	HOU	$6	24	473	.245	.304	.436	10	74	54	3	1
Marc Newfield	SEA	$10	22	400	.267	.305	.453	14	63	55	2	2
Warren Newson	CHW	$0	30	97	.256	.355	.361	2	9	15	1	0
Melvin Nieves	SD	$0	23	110	.250	.327	.391	4	15	11	1	1
Dave Nilsson	MIL	$13	25	458	.282	.344	.434	12	73	55	3	2
Otis Nixon	TEX	$25	36	509	.274	.357	.320	1	29	84	47	11
Junior Noboa	PIT	-$1	30	52	.269	.302	.327	0	5	3	1	0
Matt Nokes	BAL	$3	31	203	.259	.319	.453	10	30	20	0	0
Charlie O'Brien	ATL	$0	33	201	.234	.299	.378	5	29	24	0	0
Troy O'Leary	MIL	$0	25	98	.267	.324	.429	2	11	13	1	1
Paul O'Neill	NYY	$30	32	529	.321	.415	.543	27	105	94	6	5

HITTERS 1995 FORECAST STATS AND VALUES

NAME	TEAM	$VALUE	AGE	AB	AVG	OBA	SLG	HR	RBI	RUN	SB	CS
Sherman Obando	BAL	$9	25	328	.271	.317	.494	15	51	50	2	1
Jose Offerman	LA	$4	26	370	.240	.329	.311	1	34	45	11	6
John Olerud	TOR	$23	26	517	.316	.417	.520	20	90	76	1	2
Jose Oliva	ATL	$9	24	453	.260	.324	.448	17	57	54	1	1
Joe Oliver	FA	$1	29	214	.244	.286	.379	6	32	17	0	0
Jose Oquendo	STL	$0	31	189	.265	.358	.323	0	12	19	1	1
Joe Orsulak	NYM	$7	32	362	.270	.312	.365	8	43	48	4	3
Junior Ortiz	FA	-$1	35	93	.254	.292	.301	0	9	5	0	1
Luis Ortiz	FA	$0	24	83	.265	.296	.422	2	15	9	0	0
Spike Owen	CAL	$3	33	258	.264	.360	.372	3	30	29	2	3
Jayhawk Owens	COL	-$1	26	55	.241	.322	.364	1	5	7	1	1
Tom Pagnozzi	STL	$5	32	358	.263	.314	.383	8	48	30	1	1
Rafael Palmeiro	BAL	$29	30	539	.310	.386	.544	29	92	102	9	3
Dean Palmer	TEX	$15	26	490	.245	.306	.471	28	85	74	7	7
Erik Pappas	FA	-$2	28	104	.207	.328	.279	1	12	13	1	1
Craig Paquette	OAK	-$1	26	159	.219	.255	.358	4	14	11	2	1
Mark Parent	FA	$0	33	89	.250	.329	.393	3	13	7	0	1
Rick Parker	FA	-$2	32	50	.240	.264	.300	0	2	8	1	1
Derek Parks	MIN	-$1	26	146	.226	.260	.349	3	13	14	0	2
Lance Parrish	FA	$0	38	107	.259	.347	.383	3	13	9	1	1
Dan Pasqua	FA	$0	33	103	.222	.302	.408	4	14	13	1	1
John Patterson	SF	$2	28	181	.234	.309	.315	2	22	26	8	2
Bill Pecota	FA	$0	35	149	.240	.337	.336	2	18	18	2	0
Steve Pegues	PIT	$0	26	75	.259	.298	.373	1	5	5	2	1
Geronimo Pena	STL	$18	28	421	.261	.334	.463	18	61	64	19	5
Tony Pena	FA	-$1	37	121	.250	.304	.364	2	10	14	0	1
Terry Pendleton	FA	$8	34	484	.258	.292	.401	12	57	52	3	0
Shannon Penn	DET	$1	25	94	.251	.290	.330	1	7	11	6	3
William Pennyfeather	FA	-$2	26	52	.212	.272	.288	1	4	5	1	1
Eduardo Perez	CAL	$4	25	284	.246	.301	.387	8	36	31	5	2
Robert Perez	TOR	-$2	25	58	.241	.280	.345	1	4	5	0	0
Gerald Perry	FA	$1	34	109	.282	.392	.440	3	20	16	1	2
Herbert Perry	CLE	$0	25	80	.280	.340	.400	2	11	10	1	1
Roberto Petagine	SD	$3	23	333	.258	.315	.346	5	38	43	0	0
Jr Phillips	SF	$1	24	236	.238	.255	.364	8	30	27	1	0
Tony Phillips	DET	$20	35	564	.280	.409	.427	17	69	109	14	8
Mike Piazza	LA	$27	26	563	.306	.359	.510	29	107	79	2	4
Greg Pirkl	SEA	$0	24	71	.239	.251	.437	3	12	8	0	0
Phil Plantier	HOU	$11	26	474	.236	.315	.468	28	77	69	4	3
Luis Polonia	NYY	$20	30	464	.295	.360	.375	1	38	73	26	10
Arquimedez Pozo	SEA	$0	21	96	.240	.288	.365	2	8	11	2	1
Todd Pratt	FA	-$1	28	127	.232	.304	.378	3	14	12	0	1
Tom Prince	LA	-$2	30	50	.200	.279	.260	0	7	5	0	0
Kirby Puckett	MIN	$29	34	575	.309	.353	.506	22	116	94	8	5
Tim Raines	CHW	$20	35	490	.277	.375	.414	12	59	94	21	5
Manny Ramirez	CLE	$20	22	509	.281	.372	.511	26	92	80	5	3

HITTERS 1995 FORECAST STATS AND VALUES

NAME	TEAM	$VALUE	AGE	AB	AVG	OBA	SLG	HR	RBI	RUN	SB	CS
Luis Raven	CAL	$0	26	95	.242	.278	.411	4	15	14	1	0
Randy Ready	FA	-$2	35	50	.240	.300	.340	1	4	7	0	1
Jeff Reboulet	MIN	$1	30	237	.250	.327	.346	3	24	33	2	2
Gary Redus	FA	$0	38	50	.270	.340	.420	1	5	6	1	1
Jeff Reed	FA	-$2	32	119	.203	.284	.303	3	9	12	0	0
Jody Reed	FA	$4	32	408	.269	.350	.348	3	35	49	1	2
Rich Renteria	FA	-$1	27	83	.237	.280	.337	2	8	8	0	1
Harold Reynolds	FA	$3	34	289	.243	.324	.311	1	21	42	10	8
Karl Rhodes	CHC	$7	26	402	.244	.330	.396	12	41	57	9	6
Billy Ripken	FA	-$1	30	74	.242	.281	.338	1	6	8	1	0
Cal Ripken	BAL	$16	34	554	.280	.336	.424	17	85	81	1	1
Luis Rivera	FA	-$1	31	105	.233	.296	.381	3	9	15	1	2
Kevin Roberson	CHC	$0	27	136	.234	.272	.412	6	19	18	0	0
Bip Roberts	SD	$24	31	504	.303	.369	.383	3	38	72	30	10
Alex Rodriguez	SEA	$8	19	311	.277	.315	.424	8	39	38	6	4
Carlos Rodriguez	BOS	$0	27	146	.274	.317	.370	1	11	13	1	0
Henry Rodriguez	LA	$5	27	342	.257	.297	.398	9	50	36	1	1
Ivan Rodriguez	TEX	$19	23	511	.292	.342	.458	18	75	71	6	4
Rich Rowland	BOS	$5	28	300	.244	.311	.423	15	48	36	0	0
Stan Royer	FA	-$3	27	68	.200	.237	.324	1	5	4	0	0
Chris Sabo	FA	$6	33	293	.257	.311	.451	12	44	44	2	2
Olmedo Saenz	CHW	-$1	24	80	.235	.292	.375	2	10	10	0	0
Tim Salmon	CAL	$20	26	520	.279	.373	.512	29	94	92	3	3
Juan Samuel	FA	$4	34	182	.276	.335	.451	4	22	31	6	3
Rey Sanchez	CHC	$3	27	288	.281	.322	.330	0	24	27	2	3
Deion Sanders	CIN	$33	27	504	.288	.340	.415	8	46	83	(50)	19
Reggie Sanders	CIN	$25	27	527	.271	.340	.476	22	81	90	24	11
Benito Santiago	FA	$8	30	425	.259	.310	.407	13	50	44	4	4
Steve Scarsone	SF	-$1	29	97	.247	.304	.381	2	12	18	0	2
Gene Schall	PHI	$0	24	102	.242	.310	.363	2	14	10	1	0
Dick Schofield	FA	$2	32	315	.240	.317	.317	3	29	37	6	5
David Segui	NYM	$6	28	447	.256	.329	.387	11	55	56	1	0
Kevin Seitzer	MIL	$12	33	394	.292	.357	.414	6	58	52	5	4
Scott Servais	HOU	$1	27	335	.234	.272	.373	9	46	32	0	0
Danny Sheaffer	FA	$0	33	126	.236	.285	.325	2	15	13	1	1
Gary Sheffield	FLA	$28	26	463	.290	.372	.557	32	96	80	14	7
Craig Shipley	HOU	$3	32	214	.256	.283	.379	3	24	26	5	4
Terry Shumpert	BOS	$5	28	159	.248	.298	.415	6	20	23	10	3
Ruben Sierra	OAK	$22	29	577	.262	.307	.459	27	109	88	13	6
Dave Silvestri	NYY	$0	27	52	.250	.350	.423	2	9	7	1	1
Duane Singleton	MIL	$0	22	67	.252	.328	.343	0	7	10	3	2
Don Slaught	PIT	$8	36	406	.283	.357	.372	6	47	38	1	1
Dwight Smith	FA	$8	31	250	.285	.330	.460	9	34	39	4	4
Lonnie Smith	FA	$0	39	100	.246	.357	.370	2	10	20	3	1
Mark Smith	BAL	-$2	24	50	.230	.280	.360	1	5	5	0	0
Ozzie Smith	STL	$10	40	506	.266	.330	.338	2	41	68	14	6

NAME	TEAM	$VALUE	AGE	AB	AVG	OBA	SLG	HR	RBI	RUN	SB	CS
		HITTERS 1995 FORECAST STATS AND VALUES										
Jt Snow	CAL	$1	27	258	.233	.306	.364	9	35	30	1	1
Cory Snyder	LA	$1	32	221	.238	.299	.389	7	26	26	2	0
Luis Sojo	SEA	$3	29	237	.268	.296	.392	5	25	32	2	2
Paul Sorrento	CLE	$12	29	435	.270	.344	.441	18	74	61	1	1
Sammy Sosa	CHC	$35	26	567	.286	.328	.520	32	90	84	29	15
Tim Spehr	MON	$0	28	79	.237	.301	.418	2	10	12	3	1
Bill Spiers	NYM	$4	28	308	.256	.316	.328	2	30	40	8	4
Ed Sprague	TOR	$6	27	498	.248	.289	.382	13	59	47	1	0
Scott Stahoviak	MIN	$1	25	177	.248	.325	.412	5	21	18	2	2
Matt Stairs	BOS	$0	26	88	.272	.346	.432	3	12	11	1	1
Andy Stankiewicz	HOU	$0	30	79	.259	.342	.342	1	6	14	2	1
Mike Stanley	NYY	$15	31	391	.284	.370	.512	22	74	66	0	0
Dave Staton	FA	$1	26	283	.222	.316	.399	13	42	33	0	0
Terry Steinbach	OAK	$11	33	448	.272	.321	.415	12	62	57	3	2
Kelly Stinnett	NYM	$0	25	188	.245	.297	.351	2	18	20	2	1
Kevin Stocker	PHI	$4	25	328	.267	.353	.357	3	34	44	4	2
Doug Strange	FA	$0	30	156	.230	.285	.346	3	18	18	1	1
Darryl Strawberry	SF	$1	33	178	.229	.349	.410	8	30	24	1	3
Franklin Stubbs	DET	-$1	34	50	.220	.280	.340	1	6	6	1	0
Bj Surhoff	FA	$7	30	336	.265	.325	.405	6	48	44	5	4
Dale Sveum	FA	-$2	31	50	.210	.301	.299	1	4	6	0	0
Jeff Tackett	FA	-$1	29	86	.217	.295	.360	2	12	9	0	0
Tony Tarasco	ATL	$10	24	(316)	.273	.316	.424	11	39	42	8	3
Danny Tartabull	NYY	$12	32	468	.255	.366	.472	24	84	80	1	1
Eddie Taubensee	CIN	$7	26	372	.261	.316	.409	11	46	40	2	1
Jesus Tavarez	FLA	$0	24	92	.238	.288	.310	0	9	9	3	2
Mickey Tettleton	FA	$10	34	476	.244	.398	.458	24	79	74	1	2
Frank Thomas	CHW	$37	26	535	.329	.462	.637	41	125	121	3	3
Jim Thome	CLE	$17	24	459	.285	.377	.497	22	66	73	5	4
Milt Thompson	FA	$9	36	304	.271	.340	.359	5	37	41	11	3
Robby Thompson	SF	$6	32	301	.260	.328	.422	9	30	42	6	3
Ryan Thompson	NYM	$7	27	439	.234	.290	.428	20	60	55	3	3
Gary Thurman	SEA	$0	30	71	.242	.315	.338	0	8	12	4	2
Lee Tinsley	BOS	$3	26	196	.235	.323	.327	4	20	33	10	5
Andy Tomberlin	FA	-$1	28	50	.221	.316	.320	1	5	5	1	0
Alan Trammell	FA	$11	37	390	.278	.325	.431	11	44	57	7	3
Jeff Treadway	LA	$0	32	124	.270	.317	.347	1	11	17	1	1
Michael Tucker	KC	$2	23	175	.252	.330	.394	5	18	18	5	3
Brian Turang	FA	-$1	27	151	.216	.275	.305	1	10	16	4	2
Chris Turner	CAL	$2	26	252	.250	.297	.349	3	28	32	4	2
John Valentin	BOS	$13	28	515	.270	.352	.443	13	79	75	4	3
Jose Valentin	MIL	$6	25	301	.231	.321	.402	10	44	45	9	3
Dave Valle	FA	$0	34	100	.246	.345	.390	3	12	12	0	1
Ty Vanburkleo	FA	-$2	31	50	.227	.315	.340	1	1	2	1	0
John Vanderwal	PIT	$1	28	131	.246	.329	.397	4	18	17	3	1
Andy Vanslyke	FA	$11	34	468	.259	.342	.404	11	60	62	10	4

HITTERS 1995 FORECAST STATS AND VALUES

NAME	TEAM	$VALUE	AGE	AB	AVG	OBA	SLG	HR	RBI	RUN	SB	CS
Gary Varsho	FA	-$1	33	86	.247	.291	.395	1	7	13	1	1
Greg Vaughn	MIL	$17	29	492	.260	.352	.472	25	78	79	10	7
Mo Vaughn	BOS	$26	27	546	.297	.386	.533	31	108	87	4	4
Randy Velarde	FA	$7	32	290	.277	.331	.424	8	33	44	4	2
Robin Ventura	CHW	$19	27	551	.277	.379	.456	24	99	81	3	3
Quilvio Veras	FLA	$4	24	355	.225	.304	.300	0	26	39	19	0
Fernando Vina	NYM	$0	25	118	.247	.337	.297	0	6	18	4	1
Joe Vitiello	KC	-$1	24	71	.261	.353	.380	1	8	7	0	0
Jose Vizcaino	NYM	$5	27	493	.261	.316	.329	3	41	56	4	5
Omar Vizquel	CLE	$9	27	431	.268	.324	.318	1	35	53	13	8
Jack Voigt	BAL	$0	28	122	.241	.333	.377	3	17	14	1	0
Matt Walbeck	MIN	$1	25	412	.240	.276	.320	6	43	35	1	1
Larry Walker	FA	$30	28	513	.302	.381	.538	23	100	91	19	7
Tim Wallach	LA	$9	37	436	.255	.321	.431	18	71	60	0	2
Jerome Walton	CIN	$0	29	69	.277	.326	.377	1	7	10	2	3
Turner Ward	MIL	$5	30	384	.237	.331	.365	9	52	55	6	3
Lenny Webster	FA	$1	30	190	.260	.332	.384	4	25	19	1	0
Mitch Webster	FA	$0	35	100	.262	.325	.410	3	12	17	2	3
Eric Wedge	BOS	-$2	27	50	.212	.310	.360	2	5	6	0	0
John Wehner	PIT	-$2	27	50	.224	.304	.280	0	6	5	1	0
Walt Weiss	COL	$9	31	550	.263	.353	.309	1	45	70	12	7
Lou Whitaker	DET	$13	37	421	.287	.382	.466	14	61	80	3	1
Devon White	TOR	$20	32	556	.268	.314	.444	16	58	95	22	4
Rondell White	MON	$7	23	263	.272	.334	.456	6	37	39	7	4
Mark Whiten	STL	$17	28	471	.272	.345	.442	18	71	73	12	7
Darrell Whitmore	FLA	$0	26	114	.260	.301	.421	3	11	13	1	2
Rick Wilkins	CHC	$8	27	417	.249	.331	.436	15	56	58	4	3
Bernie Williams	NYY	$27	26	540	.285	.367	.476	20	81	97	24	11
Eddie Williams	SD	$13	30	390	.284	.341	.474	15	74	60	1	2
Gerald Williams	NYY	$2	28	134	.262	.289	.470	5	17	24	3	3
Matt Williams	SF	$25	29	583	.269	.314	.556	44	111	92	2	2
Dan Wilson	SEA	$0	26	399	.239	.271	.323	3	44	38	1	3
Nigel Wilson	FLA	$1	25	152	.250	.296	.395	4	18	18	2	1
Dave Winfield	FA	$7	43	385	.252	.321	.421	13	54	46	2	2
Tony Womack	PIT	-$1	25	50	.229	.329	.260	0	5	9	2	2
Rick Wrona	FA	-$1	31	52	.237	.283	.385	1	7	6	0	0
Eric Young	COL	$12	28	283	.270	.352	.399	6	31	45	20	9
Ernie Young	OAK	$1	25	114	.263	.303	.430	4	17	19	1	2
Gerald Young	FA	-$1	30	50	.264	.331	.400	0	3	7	2	
Kevin Young	PIT	$1	25	308	.244	.296	.367	5	36	33	1	2
Eddie Zambrano	CHC	$1	29	108	.257	.344	.435	4	16	15	2	1
Todd Zeile	STL	$15	29	526	.269	.350	.439	19	88	75	3	4
Eddie Zosky	FLA	$0	27	90	.238	.265	.367	2	11	12	1	0
Bob Zupcic	FA	-$1	28	50	.260	.308	.380	1	5	6	1	1

PITCHERS 1995 FORECAST STATS

NAME	TEAM	AGE	IP	W	L	SV	ERA	B/I	H	BB	K
Jim Abbott	FA	27	207	13	12	0	4.16	1.36	208	74	110
Kyle Abbott	PHI	27	97	5	5	0	4.87	1.44	105	35	67
Mark Acre	OAK	26	29	4	1	0	3.41	1.37	20	19	18
Rick Aguilera	MIN	33	72	2	5	29	3.30	1.21	69	18	57
Wilson Alvarez	CHW	25	201	15	9	0	3.54	1.35	182	90	167
Larry Andersen	FA	41	47	2	3	1	3.70	1.32	44	18	39
Brian Anderson	CAL	22	130	7	7	0	4.37	1.31	135	35	70
Kevin Appier	KC	27	203	15	8	0	3.45	1.30	181	83	187
Luis Aquino	FA	29	76	4	4	0	4.03	1.37	75	29	49
Jack Armstrong	FA	30	97	4	7	0	4.86	1.47	105	38	64
Rene Arocha	STL	29	78	3	6	5	3.62	1.36	80	26	52
Andy Ashby	SD	27	169	8	11	0	4.66	1.46	186	61	124
Paul Assenmacher	FA	34	44	3	3	4	3.94	1.39	43	18	43
Pedro Astacio	LA	25	185	9	10	0	3.89	1.26	175	58	130
Joe Ausanio	NYY	29	13	2	1	0	5.16	1.40	13	5	10
Steve Avery	ATL	24	189	14	7	0	3.86	1.30	183	62	149
Bobby Ayala	SEA	25	61	5	6	33	3.50	1.34	51	31	60
Cory Bailey	BOS	24	8	0	1	0	4.78	1.80	12	3	7
James Baldwin	CHW	23	80	5	4	0	4.86	1.44	81	34	65
Jeff Ballard	FA	31	43	2	1	1	5.07	1.47	50	13	22
Scott Bankhead	FA	31	54	4	3	1	4.10	1.34	51	21	39
Willie Banks	CHC	26	181	10	14	0	4.86	1.49	190	79	139
Brian Barnes	FA	28	55	1	3	1	4.56	1.67	58	35	33
Jose Bautista	FA	30	81	5	5	1	3.43	1.30	82	23	57
Rod Beck	SF	26	72	3	4	37	2.57	1.11	63	17	72
Steve Bedrosian	ATL	37	44	1	2	1	3.42	1.36	42	18	38
Tim Belcher	FA	33	225	11	17	0	4.62	1.40	230	86	145
Stan Belinda	FA	28	71	3	3	3	4.37	1.31	65	28	56
Alan Benes	STL	23	81	4	4	0	4.80	1.44	83	34	68
Andy Benes	SD	27	208	13	18	0	3.85	1.27	198	67	193
Armando Benitez	BAL	22	35	3	3	12	3.80	1.36	35	13	34
Jason Bere	CHW	23	172	14	10	0	3.92	1.41	157	86	167
Sean Bergman	DET	24	27	2	2	0	5.63	1.69	33	13	18
Mike Bielecki	FA	35	31	1	2	0	4.12	1.43	32	12	23
Bud Black	FA	38	66	4	4	0	4.41	1.34	66	22	33
Willie Blair	FA	29	121	3	7	2	4.62	1.45	133	42	83
Joe Boever	FA	34	86	4	3	3	3.75	1.45	86	39	51
Brian Bohanon	FA	26	73	3	3	0	5.11	1.40	78	24	45
Rod Bolton	CHW	26	65	3	3	0	4.44	1.50	66	31	40
Tom Bolton	BAL	32	58	3	4	0	4.80	1.64	67	28	35
Ricky Bones	MIL	25	213	13	12	0	4.14	1.32	221	61	80
Toby Borland	PHI	25	45	1	0	3	3.77	1.42	46	18	36
Chris Bosio	SEA	31	193	10	12	0	3.98	1.30	195	56	135
Shawn Boskie	FA	28	94	5	8	0	4.72	1.35	95	32	62
Ricky Bottalico	PHI	25	40	1	0	3	3.55	1.40	40	16	28
Kent Bottenfield	FA	26	119	4	4	1	4.83	1.42	128	41	56

PITCHERS 1995 FORECAST STATS

NAME	TEAM	AGE	IP	W	L	SV	ERA	B/I	H	BB	K
Denis Boucher	FA	27	86	5	4	0	4.36	1.31	88	25	44
Ryan Bowen	FLA	27	95	5	5	0	4.93	1.53	97	48	68
Jeff Brantley	CIN	31	72	5	7	17	3.60	1.33	60	36	68
Billy Brewer	KC	26	40	4	1	4	3.33	1.35	35	19	27
Brad Brink	SF	30	13	0	0	0	4.32	1.37	13	5	7
John Briscoe	OAK	27	50	4	2	1	4.65	1.55	35	42	45
Doug Brocail	HOU	28	105	4	4	0	4.47	1.40	115	32	64
Jeff Bronkey	MIL	29	28	1	1	1	4.22	1.49	29	14	16
Scott Brow	TOR	26	62	1	3	1	4.87	1.45	62	28	31
Kevin Brown	FA	30	223	14	13	0	3.73	1.33	235	61	156
Tom Browning	FA	34	77	5	3	0	4.54	1.38	87	19	38
Bary Buckels	FA	29	10	0	1	0	4.25	1.25	7	6	8
Jim Bullinger	CHC	29	72	4	3	3	4.23	1.40	70	31	50
Dave Burba	SF	28	98	6	6	0	4.38	1.42	86	53	85
John Burkett	TEX	30	218	12	10	0	3.80	1.28	228	51	136
Terry Burrows	TEX	26	22	1	0	0	5.32	1.60	22	13	15
Mike Butcher	CAL	29	40	2	1	9	4.70	1.54	37	25	32
Greg Cadaret	FA	33	63	3	2	2	4.36	1.57	62	37	46
Kevin Campbell	MIN	30	32	1	0	0	4.02	1.29	29	12	19
Tom Candiotti	LA	37	203	12	11	0	3.63	1.29	191	70	147
Cris Carpenter	FA	29	80	5	5	5	3.91	1.45	81	35	60
Hector Carrasco	CIN	25	52	7	5	15	3.37	1.25	45	20	44
Andy Carter	PHI	26	29	0	2	1	4.46	1.34	29	10	15
Larry Casian	CLE	29	59	2	5	1	5.44	1.66	80	18	26
Frank Castillo	CHC	25	110	5	4	0	4.22	1.29	112	30	73
Juan Castillo	NYM	24	10	0	0	0	4.40	1.62	11	5	5
Tony Castillo	TOR	32	65	3	2	1	3.56	1.40	63	28	47
Norm Charlton	FA	32	10	1	1	5	4.46	1.50	10	5	8
Mark Clark	CLE	26	154	11	5	0	3.95	1.32	159	44	84
Roger Clemens	BOS	32	190	15	11	0	3.59	1.30	169	78	185
Brad Clontz	ATL	23	23	1	1	2	3.91	1.26	19	10	18
David Cone	KC	32	201	18	9	0	3.56	1.28	180	77	183
Jim Converse	SEA	23	59	1	3	0	5.64	1.56	60	32	39
Dennis Cook	CLE	32	41	3	3	1	4.27	1.43	42	17	34
Steve Cooke	PIT	25	202	9	12	0	4.00	1.26	200	55	138
Rheal Cormier	STL	27	119	8	8	0	4.37	1.24	125	23	74
Brad Cornett	TOR	26	26	1	2	0	5.65	1.65	34	9	18
Danny Cox	FA	35	34	3	3	3	3.69	1.40	31	17	31
Chuck Crim	FA	33	67	5	5	2	4.51	1.38	70	23	45
John Cummings	SEA	25	57	1	3	0	5.56	1.58	61	29	30
Omar Daal	LA	24	38	1	1	0	4.29	1.48	36	20	25
Ron Darling	OAK	34	199	10	13	0	4.65	1.41	205	75	140
Danny Darwin	FA	39	149	11	8	0	4.64	1.34	160	39	97
Jeff Darwin	SEA	25	8	0	0	1	4.98	1.48	9	3	5
Mark Davis	FA	34	40	1	2	1	4.91	1.78	47	24	30
Storm Davis	FA	33	67	2	6	2	4.65	1.60	65	42	50

NAME	TEAM	AGE	IP	W	L	SV	ERA	B/I	H	BB	K
Tim Davis	SEA	24	47	2	2	3	3.78	1.45	49	19	32
Jose Dejesus	KC	30	22	2	1	0	4.72	1.50	23	11	10
Jose Deleon	FA	34	65	4	3	1	4.12	1.46	60	35	55
Rich Delucia	FA	30	30	1	2	0	4.75	1.52	31	15	27
Jim Deshaies	FA	34	174	9	15	0	5.22	1.56	207	65	96
John Dettmer	TEX	25	45	1	3	0	4.33	1.54	53	17	23
Mark Dewey	SF	30	54	2	1	3	3.52	1.45	59	20	32
Rob Dibble	FA	31	5	1	1	1	5.50	1.90	7	3	3
Jerry Dipoto	NYM	26	30	1	1	3	4.87	1.80	39	15	20
Steve Dixon	CLE	25	15	1	1	1	4.22	1.42	16	5	8
John Doherty	DET	27	178	9	10	0	4.52	1.36	198	44	60
John Dopson	FA	31	110	3	8	1	5.38	1.51	123	43	60
Doug Drabek	HOU	32	197	16	11	0	⟨3.46⟩	1.27	194	56	137
Brian Drahman	FA	28	13	0	0	0	5.28	1.60	15	6	7
Darren Dreifort	LA	22	44	1	4	5	4.19	1.43	43	20	29
Steve Dreyer	TEX	25	27	2	2	0	5.72	1.61	30	13	16
Mike Dyer	PIT	28	13	1	1	4	5.88	1.76	13	10	11
Dennis Eckersley	FA	40	67	5	5	27	3.70	1.23	65	17	63
Tom Edens	FA	33	68	5	3	1	3.90	1.40	70	25	45
Mark Eichhorn	BAL	34	71	5	5	3	3.30	1.30	71	21	45
Joey Eischen	MON	25	15	1	1	1	5.34	1.50	15	8	12
Cal Eldred	MIL	27	203	14	14	0	4.56	1.38	192	88	135
Donnie Elliott	SD	26	28	0	1	0	3.87	1.58	26	18	20
Scott Erickson	MIN	27	215	14	16	0	4.62	1.40	228	74	147
Bryan Eversgerd	STL	26	57	2	2	0	4.52	1.40	63	17	39
Hector Fajardo	TEX	24	85	4	6	0	5.62	1.33	88	25	70
Steve Farr	FA	38	43	3	1	14	4.72	1.77	51	25	32
Jeff Fassero	MON	32	162	12	7	0	3.33	1.27	152	54	140
Alex Fernandez	CHW	25	218	16	10	0	3.77	1.27	211	65	183
Sid Fernandez	BAL	32	150	10	8	0	4.36	1.31	134	63	136
Mike Fetters	MIL	30	71	3	5	18	3.33	1.42	66	35	50
Chuck Finley	CAL	32	218	14	14	0	3.97	1.38	216	85	174
Gar Finnvold	BOS	26	97	4	4	0	4.44	1.37	96	37	86
Dave Fleming	SEA	25	194	11	12	0	4.49	1.42	201	75	114
Bryce Florie	SD	24	8	0	0	0	3.90	1.40	8	3	6
Tim Fortugno	CIN	32	25	1	0	0	4.20	1.53	27	12	18
Tony Fossas	FA	37	38	2	1	1	4.49	1.39	37	16	32
Kevin Foster	CHC	26	136	9	8	0	3.79	1.39	140	49	116
John Franco	FA	34	49	2	5	33	3.26	1.41	50	19	40
Marvin Freeman	COL	31	162	10	8	1	3.64	1.31	165	48	131
Steve Frey	SF	31	53	2	1	2	3.67	1.36	48	24	34
Todd Frohwirth	PIT	32	44	1	5	1	4.69	1.39	42	19	27
Mike Gardiner	FA	29	62	2	3	9	4.68	1.45	62	28	39
Mark Gardner	FLA	33	102	5	6	0	4.74	1.32	101	34	64
Paul Gibson	FA	35	37	1	1	1	4.77	1.51	38	18	30
Tom Glavine	ATL	29	224	17	10	0	⟨3.47⟩↓	1.34	217	84	169

PITCHERS 1995 FORECAST STATS

NAME	TEAM	AGE	IP	W	L	SV	ERA	B/I	H	BB	K
Greg Gohr	DET	27	30	1	2	0	4.63	1.63	31	18	27
Pat Gomez	SF	27	38	0	1	0	4.12	1.39	30	22	20
Dwight Gooden	FA	30	60	4	3	0	4.01	1.25	56	19	46
Tom Gordon	KC	27	191	13	9	0	4.37	1.39	175	90	171
Goose Gossage	FA	43	21	1	1	1	4.29	1.40	21	9	17
Jim Gott	FA	35	63	6	5	10	4.11	1.49	67	26	52
Mauro Gozzo	FA	29	60	2	5	1	3.95	1.35	61	20	30
Joe Grahe	COL	27	50	3	5	2	4.64	1.41	55	15	30
Jeff Granger	KC	23	45	2	1	0	3.90	1.50	48	19	30
Tommy Greene	PHI	27	114	7	5	0	3.80	1.32	106	45	94
Jason Grimsley	CLE	27	69	4	3	0	4.31	1.42	71	27	49
Buddy Groom	DET	29	30	1	2	1	4.65	1.52	33	13	25
Kevin Gross	TEX	33	202	11	11	1	4.14	1.45	229	64	159
Eddie Guardado	MIN	24	90	4	4	0	5.52	1.54	109	30	43
Mark Gubicza	FA	32	155	9	11	1	4.25	1.40	177	40	116
Bill Gullickson	FA	36	115	4	8	0	5.56	1.49	145	27	57
Eric Gunderson	NYM	29	8	0	0	0	4.15	1.40	8	3	3
Mark Guthrie	MIN	29	83	4	2	3	4.39	1.35	81	31	65
Jose Guzman	CHC	31	96	7	6	0	5.00	1.44	98	41	76
Juan Guzman	TOR	28	213	15	10	0	4.32	1.40	200	99	190
John Habyan	STL	31	55	2	1	2	3.43	1.38	57	19	45
Darren Hall	TOR	31	32	2	2	15	4.20	1.50	34	14	28
Joey Hamilton	SD	24	170	10	9	0	3.50	1.28	169	48	102
Atlee Hammaker	CHW	37	15	1	1	1	4.44	1.44	15	7	12
Chris Hammond	FLA	29	146	7	8	0	3.92	1.37	151	49	81
Mike Hampton	HOU	22	138	7	5	0	4.14	1.38	150	40	74
Chris Haney	KC	26	69	5	5	0	5.03	1.56	80	28	40
Erik Hanson	FA	29	188	9	8	0	3.74	1.24	189	44	151
Mike Harkey	FA	28	175	7	8	0	4.83	1.37	188	51	89
Pete Harnisch	FA	28	167	14	8	0	3.93	1.25	148	61	136
Gene Harris	FA	30	56	2	3	6	4.08	1.39	51	27	39
Grega Harris	FA	39	87	5	7	5	5.68	1.57	91	46	79
Gregw Harris	FA	31	202	9	12	1	4.96	1.34	205	65	129
Bryan Harvey	FLA	31	38	1	2	15	2.91	1.17	33	11	37
Heath Haynes	OAK	26	3	0	0	0	4.10	1.62	3	3	2
Rick Helling	TEX	24	80	4	3	0	4.67	1.36	83	26	61
Rod Henderson	MON	24	6	0	1	0	5.15	1.50	7	2	3
Tom Henke	STL	37	53	4	7	28	3.21	1.19	44	19	53
Mike Henneman	DET	33	63	2	4	17	3.57	1.50	70	25	45
Butch Henry	MON	26	159	10	8	1	3.57	1.30	150	57	96
Doug Henry	NYM	31	49	2	4	0	4.63	1.56	51	26	35
Pat Hentgen	TOR	26	189	15	10	0	3.55	1.22	180	51	144
Gil Heredia	MON	29	85	6	3	1	3.60	1.33	96	17	66
Jeremy Hernandez	FLA	28	39	3	5	7	3.78	1.49	40	18	27
Roberto Hernandez	CHW	29	64	5	5	31	3.83	1.24	57	22	63
Xavier Hernandez	FA	30	68	4	5	14	3.80	1.29	61	27	59

NAME	TEAM	AGE	IP	W	L	SV	ERA	B/I	H	BB	K
PITCHERS 1995 FORECAST STATS											
Orel Hershiser	FA	36	197	10	11	0	3.56	1.28	192	61	133
Joe Hesketh	FA	36	127	8	6	0	4.37	1.47	133	53	90
Greg Hibbard	SEA	30	172	7	8	0	4.37	1.31	179	47	82
Bryan Hickerson	CHC	31	123	5	8	1	4.28	1.34	126	39	91
Ted Higuera	FA	36	119	5	5	0	5.14	1.46	123	51	86
Ken Hill	MON	29	191	18	7	0	3.36	1.28	179	66	126
Milt Hill	FA	29	60	1	0	1	4.96	1.50	64	26	38
Sterling Hitchcock	NYY	23	65	5	1	1	4.44	1.54	68	32	52
Trevor Hoffman	SD	27	62	4	5	30	3.13	1.29	55	25	68
Darren Holmes	COL	28	53	2	4	11	4.28	1.40	49	25	44
Rick Honeycutt	FA	40	37	1	3	1	5.37	1.57	44	15	25
John Hope	PIT	24	79	2	1	0	4.53	1.42	95	17	35
Vince Horsman	FA	28	41	1	1	0	4.44	1.44	40	19	28
Charlie Hough	FA	47	174	8	14	0	4.72	1.42	176	72	100
Christian Howard	BOS	29	31	1	0	1	4.35	1.39	32	11	18
Steve Howe	NYY	37	51	3	2	21	3.14	1.26	52	12	27
Jay Howell	FA	39	58	5	2	2	4.19	1.30	55	20	33
John Hudek	HOU	28	64	1	2	12	3.88	1.39	68	21	54
Bruce Hurst	FA	37	58	3	2	0	5.91	1.60	71	21	36
Mark Hutton	NYY	25	31	2	2	0	4.62	1.38	33	10	19
Mike Ignasiak	MIL	29	55	2	1	1	4.12	1.32	52	21	41
Danny Jackson	STL	33	211	13	9	0	3.63	1.35	215	70	146
Mike Jackson	FA	30	52	3	4	4	3.12	1.25	45	20	61
Jason Jacome	NYM	24	110	9	8	0	3.85	1.29	113	29	63
Kevin Jarvis	CIN	25	15	1	1	0	4.50	1.53	19	4	8
Domingo Jean	HOU	26	31	2	2	0	5.14	1.48	33	13	25
Miguel Jimenez	OAK	25	37	1	3	0	4.96	1.80	40	26	22
Dane Johnson	CHW	32	10	2	1	0	5.20	1.80	13	5	6
Randy Johnson	SEA	31	204	17	9	0	3.74	1.26	172	86	240
Joel Johnston	BOS	28	19	1	1	1	4.88	1.39	21	6	13
John Johnstone	FLA	26	21	1	2	0	5.92	1.80	24	14	16
Bobby Jones	NYM	25	199	12	10	0	3.77	1.35	198	71	106
Doug Jones	FA	37	76	3	5	28	2.92	1.23	80	14	62
Todd Jones	HOU	26	61	4	2	19	3.69	1.41	57	29	57
Jeff Juden	PHI	24	25	1	3	0	4.92	1.49	26	11	21
Scott Kamieniecki	NYY	30	147	8	8	0	4.02	1.46	151	64	88
Steve Karsay	OAK	23	109	5	2	0	4.18	1.38	113	37	71
Jimmy Key	NYY	33	215	18	8	0	3.19	1.24	209	58	155
Mark Kiefer	MIL	26	12	1	0	0	5.41	1.80	14	8	9
Daryl Kile	HOU	26	200	13	12	0	4.01	1.44	190	98	158
Kevin King	SEA	26	47	1	2	1	4.98	1.57	49	25	29
Scott Klingenbeck	BAL	24	6	1	0	0	3.86	1.43	5	3	4
Kurt Knudsen	DET	28	23	2	1	1	5.44	1.80	25	16	15
Bill Krueger	FA	36	94	5	6	0	5.24	1.47	103	34	67
Mark Langston	CAL	34	180	14	11	0	3.88	1.31	166	69	154
Craig Lefferts	FA	37	74	3	5	1	4.90	1.58	94	23	51

PITCHERS 1995 FORECAST STATS

NAME	TEAM	AGE	IP	W	L	SV	ERA	B/I	H	BB	K
Phil Leftwich	CAL	25	162	7	10	0	4.46	1.33	162	54	105
Dave Leiper	OAK	32	16	0	0	1	3.38	1.32	14	7	12
Al Leiter	TOR	29	80	5	8	1	4.34	1.50	81	39	60
Mark Leiter	FA	31	77	4	8	1	4.53	1.38	78	28	66
Curt Leskanic	COL	26	36	1	2	0	5.52	1.59	40	17	23
Richie Lewis	FLA	29	62	1	5	0	4.40	1.58	61	37	51
Scott Lewis	FA	29	48	1	1	1	4.18	1.31	50	13	19
Jon Lieber	PIT	24	150	8	6	0	3.85	1.26	153	36	99
Derek Lilliquist	FA	29	46	3	4	5	3.51	1.23	44	13	30
Jose Lima	DET	22	51	3	1	0	4.45	1.29	44	22	34
Doug Linton	FA	30	56	4	4	0	5.22	1.80	79	21	33
Graeme Lloyd	MIL	27	68	2	4	4	3.66	1.28	69	18	44
Brian Looney	BOS	25	25	1	0	0	4.98	1.50	27	11	19
Albie Lopez	CLE	23	136	8	7	0	4.44	1.25	135	35	93
Andrew Lorraine	CAL	22	88	6	5	0	4.64	1.50	91	41	55
Greg Maddux	ATL	28	218	20	9	0	2.47	1.14	197	51	167
Mike Maddux	FA	33	69	3	3	4	4.17	1.25	64	22	51
Mike Magnante	KC	29	101	3	4	0	4.19	1.45	112	34	43
Joe Magrane	CAL	30	90	3	9	0	5.59	1.54	94	45	54
Pat Mahomes	MIN	24	125	8	6	0	4.85	1.51	128	61	74
Josias Manzanillo	NYM	27	62	2	2	2	3.90	1.29	60	20	49
Ravelo Manzanillo	PIT	31	37	3	2	1	4.72	1.70	38	25	33
Dennis Martinez	CLE	39	204	14	9	0	3.81	1.25	194	62	124
Jose Martinez	SD	42	10	0	2	0	4.73	1.72	15	2	6
Pedroa Martinez	HOU	26	72	3	2	4	3.61	1.40	60	41	57
Pedroj Martinez	MON	23	158	13	6	1	3.82	1.32	135	73	147
Ramon Martinez	LA	27	201	13	11	0	3.90	1.38	195	82	146
Roger Mason	FA	36	78	3	7	3	4.17	1.36	75	31	49
Terry Mathews	FLA	30	36	2	1	0	3.35	1.26	38	8	18
Tim Mauser	SD	28	57	2	4	3	3.71	1.38	56	23	44
Kirk McCaskill	FA	33	77	3	6	3	4.04	1.44	80	31	52
Ben McDonald	BAL	27	210	18	12	0	3.94	1.30	197	77	156
Jack McDowell	NYY	29	242	16	12	0	3.47	1.24	239	61	172
Roger McDowell	FA	34	71	3	4	1	4.40	1.53	84	25	45
Chuck McElroy	CIN	27	65	2	3	5	3.15	1.39	63	27	55
Kevin McGehee	FA	26	46	2	2	0	5.12	1.46	48	19	27
Greg McMichael	ATL	28	75	4	6	19	3.33	1.27	68	27	67
Rusty Meacham	KC	27	43	2	3	3	3.79	1.26	44	10	30
Jose Melendez	BOS	29	39	2	2	1	3.76	1.26	36	13	29
Jose Mercedes	MIL	24	26	2	2	0	3.82	1.46	26	12	10
Kent Mercker	ATL	27	144	12	8	1	3.43	1.28	115	70	138
Brett Merriman	MIN	28	22	0	1	0	5.52	1.80	26	14	13
Jose Mesa	COL	28	114	4	4	1	5.26	1.49	128	42	80
Danny Miceli	PIT	24	56	2	1	4	4.92	1.41	57	22	40
Bob Milacki	KC	30	63	2	4	0	5.87	1.60	77	24	21
Kurt Miller	FLA	22	17	1	2	0	5.10	1.65	22	6	9

PITCHERS 1995 FORECAST STATS

NAME	TEAM	AGE	IP	W	L	SV	ERA	B/I	H	BB	K
Alan Mills	BAL	28	63	4	4	3	4.23	1.42	56	33	50
Nate Minchey	FA	25	59	2	3	0	4.27	1.38	63	18	32
Blas Minor	NYM	29	45	2	2	1	5.52	1.49	51	15	40
Angel Miranda	MIL	25	75	3	6	0	4.32	1.35	63	38	47
Mike Mohler	OAK	26	21	0	2	0	5.80	1.59	19	15	16
Rich Monteleone	FA	32	55	4	4	0	3.83	1.31	54	18	35
Jeff Montgomery	KC	33	72	3	5	33	3.26	1.23	65	24	63
Marcus Moore	COL	24	50	5	4	0	4.92	1.67	51	33	44
Mike Moore	DET	35	199	13	12	0	5.23	1.53	202	102	98
Mike Morgan	CHC	35	177	8	14	0	4.50	1.29	170	59	109
Jack Morris	CIN	39	189	13	9	0	5.55	1.59	216	84	128
Jamie Moyer	BAL	32	160	7	9	0	4.35	1.29	160	46	91
Terry Mulholland	FA	32	100	5	10	0	4.77	1.40	102	38	59
Bobby Munoz	PHI	27	94	6	5	1	3.43	1.38	91	39	61
Mike Munoz	COL	29	50	3	3	1	4.19	1.50	42	32	39
Rob Murphy	FA	34	52	4	5	2	4.60	1.35	51	19	36
Mike Mussina	BAL	26	210	18	7	0	3.50	1.24	207	53	144
Jeff Mutis	FA	28	55	2	2	0	4.98	1.50	64	19	33
Randy Myers	CHC	32	63	2	6	35	3.65	1.35	60	25	61
Chris Nabholz	FA	28	116	7	8	0	4.92	1.55	115	65	81
Charles Nagy	CLE	27	208	15	9	0	3.59	1.32	218	57	133
Jaime Navarro	MIL	28	140	7	11	0	4.90	1.61	173	52	89
Denny Neagle	PIT	26	166	9	11	1	4.74	1.37	161	66	135
Jeff Nelson	SEA	28	59	2	2	5	3.70	1.45	51	34	57
Robb Nen	FLA	25	67	5	5	19	3.95	1.38	60	32	64
Dave Nied	COL	26	184	11	9	0	4.67	1.43	190	73	111
Rafael Novoa	FA	27	81	4	4	0	4.31	1.40	81	32	44
Edwin Nunez	FA	31	41	1	2	1	5.20	1.80	55	19	35
Chad Ogea	CLE	24	81	5	5	0	4.76	1.48	85	35	55
Omar Olivares	STL	27	91	3	5	1	4.82	1.42	91	38	48
Darren Oliver	TEX	24	62	4	3	5	3.63	1.42	60	28	50
Gregg Olson	FA	28	31	2	3	5	4.50	1.42	30	14	24
Steve Ontiveros	FA	34	145	9	7	0	3.65	1.30	138	51	99
Mike Oquist	BAL	26	86	4	2	0	4.95	1.50	93	36	54
Jesse Orosco	FA	37	56	3	2	3	4.34	1.43	51	29	50
Donovan Osborne	STL	25	120	8	6	0	3.96	1.32	118	40	70
Al Osuna	LA	29	21	3	1	1	4.54	1.53	21	11	16
Dave Otto	CHC	30	47	1	3	0	4.57	1.52	51	20	25
Lance Painter	COL	27	71	3	5	0	5.09	1.40	78	21	33
Vicente Palacios	STL	31	99	3	5	1	4.44	1.25	87	36	80
Don Pall	FA	33	56	2	3	0	3.44	1.41	66	13	31
Chanho Park	LA	21	6	0	0	0	4.88	1.50	7	2	5
Bob Patterson	FA	35	52	3	4	2	4.30	1.36	53	18	45
Ken Patterson	CAL	30	23	1	1	0	4.33	1.49	20	13	14
Roger Pavlik	TEX	27	105	4	6	0	4.85	1.51	120	39	75
Brad Pennington	BAL	25	15	1	1	1	4.88	1.58	18	6	15

PITCHERS 1995 FORECAST STATS

NAME	TEAM	AGE	IP	W	L	SV	ERA	B/I	H	BB	K
Troy Percival	CAL	25	30	1	2	2	4.93	1.48	29	15	25
Melido Perez	NYY	29	163	11	9	0	4.45	1.40	160	68	150
Mike Perez	STL	30	70	3	3	4	4.04	1.45	77	25	45
Yorkis Perez	FLA	27	42	2	2	1	4.23	1.30	38	17	40
Steve Phoenix	OAK	27	36	1	0	2	3.90	1.30	35	12	25
Hipolito Pichardo	KC	25	134	7	5	1	4.24	1.45	150	44	70
Erik Plantenberg	SD	26	9	0	0	0	3.94	1.80	7	9	5
Dan Plesac	PIT	33	71	3	3	1	4.46	1.38	78	20	63
Eric Plunk	CLE	31	88	6	5	7	3.24	1.40	76	48	86
Jim Poole	FA	28	33	1	0	1	4.50	1.50	36	13	24
Mark Portugal	SF	32	188	14	8	0	3.48	1.30	179	65	119
Ross Powell	HOU	27	11	0	1	0	3.95	1.36	9	6	9
Tim Pugh	CIN	28	94	6	7	0	4.92	1.52	120	23	52
Carlos Pulido	MIN	23	71	2	6	0	5.28	1.51	73	34	27
Paul Quantrill	PHI	26	91	4	6	1	4.31	1.45	105	27	46
Pat Rapp	FLA	27	141	7	9	0	3.91	1.50	142	70	80
Rick Reed	FA	30	26	1	1	0	5.07	1.40	28	9	17
Steve Reed	COL	29	81	5	3	3	4.08	1.44	85	31	59
Mike Remlinger	NYM	29	76	3	4	0	4.86	1.54	80	37	44
Carlos Reyes	OAK	26	66	0	2	1	4.15	1.47	60	37	48
Shane Reynolds	HOU	27	188	14	10	0	3.25	1.27	199	40	165
Armando Reynoso	COL	28	139	8	7	0	4.36	1.44	148	52	77
Arthur Rhodes	BAL	25	105	6	7	0	5.52	1.54	104	57	82
Jose Rijo	CIN	29	229	15	9	0	2.84	1.23	219	63	216
Bill Risley	SEA	27	50	5	5	0	.47	1.22	40	21	49
Kevin Ritz	COL	29	62	4	5	0	5.62	1.67	74	29	45
Ben Rivera	FA	26	93	7	7	0	5.41	1.56	96	48	61
Rich Robertson	FA	26	16	0	0	0	4.84	1.80	21	7	8
Rich Rodriguez	STL	32	79	4	6	1	3.78	1.41	78	33	53
Kenny Rogers	TEX	30	203	13	10	0	4.36	1.33	205	65	143
Kevin Rogers	SF	26	56	2	1	1	3.53	1.33	52	23	42
Mel Rojas	MON	28	90	4	4	14	3.30	1.20	80	28	77
John Roper	CIN	23	104	6	3	0	4.77	1.37	106	37	61
Kirk Rueter	MON	24	159	10	9	0	4.56	1.34	176	37	90
Scott Ruffcorn	CHW	25	54	3	2	1	4.58	1.35	63	10	21
Bruce Ruffin	COL	31	80	5	6	15	4.13	1.52	83	39	75
Johnny Ruffin	CIN	23	80	5	2	4	3.40	1.25	69	31	52
Jeff Russell	FA	33	45	2	6	6	4.06	1.34	44	17	34
Ken Ryan	BOS	26	58	3	3	31	3.10	1.30	53	22	44
Bret Saberhagen	NYM	30	210	15	6	0	3.03	1.13	207	30	164
Roger Salkeld	SEA	24	144	6	4	0	4.75	1.50	152	64	114
Bill Sampen	FA	32	27	1	2	0	5.35	1.67	28	17	14
Scott Sanders	SD	26	142	7	8	1	4.69	1.38	134	62	125
Scott Sanderson	FA	38	121	9	9	0	4.75	1.33	139	22	60
Bob Scanlan	MIL	28	118	6	7	2	4.10	1.40	130	35	72
Rich Scheid	FLA	30	27	1	2	0	3.94	1.33	29	7	14

PITCHERS 1995 FORECAST STATS

NAME	TEAM	AGE	IP	W	L	SV	ERA	B/I	H	BB	K
Curt Schilling	PHI	28	162	8	10	0	3.98	1.27	160	46	119
Pete Schourek	CIN	25	150	13	9	0	4.39	1.36	157	47	133
Erik Schullstrom	MIN	26	11	0	0	1	3.87	1.38	11	4	9
Jeff Schwarz	CAL	30	30	1	1	0	4.60	1.71	22	30	27
Tim Scott	MON	28	60	5	3	1	3.65	1.35	58	23	50
Rudy Seanez	LA	26	21	1	1	0	3.19	1.47	23	8	15
Aaron Sele	BOS	24	187	12	10	0	3.62	1.38	179	79	150
Frank Seminara	FA	27	38	2	3	0	4.77	1.58	43	18	19
Scott Service	FA	27	21	1	2	1	5.55	1.42	21	8	18
Jeff Shaw	MON	28	77	4	4	1	4.01	1.26	75	22	54
Paul Shuey	CLE	24	39	2	1	16	3.65	1.42	35	20	37
Heath Slocumb	PHI	28	76	5	4	0	3.40	1.42	77	30	60
Aaron Small	TOR	23	10	0	0	0	4.90	1.70	12	5	6
John Smiley	CIN	30	208	15	12	0	3.84	1.25	206	54	131
Dan Smith	TEX	25	14	1	2	0	4.37	1.80	17	8	8
Lee Smith	CAL	37	57	2	6	38	3.45	1.17	51	16	56
Pete Smith	FA	29	178	7	11	0	4.88	1.40	191	59	99
Willie Smith	CLE	27	6	1	1	0	4.48	1.42	6	2	5
Zane Smith	FA	34	183	11	10	0	3.47	1.26	192	39	71
Roger Smithberg	FA	29	8	0	1	1	5.88	1.51	9	3	4
John Smoltz	ATL	27	211	12	13	0	3.81	1.24	184	78	179
Paul Spoljaric	TOR	24	70	4	4	0	5.10	1.50	74	31	61
Jerry Spradlin	CIN	27	21	1	0	1	5.57	1.29	23	4	11
Russ Springer	CAL	26	55	2	4	4	5.04	1.38	56	20	32
Randy St.clair	FA	30	20	2	1	1	4.85	1.50	21	9	15
Mike Stanton	FA	27	63	4	3	10	3.89	1.46	58	34	52
Dave Stevens	MIN	25	71	4	2	5	3.91	1.42	70	31	39
Dave Stewart	FA	38	80	11	10	0	5.24	1.50	83	37	60
Phil Stidham	DET	26	16	0	0	0	5.06	1.48	18	6	12
Todd Stottlemyre	FA	29	175	10	11	1	4.36	1.42	183	66	122
Rick Sutcliffe	FA	38	130	9	8	0	5.85	1.71	167	56	57
Russ Swan	CLE	31	23	1	3	1	4.94	1.80	29	13	9
Bill Swift	FA	33	165	13	8	0	3.14	1.20	153	45	110
Greg Swindell	HOU	30	188	10	13	0	4.01	1.35	218	36	115
Jeff Tabaka	SD	31	34	2	1	1	5.27	1.44	27	23	27
Kevin Tapani	MIN	31	226	14	12	0	4.34	1.34	244	59	151
Julian Tavarez	CLE	21	13	1	1	0	5.10	1.60	15	5	9
Bill Taylor	OAK	32	40	1	2	1	4.30	1.30	38	14	30
Brien Taylor	NYY	22	61	4	3	0	3.96	1.48	63	27	61
Kerry Taylor	SD	24	24	0	2	0	5.20	1.80	29	14	16
Dave Telgheder	FA	28	52	3	1	0	4.92	1.50	56	22	25
Bob Tewksbury	FA	34	201	14	12	0	4.54	1.33	237	30	101
Mark Thompson	COL	23	8	1	1	0	5.20	1.52	9	3	4
Mike Timlin	TOR	29	68	2	1	3	4.95	1.55	72	33	62
Randy Tomlin	FA	28	68	3	6	0	4.16	1.35	75	17	37
Salomon Torres	SF	23	152	7	8	0	4.96	1.51	164	65	90

NAME	TEAM	AGE	IP	W	L	SV	ERA	B/I	H	BB	K
Steve Trachsel	CHC	24	149	9	7	0	3.27	1.27	135	54	110
Ricky Trlicek	BOS	25	44	1	1	1	4.98	1.40	43	19	23
Mike Trombley	MIN	27	86	4	2	1	4.98	1.41	91	30	61
Matt Turner	CLE	28	31	2	2	1	3.64	1.32	27	14	22
Tom Urbani	STL	27	82	3	7	0	4.95	1.48	98	23	50
Ismael Valdes	LA	21	24	2	1	0	3.18	1.40	23	10	22
Sergio Valdez	FA	29	17	0	1	0	5.44	1.80	25	5	7
Fernando Valenzuela	FA	34	91	3	5	0	4.14	1.30	89	30	39
Julio Valera	CAL	26	30	2	2	0	4.94	1.49	31	14	20
Tim Vanegmond	BOS	25	32	2	2	0	5.43	1.54	32	18	18
Bill Vanlandingham	SF	24	144	11	8	0	3.75	1.40	140	62	96
Todd Vanpoppel	OAK	23	111	7	7	0	5.50	1.60	96	82	100
Dave Veres	HOU	28	34	2	2	1	3.91	1.32	32	13	23
Frank Viola	FA	34	123	7	7	0	3.58	1.42	122	53	60
Terrell Wade	ATL	22	52	5	2	0	3.86	1.46	52	24	44
Paul Wagner	PIT	27	183	10	9	1	4.46	1.48	201	70	140
Duane Ward	TOR	30	30	2	2	13	3.30	1.26	25	13	26
Allen Watson	STL	24	178	10	9	0	4.60	1.41	185	66	120
Gary Wayne	FA	32	36	2	4	1	4.61	1.47	39	14	26
Dave Weathers	FLA	25	191	10	11	0	4.98	1.51	215	73	126
Bill Wegman	MIL	32	176	10	9	0	4.29	1.38	202	41	90
Bob Welch	FA	38	145	7	9	0	5.32	1.64	169	69	77
Bob Wells	SEA	28	8	2	1	0	4.00	1.33	7	3	5
David Wells	DET	31	164	9	10	0	4.18	1.24	166	37	111
Turk Wendell	CHC	27	19	0	1	0	5.12	1.48	22	6	12
Bill Wertz	CLE	28	22	1	1	0	4.77	1.59	24	10	17
David West	PHI	30	134	9	10	0	3.49	1.36	100	82	110
John Wetteland	MON	28	70	5	6	38	3.10	1.13	53	26	81
Gabe White	MON	23	20	1	1	1	4.80	1.48	20	9	14
Rick White	PIT	26	110	8	8	1	3.74	1.26	109	30	81
Wally Whitehurst	FA	30	150	8	9	0	4.42	1.55	178	54	95
Matt Whiteside	TEX	27	77	2	2	5	4.70	1.49	83	32	50
Bob Wickman	NYY	26	81	6	5	4	4.01	1.35	74	35	60
Brian Williams	SD	26	125	8	8	0	4.98	1.52	130	60	78
Mike Williams	PHI	26	57	2	5	0	5.10	1.54	65	23	33
Mitch Williams	HOU	30	40	1	4	11	5.09	1.86	38	36	35
Woody Williams	TOR	28	61	2	3	0	3.77	1.37	49	34	54
Mark Williamson	FA	35	77	3	2	1	4.22	1.41	88	21	38
Carl Willis	MIN	34	86	3	4	4	4.93	1.53	113	18	60
Trevor Wilson	FA	28	66	5	3	1	3.81	1.36	64	26	38
Bobby Witt	FA	30	200	11	14	0	4.59	1.56	214	98	146
Mark Wohlers	ATL	25	68	6	3	11	4.21	1.43	60	37	70
Brad Woodall	ATL	25	52	5	2	0	4.70	1.38	51	21	40
Tim Worrell	SD	27	101	4	3	0	4.56	1.46	104	43	65
Todd Worrell	LA	35	60	5	5	18	4.41	1.23	56	18	59
Anthony Young	CHC	29	139	6	8	0	3.91	1.34	131	55	80

NAME	TEAM	VALUE	NAME	TEAM	VALUE
AMERICAN LEAGUE:					
Jim Abbott	FA	$8	Larry Casian	CLE	-$8
Mark Acre	OAK	$0	Tony Castillo	TOR	$2
Rick Aguilera	MIN	$32	Norm Charlton	FA	$2
Wilson Alvarez	CHW	$16	Mark Clark	CLE	$9
Larry Andersen	FA	$1	Roger Clemens	BOS	$17
Brian Anderson	CAL	$4	David Cone	KC	$21
Kevin Appier	KC	$19	Jim Converse	SEA	-$8
Luis Aquino	FA	$1	Dennis Cook	CLE	$0
Jack Armstrong	FA	-$4	Brad Cornett	TOR	-$5
Paul Assenmacher	FA	$3	Danny Cox	FA	$2
Joe Ausanio	NYY	-$2	Chuck Crim	FA	$1
Bobby Ayala	SEA	$33	John Cummings	SEA	-$8
Cory Bailey	BOS	-$3	Ron Darling	OAK	$0
James Baldwin	CHW	-$2	Danny Darwin	FA	$3
Jeff Ballard	FA	-$3	Jeff Darwin	SEA	-$2
Scott Bankhead	FA	$1	Mark Davis	FA	-$6
Brian Barnes	FA	-$5	Storm Davis	FA	-$4
Jose Bautista	FA	$6	Tim Davis	SEA	$1
Tim Belcher	FA	$0	Jose Dejesus	KC	-$2
Stan Belinda	FA	$3	Jose Deleon	FA	$0
Armando Benitez	BAL	$11	Rich Delucia	FA	-$3
Jason Bere	CHW	$7	Jim Deshaies	FA	-$13
Sean Bergman	DET	-$5	John Dettmer	TEX	-$3
Mike Bielecki	FA	-$2	Rob Dibble	FA	-$2
Bud Black	FA	$0	Steve Dixon	CLE	-$1
Willie Blair	FA	-$2	John Doherty	DET	$2
Joe Boever	FA	$3	John Dopson	FA	-$8
Brian Bohanon	FA	-$3	Brian Drahman	FA	-$4
Rod Bolton	CHW	-$3	Steve Dreyer	TEX	-$5
Tom Bolton	BAL	-$6	Dennis Eckersley	FA	$29
Ricky Bones	MIL	$11	Tom Edens	FA	$2
Chris Bosio	SEA	$11	Mark Eichhorn	BAL	$8
Shawn Boskie	FA	$0	Cal Eldred	MIL	$3
Kent Bottenfield	FA	-$2	Scott Erickson	MIN	$1
Denis Boucher	FA	$1	Hector Fajardo	TEX	-$4
Billy Brewer	KC	$5	Steve Farr	FA	$6
John Briscoe	OAK	-$2	Alex Fernandez	CHW	$19
Jeff Bronkey	MIL	-$1	Sid Fernandez	BAL	$6
Scott Brow	TOR	-$3	Mike Fetters	MIL	$18
Kevin Brown	FA	$16	Chuck Finley	CAL	$9
Tom Browning	FA	$0	Gar Finnvold	BOS	$0
Gary Buckels	FA	-$2	Dave Fleming	SEA	$0
John Burkett	TEX	$17	Tony Fossas	FA	-$1
Terry Burrows	TEX	-$4	John Franco	FA	$31
Mike Butcher	CAL	$4	Mike Gardiner	FA	$5
Greg Cadaret	FA	-$2	Paul Gibson	FA	-$3
Kevin Campbell	MIN	$0	Greg Gohr	DET	-$4
Cris Carpenter	FA	$5	Dwight Gooden	FA	$2

PITCHERS 1995 VALUES

NAME	TEAM	VALUE	NAME	TEAM	VALUE
Tom Gordon	KC	$4	Scott Kamieniecki	NYY	$1
Goose Gossage	FA	-$1	Steve Karsay	OAK	$1
Jim Gott	FA	$8	Jimmy Key	NYY	$28
Mauro Gozzo	FA	$1	Mark Kiefer	MIL	-$4
Jeff Granger	KC	-$1	Kevin King	SEA	-$4
Jason Grimsley	CLE	$0	Scott Klingenbeck	BAL	-$2
Buddy Groom	DET	-$2	Kurt Knudsen	DET	-$4
Eddie Guardado	MIN	-$9	Bill Krueger	FA	-$5
Mark Gubicza	FA	$3	Mark Langston	CAL	$13
Bill Gullickson	FA	-$10	Craig Lefferts	FA	-$5
Mark Guthrie	MIN	$2	Phil Leftwich	CAL	$3
Juan Guzman	TOR	$5	Dave Leiper	OAK	$0
Darren Hall	TOR	$11	Al Leiter	TOR	-$1
Atlee Hammaker	CHW	-$1	Mark Leiter	FA	$0
Chris Haney	KC	-$5	Scott Lewis	FA	$0
Erik Hanson	FA	$16	Derek Lilliquist	FA	$7
Mike Harkey	FA	-$1	Jose Lima	DET	$0
Pete Harnisch	FA	$14	Doug Linton	FA	-$9
Gene Harris	FA	$4	Graeme Lloyd	MIL	$6
Grega Harris	FA	-$5	Brian Looney	BOS	-$3
Gregw Harris	FA	$0	Albie Lopez	CLE	$6
Heath Haynes	OAK	-$2	Andrew Lorraine	CAL	-$3
Rick Helling	TEX	-$1	Mike Maddux	FA	$5
Mike Henneman	DET	$14	Mike Magnante	KC	-$1
Pat Hentgen	TOR	$21	Joe Magrane	CAL	-$9
Roberto Hernandez	CHW	$32	Pat Mahomes	MIN	-$5
Xavier Hernandez	FA	$16	Dennis Martinez	CLE	$18
Orel Hershiser	FA	$17	Roger Mason	FA	$3
Joe Hesketh	FA	$0	Kirk McCaskill	FA	$2
Greg Hibbard	SEA	$5	Ben McDonald	BAL	$16
Ted Higuera	FA	-$6	Jack McDowell	NYY	$27
Milt Hill	FA	-$4	Roger McDowell	FA	-$2
Sterling Hitchcock	NYY	-$1	Kevin McGehee	FA	-$4
Rick Honeycutt	FA	-$4	Rusty Meacham	KC	$3
Vince Horsman	FA	-$2	Jose Melendez	BOS	$1
Charlie Hough	FA	-$2	Jose Mercedes	MIL	-$1
Christian Howard	BOS	-$1	Brett Merriman	MIN	-$6
Steve Howe	NYY	$23	Bob Milacki	KC	-$9
Jay Howell	FA	$3	Alan Mills	BAL	$2
Bruce Hurst	FA	-$8	Nate Minchey	FA	-$1
Mark Hutton	NYY	-$2	Angel Miranda	MIL	$0
Mike Ignasiak	MIL	$1	Mike Mohler	OAK	-$5
Mike Jackson	FA	$7	Rich Monteleone	FA	$2
Miguel Jimenez	OAK	-$7	Jeff Montgomery	KC	$36
Dane Johnson	CHW	-$3	Mike Moore	DET	-$11
Randy Johnson	SEA	$20	Jamie Moyer	BAL	$5
Joel Johnston	BOS	-$2	Terry Mulholland	FA	-$2
Doug Jones	FA	$33	Rob Murphy	FA	$1

PITCHERS 1995 VALUES

NAME	TEAM	VALUE	NAME	TEAM	VALUE
Mike Mussina	BAL	$24	Lee Smith	CAL	$39
Jeff Mutis	FA	-$4	Pete Smith	FA	-$3
Chris Nabholz	FA	-$7	Willie Smith	CLE	-$2
Charles Nagy	CLE	$17	Zane Smith	FA	$18
Jaime Navarro	MIL	-$10	Roger Smithberg	FA	-$2
Jeff Nelson	SEA	$4	Paul Spoljaric	TOR	-$5
Rafael Novoa	FA	$0	Russ Springer	CAL	$0
Edwin Nunez	FA	-$7	Randy St.clair	FA	-$1
Chad Ogea	CLE	-$3	Mike Stanton	FA	$9
Darren Oliver	TEX	$5	Dave Stevens	MIN	$5
Gregg Olson	FA	$2	Dave Stewart	FA	-$3
Steve Ontiveros	FA	$11	Phil Stidham	DET	-$3
Mike Oquist	BAL	-$5	Todd Stottlemyre	FA	$2
Jesse Orosco	FA	$1	Rick Sutcliffe	FA	-$18
Don Pall	FA	$0	Russ Swan	CLE	-$4
Bob Patterson	FA	$1	Bill Swift	FA	$23
Ken Patterson	CAL	-$2	Kevin Tapani	MIN	$8
Roger Pavlik	TEX	-$6	Julian Tavarez	CLE	-$3
Brad Pennington	BAL	-$2	Bill Taylor	OAK	$0
Troy Percival	CAL	-$1	Brien Taylor	NYY	$0
Melido Perez	NYY	$2	Dave Telgheder	FA	-$4
Steve Phoenix	OAK	$1	Bob Tewksbury	FA	$6
Hipolito Pichardo	KC	$1	Mike Timlin	TOR	-$3
Eric Plunk	CLE	$11	Randy Tomlin	FA	$0
Jim Poole	FA	-$2	Ricky Trlicek	BOS	-$2
Carlos Pulido	MIN	-$6	Mike Trombley	MIN	-$2
Rick Reed	FA	-$3	Matt Turner	CLE	$1
Carlos Reyes	OAK	-$2	Sergio Valdez	FA	-$5
Arthur Rhodes	BAL	-$9	Fernando Valenzuela	FA	$2
Bill Risley	SEA	$4	Julio Valera	CAL	-$3
Ben Rivera	FA	-$7	Tim Vanegmond	BOS	-$4
Rich Robertson	FA	-$4	Todd Vanpoppel	OAK	-$11
Kenny Rogers	TEX	$8	Frank Viola	FA	$5
Scott Ruffcorn	CHW	$0	Duane Ward	TOR	$12
Jeff Russell	FA	$5	Gary Wayne	FA	-$1
Ken Ryan	BOS	$32	Bill Wegman	MIL	$4
Roger Salkeld	SEA	-$6	Bob Welch	FA	-$15
Bill Sampen	FA	-$5	Bob Wells	SEA	-$1
Scott Sanderson	FA	$1	David Wells	DET	$10
Bob Scanlan	MIL	$3	Bill Wertz	CLE	-$3
Erik Schullstrom	MIN	-$1	Wally Whitehurst	FA	-$5
Jeff Schwarz	CAL	-$5	Matt Whiteside	TEX	$0
Aaron Sele	BOS	$11	Bob Wickman	NYY	$6
Frank Seminara	FA	-$4	Woody Williams	TOR	$0
Scott Service	FA	-$2	Mark Williamson	FA	$0
Paul Shuey	CLE	$14	Carl Willis	MIN	-$2
Aaron Small	TOR	-$3	Trevor Wilson	FA	$2
Dan Smith	TEX	-$3	Bobby Witt	FA	-$8

PITCHERS 1995 VALUES

NAME	TEAM	VALUE	NAME	TEAM	VALUE
NATIONAL LEAGUE:			Brad Clontz	ATL	$0
Jim Abbott	FA	$6	Steve Cooke	PIT	$11
Kyle Abbott	PHI	-$4	Rheal Cormier	STL	$5
Larry Andersen	FA	$0	Danny Cox	FA	$1
Luis Aquino	FA	$0	Chuck Crim	FA	$0
Jack Armstrong	FA	-$5	Omar Daal	LA	-$3
Rene Arocha	STL	$5			
			Danny Darwin	FA	$1
Andy Ashby	SD	-$5	Mark Davis	FA	-$7
Paul Assenmacher	FA	$2	Storm Davis	FA	-$5
Pedro Astacio	LA	$11	Jose Deleon	FA	-$1
Steve Avery	ATL	$12	Rich Delucia	FA	-$4
Jeff Ballard	FA	-$3	Jim Deshaies	FA	-$14
Scott Bankhead	FA	$0			
			Mark Dewey	SF	$1
Willie Banks	CHC	-$7	Rob Dibble	FA	-$2
Brian Barnes	FA	-$6	Jerry Dipoto	NYM	-$4
Jose Bautista	FA	$5	John Dopson	FA	-$9
Rod Beck	SF	$43	Doug Drabek	HOU	$18
Steve Bedrosian	ATL	$0	Brian Drahman	FA	-$4
Tim Belcher	FA	-$1			
			Darren Dreifort	LA	$1
Stan Belinda	FA	$2	Mike Dyer	PIT	-$1
Alan Benes	STL	-$4	Dennis Eckersley	FA	$28
Andy Benes	SD	$14	Tom Edens	FA	$1
Mike Bielecki	FA	-$2	Joey Eischen	MON	-$3
Bud Black	FA	$0	Donnie Elliott	SD	-$4
Willie Blair	FA	-$3			
			Bryan Eversgerd	STL	-$3
Joe Boever	FA	$2	Steve Farr	FA	$5
Brian Bohanon	FA	-$4	Jeff Fassero	MON	$15
Toby Borland	PHI	$0	Bryce Florie	SD	-$3
Shawn Boskie	FA	-$1	Tim Fortugno	CIN	-$3
Ricky Bottalico	PHI	$1			
Kent Bottenfield	FA	-$4	Tony Fossas	FA	-$1
			Kevin Foster	CHC	$4
Denis Boucher	FA	$0	John Franco	FA	$29
Ryan Bowen	FLA	-$7	Marvin Freeman	COL	$11
Jeff Brantley	CIN	$18	Steve Frey	SF	$1
Brad Brink	SF	-$3	Todd Frohwirth	PIT	-$2
Doug Brocail	HOU	-$2			
Kevin Brown	FA	$13	Mike Gardiner	FA	$4
			Mark Gardner	FLA	$0
Tom Browning	FA	-$1	Paul Gibson	FA	-$3
Gary Buckels	FA	-$3	Tom Glavine	ATL	$16
Jim Bullinger	CHC	$1	Pat Gomez	SF	-$3
Dave Burba	SF	-$1	Dwight Gooden	FA	$1
Greg Cadaret	FA	-$3			
Tom Candiotti	LA	$14	Goose Gossage	FA	-$2
			Jim Gott	FA	$7
Cris Carpenter	FA	$3	Mauro Gozzo	FA	$0
Hector Carrasco	CIN	$17	Joe Grahe	COL	-$1
Andy Carter	PHI	-$2	Tommy Greene	PHI	$4
Frank Castillo	CHC	$2	Mark Gubicza	FA	$2
Juan Castillo	NYM	-$3			
Norm Charlton	FA	$1			

PITCHERS 1995 VALUES

NAME	TEAM	VALUE	NAME	TEAM	VALUE
Bill Gullickson	FA	-$11	Mark Leiter	FA	-$1
Eric Gunderson	NYM	-$3	Curt Leskanic	COL	-$6
Jose Guzman	CHC	-$4	Richie Lewis	FLA	-$6
John Habyan	STL	$1	Scott Lewis	FA	$0
Joey Hamilton	SD	$13	Jon Lieber	PIT	$9
Chris Hammond	FLA	$3	Derek Lilliquist	FA	$6
Mike Hampton	HOU	$1	Doug Linton	FA	-$10
Erik Hanson	FA	$13	Greg Maddux	ATL	$40
Mike Harkey	FA	-$3	Mike Maddux	FA	$4
Pete Harnisch	FA	$12	Josias Manzanillo	NYM	$2
Gene Harris	FA	$3	Ravelo Manzanillo	PIT	-$4
Grega Harris	FA	-$6	Jose Martinez	SD	-$4
Gregw Harris	FA	-$1	Pedroa Martinez	HOU	$3
Bryan Harvey	FLA	$15	Pedroj Martinez	MON	$10
Rod Henderson	MON	-$3	Ramon Martinez	LA	$7
Tom Henke	STL	$29	Roger Mason	FA	$1
Butch Henry	MON	$12	Terry Mathews	FLA	$0
Doug Henry	NYM	-$5	Tim Mauser	SD	$2
Gil Heredia	MON	$4	Kirk McCaskill	FA	$1
Jeremy Hernandez	FLA	$4	Roger McDowell	FA	-$3
Xavier Hernandez	FA	$14	Chuck McElroy	CIN	$5
Orel Hershiser	FA	$14	Kevin McGehee	FA	-$4
Joe Hesketh	FA	-$2	Greg McMichael	ATL	$21
Bryan Hickerson	CHC	$1	Kent Mercker	ATL	$13
Ted Higuera	FA	-$7	Jose Mesa	COL	-$8
Ken Hill	MON	$19	Danny Miceli	PIT	$0
Milt Hill	FA	-$5	Kurt Miller	FLA	-$4
Trevor Hoffman	SD	$31	Nate Minchey	FA	-$2
Darren Holmes	COL	$7	Blas Minor	NYM	-$5
Rick Honeycutt	FA	-$5	Rich Monteleone	FA	$1
John Hope	PIT	-$3	Marcus Moore	COL	-$6
Vince Horsman	FA	-$3	Mike Morgan	CHC	$4
Charlie Hough	FA	-$3	Jack Morris	CIN	-$18
Jay Howell	FA	$2	Terry Mulholland	FA	-$3
John Hudek	HOU	$9	Bobby Munoz	PHI	$4
Bruce Hurst	FA	-$9	Mike Munoz	COL	-$1
Danny Jackson	STL	$12	Rob Murphy	FA	$0
Mike Jackson	FA	$6	Jeff Mutis	FA	-$5
Jason Jacome	NYM	$6	Randy Myers	CHC	$32
Kevin Jarvis	CIN	-$3	Chris Nabholz	FA	-$8
Domingo Jean	HOU	-$4	Denny Neagle	PIT	$0
John Johnstone	FLA	-$6	Robb Nen	FLA	$17
Bobby Jones	NYM	$9	Dave Nied	COL	-$2
Doug Jones	FA	$32	Rafael Novoa	FA	-$1
Todd Jones	HOU	$17	Edwin Nunez	FA	-$8
Jeff Juden	PHI	-$4	Omar Olivares	STL	-$3
Daryl Kile	HOU	$3	Gregg Olson	FA	$1
Bill Krueger	FA	-$6	Steve Ontiveros	FA	$9
Craig Lefferts	FA	-$6	Jesse Orosco	FA	$0

PITCHERS 1995 VALUES

NAME	TEAM	VALUE	NAME	TEAM	VALUE
Donovan Osborne	STL	$4	Pete Smith	FA	-$5
Al Osuna	LA	-$2	Zane Smith	FA	$15
Dave Otto	CHC	-$4	Roger Smithberg	FA	-$3
Lance Painter	COL	-$4	John Smoltz	ATL	$16
Vicente Palacios	STL	$2	Jerry Spradlin	CIN	-$2
Don Pall	FA	$0	Randy St.clair	FA	-$2
Chanho Park	LA	-$3	Mike Stanton	FA	$7
Bob Patterson	FA	$0	Dave Stewart	FA	-$3
Mike Perez	STL	$1	Todd Stottlemyre	FA	$0
Yorkis Perez	FLA	$0	Rick Sutcliffe	FA	-$19
Erik Plantenberg	SD	-$4	Bill Swift	FA	$20
Dan Plesac	PIT	-$1	Greg Swindell	HOU	$6
Jim Poole	FA	-$3	Jeff Tabaka	SD	-$3
Mark Portugal	SF	$15	Kerry Taylor	SD	-$7
Ross Powell	HOU	-$3	Dave Telgheder	FA	-$4
Tim Pugh	CIN	-$6	Bob Tewksbury	FA	$4
Paul Quantrill	PHI	-$1	Mark Thompson	COL	-$3
Pat Rapp	FLA	-$1	Randy Tomlin	FA	$0
Rick Reed	FA	-$4	Salomon Torres	SF	-$9
Steve Reed	COL	$1	Steve Trachsel	CHC	$13
Mike Remlinger	NYM	-$6	Tom Urbani	STL	-$6
Shane Reynolds	HOU	$19	Ismael Valdes	LA	-$1
Armando Reynoso	COL	-$1	Sergio Valdez	FA	-$6
Jose Rijo	CIN	$29	Fernando Valenzuela	FA	$1
Kevin Ritz	COL	-$9	Bill Vanlandingham	SF	$5
Ben Rivera	FA	-$8	Dave Veres	HOU	$0
Rich Robertson	FA	-$5	Frank Viola	FA	$3
Rich Rodriguez	STL	$0	Terrell Wade	ATL	$0
Kevin Rogers	SF	$1	Paul Wagner	PIT	-$2
Mel Rojas	MON	$20	Allen Watson	STL	-$1
John Roper	CIN	-$2	Gary Wayne	FA	-$2
Kirk Rueter	MON	$1	Dave Weathers	FLA	-$10
Bruce Ruffin	COL	$10	Bob Welch	FA	-$16
Johnny Ruffin	CIN	$9	Turk Wendell	CHC	-$4
Jeff Russell	FA	$4	David West	PHI	$7
Bret Saberhagen	NYM	$31	John Wetteland	MON	$42
Bill Sampen	FA	-$6	Gabe White	MON	-$2
Scott Sanders	SD	-$1	Rick White	PIT	$8
Scott Sanderson	FA	$0	Wally Whitehurst	FA	-$6
Rich Scheid	FLA	-$2	Brian Williams	SD	-$7
Curt Schilling	PHI	$8	Mike Williams	PHI	-$6
Pete Schourek	CIN	$3	Mitch Williams	HOU	$0
Tim Scott	MON	$2	Mark Williamson	FA	-$1
Rudy Seanez	LA	-$2	Trevor Wilson	FA	$1
Frank Seminara	FA	-$5	Mark Wohlers	ATL	$9
Scott Service	FA	-$3	Brad Woodall	ATL	-$1
Jeff Shaw	MON	$3	Tim Worrell	SD	-$4
Heath Slocumb	PHI	$1	Todd Worrell	LA	$17
John Smiley	CIN	$16	Anthony Young	CHC	$4

1995 VALUES BY POSITION
** SEE ACCOMPANYING NOTES ON PAGES 307-311 **

AMERICAN LEAGUE CATCHERS

Ivan Rodriguez	TEX	$19
Mike Stanley	NYY	$14
Chris Hoiles	BAL	$13
Dave Nilsson	MIL	$13
Sandy Alomar	CLE	$10
Terry Steinbach	OAK	$10
Mickey Tettleton	FA	$9
Mike Macfarlane	FA	$8
Brian Harper	FA	$7
Benito Santiago	FA	$7
Jim Leyritz	NYY	$6
Rich Rowland	BOS	$4
Matt Nokes	BAL	$2
Ron Karkovice	CHW	$2
Brent Mayne	KC	$2
Pat Borders	FA	$1
Chris Turner	CAL	$1
Greg Myers	CAL	$0
Lenny Webster	FA	$0
Damon Berryhill	FA	$0
Scott Hemond	FA	$0
Matt Walbeck	MIN	$0
Joe Oliver	FA	$0
Mike Lavalliere	CHW	$0
Jorge Fabregas	CAL	$0
Lance Parrish	FA	$0
Dan Wilson	SEA	$0

NATIONAL LEAGUE CATCHERS

Mike Piazza	LA	$28
Darren Daulton	PHI	$14
Javier Lopez	ATL	$10
Mickey Tettleton	FA	$10
Mike Macfarlane	FA	$8
Brian Harper	FA	$8
Don Slaught	PIT	$8
Benito Santiago	FA	$8
Rick Wilkins	CHC	$7
Joe Girardi	COL	$7
Eddie Taubensee	CIN	$6
Darrin Fletcher	MON	$5
Tom Pagnozzi	STL	$5
Brad Ausmus	SD	$5
Todd Hundley	NYM	$5
Charles Johnson	FLA	$3
Kirt Manwaring	SF	$2
Pat Borders	FA	$2
Damon Berryhill	FA	$1
Lenny Webster	FA	$1
Scott Servais	HOU	$1
Tony Eusebio	HOU	$0
Joe Oliver	FA	$0
Scott Hemond	FA	$0

Tim Laker	MON	$0
Lance Parrish	FA	$0
Mike Lieberthal	PHI	$0
Brian Dorsett	FA	$0
Charlie O'Brien	ATL	$0
Kelly Stinnett	NYM	$0
Steve Decker	FLA	$0
Tim Spehr	MON	$0
Brian Johnson	SD	$0

AMERICAN LEAGUE FIRST BASEMEN

Frank Thomas	CHW	$38
Larry Walker	FA	$31
Rafael Palmeiro	BAL	$30
Will Clark	TEX	$27
Mo Vaughn	BOS	$27
John Olerud	TOR	$24
Cecil Fielder	DET	$18
Mark Grace	FA	$17
Wally Joyner	KC	$17
Eddie Murray	CLE	$15
Don Mattingly	NYY	$14
John Kruk	FA	$13
Bob Hamelin	KC	$12
Tino Martinez	SEA	$12
John Jaha	MIL	$12
Kevin Seitzer	MIL	$11
Paul Sorrento	CLE	$11
Troy Neel	OAK	$11
Mickey Tettleton	FA	$9
Jim Edmonds	CAL	$9
Mark McGwire	OAK	$7
Mike Blowers	SEA	$6
Ricky Jordan	FA	$5
Eduardo Perez	CAL	$3
Todd Benzinger	FA	$3
David McCarty	MIN	$1
Gerald Perry	FA	$0
Jt Snow	CAL	$0
Dave Staton	FA	$0
Dave Martinez	FA	$0
Mike Aldrete	OAK	$0
Steve Dunn	MIN	$0
Skeeter Barnes	FA	$0
Sid Bream	FA	$0
Randy Milligan	FA	$0
Tony Clark	DET	$0
Herbert Perry	CLE	$0
Tim Costo	CLE	$0

NATIONAL LEAGUE FIRST BASEMEN

Jeff Bagwell	HOU	$43
Fred McGriff	ATL	$33
Gregg Jefferies	PHI	$32

Larry Walker	FA	$31		Rich Amaral	SEA	$2
Andres Galarraga	COL	$28		Scott Hemond	FA	$0
Hal Morris	CIN	$27		Craig Grebeck	CHW	$0
Jeff Conine	FLA	$24		Rex Hudler	CAL	$0
Cliff Floyd	MON	$18		Shannon Penn	DET	$0
Mark Grace	FA	$18		Juan Bell	BOS	$0
Greg Colbrunn	FLA	$16		Norberto Martin	CHW	$0
John Kruk	FA	$13		Carlos Rodriguez	BOS	$0
Eddie Williams	SD	$13		Tim Hulett	FA	$0
Eric Karros	LA	$11				
Orlando Merced	PIT	$10				
Mickey Tettleton	FA	$10		**NATIONAL LEAGUE SECOND BASEMEN**		
Rico Brogna	NYM	$9				
David Segui	NYM	$6		Craig Biggio	HOU	$34
Ricky Jordan	FA	$6		Bip Roberts	SD	$25
Brianr Hunter	CIN	$3		Delino Deshields	LA	$23
Todd Benzinger	FA	$3		Brett Boone	CIN	$22
Phil Clark	SD	$3		Jeff Kent	NYM	$20
Roberto Petagine	SD	$2		Geronimo Pena	STL	$18
Gerald Perry	FA	$1		Carlos Garcia	PIT	$16
Dave Staton	FA	$1		Mike Lansing	MON	$15
Jr Phillips	SF	$1		Mariano Duncan	FA	$12
Kevin Young	PIT	$1		Mickey Morandini	PHI	$8
Dave Martinez	FA	$0		Ryan Thompson	NYM	$6
John Vanderwal	PIT	$0		Joey Cora	FA	$6
Skeeter Barnes	FA	$0		Roberto Mejia	COL	$6
Rich Aude	PIT	$0		Mark Lemke	ATL	$4
Sid Bream	FA	$0		Mike Gallego	FA	$4
Randy Milligan	FA	$0		Jody Reed	FA	$4
				Quilvio Veras	FLA	$3
				Rey Sanchez	CHC	$3
AMERICAN LEAGUE SECOND BASEMEN				Felix Fermin	FA	$3
				Harold Reynolds	FA	$2
Carlos Baerga	CLE	$32		John Patterson	SF	$1
Roberto Alomar	TOR	$32		Nelson Liriano	PIT	$1
Chuck Knoblauch	MIN	$31		Scott Hemond	FA	$0
Brent Gates	OAK	$16		Luis Lopez	SD	$0
Lou Whitaker	DET	$13		Jeff Branson	CIN	$0
Mariano Duncan	FA	$12		Tim Hulett	FA	$0
Mark McLemore	TEX	$11		Jeff Treadway	LA	$0
Pat Kelly	NYY	$10		Edgardo Alfonzo	NYM	$0
Bret Barberie	BAL	$10		Tony Graffanino	ATL	$0
Ray Durham	CHW	$9		Fernando Vina	NYM	$0
Joey Cora	FA	$6				
Luis Alicea	BOS	$5				
Tim Naehring	BOS	$4		**AMERICAN LEAGUE THIRD BASEMEN**		
Terry Shumpert	BOS	$4				
Jose Lind	KC	$4		Travis Fryman	DET	$22
Scott Fletcher	BOS	$4		Wade Boggs	NYY	$20
Damion Easley	CAL	$4		Robin Ventura	CHW	$19
Mike Gallego	FA	$3		Edgar Martinez	SEA	$17
Chris Gomez	DET	$3		Jim Thome	CLE	$17
Jody Reed	FA	$3		Charlie Hayes	FA	$17
Jeff Frye	TEX	$2		Dean Palmer	TEX	$14
Felix Fermin	FA	$2		Scott Cooper	BOS	$13
Luis Sojo	SEA	$2		Mariano Duncan	FA	$12
Harold Reynolds	FA	$2		Kevin Seitzer	MIL	$11
				Leo Gomez	BAL	$11

Tony Fernandez	NYY	$11
Terry Pendleton	FA	$7
Mike Blowers	SEA	$6
Randy Velarde	FA	$6
Bj Surhoff	FA	$6
Gary Gaetti	FA	$5
Jerry Browne	FA	$5
Chris Sabo	FA	$5
Ed Sprague	TOR	$5
Scott Brosius	OAK	$5
Terry Shumpert	BOS	$4
Damion Easley	CAL	$4
Dave Magadan	FA	$4
Scott Leius	MIN	$3
Russ Davis	NYY	$2
Spike Owen	CAL	$1
Scott Stahoviak	MIN	$0
Rene Gonzales	FA	$0
Herbert Perry	CLE	$0
Howard Battle	TOR	$0
Chip Hale	MIN	$0

NATIONAL LEAGUE THIRD BASEMEN

Matt Williams	SF	$25
Bobby Bonilla	NYM	$18
Charlie Hayes	FA	$18
Ken Caminiti	SD	$17
Mike Lansing	MON	$15
Sean Berry	MON	$15
Todd Zeile	STL	$15
Mariano Duncan	FA	$12
Dave Hollins	PHI	$12
Willie Greene	CIN	$10
Jeff King	PIT	$9
Jose Oliva	ATL	$9
Tim Wallach	LA	$9
Terry Pendleton	FA	$8
Steve Buechele	CHC	$7
Randy Velarde	FA	$7
Bj Surhoff	FA	$6
Gary Gaetti	FA	$6
Jerry Browne	FA	$6
Chris Sabo	FA	$5
Dave Magadan	FA	$4
Bill Spiers	NYM	$4
Scott Livingstone	SD	$2
Dave Hansen	LA	$2
Craig Shipley	HOU	$2
Lenny Harris	CIN	$2
Butch Huskey	NYM	$1
Archi Cianfrocco	SD	$0
Rene Gonzales	FA	$0
Kim Batiste	PHI	$0
Mario Diaz	FLA	$0
Bill Pecota	FA	$0

AMERICAN LEAGUE SHORTSTOPS

Cal Ripken	BAL	$15
John Valentin	BOS	$12
Jeff Blauser	FA	$12
Alan Trammell	FA	$11
Greg Gagne	KC	$11
Ozzie Guillen	CHW	$9
Alex Gonzalez	TOR	$9
Omar Vizquel	CLE	$8
Alex Rodriguez	SEA	$8
Randy Velarde	FA	$6
Mike Bordick	OAK	$6
Denny Hocking	MIN	$5
Jose Valentin	MIL	$5
Pat Listach	MIL	$4
Mike Gallego	FA	$3
Chris Gomez	DET	$3
Manuel Lee	FA	$3
Gary Disarcina	CAL	$2
Felix Fermin	FA	$2
Luis Sojo	SEA	$2
Benji Gil	TEX	$2
Pat Meares	MIN	$1
Dick Schofield	FA	$1
Derek Jeter	NYY	$0
Craig Grebeck	CHW	$0
Jeff Reboulet	MIN	$0
Carlos Rodriguez	BOS	$0

NATIONAL LEAGUE SHORTSTOPS

Wil Cordero	MON	$30
Barry Larkin	CIN	$25
Royce Clayton	SF	$15
Jay Bell	PIT	$14
Chipper Jones	ATL	$13
Jeff Blauser	FA	$12
Andujar Cedeno	SD	$11
Alan Trammell	FA	$11
Shawon Dunston	CHC	$10
Ozzie Smith	STL	$10
Walt Weiss	COL	$8
Kurt Abbott	FLA	$7
Randy Velarde	FA	$7
Jose Vizcaino	NYM	$4
Kevin Stocker	PHI	$4
Mike Gallego	FA	$4
Bill Spiers	NYM	$4
Manuel Lee	FA	$4
Jose Offerman	LA	$3
Rey Sanchez	CHC	$3
Felix Fermin	FA	$3
Ricky Gutierrez	HOU	$2
Dick Schofield	FA	$1
Vinny Castilla	COL	$1

Orlando Miller	HOU	$1
Luis Lopez	SD	$0
Mark Lewis	CIN	$0
Jose Oquendo	STL	$0
Alex Arias	FLA	$0
Ray Holbert	SD	$0

AMERICAN LEAGUE OUTFIELDERS

Kenny Lofton	CLE	$53
Ken Griffey	SEA	$43
Albert Belle	CLE	$40
Larry Walker	FA	$31
Paul O'Neill	NYY	$31
Brett Butler	FA	$30
Kirby Puckett	MIN	$30
Bernie Williams	NYY	$28
Brady Anderson	BAL	$28
Otis Nixon	TEX	$27
Chad Curtis	CAL	$25
Joe Carter	TOR	$24
Rickey Henderson	OAK	$24
Juan Gonzalez	TEX	$23
Lance Johnson	CHW	$23
Felix Jose	FA	$23
Kevin Mitchell	FA	$22
Ruben Sierra	OAK	$22
Vince Coleman	FA	$22
Devon White	TOR	$21
Luis Polonia	NYY	$21
Tony Phillips	DET	$21
Manny Ramirez	CLE	$20
Tim Raines	CHW	$20
Tim Salmon	CAL	$20
Brian McRae	KC	$20
Shane Mack	FA	$20
Stan Javier	OAK	$19
David Hulse	TEX	$19
Greg Vaughn	MIL	$17
Jay Buhner	SEA	$16
Jeffrey Hammonds	BAL	$15
Mike Greenwell	BOS	$14
Darryl Hamilton	MIL	$14
Rich Becker	MIN	$13
Alex Cole	MIN	$13
Darrin Jackson	FA	$13
Carlos Delgado	TOR	$12
Danny Tartabull	NYY	$11
Pedro Munoz	MIN	$11
Andy Vanslyke	FA	$11
Wayne Kirby	CLE	$9
Jim Edmonds	CAL	$9
Eric Anthony	FA	$8
Milt Thompson	FA	$8
Shawn Green	TOR	$8
Geronimo Berroa	OAK	$8

Kirk Gibson	FA	$8
Dwight Smith	FA	$7
Junior Felix	FA	$6
Matt Mieske	MIL	$5
Jerry Browne	FA	$5
Bo Jackson	FA	$5
Rusty Greer	TEX	$5
Danny Bautista	DET	$5
Chris Sabo	FA	$5
Wes Chamberlain	BOS	$4
Kevin Bass	FA	$4
Alex Diaz	FA	$4
Billy Hatcher	FA	$4
Juan Samuel	FA	$4
Turner Ward	MIL	$4
Jeromy Burnitz	CLE	$3
Eric Davis	FA	$3
Willie McGee	FA	$3
Kevin McReynolds	FA	$3
Lee Tinsley	BOS	$2
Mike Devereaux	FA	$2
Oddibe McDowell	FA	$2
Michael Tucker	KC	$1
Milt Cuyler	DET	$1
Chris James	FA	$1
Gerald Williams	NYY	$1
Garret Anderson	CAL	$1
Lance Blankenship	OAK	$0
Mike Huff	TOR	$0
Kerwin Moore	OAK	$0
Dave Martinez	FA	$0
Tom Brunansky	FA	$0
Greg Blosser	BOS	$0
Howard Johnson	FA	$0
Dwayne Hosey	KC	$0
Mike Aldrete	OAK	$0
Daryl Boston	FA	$0
Damon Buford	BAL	$0
Ernie Young	OAK	$0
Keith Mitchell	FA	$0
Marty Cordova	MIN	$0
Mitch Webster	FA	$0
Darren Bragg	SEA	$0
Mike Felder	FA	$0
Matt Stairs	BOS	$0
Ruben Amaro	CLE	$0
Dave Gallagher	FA	$0
Curtis Goodwin	BAL	$0

NATIONAL LEAGUE OUTFIELDERS

Barry Bonds	SF	$46
Marquis Grissom	MON	$40
Sammy Sosa	CHC	$35
Deion Sanders	CIN	$33
Moises Alou	MON	$32

Larry Walker	FA	$31		Jerry Browne	FA	$6
Dante Bichette	COL	$31		Chris Sabo	FA	$5
Derek Bell	HOU	$30		Thomas Howard	CIN	$5
Brett Butler	FA	$29		Kevin Bass	FA	$5
Gary Sheffield	FLA	$28		Henry Rodriguez	LA	$5
Roberto Kelly	ATL	$27		Alex Diaz	FA	$4
Tony Gwynn	SD	$26		Billy Hatcher	FA	$4
Reggie Sanders	CIN	$25		Mike Kingery	COL	$4
Bip Roberts	SD	$25		Juan Samuel	FA	$4
Darren Lewis	SF	$24		Lou Frazier	MON	$4
Raul Mondesi	LA	$24		Willie McGee	FA	$4
Jeff Conine	FLA	$24		Kevin McReynolds	FA	$3
Lenny Dykstra	PHI	$23		Eric Davis	FA	$3
Kevin Mitchell	FA	$23		Mike Devereaux	FA	$3
David Justice	ATL	$23		Oddibe McDowell	FA	$2
Ellis Burks	COL	$22		Billy Ashley	LA	$2
Felix Jose	FA	$22		Ray McDavid	SD	$2
Ray Lankford	STL	$22		Mark Carreon	SF	$2
Luis Gonzalez	HOU	$20		Chris James	FA	$2
Vince Coleman	FA	$20		Rikkert Faneyte	SF	$2
Shane Mack	FA	$20		Mike Kelly	ATL	$2
Cliff Floyd	MON	$18		Cory Snyder	LA	$1
Mark Whiten	STL	$17		Tom Brunansky	FA	$1
Derrick May	CHC	$17		Jim Lindeman	NYM	$0
Steve Finley	SD	$17		Howard Johnson	FA	$0
Chuck Carr	FLA	$17		Dave Martinez	FA	$0
Bernard Gilkey	STL	$16		Darryl Strawberry	SF	$0
James Mouton	HOU	$15		Eddie Zambrano	CHC	$0
Brianl Hunter	HOU	$14		Daryl Boston	FA	$0
Carl Everett	NYM	$14		Todd Hollandsworth	LA	$0
Ryan Klesko	ATL	$13		Keith Mitchell	FA	$0
Al Martin	PIT	$13		Mitch Webster	FA	$0
Darrin Jackson	FA	$13		Mike Felder	FA	$0
Eric Young	COL	$12		Melvin Nieves	SD	$0
Jacob Brumfield	PIT	$11		Dave Gallagher	FA	$0
Glenallen Hill	CHC	$11		Darrell Whitmore	FLA	$0
Andy Vanslyke	FA	$11		Jerome Walton	CIN	$0
Phil Plantier	HOU	$11		Kevin Roberson	CHC	$0
Orlando Merced	PIT	$10		Chris Jones	NYM	$0
Tony Tarasco	ATL	$10		Chris Gwynn	FA	$0
Ron Gant	CIN	$10		Keith Miller	FA	$0
Dave Clark	PIT	$9		Lloyd McClendon	FA	$0
Brian Jordan	STL	$9				
Eric Anthony	FA	$9		**DESIGNATED HITTERS**		
Milt Thompson	FA	$8				
Midre Cummings	PIT	$8		Paul Molitor	TOR	$32
Kirk Gibson	FA	$8		Jose Canseco	BOS	$23
Dwight Smith	FA	$7		Chili Davis	CAL	$20
Jim Eisenreich	PHI	$7		Edgar Martinez	SEA	$17
Joe Orsulak	NYM	$7		Eddie Murray	CLE	$15
Rondell White	MON	$7		Harold Baines	FA	$13
Karl Rhodes	CHC	$7		Dave Nilsson	MIL	$13
Junior Felix	FA	$6		Bob Hamelin	KC	$12
Bo Jackson	FA	$6		Danny Tartabull	NYY	$11
David Segui	NYM	$6		Troy Neel	OAK	$11
Robby Thompson	SF	$6		Mickey Tettleton	FA	$9

Marc Newfield	SEA	$9		Aaron Sele	BOS	$11
Sherman Obando	BAL	$8		Ricky Bones	MIL	$11
Geronimo Berroa	OAK	$8		Armando Benitez	BAL	$11
Kirk Gibson	FA	$8		Steve Ontiveros	FA	$11
Brian Harper	FA	$7		David Wells	DET	$10
Reggie Jefferson	SEA	$7		Chuck Finley	CAL	$9
Jim Leyritz	NYY	$6		Mark Clark	CLE	$9
Dave Winfield	FA	$5		Mike Stanton	FA	$9
Ron Coomer	FA	$3		Kevin Tapani	MIN	$8
Andre Dawson	FA	$3		Jim Gott	FA	$8
Damon Buford	BAL	$0		Jim Abbott	FA	$8
Darren Bragg	SEA	$0		Mark Eichhorn	BAL	$8
Lonnie Smith	FA	$0		Kenny Rogers	TEX	$8
Candy Maldonado	FA	$0		Mike Jackson	FA	$7
				Jason Bere	CHW	$7

AMERICAN LEAGUE PITCHERS

				Derek Lilliquist	FA	$7
Lee Smith	CAL	$39		Albie Lopez	CLE	$6
Jeff Montgomery	KC	$36		Graeme Lloyd	MIL	$6
Doug Jones	FA	$33		Jose Bautista	FA	$6
Bobby Ayala	SEA	$33		Bob Tewksbury	FA	$6
Rick Aguilera	MIN	$32		Steve Farr	FA	$6
Roberto Hernandez	CHW	$32		Bob Wickman	NYY	$6
Ken Ryan	BOS	$32		Sid Fernandez	BAL	$6
John Franco	FA	$31		Jamie Moyer	BAL	$5
Dennis Eckersley	FA	$29		Mike Maddux	FA	$5
Jimmy Key	NYY	$28		Darren Oliver	TEX	$5
Jack McDowell	NYY	$27		Juan Guzman	TOR	$5
Mike Mussina	BAL	$24		Greg Hibbard	SEA	$5
Steve Howe	NYY	$23		Billy Brewer	KC	$5
Bill Swift	FA	$23		Cris Carpenter	FA	$5
Pat Hentgen	TOR	$21		Dave Stevens	MIN	$5
David Cone	KC	$21		Jeff Russell	FA	$5
Randy Johnson	SEA	$20		Frank Viola	FA	$5
Kevin Appier	KC	$19		Mike Gardiner	FA	$5
Alex Fernandez	CHW	$19		Gene Harris	FA	$4
Mike Fetters	MIL	$18		Mike Butcher	CAL	$4
Dennis Martinez	CLE	$18		Jeff Nelson	SEA	$4
Zane Smith	FA	$18		Bill Risley	SEA	$4
Charles Nagy	CLE	$17		Tom Gordon	KC	$4
Roger Clemens	BOS	$17		Bill Wegman	MIL	$4
John Burkett	TEX	$17		Brian Anderson	CAL	$4
Orel Hershiser	FA	$17		Bob Scanlan	MIL	$3
Ben McDonald	BAL	$16		Joe Boever	FA	$3
Erik Hanson	FA	$16		Mark Gubicza	FA	$3
Wilson Alvarez	CHW	$16		Rusty Meacham	KC	$3
Kevin Brown	FA	$16		Kevin Gross	TEX	$3
Xavier Hernandez	FA	$16		Cal Eldred	MIL	$3
Mike Henneman	DET	$14		Phil Leftwich	CAL	$3
Pete Harnisch	FA	$14		Paul Assenmacher	FA	$3
Paul Shuey	CLE	$14		Jay Howell	FA	$3
Mark Langston	CAL	$13		Stan Belinda	FA	$3
Duane Ward	TOR	$12		Roger Mason	FA	$3
Chris Bosio	SEA	$11		Danny Darwin	FA	$3
Darren Hall	TOR	$11		Mark Guthrie	MIN	$2
Eric Plunk	CLE	$11		Trevor Wilson	FA	$2
				Dwight Gooden	FA	$2

John Doherty	DET	$2
Todd Stottlemyre	FA	$2
Gregg Olson	FA	$2
Tony Castillo	TOR	$2
Danny Cox	FA	$2
Melido Perez	NYY	$2
Kirk McCaskill	FA	$2
Fernando Valenzuela	FA	$2
Alan Mills	BAL	$2
Norm Charlton	FA	$2
Tom Edens	FA	$2
Rich Monteleone	FA	$2
Jose Melendez	BOS	$1
Tim Davis	SEA	$1
Scott Kamieniecki	NYY	$1
Denis Boucher	FA	$1
Scott Erickson	MIN	$1
Larry Andersen	FA	$1
Scott Bankhead	FA	$1
Scott Sanderson	FA	$1
Steve Karsay	OAK	$1
Steve Phoenix	OAK	$1
Mauro Gozzo	FA	$1
Jesse Orosco	FA	$1
Bob Patterson	FA	$1
Chuck Crim	FA	$1
Mike Ignasiak	MIL	$1
Luis Aquino	FA	$1
Hipolito Pichardo	KC	$1
Matt Turner	CLE	$1
Rob Murphy	FA	$1
Dave Fleming	SEA	$0
Woody Williams	TOR	$0
Don Pall	FA	$0
Mark Acre	OAK	$0
Gregw Harris	FA	$0
Russ Springer	CAL	$0
Scott Lewis	FA	$0
Tim Belcher	FA	$0
Randy Tomlin	FA	$0
Bud Black	FA	$0
Mark Leiter	FA	$0
Jose Deleon	FA	$0
Angel Miranda	MIL	$0
Mark Williamson	FA	$0
Jose Lima	DET	$0
Matt Whiteside	TEX	$0
Bill Taylor	OAK	$0
Gar Finnvold	BOS	$0
Scott Ruffcorn	CHW	$0
Tom Browning	FA	$0
Dennis Cook	CLE	$0
Rafael Novoa	FA	$0
Shawn Boskie	FA	$0
Brien Taylor	NYY	$0
Kevin Campbell	MIN	$0

Jason Grimsley	CLE	$0
Joe Hesketh	FA	$0
Dave Leiper	OAK	$0
Ron Darling	OAK	$0

NATIONAL LEAGUE PITCHERS

Rod Beck	SF	$43
John Wetteland	MON	$42
Greg Maddux	ATL	$40
Randy Myers	CHC	$32
Doug Jones	FA	$32
Bret Saberhagen	NYM	$31
Trevor Hoffman	SD	$31
Tom Henke	STL	$29
Jose Rijo	CIN	$29
John Franco	FA	$29
Dennis Eckersley	FA	$28
Greg McMichael	ATL	$21
Bill Swift	FA	$20
Mel Rojas	MON	$20
Ken Hill	MON	$19
Shane Reynolds	HOU	$19
Doug Drabek	HOU	$18
Jeff Brantley	CIN	$18
Todd Worrell	LA	$17
Hector Carrasco	CIN	$17
Robb Nen	FLA	$17
Todd Jones	HOU	$17
Tom Glavine	ATL	$16
John Smiley	CIN	$16
John Smoltz	ATL	$16
Zane Smith	FA	$15
Bryan Harvey	FLA	$15
Mark Portugal	SF	$15
Jeff Fassero	MON	$15
Tom Candiotti	LA	$14
Xavier Hernandez	FA	$14
Andy Benes	SD	$14
Orel Hershiser	FA	$14
Erik Hanson	FA	$13
Kent Mercker	ATL	$13
Kevin Brown	FA	$13
Steve Trachsel	CHC	$13
Joey Hamilton	SD	$13
Pete Harnisch	FA	$12
Butch Henry	MON	$12
Danny Jackson	STL	$12
Steve Avery	ATL	$12
Steve Cooke	PIT	$11
Pedro Astacio	LA	$11
Marvin Freeman	COL	$11
Bruce Ruffin	COL	$10
Pedroj Martinez	MON	$10
Bobby Jones	NYM	$9
Jon Lieber	PIT	$9

Mark Wohlers	ATL	$9		Bryan Hickerson	CHC	$1
John Hudek	HOU	$9		Trevor Wilson	FA	$1
Steve Ontiveros	FA	$9		Mark Dewey	SF	$1
Johnny Ruffin	CIN	$9		Heath Slocumb	PHI	$1
Curt Schilling	PHI	$8		Danny Darwin	FA	$1
Rick White	PIT	$8		Dwight Gooden	FA	$1
Mike Stanton	FA	$7		Mike Perez	STL	$1
Ramon Martinez	LA	$7		Steve Frey	SF	$1
Darren Holmes	COL	$7		Kevin Rogers	SF	$1
Jim Gott	FA	$7		Darren Dreifort	LA	$1
David West	PHI	$7		Mike Hampton	HOU	$1
Greg Swindell	HOU	$6		Norm Charlton	FA	$1
Mike Jackson	FA	$6		Danny Cox	FA	$1
Jason Jacome	NYM	$6		Gregg Olson	FA	$1
Jim Abbott	FA	$6		Jim Bullinger	CHC	$1
Derek Lilliquist	FA	$6		Ricky Bottalico	PHI	$1
Rene Arocha	STL	$5		Tom Edens	FA	$1
Chuck McElroy	CIN	$5		Kirk McCaskill	FA	$1
Steve Farr	FA	$5		Rich Monteleone	FA	$1
Bill Vanlandingham	SF	$5		Fernando Valenzuela	FA	$1
Jose Bautista	FA	$5		Rich Rodriguez	STL	$0
Rheal Cormier	STL	$5		Mitch Williams	HOU	$0
Tommy Greene	PHI	$4		Todd Stottlemyre	FA	$0
Donovan Osborn	STL	$4		Toby Borland	PHI	$0
Mike Maddux	FA	$4		Scott Bankhead	FA	$0
Bob Tewksbury	FA	$4		Denis Boucher	FA	$0
Gil Heredia	MON	$4		Larry Andersen	FA	$0
Jeremy Hernandez	FLA	$4		Scott Sanderson	FA	$0
Kevin Foster	CHC	$4		Bob Patterson	FA	$0
Bobby Munoz	PHI	$4		Jesse Orosco	FA	$0
Anthony Young	CHC	$4		Chuck Crim	FA	$0
Mike Morgan	CHC	$4		Terry Mathews	FLA	$0
Mike Gardiner	FA	$4		Mauro Gozzo	FA	$0
Jeff Russell	FA	$4		Rob Murphy	FA	$0
Cris Carpenter	FA	$3		Steve Bedrosian	ATL	$0
Pedroa Martinez	HOU	$3		Brad Clontz	ATL	$0
Chris Hammond	FLA	$3		Luis Aquino	FA	$0
Pete Schourek	CIN	$3		Yorkis Perez	FLA	$0
Gene Harris	FA	$3		Dave Veres	HOU	$0
Frank Viola	FA	$3		Denny Neagle	PIT	$0
Jeff Shaw	MON	$3		Don Pall	FA	$0
Daryl Kile	HOU	$3		Scott Lewis	FA	$0
Frank Castillo	CHC	$2		Danny Miceli	PIT	$0
Joe Boever	FA	$2		Randy Tomlin	FA	$0
Josias Manzanillo	NYM	$2		Bud Black	FA	$0
Tim Scott	MON	$2		Terrell Wade	ATL	$0
Paul Assenmacher	FA	$2		Mark Gardner	FLA	$0
Jay Howell	FA	$2				
Vicente Palacios	STL	$2				
Tim Mauser	SD	$2				
Stan Belinda	FA	$2				
Mark Gubicza	FA	$2				
John Habyan	STL	$1				
Kirk Rueter	MON	$1				
Roger Mason	FA	$1				
Steve Reed	COL	$1				

RETROSHEET

David W. Smith
6 Penncross Circle
Newark, DE 19702
(302) 731-1570

Organizational Description

Modern baseball analysis has grown increasingly sophisticated in the past decade and a number of new statistical categories have come into common usage among announcers and writers. All of these new methods require detailed play by play data for current games and several statistical organizations actively collect this information. Many fans would like to compare modern player performances to those from earlier this century but have been unable to do so, since play by play accounts have never been collected or organized in a systematic way. Therefore, a new organization, called Retrosheet, was founded in 1989 for the purpose of computerizing play by play accounts of as many pre-1984 major league games as possible (data for games since 1984 are available through the Project Scoresheet-Baseball Workshop data base).

Retrosheet's work has three distinct aspects. First is the collection of the game accounts, which have been obtained from several sources. The bulk of the collection has come from major league teams (22 to date) which have allowed us to make copies of their play by play accounts. Several sportswriters (most of them retired) have allowed copies to be made of their daily scorebooks. In addition, individual fans have donated copies of programs they scored at the park or on their own scoresheets at home. The second activity is the translation of these accounts to a unified, modern system, which is essential since there is an extraordinary variety of scoring systems which have been used. The final activity is the entry of the translated accounts into the computer.

Retrosheet has been very successful in the collection of game accounts with more than 80,000 currently in hand. A group of some 50 volunteers is actively involved in the translation work and the computer entry. However, the task ahead is enormous and we are always looking for more volunteers; any offers of help are greatly appreciated. Baseball fans interested in this historical effort are invited to volunteer their assistance in the translation and inputting efforts as well as to make available copies of game accounts they might have.

The ultimate objective of Retrosheet is to make this basic play by play information publicly available for all interested researchers. Several methods for data distribution will be followed, including depositing the material in the Hall of Fame Library in Cooperstown.

In order to volunteer or to obtain more information, contact David Smith at the address and telephone number above.

The Benson Baseball Monthly

The ultimate publication for insider tips, news before it happens, and analysis of unfolding events. The first, best largest periodical for serious fans including Rotisserie™ league enthusiasts. Benson and his network of beat writers cover the major leagues like no one else.

- not just who's going to be traded, but who else gets affected and why.
- not just who's hurt or slumping or streaking, but who gets to play more, for how long, and why.

The focus is always on the future. Benson's monthly features exclusive quotes and interviews with players, coaches, managers, GM's and agents - everyone with the most inside information and the power to make decisions.

The Benson Baseball Monthly is featured in the book *Total Baseball*, by John Thorne and Pete Palmer, as the pacesetter for the future in baseball analysis. Much too big to be called a "newsletter" *The Benson Baseball Monthly* packs every issue with 26 to 40 plus pages of tips, commentary, letters, and insights from fifty writers and analysts nationwide.

See the order form on the last page of this book to order by mail, or call 203-834-1231 for Visa/Mastercard orders.

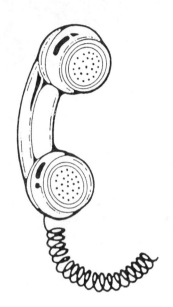

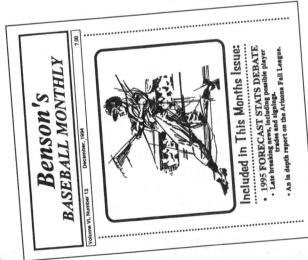

Bill James Fantasy Baseball

Bill James Fantasy Baseball enters its seventh season of offering baseball fans the most unique, realistic and exciting game fantasy sports has to offer.

You draft a 25-player roster and can expand to as many as 28. Players aren't "ranked" like in rotisserie leagues — you'll get credit for everything a player does, like hitting homers, driving in runs, turning double plays, pitching quality outings and more!

Also, the team which scores the most points among all leagues, plus wins the World Series, will receive the John McGraw Award — a one-week trip to the Grapefruit League in spring training, a day at the ballpark with Bill James and a new fantasy league named in their honor!

Unique Features Include:

- Live fantasy experts — seven days a week

- The best weekly reports in the business, detailing who is in the lead, win-loss records, MVP's, and team strengths and weaknesses

- On-Line computer system with a world of information including daily updates of fantasy standings and stats

- Over twice as many statistics as rotisserie

- Transactions that are effective the very next day!

All this, all summer long for less than $5 per week!

STATS On-Line

Catch ALL the Action!

STATS On-Line is your real-time link to the most accurate, up-to-the-minute sports information available anywhere. All you need is a computer and a modem. **STATS On-Line** will provide the rest!

ALL NEW!
STATS On-Line now provides real-time game boxscores for all sports!

STATS On-Line is the only all-sports on-line with the kind of sports information true fans need: timely updates of all player and team results as they happen, play-by-play. Plus, you'll have access to the detailed STATS, Inc. database, including exclusive STATS information, complete player info, transactions... even downloadable stat files for your fantasy league!

Timely Boxscores

Get updates from each sporting event as it happens around the country. You'll get complete player stats for every game without waiting for the morning paper!

All Sports, All The Time

Whether you follow baseball, football, basketball, hockey, or all four, **STATS On-Line** has something for you. Detailed football information, updated daily, gives fans the real story behind game day. Basketball and hockey fans have access to all players and teams. And STATS On-Line baseball coverage is unmatched!

Sign up for STATS On-Line today and experience a world of sports information you've never seen before! For info on STATS On-Line or other STATS products, send e-mail to info@stats.com.

Order from STATS INC. Today!
Use Order Form in This Book, or Call 1-800-63-STATS or 708-676-3322!

GOT A MINUTE?
A NOTE FROM JOHN BENSON - AND A REQUEST FOR HELP:

I am trying to help the official Rotisserie League Baseball Association achieve better recognition for our pastime. Information about who enjoys Rotisserie leagues will help us, and help the RLBA, attain better media coverage of the information and events that we like, for example more and better attention in national publications and more TV/radio news and analysis catering to our needs. Please take a minute or two and tell us about yourself. Feel free to copy this form for others.

1. How many Rotisserie or fantasy leagues do you play in? _____

2. A. In what year did you first play Rotisserie/Fantasy Baseball? _____
   B. How many hours a week do you spend on Rotisserie/Fantasy? _____

3. In what other fantasy sports do you have any interest? Football [], Hockey [], Basketball [], Golf [], Other [] _____

4. Which of the following terms apply to any league(s) in which you play? (Please check all that apply):
Traditional 8-category Rotisserie []   Ultra rosters []   Auction []   Straight draft []   Use of modem or E-mail []
Non-standard stat categories []   National ''challenge'' contests []
If none of these apply, please describe your league interest: _____

5. How has being a Rotisserie owner affected your:
   A. Attendance at MLB games: increased [], remained the same [], decreased []?
   B. Interest in MLB: increased [], remained the same [], decreased []?
   C. Knowledge of MLB: increased [], remained the same [], decreased []?
   D. Watching MLB on television: increased [], remained the same [], decreased []?
   E. Usage of computers: increased [], remained the same [], decreased []?
   F. Usage of on-line info services: increased [], remained the same [], decreased []?
   G. Purchase of sports publications: increased [], remained the same [], decreased []?

6. Do you currently, or would you, use a computer on-line for these purposes? (Check all that apply)
- following daily baseball stats: currently [], would consider []
- following MLB transactions/news: currently [], would consider []
- following your league standings: currently [], would consider []
- following your league transactions: currently [], would consider []
- chatting with other Roti-competitors: currently [], would consider []
- other currently_____   other, would consider_____

7. How often do you, personally, use the following publications for selecting and managing your Rotisserie/fantasy baseball team(s)? Use the following numbers to indicate how often each publication is used:
          0 = Never, 1 = Sometimes, 2 = Often, 3 = Every issue.
local daily newspaper ___   USA TODAY daily newspaper ___   The Sporting News weekly ___
USA TODAY Baseball Weekly ___   Baseball America ___   Sports Illustrated ___
Fantasy Baseball Magazine ___   Benson's Baseball Monthly ___   The Sporting News Baseball Register ___
STATS Major League Handbook ___   STATS Minor League Handbook ___   Waggoner's Rotisserie League Baseball ___
STATS Player Profiles ___   Benson's Rotisserie Annual ___   Bill James Player Ratings book ___
other publication(s) specifically:_____

8. Which of the following Official Rotisserie League merchandise would you be interested in buying, either for yourself or as gifts?
   [] Baseball Cap   [] Watch w/logo on face   [] Playing Cards   [] Baseball Jacket
   [] T-Shirt   [] Logo Pin   [] Sweatshirt   [] Ball Point Pen
   [] Tie   [] League Start-up Kit   [] Baseball in Plexiglass [] Set of Pencils
   [] National Directory of Rotisserie Owners   [] Laminated Baseball Cards of your Team
   [] Beer Mug/Glasses (12 oz. tumblers) personalized [] Annual Championship Awards
Other: _____

9. How interested would you be in a weekly Rotisserie Baseball talk / call-in show on TV or radio?
TV: very interested [],   somewhat interested [],   not very [],   not at all []
radio: very interested [],   somewhat interested [],   not very [],   not at all []

10. Do you collect baseball cards? Yes []   No []
If yes, what brand(s) ? _____

11. How interested would you be if your local newspaper had a weekly column by John Benson, featuring baseball player news and commentary?   very interested [],   somewhat interested [],   not very [],   not at all []

12. How did you get this book? Mail Order from Diamond Library [], Phone order from Diamond Library [], Bookstore []
store name _____, other: _____

13. Are you male [], or female []?

14. Year of birth? _____

15. What ethnic group or nationality best describes you? African American [],   Asian American [],   Caucasian [],
Hispanic American [],   Native American [],   Other:_____

16. Which range best reflects your total yearly household income?
Less than $25,000 [] $25-49,999 [] $50-74,999 [] $75-99,999 [] $100-149,999 []   Over $150,000 []

17. Which best describes your education?
Some High School [],   High School Graduate [],   Some College [],   College Graduate [],
Some Graduate School [],   Graduate Degree [].

18. For calculating league standings, do you or your league subscribe to a statistical service during the season? Yes[] No[]
If yes, which service?_____.

19. What motivates you to participate in Rotisserie/fantasy sports?
On a scale from 0 to 10:   not at all a factor = 0   and   10 = the main factor:
A. Entertainment: 0 - 1 - 2 - 3 - 4 - 5 - 6 - 7 - 8 - 9 - 10
B. Interest in following baseball: 0 - 1 - 2 - 3 - 4 - 5 - 6 - 7 - 8 - 9 - 10
C. Friendships/camaraderie: 0 - 1 - 2 - 3 - 4 - 5 - 6 - 7 - 8 - 9 - 10
D. Financial rewards/prizes: 0 - 1 - 2 - 3 - 4 - 5 - 6 - 7 - 8 - 9 - 10
E. Competition: 0 - 1 - 2 - 3 - 4 - 5 - 6 - 7 - 8 - 9 - 10
F. Test my knowledge of baseball: 0 - 1 - 2 - 3 - 4 - 5 - 6 - 7 - 8 - 9 - 10

20. Do you bet on baseball games? Yes []   No []

Would you like to be on the Rotisserie League Baseball Association mailing list? RLBA can send you membership information, merchandise offerings, and news about the game. We would also welcome any names and addresses from your league. You may use a separate sheet of paper. Please mail your responses to:
RLBA c/o Diamond Library, 196 Danbury Road, Suite 1; Wilton, CT 06897.

We do value your privacy and will gladly receive anonymous responses as well.
THANK YOU ! OPTIONAL INFORMATION:
Name _____
Address _____ City_____ State_____ Zip Code_____ Phone
Number (   ) _____